The Scottish Mental Health Tribunal

Practice and Procedure

For Victoria and Adam
Derek P. Auchie

To P. E. G. Di E., L. W. C. B. and M. J. C. B.
Ailsa Carmichael

The Scottish Mental Health Tribunal

Practice and Procedure

DEREK P. AUCHIE, LL.M., Dip. L.P., M.C.I.Arb.
*Senior Lecturer in Law, Robert Gordon University,
and MHTS Legal Member*

with

AILSA CARMICHAEL, Q.C., LL.B., Dip. L.P.
Advocate and MHTS Legal Member

DUNDEE UNIVERSITY PRESS
2010

First published in Great Britain in 2010 by
Dundee University Press
University of Dundee
Dundee DD1 4HN

www.dup.dundee.ac.uk

ISBN 978 1 84586 022 6

The Publishers gratefully acknowledge the assistance of the
Mental Health Tribunal for Scotland in granting permission to reproduce the
material in Appendix 4.

No natural forests were destroyed to make this product;
only farmed timber was used and replanted.

British Library Cataloguing-in-Publication Data
A catalogue record for this book is available on request from the British Library

Typeset by Waverley Typesetters, Warham, Norfolk
Printed and bound by Bell & Bain Ltd, Glasgow

CONTENTS

FOREWORD

The Mental Health (Care and Treatment) (Scotland) Act 2003, which replaced the Mental Health (Scotland) Act 1984, effected fundamental reform of mental health law in Scotland. The fact that a new legislative framework was considered necessary is not surprising. Significant advances in the understanding and treatment of mental disorder and the development of community care, with more people receiving care in the community rather than as hospital inpatients, meant that the existing legislation was out of date.

One of the principles which underpin the new Act is that of the least restrictive alternative. Care should, wherever possible, be provided on an informal basis. Any use of compulsion should only be permitted when, and to the extent that, it is absolutely necessary. Compulsion in the community is now an option in appropriate cases. A new tribunal, the Mental Health Tribunal for Scotland has been established and has replaced the sheriff in proceedings for compulsory orders and appeals. Each tribunal has a legal chair, a medical member and a general member with experience in social care, including experience as a user of services or a carer. Hearings take place throughout the country, according to need. The Tribunal is a completely new multi-disciplinary forum making its decisions with regard to the individual circumstances of the patient and what is proposed by way of a plan of care. The patient is encouraged to participate in the proceedings. The patient's wishes are to be taken into account, as are the views, needs and circumstances of carers.

The aim of this book is to provide an authoritative guide to the practice and procedure of the Tribunal. The first chapter provides an overview of the 2003 Act and explains its structure and the underlying principles, including the priority given to participation by patients in decisions about their treatment. It explains that the overriding principle governing the Rules relating to the practice and procedure of the Tribunal is to secure that proceedings are handled as fairly, expeditiously and efficiently as possible.

The second chapter describes the Tribunal and considers those who may be parties to proceedings and the role of each in proceedings before the Tribunal, by reference both to the Act and the Rules.

The third chapter deals with how the hearing should be conducted and the fourth with how the merits of the case should be assessed. The authors provide some valuable guidance as to the general approach to hearings. They do well to emphasise that, notwithstanding the obligation imposed on tribunal members to avoid formality wherever possible, tribunal members must act judicially in the conduct of hearings.

The main points of the law of evidence, as they relate to tribunal proceedings, are dealt with in the fifth chapter. The remaining chapters describe how the various types of proceedings before the Tribunal are to be initiated and progressed, the way the Tribunal communicates its various decisions, and with appeals and reviews.

The authors of this work have drawn on their extensive general professional experience and their experience as legal chair of numerous mental health tribunal hearings since October 2005. They are to be congratulated upon providing a welcome exposition of the Rules and assembling, in readily accessible form, a wealth of information as well as sound practical guidance. This work achieves its aim of providing an authoritative guide to the practice and procedure of the Tribunal. It does so in a comprehensive and easily understood fashion. Its publication should be warmly welcomed by lawyers, health professionals and all those who may come into contact with the Tribunal. I commend this book to all such persons. I am sure that it will become an invaluable *vade-mecum,* and that those who use it will be grateful to the authors for their industry in producing such a helpful work in this increasingly important area of the law.

THE RT HON LADY COSGROVE, C.B.E., LL.D.

PREFACE

The careful implementation of procedural and evidential rules within the context of any judicial process is pivotal. Following these rules (apart from being a legal requirement) offers comfort to the decision-maker. The outcome of the case is more likely to be the correct one when all the available information and arguments have been presented in a fair, comprehensive and balanced manner. Much more important than this, of course, is the experience of the participants in the judicial process, especially the parties; people will accept an unfavourable outcome more easily if they have, and can see that they have, received a full, fair and orderly hearing of their case.

In the case of the Mental Health Tribunal for Scotland, there exist, as with all judicial *fora*, features which are particular to the jurisdiction. Perhaps the most significant are: the multi-disciplinary nature of the decision-making body, the emphasis in the procedural rules on hearing informality and the complications involved in ensuring the full involvement of a mentally ill person and his anxious family in proceedings. Add to that the uncertainty of a brand-new procedure, with new and significantly reformed primary legislation, and this produces a challenging environment.

This environment has framed the operation of this new Tribunal for over 4 years, and over this period some impressive and innovative practice has developed, both in the tribunal panels and the MHTS headquarters in Hamilton. This text is designed to capture some of that practice and describe it in the context of the rules of procedure and the 2003 Act. It is designed as a reference guide for the use of tribunal members, those who appear before tribunals on a regular basis and for those who instruct and appear in the appeal courts in connection with tribunal cases.

We would like to thank a number of individuals who have assisted us in our quest to complete this text. First of all, we wish to thank those tribunal members who responded some time ago to our call for ideas on issues that the tribunal faces, and for informal discussions we have had with a number of tribunal members over the years. These discussions have been most helpful in allowing us to consider a wide range of the common problems that face tribunals up and down the country. We must also thank Mrs Eileen Davie, former MHTS President, for her agreement to allow us to access some of the earlier determinations of tribunal panels, and for her general support for this project. Stephen Kelly of MHTS must also be thanked for his help in organising the logistics of this exercise. Dr Joe Morrow, current President, has offered his enthusiastic support in general terms and in particular in making available information on the MHTS structure and organisation. Ian Kennedy, former MHTS Vice-President, assisted in identifying some of the issues that can arise for the now-entitled "in-house Conveners". Craig Murray, Advocate, spent some long hours proofreading some of the text of this book, and so is to be thanked for his time, patience and meticulous care.

The staff at Dundee University Press, in particular Carole Dalgleish and Karen Howatson, have been very supportive and understanding in the face of this long-term project and in coping with extensive changes and updates to a number of drafts of this text.

We thank Lady Cosgrove particularly for her generous and thought-provoking Foreword.

Finally, we thank our families for their perseverance.

Any errors in this book are the sole responsibility of the authors. We have tried to state the law as best we can as at 31 January 2010.

DEREK P. AUCHIE
AILSA CARMICHAEL
April 2010

TABLE OF CASES

TABLE OF STATUTES

TABLE OF STATUTORY INSTRUMENTS

Scotland

TABLE OF CONVENTIONS

LIST OF ABBREVIATIONS

AMP	Authorised Medical Practitioner
AWISA	Adults with Incapacity (Scotland) Act 2000 (asp 4), as amended
CORO	compulsion and restriction order
CT	Casework Team
CTO	compulsory treatment order
ECHR	European Convention on Human Rights
EDC	emergency detention certificate
ICTO	interim compulsory treatment order
MHO	Mental Health Officer
MHTS	the administrative function of the Mental Health Tribunal for Scotland
MHTSA	Mental Health Tribunal for Scotland Administration
RMO	Responsible Medical Officer
ST	Scheduling Team
STDC	short-term detention certificate
the "Rules"	Mental Health Tribunal for Scotland (Practice and Procedure) (No 2) Rules 2005 (SSI 2005/519), as amended
the "2003 Act"	Mental Health (Care and Treatment) (Scotland) Act 2003 (asp 13), as amended
"Tribunal"	the Mental Health Tribunal for Scotland
"tribunal"	the three members making up the tribunal panel

CHAPTER 1

INTRODUCTION AND BACKGROUND

THE PURPOSE AND NATURE OF THIS BOOK

In October 2005 a new tribunal, the Mental Health Tribunal for **1.01** Scotland ("MHTS"), was born. This Tribunal[1] is like no other that has been introduced in Scotland. It is based on a multi-disciplinary approach to decision-making involving a combination of health professionals and lawyers. The MHTS arose from the Millan Report[2] and represents a sea change in the way in which decisions are made in respect of the treatment of mentally disordered persons.

The Tribunal has been in operation now for around 4 years. It is **1.02** still, therefore, relatively young and its procedures will remain on a steep developmental incline for some time to come. However, given that hearings take place every day, up and down the country, it is fair to say that, for such a young tribunal, a considerable amount of development has already occurred.

This book seeks to provide an authoritative guide to the practice **1.03** and procedure of the Tribunal. It is not a book on the Mental Health (Care and Treatment) (Scotland) Act 2003 (the "2003 Act"), although aspects of that Act are dealt with where required. The authors, both Conveners, have drawn upon their experience of appearances before a wide variety of public courts and specialised tribunals as well as their experience of dealing with numerous Mental Health Tribunal hearings since their appointments when the Tribunal began judicial operation in October 2005. Further, the authors have relied upon the

---

[1] See the Table of Abbreviations where it will be clear that, in this book, "Tribunal" refers to the MHTS as a whole, while "tribunal" refers to the tribunal panel of three who sit on a case. This is a similar approach to that used in the definitions section of the Rules – r 2. However, the Rules themselves do not consistently employ this abbreviations scheme.

[2] For a brief explanation of this report and its influence on the 2003 Act, which in turn created the Tribunal, see below at paras 1.11 *et seq*.

anecdotal experiences of other tribunal members, in an attempt to ensure that as many as possible of the issues and problems that might come up at tribunal hearings can be covered.

1.04   The authors have also had access to hundreds of written decisions of tribunals; all of the written decisions produced from October 2005 to February 2007. These have been randomly sampled in order to pick up on issues that the Tribunal has found challenging during its early operation.

1.05   This book sets out to be a guide to Tribunal members and to all of those who might need to come into contact with the Tribunal, including lawyers, Mental Health Officers (MHOs), Responsible Medical Officers (RMOs), advocacy workers and others. It concentrates on both the law (drawing, where necessary, on the solutions offered in other comparable judicial proceedings[3]) and on practice.

1.06   Given that the Tribunal finds its origin in the radical changes brought about in the 2003 Act, a description of the Act is an appropriate place to begin examination of the practice and procedure of the Tribunal.

THE NEW MENTAL HEALTH LEGISLATION – AN OVERVIEW

1.07   The 2003 Act[4] made significant changes to mental health law in Scotland. The MHTS, with the practice of which this work is concerned, is one of the innovations of the Act.[5] Where previously decisions about compulsory treatment and detention in hospital were made by the sheriff, that jurisdiction now belongs to the Tribunal. Rather than the sheriff sitting alone, three members (one legally qualified, one a psychiatrist, one a "general" member, who may have experience of mental health issues from any one of a variety of sources[6]) sit together. The rules governing the procedure of the Tribunal[7] make it clear that the jurisdiction of the Tribunal is to be exercised without any unnecessary formality.[8]

1.08   The constitution of the Tribunal, and the manner in which its jurisdiction is to be exercised in terms of the Rules, represent an important departure from the way in which matters of mental health

---

[3] For a discussion of the relevance of such proceedings, see paras 1.31 *et seq* below.
[4] asp 13.
[5] 2003 Act, s 21 and Sch 2.
[6] See para 2.02 below.
[7] Mental Health Tribunal for Scotland (Practice and Procedure) (No 2) Rules 2005 (SSI 2005/519), as amended.
[8] Rule 63(2)(a), commented on further at para 4.02 below.

law were formerly adjudicated upon. The aim of this work is to provide those who come into contact with this new forum with legal and practical guidance as to the Tribunal's practice and procedure.

THE ACT

In the debate in the Scottish Parliament on the motion that the Mental Health (Care and Treatment) (Scotland) Bill be passed, Malcolm Chisholm, then the Minister for Health and Community Care, hailed "a landmark Bill that places patients and their welfare at its heart".[9] He went on to say that this was exemplified by:

1.09

> "a coherent set of principles to which anyone discharging functions under the Bill must have regard; a new mental health tribunal that will combine professional, legal and practical experience in deciding what is best for patients; a new compulsory treatment order, which will allow care and treatment to be tailored to the personal needs of each patient, whether in hospital or in the community; duties on local authorities to promote the well-being and social development of all persons in their area who have, or who have had, a mental disorder; additional safeguards in the use of certain medical treatments; a strengthened Mental Welfare Commission for Scotland to ensure that the mentally ill are properly protected; novel provisions to ensure that advocacy is available to all persons with mental disorder; and mechanisms for the nomination of a named person with significant rights to represent the patient's interests".[10]

The Mental Health (Care and Treatment) (Scotland) Act 2003 derives from a review of Scotland's mental health legislation carried out by a committee chaired by the Rt Hon Bruce Millan. The review was announced before devolution, by the then Scottish Health Minister, Sam Galbraith, on 8 December 1998.[11] The Millan Committee issued its first consultation paper in April 1999 and its report[12] was laid before the Scottish Parliament in January 2001. The Bill, originally entitled the "Mental Health (Scotland) Bill",[13] was introduced in the Scottish Parliament on 16 September 2002. The overall policy objective of the Bill was said to be to update the legal framework; to help deliver the best possible support and protection for patients and their families; to equip professionals with the legal tools to be able to do their jobs properly; and to provide clearer, fairer and safer

1.10

---

[9] Scottish Parliament Official Report, 20 March 2003, col 19807.
[10] *Ibid.*
[11] *Hansard*, HC, 8 December 1998, col 134.
[12] *New Directions – Report on the Review of the Mental Health (Scotland) Act 1984*, SE/2001/56 (the "Millan Report").
[13] Scottish Parliament Bill 64.

mental health legislation that underpins modern ways of delivering mental health care.[14] Malcolm Chisholm's summary provides a useful framework for an overview of the new legislative regime, and of the respects in which it innovates upon the scheme provided by its predecessor, the Mental Health (Scotland) Act 1984.

THE PRINCIPLES

1.11   As Malcolm Chisholm noted, the Act contains a statement of principles. This represents an innovation in Scottish mental health legislation. The principles derive from, and are informed by, the recommendations of the Millan Report.[15] Recommendation 3.3[16] identified 10 principles which it considered should be enshrined in the Act, namely: non-discrimination; equality; respect for diversity; reciprocity; informal care; participation; respect for carers; least restrictive alternative; benefit; and child welfare. The principles as articulated in the Millan Report do not coincide precisely with the terms of s 1 of the 2003 Act, but are substantially given effect by the enacted principles for discharging functions under the Act.

1.12   By "participation" the Millan Committee meant that:

> "Service users should be fully involved, to the extent permitted by their individual capacity, in all aspects of their assessment, care, treatment and support. Account should be taken of their past and present wishes, so far as they can be ascertained. Service users should be provided with all the information necessary to enable them to participate fully. All such information should be provided in a way which renders it most likely to be understood."

1.13   "Participation", so defined, is given a degree of priority among the principles that came to be incorporated in the Act. Section 1(1) and (2) provide that a person, other than persons mentioned in s 1(7), must have regard to the matters mentioned in s 1(3) when discharging a function under the Act in relation to a patient aged 18 years or over. Section 1(3)(a), (c) and (d) together require such a person to have regard to the present and past wishes of the patient, and to the importance of the patient's participation in the discharge of the function, and to the importance of providing information and support such as is necessary to enable the patient so to participate.

1.14   Section 1(3)(g) gives effect to the Millan Committee's principles of "non-discrimination" and "equality" in requiring a person

---

[14] Mental Heath Scotland Bill, Policy Memorandum.
[15] Millan Report, p 16.
[16] *Ibid*, pp 23–24.

discharging a function under the Act to have regard to the need to ensure that, unless it can be shown that it is justified in the circumstances, the patient is not treated in a way that is less favourable than the way in which a person who is not a patient might be treated in a comparable situation. Section 1(3)(h) requires such a person to have regard to the patient's abilities, background and characteristics, including the patient's age, sex, sexual orientation, religious persuasion, racial origin, cultural and linguistic background and membership of any ethnic group, echoing the Millan Committee's recommendation in relation to the principle of "respect for diversity". Section 3 of the 2003 Act provides, further, that functions under the Act are to be discharged in a manner that encourages equal opportunities.[17]

"Reciprocity" and "benefit" are reflected in s 1(3)(f), which   **1.15** requires a person discharging a function under the 2003 Act to have regard to the importance of providing the maximum benefit to the patient.

Very significant in informing the disposals selected by the Tribunal   **1.16** in dealing with cases before it are the provisions of s 1(3)(e) read together with s 1(4). The Tribunal, like any other person discharging a function under the 2003 Act, must have regard to the range of options available in the patient's case. After having regard to that matter, and all the other factors enumerated in s 1(3), the Tribunal must then seek to discharge its function in the manner that involves the minimum restriction on the freedom of the patient that is necessary in the circumstances.[18] This important principle reflects the Millan Committee's "least restrictive alternative".

The Millan Committee's principle of "respect for carers" is dealt   **1.17** with in s 1(3)(b), which requires a person discharging a function under the Act to have regard to the views of various individuals, including any carer of the patient. It is also reflected in s 1(5), which requires such a person (except where the function in question is the making of a decision about medical treatment) to have regard to the needs and circumstances of any carer which are relevant to the discharge of the function, and to the importance of providing the carer with such information as might assist the carer to care for the patient.

"Child welfare", the last of the Millan Committee's principles, is   **1.18** given expression by s 2 of the 2003 Act, which provides that where a function under the Act is being discharged in relation to a patient under 18 years of age, the person discharging the function shall do so in the manner that appears to him best to secure the welfare of the patient.

---

[17] As defined in s L2 of Pt II of Sch 5 to the Scotland Act 1998.
[18] 2003 Act, s 1(4), final para.

STRUCTURE OF THE 2003 ACT

1.19   Part 1 of the Act is introductory, and consists of ss 1–3 inclusive. Part 2 makes provision for the continued existence and functions of the Mental Welfare Commission. The Mental Health Tribunal for Scotland is constituted by virtue of s 21, which forms Pt 3 of the Act. Part 4 sets out the functions of local authorities in relation to mental health law.

1.20   Parts 5–7 inclusive make provision for emergency detention, short-term detention and compulsory treatment orders (CTOs). CTOs fall to be made by the Tribunal on an application by the MHO, and replace "sectioning" by the sheriff under the previous legislation. Dealing with applications relating in one way to CTOs represents the greatest proportion of the Tribunal's work. The order is considerably more flexible than its predecessor. Where compulsory treatment is required, but detention in hospital is not necessary, treatment can be delivered in the community. In that event the Tribunal is empowered to make a range of orders reflecting the particular circumstances of an individual patient. Provision is also made for "recorded matters". The Tribunal may specify medical treatment or various types of services which it considers should be delivered to the patient. If the treatment or service is not in fact delivered to the patient, the RMO will have to refer to the matter to the Tribunal.

1.21   Parts 8–11 inclusive are concerned with the orders that may be made in relation to mentally disordered offenders in criminal proceedings. The 2003 Act provides for amendment to criminal procedure legislation dealing with the disposals open where an offender has a mental disorder. The orders for which provision is made are made in the first instance by sheriffs and Lords Commissioners of Justiciary in the exercise of their criminal jurisdiction, but come before the Tribunal thereafter in a variety of ways, when extension or variation of the order is sought, and on certain applications by the patient. There is also provision for references to be made to the Tribunal in relation to certain of these types of order. Part 13 provides mechanisms for suspension of orders of the types dealt with in Parts 8, 10 and 11.

1.22   Part 12 provides for transfer of patients between hospitals, and gives the Tribunal a jurisdiction in relation to appeals against such transfers. Part 14 provides for assessment of needs for community care services. Part 15 provides for the imposition of certain duties when orders are made in relation to a patient; an MHO must be designated by the local authority and an RMO appointed by hospital managers. The MHO must also provide a social circumstances report. Part 16 makes provision in relation to medical treatment, and includes procedural safeguards in relation to giving particularly invasive types of medical treatment.

Part 17 makes provision for "Patient Representation etc", and introduces further innovations in the form of the "named person" and the right for persons with mental disorders to have access to independent advocacy services. It also imposes certain requirements in relation to the provision of information to the patient, reflecting the importance in the Act of facilitating patient participation. Chapter 3 of Pt 17 is not concerned with patient representation, but with the provision of mechanism for challenging detention in conditions of excessive security. **1.23**

Part 18 is headed "Miscellaneous". Particularly significant from the point of view of Tribunal practice are the sections making provision for a Code of Practice, and in relation to advance statements. Section 291 within this Part of the Act gives the Tribunal a jurisdiction in relation to the unlawful detention of informal patients. This important provision is designed to provide a safeguard against *de facto* deprivation of liberty where there is no lawful authority to detain.[19] **1.24**

Parts 19 and 20 deal, respectively, with powers to enter premises and to remove a patient to a place of safety, and with absconding by patients. Part 21 makes provision in relation to offences. Appeals from the Tribunal are the subject of Pt 22. Finally, Pt 23 makes certain general provisions, the most important of which being the definition of mental disorder, as well as an important interpretation section (s 329) which sets out definitions of other key words and phrases used in the 2003 Act. **1.25**

THE RULES[20]

Detailed treatment of the Rules is one of the principal aims of this work. In the context of an overview of the new legislative regime, however, certain provisions merit particular notice. The first of these is r 4, which provides that the overriding objective of the Rules is to secure that proceedings are handled as fairly, expeditiously and efficiently as possible.[21] This principle is just that: a principle. However, it is an *overriding* principle, and so is paramount to all **1.26**

---

[19] For an example of the unlawful detention of an ostensibly "informal" patient, see *HL* v *United Kingdom* (2005) 40 EHRR 32; [2004] MHLR 236 (known as the "*Bournewood* case"). See also s 291 of the 2003 Act on applications in relation to the unlawful detention of informal patients.

[20] These are the Mental Health Tribunal for Scotland (Practice and Procedure) (No 2) Rules 2005 (SSI 2005/519), as amended.

[21] On this rule, see further paras 3.08 *et seq.*

other principles that can be gleaned from the Rules. It does not, like many of the other rules, offer a specific solution in any particular instance. Its importance is much more significant than this: the application and interpretation of all of the Rules should be measured against the overriding principle, and this principle should, therefore, feature in all decisions taken by the Tribunal on points of practice or procedure.

1.27   The second provision of particular note is r 63(2) which permits the tribunal, in accordance with the overriding objective, to conduct the hearing as informally as the circumstances of the case permit, and in the manner the tribunal considers to be just and most suitable to the clarification and determination of the matters before it.[22] Certain of the Rules regarding evidence are worthy of particular note also. Evidence in written, rather than oral, form is competent, but the tribunal may require the personal attendance of any witness to give oral evidence.[23] The tribunal may of its own initiative require the production of documents.[24] As Sheriff Principal Kerr has observed:

> "it is apparent from the procedural rules of the MHTS ... that the Tribunal are given wide powers and discretions to decide what evidence they should take into account or call before them and in what form.... Under rule 63 the Tribunal are given within very broad limits an almost complete discretion as to the manner in which they conduct the hearing before them".[25]

1.28   Sheriff Principal Kerr has concluded[26] that there is an inquisitorial element in the approach that the tribunal must adopt in reaching the decisions it is called on to make; it is not merely acting as umpire in an adversarial contest.[27] The sheriff principal reaches that conclusion following his consideration of the Rules, including the wide discretion given to the tribunal as to procedure, and its powers to require the production of evidence, including oral evidence, of its own initiative. The inquisitorial role of the tribunal is one to which practitioners and the tribunal itself must be alive. It is with this in mind that the tribunal is compared with other judicial processes in an attempt further to explain the essence of the tribunal.

---

[22] On this rule, see further para 4.02.
[23] Rule 60, discussed elsewhere at para 4.67.
[24] Rule 59.
[25] *Laurie* v *MHTS* [2007] Scot SC 44; 2007 GWD 32–555.
[26] *Ibid.*
[27] For further observations on the proper style of tribunal hearings, see paras 4.01 *et seq.*

PRACTICE DIRECTIONS AND GUIDANCE NOTES

These can be issued by the President of the Tribunal in order to direct **1.29**
the practice and procedure of the Tribunal.[28] To date, two Practice
Directions and three Guidance Notes have been issued, covering the
following matters: *Granting of a CTO where Patient is Subject to
a Hospital Direction or Transfer for Treatment Direction;*[29] *Issuing
of Reasons where Interim Compulsory Treatment Order is Made;*[30]
Doctors Giving Evidence to Tribunal when RMO Cannot Attend;[31]
Same Panel Requests and Directions;[32] and *Directions.*[33] The texts
of all five are reproduced in Appendix 4. It is not clear what the
distinction is between a Practice Direction and a Guidance Note, but
presumably the former is stronger in force than the latter.

The status of the Directions and Guidance Notes is that although a **1.30**
failure to follow one will not inevitably lead to a successful appeal, it
could be used to argue that, in all of the circumstances, the procedure
adopted by a tribunal was erroneous. This argument will be stronger
in the case of failure to follow a Practice Direction.

COMPARISON OF LEGAL PROCESSES

A whole book could easily be written on the differing legal styles of **1.31**
the various judicial bodies in Scotland and in the UK. Here, we offer
a few brief but important observations.

The Tribunal is primarily a civil tribunal, partly since it is clear **1.32**
that the rules of civil evidence apply.[34] Having said this, its powers
include the power (at the behest of the State) to restrict or relax the
liberty of individuals, including the power to force a patient to reside
in a hospital or other place against his will. This makes it seem, in
one sense, rather like a criminal court: forcing the restriction of the
liberty of an individual. Indeed, unlike the regular criminal courts,[35]
the powers of the Tribunal do not stop there: the orders the Tribunal
can issue often require the patient to undergo psychiatric treatment
against his will. These features of the Tribunal's jurisdiction give it
the feeling of being a "citizen versus the State" arena.

---

[28] 2003 Act, Sch 2, para 11. See also 2003 Act, Sch 2, para 7(6), which refers to
both Guidance and Directions.
[29] MHTS Practice Direction 1/2006 of 10 November 2006.
[30] MHTS Practice Direction 1/2007 of 17 May 2007.
[31] MHTS President's Guidance 1/2007 of 17 September 2007.
[32] MHTS President's Guidance 1/2009 of 28 May 2009.
[33] MHTS President's Guidance 2/2009 of 10 July 2009.
[34] See the justification for this set out at para 5.02.
[35] By this is meant the criminal courts in which offenders are punished for criminal
behaviour.

1.33   The proceedings of two other specialised tribunals are relevant here. The first is the Asylum and Immigration Tribunal.[36] Like the Mental Health Tribunal, the Asylum and Immigration Tribunal may be concerned with the liberty of an individual; immigration judges require to consider whether bail should be granted to individuals detained under the Immigration Acts. Like the Mental Health Tribunal, its procedures are civil. It decides appeals against decisions of the Secretary of State for the Home Department regarding whether individuals should be allowed to remain in the United Kingdom. The Employment Tribunal[37] is also of importance, although there is not, of course, the same "citizen versus the State" atmosphere there since that tribunal deals with private disputes between employer and employee.

1.34   One reason for the importance of these two specialist tribunals lies in the similarities in their procedural rules, and principally the presence of a less formal procedure than in the public courts[38] and the potential for relaxation of the normal rules of evidence.[39] Added to that is the fact that their procedures are designed to deal with a particular subject-matter; their caseloads are discrete and well defined, and this influences how the rules of procedure are shaped. Public court rules of procedure require to be more general in their nature since they are designed to cater for a much broader range of subject-matter.

1.35   The main advantage of the use of the jurisprudence of these two specialist tribunals is that it exists in volume, in particular in the case of the Employment Tribunal. These bodies have grappled with the same kinds of issues with which all less formalised judicial bodies will need to deal, and there is a body of case law that can be drawn upon in Mental Health Tribunal cases.

1.36   Of course, any comparison with another judicial body is inexact and Tribunal members should use case law from these bodies with care. Having said this, as long as used with care, this body of case law can be extremely helpful, and many employment and immigration cases are cited in this text.

1.37   Although less voluminous, there is a body of case law that has developed from the English equivalent of the Tribunal, namely the

---

[36] The current rules of this tribunal can be found in the Asylum and Immigration Tribunal (Procedure) Rules 2005 (SI 2005/230).

[37] The current rules for this tribunal are set out in the Employment Tribunals (Constitution and Rules of Procedure) Regulations 2004 (SI 2004/1861).

[38] It has been said that a hearing before an Employment Tribunal is "significantly less formal" than in a public civil court: P Elias and B Napier (eds), *Harvey on Employment Law and Industrial Relations*, para T817.

[39] For a discussion on this, see paras 1.33 *et seq.*

Mental Health Review Tribunal (MHRT).[40] While some of the key aspects of this tribunal differ from those of its Scottish equivalent, the subject-matter of the cases being dealt with by the two tribunals, as well as the general relaxation in the formality of the proceedings, is comparable. Some cases and material relating to the MHRT are also therefore referred to in this text.

Then there are the public courts. While the procedure followed in these courts is markedly different from that followed in the various specialised tribunals mentioned above, the "citizen versus State" flavour of public court criminal proceedings is still relevant in Mental Health Tribunal cases. In addition, the public court jurisprudence is highly relevant in certain areas, such as the law on statutory (and statutory instrument) interpretation, the common law on fairness, the Human Rights Act 1998 case law and the rules of evidence.   **1.38**

At appropriate places in this text, examples of cases and practice from all of these judicial fora are used, in order to try to discern how, in comparable situations, the Scottish Mental Health Tribunal should behave. It should also be said that the Tribunal has been keen to acquire its own body of case law, but the number of appeal decisions that have been published is still very small – to date, around 10. Many of these decisions are referred to in this text.   **1.39**

Code of Practice[41]

This is a three-volume publication by the Scottish Executive, designed as an explanation of the often complex and opaque terms of the 2003 Act. It is of relevance to tribunals since it offers an easy-to-use summary of the provisions of the 2003 Act, often combining text with diagrammatic summaries of the provisions in a particular area. It also, in places, offers practical advice to those who may have to prepare for and appear before tribunals. However, it should not be forgotten that this work is not simply a guide; it has special statutory status, unlike its predecessor under the Mental Health (Scotland) Act 1984. Those discharging functions under the 2003 Act must have regard to the Code;[42] although this does not apply   **1.40**

---

[40] The current rules of this tribunal are contained in the Tribunal Procedure (First-tier Tribunal) (Health, Education and Social Care Chamber) Rules 2008 (SI 2008/2699). The predecessor rules were the Mental Health Review Tribunal Rules 1983 (SI 1983/942).

[41] *Mental Health (Care and Treatment) (Scotland) Act 2003 Code of Practice*, (Scottish Executive, 2005), available online at: http://www.scotland.gov.uk/Publications/2005/08/29100428/04289.

[42] 2003 Act, s 274(4).

to the Tribunal,[43] it will apply to many of those appearing before the Tribunal, such as MHOs, RMOs, social workers and advocacy workers.

---

[43] The Tribunal is specifically excluded under s 274(5)(b).

CHAPTER 2

THE TRIBUNAL, PARTIES AND RELEVANT PERSONS

The 2003 Act introduces for the first time the Mental Health 2.01
Tribunal for Scotland. It also creates a new category of party to
proceedings: the "named person". Various other persons are entitled
to receive intimation of and be given the opportunity to participate in
proceedings. The Mental Health Officer and the Responsible Medical
Officer each has a raft of statutory responsibilities in terms of the
Act. Here we consider those who may be parties to proceedings, and
the role of each in proceedings before the Tribunal, by reference both
to the Act and to the Rules.

THE TRIBUNAL

The Tribunal is constituted by virtue of s 21 of the 2003 Act. Further 2.02
provision regarding the Tribunal is made in terms of Sch 2. The
Scottish Ministers require to appoint as members of the Tribunal
three separate panels of members. These are a panel of people with
legal qualifications and experience (the "legal members"); a panel of
people with medical qualifications and experience in the diagnosis
and treatment of mental disorder (the "medical members"); and
a panel of persons having qualifications, skills and experience in
caring for or providing services to persons having a mental disorder,
or such experience as may be prescribed (the "general members").[1]
According to the website of the Tribunal, the panel of general
members includes:

- people who have experience of mental disorder and of using
  mental health services;
- carers for service users;

---

[1] Schedule 2, para 1(1).

- registered nurses with mental health experience;
- clinical psychologists on the British Psychological Society's register;
- social workers with mental health experience;
- occupational therapists with mental health experience;.
- individuals who are employed in the provision of a care service;
- individuals who are employed in the management of the provision of a care service.[2]

In addition, provision is made for a further panel consisting of all sheriffs principal, sheriffs and part-time sheriffs, to serve as sheriff Conveners.[3]

2.03   The President, also appointed by the Scottish Ministers, presides over the discharge of the Tribunal's functions, and may himself serve as a Convener.[4] The qualification requirements for the President are the same as those for legal members, namely 7 years' qualification as a lawyer.[5]

2.04   The qualifications, skills and experience required for appointment as legal, medical and general members are prescribed by regulations.[6] Legal members must have been qualified lawyers for at least 7 years. Medical members must be medical practitioners. In addition they must be members or fellows of the Royal College of Psychiatrists or have a minimum of 4 years' experience of providing psychiatric services. The experience of a general member may be drawn from a variety of sources. Service users and their carers are eligible for appointment. Registered nurses, social workers and occupational therapists all may be appointed as general members if they have experience of working with persons with a mental disorder. Clinical psychologists are eligible, as are persons employed in or managing the provision of a care service to persons having a mental disorder.

---

[2] http://www.mhtscotland.gov.uk/mhts/22.1.3.html.
[3] Schedule 2, para 2. Cases concerning patients subject to a compulsion order and a restriction order, a hospital direction, or a transfer for treatment direction must be dealt with by a tribunal chaired by the President, or a member of this panel. See paras 4.169 *et seq* below.
[4] Schedule 2, para 3.
[5] Mental Health Tribunal for Scotland (Appointment of President) Regulations 2004 (SSI 2004/155).
[6] Mental Health Tribunal for Scotland (Appointment of Legal Members) Regulations 2004 (SSI 2004/286); Mental Health Tribunal for Scotland (Appointment of Medical Members) Regulations 2004 (SSI 2004/374); Mental Health Tribunal for Scotland (Appointment of General Members) Regulations 2004 (SSI 2004/375).

The functions of the Tribunal are normally discharged by a legal   **2.05**
member (who may be the President), a medical member and a general
member.[7] The legal member or the President will be the Convener of
the tribunal.[8] Where, however, the proceedings before the tribunal
relate to a patient subject to a compulsion order and a restriction
order,[9] a hospital direction or a transfer for treatment direction
(unless the proceedings are only in relation to the named person of a
patient, under s 255 or 256 of the Act), the Convener must be either
the President or a sheriff Convener.[10]

Certain interim and preliminary matters, including any matter   **2.06**
for which specific provision is made in Pt VII of the Rules, may be
considered by a Convener sitting alone, or with such other members
as the tribunal may direct.[11]

THE TRIBUNAL CLERKS

Each hearing is administered by a Clerk.[12] The Clerk has various   **2.07**
tasks to perform, including: meeting and marshalling witnesses
to and from the hearing room; tape recording the proceedings;
and providing the tribunal panel with decision paperwork and IT
facilities. The Clerk is also responsible for sending any decision
paperwork to the MHTS headquarters for recording. There are
around 25 Clerks, split into two teams (West and East)[13] and they
can be required to travel to different venues to cover hearings,
although most Clerks will have a base from which they usually
operate. The work of the Clerk is extremely important and, if
performed well, can be instrumental to the smooth running of the
proceedings. Clerks often have to deal with patients and relatives
following the announcement of a decision, which can be a difficult
task when the decision is not as they had hoped.

---

[7] Schedule 2, para 7(3).

[8] *Ibid*, para 7(3)(a).

[9] Restricted patients are now equated for the purposes of the Act with patients
subject to a compulsion order and a restriction order, by virtue of art 20 of the
Mental Health (Care and Treatment) (Scotland) Act 2003 (Transitional and Savings
Provisions) Order 2005 (SSI 2005/452).

[10] Schedule 2, para 7(4), as amended by Sch 1, para 32 to the Mental Health (Care
and Treatment) (Scotland) Act 2003 (Modification of Enactments) Order 2005 (SSI
2005/465).

[11] Rule 43(2).

[12] The word "Clerk" in the Rules is used in a wider way: to refer to a hearings
Clerk (as it is used here) and to refer to a member of administrative staff at MHTS
headquarters: r 2.

[13] This information is drawn from the MHTS *Staff Induction Booklet* (July
2008).

THE ORGANISATION AND OPERATION OF THE MHTS

2.08   The Tribunal headquarters are based in offices in Bothwell House, Hamilton. However, hearings take place throughout Scotland, before panels of three drawn from the Tribunal's 300 or so members, all of whom work for the Tribunal on a part-time basis. By March 2008, the Tribunal had access to 90 venues across Scotland's 15 Health Board areas, 40 of which were hospital based.[14]

2.09   The Tribunal deals with a high volume of cases, literally hundreds per month.[15] Often one case is allocated to a particular tribunal panel for a particular day; however, sometimes two are fixed on the same day – one for the morning and the other for the afternoon. Where the morning hearing overruns, this can lead to a new panel being called in (perhaps from another venue, if they complete their business early) to take over the afternoon case. No more than two hearings are fixed per day per panel.

2.10   The average length of hearings from April 2006 to March 2007 was just over 2 hours where a final decision was being made.[16] However, hearings can vary widely in length and some can last a full day or even several days.

2.11   The Tribunal is headed up by the President and his office is supported by two Conveners who are known as "in-house Conveners" as well as by a Legal Secretary. The role of the "in-house Conveners" is to provide judicial and administrative support to the President. One of their main roles is to make decisions where the rules allow for these to be taken by a Convener sitting alone[17] and to decide whether a curator *ad litem* should be appointed before a hearing, where there is evidence from the application papers that such an appointment might be justified.[18] Another role is to provide advice to members of the tribunal who wish an opinion on a procedural matter during or before a hearing. It should be noted that such advice can be rejected by the tribunal member who seeks guidance from an in-house Convener; the in-house Convener may not instruct the tribunal member seeking advice (usually the Convener on the panel) on what

---

[14] *Mental Health Tribunal for Scotland Annual Report* 2008, p 19. It is possible to hold a hearing outwith a designated tribunal venue, as discussed at paras 3.41 *et seq.*

[15] The volume of Tribunal business can be tracked through quarterly statistics: *Mental Health Tribunal for Scotland Annual Report* 2008, p 28. A total of 3,215 applications were dealt with in the period April 2007–March 2008.

[16] 2008 Annual Report, p 24.

[17] There are numerous provisions in the rules where decisions can be taken by a Convener or a tribunal; the reference to a Convener effectively means an in-house Convener. See also r 43 on interim or preliminary matters.

[18] See paras 2.54 *et seq* further on this.

he should do, since this would compromise the judicial independence of the tribunal panel: the role is purely advisory. The role of "in-house Conveners" (of whom there are two) replaces the former role of Vice-President.

While the President is responsible for the strategic operation of the Tribunal, the Chief Executive of the Mental Health Tribunal for Scotland Administration (MHTSA) heads up the administration of the Tribunal. In addition, the MHTSA Chief Executive is responsible for the accountable and appropriate use of public funds for Tribunal purposes.[19]   **2.12**

The Tribunal administration comprises a number of teams.[20] The teams with which tribunal members and those dealing with the Tribunal would be most likely to come into contact are: the Casework Team and the Scheduling Team.   **2.13**

The Casework Team (CT) is responsible for the effective receipt of applications and notifications under the Act and Rules, as well as for the processing of those applications timeously. The CT must also accurately record all decisions made by tribunal panels. The CT is split into three sections, each corresponding to an area of the country: North, East and West.   **2.14**

The Scheduling Team (ST) is responsible for fixing tribunal hearings across Scotland. This task includes booking the venues and collating information on tribunal members' availability and allocating hearings accordingly.   **2.15**

PARTIES AND RELEVANT PERSONS

"Party" is defined in the Rules[21] as the person who initiated the proceedings before the Tribunal; the patient to whom the proceedings relate; the named person of the patient to whom the proceedings relate; any person whose decision (including direction, order, determination, grant of certificate, but not the decision of a court) is the subject of the proceedings; and any person added as a party under r 48. "Relevant person" is defined as a party, and any other person who sends a notice of response under the Rules indicating a wish to make representations or lead or produce evidence.[22]   **2.16**

---

[19] See the statement of the current Chief Executive in the *Mental Health Tribunal for Scotland Annual Report* 2008, p 35.

[20] The information provided here on these teams is taken from the MHTS *Staff Induction Booklet* (July 2008).

[21] Rule 2(1).

[22] Section 329(1) defines "named person" by reference to ss 250–254 and 257 of the 2003 Act. See also paras 2.18 *et seq* below.

Particular parties and relevant persons

The patient

2.17   "Patient" is defined in the Act as a person who has, or appears to have, a mental disorder.[23] For the purposes of the Rules, he is the patient to whom the proceedings relate.[24] Persons who may be in attendance in the patient's interest include curators *ad litem* appointed by the Tribunal[25] and welfare attorneys and guardians with powers in respect to the welfare of the patient.[26]

The named person

2.18   The "named person"[27] provisions of the 2003 Act replace the "nearest relative" provisions in the predecessor legislation. The policy objective was to provide a more flexible and comprehensive framework to allow a specified person to have powers to support the patient and intervene on the patient's behalf.[28] The 2003 Act provides for nomination of a named person,[29] revocation of such nomination[30] and declinature of such nomination;[31] and also makes provision for when there is no named person, or the nominated person declines to act.[32] There is provision also as to the named person in relation to a child,[33] and as to declarations by a patient that a specified person should not be the patient's named person (s 253). The Tribunal is given powers of appointment and removal of a named person in certain specified circumstances.[34] These are where the patient has no named person; or he does have a named person, but it is inappropriate that that person remain as the patient's named person.

---

[23] Section 329(1).

[24] Rule 2(1).

[25] For detailed treatment of curators *ad litem*, their role and appointment, see paras 2.54 *et seq.*

[26] Guardians and welfare attorneys are defined in s 329(1) by reference to their appointment and authorisation respectively under the Adults with Incapacity (Scotland) Act 2000. See paras 2.40 *et seq.*

[27] For a definition of "named person", see s 329(1).

[28] Policy Memorandum accompanying the Mental Health (Scotland) Bill as introduced to the Scottish Parliament on 16 September 2002 (Stationery Office, Edinburgh, 17 September 2002). This document is also available on the website of the Scottish Parliament.

[29] Section 250(1) and (2).

[30] Section 250(3) and (4).

[31] Section 250(6).

[32] Section 251.

[33] Section 252. The named person must always be a natural person, except for the named person of a child. A local authority may be the named person of a child: s 252 and s 258.

[34] Sections 256 and 257.

In terms of the Act, the named person is entitled to receive notice of   **2.19**
various circumstances relating to the patient, including the making
of an application for a CTO.[35] The named person may consent
to two medical examinations being carried out at the same time
(for the purposes of an application for a CTO) where the patient
is incapable of giving his own consent.[36] In Tribunal proceedings
the named person is a party to whom the documents relevant to
the proceedings will be sent. He may make certain applications
or appeals to the Tribunal in his own name, and pursue appeals
against the decision of the Tribunal, just as the patient may.

Although the Act gives certain rights to the named person as   **2.20**
outlined above, it does not indicate in any detail what the legislature
had in contemplation as his role. Some guidance is to be derived
from the policy memorandum mentioned above, and from the Code
of Practice published under the Act.[37] The Code of Practice states
that the role of the named person is to represent and safeguard the
interests of the patient.[38] The named person does not in practice
necessarily, however, represent the interests of the patient in the way
that a curator *ad litem* would.[39] The named person is a party separate
from the patient. While he may strive to make representations which
represent the interests of the patient, he is often a family member
who will inevitably be less disinterested than a professional curator
for an *incapax* patient would be. It follows that the presence of the
named person in proceedings does not excuse the tribunal from
considering whether a curator is required to represent a patient
who is not capable of participating in the proceedings by reason of
lack of capacity. The named person is entitled to give his own view
as to what is in the patient's interests, even when the patient is of a
different opinion.

It is open for a person to execute documents making or revoking   **2.21**
a nomination, or making a declaration as mentioned above, at any
time he is capable of understanding their effect. He may choose to
do so when well, in anticipation of a time when he might require
a named person, or may do so when the subject of an order or
application for an order is raised, provided he understands the effect
of doing so. This is clear from the language of ss 250 and 253, which
do not refer to a "patient" but, respectively, to a "nominator" and
a "declarer".

---

[35] Section 60(1)(b).
[36] Section 58.
[37] Section 274.
[38] Code of Practice, vol 1, Chapter 6, para 04.
[39] See paras 2.54 *et seq* on the curator *ad litem*.

Nomination of a named person

2.22   The relevant provision is s 250. A person who has attained the age of 16 years can nominate another person who is aged 16 years or more to be his named person. There is provision in s 250(2) for the formalities of a nomination, which must be signed by the nominator, and witnessed by a "prescribed person". In terms of s 250(7), regulations are to make further provision as to "prescribed persons". Prescribed persons are: clinical psychologists entered on the British Psychological Society's register of chartered psychologists; medical practitioners; occupational therapists registered with the Health Professions Council; persons employed in the provision of (or in managing the provision of) a care service; registered nurses; social workers; and solicitors.[40]

2.23   For the nomination to be made in accordance with the legislation, the prescribed person must not only witness the nomination but certify that, in his opinion, the nominator understands the effect of nominating a person to be his named person, and has not been subjected to undue influence in making the nomination. There is no definition of "undue influence", and reference must therefore be made to the common law as to what would constitute "undue influence". At common law, where one party naturally and reasonably relies on the advice of another person, and that other has allowed self-interest to colour his advice, a transaction between the two parties can be reduced. Close family relationships, such as those between parent and child, and relationships between solicitor and client, are among the types of relationship in which questions of undue influence may readily arise where transactions take place between the parties to that relationship.[41]

Revocation of a nomination

2.24   Provision for revocation of a nomination is made in s 250(3) and (4). As with nomination, a revocation must be signed by the person who made the nomination, and the signature witnessed with certification, in similar terms to that required for a nomination, provided by a prescribed person.

Declaration in relation to named person

2.25   Section 253 makes provision for the patient to make a declaration signed by him that a person specified in the declaration shall not be his

---

[40] Mental Health (Patient Representation) (Prescribed Persons) (Scotland) (No 2) Regulations 2004 (SSI 2004/430). "Care service" and "social worker" for this purpose are defined by reference to the statutory definitions in, respectively, ss 2(1)(a), (b), (e), (g), (h) and (k) and 77(1) of the Regulation of Care (Scotland) Act 2001.
[41] See, for example: Gray v Binny (1879) 7 R 332; Ross v Gosselin's Exrs 1926 SC 325; Honeyman's Exr v Sharp 1978 SC 223.

named person. As with nominations and revocations of nominations, a prescribed person must witness the signature and certify that the person making the declaration understands the effect of making it and has not been subjected to any undue influence in making the declaration.

Where the nominated person declines to act

Section 250(6) provides that a person nominated under s 250(1) may decline to be the named person by giving notice to the nominator and the local authority for the area in which the nominator resides. There is no provision for notice of the nomination to be given to the named person. In practice, a named person is likely to be alerted to the nomination at latest at the time when an application is being made under the Act in relation to the patient, whether that be by the patient or some other person.   2.26

The Act makes provision as to who, as a matter of law, will be the patient's named person where there is no-one nominated, or a nominee declines to act. Section 251 provides for the situation where "there is no person who is by virtue of s 250 ... the person's named person". This appears to cover not only a situation where there has never been a nomination, but one where there has been a nomination which has been revoked. Where such a situation arises, the named person will be the primary carer,[42] which failing (whether because there is no primary carer, or because the primary carer declines to act) the nearest relative of the person concerned. It is clear that the primary carer may decline to be the named person, and provision is made for the procedure by means of which he may do so.[43] The Act makes provision as to who is to be regarded as the nearest relative.[44] Where the nearest relative as defined in the Act declines to act,[45] or there is a declaration under s 253 that the nearest relative is not to be the named person, there will, in the absence of an appointment by the tribunal, be no named person. Section 253 makes provision for a declaration that a specified person is not to be the named person of the declarer. Here, again, it is clear from the language of the section that the declaration may be made by a person at a time when he is not a patient or at a time when he is a patient. As with the provisions relating to the nomination of named persons and the revocation of such nominations, the declaration must be signed and witnessed with a certification by a prescribed person that the declarer understands   2.27

---

[42] See para 2.38.
[43] Section 251(5)(b) and (6).
[44] Section 254.
[45] Provision is made in s 254(5) for the nearest relative to decline to act.

the meaning of the declaration and has not been subject to undue influence.

2.28   Particular practical difficulties can arise if a named person does not wish to participate in proceedings, but does not formally decline to act. Where there is a named person, there are circumstances in which it will be impossible for the tribunal to proceed without seeking his views, as, for example, where s 64(7) of the Act applies. In cases where it is clear that the named person does not wish to act, but has not formally declined to act, consideration may be given to an application under s 255 to remove him from the position of named person on the ground that it is inappropriate that he continue to act.[46]

2.29   In terms of the Act, there will be only one "nearest relative" for the purpose of identifying the named person of an individual. The term is defined in s 254, by reference to a list in subs (2):

- his spouse (provided the two are not separated, and one has not deserted the other);
- someone living with him as husband and wife for at least 6 months or for at least 6 months before his admission to hospital (including someone living with him in a same-sex relationship);
- his child;
- his parent;
- his brother or sister;
- his grandparent;
- his grandchild;
- his uncle or aunt;
- his niece or nephew;
- someone who has been living with him for at least 5 years, or for at least 5 years prior to his admission to hospital.

2.30   The list is in order of priority, so that where a person has a spouse and children, it is the spouse who will be his named person. The section makes further provision as to how step-relationships and relationships of the half-blood are to be treated. If the spouse declines to act[47] or is the subject of a declaration by the patient, there will be no named person since, in considering the terms of s 251(5) along with the definition of the "nearest relative" in s 254(2), it is clear that

---

[46] See r 17.
[47] 2003 Act, s 254(5), which provides that any nearest relative can decline to act by giving notice in terms of that subsection.

only the person's nearest relative can be the non-nominated named person; there can be no substitute by the next nearest relative. In other words, there is no provision whereby the list is "worked through", so that, for instance, in the event of declinature by the spouse, for example, the child will become the named person.[48] This avoids the need, in this situation, for a trawl through the nearest relatives in order to rule out each category in turn until a named person is found or all have been exhausted.

Applications to the Tribunal concerning named persons

2.31 Sections 255–257 provide for the making of and determination of certain applications to the Tribunal relating to named persons. In terms of s 255 the MHO has a duty to take such steps as are reasonably practicable to ascertain whether a patient has a named person, and who that person is.[49] If there is no named person, or the MHO cannot ascertain who the named person is, the MHO must record the steps taken to discover whether there is a named person, and who he is, and that record is to be passed to the Tribunal and the Mental Welfare Commission.[50] In such circumstances the MHO may also make an application to the Tribunal for the appointment of a named person.[51] Where he considers that it is inappropriate that the patient's existing named person should continue to act, he must make an application to the Tribunal for an order declaring that that person is not the named person of the patient.[52]

2.32 Where the patient does not have a named person, or he has a named person but it appears to be inappropriate that that person continue to be his named person, either he or a number of specified persons interested in his welfare, including his RMO, can apply to the Tribunal for an order under s 257.[53] Such an order may appoint a named person for him, declare that an existing named person is no longer his named person, or both.

The Mental Health Officer

2.33 The MHO will almost always be either a party or a relevant person in proceedings before the Tribunal. He has a right to be heard in relation to all of the proceedings that come before the Tribunal by

---

[48] See R A Franks and D Cobb, *Greens Annotated Acts: Mental Health (Care and Treatment) (Scotland) Act 2003* (2005), p 286, where this view is expressed.
[49] Section 255(2).
[50] Section 255(3) and (4).
[51] Section 255(4)(b) and s 257(1).
[52] Section 255(6) and (7) and s 257(2).
[53] Section 256.

virtue of the Act. In CTO and certain other applications, he is a party because he is the person who initiates the proceedings. Only the MHO can apply for a CTO.

2.34   The MHO is the person appointed or deemed to be appointed under s 32(1) of the Act.[54] A patient's MHO is the MHO with responsibility for his case. Local authorities have a duty to appoint persons to discharge the functions of MHOs under the Act and certain other legislation. The MHO must be an officer of a local authority, and must satisfy requirements regarding registration, education and training, experience and competence which may be the subject of directions issued by the Scottish Ministers. Directions have been made both in relation to requirements for appointment[55] as an MHO and to continuing appointment as an MHO.[56] In order to qualify for appointment as an MHO, an individual must be a social worker registered with the Scottish Social Services Council, and have obtained certain qualifications, and have completed certain courses, specified in the Direction. He must also have the equivalent of 2 years' full-time experience as a social worker. The Direction relating to continuing appointment imposes requirements regarding annual training, assessment and continuing professional development.

2.35   The MHO has a variety of functions under the Act. He must consider whether to consent where a short-term detention certificate (STDC) is in contemplation.[57] It is his duty to apply for a CTO in certain specified circumstances,[58] and he requires to prepare a report and proposed care plan in connection with the application.[59] When a "relevant event", that is the making of any one of a variety of orders under the Act and the Criminal Procedure (Scotland) Act 1995,[60] occurs, the local authority must designate an MHO as responsible for the patient's case. The MHO must, within 21 days of the relevant event, prepare a social circumstances report and submit it to the Mental Welfare Commission and the patient's RMO.[61]

---

[54] Section 329(1).
[55] Mental Health (Care and Treatment) (Scotland) Act 2003 (Requirements for appointment as mental health officers) Direction 2009 (in force on 1 April 2009).
[56] Mental Health (Care and Treatment) (Scotland) Act 2003 (Requirements for continuing appointment as mental health officers) Direction 2006 (in force on 4 May 2006).
[57] Sections 44(3)(d) and 45.
[58] Section 57.
[59] Sections 61–63.
[60] Sections 229 and 232.
[61] Section 231.

The Responsible Medical Officer

The RMO is appointed by hospital managers[62] as soon as reasonably   **2.36**
practicable after the occurrence of an "appropriate act" in relation
to a patient. An appropriate act includes "relevant events";[63] the
granting of an emergency detention certificate (EDC); the making of a
temporary compulsion order; the variation of a CTO or a compulsion
order; transfer to another hospital under specified provisions of the
Act; or return to hospital under specified provisions of the Act.[64]

The RMO must be an authorised medical practitioner (AMP).[65] An   **2.37**
AMP is a medical practitioner included in a list complied by Health
Boards and the State Hospitals Board for Scotland.[66] Like the MHO,
the RMO is almost invariably either a party or potentially a relevant
person in the context of proceedings before the Tribunal. He is often
the person whose decision, for example a determination to extend a
CTO, will be under challenge in the proceedings.[67] The RMO has a
very broad range of duties under the Act, and it is outwith the scope
of this work to detail all of these. He must keep orders such as CTOs
under review and, if appropriate, apply for variation of or extension
and variation of the order. He may revoke certain orders relating
to patients. He requires also to monitor whether the treatment
or services specified by the tribunal as recorded matters are being
delivered to the patient and, if they are not, will require to refer the
case to the tribunal.

The primary carer

In relation to various proceedings under the Act, the primary carer   **2.38**
of the patient is a person who is entitled to an opportunity to make
representations or lead evidence.[68] A carer[69] is an individual who
provides on a regular basis a substantial amount of care for, and
support to, the patient. Where the patient is in hospital, a carer is a
person who, before the patient's admission to hospital, provided such

---

[62] The "relevant managers" in relation to a particular patient will depend on the
nature of the act in question: s 230(4).
[63] Those listed in s 232.
[64] Section 230(4).
[65] Section 230(1).
[66] Section 22(4). A Health Board in this context means a board constituted by order
under the National Health Service (Scotland) Act 1978: see s 329(1). All of these
are therefore Scottish Boards, and the lists contain the names of those medical
practitioners who have been approved, in respect of training and experience, to act
in the area of the Board: *H, Applicant* 2007 SLT (Sh Ct) 5 (Sheriff J A Baird).
[67] Section 99.
[68] See, for example, s 64(2)(h).
[69] Section 329(1).

care and support. The primary carer is the individual who provides all, or most, of the care and support.[70] A person who provides such care and support by virtue of a contract of employment or other contract, or who does so as a volunteer for a voluntary organisation, is not a carer in terms of the Act. It therefore follows that ward staff who may accompany the patient to a hearing are not to be regarded as primary carers as defined by the 2003 Act. Such a person does not have any entitlement to lead evidence or make representations in the capacity of a primary carer. On occasion, nursing staff may be called as witnesses, and it is also possible that the tribunal may regard them as having a particular interest such as to entitle them to be heard.[71]

Medical practitioners who have submitted mental health reports

2.39   In relation to applications for CTOs, the medical practitioners who have submitted the reports accompanying the application are entitled to make representations and lead or produce evidence.[72] The reports must be provided by AMPs,[73] but one of the medical reports may be provided by the patient's GP, even if he is not an AMP.[74] In practice the reports are often provided by the AMP who has by the stage of the tribunal hearing been appointed as RMO, and by the patient's GP. It is rare for GPs to attend tribunal hearings, but RMOs are frequently in attendance.

Guardians and welfare attorneys

2.40   The Adults with Incapacity (Scotland) Act 2000 (AWISA 2000) makes provision in relation to guardians and welfare attorneys. What follows is a very brief summary of the law relating to such persons.[75] For the purposes of the 2003 Act, a guardian means a person appointed as a guardian under AWISA 2000 who has power by virtue of s 64(1)(a) or (b) in relation to the personal

---

[70] Section 329(1).
[71] See para 2.88.
[72] See s 64(2) and (3)(f). This is reflected in r 6(3)(f), providing for intimation to these practitioners. If they provide a notice of response, they will be relevant persons in terms of r 2(1).
[73] Section 58(2)(a).
[74] Section 58(4).
[75] For more detailed consideration of the law in relation to Adults with Incapacity, specialist works are available, such as A Ward, *Adults with Incapacity Legislation* (2008). The 2000 Act has been substantially amended by the Adult Support and Protection (Scotland) Act 2007.

welfare of a person.[76] A welfare attorney means an individual authorised, by a welfare power of attorney granted under s 16 of the AWISA 2000 and registered under s 19 of that Act, to act as such.[77]

The views of guardians and welfare attorneys require to be taken into account by those discharging certain functions under the 2003 Act[78] and they require to be given an opportunity to make representations or lead or produce evidence in a wide range of proceedings before the Tribunal.   **2.41**

Section 57 AWISA makes provision for an application to the sheriff by any person, including an adult with incapacity, who has an interest in the property, financial affairs or personal welfare of an adult, for an order appointing an individual or office-holder as guardian in relation to the adult's property, financial affairs or personal welfare. A welfare guardian is a person who is appointed as guardian in relation to the personal affairs of an adult. The conditions which must be satisfied before the sheriff will make a guardianship order are set out in s 58(1)(a) and (b) of the 2000 Act and are that the adult is incapable in relation to decisions about or of acting to safeguard or promote his interests in his property, financial affairs or personal welfare and is likely to continue to be so incapable; and no other means provided under the 2000 Act will be sufficient to enable the adult's interests in his property, financial affairs or personal welfare to be safeguarded or promoted.   **2.42**

A local authority shall make an application under s 57 where the conditions in s 58(1)(a) and (b) are satisfied; no other application has been made or is likely to be made under s 57 in relation to the adult; and a guardianship order is necessary for the protection of the property, financial affairs or personal welfare of the adult.[79]   **2.43**

So far as guardianship in relation to the welfare of an adult is concerned, AWISA 2000, s 64(1)(a) empowers the sheriff to make an order conferring on the guardian power to deal with such particular matters in relation to the property, financial affairs or personal welfare of the adult as may be specified in the order. Section 64(1)(b) provides that the order of the sheriff appointing the guardian may confer on him power to deal with all aspects of the personal welfare of the adult or with such aspects as may be specified in the order.   **2.44**

It is notable, for the purposes of proceedings before the Tribunal, that a guardian may not place the adult in a hospital for the treatment of mental disorder against his will; or consent to medical treatment   **2.45**

---

[76] Section 329.
[77] Ibid.
[78] Section 1.
[79] AWISA 2000, s 57(2).

of the type specified in AWISA 2000, s 48(1) and (2).[80] Regulations made under s 48(2) specify particular types of medical treatment, including electro-convulsive therapy for mental disorder.[81]

2.46   In the context of mental health tribunal proceedings, welfare guardians are most likely to be involved in circumstances where the patient suffers from a degenerative condition or one which is not likely to improve: dementia and Huntingdon's disease are examples.

2.47   The powers of welfare attorneys are similar to those of welfare guardians. AWISA 2000 makes provision for an individual to grant a power of attorney relating to his personal welfare.[82] The power is granted when the granter has capacity, and comes into effect when he loses capacity. Section 16(3) provides that certain conditions must be satisfied for the creation of a valid welfare power of attorney. The power becomes exercisable when the granter is incapable in relation to decisions about the matter to which the welfare power of attorney relates, and the welfare attorney reasonably believes that the granter is so incapable.[83] The welfare attorney's powers are circumscribed in relation to placing in a mental hospital in the same way as are those of the welfare guardian.[84]

2.48   The authority of a welfare attorney may come to an end in a variety of circumstances specified in s 24 AWISA 2000. Where a granter and an attorney are married to each other, unless the document conferring the power provides otherwise, the power comes to an end on decree of separation, divorce or nullity.[85] Where a guardian is appointed with welfare powers, the welfare powers of the attorney will come to an end.[86]

Advocacy workers

2.49   Advocacy workers provide assistance to patients in the course of proceedings before the Tribunal. Their participation is designed to help the patient participate as fully as possible in the proceedings, in accordance with the guidance in s 1 of the 2003 Act. "Advocacy"

---

[80] AWISA 2000, s 64(2). Section 48(1) as enacted referred to giving treatment to which Pt X of the 1984 Act applied to a patient to whom that part of that Act applied. Section 48(1) was repealed by Sch 5, Pt 1 to the 2003 Act, with effect from 5 October 2005: Mental Health (Care and Treatment) (Scotland) Act 2003 (Commencement No 4) Order 2005 (SSI 2005/161).

[81] Adults with Incapacity (Specified Medical Treatments) (Scotland) Regulations 2002 (SSI 2002/275) as amended by the Adults with Incapacity (Specified Medical Treatments) (Scotland) Amendment Regulations 2002 (SSI 2002/302).

[82] AWISA 2000, s 16; see also s 19 regarding registration.

[83] *Ibid*, s 16(5)(b)(i) and (ii).

[84] *Ibid*, s 16(5).

[85] *Ibid*, s 24(1).

[86] *Ibid*, s 24(2).

is defined in the 2003 Act as services of support and representation made available for the purpose of enabling the person to whom they are available to have as much control of, or capacity to influence, that person's care and welfare as is, in the circumstances, appropriate.[87] Every person with a mental disorder has a right of access to independent advocacy.[88] Local authorities and health boards are under a duty to secure the availability of independent advocacy services for persons with mental disorder, and to ensure that such persons have the opportunity to use the services.[89] "Independent" is defined in s 259(5). Broadly speaking, the advocacy service must not be a local authority, health board or NHS trust, or a member of any of these in the area relevant to the patient; a person providing care, treatment or welfare services to the patient; or, in relation to a State Hospital patient, the State Hospital Board or a member of the State Hospital Board.

Independent advocacy may take the form of individual advocacy,   2.50
where a patient is partnered with a worker on a one-to-one basis, or group advocacy. The latter may take the form of a patient group, which will express views on matters such as the nature and availability of services in its local area. Individual advocacy is the form which is usually more relevant from the point of view of Tribunal proceedings. A patient will work on a one-to-one basis with a worker who will help the patient to deal with the proceedings. The Scottish Executive had in mind that individual advocacy might be either professional or citizen advocacy, the latter involving long-term pairing with an unpaid person from the community local to the patient.[90] In the experience of the writers, those appearing with patients at tribunals tend to be professional advocacy workers provided by organisations which specialise in providing such services for patients.

Advocacy workers are trained and/or experienced persons whose   2.51
responsibility is to the patient. Their role is to help patients to put their position effectively to those who are making decisions which

---

[87] Section 259(4).

[88] In 2001 the Scottish Executive published *Independent Advocacy: A Guide for Commissioners*. It was intended as a guide for health boards, NHS trusts, local authorities and anyone involved with advocacy. It is instructive as it gives some indication as to what the Executive had in mind in relation to advocacy services at around the time of the gestation of the 2003 Act. See also *The New Mental Health Act: A guide to independent advocacy: Information for Service Users and their Carers* (Scottish Executive, 2005). Also of assistance are paras 90–148 of the Code of Practice, vol 1, Chap 6.

[89] Section 259(1); s 260(2)(a)(iii) makes specific provision in relation to providing information to patients about advocacy services.

[90] See *The New Mental Health Act: A guide to independent advocacy: Information for Service Users and their Carers* (Scottish Executive, 2005), p 5.

affect them. Advocacy workers may help the patient to understand the proceedings, and help them access relevant information. The advocacy worker may be a paid or a voluntary worker. Advocacy workers usually try to meet with the patient, establish a rapport with him, and find out what is the patient's own view in relation to the proceedings. They may attend the hearing with the patient, where the patient feels that support would be of value. If the patient does not wish to attend the hearing, the advocacy worker may attend and communicate the patient's views and wishes. Sometimes an advocacy worker will speak for the patient, and sometimes the patient and the advocacy worker will each speak in order to communicate the patient's views in a way that maximises the participation of the patient.

2.52   A variety of bodies provide advocacy services to patients, and there is no uniform code of professional conduct for advocacy workers.[91] Advocacy workers generally, however, see their role as to communicate the patient's view, or to assist the patient to communicate that view, to the tribunal, rather than giving to the tribunal the advocacy worker's own view as to what will be in the best interests of the patient. Practice does vary, though, and the writers do have experience of advocacy workers who provide information to the tribunal which seems to go beyond merely communicating the views and wishes of the patient.

2.53   Patients often appear with both a solicitor and an advocacy worker. The tribunal may encourage the solicitor, the patient and the advocacy worker to take time together to discuss among themselves the way in which they jointly wish to assist the patient to communicate his case to the tribunal. Without co-ordination of this sort, there could be scope for tension between what the legally qualified representative considers appropriate in presenting the patient's case, and what the advocacy worker would wish to communicate on behalf of the patient. As the Code of Practice points out, the advocacy worker is not meant to replace a legal representative, but may have a useful role in helping the patient to communicate with his legal representative.[92]

Curator ad litem

2.54   The Rules permit the appointment of a curator *ad litem* ("curator") in one of only three defined circumstances:

(1) where the patient does not have the capacity to instruct a solicitor to represent his interests in the proceedings;[93] or

---

[91] There is an umbrella organisation for advocacy workers called Scottish Independent Advocacy Alliance. See its website at www.siaa.org.uk.
[92] Code of Practice, vol 1, Chap 6, para 143.
[93] Rule 55(1) and (2)(a).

(2) where a decision has been made under r 47[94] not to disclose a document or report or part of it to the patient, and the patient is unrepresented;[95] or

(3) where the patient has been excluded from any hearing or part of it under r 68 or r 69,[96] and the patient is unrepresented[97]

The tribunal is technically not obliged to appoint a curator should **2.55** any of these three situations arise (the rule uses the word "may" – r 55(1)) but it is clear that to proceed without a curator in any of these three situations would be dangerous, and the decision of the tribunal in such circumstances would most likely be appealable.

Where none of the above three situations occurs, the tribunal **2.56** has no power to appoint a curator. The power to do so could not be derived from any of the general provisions of the Rules allowing the tribunal wide power to regulate its own procedure[98] since the rules specifically address the situations in which one might be appointed.

Situations (2) and (3) are relatively straightforward. They are not **2.57** aimed at providing a curator where the patient is unable to instruct representation, but rather are designed to allow someone on behalf of the patient to access and make representations on documentation withheld from him (situation (2)) or to allow the patient to be represented at a hearing during his absence from it (situation (3)).

In cases falling within situation (2), depending upon the reason **2.58** for the order not to disclose, it may be that a direction will be attached to that order regulating how any curator is to deal with that information *vis-à-vis* the patient. Clearly, the effect of an order not to disclose to the patient would be completely thwarted if the curator then appointed showed it to the patient.

It should be noted that the absence of representation requirement **2.59** in situations (2) and (3) means that the patient must have no representation at all; where, for example, the patient is being represented by an advocacy worker, or by someone else who is not legally qualified, this will be sufficient to take the case outwith r 55, meaning that a curator should not be appointed. The thinking behind this seems to be that the patient does not, in these situations, require a curator since his representative can read and comment on any withheld document or can represent the patient during his absence from the hearing.

---

[94] For a discussion of this rule, see paras 3.180 *et seq.*
[95] Rule 55(1) and (2)(b).
[96] For a discussion of these rules, see paras 4.128 *et seq.*
[97] Rule 55(1) and (2)(c).
[98] Rules 49(1), 52(1) and 63(2).

2.60   The most common curator appointments fall within situation (1).[99] Here, there is a mental capacity issue in that the patient does not have the ability to instruct a solicitor. In such cases, there is no requirement that the patient be unrepresented, so that a patient might have an advocacy worker who feels that the patient does have capacity to instruct him,[100] but where a curator is appointed. Before we consider how this situation is dealt with, we need to consider the law on curators more generally.

The office of the curator *ad litem*[101]

2.61   This is an old office, dating back to the Institutional writers.[102] The office is a restricted one, since the curator can only represent his ward in relation to the litigation (*litem*) in which he is appointed. Lord Hunter describes the appointment in this way in a Full Bench decision of the Inner House:

> "the position of a curator *ad litem* ... is of a special and restricted character. His duty is to protect and safeguard the interests of the *incapax* so far as they are affected by a particular ... litigation".[103]

2.62   It is also clear that the curator must act independently of the appointing judicial body and of the other litigants in the case.[104]

2.63   According to Maxwell, the curator "does not conduct the case for his ward" but is legally represented himself. While such representation is competent, it may seem odd in the context of a specialist tribunal such as the mental health tribunal, where the curator will be appointed from a list of solicitors with experience of mental health law. In most cases, the curator is (and should be) able to conduct the case himself, without legal representation. There may be a case in which a particularly complex point arises or where the evidence in a case is difficult or complicated, and where counsel (an advocate) might be employed by the curator. Such cases will, however, be extremely rare. Sheriff Principal Bowen has commented, *obiter*, that it would be more satisfactory if one legally qualified person were appointed

---

[99] Situation (2) or (3) in addition to situation (1) might apply, in which case the appointment of a curator would probably be essential, having regard to the overriding objective in r 4.

[100] For further guidance on the role of an advocacy worker, see paras 2.49 *et seq*.

[101] For a general and recent discussion of the office, see T Welsh (ed), *Macphail's Sheriff Court Practice* (3rd edn, 2006), paras 4.23 *et seq*.

[102] See J Erskine, *Erskine's Institutes of the Law of Scotland* (8th edn, 1871), vol I, Book I, Title VII, para 13.

[103] *Drummond's Trs v Peel's Trs* 1929 SC 484 at 504.

[104] *Ibid* at 496 per LP Clyde; and D Maxwell, *The Practice of the Court of Session* (Scottish Courts Administration, 1980), p 228.

to represent the interests of the patient, without the need to instruct legal representation.[105]

It is sometimes said that the curator stands in the shoes of the patient. This idea probably derives from the right of the curator to instruct legal representation. However, it is incorrect to regard the curator as a substitute for the patient, even in cases where he (the curator) is legally represented. The curator himself is a representative of the patient, so it is illogical to regard him as if he is the patient. This means that, unless excluded for some other reason, where a curator is appointed on the basis of lack of capacity to instruct, the patient should not be excluded from the hearing. Even if this is perhaps at odds with traditional conceptions of the role of the curator, the principles of patient participation enshrined in the Act should be borne in mind. A patient may not have sufficient capacity to instruct a solicitor, but that does not preclude him from any meaningful participation in the hearing.   **2.64**

This raises another important aspect about the office of the curator. He does not represent only the legal interests of the patient (even although he is a solicitor); he represents his interests *in general* within the confines of the tribunal proceedings. This is suggested by the wording of the Rules where reference is made to "[representing] the patient's interests".[106] Such interests include, but are not confined to, the legal interests of the patient. So, it is perfectly possible (and not uncommon) for a curator to argue that a CTO application, for instance, should be granted, even although the patient himself opposes the application. The curator is not a representative of the patient's views or wishes (to the limited extent that they can be gleaned in a situation of lack of capacity to instruct): he is a representative of the patient's interests in general. This is where the curator differs from a solicitor representing a patient: the solicitor is charged with ploughing the patient's furrow irrespective of whether the general interests of the patient would dictate another course (as long as the patient has a legally stateable case, of course). If lawyers in this role perceive any ethical dilemma, as where there is, for example, a legal point which they might properly take in opposition to an application, but where they regard the success of the application as being in the patient's   **2.65**

---

[105] *Hughes v Mental Health Tribunal for Scotland* [2007] MHLR 29 (Sh Pr Bowen). A curator appealed on the basis that there was not a mechanism whereby he could be remunerated for his work as curator, and that the patient was therefore denied proper legal representation by reason of lack of funding. Legal Assistance by Way of Representation (ABWOR) was available for a solicitor instructed by the curator, but not for the work done by the curator himself.

[106] See r 55(2)(a) and(5).

wider interests, they should seek advice from the Law Society of Scotland.

2.66   Where the curator is legally represented, the lawyer for the curator must also aim to promote the interests of the patient; he is not, in such a case, acting as he would if he were a lawyer for the patient.

The application of the law to a curator appointed under r 55

2.67   Although the cases and texts cited above relate to the appointment and duties of curators arising in the public courts (where the appointment of curators can be for a range of reasons, such as (most commonly) in divorce actions involving children), the office of curator itself is no different simply because the reasons for appointment are distinct in mental health tribunal proceedings.

Capacity to instruct

2.68   Where situation (1) above arises, a key question is: what does it mean to have capacity to instruct a solicitor? Where the tribunal is unsure whether the patient can instruct a solicitor, a person having appropriate skills or experience can be appointed by the tribunal to report back on the issue.[107] In practice, such a person is known as a "man of skill". The Tribunal headquarters will, in such cases, appoint a man of skill from its list. His fees for preparing a report will be paid by the Tribunal.[108] That person will be a solicitor. This suggests that, as far as the MHTS headquarters is concerned, the question of capacity to instruct is a legal one, not a medical one. This may, at first glance, seem odd. It might be thought that the question of whether a person has a particular mental capacity is a medical one; indeed, one of the questions on the proforma mental health report that the RMO will complete asks about his view on the patient's ability to arrange representation.[109] However, a solicitor would have the training and

---

[107] Rule 55(3), discussed further below at paras 2.68 and 2.78 *et seq.*

[108] Rule 55(4). Until recently, there was a dispute between the Tribunal and the Scottish Legal Aid Board over which of those organisations was liable for the expenses of the "man of skill". This led to "man of skill" reports being carried out free, on the basis that one of the solicitors in the firm from which the "man of skill" came might secure appointment as a curator, in which case legal aid cover would then become available. However, the liability of the Tribunal seems clear from r 55(4), and has now been accepted – see the Memo from the MHTS President circulated to Tribunal members on 6 November 2008, confirming that all fees and outlays of curators will be met by the Tribunal. This acceptance has led to fewer "man of skill" appointments since in practice in the past such an appointment (for funding reasons) was regarded as a necessary precursor to the appointment of a curator when of course, in terms of the Rules, a "man of skill" appointment is not, by any means, routinely required.

[109] See para 2.75 below for further discussion of this.

experience properly to assess whether he can obtain instructions from his client. This does not mean that the man of skill has the last say in such matters. The tribunal may take a different view to the view formed by the man of skill. As noted later,[110] in practice, man of skill reports are generally to be avoided, although they are still technically competent.

Patrick provides some useful guidance on the "capacity to instruct" test in the context of a mental health tribunal: 2.69

> "There is a limited amount of information that the client has to give to the solicitor that is not available from other people or documents before the tribunal ... If a solicitor is content that a client understands that he or she is in hospital, that he or she is not happy to go along with the proposed care options, and that a solicitor can help to put the case, there is probably not a need for a high degree of ability in such a case, at least to instruct the solicitor to oppose the application. It could be argued, for example, that it is not crucial to the conduct of the case that the client should be able to follow all the proceedings at the tribunal."[111]

This seems to be a sensible practical test. Indeed, there are many clients who would not be able to follow judicial proceedings. Take the example of a Debate in an Ordinary civil case in the sheriff court. It would be difficult for many clients fully to appreciate what the purpose of a Debate is. The position is even more obscure when one considers a Proof Before Answer. However, they would probably understand that a Debate is a purely legal argument without witnesses, a Proof is when witnesses give evidence about the facts and a Proof Before Answer is a mixture of both. This level of understanding would be sufficient to amount to capacity to instruct.   2.70

It is certainly true that an understanding of the content of the law (even a basic one) is not necessary for a patient (or any other client) to have capacity to instruct. So, an understanding of the statutory criteria for compulsory measures would be unnecessary in order for a patient to have full capacity.   2.71

Also, the patient would not require to be able to recall the details of any incidents relevant to the proceedings in order to have capacity to instruct. It is perfectly legitimate for a solicitor to conduct his opposition to an application for an order even although his client can offer no contradiction of any of the facts relied upon by the applicant: the case can be conducted purely on the issue of whether the unopposed facts, if accepted as true, are sufficient to justify the   2.72

---

[110] See paras 2.78 *et seq.*
[111] H Patrick, *Mental Health, Incapacity and the Law in Scotland* (2006), p 608.

establishment of the statutory criteria. Indeed, many cases are argued on this basis alone (or at least primarily so).[112]

2.73   Capacity to instruct a solicitor can come and go. A patient might demonstrate mental lucidity during interview with a solicitor, but at the hearing might be significantly less able to understand what is happening. Where the solicitor in such a case has all of the instructions he needs by the time of the hearing, properly to conduct the case, he may, it is submitted, continue to represent the patient. However, if a point arises on which he requires to take instructions and the patient is unable to provide them with sufficient clarity, he may need to consider withdrawing his services, on the basis that his client no longer has capacity to instruct, at which point consideration might have to be given to the appointment of a curator.

The appointment process

2.74   There are two ways in which a curator can be appointed:

> (1) by a Convener sitting alone (in practice an in-house Convener);[113]
>
> (2) by a tribunal panel at a hearing.

Appointments in situation (1) are more common now than at the time when the Tribunal was first operational. In cases where capacity to instruct a solicitor is not the ground for appointment, the appointment might be made by a Convener sitting alone where the ground is that a document or part of it has been withheld by a decision of that Convener. The exclusion of the patient from proceedings would almost always happen at a hearing, and so the appointment of a curator in such a case would happen there too. The curator will be appointed from a list kept by the Tribunal; the appointment is a personal one and the curator is expected to appear personally at tribunal hearings, except in exceptional circumstances.[114]

2.75   In cases where capacity to instruct a solicitor is in issue, either method of appointment is possible. Where the caseworker handling the application/appeal documentation considers that there is evidence within the papers that suggests that a curator might be appointed,

---

[112] This situation is akin to an accused person in a criminal case who admits to his solicitor that he committed the offence; the solicitor is still entitled to enter a plea of not guilty on the basis that he will argue that the Crown case is not strong enough to support a conviction.

[113] For a discussion of the role of the "in-house" Convener, see para 2.11.

[114] *Guidance to Curators ad Litem*, issued by the MHTS President, November 2008, para 2.

the papers are referred to an in-house Convener. He then decides whether or not to appoint a curator. If he decides to do so, he will issue a direction to that effect and a curator will be chosen from a list retained by MHTS in Hamilton. The most obvious evidence of the need for the appointment of a curator to be considered is where the RMO in his mental health report indicates that the patient is not capable of arranging representation in terms of s 63 of the 2003 Act.[115] Where this conclusion is reached, reasons should be provided. It would seem that the question relating to "arranging" representation is aimed not just at engaging representation, but also at properly instructing a representative. It should be noted too that this part of the mental health report does not refer only to legal representation, but to any representation. Of course, it would be possible for the Convener sitting alone to take the view that, despite the opinion of the RMO, the patient does have capacity to instruct a solicitor and to refuse to appoint a curator. This would be unusual and where the single Convener is in any doubt on the matter he should refer the question to the panel hearing, where the issue can be explored in more depth by questioning witnesses. Similarly, where the RMO takes the view that the patient can arrange representation, the Convener sitting alone could take a different view and appoint one. However, there would have to be compelling material from elsewhere to allow this to be done; it would almost always be appropriate for the Convener to refer such a case to the tribunal panel for a decision.

The benefit of the appointment of a curator by the Convener sitting alone is that, in such cases, there is usually time for the curator to be appointed, to make investigations, and to be ready to represent the patient at the first hearing of the application/appeal. Where a curator is appointed at a hearing, the case will inevitably require to be adjourned in order to allow for the appointment to take place (from the list of curators kept by MHTS in Hamilton) and to allow him to complete his investigations. This delay can be frustrating for those involved in the tribunal process, not least the patient, who will have to attend a further potentially distressing hearing.   2.76

One of the parties at the tribunal may seek the appointment of a curator, but in most cases the issue is raised by the panel as a result of information in the case papers. Since the appointment of a curator would necessitate an adjournment, this should be raised and dealt with as a preliminary issue. Where the tribunal panel is considering appointing a curator, this should be raised with the parties and their views on the proposal should be invited.[116] In most cases, the tribunal   2.77

---

[115] This part of the report appears on the final page of the proforma routinely used. On the use of proformas, see paras 3.83, 6.06 and 6.12.
[116] Rule 52(4).

will question the RMO regarding the issue of capacity to instruct. The MHO may also have a view. Indeed, the patient may be represented by a solicitor already and he would have valuable information on whether, as a matter of fact, he feels (or does not feel) properly instructed by the patient. The advocacy worker may also have an input. The opportunity for all other parties or their representative to ask questions of anyone with a view should be provided. If the solicitor is happy that he can take instructions properly, the tribunal should usually be slow to suggest otherwise.

2.78   The tribunal panel which is considering appointing a curator may be unable to decide, on the information available at the hearing, whether or not to appoint one. In such a case, as noted above, a "man of skill" can be appointed to report back.[117] However, such an appointment may be made only when the tribunal is considering the issue of capacity to instruct a solicitor, not some other ground of appointment. Although this is the position under the Rules, the practice from 1 November 2008, as directed by the President of the Tribunal, is that a "man of skill" should not be appointed and instead the tribunal should go straight to the appointment of a curator.[118]

2.79   The Convener sitting alone considering an appointment would be highly unlikely to appoint a "man of skill" to report back, since such a step would probably be premature; the tribunal panel will inevitably be able to glean more detailed information at the hearing than is in the papers on the issue of capacity, and so the question of a "man of skill" appointment should in all but the most exceptional case be left to the panel. Even then, as noted above, although technically competent such appointments should in practice be avoided.[119]

2.80   The Tribunal is obliged to provide all necessary information to the curator to enable him to represent the patient's interests.[120] This will include allowing him to have access to all relevant documentation and providing him with notice of any hearings. Effectively, he should be treated as a party to the case.

The duties of the curator *ad litem* in mental health tribunal cases

2.81   Where the appointment takes place because of the patient's lack of capacity to instruct a solicitor, the duty, as alluded to above, is to represent the general interests of the patient. In order to carry out this duty, the curator must, of course, first ensure that the patient still, after his appointment, lacks the capacity to instruct a solicitor,

---

[117] Rule 55(3). See above at paras 2.68 and 2.78 *et seq* on this further.
[118] *Guidance to Curators ad Litem*, issued by the MHTS President (November 2008).
[119] *Ibid.*
[120] Rule 55(5).

since if he thinks that the patient has now acquired that capacity (or acquires it at any other point during the period of his office) he must apply to resign office.[121] This will invariably involve a visit to the patient, which should be carried out within 3 working days of the appointment, where possible.[122] Where, as a result of that visit, the curator forms the view that the patient is capable of instructing a solicitor to represent his interests before the tribunal, the curator should confirm this in writing to the Tribunal and the appointment will be revoked.[123] This obligation persists throughout the proceedings, suggesting that the curator must continually assess the patient's capacity to instruct.[124] The next task for the curator will be to digest all of the case papers, and identify the issues that affect the interests of the patient (legal or otherwise). Here, the curator will be considering the welfare interests as well as the legal and mental health interests of the patient. These interests will comprise not only the short-term ones, but also what is in the long term interests of the patient, as long as such interests are relevant to the case in hand. In doing so, as a matter of good practice the curator should take account of the principles in s 1 of the 2003 Act, even although he is not bound to do so.[125]

To what extent the curator interviews others involved in the case prior to the hearing will depend on the time he has and on the need to carry out such interviews because of information being missing from the papers. He will have to consider to what extent obtaining such information by cross-examination at the hearing will be possible (or desirable) and to act accordingly. The curator is under an obligation to incur only reasonable expenses and fees, since he will require to lodge a professional account for the payment of fees and outlays, to be assessed on a Scale of Fees;[126] any dispute arising out of that account can be referred by the curator or the Tribunal to the Auditor of Court for taxation.[127] In addition, the curator is obliged to obtain written permission in advance before he incurs any expenditure that might be regarded as "exceptional".[128] Where a hearing date for the case has been set and the curator takes the view that it will not be possible to complete his investigations in time for the hearing, he should advise

2.82

---

[121] *Guidance to Curators ad Litem*, issued by the MHTS President (November 2008), para 6. On resigning office, see below at para 2.86.
[122] *Ibid.*
[123] *Ibid*, para 7.
[124] *Ibid*, para 8.
[125] *Ibid*, para 4.
[126] *Ibid*, para 11.
[127] *Ibid*, para 13.
[128] *Ibid*, para 12.

the Tribunal of this at least 7 days before the hearing date so that consideration can be given to adjourning the hearing.[129] This guidance comes in response to the high number of adjournments of cases on the day of the hearing caused by the curator not being ready to present his case in full. It is probable that in future where such notice is given by the curator, a decision on whether or not to cancel and adjourn the hearing will be taken by an in-house Convener, sitting alone.[130]

2.83   The curator should be allowed the same rights to present witnesses, cross-examine witnesses and deliver argument as any other party representative would have. He will rarely present his own evidence, and will usually restrict himself to cross-examination and making submissions. The curator might decide that it would be prudent to obtain an independent medical report. While such expenditure would probably not be regarded as "exceptional",[131] where the curator is in any doubt, he is best to seek advice from an in-house Convener on whether he should seek written permission before instructing such a report. The curator should, if such a report is desired, instruct the report within 5 working days of his appointment[132] and advise the Tribunal that one has been instructed and when it is likely to be available.[133] This is quite a tight deadline and so the curator will have to think fast following his first visit to the patient (which should be within 3 working days of the appointment).[134] This timescale is clearly designed to ensure that the involvement of the curator in the case does not lead to the case becoming overly protracted. The curator should be permitted to seek an adjournment to the hearing if he has only recently been appointed or if there is some other reason for not being able to conduct his representation fully on the day of the hearing. Where the patient appears at a hearing at which the curator is also presenting his case, the tribunal should deal with this situation sensitively and should ensure that the patient is allowed to participate as fully as possible.[135] This counters the notion, sometimes expressed, that the patient has no locus where a curator has been appointed: this is clearly incorrect.

2.84   It is good practice for a curator to wait until all of the evidence has been led before forming a final view on what his submission will

---

[129] *Guidance to Curators ad Litem*, issued by the MHTS President (November 2008), para 10.
[130] On adjournments, see paras 3.21 *et seq*.
[131] Requiring advance written permission in terms of *Guidance to Curators ad Litem*, issued by the MHTS President (November 2008), para 12.
[132] *Ibid*, para 9.
[133] *Ibid*.
[134] *Ibid*, para 6, commented on above at para 2.81.
[135] *Ibid*, para 5. See also 2003 Act, s 1(3)(a) and (c).

be. He may well come to the hearing with a strong idea as to his position, but the tribunal panel should not insist on his offering his concluded view until the submissions stage. This is because, given that his remit will be wider than any other party or representative, there is more scope for him being influenced by the evidence that develops at the hearing.

Cessation of the office of curator *ad litem*

This usually occurs at the end of the case, once a decision has been given. The curator has, on the face of it, no right of appeal under the 2003 Act against a tribunal decision.[136] However, given that the patient has a right to appeal, it would seem reasonable to assume that Parliament intended that the curator, as a representative of the patient, could appeal. The "no locus to appeal" issue was raised in the *Hughes* case, where the curator was the appellant.[137]   **2.85**

Where a curator wishes to resign office during a case, he will require to seek the permission of the Tribunal (or, if at a hearing, the tribunal panel) and reasons will require to be given.[138] This is because the curator is an officer of court, appointed by the tribunal. He cannot simply assume that he can resign from his office and intimate this. Such cases will be rare. However, one example of a case where the curator will require to seek to resign office is where he takes the view that the patient has acquired capacity to instruct a solicitor, where this was the reason for the original appointment. It will be a matter of discretion for the tribunal to decide, within its general powers to regulate proceedings,[139] whether such a request should be granted.   **2.86**

Curator for other parties?

The rules specifically provide for the appointment of a curator to the patient only. Of course, another party may be (or become) unable to instruct a solicitor, or may be absent from the tribunal hearing, having been excluded, or may be the subject of withheld documentation. In such cases, there seems no reason why the tribunal, under its general powers to conduct the case as it sees fit, cannot appoint a curator. In fact, given that such an appointment cannot be made under r 55, the tribunal is not limited to the three reasons for appointment provided there. However, difficult questions as to who should fund this appointment might arise.   **2.87**

---

[136] 2003 Act, Pt 22: the curator is not a "relevant person" for appeal purposes under those provisions.
[137] *Hughes* v *Mental Health Tribunal for Scotland* [2007] MHLR 29, discussed at n 105 above.
[138] See the case of *Walls* v *Walls* 1953 SLT 269, cited with approval for this proposition in T Welsh (ed), *Macphail's Sheriff Court Practice* (3rd edn, 2006), para 4.28.
[139] Rule 52(1).

Other persons appearing to the Tribunal to have an interest

2.88   This is a very broad category. It can include interested relatives of the patient who are not named persons or primary carers, and nursing staff such as the patient's community psychiatric nurse or his named nurse within a hospital setting. In relation to certain types of proceedings, including, for example, applications for a CTO, such persons must be given an opportunity to make representations or lead or produce evidence.[140] This is reflected in procedural provisions such as r 6(3)(j), providing for intimation of an application to any person appearing to the Tribunal to have an interest in the application.

---

[140] See, for example, s 64(3)(j).

CHAPTER 3

HEARING PROCEDURE I – PRELIMINARY MATTERS

In this and the next chapter, we will consider how tribunal hearings   **3.01**
should be conducted. All aspects of the hearing will be considered in
these two chapters, except for the rules of evidence, which are dealt
with in Chapter 5.

Clearly, the procedure to be followed will vary to some extent,   **3.02**
depending on the purpose of the hearing, and again depending on
who attends and on the issues the tribunal will focus on. However,
there are some general provisions in the rules on how any hearing
should be conducted. There are also some generic practical points
that can apply to most, if not all, hearings. It is these rules and generic
points that will be explained in this chapter and the next.

In this and the following chapter, unless otherwise stated, all   **3.03**
comments apply to hearings on all types of application, referral and
appeal to be heard by the tribunal.

It should be noted that although the vast majority of decisions   **3.04**
will be taken by tribunal panels of three, the rules refer in numerous
places to the power on the part of a Convener sitting alone to make
certain decisions. Such decisions will, in practice, be taken by an
in-house Convener of the Tribunal,[1] and these decisions tend to
involve issues such as misconceived cases,[2] decisions on distribution
and disclosure of documents[3] and on the appointment of additional
parties and relevant persons.[4] While, of course, such issues can
be dealt with by tribunal panels, they may arise in advance of a
hearing and a decision by a Convener sitting alone can be beneficial
in allowing the tribunal panel to deal with the merits of the case on

---

[1] See further on this position at para 2.11.
[2] Under r 44: see below at paras 3.88 *et seq.*
[3] Under rr 46, 46A and 47: see paras 3.180 *et seq.*
[4] Under r 48: discussed at para 2.16.

the day of the hearing, and not become bogged down in what are usually purely legal preliminary issues.

PROVISIONS ON PROCEDURE – GENERAL COMMENTS

3.05   It is clear that the tribunal has wide discretion in deciding how to run the hearing. The legal expertise of the Convener should be employed in making sure that the procedure in any given situation is appropriate and fair. Where he is sitting with other panel members, decisions on procedure, like other decisions, are decisions of the tribunal panel as a whole. The Convener should therefore take care to discuss procedural matters with his colleagues during the pre-hearing meeting, especially where particular procedural issues are foreseeable. Some consensus should, where possible, be reached on the approach to be taken, although it is important that procedural issues are not pre-judged, and adjournments may be necessary to allow further discussion by the panel as a whole. Given the obligation on the Convener to explain, at the beginning of any hearing, the proposed manner and order of proceedings and the procedure which the tribunal proposes to adopt,[5] it is important that the proposed order of proceedings should be agreed among the tribunal members before the hearing starts.

3.06   The Rules provide some general guidance on how the hearing should be conducted, as well as specific rules to deal with particular situations.

3.07   One of the main examples of the former type is r 52(1), which, despite its position in a rule entitled "Other case management powers", should be regarded as the starting point in any tribunal: "Subject to the provisions of [the 2003 Act] and these Rules, the Tribunal may regulate its own procedure."

3.08   This is significant, since it means that unless there is some restriction or procedure to follow in a particular situation provided for in the 2003 Act or the Rules, the tribunal has a free hand to regulate procedure as it likes. Of course, there is one caveat to that freedom: the procedure must be regulated in such a way that it is compatible with the overriding objective in r 4, and with common law and ECHR standards of fairness. Further, the fact that the rule applies to individual tribunal proceedings[6] means that the procedure need not be the same in each case: it can vary. This is sensible, since the circumstances that are relevant to the question of which procedure to follow will vary from case to case. These circumstances include: the

---

[5] Rule 63(1). See below at para 4.42 on this obligation.
[6] The use of the word "Tribunal" as opposed to "tribunal" is an error here, and this error pervades many of the rules. See the general comment on this at para 1.01, n 1.

identity and number of participants in the hearing; the attitude of the patient toward the tribunal and the other participants; the existence of sensitive material; the key issues in the case; whether the parties, or one of them, are represented; the nature of the order being sought; the existence of independent expert evidence; the need to deal with preliminary issues; and the existence of any legal arguments. This list is by no means exhaustive.

The Rules also provide that, in accordance with the overriding   **3.09** objective, the tribunal may conduct the hearing as informally as the circumstances of the case permit and in the manner the tribunal considers to be just and most suitable to the clarification and determination of the matters before the tribunal.[7] Although the rule uses the word "may" here, this should be construed purposively, and in accordance with the statutory objective of facilitating the greatest possible patient involvement. Accordingly, despite the use of the word "may", we would suggest that the tribunal is being enjoined to adopt an informal procedure so far as possible. The tribunal must, therefore, consider how to conduct the hearing as informally as is possible, while at the same time in a just and practical manner. This is a difficult balance to strike, particularly where all witnesses and parties (including the patient) are usually in the hearing together, and in a physical environment more akin to a board meeting than a court. There is a danger that if the emphasis on informality is too pronounced, the proceedings may become messy and disjointed, with participants flitting from one issue to another in no logical order. In such a circumstance, the hearing is unlikely to be being conducted in the way most suitable to the aim of clarification and determination of the issues. One of the major challenges a mental health tribunal faces is to battle against over-familiarity. Keeping order during the proceedings is critical, and is one of the obligations of the Convener.[8] Examples of how this obligation can be fulfilled will be given at various points in this chapter, and elsewhere. Indeed, in the context of employment tribunal proceedings, the Employment Appeal Tribunal (EAT) has issued guidance indicating that informality in tribunals can be taken too far. Wood J, the then President of the EAT delivering the unanimous EAT judgment in *Aberdeen Steak Houses Group plc* v *Ibrahim*,[9] said the following:

> "whilst recognising that tribunals have a wide discretion in [procedural and evidential issues] it must be remembered that the rules of procedure and evidence have been built up over many years in order to guide courts

---

[7] Rule 63(2).
[8] On these obligations generally, see paras 4.42 *et seq.*
[9] [1988] ICR 550; [1988] IRLR 420.

and tribunals in the fairest and simplest way of dealing with and deciding issues. Prolixity is to be avoided. It is possible for informality to go too far and it is important for parties appearing before any judicial body ... to know the rules normally to be applied during that hearing. It is important that there should be consistency. It is also important that any sudden change from that norm should not present a party with an embarrassing situation from which a feeling of unfairness can arise. ... Total informality and absence of generally recognised rules of procedure and evidence can be counter-productive in that parties may not feel that their cases have been fairly and appropriately dealt with. Thus ... a tribunal should be astute to prevent the tactical presentation of evidence in a way which would not normally be permitted and which can cause embarrassment or prejudice to a party".[10]

3.10   The relevance in general terms of the decisions in employment tribunal cases has been commented upon. In addition, in the *Ibrahim* case, these comments were made in the context of a consideration of the employment tribunal rule requiring that hearings should be conducted justly and in a way most suitable to the clarification of the issues, but that so far as possible formality should be avoided.[11] The equivalent mental health tribunal provision is very similarly worded.[12] In considering the acceptability of the above *obiter* comments in *Ibrahim*, it is noteworthy that the leading text on employment law refers to them as "an important review of employment tribunal procedures".[13] One aspect of the conduct of a hearing revolves around the conduct of the tribunal members, in particular the style and substance of their interventions during evidence; this subject is dealt with in a later chapter.[14]

---

[10] [1988] ICR 550 at 557–558. See also the decision of Sh Pr Sir Stephen Young in *KM* v *MHTS*, 1 August 2009, in which the sheriff principal refers to a part of the tribunal hearing during which there took place a "discussion". He comments on the impact of the discussion as having introduced "an element of confusion into the proceedings". It was said that during this discussion, evidence and submissions were "freely intermingled". In making these comments, the sheriff principal seems to be suggesting that such an approach is less desirable than the traditional approach involving these elements being separated.

[11] The rule when the *Ibrahim* case was decided was r 8(1) of the Industrial Tribunals (Rules of Procedure) Regulations 1985 (SI 1985/16). The very similar rule today is split between two regulations: Employment Tribunals (Constitution and Rules of Procedure) Regulations 2004 (SI 2004/1861), reg 14(2) on the avoidance of informality and reg 3 on resolving cases justly and expeditiously. See similar comments, again by Wood J in *Halford* v *Sharples* [1992] ICR 146 and by Morrison J (at the time President of the EAT) in *Eurobell Holdings plc* v *Barker* [1988] ICR 299.

[12] Rule 63(2).

[13] P Elias and B Napier (eds), *Harvey on Employment Law and Industrial Relations*, paras T820–825.

[14] See paras 4.103 *et seq.*

It should be remembered that tribunal members are holders   3.11
of a judicial office, and should therefore act judicially, including
demonstrating some of the key attributes of judicial behaviour, namely
independence, impartiality, integrity, honesty, objectivity, propriety,
equality of treatment, competence and diligence. There can be a
temptation to regard the proceedings as akin to a case conference,
and certainly the physical configuration of a hearing lends itself to
this as a result of the close proximity of the parties to each other,
the fact that everyone is sitting around a table, and the fact that the
hearing will almost inevitably be held on hospital property. This all
seems rather different to a traditional court setting where the judge
sits on a different level from the other participants in the hearing
(he is up on the bench) and where the furniture of a court room is
unmistakably formal. This temptation, however, must be avoided:
the proceedings are judicial. Not only is this obvious from both the
2003 Act and the Rules, it is also inherent in the powers the tribunal
holds: the power to restrict the liberty of an individual, either in the
community or in a hospital. One of the most challenging aspects of
the job of the Convener is to regulate proceedings in such a way that
this temptation is not indulged.

On the latter type (specific rules to deal with procedure in certain   3.12
situations) there are rules on a range of topics, including: on how
evidence is to be led;[15] the use of expert reports;[16] directions the
tribunal can issue on procedure and evidence;[17] the non-attendance
of relevant persons;[18] the distribution, disclosure and withholding
of documents;[19] representation at the tribunal;[20] adjournment of a
hearing;[21] excluding persons from the hearing;[22] and assisting persons
with communication difficulties,[23] to name some of the main instances.
Each of these (and others) will be covered during this (and the next)
chapter.

It should be noted that the requirement to act fairly, expeditiously   3.13
and efficiently, as outlined in the overriding principle, applies to the
conduct of preliminary matters as much as it does to the merits part
of proceedings. In addition, there are some general obligations on
members to act courteously and with respect to all involved in the

---

[15] Rules 49(1)(g), 59 and 60.
[16] Rule 62.
[17] Rules 49–51.
[18] Rules 70 and 71.
[19] Rules 46 and 47.
[20] Rules 54 and 55.
[21] Rule 65.
[22] Rules 68 and 69.
[23] Rule 53.

tribunal process. However, these obligations, although they apply to the whole hearings process including when dealing with preliminary matters, are dealt with in the chapter on the merits, since it is a duty that more commonly arises during that part of proceedings. The Statement of Principles of Judicial Ethics for the Scottish Judiciary, discussed elsewhere,[24] is also relevant here.

3.14   Finally, the tribunal is empowered to act "on its own initiative" (as opposed to at the request of a party) unless otherwise provided[25] but subject to giving any person likely to be affected by its act an opportunity to make representations.[26] The tribunal must, in such a case, take any representations into account when deciding whether to act in the manner under consideration.[27] The period and manner for any such representations should be specified,[28] but this provision is meaningful only in cases where the hearing is being adjourned to a later date or where a Convener in MHTS headquarters is considering the making of an order or direction on his own initiative. Where the tribunal seeks to act on its own initiative during the hearing, the Convener should explain the proposed act and allow parties to make representations then and there or after a short adjournment to allow the parties to consider their representations.

BEFORE THE HEARING

3.15   The hearing date will be fixed by the scheduling team at MHTS headquarters, and the intimations required will usually be made on the relevant individuals.[29] The relevant papers will usually be made available to the tribunal members electronically, and in most cases at least a week in advance, although in cases where a hearing has to be fixed urgently, less notice will be provided. The expectation on tribunal members is that the papers are read thoroughly in advance of the hearing date and that any key issues should be identified.

3.16   On the day of the hearing, the tribunal members will meet at the hearing venue around 45 minutes in advance of the start of the morning hearing.[30] The purpose of this meeting is to encourage the members to discuss among themselves the key issues that arise out of

---

[24] See para 4.04. This Statement is reproduced as Appendix 5.
[25] Rule 52(3).
[26] Rule 52(4)(a).
[27] Rule 52(4)(c).
[28] Rule 52(4)(b).
[29] See the intimation obligations for various applications, discussed in Chapter 6.
[30] The practice of fixing two hearings in one day (one in each of the morning and the afternoon) for the same panel is not uncommon. Where there are two hearings, the panel will usually discuss both at the initial morning meeting.

the papers, and to discuss how these issues will be dealt with during the hearing. In practice, this meeting is extremely useful, as it will inevitably lead to a more focused approach to the evidence by the tribunal members, who will usually, at least to some extent, take the initiative in which evidence is presented, and how it is presented.[31] It should be noted that there can be no objection to a tribunal member expressing a provisional view of the merits of the case to his fellow tribunal members. Indeed, the exchange of such views at this pre-hearing meeting is one of the benefits of the opportunity to discuss points arising from the advance case papers. This is the case as long as it is clear that this view is provisional and not final and provided that the other members understand that they are free to disagree with it.[32] As discussed later,[33] it is even quite legitimate for that provisional view to be made known to the hearing at large. Since the Convener has a role generally in the regulation of the proceedings of the tribunal, and given the specific obligation on him to explain at the outset to those attending the hearing the proposed manner and order of the proceedings,[34] these issues should be discussed among the tribunal members at the pre-hearing meeting.

The advance perusal of papers plus the pre-hearing meeting often act as a useful preparatory process for the tribunal members and this preparation will be apparent to those appearing in the tribunal, from the indications given by the panel about the procedure to be followed, and from any suggestions as to issues that are, at least provisionally, of particular concern to the panel. In addition, the hearing should be shorter, as the panel will not have to take basic details such as dates, key events and justifications offered by the mental health team for certain statutory criteria. This assumes, of course, that the papers made available to the tribunal members are complete and comprehensive.[35] Where they are, the tribunal members should require only to seek clarification of any key points. Where the

3.17

---

[31] See later at paras 4.103 *et seq* on the involvement of the tribunal members during the hearing.

[32] This was confirmed in the English Mental Health Review Tribunal case of *R(S)* v *Mental Health Review Tribunal (Department of Health, interested party)* [2002] EWHC 2522 (Admin) per Burnton J at para 23, as endorsed by Munby J in *R (on the application of RD)* v *Mental Health Review Tribunal* [2007] EWHC 781 at para 11. While these cases were decided in the context of the provision regarding the medical examination of the patient by the medical member of the tribunal shortly before the hearing and the relaying of his views to the other tribunal members, it is clear that the comments are applicable in a Scottish context.

[33] See para 5.33.

[34] Rule 63(1), explained further below at para 4.42.

[35] See below at paras 3.82 *et seq*, 3.142 *et seq* and 4.48 on the papers being presented.

patient is opposing the measure being sought by the RMO or MHO, or is appealing against an earlier decision, the process is likely to become more complex.

THE START OF THE HEARING – PRELIMINARY ISSUES

3.18 During the perusal of the papers and in the pre-hearing meeting, the panel members will identify and discuss any preliminary issues that may arise, in addition to considering the merits of the case. These preliminary issues will routinely revolve around, for example, the position of the named person, discussion of any likely request to adjourn, and consideration of what to do in the absence of any relevant individual. Such issues might be apparent from the advance papers, but others (such as issues relating to lack of attendance) may become apparent only on the day of the hearing, as a result of information relayed to panel members by the hearing Clerk.[36] In other cases, a preliminary issue might be raised in the hearing without warning. This is uncommon, but is not unheard of, particularly where the patient is legally represented. Some of the more common preliminary issues are considered in detail below.[37]

3.19 It is critical that any preliminary issue is raised at the very beginning of the hearing. It is good practice for the Convener to ask anyone present if there is any preliminary issue to be considered, and to explain what that term means. It might be best to explain the term as meaning any relevant point or issue that is not contained in the papers, or that might lead to the hearing being adjourned or shortened. The danger of not identifying such issues at the outset is that the hearing might get under way, with evidence being led, only to discover later that someone who should be at the hearing has not attended and was not told about it, or that one of the participants wishes more time to prepare. This could lead to the hearing being halted, and perhaps even adjourned, with the result that time will have been wasted and the patient will have had to endure a stressful experience needlessly, only to have it repeated by a later (possibly different)[38] panel. At the very least, the raising of such an issue part of the way through the hearing will lead to the interruption of the flow of the proceedings, causing them to become disjointed, out of order, and possibly confusing to all concerned.

3.20 Where the panel has a preliminary issue to raise, that should, for the same reasons, be raised at the outset of the hearing. The views of

---

[36] On the role of the Clerk, see para 2.07.

[37] At paras 3.21 *et seq*.

[38] On the selection of panel members for subsequent hearings of a case, see para 3.28.

the parties and any other relevant individual should be canvassed on any such issue(s). The panel members should give this some thought in the pre-hearing meeting so that, when the issue is raised, it is explained concisely and is directed at the appropriate parties.

ADJOURNING A HEARING

Where possible adjournment issues arise, these are covered in this work. However, it is appropriate here to make some generic points about adjournments.   **3.21**

The tribunal has a general power to adjourn a hearing to a different day,[39] in order that further evidence or information may be obtained, or for such other purpose as the tribunal sees fit.[40] This power is very wide indeed, although, as with any power in the Rules, it is tempered by the general provisions on the overriding objective[41] and on the manner in which the hearing should be conducted.[42] For obvious practical reasons, an adjournment request will almost always be made at the outset of the hearing as a preliminary matter. Sometimes the need to adjourn will arise only once the hearing on the merits is under way (for example, illness of a representative, relevant person or witness occurring during a hearing, or where previously unknown facts emerge during the evidence and parties require an opportunity to investigate) but this is relatively uncommon.   **3.22**

Adjournments are generally considered for the provision of additional written material in the form of reports (supplementary reports from the MHO or RMO,[43] or an independent medical report for the patient[44]) or for the attendance of a person, usually a party, witness or representative who is unable[45] or has not for some other good reason not attended.   **3.23**

The tribunal must (as with almost all applications made to it) consider any representations made by any relevant person before making a decision on whether to adjourn.[46] It is also clear that the tribunal can decide to adjourn of its own volition.[47] The tribunal can   **3.24**

---

[39] The wording of r 65 makes it clear that the provision is aimed at the power to adjourn to a different day, as opposed to the power to adjourn a hearing until later in the same day. The latter power is easily inferred from the general provisions on the conduct of the hearing: see in particular rr 52(1) and 63(2).

[40] Rule 65(1).

[41] Rule 4, discussed further at para 1.26.

[42] Rule 52(1) as tempered by r 63(2).

[43] On the need for additional documentation generally, see paras 3.110 *et seq.*

[44] On such a report generally, see para 3.31.

[45] On inability of a party and a witness to attend, see paras 3.51 *et seq.*

[46] Rule 65(2).

[47] Rule 65(1) but subject always to the limitations of r 52(3)–(4), discussed at para 3.14.

either simply adjourn any hearing (stating its reasons for doing so, usually in a decision form)[48] or it can adjourn stating reasons and also issuing directions under r 49 on the future conduct of the case, as it considers appropriate.[49] This latter provision is not necessary given the wide r 49 powers[50] but it does emphasise that the tribunal should, in any case where it decides to adjourn, consider whether directions should be issued in order to ensure that the further information it requires to enable a decision to be made is likely to be available at the adjourned hearing. Particular reference is made to the power to direct any relevant person to intimate by a specified date any information required by the tribunal.[51] Depending on the length of the adjournment and the complexity of the task set by the tribunal, there might be a requirement to lodge information in advance of the adjourned hearing (say a week in advance, for instance). The advantage of such a direction is clear: tribunal members and other relevant persons will turn up at the adjourned hearing having digested the material and this is likely to cut down on any delay at the adjourned hearing. In practice, since most adjournments are for short periods, in many cases the tribunal will order the production of the material by the hearing date, and not in advance, on the basis that such a direction will be easier to comply with.

3.25   The Rules are silent on the minimum or maximum period of any adjournment. The relevant forms encourage an adjournment of up to 28 days, but the period could be shorter than this or indeed longer, even much longer. However, the tribunal should be careful to keep any adjournment periods to the shortest possible time, particularly if the patient has to remain the subject of compulsory measures in the meantime, since a longer than necessary adjournment could be criticised as falling foul of the "minimum restriction" principle enshrined in s 1(4) of the 2003 Act. It should be remembered that where the tribunal is acting as a court for the purposes of Art 5(4) ECHR to determine the lawfulness of a patient's detention, the patient is entitled to a "speedy" determination.[52]

3.26   In at least one case, a hearing was adjourned until the following day to allow the RMO to be present for the purposes of cross-

---

[48] On decision forms, see para 7.06.
[49] Rule 65(3).
[50] On these generally, see paras 7.30 et seq.
[51] Rule 65(3).
[52] See R(C) v Mental Health Review Tribunal London South and South West Region [2001] EWCA Civ 1110; [2001] 1 MHLR 110. Where a hearing was set 8 weeks after the patient had applied for discharge, this was held to breach the requirements of Art 5(4). The 8-week period was arbitrary and applied to all cases, and was not based on any assessment of the time reasonably necessary to allow the tribunal to adjudicate fairly on the case.

examination. In that case, since the STDC was still running until after the end of the following day, the tribunal made no order other than for an adjournment. This case highlights the point that an adjournment need not accompany any interim order, particularly when the *status quo* will be preserved without one.

It should be noted that the granting of an ICTO, along with the necessary postponement of the hearing on the full CTO application, is not an example of an adjourned hearing, since the full CTO application hearing is *automatically* postponed until towards the end of the ICTO; in such a case, r 65 does not apply since the tribunal has no discretion – it cannot consider the full CTO application on the same day as the ICTO is granted.[53] However, the ICTO could be granted for a shorter period, necessitating that the postponed CTO application hearing occur earlier.[54]

3.27

In cases where a final decision on the application/appeal is not being made that day, it is important that the tribunal members, during the deliberation stage, consider whether they will recommend to the MHTS headquarters that the same panel members should attend at the adjourned or further hearing of the case. The papers prepared by the panel at the end of each hearing ask whether the panel recommends that the further hearing take place before the same panel, with some of the same panel members, with entirely different panel members or as available. In cases where more than a minimal amount of evidence has been heard (for instance where an interim CTO has been granted) it would be wise for the panel to consider recommending that the same panel sits in the later hearing. If this happens, or at least if one or two of the same panel members sit in the later hearing, this can improve consistency since there will be familiarity on the part of at least one panel member with what has gone on at the previous hearing. Where only one or two members of the previous panel are available, however, care must be taken to ensure that the new members rely only on the evidence actually available to them. Recently, Guidance to Tribunal Members No 1/2009 on Same Panel Requests and Directions has been issued, setting out the circumstances in which a request (or even a direction) for the same panel should be made. This guidance, reproduced in Appendix 4, should be folllowed in any case where a hearing is being adjourned.

3.28

Although the written decision of the previous panel will be available, there is often other information or an understanding of

3.29

---

[53] This interpretation is supported by the terminology of r 8 (dealt with elsewhere at paras 3.130 and 6.08) where reference is made to a "first hearing" and a "further hearing".

[54] Under the 2003 Act, s 65(2) the *maximum* period of an initial ICTO is 28 days.

certain issues that can benefit a later panel, but that are not to be found in the written decision. In addition, this continuity can benefit the participants in the hearing, since it can be daunting facing a fresh panel who may come to the case with a slightly different attitude to that of the earlier panel. Where the written decision from the previous hearing is not comprehensive, this can even lead to old ground being covered again by a new panel, to the discomfort and frustration of all participants; such a situation does not enhance the reputation of the Tribunal as a whole. On the other hand, as pointed out in the above-mentioned Guidance, patients could feel better served if a fresh panel considers the case at the adjourned hearing, avoiding the perception of pre-judgment (para 3 of the note). Where a party feels that the panel at the adjourned hearing should (or should not) consist of the same members, this should be made clear, with reasons, ideally before deliberations begin. In such a case, the panel should consider the request and orally intimate its views on that matter when intimating the decision. This issue should also be dealt with in the written decision of the tribunal. There is no guarantee that if a "same or similar panel" request is made that it will always be possible to avoid a fresh panel being appointed, since much depends on the length of the adjournment and the availability of the panel members for the adjourned hearing, but in the authors' experience the MHTS administration does make every effort to honour any such request, as long as the report of the proceedings records the request and a reason for it.

3.30   Finally, the tribunal can announce the date of the adjourned hearing at the tribunal hearing, in which case, as long as all relevant persons have been notified in this way, no further notification is needed.[55] In practice, the hearing date will rarely be fixed there and then, since MHTS staff will need to line up a slot at the same venue with three tribunal members who are available. Unless a very short adjournment period is granted, the date will be issued later by MHTS staff.

Adjournment to obtain an independent medical report

3.31   Where such an adjournment request is made, it should be treated in the same manner as any other request: it should be considered on its merits. The practice that has developed, however, seems to be that such a request should be granted under any circumstances. In some cases it will be necessary to obtain an independent medical report because the mental health reports accompanying the CTO

---

[55] Rule 65(4).

application do not address a particular point in favour of one of the criteria being met, or even where there is some charge that there has been ill feeling between the mental health report authors and the patient and/or his family. However, often the reason cited is that the patient does not accept that he is mentally ill. It must never be assumed by the tribunal that the patient has a mental illness, and that his denial of this is evidence of a significant impairment of his decision-making ability. The patient's solicitor, if he has one, cannot advise the patient properly as to whether the statutory criteria are met unless he has obtained a medical report addressing these issues. Such requests should be viewed as requests to adjourn in order to prepare the case further by employing an expert witness to examine the patient and prepare a report.

This leaves the question: can such a request for an adjournment ever be refused? Since it is a request and not a demand, the logical answer is that it must be capable of refusal, but on which grounds? Perhaps where the patient has capacity and where he does not disagree with anything said on the mental health reports, a request for an adjournment for an independent medical reports could be said to lack any real basis. However, where there is something in the medical reports that the patient does not accept, the patient or his representative should be able to demonstrate that it is a point on which an independent expert could legitimately express a view in evidence, not a disagreement on a matter of fact, which should be resolved by the tribunal without the aid of expert evidence.[56] It should be said that requests for adjournments for independent reports are rarely opposed by the MHO/RMO who is the other party in the application/appeal before the tribunal. Indeed, there is some evidence to suggest that in practice some RMOs welcome such independent reports since they can put the mind of the RMO at ease in a difficult case, or they may even be of therapeutic value in offering encouragement to the patient to become more accepting of the care being offered.[57] However, the tribunal should not feel tempted to grant such a request which it would not otherwise grant, simply on the basis of a lack of opposition from the other party(ies) in the case. The tribunal has an obligation to act expeditiously under the overriding principle in r 4 of the Rules and granting an adjournment that is not needed to allow the tribunal properly to decide the case would cut across that obligation.

3.32

---

[56] On the restrictions on the content of expert evidence, see paras 5.106 *et seq* and 7.27.
[57] See the case of *Byrne v Mental Health Tribunal for Scotland* [2007] MHLR 2, a decision of Sh Pr Taylor, where the sheriff principal notes that the lack of opposition by the RMO to the adjournment request was motivated by such a train of thought.

3.33   In the only judicial pronouncement on this issue to date, Sheriff Principal Bowen comments, very briefly and *obiter*, that:

> "An opportunity to ... obtain that separate opinion was one which should have been provided in accordance with the principles contained in s 1 of the Act which I need not cover in detail."[58]

3.34   The suggestion here seems to be that the principles in s 1 of the 2003 Act confer a right to obtain such a report. It may be difficult to see how the patient could participate in opposed proceedings in any meaningful way without the opportunity to see whether he could obtain expert opinion to support his position. It remains the case, however, that the obtaining of such a report almost inevitably will involve a request for an adjournment and this is where the discretion of the tribunal applies, albeit that the circumstances in which an adjournment would be refused would be limited to those in which the patient or his lawyer could not indicate any area in issue on which further light might be shed by an independent medical report.

3.35   It may be that in the future some further judicial guidance will be given on the extent of the tribunal's discretion in this area but, for the moment, tribunals should adopt the practice of asking for specific reasons for the perceived need for an independent report, even in the absence of opposition to the request.

Adjournment to prepare a case

3.36   Ideally, all parties should be given ample notice of the tribunal application/appeal so that everyone is ready to present their arguments and witnesses at the hearing. However, this is not always the case. Usually the MHO/RMO will be prepared in a CTO application or application to vary/extend and vary since they will have considered the statutory grounds and the papers they intend to rely on will be prepared and lodged. It is conceivable in the case of a patient's appeal/application that the MHO/RMO might argue that more preparation time is required, but this would be rare given the ongoing day-to-day control that person has over the patient's care and medical records. Sometimes a named person might need more time to prepare his case, but this too is rare.

3.37   More commonly, the patient may ask for more time to prepare when he is the subject of a CTO application or an application connected with a CTO. It may be that the patient has only recently

---

[58] *McGlynn v Mental Health Tribunal for Scotland* [2007] MHLR 16 at para 4 of the judgment.

received the documentation or wishes to investigate the availability of witnesses. It is not unusual for the patient to have instructed legal representation late in the day; the timescales for CTO applications are tight and unless the instruction of a lawyer comes early on in the process, it can be difficult for a lawyer to digest the papers, interview his client and other potential witnesses and prepare his arguments. A lawyer who is not sufficiently prepared to conduct the patient's case should seek an adjournment of the case, and the tribunal should be sympathetic to this. The question of whether the lawyer has had sufficient time to prepare will be a matter for him as an officer of court. The tribunal should be slow to decide that the lawyer has, contrary to his assertions, had sufficient time.[59] This is not to say that the lawyer should be permitted more time by the request for an adjournment being granted simply because it is asked for; the tribunal is entitled to make enquiries as to the time when the lawyer was instructed and progress made since then. However, even in cases where it could be said that the lawyer could have been prepared to proceed without an adjournment had he been more organised/ dedicated to the case, it would be an exceptional situation where the patient could be punished for this by denying him effective representation.

There could arise a case where the client of a lawyer is partly 3.38 or wholly to blame for the lack of preparation by his lawyer, for instance where he has withheld information from the lawyer until late in the day or where the instruction of the lawyer has, without good reason, taken place very late in the day. Where this situation arises with regard to the patient, account must be taken by the tribunal of the patient's possible mental state during the relevant period and, again, it may well be regarded as procedurally improper to refuse a patient an adjournment as a result of his own conduct, given the particular difficulties facing a mentally ill client.[60] In the case of a named person, there might be a different outcome, but again careful consideration would have to be given before refusing an adjournment to allow a lawyer to represent a party. Where the lawyer for the named person is seeking the adjournment for further time to prepare but where the patient wishes to proceed on that

---

[59] This was the view expressed by Sh Pr Taylor in *Byrne v Mental Health Tribunal for Scotland*, n 57 above.

[60] See the decision of Sh Pr Taylor in *Byrne v Mental Health Tribunal for Scotland*, n 57 above, where the sheriff principal refers to the patient's "impaired intellectual functions" as relevant to the question of whether a very short period of notice of a CTO hearing (48 hours) was enough to allow proper preparation to take place. It would seem logical to apply that line of reasoning to the conduct of the patient generally, for instance in considering whether he acted quickly enough in appointing a lawyer.

day, this could lead to the motion to adjourn being refused, since the result of the adjournment may be the granting of an interim order (see below) causing a restriction of liberty of the patient for the period of the adjournment.[61]

3.39   In cases where an order is being sought, the party seeking the adjournment will usually consent to an interim order being put in place (where needed)[62] to cover the period of the adjournment. Where that order is an interim CTO, for example, as noted elsewhere,[63] evidence will require to be led and a decision made on the statutory criteria, without reference to the adjournment since the question of the adjournment and the interim order are separate, even although one leads to the other.

3.40   It has been made clear that the "full participation" principle in the 2003 Act[64] demands that a patient be afforded an opportunity to have the benefit of fully prepared legal representation, since any such participation must be meaningful; the "mere presence" of a lawyer will not be enough to satisfy this requirement.[65]

THE LOCATION OF THE HEARING

3.41   As a matter of practice, hearings must take place at one of the recognised MHTS tribunal venues which, as noted earlier,[66] are located around Scotland. However, in a particular case, there may be an argument for holding the hearing elsewhere. The tribunal members will gather at the hearing venue, and the hearing should start there, but it may become apparent, for whatever reason, that the hearing would be best held somewhere else. For example, in one case, the RMO expressed concern about bringing the patient to the hearing venue which, although being located in the grounds of the hospital where the patient was being held, was a few hundred yards away from the ward in the building where the patient was being held. The RMO expressed concerns regarding security since the patient

---

[61] This would be the case whether an interim hospital or community order would be under consideration since both represent a restriction on the liberty of the patient. Community-based interim CTOs are rare, however.

[62] In some cases the adjournment period might fall within an order currently running, even an STDC or, more likely, an ongoing CTO in the case of an application to extend and vary/vary by the RMO.

[63] See para 4.38.

[64] 2003 Act, s 1(3)(c) and (d).

[65] See the comments to this effect by Sh Pr Taylor in *Byrne* v *Mental Health Tribunal for Scotland*, n 57 above, where it was held that a refusal to grant an adjournment to allow a lawyer further time to prepare the patient's case was wrong where the patient had been informed of the hearing only 48 hours in advance and where her lawyer had perused the papers only 10 minutes in advance.

[66] For more on the tribunal venues, see para 2.08.

had attempted to abscond from a previous hearing while being taken back to the ward, and since the patient had a history of violence. In the circumstances, the tribunal agreed to reconvene in a meeting room on the patient's ward, although technically that room was not in an MHTS venue. There is no legislation prescribing the use of MHTS venues only, so the use of such facilities arises only as a matter of convention. In fact, the application of a particular provision in the Rules has led to, in some cases, the patient being visited on the ward where he is being held, and taking his views there;[67] this constitutes holding part of the hearing outwith a tribunal venue.

The power to hold a hearing other than in a tribunal venue could (depending on the circumstances of the case) spring from the tribunal's general power to regulate its own procedure[68] or the duty to conduct the hearing as informally as the circumstances of the case permit[69] and in a manner the tribunal considers to be just and most suitable to the clarification and determination of the matters before it.[70]   **3.42**

Of course, holding the hearing in a venue other than one on the MHTS list should be resorted to only in exceptional cases for good reason, since the venues on the list have been chosen for their suitability and size for a hearing. Also, any such proposal should be canvassed fully with all parties before a decision is made on any relocation request.   **3.43**

"LIMITED HEARING" ON PRELIMINARY MATTER(S)

In some cases, it might be prudent to invite into the start of the proceedings only those individuals who might have something to say on a particular issue that requires to be discussed.[71] Consideration should be given, for instance, to whether or not the patient needs to attend personally during discussion of the issue(s). Where the patient is represented (legally or by an advocacy worker) and where the issue to be discussed is technical in nature, consideration should be given to whether the patient's representative should be asked to attend on behalf of the patient. This might be wise where the advance papers suggest that the patient might be nervous or reluctant to attend for a long period at the hearing, or simply on the basis that the discussion will be so technical that no patient without legal training would fully understand at the time what was being discussed. Of course,   **3.44**

---

[67] Rule 70(3), discussed at paras 3.70 *et seq.*
[68] Rule 52(1), discussed at paras 3.07 *et seq.*
[69] Rule 63(2)(a), discussed at para 4.02.
[70] Rule 63(2)(b), discussed at paras 1.26 *et seq* and 3.09.
[71] Where not all relevant individuals who have attended the venue to take part in the hearing are invited into the hearing at the outset, this will be known, for convenience, as a "limited hearing".

many patients will be nervous, for obvious reasons, but there may be particular concerns relating to the patient that might point to the need to avoid an unnecessarily prolonged hearing.

3.45   In addition, the role of the ward staff and even the RMO might be limited, depending on the preliminary issue, and simply calling in the MHO and/or his lawyer and the patient's representative(s), might be prudent. It should be remembered that many of those in attendance will be witnesses as to fact and will not have any role in the preliminary issue in hand.

3.46   Where the panel is considering holding a limited hearing, those concerned should be given advance warning of this by indicating this intention to the hearing Clerk and asking him to inform the parties of this. This will give the parties the time to tell those not being invited in of that fact and, where a lawyer(s) is present, this will give him time to seek the view of his client on the proposal of the panel to exclude certain individuals from this part of the proceedings.

3.47   In the event of a limited hearing taking place, the parties should be told what the preliminary issue(s) is/are and why certain individuals have been excluded, and those present should be afforded an opportunity to state their view on whether the issues should be heard only in the presence of those invited in. The panel will require to consider such representations and should decide whether to proceed as planned or to reconvene the hearing with a different membership. The panel may even need to adjourn briefly to make that decision. In most cases, however, the parties will be content to have the preliminary issues discussed in a limited hearing, and to relay the content of that discussion to the other relevant individuals. Where a limited hearing is held, a summary of what was discussed, as well as the decision, should be intimated orally by the Convener to the tribunal participants once the tribunal as a whole reconvenes. The proceedings during limited hearings should, as with all tribunal proceedings, be tape recorded. This applies even where the issues discussed in the limited hearing are sensitive since it is someone else's decision whether to transcribe; the decision on whether to tape record does not allow automatic access by any party to the transcript later.[72]

ABSENCE OF A TRIBUNAL MEMBER

3.48   The tribunal system is designed to ensure that, except where the Rules allow for a decision to be taken by a Convener alone, all decisions are taken by a panel of three members consisting of a Convener, a

---

[72] On the tape recording of proceedings generally, and the issue of transcripts, see paras 3.175 *et seq* below.

medical member and a general member. The question arises: what happens if one or more of the members allocated to a case cannot, for some reason, attend at the hearing, or for the duration of the hearing? The Rules provide that a decision shall not be taken unless all members of the panel are present.[73] However, certain solutions are provided for in this situation:

(1) Where the absence issue arises only on the day of the hearing (for example illness or travel difficulties for the panel member) the case could be adjourned to a later date to allow the full panel (or a different full panel) to take the decision:[74] this would be the last resort since it would involve delay and the tribunal is obliged to act as expeditiously and efficiently as possible.[75]

(2) Where the absence issue arises only on the day of the hearing, the case could be referred to another tribunal panel to allow the decision to be taken that day.[76] This solution might involve another panel or panel member travelling to cover the case on the same day once their scheduled case(s) have been dealt with. There seems no reason why the reformed panel needs to consist entirely of new members, it might be a mixture of the original panel members and (a) new member(s). In fact, such a mixture seems sensible, since the members who were allocated the case originally will be likely to have carried out some preparatory work; it would be undesirable for the substitute panel to all be coming to the case entirely fresh and at short notice. The alternative would be to draft in a suitable member who is based locally and who can reach the venue at short notice.

(3) Where the absence issue arises before the day of the hearing, due to a member ceasing to be a member of the tribunal or being unable otherwise to act as a tribunal member at the hearing, the President (in practice, the MHTS scheduling staff) is permitted to allocate the hearing to a differently constituted tribunal.[77] Much here will depend on the timescale involved, but any new panel should, for the reason identified in para (2) above, consist of a mixture of some of the original panel members plus a substitute for the missing member(s). This situation may arise due to a member taking an illness or being incapacitated in some way in advance of the hearing so that some warning is able to be given of the inability to attend.

---

[73] Rule 64(1).
[74] *Ibid.*
[75] This is part of the overriding objective in r 4.
[76] Rule 64(1).
[77] Rule 64(2).

(4) Where the hearing commences, and a member (not the Convener) is absent for any reason during it, the remainder of the case may be heard by the other two members, as long as all parties consent to this. Such a hearing will be regarded as properly constituted.[78] The most likely explanation here would be where a tribunal member becomes ill during the hearing and cannot continue to sit until the decision is made. Where all parties do not consent to the two remaining members sitting, or where the absent member is the Convener, the general rule applies, and a decision cannot be made: the hearing will have to be adjourned or referred to another tribunal.[79] This could cause some extreme difficulties where, for instance, the hearing of a CTO application is held on the last possible day, and where another panel (or another panel member) is not available to sit in the case. Such a course of events would be, of course, very unlikely to occur, and there will almost always be a substitute member(s) available, even if this means a hearing taking place into the evening.

3.49   Where the solution resorted to is to draft in another member(s) to plug the gap in the panel caused by the absence, that member would have to be of the same type (medical, general or Convener) as the missing member he replaces.

3.50   Where the absence of a member is temporary, the hearing can be started late (or adjourned until a later time in the same day) in order to avoid triggering the rules above. In practical terms, any fresh allocation/re-allocation of members to cover a gap would be directed by MHTS headquarters, under the guidance of the Clerk.

ABSENCE OF A "RELEVANT PERSON"

3.51   This should always be dealt with as a preliminary issue. The rules define "relevant person" as including a party or any other person who sends a notice of response under the Rules.[80] The word "party" is further defined[81] and for the most part will comprise the patient, the MHO or RMO (depending on which is the applicant) the named person, and any person who has been added as a party following an application under r 48 of the Rules.

3.52   From a practical point of view, the tribunal will usually enquire with those who are present (particularly any representative of the missing person) as to the likelihood of the person attending. Where

---

[78] Rule 64(3).
[79] Rule 64(1), which would apply where all of the conditions in r 64(3) are not satisfied.
[80] Rule 2(1). On the definition generally, see para 2.16.
[81] *Ibid.*

no information on this is available, or where such information is incomplete, the tribunal Clerk should be asked to try to contact that individual by telephone. There is no obligation on the tribunal to follow this course of action but, in the context of employment tribunal proceedings, it has been held that the tribunal should at least consider such a course and in cases where there is some information available to the tribunal that the party intended to appear, but has perhaps forgotten to do so or has potentially been delayed in arriving, very good reasons would have to be given for not attempting to contact that person by telephone.[82] A similar course of action has been urged in the context of immigration tribunal proceedings.[83]

There are two main categories of reason for the absence of such   **3.53**
a person: (1) inability to attend; and (2) other reason for non-attendance.

Inability of relevant person to attend: r 71

This occurs where there is evidence, either in the papers, or provided   **3.54**
orally by someone who is present, that a relevant person is unable to attend. This may be as a result of illness, age, incapacity or other sufficient cause.[84] Where any of these reasons applies, the Convener may make arrangements for deciding the case fairly and may, in particular, arrange for the provision of a signed statement by the absent relevant person or for the provision of evidence in any other form as seen fit by the tribunal,[85] or to enable the relevant person to make representations on the evidence.[86] These provisions are very wide, and allow the tribunal a significant discretion to take evidence in almost any way, as long as the method of taking evidence will allow the tribunal's decision to be made fairly, and as long as the measures adopted comply with the overriding objective in r 4. So, the taking of evidence over the telephone might be permitted, as long as the evidence can be heard by all other relevant persons in the room and as long as there is sufficient opportunity for cross-examination of the witness to take place. There are numerous examples in the determinations of

---

[82] See the cases of *Cooke v Glenrose Fish Co Ltd* [2004] IRLR 866 and *Southwark LBC v Bartholomew* [2004] ICR 358.
[83] *R (on the application of Karagoz) v IAT* [2003] EWHC 1228 and *R (Simeer) v IAT* [2003] EWHC 2683.
[84] Rule 71(1). On the definition of "sufficient cause" generally, see para 3.59.
[85] Rule 71(1)(a).
[86] Rule 71(1)(c). The rule (unlike r 70) refers to the Convener being satisfied. This means that the rule could be triggered by the actions of an in-house Convener (see para 2.11) and, technically, if the rule is being considered at a hearing, only the Convener needs to be satisfied. In practice, in the latter situation, the decision as to the application of r 71 will be taken by the tribunal panel. Reference is therefore made here to the tribunal being satisfied.

evidence being taken over the telephone, and this should be considered where there has been an inability to attend. However, care should be taken in such cases to alert the relevant person in advance of the impending telephone call, to allow the tribunal to seek his permission to take evidence in this way (the tribunal has no power to force such a procedure on the witness) and to ensure that the quality of any speaker on the telephone being used is sufficient to allow everyone in the hearing actually to hear the content of the evidence being given. If this is not the case, this could lead to an argument later that r 71(1) was breached since the arrangements made were not such as to allow a decision to be made fairly. In addition, it could be argued that the overriding objective was not met in such a case.[87] The same opportunity to cross-examine the witness over the telephone should be available to all parties as would be the case if the witness were giving his evidence live. It could be argued that the stilted, interrupted, unclear or confusing nature of a telephone session hindered this process, again leading to arguments of a breach of r 71(1) and/or r 4 of the Rules. Also, representations should be heard on whether, in the absence of a relevant person, his evidence should be taken by telephone. If the tribunal simply makes that decision without reference to the parties present, there could be an argument that the hearing was conducted unfairly, in contravention of r 4 of the Rules. Care should be taken to explain to the recipient of the telephone call that the proceedings are being recorded.

3.55   Another method of taking evidence from a relevant person unable to attend is via video-conferencing equipment. From the tribunal determinations examined by the authors, it is clear that evidence has been taken by this method where one or more of the parties is situated in a remote area, and where attendance at a tribunal venue would be costly and inconvenient. In such cases, the tribunal could make the decision that non-attendance of a relevant person because of cost of travel and inconvenience represents "sufficient cause" in terms of r 71(1) of the Rules. The Rules explicitly envisage the use of video-conferencing in the context of r 71.[88] As with a proposal to take evidence by telephone, representations on this proposed method should be taken, and (again as with telephone evidence) care should be taken on how the evidence is delivered, and that the technology does not significantly impair the process that would usually apply were the evidence to be given live. For obvious reasons, the application for evidence to be led in this way will have to be made in advance of the hearing, so that advance arrangements can be made for the equipment

---

[87] Rule 4. On the overriding objective generally, see para 1.26.
[88] Rule 71(2). The reference there is to evidence by "video link", but it seems clear that this would include video-conferencing.

to be set up, assuming of course that the tribunal agrees that evidence should be led in this way. Any such application, if granted, would lead to a direction being issued by the tribunal under r 49(1)(g)(iii) of the Rules. Video-conferencing has been used extensively in immigration appeal proceedings, with parties' representatives appearing in Glasgow and addressing a tribunal located in London.

There might be other methods of enabling the relevant person who   3.56
is absent through inability to attend to make representations, such as by taking these from a representative, for example a lawyer, advocacy worker or other person nominated by the relevant person. Such an arrangement would probably be limited in its effectiveness, as the opportunity for clarification of any points, cross-examination of the relevant person and for dealing with points not covered by the script provided to the representative might be diminished in comparison with the situation where the relevant person is personally present. However, it might be that such a method of taking evidence is, in the circumstances of the case, best suited for deciding the case fairly.

The Rules envisage a decision being made by the tribunal simply to   3.57
decide the case "in the absence of" the relevant person.[89] Given that this provision is one option that applies only where the relevant person is unable to attend the hearing, this should be taken as a reference to the absence of any measure taken under r 71(1)(a)–(c) or under the first para of r 71(1). The tribunal must still be satisfied that it can reach a decision in the case fairly[90] and that the overriding objective in r 4 can be complied with.[91] The tribunal might be satisfied that such a course of action is appropriate in a number of circumstances. For instance, the views of the relevant person might be adequately represented in the advance papers, for example by the MHO in his application. Alternatively, someone who is present may be able to give evidence as to the views of the missing relevant person. As long as the tribunal is satisfied that these views are being reliably represented as the comprehensive and current opinions of the relevant person on all pertinent issues, this could be a reason for proceeding down the r 71(1)(d) route.

Where the tribunal is considering making a decision in the absence   3.58
of a relevant person who is unable to attend, it should consider what the alternative is. If, by adopting a measure under r 71(1), first paragraph or r 71(1)(a)–(c), this would lead to a delay in determining the application before it, the consequences of such a delay should be considered as part of the fairness criterion. The need to provide a speedy hearing where Art 5(4) ECHR applies is also of some

---

[89] Rule 71(1)(d).
[90] Rule 71(1), first para.
[91] For a discussion of the overriding objective generally, see para 1.26.

importance here. "Fairness" here would refer to fairness to all of the parties, including the MHO/RMO and the named person, as well as the patient. It might be that an interim order could be put in place to maintain the *status quo*, and that it would be fair to the MHO/RMO making the application that this happens.

3.59   In appropriate cases, the tribunal will require to decide whether the reason advanced for the absence constitutes "sufficient cause" and this will vary from case to case. It seems sensible to include within this phrase any mishap which is not due to the fault of the party, or any other commitment (such as a work commitment) which the party could not cancel or re-arrange. The cost and/or inconvenience of travel to the hearing venue might also be accepted as sufficient cause. It has been held, in the context of employment tribunal proceedings, that where a party cannot attend through no fault of his own, this should usually lead to an adjournment "however inconvenient it may be to the tribunal ... and to the other parties".[92]

3.60   It should be noted that the options set out in r 71(1)(a)–(d) are not exhaustive, and where the tribunal wishes to adopt a method which cannot be fitted into any of these options, but which still is the best arrangement in the circumstances for deciding the case fairly, it is free to adopt that course of action.[93] Of course, as ever, representations should be invited on the proposal first.

3.61   The application of r 71 is predicated on the tribunal being satisfied that the inability to attend is for one of the reasons set out there. This means that there should be some evidence before the tribunal to suggest that r 71 applies. Again, in the Court of Appeal case of *Teinaz* v *London Borough of Wandsworth* it was emphasised that the tribunal "is entitled to be satisfied that the inability of the litigant to be present is genuine"[94] before granting an adjournment even in a case where the reason advanced does not, on the face of it, suggest any fault on the part of that litigant. The court goes on to stress that the burden of proof of such genuineness lies with the party seeking the adjournment. Where the initial evidence provided is insufficient, an opportunity to provide such evidence should be given before the case is proceeded with.[95] In addition, it has been

---

[92] Gibson LJ in the Court of Appeal case of *Teinaz* v *London Borough of Wandsworth* [2002] EWCA Civ 1040; [2002] IRLR 721 at para 21.

[93] This is clear from the use of the words "and in particular may arrange" in r 71(1).

[94] Note 92 above, at para 21 per Gibson LJ.

[95] This is taken from the events that unfolded before the employment tribunal in *Andreou* v *Lord Chancellor's Department* [2002] EWCA Civ 1192; [2002] IRLR 728, where the tribunal was held by the Court of Appeal to have acted fairly in allowing the missing party two opportunities to satisfy it on the medical evidence before striking out the claim.

held that medical evidence should be presented when a party cannot attend for medical reasons and that the medical evidence should refer to an inability to attend the tribunal; evidence of an inability to work may not suffice, unless it is obvious that the medical condition preventing the party from working would also, necessarily, prevent attendance at the tribunal.[96]

Where the tribunal is not so satisfied, it may deal with the absence under r 70 (see below). However, even where the tribunal is satisfied that the relevant person cannot attend for one of the reasons set out in r 71(1), this does not seem to compel the application of that rule, since the wording of the rule is permissive (the use of the word "may" in line two as opposed to "shall"). However, it is submitted that the first use of the word "may" in that rule should effectively be read as "shall" since the rule must be placing an obligation on the Convener to make such arrangements as may appear best suited in all the circumstances of the case. The second use of the word "may" is permissive, since it refers to a number of suggested measures, but this is not an exhaustive list (indicated by the use of "in particular"). Of course, the arrangements that best suit the situation may involve simply proceeding with the case in the absence of that relevant person, without resort to any other measure. While this is a competent course of action under the rule (as long as the tribunal considers the situation and makes that decision, without ignoring the rule) it would be appropriate only in the most extreme cases, for example where a decision must be made that day and where there is no other way the views of the relevant person can be obtained that day.   **3.62**

Where there is no alternative way to take the evidence of the missing relevant person on the day of the hearing, and the tribunal does not wish to proceed in the absence of that person, the only alternative will be to adjourn the hearing until a later date under r 65. The general comments on the power to adjourn in that rule, above, apply here. More specifically, it is clear that where the tribunal is aware that a relevant person intends to appear but cannot for some reason beyond his power (such as bad weather, but not illness, which is dealt with above) an adjournment should usually be granted.[97] One not uncommon situation arises where the RMO or MHO is   **3.63**

---

[96] See the Court of Appeal decision in *Andreou v Lord Chancellor's Department* [2002] EWCA Civ 1192; [2002] IRLR 728. In that case the medical condition was anxiety and stress. See also the immigration tribunal case of *R v IAT, ex p Baira* [1994] Imm AR 487 and the Court of Appeal case of *Deen-Koroma v IAT* [1997] Imm AR 242.

[97] For a case involving inability to attend due to bad weather, see *Priddle v Fisher & Sons* [1968] 3 All ER 506, a decision on an employment tribunal case.

unable to attend personally, sending someone who is less familiar with the case, or sending no one since no one else is familiar with it. The latter situation should, in all but the most exceptional cases, be avoided, but, depending on the reason for the non-attendance of the party, and the extent of the written evidence of that party that is available, if the tribunal does not want to proceed in the absence of that party, an adjournment should be allowed.[98]

Failure of a relevant person to attend: r 70

3.64   Where a relevant person does not attend, and where r 71 does not apply, the absence of that person should be dealt with in accordance with r 70 of the Rules. The first point to note is that the case can be decided in the absence of any relevant person. However, this may be done only where the following conditions are met:

(1) where the tribunal is satisfied that the relevant person was duly notified of the hearing;[99] and

(2) that there is no good reason for the absence of the relevant person;[100] and

(3) that any written representations submitted by the absent relevant person in response to the notice of hearing must be considered.[101]

3.65   Where the relevant person is also a party,[102] these three conditions apply, but in addition the tribunal requires to afford the party an opportunity to be heard either by the Convener alone or with such other members as the tribunal may direct to explain his absence and to advise whether the party wishes to proceed.[103]

3.66   Before we deal with these conditions, it is worth considering what the rule means when it refers to "hear and decide the proceedings" in r 70(1), and "before deciding any case" in r 70(2). It is submitted that these phrases refer to a final decision on the application/appeal before the tribunal, and not an interim one. So, where the tribunal wishes to adjourn the hearing to allow a relevant person to attend, it could decide to grant an interim order in the meantime, assuming

---

[98] A not dissimilar situation arose in the Employment Appeal Tribunal case of *Masters of Beckenham Ltd* v *Green* [1977] ICR 535. See also the President's Guidance 1/07, reproduced in Appendix 4.
[99] Rule 70(1).
[100] *Ibid.*
[101] Rule 70(2).
[102] As defined in r 2(1). See para 2.16 above.
[103] Rule 70(3).

that one is competent, and assuming that it is satisfied that one is appropriate. This interpretation is not only sensible from a practical point of view, but it also is a reasonable interpretation of the words used, since "the proceedings" and "any case" seem to refer to the whole application/appeal, and not just the decision at the end of one hearing. To put it another way, r 70 will not apply unless the tribunal is making a final decision on the application/appeal.

Dealing with each of these conditions in turn, it is clear that the word "duly" in r 70(1) refers to adequate notice. Where there is some evidence that notice of the hearing was sent to the relevant person, but outwith the prescribed notice period in the relevant rule,[104] the tribunal will have to consider carefully whether to proceed to make a final decision in the absence of the relevant person. However, it may still do so as "due" notice in this context means, it is submitted, adequate notice, and this could be less than the prescribed period, depending on the circumstances. Where the relevant person has been in touch with the Tribunal headquarters or with someone else who attends the hearing to advise that he will not be able to attend, clearly notice of the hearing has reached that person and, depending on the explanation given for the intended absence, the issue might have to be determined under r 71. Clearly, where there is some doubt over whether the relevant person has received notice at all, the tribunal must tread very carefully indeed, and any final decision on the application/appeal in these circumstances would be vulnerable to appeal.[105]

3.67

On condition (2), the tribunal will have to consider whether there is a good reason for the absence of the relevant person before making a final decision in the case. Clearly, if no reason at all is advanced for the absence of the relevant person, either by that person (for example in writing) or by anyone else on his behalf, the tribunal can be satisfied that there is no good reason for the absence, assuming that any efforts made to contact the missing person have been fruitless.[106] However, where a reason is advanced, the tribunal will require to assess whether or not it is a "good" one. If the decision is that the reason advanced is "good" then the tribunal will be in breach of r 70(1) if a final decision in the case is made at that hearing. In such circumstances, the decision will be vulnerable to an appeal. If the reason advanced is not "good", the tribunal may simply proceed to make a final decision even in the absence of the relevant person. It is difficult to say with any degree of precision what will constitute a

3.68

---

[104] On the notification requirements generally, see paras 6.05 *et seq*.
[105] On appeals generally, see Chapter 8.
[106] Such efforts should usually be made: see the comments at paras 3.52 and 3.78.

"good reason", but any reason which is influenced to a significant degree by the fault of the relevant party might not be regarded as a "good reason"; anything else probably does qualify as a "good reason".

3.69   Condition (3) is largely self-explanatory; any written response should be considered by the tribunal, although the weight to be afforded to it in the absence of an opportunity to clarify any points, and in the absence of any cross-examination, might be minimal.

3.70   The additional requirement in r 70(3) applies where the absent relevant person is also a party. This provision seems to require the tribunal to give that person the opportunity to explain why they were absent and to indicate whether or not they intend to take part in the proceedings, presumably before a final decision is made in the case. This is rather confusing, as this cuts across the facility in r 70(1) to proceed to hear the case in the absence of the relevant person (including a party who is a relevant person, as parties are not excluded from r 70(1)). The only way to make sense of r 70, when taken as a whole, is to apply r 70(1) to any relevant person who is not a party, to apply r 70(2) to all relevant persons, whether or not a party, and to apply r 70(3) only to a relevant person who is a party. If this interpretation is not adopted, r 70(1) and (3) do not correspond.

3.71   In a case where r 70(3) applies, and where the party is a patient who is in the community or someone who is not the patient (such as a named person or MHO) the strict application of the rule would necessitate an adjournment of the case, perhaps with the imposition of an interim order. If this approach were to be adopted, this could cause the adjournment of many hearings, since although the MHO and the patient are usually present, the named person is often not. It should be remembered that the named person is a party under the rules.[107] The problem is that r 70(3) uses the word "shall", which seems to make such a procedure mandatory. However, there is a way to interpret r 70(3) which would avoid an adjournment in a large number of cases. Rule 70(3) could be regarded as a provision which applies only where it can be followed on the day of the hearing. So, where the missing party (for instance a named person) can be contacted by telephone, the provision could be complied with. However, where there is no opportunity to contact the missing party on the day of the hearing, r 70(3) flies off. The wording of r 70(3) would support this interpretation, as it refers to the possibility of the party being heard "by the Convener alone or with such other members as the Tribunal may direct". The tribunal members only gather on the day of the hearing, and may never sit together again

---

[107] See the definition of "party" in r 2(1).

on the same case.[108] This points to the application of that provision being restricted to the day of the hearing. This would avoid the need to adjourn in every case to allow the rule to be complied with. However, this does not mean that an adjournment to comply with r 70(3) would never be justified. For instance, such an adjournment might be appropriate where the patient, who is in the community, was expected to attend, but could not and where he is not contactable on the day. Another such situation might be where a named person has expressed views either in writing to the tribunal or via another person, such as the MHO, and where the tribunal wishes the named person to clarify certain points, and where he is not contactable on the day. In any such case consideration will, of course, be given to whether an interim order is competent and appropriate.

Perhaps the most common application of r 70(3) is where the patient has not attended and where he is, at the time of the hearing, in hospital, perhaps under an STDC. It is not unusual to find that a patient refuses to attend the hearing in person. This might be for a variety of reasons, such as a mistrust of the tribunal system, a failure to understand the importance of the hearing or simply that the patient is too stressed and frightened to attend. Of course, a tribunal hearing is a stressful event for all concerned, but perhaps in particular for the patient, whose liberty is often at stake. The strict application of r 70(3) would suggest that the Convener (or another tribunal member, all of the tribunal members or some of them) should descend on the patient in the ward where the patient is and ask him to explain why he does not wish to attend and to explain what his position is on the application/appeal being decided upon. The trouble with the wording of the rule is that it suggests that such a visit is compulsory. However, this is not the case. The rule only requires that the patient be *given an opportunity* to be heard by the tribunal. The minimum required to comply with this rule is that a message be sent by the tribunal via the MHO, RMO, patient's representative or other person present that the tribunal wishes to visit the patient to speak with him. If the patient refuses, or if the patient does not consent to such a visit, the tribunal could be satisfied that r 70(3) has been complied with. The tribunal may take the view that a sufficient opportunity to attend has already been afforded to the patient and that any further attempt might be pointless or even counter-productive. This would technically be a breach of r 70(3), although the tribunal could explain that, in doing so, it was furthering the overriding objective. 3.72

Where the patient has expressed the view that he would consent to such a visit, this does not mean that the tribunal is obliged to 3.73

---

[108] On the issue of continuity of panel members in subsequent hearings in the same case, see paras 3.28 *et seq.*

carry one out, although it would have to be very careful in refusing to comply with the rule in such circumstances. In considering the question of what to do in the absence of a patient who is in hospital, it would be appropriate to find out from the MHO and RMO why the patient does not wish to attend/cannot attend. It may be that the patient is so ill that any attendance would be pointless, since the patient would not be able to participate in any meaningful way in the hearing. In such a case, it may even be appropriate to deal with the situation as one falling under r 71(1). In that provision, discussed above, "illness" could encompass mental illness and "incapacity" could include mental incapacity. In addition, there is the possibility of relying on "other sufficient cause". However, r 71 applies only where the situation of the patient would cause the patient to be *unable to attend*, not unable to participate, so the tribunal would have to be selective in the use of this rule. It might be possible to argue that the physical state of a patient makes attendance impossible. Whatever the reason(s) is/are, these should be established first. In addition, it is relevant to know whether the view has been formed that the patient has capacity to enable him to take part in the proceedings. The RMO will have expressed his view on capacity as part of the CTO application. If it is not a case where a CTO application is under consideration, the RMO could be asked to express a view on the capacity issue. Again, the answer might trigger the application of r 71(1), but once again that rule is triggered where there is an inability to attend. Finally, the impact of any visit by the tribunal panel (or some of them) should be considered; the RMO and MHO might well have views on this. For instance, they may view such a visit as being pointless, since the patient has clearly indicated over a period of time that he does not wish to attend. It may be that such a visit might, in the view of the RMO, cause distress to the patient. After considering these questions, and after taking representations on the question of whether such a visit is wise, the tribunal will require to decide whether it would like to try to carry such a visit out.

3.74   Where the patient does not consent to such a visit, the tribunal will require to consider whether to proceed to make a final decision on the application/appeal that day. Of course, the tribunal could adjourn the hearing in the hope that at the next hearing the patient will be able and willing to attend. However, this step should be taken only where there is evidence to suggest that there is a real chance of this happening, and should not be a step taken in hope.

Where there is no named person

3.75   In all cases where there is no named person present, enquiries must be made by the tribunal to ascertain whether a named person has been identified under the 2003 Act; if not, why not; and, if so, who that person is and why he is not in attendance. The tribunal should not be tempted simply to ignore the absence of a named person, even in cases where it is clear that no one wishes the named person to be involved in the case; such involvement or lack of it is not in the gift of any of the parties (or all of them collectively); the named person is a party and so the tribunal must make the appropriate enquiries, otherwise its decision could be open to appeal later by the named person or even by the patient.

A full discussion of the provisions relating to the named person **3.76** is not properly within the scope of this work, although there are some very useful sources of information on this subject.[109] However, one common situation involving the named person deserves some coverage here. Sometimes, where a patient has not nominated a named person, he will have no default named person, in which case the tribunal should simply note this and proceed. There is no need for someone to have a named person at all. However, very often the patient will not have nominated a named person and there will be a default named person in place. It is not uncommon in this situation to find that the default named person does not wish to be involved in the case and/or the patient does not wish that person to have the role of named person. It may be the case that the relationship between the patient and the default named person is a distant or even acrimonious one or that the default named person has lost touch with the patient, due perhaps to the geographical distance between them. Whatever the situation, the view might be formed by the MHO and/or the patient that the default named person is not an appropriate person to be in that role. In such cases, an application can be made to the tribunal by any one of a number of persons, including the MHO and the patient, for a declaration that the default named person (in this situation referred to as the "apparent named person" in the 2003 Act) is not the named person.[110] The tribunal, if satisfied that such an order should be granted, can either do so and make no further order (leaving the patient with no named person) or grant the order with a further order appointing another default named person in place of the one just removed.[111] In many cases, there is no obvious substitute

---

[109] Code of Practice, vol 1, pp 82–93. See also the following publications by the Scottish Executive/Government: "The New Mental Health Act: A Guide to Named Persons" (2004); "The Mental Health (Care and Treatment) (Scotland) Act 2003: Are you a named person? A Guide Supporting the Role of the Named Person" (2008); and A Dawson *et al*, "An analysis of the operation of the 'named person' in the operation of mental health legislation" (2009).

[110] 2003 Act, s 255(6), (7)(b)(ii), s 256(1)(b) and s 257(2).

[111] *Ibid*, s 257(2)(b).

candidate, so the former situation is more common than the latter. The legislation does seem to require that a request for such an order is made, rather than a decision coming from the tribunal acting on its own initiative. It is rare for a patient or an MHO to come to the hearing prepared to make a request for such an order with reference to the legislation, but there is nothing to prevent the tribunal from suggesting to the MHO that a request for such an order can be made, as long as all parties are heard on such a request. Such a prompt from the tribunal should occur only once the tribunal has ascertained that there are good arguments in favour of such an application being made.

ABSENCE OF A WITNESS OTHER THAN A RELEVANT PERSON

3.77   The Rules do not specifically deal with the absence of someone who is not a relevant person.[112] This does not mean that the tribunal should simply ignore the absence of someone who might be expected to have relevant information. Where a party is of the view that someone who is not in attendance should be heard before a final decision on the application/appeal is made, the tribunal will require to hear representations on whether or not to adjourn to allow evidence to be taken from that person and, if not, whether the evidence can be taken in some other way. In order to consider whether the tribunal should take any steps to secure the evidence of the witness, it will be relevant to know, of course, the reason for his non-attendance. It will also be highly relevant to know whether the evidence of the witness is truly essential to the disposal of the case. For example, the view might be taken that the evidence, while relevant, might simply repeat evidence already available to the tribunal either from another witness or in the advance papers. Alternatively, the tribunal could form the view that while the evidence would be relevant and not repetitive, it would have little bearing on the case in hand. In such cases, the tribunal could simply refuse to adjourn the case or attempt to have the evidence of the witness taken in any other way. The tribunal is given wide discretion to exclude evidence for a number of reasons, and these powers are discussed elsewhere.[113] It should be noted that rr 70 and 71 do not apply to such a witness, so the tribunal has a wide discretion as to what to do in such cases. Of course, that discretion is tempered by the need to comply with the overriding objective in r 4, and in particular the need to secure that proceedings are handled as fairly as possible.

---

[112] Unless that person has been cited as a witness by the tribunal, in which case the provisions in r 59 apply.
[113] See r 49(1)(g) and the discussion on it at para 5.03.

On the other hand, this objective also refers to the importance of being expeditious and efficient, and to delay proceedings (even on the day, and certainly in the form of an adjournment to another day) might cut across these imperatives. As ever, the question is a balancing act.

If the tribunal considers that the evidence of the witness should be heard, it could grant an adjournment. Where an adjournment is granted for this purpose, the tribunal will need to consider whether or not to make an interim order. Alternatively, the tribunal could canvass views on whether the witness can be and should be contacted to give evidence by telephone that day. The dangers inherent in such evidence are discussed above and apply here with equal force.[114] Another alternative might be to explore the possibility of contacting the witness to find out if he can attend later in the day. This will depend upon whether the witness is within easy travelling distance and if he is available to attend. In any event, some effort should always be made to contact the witness where he was expected to attend and where his evidence is deemed important to the resolution of the issues in the case.[115] The tribunal may even "part hear" the case: in other words, take all other evidence that day and adjourn the case to another day (perhaps even the following day) to take the evidence of the missing witness. This may seem a superficially attractive option, since it avoids everyone who is present coming back another day, and avoids the cost of having another full tribunal hearing. However, such an approach is beset with problems. The tribunal members will all have to be available for the adjourned hearing. The other attendees will arguably have to attend again at the adjourned hearing since the tribunal or a party may wish to ask supplementary questions arising from the evidence of the new witness. Then there is the difficulty that the new witness will not have heard at first hand the evidence of the other witnesses, and again this could lead to a disadvantage to the party seeking to call that witness. The tribunal would have to be very careful indeed before going down the route of a "part-heard" hearing, although such a hearing would be competent under the wide powers of the tribunal to regulate its own procedure.[116]

3.78

Where the evidence due to be given is expert evidence, the tribunal must tread especially carefully in considering whether it should be heard. The most common situation in this area is where the

3.79

---

[114] See above at para 3.54.

[115] See the cases of *Cooke*, *Bartholomew* and *Karagoz*, all discussed above at para 3.52 in the context of contacting a party by telephone who has not turned up. It would be good practice for tribunals to adopt the same procedure where an important witness is missing.

[116] See rr 49(1), 52(1) and 63(2) for the main examples of this wide power.

patient has (usually through his lawyer) instructed the preparation of an independent psychiatric report. Although this is not strictly consideration of a missing witness situation (since the independent expert will not usually attend to speak to his report) the situation is akin to that of a missing witness. Where the tribunal has previously adjourned the case for such a report to be prepared and lodged and it is not yet ready at the adjourned hearing, unless the tribunal decides to "part hear" the case (probably unwise in this situation – see above) it is virtually inconceivable that the tribunal would decide not to adjourn again, unless, of course, a significant reason for the non-production of the report is the fault of the party himself. It is hard to envisage such a situation, and the safer course would be to adjourn again, and give consideration to whether an interim order is needed in the meantime. The view should not be taken that since there is expert evidence available on the points in question already, from the RMO, further expert evidence is unnecessary; in this sense, expert evidence is distinct from factual evidence, as it cannot, in the same way, be repetitive, since it is opinion evidence. The whole point of such evidence is that it is the opinion of a particular skilled person.[117]

3.80   The tribunal's case management powers should also be borne in mind here. The tribunal can, either on the application of a relevant person or on its own iniative, issue a citation to a witness.[118] This may be necessary if there is evidence to suggest that the witness will not co-operate by attending voluntarily. It is an offence to fail without reasonable excuse to comply with such a citation.[119]

WHERE THE APPLICANT/APPELLANT FAILS TO APPEAR

3.81   From the determinations reviewed by the authors as well as from their own experiences, it is clear that there have been cases in which the applicant has not appeared, namely (to cite the main examples) the MHO in connection with a CTO application; the RMO in connection with an application to extend and vary a CTO; or the patient in connection with an appeal or a review application. Where information is available to the tribunal that there is a reason for the non-attendance of such a party, r 71 might apply.[120] If not, r 70 will apply.[121] Where there seems no good reason for

---

[117] On opinion evidence generally, see paras 5.102 et seq.
[118] Rule 61(1).
[119] Schedule 2, para 12(3) to the 2003 Act. These provisions are discussed elsewhere at para 3.80.
[120] See paras 3.54 et seq above on this.
[121] See paras 3.64 et seq above on this.

the non-attendance of the applicant/appellant, one view is that the application or appeal should simply be refused. However, r 70(1) indicates that even where that provision is triggered, the tribunal can "hear and decide" the application in that person's absence. It is submitted that this should be done in all such cases where an adjournment is not allowed, unless there is no information before the tribunal from which a decision can be made. It would be rare for a tribunal hearing to take place in circumstances where no one attends. However, in at least one case, only a member of ward staff attended in an application to extend and vary a CTO. The tribunal took the view that, from the papers and the information provided by the member of ward staff, an interim order extending and varying the CTO should be granted. This is a perfectly sensible approach where there is sufficient information available to allow such a decision to be made, although the interim order should be as short as possible while allowing an adequate opportunity for the applicant to appear; in the case cited, the interim order was granted for 14 days.

FURTHER DOCUMENTS REQUIRED

Sometimes, it will be apparent from a perusal of the advance papers   3.82
that insufficient information is available to enable the tribunal to decide the case on the hearing date. It is important that such a matter is dealt with as a preliminary matter since the hearing may have to be adjourned to another date (or at least until later in the day) to allow further documentary evidence to be produced. Such deficiencies in the papers available might take one of three forms.

In the first form, there will be papers missing from those made   3.83
available to the tribunal. It is important to note that there are regulations prescribing the documentation that should accompany certain applications, namely applications under ss 92, 95 and 96 of the 2003 Act, in relation to CTOs[122] and applications under ss 149, 158 and 161 of the 2003 Act in relation to compulsion orders.[123] Where the documents specified in any of these regulations are not present with the advance papers, the tribunal could order their production. This might not necessitate an adjournment since the documents might be available then and there, or perhaps later in the day, from the MHO or RMO. Of course, a CTO application must be accompanied by two mental health reports, covering the relevant

---

[122] Mental Health (Compulsory treatment orders – documents and reports to be submitted to the Tribunal) (Scotland) Regulations 2005 (SSI 2005/366).
[123] Mental Health (Compulsion orders – documents and reports to be submitted to the Tribunal) (Scotland) Regulations 2005 (SSI 2005/365).

material.[124] However, it should be borne in mind that although the relevant proformas[125] are invariably used, they do not have statutory status and so are not compulsory.

3.84   In the second form, although there are no prescribed papers missing from those before the tribunal, the view might be taken that certain papers that exist should be made available before a decision is taken in the case. Where such additional papers can be provided on the day, and where they are not voluminous, it may be that this difficulty can be overcome by the holder of those papers (usually the MHO or RMO) simply handing over copies to the tribunal. In such a case, the obligation to conduct proceedings fairly would dictate that a short adjournment should take place to allow those without access to the papers an opportunity to be given copies (usually by the Clerk) and to read and digest them. Where such a party is legally represented, this will necessitate an adjournment long enough to allow proper instructions to be taken on any newly available information in the documents. Where the material that is available is voluminous, the tribunal may decide to adjourn the hearing to another day, since it would not be efficient or fair to expect parties (and the tribunal members themselves) to digest and prepare the same day for a hearing where the documents would be tabled. In some cases, the material requested might not be available on the day, and here the tribunal may have to be adjourned to allow them to be made available, unless the tribunal decides to "part hear" the case, but as commented on above,[126] there are various pitfalls in such a course of action. In such a case, the tribunal will require to consider whether to make an interim order, and the adjournment would be made under r 65.[127] It would also be wise for the tribunal to issue a direction specifying the title and date of the document to be lodged, to ensure that there is no confusion over which document is required, as well as a deadline for lodging it and a requirement to intimate it by that deadline to all other parties. Ideally, this deadline should be at least one week prior to the adjourned hearing, to allow those receiving it (including the tribunal members; a copy should be ordered to be lodged at MHTS headquarters) a chance to read and digest it.

---

[124] See s 57(4) of the 2003 Act for the constituent ingredients of a mental health report.

[125] These are available on the website of the Scottish Government, Health and Community Care Department at: http://www.scotland.gov.uk/Topics/Health/health/mental-health/mhlaw/mha-Forms. The use of these forms is recommended by the Code of Practice at vol 1, introduction, para 21. On the status of the Code, see para 1.40.

[126] See para 3.78.

[127] On the application of this rule generally, see paras 3.21 et seq.

In the third type of missing documents scenario, the tribunal could   **3.85**
decide that more written information is required to allow it to be in a
position to make a decision on the case. Here, the tribunal is ordering
the preparation of fresh reports. This might be in order to obtain an
up-to-date report on the progress of the patient. In one tribunal case,
the information presented by the MHO and RMO was around a year
old, and the patient had been a long-term compulsory resident in
hospital. Although the argument was made that the patient's position
had not altered since the last time reports had been obtained, the
tribunal insisted that up-to-date information was required in order
to determine the case, and fresh reports were ordered. The view was
taken by the tribunal that it would be inefficient and potentially unfair
to attempt to take such a volume of information (developments over
a year) orally in the heat of the tribunal hearing. Various powers
are available to the tribunal authorising such a move. First of all,
where the tribunal wishes to order an expert report (for example
from an independent psychiatrist) it may do so under the provisions
of r 62(1)–(4).[128]

Alternatively, the tribunal could issue a direction requiring the   **3.86**
production of a report under r 49(1)(a). The direction would need
to specify exactly what should be included in the report, as well as
a deadline for lodging it and a requirement to intimate it by that
deadline to all other parties. Ideally, this deadline should be at least
one week prior to the adjourned hearing, to allow those receiving
it (including the tribunal members; a copy should be ordered to be
lodged at MHTS headquarters) a chance to read and digest it.

Perhaps the best route to be followed by the tribunal would be to   **3.87**
make use of the powers set out in regulations made under the 2003
Act. These regulations provide the power to order certain additional
information in the form of a report where certain applications are
before the tribunal, namely applications under ss 92, 95, 96, 98(2),
99(1), 100(2) or 101 of the 2003 Act, in relation to CTOs;[129] and
applications under ss 149, 158, 161, 163(1), 164(2) or 165(2) of the
2003 Act in relation to compulsion orders.[130] Although the regulations
derive from provisions in the 2003 Act, it would be prudent to carry
the requirements in a direction issued under r 49(1), but with direct
reference to the relevant regulation. In fact, the regulations offer
a useful tool for the framing of a direction, since the information
to be included in the relevant report is listed in the regulations, so

---

[128] On the application of these provisions, see paras 4.165 *et seq.*

[129] Mental Health (Compulsory treatment orders – documents and reports to be
submitted to the Tribunal) (Scotland) Regulations 2005 (SSI 2005/366).

[130] Mental Health (Compulsion orders – documents and reports to be submitted to
the Tribunal) (Scotland) Regulations 2005 (SSI 2005/365).

that a direction could simply refer to the relevant regulation number as opposed to setting out the specifics of the report in the decision form.[131] In addition, as with a plain r 49(1) direction, the deadline for production of the report should ideally be at least one week prior to the adjourned hearing, to allow those receiving it (including the tribunal members; a copy should be ordered to be lodged at MHTS headquarters) a chance to read and consider it.

COMPETENCY OF THE APPLICATION/APPEAL

3.88   Where there is an issue regarding whether the application or appeal is competent, this should be dealt with as a preliminary issue, and almost certainly as the first such issue. If there is a competency problem, this might lead to the proceedings ending then and there. The provision in the rules covering a misconceived case[132] seems, at first glance, to be aimed at a case where any competency problem has been noticed while the papers for the case are being processed, as opposed to at the hearing. However, the "Clerk" refers to a member of the administration at the Tribunal as well as to the clerk at the hearing.[133] So, the rule applies also to competency problems discovered for the first time by the tribunal members, or brought to their attention during the hearing by one of the parties. Although there is reference to a misconceived case being brought to the attention of the Convener by a Clerk,[134] and to the Convener having the opportunity of deciding alone whether the case is misconceived,[135] these parts of the rule will apply where a competency problem is discovered from the papers prior to the hearing.[136] In such cases, the papers will be referred to one of the in-house Conveners for a decision. Where the problem is discovered at a hearing, it will be dealt with simply as a preliminary issue. It is possible for a hearing to be fixed before a full panel on a preliminary issue such as competency,[137] but in the normal course of events the in-house Convener will simply make the decision himself.

3.89   The first ground on which an application might be regarded as misconceived is where it is outwith the jurisdiction of the tribunal. This will rarely arise and, where it does, it is likely to be picked up by

---

[131] On decision forms generally and how they are different from determinations and directions, see para 7.06.

[132] Rule 44: see a discussion on this rule at paras 3.88 *et seq.*

[133] See the definition of the "Clerk" in r 2(1).

[134] Rule 44(2).

[135] Rule 44(3).

[136] On such cases, see para 2.11.

[137] Rule 43(3) which refers to both the Convener sitting alone and the tribunal as a panel. Given that there is a defined procedure under r 44, it is arguable that such a decision is not one made under r 43, although r 43(1) covers a matter "including any matter for which specific provision is made in this Part".

the MHTS staff when the papers are processed. Applications in this category would include those which the tribunal cannot hear, such as those which do not fall under the provisions of the 2003 Act, in terms of either the subject-matter or the geographical application of the Act. Also included might be an application which is made out of time, usually because of a date calculation error (for example where an extension of an order is being sought, but the order has already expired) or where the wrong section of the 2003 Act is used, leading to the wrong proforma application[138] being filed. In such a case, the application is unlikely to be able to be rescued since the forms follow the relevant statutory provisions, and so the wrong form is unlikely to be substantively sound. Again, such applications are unlikely to reach a tribunal hearing. It may be, however, that a time limit problem will not be fatal to the competence of the application, in accordance with the *Soneji* decision, discussed elsewhere.[139]

Another possible argument on lack of jurisdiction might be that the application is not an application of the type it bears to be. Although there are no prescribed forms for any application under the 2003 Act, the Act does stipulate that applications of a certain type must contain or be accompanied by certain information. To take an example, a CTO application must be accompanied by two mental health reports.[140] Where there is only one (or none), the application is not an application under the 2003 Act at all. In such a situation, the tribunal has, on the face of it, no jurisdiction to entertain it. However, it could be argued that in applying the overriding objective, an adjournment should be granted in such a situation, in order to allow this problem to be cured by the lodging of the missing report.[141] If this course of action is followed, however, no interim order could be granted, since two mental health reports are required to support an application sufficient even for this.[142] It could be argued that even an adjournment cannot be granted and the application should be dismissed outright. This would be on the basis that it is not an application under the 2003 Act, so the tribunal has no jurisdiction at all to do anything with it (other than dismiss it). This is a very strict view, and the tribunal/Convener sitting alone in reaching that view would have to be satisfied that in doing so it was

3.90

---

[138] On the various proformas that are routinely used (but not prescribed), see paras 6.06 *et seq.*

[139] See below at paras 3.127 *et seq.*

[140] Section 63(3)(a) of the 2003 Act.

[141] This assumes that another report exists and has simply been omitted from the papers.

[142] An interim CTO can be made only where there is an application before the tribunal under s 63 of the Act: s 65(1). Section 63(3) of the Act requires such an application to be accompanied by two mental health reports (as defined in s 57(4)).

acting in accordance with the overriding objective, since it must do so when invoking any of the Rules, even a rule on dismissing a case which is outwith its jurisdiction. In such a case, unless the applicant offers to withdraw the CTO application altogether and start again, the tribunal should very carefully consider whether it would be more in keeping with the rules, and in particular the overriding objective, to allow the defect to be cured.[143]

3.91   Another problem may be that although all of the papers are before the tribunal, they may not contain the prescribed information.[144] For example, the 2003 Act requires that a CTO application and the accompanying mental health reports must contain certain information.[145] Again, the argument could be made that where one of these documents does not contain the essential information (perhaps because a box has been left blank or where it has been completed but not to the extent that it provides a bare minimum of the necessary information) the application is not a proper application at all, is outwith the jurisdiction of the tribunal and should be dismissed.[146] There is an even stronger argument here for not following this course of action, given that, unlike in the previous example of a missing mental health report, the appropriate papers are before the tribunal, but are deficient only to a limited extent. Where an adjournment is granted to provide a substitute document or to expand on the detail in the current one, an interim order could be considered where the missing information could be provided orally at the hearing. Indeed, it may even be possible to avoid an adjournment to another day where the author of the deficient document is present and is willing to amend or expand upon its content, in order to cure the problem. It would be difficult to see how the party seeking to rely on the lack of jurisdiction point could argue that any prejudice (and therefore unfairness) is caused to him, as long as sufficient time is allowed for that party (as well as all other parties) to consider the amended document before the hearing resumes.

3.92   The second basis on which a case might be said to be "misconceived" is where it is: "made otherwise in accordance with these Rules and has no reasonable prospect of success".[147] It is difficult to see what

---

[143] See later at paras 3.142 *et seq* for a fuller discussion of the consequences of problems with statutorily required documents

[144] This particular problem is discussed in more detail at paras 3.145 and 3.147 *et seq*.

[145] See s 63(3) on the documents to accompany the CTO application, as well as s 63(2) on the content of the application.

[146] See the discussion on statutorily required documents later at paras 3.142 *et seq*. This was the argument made in the case of *M v Murray* 2009 Scot (D) 8/5, although it was not successful there.

[147] Rule 44(1)(b).

this provision is aimed at. The reference to a case that falls outwith the Rules might refer to one which is defective in some way, perhaps having been lodged after the deadline set in the Rules or where it is not accompanied by certain documentation as required in the Rules. It should be noted that this ground does not cover cases where there has been some failure to follow the requirements of the 2003 Act; it refers to the tribunal Rules. On the question of what constitutes an application that has no reasonable prospect of success, this is difficult to define any further. Clearly, where there is any doubt about whether this standard is met, the safer course would be to put the case to a hearing, or proceed to deal with the case, where it is already at a hearing. What can be said is that the application/appeal does not have to be one which has no prospect of success at all, in order to satisfy this part of the provision; it simply has to lack a reasonable prospect of success. Presumably, where the application/appeal is made in accordance with the Rules, this ground of dismissal does not apply, as it contains two parts, both of which must be triggered.

The final ground for a decision that a case is misconceived is that   **3.93**
it is "frivolous or vexatious".[148] Such cases will be extremely rare, but might cover, for example, an application for appeal by a patient where the application seeks a review of a previous order on grounds that are illogical, nonsensical or irrelevant to any consideration the tribunal would be able to take account of in deciding on such an appeal. Again, cases such as this might be picked up by the MHTS prior to any hearing being fixed.

The decision that a case is misconceived on any of these three   **3.94**
grounds can be taken only by a Convener alone or by the tribunal at a hearing.[149] The MHTS staff member cannot take that decision; he must refer such a case, where suspected, to a Convener for a decision.[150] In practice, as mentioned above, this would involve a referral to an in-house Convener to take a decision.

The Convener should allow all relevant persons the opportunity   **3.95**
to be heard before making a decision on whether a case is misconceived. This can take two forms: (1) where a Convener sitting alone intends to make the decision, he should send a notice of the proposed dismissal, inviting the relevant persons to make written representations on the proposal within a specified period;[151] or (2) where the decision is being made at a tribunal hearing, all relevant persons must be heard before the decision is made.[152] In the case

---

[148] Rule 44(1)(c).
[149] Rule 44(3).
[150] Rule 44(2).
[151] Rule 44(4)(a).
[152] Rule 44(4)(b).

of option (2), where all relevant persons are not in attendance, the tribunal should adjourn and perhaps intimate in terms of situation (1) on all of the relevant persons prior to the reconvened hearing. There is no strict obligation to follow these intimation procedures prior to making such a decision, since the notice provisions (r 44(4)) are framed in permissive language ("may" and not "shall"). However, given that these procedures are set out in the Rules, an appeal against the decision on the grounds of procedural impropriety is a strong possibility, where they are not implemented.

3.96   The Convener may refer a case to the Mental Welfare Commission (MWC) where the decision is to dismiss the case; he may do so "where appropriate".[153] It is difficult to provide any generic guidance on when such a referral should be made, but where there is some issue that concerns the tribunal or in-house Convener about how the case (or preparations for it) have been conducted, and where there are issues that might merit further investigation, the Convener might consider a referral. In such cases, the issues might be matters which would have fallen under the jurisdiction of the tribunal, had the case not been misconceived, and might be issues that could have led to the making of recorded matters.[154] The tribunal, when considering making such a referral, will require to consider the scope of the MWC's jurisdiction.

REPRESENTATION

3.97   No one who appears before the tribunal (whether or not a relevant person) requires to be represented in order to be permitted to take part in the proceedings. The right of a relevant person to be represented (whether by someone legally qualified or not) or to conduct his case personally is enshrined in the Rules.[155] Where a person appearing chooses to be represented, there are, generally speaking, two main options: representation by a lawyer or by an advocacy worker.[156] Advocacy workers are discussed elsewhere.[157] The role of a legal representative is the same role as he traditionally serves in any other judicial forum, although he will have to carry out his duties in accordance with the Rules, and in particular with the overriding objective. There is a third possibility expressly recognised in the

---

[153] Rule 44(5).
[154] On recorded matters generally, see para 1.20.
[155] Rule 54.
[156] The other possible form of representation is that provided by a curator *ad litem*, but this is not representation in the usual sense of that word, and so curators are dealt with elsewhere – see paras 2.54 *et seq*.
[157] See paras 2.49 *et seq*.

Rules: representation by someone who is neither legally qualified nor an advocacy worker.[158] This will be rare in practice, but might be considered where the relevant person is nervous and perhaps not accustomed to public speaking and where he has a friend or relative who is better able and is willing to state that person's viewpoint before the tribunal. In such cases, the tribunal would be wise to check directly with the relevant person that the representative is fully authorised; this will not be a problem where the relevant person is present, but where he is not and has sent a representative, something in writing from the relevant person should be available on the day, otherwise the tribunal could be acting irregularly in assuming that the view being expressed is genuinely that of the relevant person. Of course, the tribunal should be careful, in any situation where a representative is stating the views of a relevant person, to prevent that representative from straying into evidence rather than simply representing the views of the relevant person. This is a danger that, in practice, will arise only in cases involving non-legally qualified representatives.

The Rules contain some notice provisions on representation, but these are largely ignored in practice. So, technically speaking, a relevant person should, as soon as possible, give notice of the name and address of any representative appointed.[159] Where one is not appointed, notice should be given by the relevant person of whether or not he or she intends to do so.[160] Any change of representative should be intimated to the Tribunal.[161] In practice, the tribunal will hear about any representative on the day of the hearing, particularly at a first hearing on the application or appeal. This will usually happen as those in the tribunal room introduce themselves. The authors cannot imagine any practical impact from a failure to follow these notice provisions, and as long as oral intimation is given on the day, it is difficult to see what possible prejudice can arise. The only real purpose of r 54(1) is to make sure that the Tribunal has the details of any representative so as to allow it to correspond with the representative. The dispensing power is always in any event available where an argument is made that the Rules in such a case have not been followed.[162] It would probably not be a good enough argument for an adjournment to complain that had the objector known that another relevant person had legal or other representation, that

3.98

---

[158] Rule 54(3) simply refers to the possibility of someone who is not legally qualified, so this would cover anyone in that category, including an advocacy worker.

[159] Rule 54(1).

[160] *Ibid.*

[161] Rule 54(2).

[162] On the dispensing power generally, see paras 7.48 *et seq.*

person would have obtained it also. While this might be an argument (albeit a thin one) in the public courts in a case where one party unexpectedly turns up with an advocate as a representative, relevant persons in tribunal proceedings must be taken to be aware that legal representation at least is a possibility, and this includes the patient, assuming, of course, that in the latter case, the duty under s 61(2)(c) of the 2003 Act has been complied with.

3.99   The Rules make specific provision allowing the tribunal to refuse to permit a particular person to represent a relevant person during a hearing.[163] The use of the phrase "particular person" indicates that this provision is designed to allow the tribunal to refuse to permit a particular individual to represent someone, as opposed to refusing a certain type of representation, such as non-legal representation. Where the tribunal wishes to refuse an adjournment request seeking time to obtain representation, this provision is not apposite. Instead, a request for an adjournment under r 65 should be made.[164] While cases in which the issue of the suitability of a representative will rarely arise, the informality of tribunal proceedings, and in particular the reduced involvement of legal representation in comparison with public court cases, makes this power a sensible one to have. The sole test for the exercise of this power is that the order must be made only where there is "good reason". Given the generality of this test, the discretion available to the tribunal is wide. For instance, the view might be taken that a non-legally qualified representative is too aggressive or meandering or in some other way obstructive or unhelpful to the proper conduct of the proceedings. Of course, in such cases, one would expect to see evidence of warnings and opportunities being given to behave appropriately, but where such reasonable warnings are not heeded, the power under r 54(4) might justifiably be invoked. Such a course of action might even be combined with an order excluding the representative from the proceedings.[165]

3.100   At a more general level, the power might be used to avoid a conflict of interest situation. For example, a representative who is a friend of the patient might have personal knowledge of some of the facts being spoken to in evidence. Where this happens, it may well be deemed inappropriate for that person to act as the patient's representative, whether or not he plans to give evidence, particularly where the representative uses that personal knowledge in some way to gain an

---

[163] Rule 54(4).
[164] See paras 3.21 *et seq* on the power to adjourn generally. See below on an adjournment request for this reason.
[165] Such an order can be generated under r 68, discussed elsewhere at paras 4.128 *et seq.*

advantage in his role. In the case of a legal representative, the same comments apply, although obstructive or unhelpful behaviour would be rare. However, r 54(4) applies to legal representation as much as to other types of representation. Similarly, most lawyers are acutely aware of the need to avoid a conflict of interest (for example, where a witness who will be cross-examined by the lawyer is a current or former client and where the lawyer has, as a result of representing that witness, gained some information relevant to the case) and so this will not usually be a problem. However, there can be cases where the question of whether a lawyer's interests are in conflict is open to debate. In such cases, the tribunal should encourage the lawyer to seek (and follow) advice from the Law Society of Scotland on his position and that advice could even be obtained during a short adjournment to the hearing. Where the lawyer refuses to obtain such advice or where he insists on continuing to act having obtained guidance and refuses to disclose it,[166] the tribunal might be justified in obtaining advice on the situation from the Law Society. This action could not be regarded as "evidence gathering" by the tribunal,[167] or as over-involvement in the case, given the specific power in r 54(4) and given the inquisitorial bent properly applicable to tribunal proceedings generally.[168]

There is no indication of a restriction on who may seek such an   **3.101** order, and this leaves the way open to any relevant person, as well as for the tribunal itself, where a concern arises, always, in the latter case, subject to the tribunal's duty to canvass views from all relevant persons in advance.[169]

Where an order is made under r 54(4), it would seem sensible   **3.102** that it applies from the point in time when it is announced; any representations previously made by the now removed representative (whether in writing or orally during the hearing up until that point) would have to be taken account of in the decision to be made. The tribunal should refrain from trying to eliminate any such representation from its collective mind since this would expose the decision to attack on appeal on the basis of a procedural impropriety. Of course, the person who, following such an order, is left without representation may wish to obtain an alternative representative. The tribunal will have to consider very carefully any consequent request

---

[166] He could not be ordered by the tribunal to disclose details of his communication with the Law Society of Scotland since this communication would be privileged under the lawyer–client communications privilege – see paras 5.82 *et seq* for a discussion of this privilege.

[167] For a discussion of this concept, see paras 5.22 *et seq.*

[168] On the general tenor of tribunal proceedings, see paras 1.26 *et seq.*

[169] See the general duty to do so in r 52(3)–(4), discussed generally at para 3.14.

to adjourn the hearing to a later date, and should be slow to deny such a request in any case except where the relevant person is wholly culpable (an unlikely scenario) given the importance placed on the right to representation.[170]

3.103   Rule 54(4) refers to assisting or representing. This then brings into focus the nature of representation. As discussed in relation to the role of the advocacy worker, "support" and "representation", both mentioned under the 2003 Act,[171] are clearly distinct. The same logically would apply to "assistance" and "representation" in r 54(4). In the absence of a definition of "assistance" (or "support", which might have been useful in determining the scope of "assistance") it would seem that "representation" consists of putting the case of a relevant person to the tribunal. This might simply involve stating his views without adding any additional material, or it might involve making arguments on behalf of the relevant person, where there is an element of skill on the part of the representor beyond the mere parroting of the views of the representee. Further along the scale would be full-blown legal representation. "Assistance" would seem to denote something altogether different in nature. It might mean simply helping the relevant person to prepare for the hearing by discussing with him the likely procedure and the likely issues to arise. However, only where assistance continues into the hearing itself will the tribunal be likely to become aware of it. During the hearing, someone may simply offer emotional assistance, in the sense of being an escort. Alternatively, assistance might be available to overcome or reduce any oral communication difficulties a participant in the hearing is likely to have, and there are both statutory duties[172] and provisions in the Rules[173] dealing with such difficulties. Although such assistance may not be classified as representation, r 54(4) could be invoked. This is despite the heading in the rule referring to "Representation".

3.104   Where one party (or the tribunal) notices an issue that may give rise to a discussion of a r 54(4) order, this should be canvassed as a preliminary issue as there is no point in allowing the representation to affect the merits part of the hearing in circumstances where the party representing or assisting may be refused permission to continue

---

[170] This right is well recognised as a cornerstone of the rules of natural justice, applicable in all judicial proceedings in the civilised world. However, more specific recognition is implicit in the principles in s 1 of the 2003 Act and in particular the need to take account of the views of various participants (s 1(3)(b)) and of the importance of the patient participating as fully as possible in the process (s 1(3)(c)).

[171] See the definition of "advocacy services" in s 259(4) of the 2003 Act, and the discussion of the advocacy worker at paras 2.49 et seq.

[172] 2003 Act, s 261.

[173] Rule 53, which applies only where s 261 does not. See para 4.35 on r 53.

to do so. This will depend, of course, on whether the potential issue can be foreseen; it may only become apparent during the course of the hearing, it which case it should be dealt with there and then.

Any matter falling short of an issue under r 54(4) should also, where possible, be dealt with as a preliminary issue. The most common example of such an issue is where one party wishes representation but for some reason does not have it, and wishes an adjournment in order to obtain it or to arrange for an already hired representative to attend. Such requests will have to be dealt with on a case-by-case basis. However, given the power in almost all cases to grant an interim order of some kind, allowing the *status quo* to be maintained, and given the importance of the right to be represented,[174] the tribunal would have to tread very carefully in refusing to adjourn a hearing to allow representation to be made available.

3.105

Where an adjournment request is made in order to seek or obtain legal representation, whether a lawyer is already engaged (and perhaps cannot attend due to other commitments or short notice) or not, the tribunal should be slow to refuse it, as to do so might be regarded as cutting across the principle of maximum patient participation, enshrined in s 1(3)(c) of the 2003 Act, and the requirement in the overriding objective to act fairly. The tribunal would be particularly hard pressed to refuse such an adjournment request where it could take steps to maintain the patient's current legal position in the meantime, for example by an interim order. On the other hand, the extent of efforts to find representation and any delay, without good reason, in embarking on a search for such representation could influence the tribunal's decision on this matter. The comments earlier on the power to adjourn generally under r 65 are relevant here.[175]

3.106

There has been some discussion as to whether representation need be by a lawyer in the context of the patient's rights under Art 5(4) ECHR. The Strasbourg Court summarised the law as follows in *Megyeri v Germany*:[176]

3.107

- A person of unsound mind who is compulsorily confined in a psychiatric institution for an indefinite or lengthy period is in principle entitled, at any rate where there is no automatic periodic review of a judicial character, to take proceedings "at reasonable intervals" before a court to put in issue the "lawfulness" – within the meaning of the Convention – of his detention (see, *inter alia*,

---

[174] See n 170 above on this.
[175] See earlier at paras 3.21 *et seq*.
[176] (1993) 15 EHRR 584, para 22.

the X v *United Kingdom* judgment of 5 November 1981, Series
A no 46, p 23, para 52[177]).

- Article 5(4) requires that the procedure followed have a judicial
  character and give to the individual concerned guarantees
  appropriate to the kind of deprivation of liberty in question;
  in order to determine whether a proceeding provides adequate
  guarantees, regard must be had to the particular nature of the
  circumstances in which such proceeding takes place.

- The judicial proceedings referred to in Art 5(4) need not always
  be attended by the same guarantees as those required under
  Art 6(1) for civil or criminal litigation. None the less, it is essential
  that the person concerned should have access to a court and the
  opportunity to be heard either in person or, where necessary,
  through some form of representation. Special procedural safeguards may prove to be called for in order to protect the interests
  of persons who, on account of their mental disabilities, are not
  fully capable of acting for themselves (see the *Winterwerp* v
  Netherlands judgment of 24 October 1979, Series A no 33, p 24,
  para 60).[178]

- Article 5(4) does not require that persons committed to care
  under the head of "unsound mind" should themselves take the
  initiative in obtaining legal representation before having recourse
  to a court (see the same judgment, p 26, para 66).

3.108   The reference to "some form of representation" might be taken
to suggest that representation other than legal representation will
suffice. That suggestion was discussed in the tribunal case of *Paterson*
v *Kent*.[179] At para 56, Sheriff Principal Dunlop relied on the following
quotation from *Megyeri* v *Germany*:[180]

> "where a person is confined in a psychiatric institution ... he should – unless
> there are special circumstances – receive legal assistance in subsequent
> proceedings relating to the continuation, suspension or termination of his
> detention. The importance of what is at stake for him – personal liberty –
> taken together with the very nature of his affliction – diminished mental
> capacity – compels this conclusion."

3.109   In *Megyeri*, the court's observations related to a person who was
confined in a psychiatric institution because of acts which would, but
for his mental illness, have been regarded as criminal; it may be that

---

[177] (1982) 4 EHRR 188.
[178] (1979–80) 2 EHRR 387.
[179] 2007 SLT (Sh Ct) 8; [2007] MHLR 20.
[180] See n 176 above.

the observations regarding the need for legal assistance apply with particular force to patients who are subject to compulsion orders or compulsion orders and restriction orders imposed by the criminal courts. The observations relating to what is at stake for the patient, however, seem equally apposite where purely "civil" orders are in question.

SUBMISSION OF ADDITIONAL DOCUMENTARY EVIDENCE

Sometimes a party (usually the MHO) will arrive with additional written material on the day of the hearing. This might consist of an updated care plan or an additional report from a support service representative, or some other information seen as relevant to the case. The rules require that any documents be lodged and intimated within 7 days prior to any hearing,[181] so the tribunal should seek an explanation for any documents lodged within the 7-day period, or at the hearing itself. In doing so, the tribunal will be considering whether or not to use its dispensing power to excuse the late arrival of the documents, and so there must be some "mistake, oversight or other excusable cause" available.[182] There is an alternative test, which is that under the rule relating to lodging and intimating documents there is the power to allow these to be lodged late "where good reason is given".[183] It seems that these are alternatives, since the dispensing power applies to "any provision" of the Rules.[184]   **3.110**

The rule envisages that the tribunal explores the reason for the non-lodging or intimation on time. Often, there will be a simple explanation, such as that the document was not available 7 days before the hearing, or that it should have been lodged before that deadline but was not, because of an error or ignorance of the rule. It will be for the tribunal to consider whether, in the circumstances of the case, at least one of the alternative excusal tests has been satisfied.   **3.111**

If the tribunal is satisfied with the explanation for the lateness of the arrival of the documents, it seems that it could still refuse to receive them where it is satisfied that the evidence is irrelevant or inadmissible for some other reason. Where a relevant person has lodged/seeks to lodge documents late, it would seem logical that a "good reason" under r 45(2) would not exist in relation to   **3.112**

---

[181] Rule 45(1).
[182] The dispensing power is contained in r 75 and is discussed in detail at paras 7.48 *et seq.*
[183] Rule 45(2).
[184] Rule 75(1). This raises the general issue of multiple excusal tests, dealt with at para 7.52.

documents that fall foul of the rules of evidence relating to relevancy or admissibility. This is particularly so when regard is had to the obligation in the rule to consider whether it is "fair in all the circumstances" to allow late lodging.[185] In any event, the tribunal has the power to exclude such evidence in terms of its power to issue a direction under r 49(1)(g), where it is seen to be "irrelevant, unnecessary or improperly obtained".[186]

3.113   Where the tribunal is satisfied that there is a good reason for the lateness of the arrival of the document and that there is no legal impediment to its acceptance, it might still refuse to allow it to be lodged, since to do so might prejudice the rights of another participant or would contravene the overriding objective under r 4; these would be key considerations in determining whether the late lodging should be permitted as being "fair in all the circumstances". So, where any prejudice can be overcome by adjournment, the documents should usually be permitted to be lodged late. The tribunal will generally want to be as well informed as possible in relation to all the issues in the case, and will not wish to exclude potentially relevant material, if that can be avoided. It might be argued, however, in some cases, that an adjournment of the case to a later date would not be fair in all of the circumstances, particularly where that argument is being made by a patient who would face an interim hospital-based order during the adjournment. In most cases, the tribunal can adjourn the hearing for a short period to allow the other parties to consider the documentation before resuming the hearing. The tribunal would, in such a case, be careful to establish that the parties who need to examine the documents during such a short adjournment feel able to continue with the case that day. It might be that the case has to be adjourned to another day, for example if the documentation is too voluminous or complex to be digested and responded to during the same day, or the content of the documents may give rise to the need for further investigation and/or witnesses, which would, of course, necessitate an adjournment to a later date.

3.114   All of the above would be dealt with as a preliminary matter since at the outset the party seeking to lodge the documentation late should present it before the hearing on the merits begins.

OBJECTIONS TO ANY PROPOSED EVIDENCE – DOCUMENTARY OR WITNESS EVIDENCE

3.115   Where a relevant person knows in advance that he wishes to object to the tribunal considering a document or hearing evidence from a

---

[185] Rule 45(3).
[186] This provision is discussed later at paras 5.02 et seq and 5.49 et seq.

witness, that objection should be raised and dealt with as a preliminary matter. In the case of oral evidence, it should only be raised at this point where the argument relates to the exclusion of the evidence of the witness in its entirety, which will probably be a relatively unusual event. In the case of an objection to part of the evidence of a witness, the objection need only be raised to an individual question or line of questioning when it arises. This is not to say that an objection at the outset to an anticipated line of questioning should not be taken as a preliminary matter; it may be sensible to narrow the focus of the oral evidence from the beginning of the hearing. However, a tactical decision presents itself here: where the issue being objected to is not canvassed in the written evidence, it might never arise during oral evidence, meaning that the tribunal will be unaware of it. By raising the anticipated line, this brings the issue to the attention of the tribunal. In such cases, close consideration should be given to whether to wait until the issue is raised before objecting.

In cases where the objectionable material is contained in documen-   **3.116**
tation that is before the tribunal (usually within the application documents) the tribunal members will have read it already. The appropriate request in such cases would be to ask the tribunal to ignore the relevant material during deliberations. This would be a request best dealt with as a preliminary matter; there is no point in leaving the matter until later, since the evidence may be in the mind of the tribunal, even if it not referred to directly during the oral evidence. In such a case, the tribunal should either decide, after hearing representations, to exclude or take into account the material, or consider the objection "under reservation"[187] until the oral evidence and submissions are over.

NON-COMPLIANCE WITH STATUTORY REQUIREMENT

Given the relative novelty of the current procedure (as well as its   **3.117**
complexity) it is perhaps unsurprising that not uncommonly a tribunal has to consider a failure by a relevant person to comply with a provision in the Rules or the 2003 Act. Some such failures are mere slips with little or no consequence, while others are more serious. Any debate in this area between tribunal members often focuses on the balance between, on one hand, the need to follow the legislation to the letter given the serious consequences of the tribunal's jurisdiction for the patient; and, on the other hand, the need to avoid injustice simply on the basis of an accidental failure to comply with a technical requirement of the Rules or the Act.

---

[187] See para 4.74.

The irrelevant "technicality"

3.118 The tribunal must consider at the outset whether the failure to comply with a requirement of the Act or the Rules is relevant to its consideration of the case before it. A situation which sometimes arises is that the tribunal is considering a CTO application and the tribunal members notice that there is some procedural defect affecting a previous (or still in force) STDC or EDC. We would suggest that defects of this sort do not impact on the tribunal's jurisdiction to consider the application before it. The tribunal's jurisdiction is to decide the CTO application and so any defect in an STDC, for example, is irrelevant to the tribunal's function. In any event, the previous order, if *ex facie* (on the face of it) good, stands as such until it is declared not to be, for example on appeal or judicial review.

3.119 The CTO application does not need to be preceded by any other order or certificate, far less a technically competent one. This is demonstrated by the fact that where an STDC expires and where the patient is still in hospital, ostensibly under the authority of the STDC, and the related CTO application comes before the tribunal, the expiry of the STDC has no impact on the CTO application. The reality is that the patient is being (and has been since the STDC expiry) held unlawfully and has a right to claim damages for such an unlawful detention. However, that is not something on which the tribunal can adjudicate, and the tribunal must simply consider the CTO application itself.

3.120 Even where the terms of s 69 of the 2003 Act have not been complied with, and the hearing is taking place more than 5 days after what would be the "normal" expiry date of an STDC, it might be competent for the tribunal to consider the application, depending on the impact of the *Soneji* case (see below on this).[188] There is no inherent connection between the STDC and the CTO application, which means that where the former is defective, this should have some effect on the latter. This point could apply in other situations. The tribunal must consider the case before it and not the history of compulsory measures as a whole. Another example might be consideration of an application to extend and vary or to vary a CTO. The tribunal panel should refrain from examining any technical defect that may have existed and that should arguably have led the earlier tribunal to refuse the CTO application.

Types of "technicality": 2003 Act or tribunal rules?

3.121 Before considering this area further, it is important to note that there are two types of requirement: (1) those arising out of the tribunal

---

[188] *Paterson* v *Kent* 2007 SLT (Sh Ct) 8; [2007] MHLR 20 per Sh Pr Dunlop, discussed below at paras 3.127 *et seq.*

rules; (2) those arising out of the 2003 Act or a statutory instrument. Each of these must be dealt with separately.

In the case of a failure to follow a requirement in the Rules, there   **3.122** is an a mechanism for relief available in the form of the dispensing power in r 75.[189] In addition, some individual rules will contain an excusal provision; in such cases the dispensing power applies as an additional, alternative mechanism to that contained in the rule.[190] This must be so as the dispensing power applies to "any provision of the Rules",[191] not just those without an individual dispensing facility built in. Where the tribunal is considering whether the dispensing power or individual rule test has been met, consideration should, in a wider sense, be given to the tension between strict adherence to all requirements and allowing justice in a general sense to be done. This balancing act is, of course, not a new one, and in particular in criminal cases has had to be considered where, for instance, the courts have had to decide whether a confession is admissible given the circumstances in which it was extracted, or whether the fruits of a search of a suspect should be admitted into evidence, given the circumstances under which the search was conducted. Given the power of the tribunal to restrict or deprive a patient of his liberty, the criminal analogy may be appropriate. In addition, as mentioned earlier, mental health tribunal proceedings are more akin to "citizen versus state" disputes than "party versus party" cases,[192] and this offers some further justification for the use (where appropriate) of criminal procedural law analogies. In the landmark, Full Bench criminal case of *Lawrie* v *Muir*,[193] this dilemma between the need to protect the citizen from irregular conduct on the part of the State and the desirability of not excluding evidence in serious criminal cases was addressed:

> "Whether any given irregularity ought to be excused depends upon the nature of the irregularity and the circumstances under which it was committed ... to take an extreme instance ... it would usually be wrong to exclude some highly incriminating production in a murder trial merely because it was found by a police officer in the course of a search authorised for a different purpose or before a proper warrant had been obtained."[194]

---

[189] See a detailed discussion of the dispensing power at paras 7.48 *et seq.*
[190] See the discussion of the effect of multiple excusal tests at para 7.52.
[191] Rule 75(1).
[192] See a general discussion of a comparison of mental health tribunal proceedings with other types of judicial process at paras 1.31 *et seq.*
[193] 1950 JC 19; 1950 SLT 37.
[194] LJ-G Cooper, delivering the unanimous opinion of the Full Bench at (JC 19 at 27).

3.123   In other words, the nature of the irregularity itself and the circumstances of its commission (including the reasons for it) should be
examined. In the extreme instance cited by the court, there seems
to be some emphasis in this exercise on the consequences of non-
admission of the evidence, and this would seem sensible in a tribunal
context too. Of course, these considerations should not replace the
test in the dispensing power or excusal provision being relied upon,
but they do provide some additional pointers to the sort of factors
the tribunal should be considering. The further comments on the use
of the dispensing power in particular cases should be referred to for
further guidance.[195]

3.124   The second situation occurs where there has been a failure to
follow a requirement in the 2003 Act or in a Scottish statutory
instrument (SSI) made under the Act.[196] There is no dispensing
power in the Act, and rarely is there one in an SSI. This means
that any failure to follow a requirement in the Act or SSI cannot be
excused, as is often the case with such a failure under the Rules. The
focus then in such cases is not on the question "Can we overlook
this failure?" (since the answer is that it cannot be overlooked) but
rather: "What are the consequences of the failure?" The answer
here is not straightforward. One would have thought that where
a statutory provision says that something shall be done, where it
is not, there must be consequences for the party who has failed to
comply. This is not necessarily the case. The question for the court
or tribunal is what Parliament intended to be the consequence of
non-compliance with the particular requirement.

3.125   Generally speaking, requirements under the 2003 Act and any SSI
fall within one of two types: (1) requirements relating to the fulfilment
of deadlines; and (2) requirements relating to compulsory content of
certain statutory documentation. There are many examples of each.
We will deal with each in turn.

Requirements on deadlines

3.126   The whole framework of the compulsory powers in the 2003 Act
is built around a series of timeframes and deadlines. Where these
deadlines are complied with, there is not an issue. It will usually
be obvious where a deadline has been breached, but this might not
be so. For example, the papers before the tribunal might disclose
what seems to be a breach of a statutory deadline. However, the
question is whether *in fact* there has been a breach, or whether the

---

[195] See the discussion on the dispensing power generally at paras 7.48 *et seq.*
[196] The tribunal rules SSI is an example of such a statutory instrument, but reference
is being made here to others.

documentation is misleading. Given that there are no prescribed statutory forms for any of the documentation required under the Act or regulations under it, meaning that an error in any documents cannot be determinative,[197] the tribunal may have to take oral evidence from those at the hearing to establish whether there really was a failure to comply with a time limit. In addition, there can be issues over the calculation of deadlines, such as whether the reference is to working days or days. Care should be taken in such cases to check that there has been a breach since, if there has not, the tribunal need not go on to consider whether any consequence flows from the breach. There is some useful guidance on the interpretation of timescales in the Code of Practice to the 2003 Act.[198] Assuming that there has been a failure to comply with a time restriction, the *Soneji* formula (see below on this) should be applied to consider whether that failure is fatal. We will now consider some of the main examples of such time restrictions.

One such restriction is that contained in s 68 of the 2003 Act, which extends a short-term detention certificate pending a hearing of an application for a CTO.[199] The provision effectively extends the certificate for 5 working days beyond its natural expiry, in order to allow a hearing on a CTO application (assuming that one has been lodged before the expiry of the certificate) to take place. Where the 5-day extension applies, s 69 requires that the tribunal should decide, within that 5-day period, whether or not an interim CTO should be granted. In the case of *Paterson* v *Kent*[200] Sheriff Principal Dunlop (Sheriff Principal of Tayside, Central and Fife) considered the consequences of failure to adhere to this 5-day deadline. The patient argued that the CTO that was granted at a hearing held after the 5-day period had expired was invalid, since the tribunal by that time had no jurisdiction over the application. The court heard detailed submissions on the line of case law dealing with the consequences of failure to comply with statutory provisions and ultimately the sheriff principal relied on the line of authority culminating in the English House of Lords decision of *R* v *Soneji*.[201] Although a full discussion of that case and the Scottish and English cases that are in the line of authorities

3.127

---

[197] For a further discussion of the lack of prescribed documentation, please see below at paras 3.142 *et seq.*

[198] See vol 2, introduction, paras 22–27. On the Code generally, see para 1.40.

[199] The heading for this section refers to the extension of the certificate "pending determination of [the] application" but this should be taken to refer to pending a hearing on the application, since the application is often not determined until later, well beyond the expiry of the additional 5-day extension. This distinction is discussed later at paras 3.132 and 3.134.

[200] 2007 SLT (Sh Ct) 8; [2007] MHLR 20.

[201] [2006] 1 AC 340; [2005] 3 WLR 303.

leading up to it is beyond the scope of this work, the key point in that case is that the test for determining whether any consequences are to flow from non-compliance with a statutory requirement has changed. That case is the main recent authority that signals a move away from the previous classification of statutory requirements as being either mandatory (failure to follow is fatal) or directory (failure to follow is not fatal). The test is now whether Parliament has intended that a failure to follow the statutory requirement leads to the invalidity of the procedure.[202] In endorsing this approach, the court in *Soneji* referred to the earlier authority of *Wang v Commissioners of Inland Revenue*[203] in which the following was said by Lord Slynn in the Privy Council:

> "when a question like the present one arises – an alleged failure to comply with a time provision – it is simpler and better to avoid these two words 'mandatory' and 'directory' and to ask two questions. The first is whether the legislature intended the person making the determination to comply with the time provision, whether a fixed time or a reasonable time. Secondly, if so, did the legislature intend that a failure to comply with such a time provision would deprive the decision-maker of jurisdiction and render any decision which he purported to make null and void?"[204]

3.128   The *Soneji* court also cited with approval some similar pronouncements from courts abroad, including the following comments from the Australian High Court case of *Project Blue Sky Inc v Australian Broadcasting Authority*:[205]

> "A better test for determining the issue of validity is to ask whether it was a purpose of the legislation that an act done in breach of the provision should be invalid ... In determining the question of purpose, regard must be had to 'the language of the relevant provision and the scope and object of the whole statute'."[206]

Coming back to the *Paterson* case, Sheriff Principal Dunlop concludes:

> "In my opinion the purpose of the time limit in section 69 is that suggested by counsel for the Tribunal. If the hearing is not held before the expiry of the five-day period of 'grace' there will be a break in the patient's detention which, on the hypothesis that this is a person who requires to be detained in hospital, is undesirable, not just in the interests of the patient but in the interest of the public as well. The avoidance of

---

[202] See para 23 of the *Soneji* decision.
[203] [1994] 1 WLR 1286.
[204] *Ibid* at 1296.
[205] (1998) 194 CLR 355.
[206] *Ibid* at para 93.

that state of affairs is in my opinion the objective sought to be achieved by the provision of a time limit and was recognised by Lady Smith in *Smith v Mental Health Tribunal for Scotland* as a compelling reason for holding the Tribunal to its obligation to comply with it. Thus a balance is struck between the need to protect the patient's right to liberty on the one hand and the avoidance of an inappropriate release from detention on the other. When one sets section 69 in the context of the scope and object of the Act as a whole, particularly Part 7, it seems to me that the Tribunal has a duty to entertain and determine all applications for a compulsory treatment order and, in relation to those cases in which the provisions of section 68 apply, to do so within the time limit prescribed by section 69. In those latter cases however it does not follow that the Tribunal's duty is to determine the application within that time limit or not at all ... Whether or not the Tribunal complies with the time limit, the essential foundation of the application remains and in my view Parliament cannot fairly be taken to have intended that the Tribunal's duty to determine that application should disappear on the mere expiry of the five-day period of 'grace' allowed by section 68. Accordingly, subject to the possibility of discretionary control by the court to which I refer hereunder, I am satisfied that in convening the hearing outwith the period of five working days the Tribunal was not acting outwith its jurisdiction."[207]

In reaching that decision, Sheriff Principal Dunlop dismissed the argument that the purpose of the time limit is to protect patients against unnecessarily long periods of detention. He held that a patient would have to be released if the hearing was not held within the 5-day period (although that had not happened in this case). This is not the same as saying, he held, that the whole application must fall. While this reasoning seems attractive at first glance, it is submitted that a different view might legitimately be taken. It is perhaps not entirely accurate to say that the argument was being made that the "mere expiry of the five day period of 'grace' allowed by section 68" justified the conclusion that the tribunal had no jurisdiction beyond it; the argument was made with reference to both ss 68 and 69. It is certainly true to say that s 68 has no bearing on the validity of the application when looked at in isolation: that section does not deal with the requirement to present an application within a particular time, but instead is concerned with the extension of the certificate. However, s 69 squarely addresses the issue of the time limit. It is submitted that two particular points about s 69 are relevant here.   3.129

First of all, that section places an obligation on the tribunal to reach a decision on the merits of the application within the 5-day period: to grant an interim compulsory treatment order (ICTO) or to determine the application finally. Sheriff Principal Dunlop's   3.130

---

[207] At paras 33–34 of his judgment.

reference to the proper interpretation of "first hearing" in r 8 of the Rules is, arguably, unconvincing. Rule 8 is designed simply to provide a specific procedure where ss 68 and 69 of the 2003 Act apply. Sheriff Principal Dunlop argues that the reference in s 69 to an "interim compulsory treatment order" must mean an order pending full consideration of the CTO application. There is room for a contrary view. Section 69 carries a definitions list which includes a definition of an "interim compulsory treatment order" which refers back to the definition of that order in s 65(2) of the Act. If this is correct, it follows that Parliament is envisaging that a decision on the merits of the application (albeit possibly an interim one) is made within the 5-day extension period. It is also envisaged that, given the limited timescale for preparation from the patient's point of view, if an order authorising further detention is to be made, it is likely to be of an interim nature. In these circumstances, it is arguable that Parliament should be taken to have intended that the application, having not gone through this necessary consideration on its merits, should fall.

3.131   Sheriff Principal Dunlop considers the aim of ss 68 and 69, and in doing so concludes:

> "In my view [the aim of the five working days prescribed by s 69] cannot be the protection of persons against unnecessarily lengthy periods of detention because nothing in the Act, least of all s 69, authorises detention beyond the five-day period specified by s 68. On the expiry of that period, and in the absence of a compulsory treatment order [or such an interim order] having been made, the [patient] cannot lawfully be detained further, at least without some intervening period of liberation."[208]

3.132   Sheriff Principal Dunlop is undoubtedly correct where he says that detention will be unauthorised after the expiry of the 5-day period. There is room, however, for a more nuanced view in relation to the interaction between ss 68 and 69. Section 69 explicitly requires a determination of the application to be made within the 5-day period set out in s 68(2)(a). If such a course of action is followed, this could lead to a decision which involves the release of the patient from detention within that 5-day period. This suggests that the aim of Parliament in enacting s 69 is, at least in part, that ruled out by Sheriff Principal Dunlop: to protect against unnecessarily lengthy periods of detention. In other words, although s 69 does not authorise the continued detention of the patient beyond the 5-day period, if the section is complied with, it could lead to the release of the patient from detention within that period, thereby, in an appropriate case,

---

[208] Paragraph 32 of the judgment.

ending what would otherwise be an unnecessarily lengthy period of detention.

A contrary view is that the period of detention would be shortened only marginally in the event of an application heard and refused during the 5-day period. It might not be shortened at all in the event that the hearing took place on the last of the 5 days.

Second, the headline of s 69[209] throws some light on Parliament's view of the nature of the section: "Time limit for tribunal's determination: special case." Parliament carried the reference to "special case" through to the corresponding rule, r 8. The use of the words "special case" is instructive, since it indicates that Parliament is well aware of the fact that in no other circumstances is there an obligation to *determine* (not just hold a hearing on) an application within a set period. This suggests that Parliament regards the position of a patient who has just endured a short-term certificate and is in the midst of being in detention for possibly another week (5 *working* days being the extension period) as "special" and as such should have his case determined within a time limit. Again, if this interpretation is correct, it lends weight to the argument that Parliament would have intended that the application that is not dealt with in accordance with these special circumstances should fall.

The Australian High Court in the *Project Blue Sky* case (above) referred to the "scope and object of the whole statute" as being relevant as well as the language of the provision, in determining whether Parliament had intended invalidity to follow from non-compliance. Sheriff Principal Dunlop in the *Paterson* case touches on the scope and object of the Act as a whole and particularly in Pt 7, and is of the view that:

> "the Tribunal has a duty to entertain and determine all applications for a compulsory treatment order and, in relation to those cases in which the provisions of s 68 apply, to do so within the time limit prescribed by s 69".

He goes on to explain, however, that this does not mean that failure to comply deprives the tribunal of its jurisdiction. There is no reference in the case, in the context of s 69, to the principles set out in s 1 of the Act. It may be that the principle requiring any function to be discharged with the minimum restriction on the freedom of the

3.133

3.134

3.135

3.136

---

[209] This is a reference to the heading in italics used by the framers of the legislation for that part of the Act. This is confusing as there is only one section within that part, s 69. Section 69 has its own title. It is, however, an indication of the view Parliament takes of the nature of the section within that part.

patient is relevant to a consideration of what should happen in the event of a failure to comply with s 69. It is relevant to determining the purpose of s 68 and s 69. It could be said that Parliament, in making provision for a rapid judicial determination of an application in respect of a patient who is in detention already, is implementing the principle that the function (in this case the determination of the application by the tribunal)[210] is discharged "in the manner ... that involves the minimum restriction on the freedom of the patient that is necessary in the circumstances". Given that the object and purpose of the Act is relevant to the question of validity, this point could lend further weight to an invalidity argument.

3.137   Of course, the discussion above deals with only one statutory time restriction; there are many in the 2003 Act and in subsidiary legislation. In connection with a CTO application, for example, there are time restrictions relating to the lodging of an application with the Tribunal (within 14 days of the latest of the two mental health reports: s 57(7)) and the period between the two mental health report examinations (no more than 5 days: s 58(3)).

3.138   In each of these cases, a tribunal will have to consider whether (in line with the *Soneji* test – see above) it is the intention of Parliament that, where not complied with, the whole application should fall. In the case of the submission of the application deadline, again, the minimum restriction principle in s 1(4) is relevant: if the application is submitted late, it will take longer to determine, meaning that the patient may be in detention for longer or, in a case where the patient is in the community, will have to be the subject of compulsory measures for longer (this in itself is a restriction on freedom). On the other hand, where it is submitted 1 or 2 days late, it could be said that Parliament would not have intended that the whole application should fall. This raises the interesting, but as yet unanswered, question of whether, when considering the invalidity issue, the extent of the error is relevant. It could be argued that it is not: invalidity follows non-compliance to any extent. However, it is thought that the better view, with regard to the application lodging deadline at least, is that the extent of non-compliance is relevant in considering whether or not Parliament would have intended that such non-compliance must lead to the application falling.

3.139   The same would seem to follow in the case of the provision on the maximum time period between the medical examinations of the two practitioners. The purpose of the requirement for two medical opinions is clearly to allow for corroboration of the diagnosis of the patient's condition as well as of the view on how the patient should be

---

[210] The tribunal is a "person" for the purposes of s 1, since it is not excluded in terms of s 1(7).

treated for it. Given the propensity of a mental disorder to change in severity and presentation very quickly, if a long period were allowed to elapse between the two medical examinations, this would lead to less reliable corroborative evidence. Once again, where the time gap is wider by only a day or two, the view might be taken that the breach of this statutory requirement is not fatal to the application; Parliament did not intend this to happen. Where the gap is wider, the invalidity argument becomes stronger.

In the case of a STDC, a time limitation of 3 days between the medical examination and the granting of the certificate applies.[211] It is likely that any STDC granted outwith this 3-day period will be invalid. While this 3-day period is less than the 5 days that might elapse between the medical examinations in connection with a CTO application, it is clear that in the case of an STDC, speed is of the essence. The wording of the section suggests that compliance with the 3-day period is a prerequisite of a valid certificate. In addition, the STDC often represents the first prolonged detention of the patient (who may have been under an EDC for up to 72 hours). Further, the certificate is not, as with a CTO application, the culmination of a detailed examination of the patient's whole circumstances by an MHO, with the assistance of two concurring medical opinions. It is the result of an examination by one medical professional (the same one who then grants the certificate), albeit with the approval of the MHO. Given that the procedure, then, is more truncated and with fewer safeguards built in than a full CTO application, it could be said that there is a stronger case for arguing that any time requirement in the legislation would be intended by Parliament to be followed on pain of invalidity of the certificate if not. Finally, the time limitation in the case of an STDC is more important in many cases than any attached to the CTO application procedure, since the granting of an STDC will invariably lead to the restriction of the liberty of the patient. In the case of the CTO application, the patient is usually in hospital under a valid STDC, and so any failure to comply with deadlines such as those discussed above, will not directly lead to an initial depravation of liberty. In these circumstances, using the *Soneji* analysis, it would seem that failure to follow this 3-day deadline would be fatal to the validity of the STDC since this is what Parliament would have intended. In such cases, an appeal against the STDC should be allowed.[212]

3.140

Finally, it should be noted that there is a statutory interpretation presumption in favour of liberty, which was not touched upon by the

3.141

---

[211] 2003 Act, s 44(1).
[212] On such appeals, see para 3.158 and para 6.07, n 16.

sheriff principal in *Paterson*. This presumption was commented on, however, in a pre-2003 Act mental health case which finds favour in the *Paterson* judgment:

> "the general presumption is in favour of freedom of the individual and that may quite properly be used as an aid to construction where necessary. No one should be detained for a moment longer than is justified by the warrant to detain and such warrant should be construed strictly".[213]

There are, of course, numerous other statutory deadlines, but the main ones have been considered above. In any such case, the tribunal will have to make a decision on the *Soneji* test, guided by the comments in some of the case law cited above.[214]

Requirements on content of statutory documentation

3.142   There are numerous obligations in the 2003 Act and in statutory instruments relating to the content of key documents. Unlike under the former legislation, where there were some examples of prescribed forms,[215] no prescribed forms exist under the 2003 Act regime. As a matter of course, the forms issued by the Scottish Executive are used.[216] However, technically, they could be ignored and substitute forms could be used. This means that an adverse consequence cannot come from the failure properly to complete the forms routinely used by MHOs, RMOs, patients and the tribunal. However, this applies only to the form of the document concerned; there are still statutory provisions on content. The best examples are the provisions on the

---

[213] Lord MacLean in the judicial review case of *R v Lothian Health Board (No 2)* 1993 SLT 1021 at 1025. The sheriff principal in *Paterson* cites this case with approval (para 32), but does not specifically deal with this passage, or the presumption referred to in it. This presumption is also accepted by Sh Pr Lockhart in the mental health tribunal appeal of *Beattie v Dunbar and Mental Health Tribunal for Scotland* 2006 SCLR 777; [2007] MHLR 7 at para 16, where the sheriff principal refers to various additional authorities.

[214] See also the example of non compliance with the conflict of interest regulations, dealt with at paras 3.152 *et seq.*

[215] These were set out in the now-revoked Mental Health (Prescribed Forms) (Scotland) Regulations 1984 (SI 1984/1495) and the Mental Health (Prescribed Forms) (Scotland) Regulations 1996 (SI 1996/743) (which remains in force).

[216] These are available on the website of the Scottish Government, Health and Community Care Department at: http://www.scotland.gov.uk/Topics/Health/health/mental-health/mhlaw/mha-Forms. The use of these forms is recommended by the Code of Practice at vol 1, inroduction, para 21. On the status of the Code, see para 1.40.

content of CTO applications,[217] care plans,[218] mental health reports[219] and social circumstances reports.[220] Although the standard forms could be ignored, they carry significant benefits in that they take the author through the statutorily required information, lessening the chances that something is missed.

In connection with a CTO application, s 63(2) of the 2003 Act sets out the material that must be included. The standard form CTO application which is routinely used will take the MHO through this material. The application must be accompanied by the documents set out in s 63(3) (mental health reports, proposed care plan and a report under s 61). Again, there are standard forms for mental health reports[221] and the standard form CTO application will take the MHO through the other parts of s 63(3). Where the RMO decides to extend a CTO, he must prepare a determination and the standard form used for that determination will take the RMO through the requirements set out in s 86 of the 2003 Act. Similarly, the relevant standard form covers the requirements in connection with an application to extend and vary a CTO (s 92 of the 2003 Act) and likewise for an application to vary only (s 95 of the 2003 Act). Similar forms exist, taking the RMO through the application to extend a CO following a first mandatory review (s 149 of the 2003 Act), the determination extending the CO thereafter (s 153 of the 2003 Act), any application to extend and vary a CO (s 158 of the 2003 Act) and in any application to vary a CO (s 161 of the 2003 Act).

3.143

It should also be borne in mind that in addition to the requirements in the 2003 Act as to the content of these applications, there are regulations prescribing the content of documentation in relation to both a CTO[222] and a CO.[223] However, it should be pointed out that these regulations are largely concerned with either the lodging of additional documents (where the 2003 Act allows regulations to prescribe this) or with providing the tribunal with the power to

3.144

---

[217] Section 63(2)–(3) of the 2003 Act.

[218] Section 62(5) of the 2003 Act for CTOs, supplemented by s 76 and the Mental Health (Content and amendment of care plans) (Scotland) Regulations 2005 (SSI 2005/309); and s 137, referring to a "Part 9 care plan", supplemented by the Mental Health (Content and amendment of Part 9 care plans) (Scotland) Regulations 2005 (SSI 2005/312).

[219] Section 57(4) of the 2003 Act.

[220] Section 231 of the 2003 Act, supplemented by the Mental Health (Social Circumstances Reports) (Scotland) Regulations 2005 (SSI 2005/310).

[221] This report is as described in s 57(4) of the 2003 Act.

[222] Mental Health (Compulsory treatment orders – documents and reports to be submitted to the Tribunal) (Scotland) Regulations 2005 (SSI 2005/366).

[223] Mental Health (Compulsion orders – documents and reports to be submitted to the Tribunal) (Scotland) Regulations 2005 (SSI 2005/365).

order supplementary documentation where it does not feel that it has sufficient information to allow it to make a decision.[224] This leaves the 2003 Act provisions with the job of specifying the content of the key documents.

3.145   Where there is some information missing from a statutorily required document and where that information is prescribed, the consequences will depend on the seriousness of the error, and how easy it might be to rectify. It will often be possible to adjourn the hearing in order to allow the document to be re-submitted with the correct information. The tribunal would, in such a case, issue a direction to the appropriate relevant person.[225] In fact, only if there existed very good reason would the tribunal refuse to adjourn a hearing in these circumstances. This might be the best course of action with documents such as a proposed care plan as part of a CTO application, or a social circumstances report. The tribunal, in such cases, would consider whether, in the meantime, to grant some kind of interim order. Where the tribunal is considering a CTO application, it would seem that it could grant an interim compulsory treatment order (ICTO) pending the rectification (following adjournment) of an omission or error in the application documentation, so long as that error or omission could be rectified. Under s 65, all a tribunal must be satisfied of when granting an ICTO is that the conditions set out in s 64(5)(a)–(d) are met and that such an order is necessary.[226] In fact, since an ICTO can be made by the tribunal on an *ex proprio motu* (of its own volition) basis,[227] it must be the case that a formal written application for one is not required. However, since s 65 only applies where an application is made under s 63,[228] the essential elements of such an application would have to be before the tribunal, namely an application under s 63(1) accompanied by a report under s 61, two mental health reports and a proposed care plan.[229]

3.146   In cases where statutorily required information is missing, there would be nothing to prevent the tribunal seeking to obtain oral evidence from those present as a substitute for the absent written information, where that information might be relevant to consideration of whether to grant an interim order. It may even be possible to secure an amended document that day, following a short adjournment. In many such cases, the relevant persons who would stand to be disadvantaged by the absence of essential content in

---

[224] These regulations are discussed later at paras 3.82 *et seq.*
[225] On directions, see paras 7.30 *et seq.*
[226] 2003 Act, s 65(2) and (6).
[227] *Ibid*, s 65(2).
[228] *Ibid*, s 65(1).
[229] *Ibid*, s 63(2) and (3).

documentation will agree that it can be provided orally at the hearing, rather than delay the process by adjourning the case. It would seem pointless and against the spirit and letter of the overriding objective in the Rules[230] to insist on adjourning when no one wants to do so and where the information is available orally. Sometimes, however, the missing information will be significant in terms of both importance and volume, and here the tribunal should closely consider whether to adjourn, since all relevant persons will need time to consider the information and it may not be fair to expect those at the hearing to do so then and there.

It can be problematic where there is information missing from one of the mental health reports. There are several reasons for this. First of all, it is unusual for both authors of the mental health reports to be available at the hearing. This makes oral clarification more difficult, although not impossible if the author can be reached by telephone.[231] The second problem is that the reports are prepared at a certain point in time, following an examination of the patient, and so any clarification sought much later might be being provided on the basis not of the examination only, but on the basis of the author's view at the time when he is asked. In this sense, clarification at the hearing is an artificial (and perhaps unreliable) exercise. Third, the mental health reports are the main foundation for any CTO application. The duty on the MHO to apply for a CTO does not arise until two mental health reports, containing certain specified material, are available.[232] In addition, the reports take centre stage as the key expert evidence on the existence of the CTO statutory criteria. The importance of the mental health reports in the context of the statutory framework cannot be overstated. It could be argued, then, using the *Soneji* test, discussed above,[233] that Parliament intended that an application that did not carry two properly formulated mental health reports should fall as invalid.

3.147

However, even in the case of mental health reports, there are two points to make which mean that only the most defective examples of such documents would be fatal to an application. The first is that the required minimum content of the mental health report under the 2003 Act is general: it need only contain the information set out in s 57(4). This means that as long as all of the boxes in the non-statutory proforma report are, to some extent, completed, the statutory content criteria are likely to have been met. This does not mean that the tribunal will be satisfied that the information in the reports will be sufficient to

3.148

[230] Rule 4: see para 1.26 on this.
[231] On evidence taken over the telephone generally, see para 3.54.
[232] 2003 Act, s 57(1) and (4).
[233] See paras 3.127 *et seq*. See also para 3.90.

allow it to dispose of the application – further clarification might be required – but it does make it a mental health report in terms of the legislation. The second point is that it has been held recently that the existence of the minimum content of such reports can be *inferred* by considering the report as a whole. In the case of *Beattie v Dunbar*,[234] a decision of Sheriff Principal Lockhart (Sheriff Principal of South Strathclyde, Dumfries and Galloway), it was argued that there was no proper mental health report before the tribunal from one of the medical practitioners since the report lodged did not comply with the terms of s 57 of the 2003 Act in two respects: (1) the author of the report had failed to shade a circle in the proforma against the phrase "I am satisfied that the making of a compulsory treatment order is necessary for the following reasons", and this omission meant that s 57(3)(e) of the 2003 Act had not been complied with; and (2) a page was missing from this report, p 9, and so there was no view stated in the report as to the opinion of the practitioner as to which measures should be authorised by the tribunal; in these circumstances, it was argued that there was no coincidence between the reports on this matter, as required by s 57(5)(b) of the 2003 Act. It was argued by the patient that, as a result, there was no proper CTO application before the tribunal (in the absence of proper mental health reports, a key ingredient of a competent CTO application: s 63(3)(a)) and so the tribunal had no jurisdiction to grant a CTO as it did. Sheriff Principal Lockhart refused the appeal. On the issue of the failure to shade in the circle in the form (issue (1) above), he looked to the content of the remainder of the mental health report, from which it could be inferred that the author was satisfied that the making of the order was necessary. For example, the author had completed the box requiring reasons as to why treatment could not be provided on an informal basis; he would not have done so, it was held, if he did not think the order sought (a hospital-based CTO) was necessary. The sheriff principal also relied on the author's completion of the part of the form authorising the giving of notice of the application on the patient; this would not have been done if the practitioner did not feel that a CTO in the terms being sought was appropriate. In connection with the argument of lack of coincidence between the reports (point (2) above) the sheriff principal took the view that they did coincide. Again, although p 9 was missing, the court looked to the remainder of the report, and it was clear that the author supported the detention of the patient in a hospital and treatment in accordance with Pt 16 of the 2003 Act. For instance, the court focused on the opinion of the author, expressed elsewhere in the report, to the effect that the relevant treatment required for the patient could not be provided "without admission".

---

[234] 2006 SCLR 777; [2007] MHLR 7.

This decision is important, as it confirms the position that the incorrect or incomplete condition of the proforma documents need not lead to the conclusion that such documents are not before the tribunal. Instead, the court should read the document as a whole and decide whether the statutorily prescribed information is present or can be inferred from the content of the document. This approach seems correct since, in the case of oral evidence, content can be inferred, and, in the case of documentary material, the courts are permitted to apply rules of interpretation to discover the true intention of the author.[235] Despite this, it will always be a question of fact and degree in any particular case as to whether there is sufficient material in the document to infer that the required material is there. As discussed above,[236] even where the material is not there, it might be possible to adjourn to correct the material but, in the case of mental health reports, this poses special problems due to the timing constraints imposed in the Act.

3.149

One further point should be highlighted here. Although a CTO application specifies that certain measures are sought under s 64(4) of the 2003 Act, the tribunal can grant a CTO specifying different orders, but only after stating what those measures are and informing a number of specified persons of what it proposes to do.[237] Those persons must be given the opportunity to make oral or written representations and to lead evidence.[238] Where those participants are at the hearing, this can be done orally then and there;[239] however, where one or more of the specified persons are not present, or where a party or relevant person who is present argues that he needs time to lead additional evidence or prepare argument on the issue, the tribunal will require to adjourn the hearing until a later date. One of the persons listed who will usually not be present is a GP who is an author of one of the mental health reports.[240] This means that

3.150

---

[235] It is notable that the sheriff principal in this case accepted and had in mind the principle that prescribed conditions should be strictly complied with when the liberty of an individual is at stake – see para 15 of the judgment. On this subject, see para 3.141. See also the recent case of *M v Murray* 2009 Scot (D) 8/5, where Sh Pr Lockhart held that a mental health report was adequate since it complied with the requirements of ss 57 and 58, even although it was sparse in detail. He stated that mental health reports "did not require to be spelt out with the precision of a legal document". He also took the view that the tribunal was entitled to look at the CTO application as a whole, as well as the evidence led, in considering whether the Act had been complied with.

[236] See para 3.90.

[237] 2003 Act, s 64(7)(a). The list of those who need to be informed is contained in s 64(3).

[238] *Ibid*, s 64(7)(b).

[239] *Ibid*, s 64(8).

[240] He is one of the specified participants: s 64(7) and s 64(3)(f).

in practice in almost every case, the question of an adjournment will arise. However, one way around this would be to telephone the GP and discharge the duty to explain over the telephone.[241] Where the change in measures being proposed involves a change from a hospital application to a community one or vice versa, this will almost certainly necessitate an adjournment (and therefore possibly an interim order) since a written care plan that matches the measures is required,[242] and this will not be available within the application as presented. The proposal might, on the other hand, be to change the measures sought only in a minor way, in which case a new care plan may not be necessary. Even where a new care plan is required, it can be prepared on the same day as the hearing, during an adjournment for that purpose, as happened in one hearing where a community order was sought and the application had been prepared at a time when a hospital order was deemed necessary; the community care plan was very simple and so was prepared and delivered on the same day, allowing a community CTO to be granted.

THE PRESENCE OF THE MINIMUM STATUTORY DOCUMENTATION

3.151   As stated earlier, there is certain information that is required in order to give rise to a proper application before the tribunal. Where the tribunal is faced with a complete absence of a prescribed document (as opposed to having the document but finding that it is inadequate in is content) this might be a fundamental problem, depending on the nature of the document. Clearly, where there is no written application for a CTO, for instance, the tribunal cannot grant an interim or a full CTO. It could be argued that a document that purports to be a CTO application or a mental health report or an application to extend and vary a CTO or CO, does not qualify as such a document in cases where some prescribed information is missing; in other words, it could be argued that the document before the tribunal is masquerading as, for example, a CTO application. However, it is submitted that such an argument is unlikely to succeed unless the document is so lacking in prescribed information that it hardly resembles the document it is purporting to represent; this is a highly unlikely scenario, given the existence and prevalence of the standard forms for most statutorily required documents. Where a document is simply missing some key prescribed component, the tribunal should always consider whether

---

[241] On taking evidence over the telephone generally, see para 3.54.
[242] 2003 Act, s 62(6) refers to the MHO signing the care plan, which suggests that it must be in written form. The reference to the care plan being prepared (s 62(2)) also suggests that it must be in writing.

this situation can be resolved other than by way of refusing the application as incompetent.[243] In the case of a missing mental health report (in the sense of one that does not exist) clearly this would be a fundamental error that, given the time constraints in the Act, could not be rectified, and the application should, in such a case, be refused as incompetent.[244]

CONFLICTS OF INTEREST

Provisions on conflicts of interest can be found in relation to both STDCs and CTOs. In the former case, s 44(3)(a) and s 47(2)(a) (the latter dealing with STDC extension certificates) stipulate that there must be no conflict of interest in relation to the medical examination. Where there is such a conflict, it is clear from the wording of s 44(1)(c) combined with s 44(3)(a) that the AMP may not grant an STDC. In the latter case (CTO applications) the 2003 Act provides, in s 58(5), that except in cases where regulations provide, there "must not be a conflict of interest in relation to the medical examination". All three sections indicate that the circumstances in which such conflicts might arise are to be provided for in regulations.[245]   **3.152**

The regulations that set out these circumstances are the Mental Health (Conflict of Interest) (Scotland) (No 2) Regulations 2005.[246] It is clear from the tribunal decisions examined by the authors that the application of these regulations has created some difficulty, not to mention clear contradictions, in the practice of the tribunal.   **3.153**

STDC or extension certificate conflicts

Dealing with the conflict situation in connection with an STDC or an extension certificate first of all, reg 2 indicates that there is taken to be a conflict where at least one of two situations arises: **3.154**

(1) where the AMP is related to the patient in some specified way[247] (see below on CTO application conflicts); or

(2) where the patient is liable, by virtue of the proposed STDC or extension certificate, to be detained in a hospital where the AMP is employed by or contracted to provide services in or to an independent health care service.[248]

---

[243] See above at para 3.90 for further guidance on how this might be achieved.
[244] Such extreme cases should be picked up as misconceived cases anyway: see paras 3.88 *et seq* on such cases.
[245] Section 44(8), s 47(5) and s 58(5).
[246] SSI 2005/380.
[247] *Ibid*, reg 2(a).
[248] *Ibid*, reg 2(b).

The term "independent health care service" is defined in s 2(5) of the Regulation of Care (Scotland) Act 2001,[249] as follows:

"(a) an independent hospital;
(b) a private psychiatric hospital;
(c) an independent clinic; and
(d) an independent medical agency, but a service may be excepted from this definition by regulations."

3.155   So, it is clear that where the patient is liable, as a result of the STDC or extension certificate (if granted) to be detained in a hospital which does not fall within the definition of "independent health care service" (such as an NHS Trust hospital), the second conflict situation does not apply, leaving situation (1) as the only potential conflict situation in such cases.

3.156   However, reg 3 provides that even where a conflict of either type arises, there is *not taken to be*[250] such a conflict where:

"failure by the [AMP] to carry out the medical examination would result in a delay which would involve serious risk to the health safety or welfare of the patient or to the safety of other persons".

3.157   In the case of an STDC or an extension certificate, the minimisation of delay is, by definition, important. Although the AMP might take the view that the conditions in s 44(4)(a)–(d) of the 2003 Act are met, and in particular s 44(4)(d), this will not allow a conflict to be overlooked under reg 3, since there has first to be a causative connection between the delay caused by failure of *that particular AMP* to carry out the examination and the serious risk of harm. Where another AMP could carry out the examination without such delay, this course of action must be adopted, otherwise reg 2 (and therefore s 44(3)(a) and s 47(2)(a)) has been breached. Of course, where any potential replacement AMP would attract the application of reg 2, his substitution would be pointless, and reg 2 would continue to apply. In cases where the patient is already in hospital under compulsory measures (for example under an EDC or, in the case of an extension certificate, an STDC) or informally, and where there is little or no evidence of an intention imminently to abscond or, in the case of an informal patient, a refusal to accept medical treatment, it would seem that the AMP who is at the centre of a reg 2 conflict should make efforts to find an alternative AMP to grant the certificate. In such cases, the delay caused by his failure

---

[249] Mental Health (Conflict of Interest) (Scotland) (No 2) Regulations 2005 (SSI 2005/380), reg 1(2).
[250] The italicised wording derives from that used in the 2003 Act, s 44(8) and 47(5).

to conduct the examination himself is unlikely to have any adverse effect on the patient, since the *status quo* could be maintained, either voluntarily or under the powers of the compulsory measures in place. It will be easier for the AMP to argue the application of the reg 3 exception where the patient is either in the community and in urgent need of hospitalisation or on an EDC and in need of a longer period in hospital, than in the case where the patient is already in hospital on an STDC, and where an extension certificate is being considered. In the latter case, the AMP will have had the benefit of being able to consider, during the running of the STDC, whether there is a conflict situation in terms of reg 2, and to avoid it.

In the event that there is a conflict and where reg 3 arguably does not apply, it appears that there is no suitable remedy available under the Act to rectify the situation. Although the patient can apply to the tribunal for an order revoking the STDC or extension certificate, the only grounds on which such a revocation may be ordered are that one or more of the conditions in s 44(4)(a), (b) and (d) are not satisfied at the date of the revocation hearing, and where at that time the tribunal takes the view that it is not satisfied that the continued detention of the patient is necessary.[251] The only remedy would appear to be an application for judicial review to the Court of Session for the reduction of the certificate.[252] This course of action is, in practice, extremely unlikely to take place, given the timescale involved in the certificates.

3.158

CTO *application conflicts*

The position here is more complex. However, the general structure of the provisions is similar to those that apply to STDCs and extension certificates: there are certain situations where there is taken to be a conflict of interest but, where such a conflict exists, the medical examination can still be permitted, in certain circumstances. The provisions in the regulations,[253] namely regs 4 and 5, are concisely summarised in the Code of Practice as follows:

3.159

"The Mental Health (Conflict of Interest) (Scotland) (No 2) Regulations 2005 specifies the circumstances where there is or there is not to be considered a conflict of interest in relation to compulsory treatment orders. Considered a conflict when:

---

[251] 2003 Act, s 50(4). Although in s 50(4) the word "or" is used between conditions (a) and (b), these are not alternatives but are cumulative since the reference in the first part of s 50(4) is to the tribunal *not* being satisfied of (a) or (b). See also para 6.07, n 16.

[252] A judicial review application on proceedings under the 2003 Act is, in principle, competent: see para 8.23.

[253] Mental Health (Conflict of Interest) (Scotland) (No 2) Regulations 2005 (SSI 2005/380).

- either medical practitioner is related to the patient in any degree specified (see list of prohibited degrees of relationship below);
- the two medical practitioners are related to each other in any degree specified (see list of prohibited degrees of relationship below);
- where the CTO proposes the detention in an independent health care service and either medical practitioner is employed by or contracted to provide services in or to that health care service;
- where the CTO authorises detention in an NHS hospital and both medical practitioners are employed or contracted to provide services in or to that hospital;
- prohibited degrees of relationship are – child, grandchild, parent, grandparent, wife, husband, sister, brother, daughter-in-law, son-in-law, mother-in-law, father-in-law, sister-in-law, brother-in-law, cohabitee and any child, grandchild, parent, grandparent, sister or brother of a cohabitee.

An examination is permitted to be carried out even where there is a conflict of interest if:

- the conflict of interest is in terms of regs 4(1)(c) or (d) (see third and fourth bullet points of para ... above);
- failure to carry out a medical examination would result in delay which would involve serious risk to the health, safety and welfare of the patient or to the safety of other persons; and
- if one of the medical practitioners is a consultant and the other practitioners does not work directly with or under the supervision of that consultant."[254]

3.160   As with an STDC or extension certificate, there are two stages in any conflict situation. First of all, the question of whether a conflict of interest is to be "taken" to arise must be decided; if not, the regulations do not apply and the examination can legitimately proceed. Where there is a conflict situation under reg 4, the examination may still properly proceed, but only if the conditions in reg 5 are satisfied. There are two exceptions to this: where the conflict arises out of the relationship between a practitioner and a patient or between the two authors of the mental health reports, there is no second stage. In other words, the conflict cannot be "excused" and the examination should not proceed under any circumstances.[255]

3.161   It is usually clear whether or not a conflict situation in terms of reg 4 arises. It is worth noting that where the proposed detention would be in an independent health care service (see above for the

---

[254] Code of Practice, vol 2, p 64, paras 14 and 15. On the status of the Code, see para 1.40.
[255] This is different to the equivalent situation where there is an STDC, in which case a conflict based on an AMP–patient relationship can be excused.

definition) *neither* medical practitioner should be employed by or contracted to provide services there, otherwise a conflict situation arises;[256] such a conflict does not arise where the proposed detention is in an NHS (or other non-independent) hospital unless *both* medical practitioners are so employed or contracted.[257] The phrase "employed by or contracted to provide services in or to that hospital" applies only where the medical practitioner works "wholly or mainly" in that hospital.[258] This will be a question of fact and degree to be decided in each case.

There is more difficulty surrounding whether or not the conflict can be overlooked in terms of reg 5. It is unusual but by no means unheard of for a potential conflict situation to arise where the patient does not have a GP or where the patient's GP is unwilling or unable to provide a mental health report to support the application. In these cases, usually the RMO will ask a colleague who is an AMP from another department within the hospital to author the report. This is where a problem might arise.   **3.162**

It is important to note that all three parts of reg 5(1) must apply in order for the conflict to qualify as a permitted one. The condition in reg 5(1)(a) provides that the conflict must be one that does not involve a relationship between the patient and the medical practitioner or between the practitioners; such conflicts are not permitted under the regulations. The other two conditions in reg 5 have been adjudicated upon in some tribunal hearings, and this has caused some disparity of approach. The first requires that, in order to be a permitted conflict, it has to be established that failure to carry out the medical examination would involve serious risk to the health, safety or welfare of the patient or the safety of others. As with the similar test in the case of an STDC, the comments about attempting to find an alternative practitioner to write the report (one in respect of whom there is no conflict) apply here.[259] The most obvious course of action here would be for the RMO to seek the assistance of an AMP who is at another hospital and who would therefore not attract the application of the conflict regulations. In the case of a CTO application, the timeline is more favourable for this kind of evasive action than in the case of an STDC, since the RMO will usually have the period of the certificate (plus possibly the automatic extension to it if a CTO application is being presented)[260] to source and line up such an alternative AMP. Of course, it is fair to say that from a   **3.163**

---

[256] Regulation 4(1)(c).
[257] Regulation 4(1)(d).
[258] Regulation 4(2).
[259] See the comments at para 3.157 above.
[260] 2003 Act, ss 68 and 69.

practical point of view, this course of action might prove difficult since it would involve cross-hospital co-operation. However, there is no explicit qualification by reference to practicability or reasonable practicability here, as there is with some of the obligations under the 2003 Act. Where efforts are made to source an alternative, and these prove fruitless, the MHO could, however, then argue that reg 5(1)(b) is triggered since, if the on-site AMP does not conduct the examination with a view to producing the second mental health report, the CTO application would not be able to be made on time, meaning that the patient would have to be released, and this, it could be argued, would satisfy the "serious risk" test. Given that the test is very similar to the wording of the criterion in s 64(5)(c),[261] the same arguments as would be employed in the CTO application against a release into the community (assuming a detention order is being sought) could be employed to explain the inability to avoid a conflict under the regulations.

3.164   Where the MHO assumes that he will not be able to source an alternative AMP from outwith the hospital, and so does not try, there arises a question over whether it can be said that reg 5(1)(b) has been brought into play, since it could not be said that the failure by the on-site AMP to carry out the examination is the cause (and sole cause) of the serious risk of harm. It might be possible for the RMO to argue that he has tried to source an alternative in previous cases, and that to try to do so again would be pointless, since (for example) the other hospital in question has indicated that it will not assist in such cases. If such an argument is advanced, the tribunal might be convinced that reg 5(1)(b) is triggered. The MHO would not, it is submitted, require to scour the country in the hope of finding an AMP who might assist; it would seem sufficient that attempts have been made to do so with the nearest hospital and have either been fruitless on the occasion in question or where a general refusal to assist has been issued previously.

3.165   The authors have noted that there is a particular problem with obtaining a second report from another hospital in the Highland area. This can often lead to Highland applications giving rise to permitted conflict situations. The problem is partly caused by the

---

[261] The only difference is that the Act refers to "significant risk" and the regulations to "serious risk" but this is an unimportant difference. In this context, see the recent decision of Sh Pr Sir Stephen Young in *KM v MHTS*, 1 August 2009 (unreported), available on the Scottish Courts website at www.scotcourts.gov.uk and on the legal database Westlaw. In that case, the tribunal was held to have erred in finding that reg 5(1)(b) had been complied with, since there were insufficient findings-in-fact from which this could be inferred. This decision provides useful guidance on the questions to be asked by the care team (and the tribunal) in order to reach a conclusion on the applicability of reg 5(1)(b) (see para 20 of the judgment).

large geographical area that the Highland Trust covers, and the difficulty in persuading someone from another and often distant hospital to travel in order to carry out a medical examination of a patient. In such cases, a GP can be the answer but, in at least one tribunal case, the patient's GP was based in a town some distance from the hospital where he was being held under the STDC. The GP was not asked, in this case, to prepare a report and instead two reports were obtained from doctors in the hospital where the patient was. The tribunal asked the MHO to contact the GP who confirmed that he would not have been able to provide a report if asked, partly due to the travelling distance. In that case, it was accepted that reg 5(1)(b) was triggered, since the MHO would not have been able to secure the second report without serious risk of harm (risk of running out of time to apply for a CTO, in turn risking the release of the patient). However, much will depend on the circumstances of each case, and in all cases where there is a GP and a potential conflict would otherwise arise, the GP should always be asked to provide the report. If he refuses, and if the MHO has no other option, he can turn to another s 22-approved doctor in the hospital, and have a good case later for arguing that the conflict is a permitted one.

This brings us to reg 5(1)(c) which has also featured in a **3.166** number of tribunal decisions. The issue here is that certain types of professional relationship between the mental health report authors should be avoided. The aim here is to remove the suspicion that a lower-ranking practitioner may be simply "rubber stamping" the diagnosis of the higher-ranking practitioner, or at least may be fearful of questioning that diagnosis, or may simply take less care in conducting the examination since a more senior and experienced practitioner has reached a particular view. There is no requirement for the practitioners to carry out the examination in any particular order, nor is there a rule preventing the disclosure of the first completed mental health report (or an oral description of its findings) to the author of the second, in advance of the second medical examination. Of course, in arguing that a conflict has arisen and is not permitted, the challenger does not require to argue that there has been some complacency or pressure or foul play involved; it is the possibility of such a situation arising that the regulations are aimed at. This is why the 2003 Act does not talk of a conflict arising, but of regulations prescribing where one is "taken to" have arisen;[262] in other words, where one is assumed to have arisen. Similar protections are in place in cases of apparent

---

[262] This wording is used for STDCs, extension certificates and CTOs: see the 2003 Act, ss 44(8), 47(5) and 58(5) respectively.

bias on the part of a judicial body.[263] When a tribunal considers how the regulations are to be interpreted here, this purpose should be borne in mind.

3.167   As long as one of the medical practitioners is a consultant, the other should not "work directly with or under the supervision of that consultant".[264] There are two alternatives here: (1) working with; or (2) under the supervision of. There is an argument that the word "directly" applies to both alternatives, but it seems likely that it applies only to the "working with" part, on the basis of the structure of that paragraph and since it would make sense for regulations of this nature to strike at any relationship of supervision, direct or otherwise.[265] In the case of the "working directly with" part this should be clear, as this refers to a day-to-day working relationship. It implies that the relationship is ongoing, so where the practitioners no longer work together but have in the past, reg 5(1)(c) would apply. Similarly, where the practitioners have worked together recently, but sporadically, this would not seem to constitute "working directly with". Of course, as ever, the answer in any particular case will depend on fact and degree.

3.168   The question of whether one practitioner works "under the supervision of" the other is more difficult. Unlike "working directly with", a relationship of supervision implies that there is a hierarchy between the two practitioners. However, a difference in the "rank" of the practitioners would not be enough; there has to be some kind of responsibility on the part of the superior-ranking practitioner for the work of the other. Given the omission of the word "directly" in relation to supervision (see above), it is reasonable to infer that supervision in any sense, whether direct or indirect, would qualify as supervision for the purposes of this part of the regulation. For example, in one tribunal case, it was decided that condition 5(1)(c) did not apply where the author of the second mental health report was ultimately responsible for any disciplinary action against the RMO, and for his general strategic management (but not his day-to-day management). It was decided there that a conflict arose and that it was not a permitted one. Once again, much will depend on the circumstances of the case.

---

[263] The law relating to bias, actual and apparent, is discussed further at paras 4.13 et seq.

[264] Regulation 5(1)(c) would potentially apply where both medical practitioners are consultants, since the wording suggests (although does not specify) that at least one must be a consultant for it to apply.

[265] This could be an important point, since working under the supervision of someone and working directly under their supervision are quite different. This point may have to be decided in an appropriate case. It was considered by at least one tribunal, and the interpretation favoured here was adopted.

In cases where a permitted conflict arises, a request by the patient   **3.169**
for time to seek an independent medical report will be difficult to
refuse, since at least this will involve the input of a psychiatrist
from outwith the trust involved in seeking an order in respect of the
patient.

Consequences of a conflict of interest

Where a conflict arises and it is not one that is not taken to be a   **3.170**
conflict under reg 3 (in the case of an STDC or extension certificate)
or it does not satisfy all three branches of reg 5(1) and so is not a
permitted conflict (in the case of a CTO application) the question
arises as to what the consequences are for the process. There are
two possibilities: (1) the conflict has no effect on the process and
the STDC, extension certificate or CTO application can proceed/
stay in place; or (2) the conflict is fatal to the process, and can lead
to the revocation of the STDC or extension certificate (but only
upon judicial review: see above at para 3.158) or the refusal of the
CTO application. This brings us back to the interpretation of the
Soneji guidelines discussed above.[266] We refer to the authorities and
principles discussed already here. The key question, then, is: did
Parliament intend that, in such a situation, the conflict be fatal to
the process? It is submitted that the answer is that it did so intend.
This is for several reasons:

(1) The opinion of the medical practitioner(s) is a key part of the
     process for the detention of a patient against his will under the
     2003 Act. In particular, in the case of an STDC or extension
     certificate, there is no independent check on the opinion of
     the medical practitioner, and his view as expressed following
     the medical examination is therefore the sole mechanism for
     detention. There is, of course, a requirement that the MHO
     consents to the granting of either certificate,[267] and this is
     an important check on the process, but there is no medical
     professional diagnostic check on the view of the psychiatrist
     issuing the certificate. Where there is taken to be a conflict,
     therefore, in terms of the regulations, this erodes a process
     which is already, arguably, lacking in external checks, leading to
     a deprivation of liberty for a substantial period. In the case of a
     CTO application, the second check on the mental health report
     author is, in a sense, even more important, since although there
     is more protection than in the case of an STDC or extension

---

[266] See paras 3.127 *et seq.*
[267] Section 44(3)(c)–(d) (STDC) and s 47(3)(c) (extension certificate).

certificate (at least there requires to be two opinions) in the case of a CTO, the potential deprivation of liberty is for a much longer period: up to 6 months. It is worth remembering that this is the equivalent of a 1-year sentence in the case of a convicted person. In fact, given the power to extend the CTO for a further 6-month period without the need for recourse to the tribunal, and given that the power to extend lies principally in the hands of the RMO (who will usually have written one of the original mental health reports) the significance of the initial reports is all the greater.

(2) The requirement to avoid a situation in which there is taken to be a conflict of interest takes pride of place among the key prerequisites for the granting of a certificate or the proper preparation of mental health reports for a CTO application. In ss 44 and 47, the power to issue a certificate applies only where *inter alia* there is no conflict of interest.[268] In the case of a CTO application, there "must not be" a conflict of interest except as specified in regulations.[269] This latter provision is in a section entitled "Medical examination: requirements". In fact, the requirements provided in s 58 are explicitly referred back to the MHO's duty (and therefore power)[270] in s 57 to apply for a CTO;[271] it seems that that duty (power) does not even arise unless the requirements in s 58 are fulfilled (including the requirement that there be no conflict of interest).

(3) Parliament has already turned its mind to the situations in which there is not taken to be a conflict of interest (or, in the case of a CTO application conflict, where a permitted conflict arises)[272] by setting these situations out clearly in detailed regulations. This impression is bolstered by the way in which, in particular, s 58(5) is framed: "Except in circumstances specified in regulations, there must not be a conflict of interest in relation to the medical examination." Parliament has considered that there may be exceptions, and has legislated on them. It would be odd, then, to take the view that Parliament intended that a

---

[268] 2003 Act, s 44(1)(c) and (3)(a) and s 47(1)(c) and (2)(a).

[269] *Ibid*, s 58(5).

[270] The two are, from a practical point of view, the same since there is no power on the part of the MHO to apply for a CTO unless he is duty bound to do so in terms of s 57.

[271] See 2003 Act, s 58(1) referring back to s 57(2).

[272] It is not clear why the conflict regulations refer to there being not "taken to be" a conflict in the case of an STDC or extension certificate, therefore following the wording of the corresponding provisions in the 2003 Act (ss 44(8) and 47(5)) while abandoning similar wording in the case of a CTO application (s 58(5)) in favour of a different formulation, namely permitted conflicts of interest.

situation not falling within the exceptions could nonetheless be overlooked, allowing the certificate to stand or the application to be granted.

(4) Parliament has focused on situations in which there is "taken to be" a conflict of interest. As mentioned above, this suggests that the concern is not on actual conflicts, where there can be proven to have been some pressure, complacency or compliance which could not be avoided without serious risk of harm to the patient or someone else, but on situations where there is assumed to be a conflict. This enhances the impression that Parliament took the question of conflict of interest very seriously. As alluded to earlier, in this sense, Parliament is adopting a similar stance to that taken by the courts to the presence of apparent bias in judicial decision-making;[273] the real possibility of bias (even if actual bias is not regarded as a serious possibility) is fatal to the judicial process in such cases. While the comparison is not exact, this is a further indication that such consequences were intended by Parliament where a conflict that cannot be excused occurs.

We would submit that it is plain that a conflict of interest is a matter **3.171** that Parliament has intended should have certain consequences. In the case of an STDC, the purported STDC will be invalid, although, as noted earlier, the only remedy is a declaration of invalidity arising out of judicial review proceedings. If there has been a non-permitted conflict of interest in relation to the preparation of the reports associated with the CTO application, then there is no proper application for a CTO before the tribunal, and the application should be refused. This is in accordance with the principle that statutory provisions which allow for deprivation of liberty of should be constructed strictly.[274]

Conflict of interest between tribunal members and other professionals[275]

In the case of tribunal members, it is clear that, as is the case with **3.172** any judicial office-holder, actual or potential conflicts of interest must be avoided. This danger is probably more acute in relation to medical and general members than with legal members. The Rules

---

[273] For a fuller discussion of apparent and actual bias and their impact in tribunal cases, see paras 4.13 *et seq.*
[274] See the discussion on this principle at para 3.141 above.
[275] For a discussion of the general law on the requirement of the tribunal to be independent, see paras 4.09 *et seq*; the law there might be relevant in considering any conflict of interest allegation aimed at a tribunal member.

do provide for certain relatively obvious cases where the member is automatically disqualified from sitting in the case, and these provisions are considered elsewhere.[276] However, for the most part, medical and general members do not accept cases in jurisdictions where they currently work or have in the past worked (although, in the latter case, the time gap is important in determining whether the member should take cases in the area). This means that, in reality, medical and general member conflicts (or potential conflicts) rarely arise. In the case of the legal member, he has more freedom to sit in his local area of operation, either current or in the recent past. However, there will be cases where the legal member has acted as a solicitor for a patient, or indeed for a witness, and, in the former case, there will almost always be a potential conflict; in the latter, it depends on the circumstances. Where a member comes across a good friend or current or recently former close colleague who is appearing as a witness or a representative of a party, serious consideration should be given to whether a potential conflict arises. This does not refer to cases where the witness or representative is a current or former professional acquaintance, in the sense of being known to the member professionally; something deeper than this will be required before the member needs to consider closely whether to sit in the case. It will, in all cases, be a matter of degree.

3.173   Where there is any doubt about whether a conflict arises, a member should always err on the safe side and refuse to sit in the hearing. It would be most unwise for the member to simply take the risk and to hope for the best; if the potential conflict comes to light, even if it has no bearing on the case, such action could amount to a disciplinary issue for the member concerned.[277] In addition, the member may have to consider the terms of any code of conduct or other similar guidelines issued by his employer and/or professional body, as to general conduct, since accepting a case where there is an actual or potential conflict of interest might breach such a code, leading to action being taken. In cases where a potential or actual conflict of interest arises, the tribunal member should contact MHTS as soon as it is spotted, in order that there might be time before the hearing to substitute that member, thereby avoiding a cancellation and re-scheduling of the hearing. Since case papers are made available in advance to members (usually at least several days in advance) these should be checked straight away, even if only to satisfy the member that no actual or potential conflict arises. While the tribunal member should always be alive to any actual or

---

[276] Rule 42, discussed at para 4.11.
[277] The regulations providing for disciplinary action against members can be found in the Mental Health Tribunal for Scotland (Disciplinary Committee) Regulations 2004 (SSI 2004/402), made under Sch 2, para 5 to the 2003 Act.

potential conflict of interest, like everyone else, tribunal members are not infallible. A participant in the hearing might notice such a conflict, and should, in such cases, draw this to the attention of the tribunal. Often, this will have to be done at the hearing itself, since those appearing will not be aware of the identity of the tribunal panel until then. Even so, it is better that a conflict situation is dealt with then so that the tribunal members can decide how to deal with the situation. Where such an issue is raised at a hearing, the tribunal should hear it as a preliminary matter (since the hearing may have to be adjourned) and should hear all parties before making a decision on whether the hearing can proceed that day.

There might arise a conflict of interest (actual or potential) which   3.174
does not involve the tribunal members at all, but which might arise as a result of a family, friend or professional relationship between two people appearing at the tribunal, as witnesses, parties or representatives or as a combination of two such categories. Again, it is always best to air such concerns before the tribunal since, if a decision is made in ignorance of the connection, and it is later discovered, the decision will be vulnerable to appeal on the ground of procedural impropriety.[278]

TAPE RECORDING OF PROCEEDINGS

Clearly, any issue regarding the recording of proceedings should be   3.175
raised as a preliminary issue. The proceedings before the tribunal are routinely recorded in an electronic sound file. It has been noted that: "There does not appear to be any authority in primary or subordinate legislation for the tape recording of proceedings before the Tribunal."[279]

This is, strictly speaking, incorrect, since there is an implied   3.176
power to do so in the Rules. In r 49(1)(f) there is a specific power allowing the tribunal to issue directions restricting *inter alia* the recording of any hearing. If there is the power to restrict the recording of any hearing, there must be the power to record it in the first place. That power is not specified, but can easily be implied from the general power to conduct the hearing in the manner the tribunal considers to be just and most suitable to the clarification

---

[278] On appeals, see Chapter 8. The Code of Practice, vol 2, pp 64–65, para 16 identifies one such possible conflict as being between the MHO and the patient and stresses that such a conflict be avoided as a matter of good practice. On the status of the Code, see para 1.40.
[279] Sh Pr Bowen of Lothian and Borders in *AG v Mental Health Tribunal for Scotland* [2007] MHLR 1, at para 5 of his Note.

and determination of the matters before the tribunal.[280] It could be said to be just in the sense that the parties should be able to access a full record of what was said at the hearing, in the event of any later challenge. Indeed, an argument in the *AG* case was made for the ordering of the transcription of the recording, since a concern was expressed that the written determination issued by the tribunal was inaccurate. This ability is even more pronounced in cases (not unusual) where the patient or a representative is not present and where, for instance, an interim CTO is granted. In addition, it might be said to be just to enable the tribunal members to access a certain part of the recording of the hearing during deliberations, where there is some uncertainty about what a witness has said, and where that uncertainty is relevant to the decision in the case. For the same reasons, the power can be said to be implied as one which is suitable for the clarification and determination of the matters before the tribunal.

3.177   The sheriff principal in the *AG* case takes the view that since the recording of proceedings is "voluntary", an order to transcribe any tape recording probably cannot be made. If it is correct that there is an implied power to record proceedings, this would suggest that there is power on the part of the appeal court to order a transcript. The sheriff principal does raise the possibility that a power to order a transcript of the proceedings may derive from a provision in the rules that applies mainly to summary applications in the sheriff court.[281] It might also be argued that the recording could be recovered under s 1 of the Administration of Justice (Scotland) Act 1972.

3.178   Given that there is the power to issue a direction restricting the recording of proceedings;[282] it is clear that the tribunal can, in any particular case, decline to do so. A specific request will have to be made otherwise, as a matter of routine, the hearing proceedings will be audio recorded. A request not to audio record may be made where the patient feels uncomfortable with such a recording being made; it may even be argued that the patient's paranoid state might be detrimentally affected by the presence of audio equipment. Where such an objection is raised, the views of all other parties must be canvassed, and a decision made.

---

[280] Rule 63(2).

[281] This is r 2.31 of the Act of Sederunt (Summary Applications, Statutory Applications and Appeals etc Rules) (SI 1999/929) which provides that: "The sheriff may make such order as he thinks fit for the progress of a summary application ...". On the application of this Act of Sederunt to appeals from tribunal decisions, see para 8.11.

[282] Rule 49(1)(f).

It is submitted that unless there exist exceptional circumstances, **3.179** all parts of the hearing proceedings should be recorded. This applies even to limited hearings where only some of the parties are present. Where the purpose of the part of proceedings in question is to decide whether to admit certain persons to the hearing or whether to exclude certain evidence, and where there is a sensitive issue which has led the tribunal to exclude certain parties from that part of the proceedings, even here the proceedings should be recorded. It is particularly important that such proceedings are recorded since one of the parties who has been excluded might later argue that the decision to hold a limited hearing on a certain issue represented a procedural impropriety; in order to make such an argument properly, a transcript of what was discussed may be necessary. It is important for the tribunal in such a situation to note that it is not deciding whether or not the tape should be transcribed, and its contents made available to the party it was trying to prevent from hearing the proceedings; that will be a decision for the appeal court, and at that stage the sensitivities of the situation can be considered and weighed against the rights of the excluded party. Even where the excluded party is represented in the limited hearing, the tribunal should still usually record it, since the party concerned may change representative and any new representative will naturally wish to know what was discussed during the limited hearing, and not necessarily rely on the notes or recollection of the previous representative. It is important in this context to bear in mind that where proceedings are recorded, this does not mean that everyone, or indeed anyone, will gain access to that recording at a later date. It seems that such access would be possible only where the tribunal or an appeal court directs that a transcript be made. Such a power would almost always be exercised in the context of appeal proceedings,[283] not by the tribunal itself.[284]

REQUESTS FOR NON-DISCLOSURE OF DOCUMENTS

Rule 46 provides that, except as otherwise provided for in the Rules, **3.180** the Clerk shall as soon as reasonably practicable send to the parties a copy of any document received in relation to the proceedings.[285] Whether at the request of a relevant person, or on its own initiative, the tribunal sitting as a panel or a Convener sitting alone may determine

---

[283] Such as in the *AG* case, discussed above.
[284] The tribunal would probably technically have the power to order a transcript under the general r 49 power to issue directions and the very wide power to regulate its own procedure under r 52(1). A review is being conducted, at the time of writing, into whether or not to continue the practice of tape recording all hearings.
[285] Rule 46(1).

whether a document should also be sent to any other person.[286] For example, the RMO is not a party in an application for a CTO, but he is a person with a right to be heard and to lead evidence.[287] In order for him to exercise that right, it may be necessary for him to have notice of the content of a document that the tribunal has received in connection with the application. Rule 46(2) allows for the tribunal to determine that the document should be sent to him.

3.181   Requests for non-disclosure of documents are dealt with in r 46A. A request is to be made in writing by the person sending the document to the Tribunal, at the time when the document is sent to the Tribunal. The request must specify the words and passages for which non-disclosure is sought, and giving reasons for the request. The rule does not specify that the request must indicate to whom the document is not to be disclosed; it is, however, essential that the Tribunal be made aware of this.

3.182   On receipt of a request under r 46A, the tribunal or a Convener is to decide whether the request is to be intimated to any person.[288] That person is then to be invited to make representations either in writing or at a hearing. It is not clear from the Rules what information is to be disclosed with the request. Clearly, it is possible that the purpose of the request might be undermined if intimation of the terms of the request disclosed the information in respect of which non-disclosure was sought. Equally, if insufficient information is provided, it may be difficult for the party to whom intimation is made to make any meaningful submissions about the matter. There is no provision whereby the request can be intimated, for example, to a patient's curator or a patient's solicitor rather than to the patient personally.[289] Rule 55(2)(b) applies specifically where a decision not to disclose a document to a patient has been made under r 47, and not at a stage where the decision whether or not to disclose the document is being made under r 46.

3.183   Rule 46A(4)(a) provides that after considering the request and any representations, the tribunal may direct that all or any part of the document should not be disclosed. Rule 46A(4)(b) provides that the

---

[286] Rule 46(2). On Conveners sitting alone (namely in-house Conveners), see para 2.11.

[287] 2003 Act, s 64(2) and (3).

[288] Rule 46A(3).

[289] Contrast with r 47(4). See also the English Mental Health Review Tribunal Rules, which provide that where the tribunal is minded not to disclose a document, it may disclose it to a patient's appointed representative, where disclosure would be in the interests of the party and where the representative will refrain from disclosure to anyone else (including his client) unless with the Tribunal's consent. See r 14(2), (5) and (6) of the Tribunal Procedure (First-tier Tribunal) (Health, Education and Social Care Chamber) Rules 2008 (SI 2008/2699).

tribunal may direct that where a redacted and disclosable version has been provided under para (2), that version is to be disclosed in place of the original document. Rule 46A, unlike r 47, does not set out a test such as "serious harm to the patient", which must be met before a decision not to disclose a document can be taken. It is possible to envisage a document parts of which might be subject to confidentiality or legal professional privilege.[290] It may contain details about another patient which are irrelevant to the case. In order to respect the rules of law regarding confidentiality and privilege, the tribunal might require to have the document redacted. In cases such as this, the tribunal would have to consider only the disclosable part of the document in determining the application before it.

It is plain from r 47 that the tribunal may consider a document all   **3.184** or part of which is not to be disclosed only in circumstances where:

- disclosure may cause serious harm to the patient or any other person such that it would be wrong to disclose it to the patient or another person; but
- in the circumstances it would not be unfair if the document or report or the undisclosed part of it were considered by the tribunal.[291]

The Convener or the tribunal may appoint a person having appro-   **3.185** priate skills or experience to report on whether disclosure may cause such serious harm.[292] Rule 47, as substituted by r 2 of the Mental Health Tribunal for Scotland (Practice and Procedure) (No 2) Amendment Rules 2008[293] (with effect from 20 December 2008) omits the unworkable provision in its predecessor which required parties to be given an opportunity to make representations about documents they had not seen.[294] The Convener or the tribunal is then, having taken into account the report of any expert appointed under r 47(2), to decide how much, if any, of the document is to be disclosed, and may direct that the document may be considered by the tribunal, and that all or part of its contents is not to be disclosed to specified persons.[295] It is suggested that as the usual presumption is in favour of disclosure of the evidence on which the tribunal intends to rely, only such material as the tribunal is satisfied, on the basis of evidence, may cause serious harm, can be withheld.

---

[290] For a discussion of this privilege, see paras 5.82 et seq.
[291] Rule 47(1).
[292] Rule 47(2).
[293] SSI 2008/396.
[294] Rule 47(4) as in force prior to 20 December 2008.
[295] Ibid.

3.186   In terms of r 47(5), the Tribunal is to notify the representative or the patient or other person to whom the document is not to be disclosed that such a decision has been made, and of the reasons for it. The decision, and the reasons for it, are presumably to be recorded in writing, as with any other decision of the Tribunal. This suggests that the drafter intended that the patient or other person should not personally receive the decision on this matter. There is no provision specifically prohibiting the representative from communicating the terms of the decision to his client.[296] It may be that a direction under r 47(4) prohibiting disclosure of the content of the document itself would prevent communication of any part of the decision or reasons which would in turn disclose the content of the document.[297] Where a patient does not have a representative, a curator may be appointed under r 55(1) where a decision has been taken not to disclose a document or any part of it to the patient.[298] It is not clear how the interests of any other party, such as a named person, who is unrepresented, are to be protected where a decision has been taken not to disclose a document to him. It is also unclear how the provisions of the Rules regarding intimation of a decision about this type of matter are intended to interact with the statutory provisions regarding the intimation of written decisions.

3.187   The interaction of rr 46A and 47 seems to be as follows. Rule 46A is intended to be used where the document or part of it is not to be disclosed, and there is no question of the Tribunal considering any non-disclosed part of it in reaching its decision. Non-disclosure under r 46A might be appropriate as a result of the operation of any one of a variety of legal rules which would result in the withholding of part of the contents of a document. Rule 47 is intended to apply where non-disclosure can be justified on the ground that serious harm would be caused to the patient or another person, but the Tribunal nevertheless considers it would be fair to consider the whole document. In that latter situation, the safeguard for the patient or other person is provided by the disclosure of the decision and the reasons for it to a representative or curator. There is also the potential for a direction that the report is not to be disclosed to the patient, but may be disclosed to his representative or curator.

3.188   Although a single Convener or the tribunal can deal with a request for non-disclosure, in practice most such requests are sent to the MHTS headquarters in advance of the hearing in order to be actioned so that by the time of the hearing the request has been dealt

---

[296] Again, contrast with r 14(2), (5) and (6) of the English Rules: see n 289 above.
[297] On directions generally, see paras 7.30 et seq.
[298] Rule 47(6).

with. Where the request is sent to MHTS headquarters in advance of a hearing, one of the in-house Conveners will deal with it.[299] On some occasions, a request has been made to order non-disclosure of the fact of an application. However, rr 46A and 47 do not permit the granting of such an order, since they both relate specifically to the non-disclosure of documents. In addition, an advance application for non-disclosure should state the grounds for non-disclosure clearly, with reference to the appropriate rule being relied upon. In some cases, applications under either of the rules have been sparsely justified, and this is likely to lead to a rejection of the application. Additional evidence, for example in the form of medical evidence which addresses the likelihood of serious harm under r 47, should be included where possible. Similarly, where a request is made to the tribunal at the hearing, it should be well reasoned and should come with supporting evidence where available.

An application under either r 46A or r 47 made at the hearing **3.189** presents practical difficulties as the Convener will have to ensure that the application is heard outwith the presence of the person who it is desired should not see the document. This power is available in terms of r 66(7), a provision which applies exclusively to r 47 proceedings.[300] As already mentioned, while, for r 47 applications, the tribunal can appoint a curator,[301] such a step is not available with regard to r 46 applications and, in such a case, a direction to the representative not to disclose a document to his client would be the obvious (if awkward) way around the need to ensure that representations are taken from the party who might be affected, while ensuring that the document content is not disclosed by the representative in the event of the request for non-disclosure being granted. This puts the representative of the party concerned (usually the patient) in a very difficult position since his client will (naturally) wish to know why he was not invited into the tribunal room and what the outcome of the discussion was. The position might become even more complex where the person concerned acquires fresh representation or becomes unrepresented; there is an issue over the application of the direction to any new representative (this might depend on how it is worded) and to the patient. In the latter case, presumably the direction does not apply. These practical problems have not, to the knowledge of the authors, yet arisen, but they may in the future. This is why, in all such cases, an advance application, to be dealt with by an in-house Convener, is by far the preferable

---

[299] For a discussion of the role of the in-house Conveners, see para 2.11.
[300] This provision is commented on further at para 4.155. As noted there, it seems odd that this provision is to be found in r 66 and not r 47.
[301] Rules 47(6) and 55(2)(b).

course. An added advantage is, of course, a saving in time at the hearing since the disclosure decision will have been taken.

3.190   A decision not to intimate a medical report to a patient might be regarded as infringing his right to respect for his private and family life.[302] Where that decision is based on a risk of serious harm to himself or another person, however, the protection of "health or morals" or the prevention of disorder and crime might be prayed in aid as legitimate aims justifying the non-disclosure. So far as procedures are concerned which permit the patient's representative, but not the patient personally, to have access to the evidence relating to decisions to detain him because of a mental disorder, these find some support in the reasoning of the Commission in *Winterwerp v Netherlands*, in the context of compliance with the requirements of Art 5(4):[303]

> "The Commission considers that, in deciding on the merits of the detention or release of a person of unsound mind, it may indeed be necessary, in the interests of the patient, for the proceedings not to take place in public, and for the patient not to be personally informed of all the evidence on which the competent authority has to base its decision ... In the present case, the fact that the applicant was not allowed access to the medical records relating to him is not incompatible with the requirements of a judicial procedure.

> "On the other hand, no procedure can be described as judicial which provides no opportunity for both sides to express their views in some way or other. In the opinion of the Commission, the right of the person to present his own case and to challenge the medical and social evidence adduced in support of his detention constitutes, in the case of a person of unsound mind, the absolute minimum for a judicial procedure.

> "It is naturally the responsibility of the national legislature or of the judge dealing with a particular case to arrange for these rights to be exercised in whatever way is considered most suitable, eg: the hearing by the court either of the person concerned himself or of his representative (lawyer, guardian etc,); for the appointment of an independent expert by the court; the right for the person concerned to submit the findings of a doctor of his choice."[304]

3.191   It is worthy of note that the House of Lords has specifically disapproved of a procedure, in the context of documents for which

---

[302] See comment on r 12 (now repealed) of the English Mental Health Review Tribunal Rules 1983 (SI 1983/942) in Jones, *Mental Health Act Manual* (10th edn, 2006), p 652. The equivalent provision is now found in the current rules: r 14(2), (5) and (6) of the Tribunal Procedure (First-tier Tribunal) (Health, Education and Social Care Chamber) Rules 2008 (SI 2008/2699) – see n 289 above.

[303] App No 6301/73, Commission Report adopted 15 December 1977.

[304] *Winterwerp v Netherlands*, Commission Report cited above, paras 101 *et seq*.

public interest immunity has been asserted, whereby counsel only were allowed to view the documents in question. It was noted that this put counsel in an invidious position as regarded his client, to whom he could not disclose the contents of the document.[305] The House of Lords indicated that if, exceptionally, documents could not be discussed in open court, independent counsel should be appointed to deal with the matter. With that in mind, it is open to question whether even the provisions of the former English rules deal with the difficulty which arises for an instructed representative where there is something that he is directed not to disclose to his client. What is said by the Commission in *Winterwerp*, however, does indicate that a distinction may properly be drawn in relation to the disclosure of information to the representative of a patient suffering from a mental disorder.

---

[305] *Somerville v Scottish Ministers* 2008 SC (HL) 45, per Lord Mance at paras 203 and 204.

CHAPTER 4

HEARING PROCEDURE II – THE MERITS
OF THE CASE

THE GENERAL APPROACH

In this chapter we consider how the merits of a case should be dealt   **4.01**
with by the tribunal. This stage begins once all preliminary matters
have been dealt with. It is not possible to lay down an absolutely
fixed procedure, since much will depend on the facts of the case
and its procedural history. However, we consider, in the usual order,
some of the main parts of a standard hearing on the merits, so as to
give a general impression of how a typical tribunal case should be
conducted.

As has already been mentioned, tribunal members are under   **4.02**
an obligation to avoid formality wherever possible.[1] While this
obligation exists for all parts of the hearing, including discussions
on preliminary matters, it is perhaps more relevant where the merits
of the case are under consideration, since at this stage evidence on
the merits of the application or appeal will be led.[2] One of the major
ways in which such informality is demonstrated (when compared with
public court hearings) lies in the emphasis during tribunal hearings
on interventions and questioning by tribunal members.[3] However,
the obligation to conduct the hearing as informally as possible should
not be seen as a blank cheque simply to deal with the arguments and
evidence presented in a completely arbitrary and relaxed way.

Users of the tribunal are entitled to expect patience, courtesy and   **4.03**
respect from tribunal members, as from any other judicial body.
Overbearing or aggressive behaviour is particularly out of place in a
setting where some of the key participants are vulnerable by reason
of mental disorder.

---

[1] Rule 63(2)(a).
[2] See paras 3.09 *et seq* for the content of this informality notion, and those comments are equally applicable here.
[3] These are covered below in detail at paras 4.103 *et seq* and 4.114 *et seq.*

4.04   Drawing the line between behaving informally, thereby putting participants at their ease (leading often to a more productive hearing), and keeping the hearing within the bounds of proper judicial process is one of the major challenges all tribunal members face. It is this balancing act that characterises much of the way in which a hearing on the merits should take place. It is particularly important that the structure and tone of the proceedings are judicial in character. Many of the participants, whether patients, family members or social work or medical staff, are used to working in case conferences. It is important, however, that the judicial character is not diluted by following the approach of a case conference in the tribunal hearing. It is notable that the Tribunal has recently adopted the Statement of Principles of Judicial Ethics for the Scottish Judiciary (produced by the Judicial Council for Scotland) as applicable to tribunal proceedings. This Statement is reproduced as Appendix 5 and should be referred to in considering any question of judicial conduct. Clearly, it is not as influential as the common law or the rules in any particular area, but it does offer a more general flavour of the standard of conduct expected of tribunal members.

4.05   It should be noted that certain material in this chapter can be applicable to the way in which the hearing is conducted throughout, not just at the merits stage. So, for instance, the law on fairness[4] and comments below on interventions and questions from tribunal members[5] apply equally to the whole tribunal hearing process. However, these issues often arise more acutely during consideration of the merits of the case, and so are dealt with here.

THE GENERAL LAW ON FAIRNESS

4.06   Before we consider the various stages in the tribunal's consideration of the merits of the case, we should deal relatively briefly with the law on fairness of judicial proceedings. The overriding objective[6] requires the tribunal to act fairly in carrying out its duties, but what does this mean in practice? All judicial bodies must abide by certain basic rules of fairness. This does not mean that all judicial bodies must react in the same way in similar situations. What fairness demands may differ in practice as between public courts and specialist tribunals. An important example is practice in judicial questioning of witnesses: in the public courts, judges are expected to

---

[4] Below at para 4.06.
[5] Below at paras 4.103 *et seq* and 4.114 *et seq*.
[6] Rule 4. See generally on this principle para 1.26.

intervene less than in specialist tribunals[7], and this certainly applies when comparing the public courts with the mental health tribunal.[8] The reason for this difference in approach arises from the prevalence of the adversarial atmosphere in the public courts, compared with the more inquisitorial expectation which prevails in the specialist tribunals.

Although differences exist, in all judicial bodies, two basic rules of fairness prevail: (1) all parties should be given a full opportunity to put their case; and (2) all parties are entitled to have their case heard by an impartial and independent body. These two principles are fundamental to all fair processes. There is a large body of case law that has developed over a long period, from both the public courts and specialised tribunals, setting out the parameters of these fundamental rights. This case law is relevant when examining a situation wherever it is alleged that a tribunal has acted unfairly. There is insufficient space to consider these principles in full here,[9] but some of the main points will be covered, in order that mental health tribunal members and those appearing before them can be aware of the significance of these more general authorities.   **4.07**

Full opportunity to present case

The obligation to allow parties a full opportunity to put their case can be dealt with relatively shortly, since the principle can be demonstrated only by examining particular examples, many of which we deal with later in this chapter. So, the tribunal must, for example, allow all relevant persons to call any witnesses they want to lead, unless there are exceptional circumstances.[10] The tribunal must usually allow submissions to be delivered without curtailment.[11] Any interruptions should be kept to a minimum and should not have the effect of inhibiting the presentation of a party's case or unduly restricting the evidence of a witness.[12] Where a reasonable alternative course is available, perhaps by adjourning a case,[13] the tribunal should adopt   **4.08**

---

[7] In the sheriff courts, for example, it is said that a sheriff must question witnesses "with caution, usually only when it is necessary to clear up any point which has been overlooked or left obscure": T Welsh (ed), *Macphail's Sheriff Court Practice* (3rd edn, 2006), para 16.39. See the authorities cited there at nn 55 and 56.

[8] This issue is dealt with below at paras 4.114 *et seq.*

[9] For an excellent discussion of the authorities in a tribunal context, see P Elias and B Napier (eds), *Harvey on Employment Law and Industrial Relations*, paras T901–T924.

[10] See below at para 4.44.

[11] See below at paras 4.93 *et seq.*

[12] See below at paras 4.103 *et seq.*

[13] See below at paras 3.21 *et seq.*

that course, rather than restrict an opportunity to present evidence or argument.[14] The tribunal could be criticised where it relies on an argument or legal authority it has not canvassed with the parties in advance.[15]

Independence and impartiality generally

4.09   The work of the Tribunal is principally concerned, from the point of view of human rights law, with making determinations which impact on the patient's right to liberty under Art 5 ECHR.[16] The question as to whether liberty is a civil right, and Art 6 engaged, is not settled in Strasbourg case law.[17] The common law, however, has long required that parties be given a fair hearing, and the standards of fairness required of a tribunal by the common law have become increasingly aligned in recent years with those required by Art 6 EHCR.[18] Indeed, the domestic case law in this area has now been developed to such an extent that it has been said in the House of Lords that: "there is now no difference between the common law test of bias and the requirements under Article 6 of the Convention of an independent and impartial tribunal".[19]

4.10   Whether or not Art 6 is engaged, the Tribunal must meet the standards of a court for the purposes of Art 5(4) ECHR, when it is

---

[14] See below at para 3.23.

[15] See below at paras 4.97 *et seq.*

[16] The tribunal may be depriving a person of liberty, by making an order such as a CTO. Such deprivation of liberty must be in accordance with a procedure prescribed by law. It must also be for a purpose permitted by the Convention. The lawful detention of persons of unsound mind is permitted by Art 5(1)(e). Where the tribunal is considering an application for revocation of a decision to detain, whether of the tribunal, or of medical personnel, it is acting a court for the purposes of Art 5(4) ECHR. Everyone who is deprived of his liberty is entitled to take proceedings by which the lawfulness of his detention shall be decided speedily by a court.

[17] See, for example, *Aerts v Belgium* (1998) 29 EHRR 50, *Aldrian v Austria* 65 DR 337 and *Brown v United Kingdom* (Application 968/04). Silber J appears to have accepted that liberty was a civil right for the purposes of Art 6 in *R (PD) v West Midlands and North Mental Health Review Tribunal* [2004] 1 MHLR 25, but in doing so he goes further than the Strasbourg authorities: see discussion in *R (West) v Parole Board* [2005] 1 WLR 350. In *R (PD)* the Court of Appeal similarly seems to have accepted without any active discussion of the point that Art 6 applies: [2004] 1 MHLR 183. Whether or not it applies, the standards of fairness required today at common law do not differ from those required by Art 6.

[18] For example in the field of apparent bias: see *Porter v Magill* [2002] 2 AC 357; *Singh v Secretary of State for the Home Department* 2004 SC 416.

[19] *Lawal v Northern Spirit Ltd* [2003] UKHL 35; [2004] 1 All ER 187; [2003] ICR 856 at para 14. For a Scottish perspective on these authorities, see R Reed and J Murdoch, *A Guide to Human Rights Law in Scotland* (2nd edn, 2008).

determining the lawfulness of the detention of an individual which include the requirements of fairness at common law.[20] The tribunal in making any decision would act unlawfully if it did not comply with the requirements of fairness at common law.

Lack of independence and impartiality

The necessity for independence would tend to preclude any connection between a tribunal member and a party or witness involved in the case in question, or perhaps between a tribunal member and some organisation or cause that might benefit from the outcome of a case. The Rules deal with certain situations that arise here, namely where a member is employed or contracted to provide services in or to the hospital or independent health care service in which the patient is or may be detained;[21] where a member is directly involved in providing medical treatment, community care services, relevant services or any other treatment, care or service to that patient;[22] or where the member has a personal or professional connection with the patient.[23] In any of these situations, the member is automatically disqualified from serving on the tribunal deciding the case.[24] In the event that this rule is breached, this will certainly constitute a procedural impropriety. In the case of a personal connection, this will usually be obvious, and would include friendship, even where that friendship has developed from what was initially a professional relationship. We would suggest that any professional connection with the patient, even in the past, would disqualify a member from sitting.[25] This part of the rule uses the word "connection"[26] as opposed to "relationship", suggesting that even a brief encounter will disqualify the member; a lengthy relationship (personal or professional) is not required to trigger this part of the rule. Of course, even where the rule is not technically triggered, a member will usually be wise to decline to sit in a case even where the personal or professional connection is in the past, to avoid any awkward scenes or any accusation later of lack of independence. Any professional ethical rules covering the member should be complied with, of course, even in cases where they are stricter than r 42.

4.11

---

[20] R (West) v Parole Board [2005] 1 WLR 350.
[21] Rule 42(1)(a). This provision is triggered only where the member works wholly or mainly for the hospital or independent health care service (r 42(2)).
[22] Rule 42(1)(b).
[23] Rule 42(1)(c).
[24] Rule 42(1), first line.
[25] The English Mental Health Review Tribunal's Conflict of Interest Guidelines, reproduced in R (PD) v West Midlands and North MHRT [2004] MHLR 174 at para 48 are instructive here.
[26] Rule 42(1)(c).

4.12   Most claims of a lack of independence or impartiality come to be framed as apparent, rather than actual, bias. Apparent bias may arise where, for example, a judge has some connection to a litigant which might call into question his impartiality, or may be pled on the basis of a want of "structural" independence and impartiality. There have been a number of high-profile examples of the latter type of challenge in recent years (mainly under the independence obligation contained in Art 6 of the ECHR) such as those arising out of the relationship between the Crown and the re-appointment of the now abandoned office of temporary sheriff;[27] between the Scottish Ministers and Historic Scotland in a planning context;[28] and between members of the Children's Panel and the Scottish Ministers.[29]

Actual and apparent bias

4.13   There are two types of impartiality argument. The first involves an accusation of *actual* bias. Such cases are rare since, in order to succeed, it has to be shown that the judicial office-holder has indicated in advance of the announcement of the decision and in clear terms a preference for the case of one party over the other. Such cases are not unknown,[30] but most judicial office-holders are acutely aware of the need to reserve their opinion (and certainly not to express a final view) until deliberations are under way. As noted below, a provisional view is permitted and so would not be classed as an example of the exhibition of actual bias.[31]

4.14   The second type of impartiality is more common, and there is plenty of scope for the application of the law in this area in the inquisitorial atmosphere of a mental health tribunal hearing. This form of impartiality involves what is known as *apparent* bias. There are two situations in which such bias might arise:

---

[27] See *Starrs v Ruxton* 2000 JC 208.
[28] *County Properties Ltd v Scottish Ministers* 2002 SC 79 and *Lafarge Redland Aggregates Ltd v Scottish Ministers* 2001 SC 298.
[29] *S v Miller (No 1)* 2001 SC 977.
[30] See the extraordinary comments made by the arbitrator in *Catalina and Norma MV* (1938) 61 Lloyd's Rep 360 where he expressed views about the credibility of witnesses based upon their nationality. The decision in this case was overturned on appeal as a result of a display of actual bias. The majority of challenges are framed as apparent bias. If conduct from which actual bias might be inferred takes place, then the test for apparent bias will readily be met. It is notable that in *Bradford v McLeod* 1986 SLT 244, where a sheriff had expressed a view to a solicitor at a social occasion that striking miners should not be given legal aid, the challenge succeeded on the basis of apparent bias.
[31] See below at para 4.13.

(1) where there is a connection between a tribunal member and a party or witness involved in the case in question, or perhaps between a tribunal member and some organisation or cause that might benefit from the outcome of a case; and

(2) where the conduct of the tribunal member during the hearing gives rise to concern

The test in any case arising under either category is:

"whether the fair minded and informed observer, having considered the facts, would conclude that there was a real possibility that the tribunal was biased".[32]

The critical point about apparent bias is that the correct question is   **4.15**
not whether the tribunal member was in fact biased, or whether there was any evidence that he was biased. Nor is it relevant to consider whether the parties, or one of them, thought the tribunal member in question was biased. Any suspicion of bias on the part of a losing party must be objectively justified, and there must be a demonstrable and rational basis for it.[33] The test is objective, and the fictitious person who is used in that test is the fair-minded and informed observer.[34] The reference to an observer who is informed is important, especially in relation to apparent bias type (2) above; this fictitious person is not the casual observer, parachuted into the hearing in question at the point at which it is said that the behaviour occurred, but someone who, it is imagined, has witnessed the whole hearing and who is aware of all of the evidence and issues in the case. In cases of type (1), the knowledge with which the informed observer is *endowed* is of the general nature of the tribunal proceedings and of the connection the member is said to have. The reference to a "real possibility" means that the conduct or connection has to be substantial, and trivial or minor examples will not lead to an established case of apparent bias. The observer mentioned in the test will be neither complacent nor unduly sensitive or suspicious.[35]

The Court of Appeal has issued some general guidance on apparent   **4.16**
bias type (1) in *Locabail Ltd* v *Bayfield Properties Ltd*:

---

[32] *Porter* v *Magill* [2002] UKHL 67; [2002] 2 AC 357 per Lord Hope at para 103 in the House of Lords. The adoption of this test by the English courts brought the English law into line with the standard required by Art 6 ECHR, and also with the Scottish test for apparent bias, as enunciated by the High Court of Justiciary in *Bradford* v *McLeod* 1986 SLT 244.

[33] *Hauschildt* v *Denmark* (1990) 12 EHRR 266 at para 48.

[34] See discussion by Lord Hope of Craighead in *Helow* v *Secretary of State for the Home Department* [2008] UKHL 62; 2008 SLT 967 at paras 1–3.

[35] *Johnson* v *Johnson* (2000) 201 CLR 488 per Kirby J at para 53.

"Everything will depend on the facts, which may include the nature of the issue to be decided. We cannot, however, conceive of circumstances in which an objection could be soundly based on the religion, ethnic or national origin, gender, age, class, means or sexual orientation of the judge. Nor, at any rate ordinarily, could an objection be soundly based on the judge's social or educational or service or employment background or history, nor that of any member of the judge's family; or previous political associations; or membership of social or sporting or charitable bodies; or Masonic associations; or previous judicial decisions; or extra-curricular utterances (whether in textbooks, lectures, speeches, articles, interviews, reports or responses to consultation papers). By contrast, a real danger of bias might well be thought to arise if there were personal friendship or animosity between the judge and any member of the public involved in the case; or if the judge were closely acquainted with any member of the public involved in the case, particularly if the credibility of that individual could be significant in the decision of the case; or if, in a case where the credibility of any individual were an issue to be decided by the judge, he had in a previous case rejected the evidence of that person in such outspoken terms as to throw doubt on his ability to approach such person's evidence with an open mind on any later occasion; or if on any question at issue in the proceedings before him the judge had expressed views, particularly in the course of the hearing, in such extreme and unbalanced terms as to throw doubt on his ability to try the issue with an objective judicial mind or if, for any other reason, there were real grounds for doubting the ability of the judge to ignore extraneous considerations, prejudices and predilections and bring an objective judgment to bear on the issues before him. The mere fact that a judge, earlier in the same case or in a previous case, had commented adversely on a party or witness, or found the evidence of a party or witness to be unreliable, would not without more found a sustainable objection. In most cases, we think, the answer, one way or the other, will be obvious. But if in any case there is real ground for doubt, that doubt should be resolved in favour of recusal. We repeat: every application must be decided on the facts and circumstances of the individual case."[36]

4.17   Another case where a type (1) connection had to be considered was that of *R v Bow Street Metropolitan Stipendiary Magistrate, ex p Pinochet Urgarte (No 2)*[37] where a connection between a House of Lords judge and a subsidiary of Amnesty International, an organisation which had intervened in the case, was fatal to that judge's impartiality. The case had to be re-heard before a new House of Lords bench. In this case, the House of Lords court that decided

---

[36] [2000] QB 451; [2000] 1 All ER 65 at 77f–78c per Lord Bingham. Although the "real danger" test in *Locabail* has been replaced by the "real possibility" test in *Porter* above, the considerations set out by the Court of Appeal still afford useful guidance.
[37] [1999] 1 All ER 577.

the judge's connection was fatal made it clear that it was satisfied that the connection made no difference to that judge's decision in the case (the case had been decided by a 3–2 majority, with the judge in question being part of the majority). This highlights the fact that the actual impact (if any) of such a connection is irrelevant; it is the possibility of an impact that the law protects against. The *Pinochet* case was decided before the adoption by the English courts of the test in *Porter* v *Magill*. It was decided not on the basis of apparent bias, but on the principle that a judge must not act as the judge in his own cause. It is likely, however, that with the adoption of the *Porter* test, a challenge of this sort would now be made on the basis of apparent bias.[38]

So far as the "structural" impartiality of the tribunal is concerned, there might be thought to be scope for challenge along similar lines to the successful one in *Lawal* v *Northern Spirit Ltd*.[39] In *Lawal*, in proceedings before the Employment Appeal Tribunal, the employer was represented by counsel who also sat as a recorder (part-time judge), and in that latter capacity chaired the Employment Appeal Tribunal. He had previously sat along with one of the lay tribunal members before whom he was appearing in *Lawal*. The argument was that this contravened the right to an independent and impartial tribunal, because the counsel concerned had previously sat in a position where the lay members would have tended to rely on his views so far as the law was concerned. The fair-minded and informed observer would therefore conclude there was a real possibility that the lay member concerned would be subconsciously biased in favour of the counsel concerned. This argument succeeded in the House of Lords.   **4.18**

Where mental health tribunal Conveners appear in front of tribunals as lawyers for patients or for other parties, similar issues might be thought to arise. Given the multi-disciplinary nature of the tribunal, it could be argued also that the legal and medical members may rely on the general member's expertise in relation to some matters, and that the legal and general members rely on the medical member's expertise. Although general members (particularly those who work as MHOs) and medical members are more likely to be parties, or witnesses in proceedings, rather than representatives, it is difficult to see much distinction between a situation where a medical member comes before the tribunal as an RMO, having previously been the source of medical expertise on which one or more panel members have relied, and that in *Lawal*. In a small jurisdiction it might be difficult, as a practical matter, to run a multi-disciplinary   **4.19**

---

[38] See the comments of Lord Hope of Craighead in *Meerabux* v *Attorney-General of Belize* [2005] 2 AC 513 at para 22.
[39] [2003] ICR 856.

tribunal system without engaging members whose professional lives bring them into contact with the tribunal when they are not sitting in a judicial capacity.[40]

4.20   One of the key aims of the multi-disciplinary nature of the tribunal is to involve members with expertise in the process in which the tribunal is involved, and by definition such a person will come with their experience (or baggage) in a particular area. The important point here is that members are required to put aside their professional feelings and act judicially. Tribunal members will, however, require to be careful in stating any general views in public, such as during training events, in any published material or seminars or at conferences, since such utterances could, if heard or relayed to the lawyer for a future relevant person, form the basis of an apparent bias argument. Much will depend on the tone and content of the extra-judicial utterance.[41] The other area which might present a type (1) problem is where a tribunal member has had some professional[42] or personal[43] connection with a witness or party appearing before the tribunal. Situations in which a conflict of interest may arise involving a tribunal member have already been dealt with,[44] and most members are acutely aware of the likelihood of (and dangers inherent in) such connections, particularly where the professional pools involved are usually small. Finally, an argument that a medical member who provides the MHTS with independent expert reports is apparently biased is doomed to failure since even where a tribunal member is employed (albeit via an independent agency) *by one of the parties in a case* to provide independent expert reports (although not, of course, on a case in which that expert sits) it has been held that there is no apparent bias.[45]

---

[40] In *R (PD)*, n 17 above, the Court of Appeal, at para 11, considered that, in an extreme case, it might be a relevant consideration that it would be practically impossible to find a qualified tribunal free of connections which might give rise to an apprehension of bias, under reference to *Piersack* v *Belgium* (1982) 5 EHRR 169.

[41] For a case where a press article by a High Court judge in which he was highly critical of the ECHR (in particular Art 6) led to a finding of apparent bias in connection with an earlier judgment on an appeal based on Art 6 of the Convention, see *Hoekstra* v *HM Advocate (No 2)* 2000 JC 391.

[42] See the rather stark example of *Halford* v *Sharples* [1992] ICR 146, an employment case that, surprisingly, had to go to the Court of Appeal before the apparent bias argument succeeded.

[43] For an example of a personal connection in a tribunal context, see the employment case of *University College of Swansea* v *Cornelius* [1988] ICR 735, a decision of the Employment Appeal Tribunal.

[44] See paras 3.172 *et seq.*

[45] *Gillies* v *Secretary of State for Work and Pensions* 2006 SC (HL) 71; 2006 SLT 77, a decision involving the medical member of a disability appeal tribunal and his connection with the Benefits Agency.

Type (1) apparent bias cases will not be common. Type (2) **4.21** cases will be more common, although by no means common in themselves. The informality of the mental health tribunal hearing can be a curse as well as a blessing. Tribunal members must be acutely aware of the need to behave professionally and with patience even although that patience can sometimes be tested in what can be a fraught atmosphere. Even in tribunals where the issues are perhaps of a less emotive nature than those inevitably presented in mental health tribunals, tribunal members have found it difficult to maintain composure and concentration. This has given rise, in the context of employment tribunals, to apparent bias arguments based around allegations of drunkenness, leading to the tribunal member sleeping,[46] or simply falling asleep,[47] aggressive behaviour[48] and irritation and intemperate remarks.[49] It can be seen from these examples that apparent bias cases usually do not concern themselves with a tribunal member expressing a view in favour of one argument or case against another; the bias is implied from the behaviour of the tribunal member. It is clear that the this behaviour need not be morally reprehensible, unprofessional or in some way sloppy in order for a finding of apparent bias to be reached. The conduct might, on the face of it, be entirely innocent. For example, where a tribunal member makes a jocular comment of some kind, perhaps designed to lead to a more relaxed atmosphere at the hearing, this could lead to an argument of apparent bias, where the comment indicates that the member in some way does not treat an issue before the tribunal seriously, or where the comment discloses that the member concerned has formed a particular view on the matter.[50] This is not to say that in such cases this is the case; as

---

[46] *Stansbury* v *Datapulse plc* [2003] EWCA Civ 1951; [2004] IRLR 466.

[47] *Fordyce* v *Hammersmith and Fulham Conservative Association* [2006] All ER (D) 10.

[48] *Docherty* v *Strathkelvin District Council* 1994 SC 395. The conduct of the employment tribunal member was described as "quite animated", aggressive and hostile, but the decision of the Employment Appeal Tribunal to the effect that a case of bias had been made out was reversed by the Inner House. This case is also dealt with below at para 4.126.

[49] *Kennedy* v *Commissioner of Police for the Metropolis, The Times*, 8 November 1990. See also *IS (Fair hearing, natural justice) Belarus* [2004] UKIAT 00114, a decision of the Immigration Appeal Tribunal, where the adjudicator was said to have asked questions in an "angry voice" and to have said "Just answer the question!". However, the proceedings were found, on appeal, to have been fair, when considered as a whole.

[50] For a particularly unfortunate recent example where judicial jokes in poor taste, and of a potentially racially insulting nature, were held to found an apparent bias challenge, see *El-Farargy* v *El-Farargy* [2007] EWCA Civ 1149.

long as the fair-minded and informed observer, having considered the facts, would conclude that there was a real possibility that the tribunal was biased, the test will be satisfied.

4.22   In addition, tribunal members should refrain from commenting on the evidence of a witness while the case is under way, although it should take care to draw to the attention of parties matters which concern it, and about which it would wish to be addressed.[51] The general point here is that the tribunal should not behave in such a way that it seems its mind is closed on a particular issue. The tribunal could be accused of apparent bias where it creates:

> "the appearance of a closed mind against a party on a matter which calls for decision by the tribunal when that party has not yet presented all his evidence relevant to the point or had the opportunity of addressing the tribunal on that evidence".[52]

4.23   There is no harm in the tribunal indicating its preliminary views on a case before the evidence is over, as long as it is clear that the view is not a final one and that the tribunal's mind on the case remains open. Clearly, a tribunal would be most unwise to adopt this perilous course unless there was some good reason to do so. It might be sensible to adopt this course where, for instance, the tribunal wishes to focus the mind of the parties on its concerns about the case where the evidence being led is not concentrating on those points. It is clear that, in expressing such a view, tribunals will be given some latitude. In *Southwark London Borough Council* v *Jiminez*[53] an argument

---

[51] See the criminal case of *Milton* v *McLeod* 1999 SCCR 210 where the sheriff passed comment on the evidence of a witness, which indicated that he had formed a view on the evidence before the end of the case. The High Court quashed the conviction for theft on the basis that justice had not been done. See also another High Court case: *Millar* v *Lees* 1991 SCCR 799, where the sheriff had commented on the strength of the Crown case before all of the evidence was over. Even although this was in response to a direct question from the Crown to the sheriff, the comment was inappropriate and led to a miscarriage of justice, although authority to launch a fresh prosecution was granted. See also the case of *XS (Kosovo – Adjudicator's conduct – psychiatric report) Serbia and Montenegro* [2005] UKIAT 00093 at para 29 on a premature expression of a view on credibility in an immigration case. The IAT in that case also criticised what it saw as the Adjudicator's "expressions of disbelief" at certain answers from a witness.
[52] *Peter Simper & Co Ltd* v *Cooke (No 2)* [1986] IRLR 19 per Mr Justice Gibson at para 10. This case was applied in connection with comments by a tribunal member on the prospects of a claimant's case where he said she had "a mountain to climb" and where the Employment Appeal Tribunal accepted that these comments displayed apparent bias: *Dumfries and Galloway Acute and Maternity Hospitals NHS Trust* v *Fraser, Independent*, 11 June 2001 (full transcript available on the Westlaw legal database).
[53] [2003] EWCA Civ 502; 2003 ICR 1176.

of apparent bias was rejected, even although the chairman of the employment tribunal had referred to the employer's treatment of the employee as "appalling" and had encouraged the parties to settle. However, the circumstances of the case are rather unusual and, although rejecting the apparent bias argument, Gibson LJ said this:

> "I would add a word of caution for tribunals who choose to indicate their thinking before the hearing is concluded. As can be seen from this case, it is easy for this to be misunderstood, particularly if the views are expressed trenchantly. It is always good practice to leave the parties in no doubt that such expressions of view are only provisional and that the tribunal remain open to persuasion."[54]

Finally, the following guidance on this issue of expressing a preliminary view has been issued by the Court of Appeal:

> "In some jurisdictions the forensic tradition is that judges sit mute, listening to advocates without interruption, asking no question, voicing no opinion, until they break their silence to give judgment. That is a perfectly respectable tradition, but it is not ours. Practice naturally varies from judge to judge, and obvious differences exist between factual issues at first instance and legal issues on appeal. But on the whole the English tradition sanctions and even encourages a measure of disclosure by the judge of his current thinking. It certainly does not sanction the premature expression of factual conclusions or anything which may prematurely indicate a closed mind. But a judge does not act amiss if, in relation to some feature of a party's case which strikes him as inherently improbable, he indicates the need for unusually compelling evidence to persuade him of the fact. An expression of scepticism is not suggestive of bias unless the judge conveys an unwillingness to be persuaded of a factual proposition whatever the evidence may be."[55]

A not uncommon (and perfectly legitimate and useful) judicial tactic   **4.24**
is to play "devil's advocate", in other words, taking a position (one not necessarily held by the propositioner) for the sake of argument. This tactic allows a theory or an idea to be put by a tribunal member to a witness or lawyer in order to test the strength of the evidence/ submission in question. If this tactic is to be used, the member should be careful to express the proposition being put as one being put in order to test the argument, not as the member's final, considered (and therefore prematurely formed) view.

---

[54] [2003] EWCA Civ 502; 2003 ICR 1176 at para 40.
[55] *Arab Monetary Fund v Hashim (No 8)* 1994 6 Admin LR 348 at 356 per Sir Thomas Bingham MR. See also the comments in *Harada Ltd v Turner (No 1)* [2002] EWCA Civ 599 per Pill LJ at para 31.

4.25   It is clear that in multi-member tribunals, any argument of lack of independence or of bias (apparent or actual) needs only to be directed at one tribunal member in order to succeed. Where the argument comes to the attention of a party (especially a legally represented one) before or during the hearing, usually the law expects that the issue is raised with the tribunal during that hearing (or even before the hearing, with the MHTS administration staff),[56] and not afterwards on appeal. However, depending on the circumstances, an argument might not be time barred if raised for the first time on appeal.[57] In the event that any lack of independence or bias argument is raised at the hearing, it may be that the situation can be resolved by that tribunal member standing down; in such a case, as long as that member is not the Convener, the hearing can continue before the two remaining members, but only with the consent of the parties.[58] If the member concerned is the Convener, and he seeks to withdraw (or if the parties do not all agree that the hearing should continue before the remaining two members) the usual rule applies, and the tribunal hearing should be adjourned and the case referred to a different tribunal,[59] certainly one which does not include the Convener, but possibly to an entirely different panel, depending on the circumstances.

4.26   Where an argument involving lack of independence or bias is made during the hearing, a clear decision should be reached and recorded by the tribunal. If the argument is rejected and the hearing continues before the tribunal, the aggrieved party can appeal against the decision on the ground of procedural impropriety or error of law.[60]

The start of the hearing

4.27   At the outset, the Convener should introduce the tribunal members (or introduce himself and let the others do likewise), clearly stating who are the legal, medical and general members respectively. Everyone in the hearing should then be asked to state their names. This is essential as the tribunal members will not necessarily know everyone around the table, and will need to direct particular questions to particular individuals during the hearing. Also, it should not be assumed that those around the table will know each other; a lawyer for the patient may never have met the MHO or RMO and he will probably wish

---

[56] For an overview of the administrative operation of the MHTS, see paras 2.02 et seq.

[57] See the judgment of Gibson LJ in *Stansbury* v *Datapulse plc* [2003] EWCA Civ 1951; [2004] IRLR 466 at paras 23–24.

[58] Rule 64(3).

[59] Rule 64(1). This rule refers to an adjournment or a referral, but both would seem likely in a case where a member stands down and where r 64(3) is not activated.

[60] On appeals, see Chapter 8.

to cross-examine them in due course. In addition, it is important for the purposes of recording the evidence (and the recording may later have to be transcribed) that all of those present introduce themselves on tape.

It is important at this stage that the tribunal identifies in its   **4.28** collective mind which of the participants are parties in the case and which are witnesses. This is important in order that the tribunal knows to whom to address the next part of the hearing. At this stage, any comments by witnesses should be fed through the party/representative who is responsible for that witness. This is not as obvious as it might at first seem. For instance, in a CTO application the RMO has a right to be heard, not just as a witness, but in his own right,[61] as does any medical practitioner who submitted the mental health report which accompanies the application.[62] This right comprises the right to lead or produce evidence and to make oral or written representations.[63]

Once the introductions are over, the Convener should ask whether   **4.29** there are any preliminary issues anyone wishes to raise, and these should be dealt with. Any such issues the tribunal members have identified should also be dealt with. As stated earlier,[64] the Convener should ask anyone if there are any such issues and should explain what a preliminary issue is. Before a decision is made on any preliminary issue, the tribunal will normally have to be adjourned so that the tribunal members can deliberate in private, unless it requires such brief discussion that deliberation can be carried out adequately there and then in the tribunal room: irrespective of the nature of the preliminary issue, all three tribunal members must have an opportunity to contribute to the decision-making process.[65]

One issue that should be dealt with at this stage (unless it has   **4.30** arisen already while any preliminary matters are being considered) is the issue of communication difficulties on the part of any of the witnesses who are due to give evidence. This might be an issue where the patient has a learning difficulty and so cannot communicate in the usual way. Alternatively, the patient may be hard of hearing or deaf or might be partially sighted or blind. The communication difficulty might not be oral; an individual might have problems expressing himself in writing, and this can hamper communication where a

---

[61] 2003 Act, s 64(3)(g).
[62] *Ibid*, s 64(3)(f).
[63] *Ibid*, s 64(2)(a) and (b). See also similar provisions in s 50 of the 2003 Act in connection with STDC revocation applications by the patient.
[64] See para 3.19.
[65] See a discussion of the deliberation process at paras 4.96 *et seq.*

witness might prefer to give evidence by signed statement[66] rather than by giving oral evidence during the tribunal.

4.31   There are two points at which communication problems may become an issue: during a process prior to a tribunal hearing, where the tribunal is later considering that process; or during the tribunal hearing itself. The former situation is dealt with under s 261 of the 2003 Act, the latter under r 53 of the Rules.

4.32   Under s 261 of the 2003 Act, the "appropriate person"[67] has certain duties in connection with a patient under an order where: (1) the patient has difficulty in communicating or generally communicates in a language other than English;[68] and (2) where there is to be a medical examination of the patient for the purposes of assessing his mental disorder or where there is to be a statutory review of the patient's detention or in any proceedings before the tribunal.[69] These duties consist of taking all reasonable steps to enable the patient to communicate during the examination, review or tribunal proceedings by making arrangements appropriate to the needs of the patient and by providing assistance or material appropriate to the patient's needs. This section might be relevant to tribunal proceedings in two ways. First of all, there might be evidence that the duties contained in it were not complied with during a medical examination or the review process, such that the patient has been unable to communicate his views during the examination or review. In such a situation, the tribunal will require to put in place steps to counteract any resulting disadvantage, for example by taking the views of the patient during the tribunal process.

4.33   In an extreme case, failure to comply with the duty in s 261 might even fatally affect the tribunal process, for example where the examination was for the purpose of providing CTO mental health reports and where there is a jointly held examination involving both practitioners but where the patient has not consented to the

---

[66] Evidence can be given in this manner in terms of r 60 of the tribunal rules.

[67] This person is generally the managers of the hospital where the patient is detained or the managers of the hospital where the patient's care is based, where he is not detained. See s 260(5) of the 2003 Act for the definition of "appropriate person" for the purposes of s 261, as applied by s 261(5).

[68] 2003 Act, s 261(1)(b). The s 261 duty of assistance is applicable where the patient generally (which means usually) communicates in a language other than English. It seems that there is no need for that person to have a particular level of English language ability only that they do not generally communicate using it. Where a non-native English-speaking patient asks for assistance that falls within s 261, it appears that the duty will kick in, even where the appropriate person takes the view that the patient can communicate perfectly well in English.

[69] *Ibid*, s 261(3).

examination being held jointly,[70] and instead consent has been taken from another,[71] but where the patient's lack of consent results not from a lack of ability to give it but from a difficulty in expressing his view. In such a case, it could be said that the "appropriate person"[72] failed in his duty to take steps under s 261, and failed to follow the appropriate procedure on jointly held medical examinations. A similar situation might arise where, for instance, the MHO is interviewing the patient in connection with a mandatory review of a CTO[73] and the patient has difficulty in communicating with the MHO. The "appropriate person" (usually the hospital managers) would have to take appropriate steps to ensure that the patient could express himself properly during that interview. The obligation is not on the MHO, since he is not an "appropriate person"[74] although in practice the request for assistance might come from the MHO.[75] However, the refusal of the CTO would be a last resort even in such cases and the tribunal should always strive to counteract the disadvantage rather than allowing the application to fall.

The second way in which a s 261 issue might arise in tribunal proceedings is where the patient complains (or the tribunal notices) that the "appropriate person"[76] has failed to make available assistance to allow the patient to communicate during the hearing. In such a case, the tribunal will require to consider whether such assistance can be made available that day or whether an adjournment will be required to allow the s 261 duty to be complied with. In any case involving a s 261 issue the tribunal will, of course, require to decide whether s 261 has been breached at all. It may be that the "appropriate person"[77] has taken "all reasonable steps"[78] to provide assistance to the patient; the obligation is not to have taken all possible steps. It might be argued, for example, that the necessary steps could not reasonably have been taken where this would lead to delay in the process and would therefore involve missing a crucial statutory deadline. The steps might incur extraordinary expense which is disproportionate

4.34

---

[70] Such consent is usually required under s 58(6)(a) of the 2003 Act where the patient is capable of consenting.

[71] This can be the named person, guardian or welfare attorney of the patient where the patient is incapable of consenting to the examinations: s 58(6)(b).

[72] Defined in s 260(5).

[73] Such an interview is mandatory in terms of s 85(2)(a) of the 2003 Act, unless it is impracticable to do so: s 85(3).

[74] Defined in s 260(5).

[75] The MHO has an escape valve in terms of s 85(3) where compliance with s 85 or part of it is "impracticable" but this would not affect any duty under s 261.

[76] Defined in s 260(5).

[77] *Ibid.*

[78] 2003 Act, s 261(2).

to the communication difficulty in question. Where there has been no s 261 breach, the tribunal should turn to consider the impact of r 53 since assistance in such cases will not be required under s 261.[79] Where steps are taken under s 261, a written note should be made of them as soon as practicable.[80] The steps that might be taken under s 261 are not limited, but might consist of, for example, provision of a translator for someone who does not usually speak or write in English;[81] a scribe for someone who wishes to present his views in writing but cannot write; a sign language interpreter for someone who has a speech impediment or who is dumb; or some physical material to allow expression such as a hand gesture key or flashcards. The latter devices might be suitable for someone who has a learning difficulty leading to problems in communicating his views or a lack of understanding of the process or the need for a break, in the heat of a tribunal.

4.35   Turning to r 53 of the Rules, it is important to note that it applies to any person taking part in tribunal proceedings,[82] not just the patient, as is the case with s 261 of the 2003 Act. This is not to say that r 53 cannot apply to the patient; it does so apply where s 261 does not,[83] for example where the view is formed by the tribunal that a s 261 duty does not arise. Where such a duty does arise, however, it would appear that r 53 does not apply. The person who requires assistance to communicate must inform the tribunal of this at the earliest opportunity.[84] There is a similar duty on any relevant person to inform the tribunal in similar circumstances.[85] Often, however, any issue of communication problems will arise at the hearing, without prior warning. The tribunal is under an obligation in cases where r 53 applies to take all reasonable steps to secure that arrangements appropriate to that person's needs are met.[86] This obligation is not, then, to take all possible steps to meet those needs, only those that are reasonable. This is a wide test, and factors that the tribunal will be considering will include: any delay in the proceedings that would be caused by taking such steps, and the possibility of a resulting adjournment; the benefit the steps are likely to reap compared with the effort and time required to put them in

---

[79] This will mean that r 53 applies: r 53(1)(b).
[80] 2003 Act, s 261(4).
[81] The s 261 duty in connection with such a patient would appear to apply even where the patient is regarded as someone who can speak good English, as long as they do not generally (usually) speak English – see n 68 above further on this.
[82] Rule 53(1)(a).
[83] This is made clear in r 53(1)(b).
[84] Rule 53(2).
[85] Rule 53(3).
[86] Rule 53(4).

place; the existence of alternative material from that person, such as a prior written statement or the existence of an advocacy worker or other representative who can put the views and/or evidence of the person concerned; the impact from a fairness perspective on the proceedings as a whole if the steps are not taken. The kind of arrangements a tribunal might consider taking under r 53 are similar to those described above as typical under s 261, such as a translator, scribe, sign language interpreter or flashcards. Of course, the tribunal itself is not providing these facilities; it would be adjourning with a direction that such arrangements be provided by others. There are some arrangements that could, in certain cases, be made by the tribunal on the day of the hearing, such as devising a method of communication by the person other than oral communication, re-arranging the physical configuration of the tribunal room and the places where the panel members sit (as happened in one case where the patient was substantially blind and deaf and the Convener sat beside the patient, so that he could relay to her the progress of the proceedings) or taking evidence from the person on his own, where the communication difficulty arises not from a physical or mental difficulty but from fear of speaking about the case in front of others, or in front of a particular person.[87] The tribunal does have an overriding duty to provide a fair hearing, and also, in terms of s 1 of the 2003 Act, to facilitate the greatest possible participation by the patient, and it is difficult to see how either of these duties can be discharged adequately where a patient is deprived of facilities which would enable him to communicate more effectively.

In addition, in relation to CTO applications, the tribunal should, at this stage, consider whether an interim CTO is to be granted.[88] This obligation arises where s 68 of the 2003 Act applies, triggering, in turn, the application of s 69 and of r 8 of the Rules. These provisions apply in cases where the 5-day automatic extension to an STDC is triggered. Given the usual timings of hearings on CTO applications, and the prevalence of STDCs, such consideration will be required in most cases. In one tribunal case, it was clear from the decision that consideration had not been given to whether to grant an interim order before considering the full application and this led to a successful appeal.[89] It seems, then, that in the unusual cases where a decision

4.36

---

[87] In any case where it is deemed appropriate evidence can be taken outwith the presence of others: see para 4.90 on this.

[88] Any application for an ICTO can be made orally at the hearing or in advance in writing: r 7.

[89] *McGlynn v Mental Health Tribunal for Scotland* [2007] MHLR 16, a decision of Sh Pr Bowen in which the appeal was conceded, but where the sheriff principal offered some comment on the merits of the appeal.

is made on the CTO application prior to the expiry of the STDC, or where there is no STDC in place, the obligation to consider granting an interim CTO does not apply. In such cases, where a request for consideration of an interim CTO is not made, the tribunal does not need to consider whether or not to grant one.

4.37   Where s 69 and r 8 apply, the tribunal should always note that it has considered whether to grant an interim order, and record its reasons for not granting one, even where there is no issue that could give rise to the possibility of an interim order, either in the documentation before the panel or in the evidence/submissions delivered by any party. This may seem pointless, but the legislation and rules are clear.

4.38   In cases where a possible interim order issue does arise, the best practice is to hear the arguments in connection with the possible interim order and then to hear all relevant evidence on the merits of the case. The tribunal should then adjourn to deliberate on both questions (whether there should be an interim order at all and, if so, whether one should be granted in this case) at the same time. The reason for hearing all of the evidence on the merits is that the criteria applicable to consideration of an interim order are identical in substance to those for the granting of a full CTO.[90] This means that in order to consider whether to grant an interim CTO, a full CTO or to refuse to grant any order, all admissible evidence available on the day of the hearing will require to be heard and considered. Of course, where the tribunal is considering adjourning the case and no order is necessary (for example where there is already an order in place that would maintain the *status quo* until at least the date of the adjourned hearing) or where the tribunal is considering refusing the application as incompetent or in some other way fatally flawed, there will be no need to hear such evidence before making this decision. In most cases, however, this will not be the case and so full evidence will have to be heard. In considering whether or not to grant an interim order, the tribunal should avoid the temptation to "water down" the standard of evidence required on the basis that the interim order will last for a much shorter time than a full order, and therefore be less of an imposition on the freedom of the patient. If there is any suggestion of this approach in either the written decision or anything said or done by the tribunal during the hearing, this will represent an error of law, as there is nothing in the statute to warrant such a construction. There is no suggestion in the 2003 Act or the Rules that the criteria should be examined any less rigorously in a case

---

[90] 2003 Act, s 65(6) on the criteria for an interim CTO refers back to s 64(5)(a)–(d) (s 65(6)(a)) plus an interim order necessity criterion (s 65(6)(b)) which is identical in import to s 64(5)(e).

where an interim order is being considered than in a full order case. The only matter that sets an interim order apart from a full one is that the interim order is granted for a shorter period of time, in order to obtain further information. Surprisingly, the 2003 Act and the Rules are silent on the range of discretion or test to be applied in considering whether or not an interim order is necessary, but the Code of Practice provides some guidance:

> "[an ICTO might be granted] where, for example, the Tribunal does not feel it has enough information on which to base their [sic] decision about the full CTO; where it wishes to seek further evidence from another party such as a medical practitioner, psychologist, social care provider, carer or relative; or where the patient and his or her representatives require further time in which to prepare their evidence".[91]

These are merely examples of some of the cases in which an ICTO might be considered, there is no limit on the circumstances, although the tribunal will have to justify that one is necessary, as opposed to simply convenient or advisable.[92]   **4.39**

Where an ICTO is granted in circumstances where ss 68 and 69 of the 2003 Act apply (see above) then a further hearing must be fixed for consideration of the full application.[93] Clearly, that hearing will fall within the period of the ICTO, although it does not require to.[94] On fixing the further hearing, the tribunal has very wide powers to give directions on a number of matters in relation to that further hearing.[95] Before a further hearing is fixed (whether the tribunal is considering making any accompanying directions or not) all relevant persons require to be given an opportunity to be heard.[96]   **4.40**

---

[91] Vol 2, p 92, para 94. On the status of the Code, see para 1.40.

[92] 2003 Act, s 65(6)(b).

[93] Rule 8(3). The wording of this part of the rule is rather confusing but in essence it applies to any case where an interim CTO is being granted.

[94] From a practical point of view, the tribunal will wish the interim order to still be in place by the time of the further hearing since, if the interim order falls, this would mean that until the full hearing the patient is under no compulsory measures, unless a further EDC is applied. However, there is no requirement for the further hearing to take place within any timescale, either in r 8 or in the 2003 Act. In other words, the fall of the interim order does not automatically bring the CTO application to an end; in theory the further hearing could be much later, although a tribunal faced with a delayed further hearing would have to consider whether the application should be refused and started again since the information would be out of date. A further consequence of the omission by the 2003 Act to specify a timescale for the holding of a final CTO application hearing is that where there is no STDC in place, there are no indications at all as to when the CTO application hearing should take place, despite strict time limits for the preparation of mental health reports and for the submission of the application.

[95] Rule 8(4).

[96] Rule 8(5).

4.41   Once the preliminary issues have been disposed of, the tribunal can begin examining the merits of the application/appeal.[97] The Convener should, first of all, establish whether the applicant wishes to insist on the application, and what the respective positions of the other relevant person(s) are to the application/appeal. The purpose of this brief canvassing of views is to ensure that everyone is aware, at the outset, of the very basic stance to be taken by each relevant person. This may already be clear if any preliminary issues have been dealt with, but even in such cases this should be clarified again, since some time may have passed since the hearing started, and in any event the preliminary issues may have led to a party altering his position. The Convener should be careful to extract a simple answer to this question, and not allow the participant to launch into a full exposition of his case. This process can lead to the discovery of the key areas of contention and agreement between the parties. So, for example, the patient might accept that he has a mental disorder and that he needs to be the subject of a CTO; his argument might lie in the question of whether the CTO should be hospital or community based. It would be useful to know this at the outset, since this will allow the tribunal to focus the hearing principally on that issue, assuming, of course, that the tribunal itself does not have any other areas of concern.

Explanation of the proposed order, manner and procedure of the hearing

4.42   Once the position of the parties has been established, the Convener should comply with the obligation to explain the manner and order of the proceedings and the procedure which the tribunal intends to adopt.[98] This explanation should be tendered in such a way as is likely to be understood by all around the table. Of particular importance is an explanation of the order in which the participants will be asked to speak. The Convener should also take the opportunity to explain that, where possible, participants should not speak out of turn or speak over one another, since not only can this make the hearing difficult to follow, it can cause problems should the tape recording of the proceedings ever require to be transcribed. The Convener should check with everyone that the proposed order, manner and procedure are agreeable to all. One of the parties may have an objection to it and, if so, it should be heard and a swift decision made. As part of this explanation, the Convener should be

---

[97] This assumes, of course, that the application/appeal has not been brought to an end or adjourned as a result of a decision on a preliminary issue.
[98] Rule 63(1).

careful to include a brief description of the alternative courses of action available to the tribunal, such as: to make no order; to grant a hospital-based CTO for up to 6 months; or to grant an interim order for up to 28 days. The importance of this part of the explanation can be seen in one tribunal hearing where the patient (who was unrepresented) seemed surprised at the possibility of an order for up to 6 months being granted. Despite explanations from the RMO that the order need not last 6 months, and could be ended at any time, depending on the patient's progress, the patient was unaware of the possibility of an order of up to 6 months' duration being made that day. The outcome of that hearing was an adjournment to allow the patient to seek legal representation and an interim order was, in the meantime, granted. Of course, the tribunal is not there to provide legal advice to any of the parties, but everyone at the hearing should be aware of the options before the tribunal, whether represented or not.

The taking of oral evidence generally

The order and manner in which evidence is taken by the tribunal should usually mirror that used in the public courts, but with some adjustments. For instance, while evidence in the public courts must be given on oath or under affirmation, this will rarely happen in a tribunal hearing.[99] There is the provision for taking evidence under oath,[100] so it is competent. The taking of evidence on oath in a tribunal setting is usually not appropriate, given that there is an obligation on the tribunal to conduct the hearing as informally as the circumstances of the case permit.[101] The use of an oath would serve to add to the formality. The issue of whether to take evidence on oath does not usually arise as a matter of course, and will be an issue only where a party asks that an oath be administered with certain witnesses or where the tribunal raises such a possibility. In either case, the tribunal should canvass the views of all of the parties (not the witnesses) on whether an oath would be appropriate. As ever, not only would the tribunal, in making such a decision, have regard to the provisions of r 63(2); the overriding objective in r 4

4.43

---

[99] This is also the position in England, where taking evidence on oath has been described as "not normally done": R Jones, *Mental Health Act Manual* (10th edn, 2006), para 3–071; and "virtually unheard of": A Eldergill, *Mental Health Review Tribunals Law and Practice* (1997) at p 815. The provision being commented on here is the Tribunal Procedure (First-tier Tribunal) (Health, Education and Social Care Chamber) Rules 2008 (SI 2008/2699), r 15(3).

[100] Rule 63(6).

[101] Rule 63(2)(a).

should be taken account of. Given that the oath/affirmation is a solemn statement to tell the truth, it would seem appropriate to sanction its use only in cases where there is likely to be a dispute over the facts, and where one party will be accusing a witness of being dishonest in his evidence (whether oral or documentary). In one tribunal hearing, it was argued that one particular witness (the RMO) should give her evidence under oath, since the patient's lawyer (who made the request for the use of the oath) was planning to cross-examine the RMO on an allegation that she had tried to persuade the patient to abandon his appeal to the tribunal. However, the tribunal decided that it would decline to administer the oath since the patient's lawyer confirmed that he would not be suggesting during his cross-examination of the RMO that she had behaved inappropriately.[102]

4.44   It is clear that a party has a right to call any witness he wishes, subject always to objections on the admissibility of evidence;[103] however, it would be very unusual (although not impossible) for an admissibility objection to affect the entirety of the evidence of a witness, so it is likely that some of the evidence of each witness offered will be admissible and so will have to be heard.

4.45   It is not unusual for evidence to be interrupted during mental health tribunal hearings. The issues that are discussed are emotive and controversial, and often evidence will be given with which one or more of the participants will not agree. In particular, the RMO might give evidence about the past behaviour of the patient with which the patient profoundly disagrees. Such evidence can lead to interruptions, since patients in particular might find it difficult to wait until they can have a chance to respond to the point with which they take issue. This is a hearing management issue and so is one that lies squarely within the remit of the Convener. Although he may have explained at the outset of the hearing the order the procedure is to take, by the time the hearing is well under way, that guidance may have been forgotten. In the case of such interruptions, the Convener will have to decide how best, in the circumstances of the case, to handle them. He may decide to ignore the interjection, and allow the evidence to continue. He may allow the interruption to run its course, and may even turn away from the witness who was giving evidence and allow the point to be made in full, with supplementary questions. The view might be taken that this course should be followed where the patient is unlikely to take advice to

---

[102] The tribunal in question did not need to pronounce on the issue since the patient withdrew his request before a decision was announced.
[103] On such objections, see paras 4.71 et seq.

stop interrupting or where the point would be best explored before the evidence of the witness who has been interrupted is completed. He may explain to the person interrupting that he will have a chance to put his point later; this course of action might be more appropriate where the interruption is by a professional participant rather than by the patient or an anxious or angry relative. A further option would be to adjourn the case briefly in the hope that the evidence can be resumed uninterrupted. It is important for the Convener in all such cases to keep his composure, even in cases of continuing interruptions, as any lack of composure could lead later to an accusation of apparent bias.[104] If possible, Conveners should try to find ways of encouraging participants to wait to make their point at the appropriate time. There can be a danger, if interruptions are allowed, that the procedural structure which allows witnesses to put their positions, and then be open to challenge by parties, can break down.

It is worth mentioning here that although the Convener might suggest a short adjournment during the evidence for a number of obvious reasons, such as a disruption, the patient leaving the hearing unexpectedly, or lunchtime, the Convener should also consider whether in any particular case a short adjournment should be taken due to the general complexity and volume of the evidence being led, both in the interests of tired and/or confused participants, but also for the benefit of tribunal members. There is no need for the tribunal to feel constrained in discussion of the evidence led/presented so far during any break in the proceedings for fear of being accused of prejudging the case. Indeed, even in non-complex cases, a short break can allow the tribunal members to discuss the evidence so far, and allow a more focused approach to be taken after the adjournment, particularly where new issues have arisen or where the evidence is taking a track that was not expected by the tribunal members when discussing the case before the hearing begins. Of course, the tribunal members should be careful during any such adjournment not to allow the discussion to progress to a point where a concluded view has been formed on any issue, or on the tenor or weight of any of the evidence heard/presented to that point; any such conclusions can only properly be reached after the end of the evidence. **4.46**

As in the public courts, evidence should be given by each witness in a particular order, namely: examination-in-chief, cross-examination and lastly, where appropriate, re-examination. Each of these will now briefly be considered. **4.47**

---

[104] On apparent bias, see paras 4.13 *et seq.*

4.48   Examination-in-chief has been defined as: "the process whereby counsel or the solicitor for a party elicits from a witness called by that party evidence which it is believed will be favourable to that party's case".[105]

Of course, this definition will apply not only where a party is legally represented but also where the examination is being conducted by a party himself or by a tribunal member. The examination should begin by asking the MHO/RMO to confirm that he has submitted an application/report(s) and these should be identified and the witness should adopt them formally into his evidence. This process will significantly reduce the need to take the witness through his personal details, qualifications, involvement in the case and the history of the case. This assumes that all of these matters are addressed in the application/report lodged by the MHO/RMO. Where such basic information is missing from the papers or is in short supply, this material should be covered with the MHO/RMO during the examination-in-chief. This adoption of the papers authored by the MHO/RMO will lead to the principal points in support of the statutory criteria being adopted into the evidence in one stroke. This assumes that there is no factual matter recorded in the documents in question on which a contrary finding is made by the tribunal; should this occur, such an adoption will not apply to those facts and the tribunal finding will take priority. This will allow the examiner to concentrate his questions only on the key areas of the case, usually the areas where there is some contention or concern.[106]

4.49   It is important that the questions are short, uncomplicated and incremental. Long questions with more than one proposition to answer are confusing and may ultimately be worthless. Questioners should plan their examination so as to try to elicit one fact from the witness per question asked. The witness should be taken gradually through his evidence and should not be allowed to "run away" with a narrative of events. Controlling even one's own witness can be difficult – sometimes he will, perhaps due to his natural anxiety, wish to give all of his evidence at once. The witness should be stopped

---

[105] F Raitt, *Evidence: Principles, Policy and Practice* (2008), para 16.10.

[106] Such adoption has been held to be unnecessary in order to allow the evidence to be taken into account: see the comments of *B v MHTS*, a decision of Sh Pr Sir Stephen Young, 2008 GWD 36–543 (full judgment is available on the Scottish Courts website at: www.scotcourts.gov.uk and on the Westlaw legal database) at para 34, in relation to the evidence of an RMO referring to her mental health report. This seems logical when one considers the terms of r 60, which allows a signed statement to be regarded as evidence (although r 60 is not cited as the reason for this conclusion reached in the *B* case).

and taken back through what he has said, step by step, and at a pace the tribunal can follow. Interruption of a witness, although usually frowned upon, will be tolerated in order to break a fast flow of evidence. Of course, the questions themselves should be framed so as to invite short answers. So, questions such as "What happened?" or "Explain the history of the patient's mental illness" can, without further context, be unhelpfully broad, and should probably be avoided. More focused questions, such as "What happened on the ward on Monday 21 March?" or "Describe the symptoms that you observed when the patient was admitted on 21 March", might be more likely to elicit responses focused on the matters which the questioner wants to bring to the attention of the tribunal. On the other hand, sometimes fairly general questions can be helpful, particularly those which have the aim of securing an update on the patient's condition since the preparation of the application or the last hearing.

There can be no objection to a lawyer, advocacy worker or other   **4.50** representative advising a witness in advance of the hearing in general terms on how he will be expected to give evidence, but this must not involve "briefing" the witness on what he is likely to be asked or how he should answer.[107] He can be advised, therefore, on the order of questioning and on general "tips" such as keeping answers short and courteous. While a representative is taking details of the evidence a witness is likely to give, the witness could be asked questions expected in cross-examination, but this should not be presented as a "practice run" for the case, since this might amount to briefing a witness. Solicitors in particular must tread carefully here and, if in doubt, guidance should be sought from the Law Society of Scotland before adopting a particular course of action with a witness during statement taking or pre-hearing. These comments apply just as strictly to a party who is to give evidence as they do to a witness who is not a party to the case.

Leading questions[108] are usually not permitted during examination-   **4.51** in-chief. Even if no objection is taken, the answers to leading questions tend to be of rather less value to the tribunal as evidence. Answers to such questions will often be simply "yes" or "no". The tribunal is therefore deprived of hearing the witness's evidence in his own words.

---

[107] For a more detailed and very clear explanation of the difference between "coaching" a witness and preparing him to give evidence, see C Hennessy, *Practical Advocacy in the Sheriff Court* (2006), paras 8–10.

[108] These are questions which are phrased in such a way that they suggest what the answer should be. An example would be: "The patient relapsed due to a failure to comply with instructions on medication, didn't he?".

4.52   Each witness, after being examined in chief, may then be cross-examined by all other parties who wish to do so. Cross-examination has been defined as consisting of:

> "questioning an adverse witness in an effort to break down his evidence, to weaken or prejudice his evidence, or to elicit statements damaging to him and aiding the case of the cross-examiner".[109]

4.53   As John Munkman QC notes and illustrates, cross-examination rarely fulfils the purpose portrayed in television courtroom dramas.[110] There is rarely the devastating, case-winning question causing a sigh of surprise from those in attendance. The best cross-examination technique can seem relatively mundane to the casual observer. Other texts ponder this important part of the examination process in some depth and the interested reader is referred there.[111] However, a few important points should be grasped.

4.54   It is important for representatives to remember that if they have led evidence, or intend to go on to lead evidence which differs from that of the witness who has just given evidence-in-chief, they should put the point of difference to the witness in cross-examination. If they fail to do so, the evidence which they rely on will be regarded as being of less weight, because the witness putting the opposing position has not been given any opportunity to comment on it.[112]

4.55   Second, the cross-examiner should have in mind not only the questions which he intends to ask, but the technique he intends to adopt with each witness. Some witnesses will require patient, deferential, gentle cross-examination while others will need to be dealt with robustly, even aggressively. Expert witnesses should almost always be treated with respect. It will often be worth considering whether the conclusion of an expert has been reached on the basis

---

[109] Lord Avonside in *Hartley v HM Advocate* 1979 SLT 26 at 28. This is a case on the admissibility of police statements and the definition is given in the context of cross-examination of a suspect by a police officer but it was approved in F Raitt, *Evidence: Principles, Policy and Practice* (2008), para 16.23 as applicable to examination of witnesses in court.

[110] J Munkman, *The Technique of Advocacy* (1991) at p 60.

[111] See, for example, *ibid*, Chaps 3–7; J M Lees, *A Handbook on Written and Oral Pleading in the Sheriff Court* (2nd edn, 1920, reprinted 1988), pp 84–102; M Stone, *Cross-Examination in Criminal Trials* (2nd edn, 1995). Although the latter text focuses on criminal trials, some of the general analysis of the stages of examination of a witness are equally pertinent in a tribunal context.

[112] See the comments to this effect by LJ-C Cooper in *McKenzie v McKenzie* 1943 SC 108 and *Bryce v British Railways Board* 1996 SLT 1378 for a case in which it is stated that the failure to cross-examine in this way might not be fatal to the admissibility of the later contradictory evidence.

of an erroneous assumption about a matter of fact, and questions should be formulated to clarify which factual matters the opinion is based on, and how it might differ if the factual assumptions made were not in fact correct. These matters should be dealt with carefully and systematically in cross-examination, as they may enable the questioner to undermine the conclusion of the expert.

Third, the cross-examiner must be flexible. It is not uncommon   4.56
to expect a witness (perhaps as a result of information given by a client) to be a quivering wreck or unreliable or shifty, only to find that during examination-in-chief they are well presented, eloquent, even convincing. What started as a planned robust, hard-hitting ride in cross might have to become a clever, trap-setting gradual attempt to erode the witness or break down the alleged façade. Of course, the opposite situation could present itself: for example, the nervous, uncertain, defensive expert witness. Whatever the situation, the cross-examiner might find himself having to alter his intended course. He will not have much time to think about this, but he must be prepared to do so. There is nothing more destructive to a case than using the wrong tactic with the wrong witness.

Why is it that witnesses should be treated so carefully in cross-   4.57
examination? The reason is simple. The vast majority of witnesses will come to the tribunal with the intention of giving their evidence in a particular way. The cross-examiner is usually trying to persuade the witness to alter course or change his mind or concede some ground. In attempting to do so, the cross-examiner is fighting an uphill struggle. The witness has just finished giving his evidence-in-chief and usually that will have gone to plan. The cross-examiner (whose role in the proceedings will be understood by most witnesses) will have to alter the *status quo*. It will be difficult to persuade most witnesses, particularly those with a vested interest in the outcome of the case, that their point of view, honed and justified over a long period and just confirmed during the benign, friendly, encouraging circumstances of examination-in-chief, is in fact wrong, even to a small extent.

Where the evidence is being taken from a witness by the tribunal   4.58
in circumstances where none of the parties is legally represented, no cross-examination as such will take place. The questioning techniques adopted by the tribunal members in such a case might be more robust than in the situation where the witness will be cross-examined by a legal representative for another party, but, as explained elsewhere,[113] the role of the tribunal is not to step into

---

[113] See para 4.78.

the shoes of that legal representative and carry out a full-blown cross-examination. The tribunal will, however, have to do what it considers necessary in order to satisfy itself as to aspects of the evidence which may cause it concern. Where the witness is being called by a party who is represented (or where the witness is himself a represented party) and there are no other legally represented persons, again, the same point applies.

4.59   Finally on cross-examination, it would be possible to argue that a witness should not be cross-examined at all, but very good reason would have to be offered. This might be that the witness is too emotionally frail or frightened to be subjected to difficult questions. If such an argument is made, it should be substantiated ideally by medical evidence, although such evidence would not, strictly speaking, be necessary. The tribunal would have to hear representations from all parties on a request to excuse a witness from the cross-examination process, and would have to consider whether a direction on that evidence should be issued.[114] Consideration should be given to whether arrangements could be made to allow a cross-examination to take place which would obviate the problems cited, such as taking the evidence in the absence of other witnesses and parties, or issuing a direction restricting the subject-matter of the cross-examination or its general tone.[115] In such cases, the tribunal may take the view that all that is required is the careful monitoring of the cross-examination process, which can be stopped at any time in the event of undue distress, perhaps to be resumed after a break. Much will depend on the circumstances of the case, but the right to cross-examine a witness is a fundamental one in the context of fairness[116] and this right should be curtailed or denied only in the most extreme cases.

---

[114] Such a direction would be under the power to direct the way in which the evidence is to be led under r 49(1)(g)(iii).

[115] *Ibid.*

[116] The right to cross-examine witnesses is enshrined in the ECHR, Art 6(3)(d). Although this right is applicable only in criminal cases, it is submitted that such a right exists in mental health cases which are, as stated earlier, "citizen versus state" type proceedings, where the liberty of an individual is at stake and so are broadly comparable to criminal proceedings. To put it another way, the scope of the right to a fair trial under Art 6(1) in mental health cases can be influenced by the tenor of the Art 6(3) rights, albeit that those rights are not directly applicable outwith criminal cases. For a discussion of this Convention right, see R Reed and J Murdoch, *A Guide to Human Rights Law in Scotland* (2nd edn, 2008), paras 5.133 *et seq*. On the application of the ECHR in the context of fairness of tribunal hearings, see above at paras 4.09 *et seq*. In addition, the right to cross-examine is recognised as a fundamental one in domestic Scots law, and has been for some considerable period.

The third stage in the process of the examination of a witness is   **4.60**
re-examination. As with cross-examination, the party who is offered
the chance to re-examine need not take it. The tribunal might take
the view that the cross-examination process has not given rise to any
material that would benefit from re-examination. The wide powers
the tribunal has to regulate its own procedure[117] as well as the power
to give directions about the way in which the evidence before the
tribunal is led[118] or on the exclusion of irrelevant evidence[119] could
all be used to deflect a request to re-examine where the tribunal
thinks that one is not required. In addition, the overriding objective
of ensuring that cases are handled as efficiently as possible[120] could
lead to such a refusal. If a party (or more specifically a representative
of a party) is aggrieved at the lack of an opportunity to re-examine,
this should be raised at the hearing, since later, in the context of
an appeal on the point, he may be criticised for not doing so. In
addition, where there are any points of clarification arising out of
cross-examination, these may well be picked up by the tribunal, who
can put those questions themselves, particularly as they will be asking
non-leading questions[121] which are the only kind that can be put in
re-examination. Having said this, the tribunal may decide of its own
volition, or faced with a cogent request from a party seeking to re-
examine, that such an opportunity should be permitted, so some
general comments are offered here.

This stage of the process has been defined as: **4.61**

> "[giving the party] who has adduced the witness an opportunity of
> clearing up difficulties or ambiguities which may have emerged from cross-
> examination or to seek to repair the damage which cross-examination
> may have done".[122]

Where cross-examination has not gone well for a party's witness, that
party should seriously consider re-examination. At this stage in the
process, which is basically an extension, within certain limits, of the
examination-in-chief, leading questions are again not permitted. Also,
re-examination must involve only issues raised in cross-examination
(although the issues need not have been raised in examination-in-
chief). Where new issues are strayed into, an objection should be
taken. To put it another way, re-examination should not be used
to cover ground the examiner-in-chief has forgotten to cover, or

---

[117] Rule 52(1), discussed generally at paras 3.07 *et seq.*
[118] Rule 49(1)(g)(iii).
[119] Rule 49(1)(g)(iv).
[120] Rule 4, discussed generally at para 1.26.
[121] On leading questions, see para 4.51.
[122] A B Wilkinson, *The Scottish Law of Evidence* (1986), p 161.

to raise an issue that has occurred to the examiner-in-chief during cross-examination. It is a process whereby ground lost *during cross-examination* may be regained. However, even where an objection is made on this ground, the tribunal might decide to allow the questioning anyway, subject to a right of further cross-examination on the point being explored, where the view is taken that the issue should be explored in order to clarify the issues in the case.[123] Given the wide powers of the tribunal on the regulation of procedure[124] and the relative informality of the tribunal procedure generally compared with the public court process,[125] it would seem that a good reason for not raising the point earlier would not need to be advanced as long as the case for a re-examination itself is a good one.

4.62   Tactically speaking, parties should consider carefully, in connection with each witness, whether to exercise the right to re-examine. Too often, this right is exercised simply because it exists. The danger of doing so unnecessarily is that the witness may make concessions which were not given under cross-examination. Occasionally, cross-examination has been so devastating that re-examination serves only to compound the situation. Where ground seems unrecoverable, an attempt to do so will be futile and may be counter-productive. Where such a situation exists, the representative would be well advised to allow the witness to complete his evidence as quickly as possible and move on to other, hopefully more promising, witnesses.

The right not to give/lead oral evidence

4.63   The tribunal cannot, of course, physically force a witness to give evidence. Where a witness has been cited to attend to give evidence and refuses to do so, he may be guilty of an offence.[126] However, citations by the tribunal for a witness to attend will be rare. The tribunal can require someone to be personally present in order to give oral evidence,[127] but no sanction is attached if such a requirement is not complied with. A witness who refuses to give evidence could conceivably be directed to do so,[128] but the sanction for failing to

---

[123] Rule 63(2)(b)(ii).
[124] See r 52(1) and the power to issue directions across a wide procedural range in r 49.
[125] On the comparison between these processes generally, see paras 1.31 *et seq.*
[126] 2003 Act, Sch 2, para 12(3)(a)(ii).
[127] Rule 60.
[128] Rule 49(1)(a), where reference is made to a relevant person providing "further particulars" could be construed as a reference to oral evidence or r 49(1)(g)(iii) on the way in which evidence is to be given; an instruction that oral evidence should be given could fall within this provision.

follow the direction is that the tribunal can direct that the person take no further part in proceedings[129] – the very consequence the tribunal would be seeking to avoid in issuing such a direction. The fact that this is the only sanction available suggests that those who framed the directions provisions did not have this use of those powers in mind. This would suggest that such a direction might not be competent. Of course, where a witness who is present refuses to give evidence, there will usually be some good reason for this; those who simply do not wish to participate would presumably simply refuse to attend in the first place.

A slightly different but related situation arose in one tribunal hearing. The lawyer for the patient indicated that the tribunal should not ask him questions directly and that since he was representing the patient, he would ask the patient any questions, and offered to put questions from the tribunal to the patient and relay any answers back to the tribunal. The tribunal permitted this to happen. Although such an arrangement seems cumbersome, it is perfectly competent. There might be good reason for a lawyer wishing to adopt this course, for instance where he fears that his client will be unable to resist making comments detrimental to his case when asked certain questions, or where he fears that for some other reason his client will not make a good witness or will damage his own case. Such matters must ultimately be left in the judgment of a legal adviser. Also, given that the patient's liberty is at stake, it is reasonable to conclude that he has a right to silence in the same way as a person has when faced with a criminal charge and, in any event, in civil proceedings, a party cannot be forced to give evidence. It is submitted that patients in mental health tribunal cases can scarcely have less entitlement than all civil litigants and accused persons. In these circumstances, where a tribunal ignores the wishes of a party or witness (or his representative) and asks the witness questions, this may give rise to an argument of unfairness leading to a procedural impropriety. The offer made by the solicitor in the case referred to earlier in this paragraph went beyond what was required as a minimum; he could legitimately have told the tribunal that his client was not giving evidence and that the tribunal should not ask him any questions, directly or through his representative. **4.64**

However, in a situation where the patient has already given evidence, it would be unfair to the other parties (and would unduly hinder the business of the tribunal) if an attempt was made to deny access to the patient; the tribunal could refuse that attempt and legitimately question him directly.[130] **4.65**

---

[129] Rule 51(1).
[130] The tribunal here could rely on its power in terms of r 63(2)(b)(i) and (ii).

Evidence in non-oral form

4.66   The comments above are directed at the taking of oral evidence since
this is the most common way that the evidence of a witness is given.
However, in extreme cases, a witness might be too nervous or frightened
to answer questions and there would be no objection in principle to
a witness giving his evidence by reading a prepared statement. Such
a course of action is permitted in employment tribunals in respect
of a party who is unrepresented,[131] but in mental health tribunals
there seems no reason why this course of action cannot be followed
even where the party is represented. It is imperative in such cases
that the statement is signed by the author.[132] Further, this method
of giving evidence-in-chief could apply to any witness, not just a
party to proceedings. In any case where such a course is urged, the
tribunal should hear the views of all parties before deciding whether
to depart from the usual course of an oral examination of he witness.
It should be borne in mind that oral evidence direct from the witness
is preferable in general terms since the tribunal (and anyone seeking
to cross-examine)[133] would be better able to gauge the reliability[134]
of that evidence from an oral recital, particularly one in response
to certain pointed questions, than is possible from a flat statement,
particularly where that statement is to be read out by a representative
and not the party/witness himself. It may be possible to argue that
a witness has difficulty in communicating orally, and in such a case
a written statement, so long as it is signed, might be acceptable.[135]
Finally, where a witness will not be personally present at the hearing
but where he wishes his views to be recorded, a signed statement
can be submitted,[136] but the tribunal will require to approach such
an account with caution since it will not be able to be challenged
by cross-examination, and so its value may well be severely limited,
depending on how controversial the content of the statement is in the
context of the case.

4.67   It should be noted that although the tribunal will rely heavily
on the content of the application, mental health reports and on
supplementary reports and documentation, the terms of a document

---

[131] *Hardisty* v *Lowton Construction Group Ltd* (1973) 8 ITR 603.
[132] Rule 60 refers to any evidence being given orally or by "signed statement".
[133] On an argument that someone should not be subjected to cross-examination,
see para 4.59.
[134] On the reliability of evidence generally, see paras 5.121 *et seq.*
[135] The tribunal has an obligation to take all reasonable steps to secure appropriate
arrangements are made for the needs of such a person – r 53(4), commented on more
generally at para 4.35. Cross-examination in such a case might be problematic: see
above at paras 4.52 *et seq.*
[136] Rule 60.

may not represent evidence until someone "speaks to" the document (refers to it during oral evidence). Where the witness who refers to the document is not its author, some reference to how the document came to be compiled or delivered to the tribunal will be necessary. Where the witness is the author of the document, he will need to adopt it as part of his evidence. This should be done by asking the author if he is relying on/adopting the content of the document as part of his evidence and asking if there is anything in the document he would wish to retract/no longer reply upon. This avoids the cumbersome and rather pointless process that would otherwise apply: the witness reading out the terms of the document word for word. If a document is not referred to by a witness at all, it may still be possible for the tribunal to take account of it, if it can be classified as a "signed statement", and this may include signed reports.[137] Given the emphasis in the rules on informality,[138] it is submitted that this phrase should be given a wide meaning and will include most documents produced to the tribunal. The phrase would include a document with an electronic signature (as opposed to an ink one, which is clearly covered) as well as a document which carries the name of the author (whether the name is signed or typed). If it cannot be so classified and is not referred to by a witness, it is not evidence and so must be left out of account by the tribunal.[139] Despite the possibility of reliance on r 60, the safer course is to have a witness who is present at the hearing adopt the document into his evidence, wherever possible.

The order in which evidence is to be taken: application by the MHO or RMO

When considering the order in which evidence should be taken, the Convener should consider, with the other members, which order would be the best in the particular case, always bearing in mind the overriding objective in r 4.[140] From a pragmatic point of view, it can be useful to take from the patient a brief statement of his position at

4.68

---

[137] In terms of r 60, such a document constitutes evidence.

[138] Rule 63(2)(a).

[139] This is the position in the rules of civil evidence in public courts: see the comments of Lord Nimmo-Smith in *McTear* v *Imperial Tobacco Ltd* 2005 2 SC 1, para 1.37: "I do not regard it as open to me to take account of any passage in any document, the terms of which were not agreed, and to which reference was not made in the course of the evidence of any witness. This is because of the fundamental rule that I must decide the case on the basis of the evidence led before me." Given the application of the public court civil rules of evidence in tribunal cases (see paras 5.02 *et seq* on this) there seems no reason why this statement should not apply in mental health tribunal cases.

[140] Discussed further at para 1.26.

the outset (that is something more than simply saying whether or not he is opposing the application) before taking any detailed evidence from the applicant; otherwise, by the time evidence is taken from the patient he might have become bored, frustrated or might simply feel left out. This is particularly important in cases where the patient is unrepresented, since a representative is at least a point of contact and comfort for the patient. On the other hand, expecting the patient to give evidence in full first is probably not a good idea, even where it is intended to given him a further right to give evidence at the end, since it might create the impression that the patient has something to prove. The evidence should, where possible, be taken in the order suggested by the burden of proof, which, as commented on earlier, does not lie with the patient even in cases where he is the applicant or appellant.[141]

4.69   On the question of the order in which a party leads his witnesses, it seems that the party makes that decision,[142] although there is no reason why the tribunal could not, of its own volition or at the request of another party, seek to offer guidance to a party on that order, for practical reasons. Ultimately, however, the order is the prerogative of the party calling the witnesses.

Evidence and argument: the distinction

4.70   It is important that the tribunal ensures that only evidence is given at this stage. This can mean curtailing the flow of information from the MHO/RMO, as there is a temptation for the entire case to be put in one long speech in answer to a specific question. That question may well be one which requires a detailed answer, of course, such as one seeking an update on the progress of the patient since the last hearing or since the CTO application was framed. However, witnesses should restrict themselves to factual information only, not argument about whether certain statutory criteria apply; the latter should come at the submissions stage.[143]

Making an admissibility objection

4.71   Where a party to tribunal proceedings takes the view that evidence that is likely to be led is inadmissible, an objection should be taken to the admission of that evidence. Of course, if the material objected

---

[141] See the burden of proof in such cases being discussed at para 5.09.

[142] This is the position taken in employment tribunal cases: *Barnes v BPC (Business Forms) Ltd* [1975] IRLR 313, approved in *Aberdeen Steak Houses Group plc v Ibrahim* [1988] ICR 550; [1988] IRLR 420.

[143] On this stage in proceedings, see below at paras 4.93 *et seq.*

to is contained in written evidence that is already before the tribunal (for example in a CTO application) it will already have been digested by the tribunal members before the hearing.[144] In such a situation, the objector could raise the matter as a preliminary point at the outset of the hearing.[145] The tribunal should then rule on the objection and, where the objection is upheld, issue directions on the restriction of the inadmissible evidence. In the case of oral evidence, this should be treated in the same way as an objection made to oral evidence in court. This essentially means that the objection should be made timeously (before the answer has begun, ideally, but at least before it is over). However, it might be possible to persuade the tribunal to consider an objection to evidence once it has been given, since the proceedings in the tribunal are not as formal as they are in a public court, and should be conducted as informally as the circumstances of the case permit.[146]

As discussed elsewhere, on the procedure for issuing directions generally,[147] it would seem that a direction on a request to exclude evidence (as with any other direction) can be issued in advance of a tribunal hearing (usually by an in-house Convener sitting alone)[148] or by the panel at the hearing itself. The main grounds for the objection of the admissibility of evidence in tribunal cases are discussed elsewhere.[149] Of course, where the objection is to be taken to oral evidence, this will have to be taken, argued and determined on the day of the hearing, by the tribunal panel. However, careful consideration should be given to the question of whether material in the tribunal papers should be objected to in advance of the hearing. The main advantage of following this procedure is that time will not be taken up by the Tribunal panel having to hear and deliberate on the request for such a direction. A further advantage is that if the direction request is assented to, the inadmissible material should be removed from the papers that are sent out to the tribunal members, so that there is no question of those members being unconsciously influenced by them.[150] There is no provision dealing

4.72

---

[144] For the pre-hearing activities of tribunal members, see paras 3.15 *et seq.*
[145] On preliminary points generally, see Chapter 3.
[146] Rule 63(2)(a).
[147] On this question surrounding directions generally, see the explanation at paras 7.31 *et seq.*
[148] On the role of such Conveners, see para 2.11.
[149] At paras 5.47 *et seq.*
[150] This assumes that the papers have not been sent out to the tribunal members already, of course, and that it is physically possible to remove the objected to material while keeping the documents intact. Where the direction relates to one whole document, then the entire document should be removed, where possible, prior to distribution of the papers.

with such removal, but this seems a sensible approach to take in such circumstances, and the removal of material from papers would best be authorised under a direction in terms of r 49(1)(g)(iv). Of course, the main problem with seeking an advance direction of this nature is that there will often be little time between the issue of, typically, a CTO application, and the hearing. This situation is compounded by the requirement that all requests for a direction on the exclusion of evidence require to be made in writing, with a 14-day notice period being allowed for representations on the request.[151] The timing issue means that in practice the vast majority of such requests will be dealt with at the hearing orally, and with notice there and then, whether the objection relates to oral or written evidence. In any such case, the plea for exclusion should be accompanied by a plea in terms of r 75 of the Rules[152] to dispense with the prescribed procedure for any direction.[153]

4.73   Of course, in order to determine whether certain evidence is admissible or not, the tribunal will require to know something about its likely content. Where the request for exclusion is made in advance in writing, the reasons for the exclusion will, naturally, refer to the evidence anticipated, and the procedure for considering the request for issuing a direction set out in r 49 will follow from there. In the by far more common case of an admissibility objection made orally at a tribunal hearing itself, the Rules do not provide for the precise procedure to be followed, only that certain evidence might be excluded for certain reasons. However, there is an established procedure in use in civil public court cases, and there seems no reason to use a different procedure in tribunal cases. Indeed, the obligation on the tribunal to act fairly would suggest that a careful and methodical approach to a question of the exclusion of evidence should be taken. The procedure in such cases will be influenced by the source of the admissibility objection. It will come either from a relevant person or from a tribunal member (usually the Convener). In the case where the objection comes from a relevant person, the usual course would be for the objector to explain briefly and in outline what the content of the evidence would be, if declared admissible. In the event of the evidence being ruled as inadmissible, the tribunal will simply put out of its mind the information contained in the explanation offered, and place no reliance on it at all. This applies whether the anticipated evidence is oral, and so is never heard in its pure form; or whether it is written and so has probably already been

---

[151] Rule 49(3).
[152] On the dispensing power in the rules generally, see paras 7.49 *et seq.*
[153] That procedure is set out in r 49(2)–(7) and is discussed in more detail at paras 7.30 *et seq.*

read by the panel members. In the latter case, the tribunal's task is more difficult, but is clear.

In most cases where an admissibility objection is made at the hearing, the tribunal will hear/read the evidence under reservation. This means that the evidence is allowed to be presented in full and a decision on whether the evidence is to be admissible is made after hearing arguments on the point during the submissions stage. Where it is decided that the evidence is admissible, the tribunal will simply take account of it. Where it is decided that the evidence already presented is inadmissible, the tribunal will be obliged simply to leave it out of account. 4.74

An alternative approach to hearing the evidence under reservation would be to exclude the evidence after hearing admissibility argument at the point when the objection is taken. This course of action might be appropriate where the objection is to a line of evidence (as opposed to a single question) and where the evidence in that line is likely to be substantial. In such cases, hearing the evidence first and deciding on admissibility later might not be the most expeditious way to proceed[154] since it might involve the hearing of significant evidence that may later be excluded as inadmissible. Indeed, in order to avoid breaking the flow of evidence, where a party wishes to raise an admissibility objection which is likely to affect a major issue in the hearing, it would seem sensible to raise it as a preliminary matter, and not as an objection to a specific question; that said, there may be a tactical decision for the objector to make here: unless the evidence is in written form and already before the tribunal (in which case an objection will be necessary in order to have any hope of having it excluded) the objector might be best to wait and see if the evidence he wishes to have excluded appears during the oral part of the hearing. If it does not, no objection was necessary; if it does, the objection can always be taken at the time when the evidence arises. There is a danger, in other words, that an early objection may be counter-productive in that the issue the objector seeks to avoid is drawn to the attention of the parties and witnesses present, so that if the objection is repelled, the evidence will almost certainly come out when it may not have done. 4.75

The case for the MHO/RMO as applicant

After taking a short statement of the patient's view, the tribunal should allow the MHO or RMO to present his evidence. It is critical for the tribunal and the parties to bear in mind which attendees are parties and which are witnesses. It is for the applicant (in most cases 4.76

---

[154] The obligation to act expeditiously springs from the overriding objective in r 4, discussed elsewhere generally: para 1.26.

the MHO) to make representations, and to offer witnesses. Witnesses should be restricted to giving evidence only.[155]

4.77   In most cases, the MHO/RMO as applicant will be unrepresented. This is perhaps surprising given that, under the former procedure, which in many ways was simpler, the MHO was always represented.[156] However, this is probably because of the tribunal environment: many MHOs would not have dreamt of presenting an application without the assistance of legal representation in the sheriff court.

4.78   Where the MHO/RMO is unrepresented, the tribunal members will conduct the examination-in-chief of the MHO and RMO, and attention will usually focus on the RMO, at least for the most part. Other witnesses might include ward staff and, again, the tribunal will be responsible for the oral examination of such witnesses. The tribunal, when taking evidence in this way, should be careful to avoid asking leading questions, and should generally conduct the questioning as though it is acting as a lawyer taking his client through examination-in-chief. The reason for this is that it is not the job of the tribunal (at least at this stage) to conduct a full examination of the witness; cross-examination should be left to the legal representative(s) present. Where there are no other legal representatives, the tribunal may adopt a more rigorous questioning approach, since there is no-one legally qualified there to cross-examine the witness. However, even in such cases, the tribunal members should test the evidence in relation to the matters they need to be satisfied about with courtesy, rigour, and appropriate restraint.[157] Where cross-examination has taken place for another party by a lawyer, the tribunal is entitled to follow up the cross-examination with further questions, again being careful to avoid leading questions where possible and being mindful of the duty not to take the questioning too far.[158] At this stage, the role of the tribunal would be to clarify issues, or indeed to raise pertinent issues that have not been raised before. The tribunal is not, at this stage, restricted to the rules on re-examination, since the role of the tribunal as an inquisitorial judicial body is to seek information relevant to the disposal of the case, while allowing the evidence to be brought out, where possible, without its intervention. It is important to note that other parties must be given an opportunity to ask further questions arising out of enquiries put by tribunal members. This opportunity should be afforded soon after those enquiries have been put.

---

[155] However, note the position of the RMO and other mental health report authors in CTO applications and s 50 STDC revocation applications – they have similar rights as parties: see para 4.28.

[156] This was under the Mental Health (Scotland) Act 1984, principally under s 18.

[157] On the questioning limits of tribunal members, see paras 4.114 et seq.

[158] Ibid.

In the rare cases where the MHO/RMO is represented, the tribunal   **4.79**
should leave the lawyer for that party to take the witnesses through
their evidence. Again, the role of the tribunal thereafter will depend
on whether there is other legal representation available, and the
comments in the preceding paragraph apply here where there is not.
Where there is other representation, once again, the tribunal should
leave most of the work to the lawyers. After the lawyers have been
able to examine, cross-examine and re-examine (where appropriate)
the tribunal should restrict itself again to the clarification of issues
arising, the raising of pertinent issues not already covered, and
the avoidance of leading questions in the process. Sometimes, the
tribunal can intervene to make it clear that evidence can be led in a
particular way. For instance, some tribunals prefer questioning of the
MHO/RMO to focus on the key issues arising in the case. Part of the
advantage of having advance detailed papers available is that there is
no need for the MHO and RMO to be taken through the entire terms
of the report in their evidence; they can simply adopt their report/
application into their evidence, allowing the oral evidence thereafter
to be more focused and take less time.[159] Where appropriate, there is
no difficulty in the tribunal indicating that this course of action may
be adopted, either at the outset of the case of the MHO/RMO or by
intervening where it looks as though the lawyer for the MHO/RMO
will adopt a longhand approach; this intervention could be justified
on the basis of the overriding objective, which includes the duty to
handle proceedings as efficiently as possible.[160]

The tribunal should then allow the patient an opportunity to   **4.80**
present his case and the process above should be adopted. The same
will apply to the evidence to be presented by any other party, for
example the named person, although in the case of a named person,
usually he will be unrepresented and will be calling no additional
witnesses, in which case the examination of the named person should
be conducted by the tribunal, and the comments above apply as they
do to the MHO/RMO and patient. The tribunal should be careful
to check that all witnesses intended to be called by a relevant person
have been allowed to give evidence, before moving to the case of the
next party.

The case for the patient as applicant/appellant

The case for the patient as an applicant/appellant is conducted   **4.81**
in much the same way as occurs where the MHO/RMO is the
applicant. In such cases, the basis of the patient's case should be

---

[159] On adoption of reports into evidence, see para 4.48.
[160] Rule 4.

clarified at the outset; unlike in the case of a CTO application, the basis of the patient's case will often not be in writing, even where the grounds of the application/appeal are supposed to be provided in writing in advance of the hearing.[161] However, where the patient is seeking to challenge the position of the MHO/RMO, for example in a hearing where he is seeking to have the STDC revoked, there will be no evidence from the patient as such, and the RMO/MHO should be asked first to justify his position, usually by cross-examination of them (and their witnesses) by the patient or his representative, followed by evidence from or on behalf of the patient. This follows from the fact that the burden of proof even in such cases lies on the State.[162]

4.82   The advocacy worker, if one is present, should be allowed to tender his views, even where the patient has given evidence, but he may decline to do so on the basis that everything he intended to say has been covered.[163]

Evidence from any other party

4.83   The evidence of the named person will usually follow the case for the MHO/RMO and the patient, and the same general rules and protocols follow as with any other party. There should then follow, finally, the evidence of any other party to proceedings.

Role of the advocacy worker in the witness examination process

4.84   Depending on the proper view of the role of the advocacy worker,[164] it may be that he should be permitted to cross-examine any witness for the MHO/RMO. He is not a party and so should not be permitted to call any witnesses, but he may have cross-examination rights, if he is to be regarded as a representative. It is safest to invite the advocacy worker to cross-examine each witness, although, in the vast majority of cases, this invitation will be declined. Where the advocacy worker simply puts the position of the patient to the tribunal, this is likely to consist of a mixture of evidence and submissions, and any part of his contribution which is regarded as evidence should be treated as such and where any new evidential material is introduced by him, the relevant persons should be given an opportunity to comment on that evidence.

---

[161] For example, r 5(2)(e). In such cases, the grounds will not be stated at all, or if they are will be in very bald terms.
[162] This has been discussed already at para 5.09.
[163] On the role of the advocacy worker, see paras 2.49 et seq.
[164] Ibid.

Unrepresented relevant person: right to cross-examine

It is often forgotten, in the absence of a lawyer, that a party to   **4.85**
proceedings before the tribunal should usually be given the opportunity to cross-examine the witnesses of his opponent(s). The right
of that party to cross-examine his opponent's witnesses should not
be forgotten; however, the tribunal might in an extreme case take
the view that any cross-examination might be counter-productive
to the efficient running of the proceedings, with little hope of any
clarification of the issues. This may apply in particular where the
patient is less than coherent in his presentation at the hearing, and
where the provision of the right to cross-examine would exacerbate
this situation. The tribunal would have to make sure, however, that
adequate opportunity is given to permit the evidence of the opponent
to be challenged on the points with which the patient disagrees. The
tribunal should always offer the opportunity to cross-examine and,
if the offer is taken up, the tribunal can always control the flow and
relevancy of questions by intervening (see below). If a right to cross-
examine is not provided, and should have been, this could amount to
a procedural impropriety, since the right to cross-examine witnesses
is fundamental to the fair and just conduct of judicial proceedings.[165]
If the offer is declined, the tribunal may wish to ask whether there
are any questions that the patient would like the tribunal to ask the
witness, in case the patient feels inhibited personally from cross-
examining his medical advisers.

The attendance of witnesses during the hearing

In the public courts, and in some specialised tribunals, witnesses are   **4.86**
routinely excluded from the hearing during the evidence of other
witnesses, with two exceptions,[166] unless a special application is
made. In mental health tribunals, the standard procedure is to have
everyone in the hearing for the whole of the evidence.

Although this is the standard procedure, there are various situations   **4.87**
in which a witness might not be present throughout. First of all, the
patient may leave during the hearing; this is not uncommon where
he is finding the experience stressful or where he objects to some
of the evidence he hears. Where the patient unexpectedly leaves the
hearing, it is good practice for the hearing to be briefly adjourned in
order to find out whether the patient will return; the tribunal should

---

[165] See further paras 4.52 *et seq.*
[166] These are: the parties to the litigation are permitted to be present throughout
(in criminal proceedings the accused *must* be so present) and expert witnesses, who
may listen to evidence as to fact which is relevant to their own evidence, to be given
later.

not simply continue in his absence until that step is taken. Once the intention of the patient is established, the hearing can continue, preferably with him in attendance but, if he refuses to attend, the hearing should proceed in his absence. This process is easier where the patient is represented, since at least he will retain a voice in the resumed hearing. Where the patient has no representation, the tribunal may consider whether to offer to visit the patient (where he is on a nearby ward) in order to take his views further.[167] If that step is being considered, the tribunal will have to decide whether to take that step before resuming the hearing proper or whether to wait until after the evidence is over, so that the patient can have a chance to comment on the evidence he has not heard. Any such decision (if, and if so when) should only be taken after the options have been canvassed with all relevant persons present.[168]

4.88   Another not uncommon situation arises where a witness indicates that he has other business and wishes to leave after giving evidence. This is most common in relation to an RMO during a CTO application hearing. As long as there is no objection from any other relevant person (and if there is, that objection will be heard and a decision will have to be made) there will usually be no reason to detain such a witness longer than necessary, and an early excusal may be sensible. However, much will depend on the circumstances of the case. It may not be wise to excuse the RMO in particular, where the hearing is closely contested or where other witnesses to medical matters have still to give evidence. If the patient is to give evidence after the RMO (as will usually be the case in CTO applications) and where there are likely to be disagreements as to events and accounts, the RMO should be asked to stay, in order that he can have an opportunity to comment. Essentially, the tribunal should consider whether the witness concerned is likely to be needed later, as a result of evidence arising from other witnesses. Sometimes, of course, it is not easy to predict what evidence will be led, and a possible compromise in cases of doubt is to allow the witness to be excused, on the basis that he will be available later to return and supplement his evidence if necessary. This solution may be apt where the witness is a medical professional who works in a ward near to the tribunal venue. Again, it is important that any decision is taken against the background of the views of all relevant persons.

4.89   Where the person seeking early excusal is a party to the proceedings (for example the MHO, but could be the RMO) the request should,

---

[167] Such a step is usually required under r 70(3) but r 70 only applies where a relevant person does not attend at all, not where he does not attend for the whole hearing.
[168] See r 52(3)–(4), discussed in detail at para 3.14.

save in the most exceptional of cases, be refused, since the parties should be present to deliver submissions after the evidence is over.

There is nothing to prevent the tribunal from hearing the evidence **4.90** of each witness in the absence of other witnesses. The power to take such a step can be found in the tribunal's general discretion to regulate proceedings as it sees fit,[169] on the basis of the tribunal's power to conduct the hearing in the way considered most suitable to the clarification and determination of the matters before it[170] and from the power of the tribunal to issue directions on the way in which evidence is to be led.[171] In addition, there is a specific power to exclude any person who is to appear as a witness until they given evidence if it is considered fair to do so.[172] However, this process can be cumbersome and time-consuming, and where the tribunal has two full hearings to conduct in a day (including writing the determinations) such a course of action is usually impractical. Having said this, in certain cases, there may be a reason for adopting this course, for instance where a witness does not wish to give evidence in the presence of another, for fear of embarrassment or because this would give rise to distress on the part of the witness. Also, where there are important issues of credibility, it might be preferable if witnesses are heard separately, in case they are influenced by what others say in their presence. Where a witness is likely to be fearful of giving evidence in the presence of another witness, the tribunal should consider hearing the evidence separately. Sometimes, there is evidence of undue influence by the patient on a relevant person, most notably the named person who is also a close relative. This can arise when the named person supports the granting of the order being sought (usually a hospital-based CTO) while the patient strongly opposes the order. This can make the evidence-giving process for the named person very awkward and can lead either to the evidence being more muted than would otherwise be the case or, in extreme cases, to confrontation between the named person and the patient which might damage their relationship. Sometimes a case of this kind can be picked up from the papers, but often the tribunal members will only discover such a situation during the hearing. In the latter case, the tribunal can still put in place arrangements to hear the relevant evidence separately, but may have to use discretion in doing so.

Where the evidence of a witness is heard outwith the presence **4.91** of some or all of the other participants at the hearing, the tribunal should consider whether, in the interests of fairness, there should

---

[169] Rule 52(1).
[170] Rule 63(2)(b)(ii).
[171] Rule 49(1)(g)(iii).
[172] Rule 63(7).

be some disclosure of that evidence to the excluded participants. Where such a step is not taken, this could give rise to an argument that the excluded participant has not had an opportunity to present his case,[173] or (where the person excluded is not a party) that, had the excluded participant known of the content of the evidence, the remaining evidence might have been different. Where the excluded participant is a witness who is unlikely to have anything to say about the evidence in question, the tribunal need do nothing to redress the situation. However, where the witness has given evidence outwith the presence of any other party the tribunal would only in the most exceptional case take no steps to inform that party of the content of that evidence. This can most obviously be done by summarising the evidence for that party, and offering him an opportunity to comment on it. This may even lead to that party seeking to lodge new evidence, call new witnesses or recall witnesses who have already given evidence, in order to counter or explain the evidence given outwith his presence, and such a request will have to be dealt with carefully by the tribunal.

4.92   Where the person excluded is a party who is legally represented, the best course of action would usually be to allow that representative to be present during the questioning, since he could relay the content of the evidence back to his client, and would be able to cross-examine the witness. This arrangement could lead to the lawyer seeking permission to take instructions from his client before cross-examination of the witness, and a brief adjournment for this purpose should be allowed.

Submissions

4.93   After all of the evidence is over, the tribunal should invite all parties to present submissions. The difference between evidence and argument has already been commented upon.[174] Parties or representatives who are not lawyers will usually understand their role when asked to offer "closing arguments" or to "sum up", since the word "submissions" is usually understood only by lawyers. This is the opportunity for the party to explain why, given the evidence led, the order sought should or should not be granted. Lawyers will be expected to deliver submissions with reference to the statutory criteria, and to identify the key points in support of their argument. Where a party is unrepresented, some latitude is expected from the tribunal and tribunal members would probably not be criticised for intervening to seek to clarify where the

---

[173] On this key part of the fairness right, see para 4.08.
[174] See para 4.70.

party stands on a particular point, since this kind of intervention is not uncommon during submissions being delivered by lawyers in the public courts. Such interventions may be justifiable on the basis of the tribunal's power to conduct the hearing in the way considered most suitable to the clarification and determination of the matters before the tribunal.[175] In addition, it should be remembered that the hearing should be conducted as informally as the circumstances permit, suggesting that submissions should not be treated with the same formality as public court submissions.[176] However, as discussed later, such interruptions should be handled carefully.[177]

There is some lack of clarity over the status of any comments   **4.94**
made by advocacy workers.[178] As has already been noted,[179] their contribution is likely to consist of a mixture of factual material and submissions. It is probably unwise, therefore, for the tribunal to turn to him as late on as at the submissions stage, since by that time the evidential part of the hearing will have concluded. Since any evidential material in the advocacy worker's submission would have to be put to the other parties (and perhaps non-party witnesses) this could lead to an interruption of submissions to go back into evidence, which would be untidy. Even more problematic would be a case where, by the time this happened, a witness to whom this new material should be put has left, perhaps with the permission of the tribunal.[180] For these reasons, the advocacy worker's representations should be invited before the end of the process of examination of witnesses and as early on in the process as possible.

Any outstanding points of law should be dealt with at the submis-   **4.95**
sions stage also. Where evidence is heard under reservation[181] the tribunal should hear submissions on whether it is admissible or not, so that it can decide whether to take account of the evidence or discount it during deliberations.

Procedure post-submissions

Once the submissions stage is over, the tribunal will be ready to   **4.96**
deliberate and reach a decision. The Convener should make it clear to the parties that the participative part of the hearing is over, in case there is any last-minute issue a party wishes to raise. Clearly, at this

---

[175] Rule 63(2)(b)(ii).
[176] Rule 63(2)(a).
[177] On interruptions to submissions, see paras 4.112 *et seq.*
[178] On the status of the advocacy worker generally, see paras 2.44 *et seq.*
[179] See the discussion at para 4.84 above.
[180] For a discussion of the excusal of witnesses before the end of the hearing, see paras 4.88 *et seq.*
[181] This is discussed further at para 4.74.

stage, any new evidence is unlikely and the tribunal should not hear any further evidence or submissions unless with the consent of all parties, or, without it, where it is satisfied that it is just and is suitable to the clarification and determination of the matters before it that it should do so.[182] After submissions have been heard, the tribunal should adjourn to consider its decision, indicating to the participants roughly how long it might take to deliberate.

4.97   While deliberating on their decision, the tribunal members may discover some point that has not been covered during the evidence, and which they wish to rely on in reaching a decision. For instance, there may be an incident referred to in a CTO application or mental heath report, but which has not been canvassed during the hearing, and is not covered by a general acceptance of the content of the application or report. If it is possible that any of the witnesses may have a view on that matter, it might be wise for the tribunal to reconvene briefly to allow the issue to be put to relevant witnesses. The tribunal may call back the parties under its general power to regulate proceedings as it sees fit[183] and its obligation to conduct a hearing in the way most suitable to clarification and determination of the matters before the tribunal.[184] If this step is not taken, and the tribunal takes account of this matter in making a finding-in-fact or deciding a legal or procedural point, there is likely to have occurred an appealable procedural impropriety.[185] In this process, the questions will be asked by the tribunal members, but, as in all cases where questions are put by a panel member, an opportunity for the other parties or representatives to ask any follow-up questions on the subject raised should be afforded.[186] The question of whether the issue is one that requires the hearing to be reconvened is a matter of judgement for the tribunal. Ultimately, whether a decision in these circumstances will survive an appeal will depend on the appeal court's assessment of what would have been likely to happen had the hearing been reconvened. There is employment tribunal case law to the effect that where the relevant finding-in-fact would not have been altered on a re-hearing, an appeal against the decision should fail.[187] Where the tribunal is in any doubt on the matter, the safe course would be to reconvene the hearing and

---

[182] Rule 63(2)(b).

[183] Rule 52(1), discussed elsewhere in general terms at paras 3.07 *et seq.*

[184] Rule 63(2)(b)(ii), discussed elsewhere in general terms at para 1.27.

[185] An example of such a situation in the employment tribunal context is making a contributory finding of fault in a case where the tribunal has omitted to canvass that possibility during the hearing: see P Elias and B Napier (eds), *Harvey on Employment Law and Industrial Relations,* para T901 and the cases cited there.

[186] On this requirement generally, see para 4.78 below.

[187] See the Court of Appeal decision in *Judge v Crown Leisure Ltd* [2005] EWCA Civ 571; [2005] IRLR 823.

take the additional evidence as a precaution. Such a step is usually logistically possible, since most parties and witnesses will wait to hear the oral decision of the tribunal being announced, and so will still be in the vicinity of the tribunal venue.

The tribunal members may discover during deliberations that   **4.98** some matter covered in the evidence is unclear. This might arise from a disagreement between the members as to what was said on a particular point, or it may simply become clear that the evidence given on a particular matter is not sufficiently comprehensive to allow a particular finding or conclusion to be reached. In such cases, the tribunal may decide to reconvene the hearing to clarify the position, in which case the guidance in the preceding paragraph applies. However, this will not always be the appropriate course of action, especially where the witnesses who could have clarified the point failed to do so where there was ample opportunity during the hearing: reconvening and giving that witness a chance to give his evidence on the point again might even constitute apparent bias on the part of the tribunal.[188]

A slightly different but analogous scenario might occur where the   **4.99** tribunal decides to rely on an authority (statutory provision, case law or legal text) where that source was not discussed during the hearing. It is not incumbent on the tribunal to ensure that *every* legal source relied upon has been canvassed during the hearing. In an employment tribunal context, it has been held that:

> "the authority [which was not discussed at the hearing] must alter or affect the way the issues have been addressed to a significant extent so that it truly can be said by a fair-minded observer that the case was decided in a way which could not have been anticipated by a party fixed with such knowledge of the law and procedure as it would be reasonable to attribute to him in all the circumstances. ... The vital question, in my judgment, is whether it would have made any difference to the outcome if [the authority had been available to the parties at the hearing]".[189]

It will, however, if possible, be wise to try to give parties an oppor-   **4.100** tunity to address the tribunal on the authority in question. Once a decision has been reached, the participants will be invited back into the tribunal room and told the result. Strictly speaking, only the parties need attend this part of the proceedings, and witnesses have no locus. However, in practice, witnesses will usually wait for the

---

[188] On apparent bias generally, see paras 4.13 *et seq.*
[189] Per Ward LJ in the Court of Appeal in *Stanley Cole (Wainfleet) Ltd* v *Sheridan* [2003] EWCA Civ 1046; [2003] ICR 1449 at paras 32 and 38. See also the immigration case of *R v Immigration Appeal Tribunal, ex p Sui Rong Suen* [1997] IAR 355.

announcement and attend. Having said this, the tribunal, in certain cases, may wish to limit the attendance at the announcement of the result, where there is good reason to do so, for example if the tribunal fears an adverse (or even violent) reaction to the decision, or where the view is taken that a party or witness (for example the patient) would be caused distress by the announcement. This power would fall within the power to regulate proceedings as the tribunal sees fit.[190] Where a party does not wish to attend this part of the proceedings, the tribunal should not insist on his attendance, as this will slow the proceedings and may cause additional distress or discomfort. In very extreme cases, where a party or witness refuses to accept a decision that he should not attend the announcement, the tribunal could issue a direction that he be excluded.[191]

4.101   The Rules require that the decision be "given" at the end of the hearing,[192] which means that it should be issued. The written decision will be signed and intimated at the end of the hearing by the Clerk, even where the findings-in-fact and reasons are issued later. Where any recorded matters are being issued, these should be intimated briefly during the oral announcement of the decision. It should be made clear to the participants that a full decision, in writing and with reasons, will be issued. It is usually expected that the Convener will offer some general indication of the reasons for the decision, even if this is just to say that certain evidence was preferred and the criteria were found to be satisfied. On the other hand, sometimes the intimation of the result will provoke an adverse reaction from some of those attending. Where the tribunal thinks this might happen, consideration should be given to whether to dispense with the giving of any oral reasons, to avoid disruption or any attempt to open up the issues again or argue with the decision. In the event of no one attending to hear the decision, there is no need, of course, to announce it orally.

4.102   It is clear that the written decision takes precedence over the oral pronouncement, even in cases where the orally announced result is contradicted later in the written decision.[193]

---

[190] Rule 52(1), discussed elsewhere in general terms at paras 3.07 *et seq.*

[191] Such a direction could be issued under r 49(1)(g)(iii) or under r 68 or r 69 (see paras 4.128 *et seq*, and paras 4.139 *et seq*, respectively), depending on the circumstances.

[192] Rule 72(1). This rule permits the reservation of the decision but this is virtually unheard of in practice.

[193] See the immigration case of *R v Special Adjudicator, ex p Bashir* [2002] IAR 1. The procedural provisions that applied to the issuing of a written decision in such cases (at the time of the decision, rr 2(3) and 11 of the Asylum Appeals (Procedure) Rules 1996, now rr 22 and 23 of the Asylum and Immigration Tribunal (Procedure) Rules 2005 (SI 2005/230)) are similar in their import to the equivalent mental health tribunal provision, namely r 72(7), so this case is analogous.

Interventions by tribunal members during hearing

It may become necessary for a tribunal member, in particular the   **4.103**
Convener, to intervene during the taking of evidence or submissions
to keep the hearing on track and ensure order is maintained.[194] Such
interventions are justifiable as long as they are kept to the minimum
necessary to fulfil these important aims; the evidence and submissions
should, as far as possible, be allowed to unfold naturally. Interventions
during the examination of witnesses where the examination or cross-
examination is being conducted by a lawyer should take place only
in order to ask necessary questions (see below) or to protect a witness
from over-zealous, rude or aggressive questioning. Alternatively,
the Convener may form the view that the line of questioning being
adopted is irrelevant or repetitive or unhelpful to the issues the
tribunal is trying to determine. This should be pointed out to the
questioner, and his response to the point (if any) should be taken into
account.[195] Assuming that response does not persuade the tribunal
that the questioning should continue, ultimately, the line being
adopted can be stopped by the tribunal directing that the questioning
moves onto new ground. Such a course should be adopted with great
care, and certainly only once the questioner has had an opportunity
to defend his techniques; without that opportunity, a curtailment
of questioning could be attacked on appeal as being procedurally
improper. Interventions of this nature can be justified by a number of
provisions in the rules, depending on the situation:

- ability to take evidence in writing under r 60: could be used
  to prevent repetition of evidence already before the tribunal in
  writing;
- obligation to conduct hearing as informally as possible under
  r 63(2)(a): could be used to justify intervention, breaking the
  traditional adversarial flow;
- obligation to conduct hearing in a just way under r 63(2)(b)(i);
- obligation to conduct a hearing in a the way most suitable
  to clarification and determination of the matters before the

---

[194] The duties of the Convener in regulating procedure are discussed in general
terms at para 3.05.
[195] See the Immigration Appeal Tribunal case of *K v Secretary of State for the
Home Department (Côte d'Ivoire)* [2004] UKIAT 00061 where the Tribunal refers
to "a line of questioning that is irrelevant or valueless or repetitious or is going
nowhere". In such cases, it is "necessary and proper" for such questioning to be
interrupted and the problem pointed out, although it is also said that any response
from the questioner should be taken into account when deciding what to do next.
See the judgment at para 42.

tribunal under r 63(2)(b)(ii): could be used to cut out repetitive or unnecessary evidence;

- power to give directions under r 49(1)(g) on evidential issues, nature of evidence, method of leading evidence and the exclusion of evidence;[196]
- general power to regulate its own procedure under r 52(1);
- the overriding principle in r 4.

Where such an intervention leading to a curtailment of questioning does take place, this decision should be taken by the tribunal members after consultation (and not by the Convener alone)[197] and the decision should be issued orally (and later in writing).[198]

4.104   The power of the Convener in particular to intervene in such cases is justified also with reference to the provisions on the role of the Convener as the tribunal member responsible for regulating procedure at the hearing.[199] Conveners should be careful in conducting such interventions that they do not appear to be favouring one party over the other, nor should they be seen to be assisting one side or the other with their interventions. If such an impression is created as a result of interventions, this could constitute apparent bias.[200] These interventions should also avoid altering the nature of the hearing by allowing it to become more akin to a meeting or case conference than a judicial hearing.

4.105   In practical terms this means the hearing should be conducted as closely as possible to the traditional adversarial model, with examination, cross-examination and re-examination followed by submissions, with interventions from the tribunal coming only where necessary.

4.106   Where a party is not present and has no representation, however, and where, therefore, the tribunal takes the lead in questioning witnesses,[201] the tribunal is not obliged to take on the role that would have been fulfilled by the party or representative had he been present. This is made clear in a number of authorities, including the Inner House immigration case of *Koca* v *Secretary of State for the Home Department*.[202] In that case, the court repeated the sentiment expressed in earlier cases that a tribunal is not obliged to go out of

---

[196] On directions generally, see paras 7.30 *et seq.*
[197] See further on this at para 3.48.
[198] On directions generally, see paras 7.30 *et seq* and on a direction in this situation, see para 7.38.
[199] On the duties of the Convener, see para 3.05.
[200] On apparent bias, see paras 4.13 *et seq.*
[201] On this role in such cases, see paras 4.114 *et seq.*
[202] 2005 1 SC 487.

its way to seek out evidence that is not presented by the parties, even when it is referred to.[203]

However, in such a situation, the tribunal should be careful to put any discrepancy in the evidence before it to any witnesses who are present and can comment on such a discrepancy and where the discrepancy is going to be a significant factor in the tribunal's decision.[204] This does not mean that every discrepancy should be put by the tribunal. In cases where the discrepancy will not be a significant factor, it is the job of the party affected by the discrepancy to address it if he wishes, whether or not in the absence of a "contradictor" (opposing party); he cannot remain silent on the matter and then claim later, when the discrepancy is relied upon by the tribunal to his disadvantage, that he assumed the tribunal would not do so since it was not canvassed at the hearing.[205]   **4.107**

It is clear that the tribunal should not reach a finding-in-fact[206] where that fact is not one in issue in the evidence before it. Where a tribunal member thinks there is a factual matter which has not been covered in the evidence, it should be raised with the parties before a decision on the case is made. Smith LJ had this to say on the subject in an employment case in the Court of Appeal: **4.108**

> "It is highly desirable that if a tribunal foresees that it might make a finding of fact which has not been contended for, that possible finding should be raised with the parties during closing submissions. If the Tribunal does not realise what its findings of fact are likely to be until after the hearing has finished, it will usually be necessary to give the parties the opportunity to make further submissions, at least in writing, although not, in my view, necessarily by oral argument."[207]

---

[203] 2005 1 SC 487 at para 17. In doing so it relied on the Court of Appeal case of *R v Immigration Appeal Tribunal, ex p Keziban Kilinc* [1999] Imm AR 588.

[204] See the Inner House decision in the immigration tribunal case of *Koca v Secretary of State for the Home Department* 2005 1 SC 487, para 20. This case concerned, in part, an argument that a credibility discrepancy should have been put by the adjudicator to the asylum applicant, but it would probably apply to a discrepancy of another nature, as long as it is a significant factor in the decision. The Inner House decided that the adjudicator had failed in that duty and allowed the appeal.

[205] See the Immigration Appeal Tribunal decision of *WN v Secretary of State for the Home Department* [2004] UKIAT 00213, para 28. The appeal tribunal in this case relied on Lord Carloway's judgment in the Outer House case of *Koca v Secretary of State for the Home Department*, but his reasoning on this point was criticised by the Inner House on appeal (2005 1 SC 487 at para 20) who reversed his decision. The Inner House decision was not issued until after the *WN* decision, so the reliance on *Koca* in that case should be ignored, although *WN* is still good authority for the point being made here.

[206] On findings-in-fact generally, see para 7.21.

[207] *Judge v Crown Leisure Ltd* [2005] EWCA Civ 571 at para 20.

4.109   There is something of a fine line between an inference to be drawn from a fact that is found as a result of evidence before the tribunal and a bare finding-in-fact that cannot be justified as inferential.[208] However, if in doubt, the tribunal should err on the side of caution and canvass views on the proposed finding, if necessary by briefly reconvening the hearing if the issue becomes apparent during deliberations.

4.110   A tribunal would have to have very good reason for curtailing the submissions of a party at the end of the case. This happened in the case of *Katrinak* v *Secretary of State for the Home Department*,[209] where the Immigration Appeal Tribunal prevented a representative from continuing with submissions since it did not feel that it needed to hear from him further, and that it was not persuaded on the particular issue on which the submissions were based. Schiemann LJ in the Court of Appeal was unimpressed:

> "While not wishing to circumscribe the way in which the tribunal organises its own hearings, I have to say that if it stops an appellant's advocate from developing his client's case it needs to be very sure of its ground."[210]

4.111   The decision of the IAT in this case was quashed, partly on the basis of this curtailment of submissions. It should be pointed out that the representative in this case was not legally qualified. This is not to say that stopping submissions will never be justified. Schiemann LJ refers later in his judgment to the situation where a representative abuses his position.[211] In such a case, stopping submissions might be in order. In terms of the mental health tribunal rules, the tribunal is under an obligation to behave as expeditiously and efficiently as possible (while acting fairly).[212] This duty could be used to justify curtailing submissions where the points being made are repetitive or irrelevant to the issues, whether those submissions are being made by parties without representation or by lay or legally qualified representatives. However, such a course of action could only be justified in extreme cases.

4.112   On the question of interruptions by the tribunal during the course of submissions in order to clarify or raise points, this is perfectly permissible:

> "it is quite wrong to suppose that there is an obligation on an Adjudicator merely to keep silent during submissions, noting them down regardless of whether they are words of wisdom or irrelevancies, failing to deal with

---

[208] On inferences from facts generally, see paras 5.123 *et seq.*
[209] [2001] EWCA Civ 832.
[210] *Ibid*, para 13.
[211] *Ibid*, para 25.
[212] Rule 4.

the points which trouble the Adjudicator. An Adjudicator is entitled also to intervene to ensure that an advocate responds, if he is not otherwise doing so, to points which his opponent has made. There is no reason for the number of questions to be asked of one side to equal the number of questions asked of another. The degree of intervention will depend entirely upon the focus and relevance of the submissions made, their helpfulness and their succinctness".[213]

It is also perfectly valid to move submissions on where the point being made has been understood by the tribunal or in order to curtail or prevent irrelevant points being made.[214] Once again, as with all interruptions, caution should be exercised, and any protestations from the party being told to move on should be listened to and taken into account in considering what to do next.   **4.113**

Questioning by tribunal members during evidence

Asking questions is one of the main roles of mental health tribunal members. However, caution must be exercised when questions are put, since there is a body of relatively well developed case law from immigration and employment tribunals which warns of the pitfalls in taking the wrong approach during such interventions. It has been said that: "Questions can be unfair, both by what they ask and by the way, including tone, length and overall manner, in which they are asked."[215]   **4.114**

It is clear from the mental health tribunal rules that the Convener, or another tribunal member with the permission of the Convener, may put questions to any relevant person or witness.[216] The relevant provision makes it clear that such questions must be put for the purposes of assisting the resolution of any disputed fact.[217] The wording of the provision suggests that before putting any such questions, or permitting another member to do so, the Convener should first consider "the circumstances of the relevant persons and whether (and to what extent) they are represented".[218] Dealing with the circumstances of the relevant person, this suggests that where the relevant person is unrepresented, but able to conduct the presentation of his case perfectly well, the tribunal should be careful not to overstep its role in seeking to clarify any issues which the relevant person might   **4.115**

---

[213] *K* v *Secretary of State for the Home Department (Côte d'Ivoire)* [2004] UKIAT 00061 at para 45, a decision of the Immigration Appeal Tribunal.
[214] *Ibid.*
[215] *SW* v *Secretary of State for the Home Department (Adjudicator's questions) Somalia* [2005] UKIAT 00037 at para 30.
[216] Rule 63(5).
[217] *Ibid.*
[218] *Ibid*, first sentence.

be capable of clarifying himself. The reference to representation is similarly meant to temper any tendency of the tribunal to intervene too much, where the relevant person is perfectly well represented, usually by a lawyer. However, this is not to say that the Convener or any other member is not permitted to ask any questions of a relevant person or his witness where that relevant person is represented, always assuming that the person in question has made himself available to give evidence[219] or appears by compulsion[220] to do so. Such questions may fall within the remit of r 63(5)(a) where they seek to clarify an issue that has not been fully or clearly discussed in evidence so far, or has been missed in the evidence. The role of the tribunal member here might be best described as one where he would ask questions, make enquiries and test the evidence. This role takes on a particular significance where the patient is unrepresented.

4.116   Rule 63(5)(a) suggests a heavier role for the tribunal in asking questions where the patient is not represented, and suggests an investigatory role. This means that the tribunal members are free to raise matters that have not been raised before and to seek answers to questions even although there is no obvious live issue arising from the written or oral evidence. In the context of employment and immigration tribunals, there are some strong judicial statements to the effect that the tribunal should not adopt the role of seeking out new evidence or points in favour of a party, whether represented or not.[221] In fact, the point has been made by the Court of Appeal in the context of medical evidence.[222] It is probably the case that there is more scope for seeking out new evidence from witnesses in a mental health tribunal than an employment tribunal, so these authorities may not be *directly* applicable. However, they are a useful reminder that the tribunal must be careful not to become a fact finder or to effectively act as if it is a representative of one of the parties, even where there is none available. To put it another way, there is a distinction between

---

[219] The situation where the patient refuses to give evidence is discussed at para 4.64. The same comments would apply to any party or relevant person.

[220] See the discussion on the powers of compulsion the tribunal has at para 3.80.

[221] *Rugamer v Sony Music Entertainment UK Ltd; McNicol v Balfour Beatty Rail Maintenance Ltd* [2001] IRLR 644 per Commissioner Howell at para 47 (employment case) upheld and approved by the Court of Appeal in *McNicol v Balfour Beatty Rail Maintenance Ltd* [2002] EWCA Civ 1074; [2002] IRLR 711 at para 26 (the *Rugamer* and *McNicol* cases were heard before the EAT as conjoined, but only *McNicol* pursued his appeal to judgment in the Court of Appeal) and *Koca v Secretary of State for the Home Department* 2005 1 SC 487, discussed above at paras 4.106 and 4.107.

[222] See the Court of Appeal employment case of *McNicol v Balfour Beatty Rail Maintenance Ltd* [2002] EWCA Civ 1074; [2002] IRLR 711 per Mummery LJ at para 26. See generally P Elias and B Napier (eds), *Harvey on Employment Law and Industrial Relations*, para T–826.02.

pursuing an issue not put squarely before the tribunal, but which arises from the material available to it (which is generally permitted) and adopting a proactive role[223] in encouraging and seeking out arguments or evidence along a particular line (which might constitute apparent bias).[224] One of the clearest judicial statements in this area comes from Commissioner Howell in the Employment Appeal Tribunal:

> "the tribunal is obliged, as indeed is expressly recorded in rule 9 of the tribunal Procedure Rules, [and as required in terms of rule 4 of the mental health tribunal rules as part of the overriding objective] to conduct the hearing in a fair and balanced manner, intervening and making its own enquiries in the course of the hearing of such persons appearing before it and such witnesses as are called before it as it considers appropriate, so as to ensure due consideration of the issues raised by, or necessarily implicit in, the complaint being made. However, the role of the tribunal is not thereby extended so as to place on it the duty to conduct a free-standing inquiry of its own, or require it to attempt to obtain further evidence beyond that placed in front of it on the issues raised by the parties, or to cause the parties to raise additional issues they have not sought to rely on at all".[225]

Having said this, the tribunal is perfectly *entitled*,[226] even in cases where all parties are represented, to put questions to witnesses in order to cover matters relevant to the case but not covered (or adequately covered) by the examination of witnesses by those representatives.[227]

4.117

---

[223] Indeed, Mummery LJ in the employment case *McNicol v Balfour Beatty Rail Maintenance Ltd* [2002] EWCA Civ 1074; [2002] IRLR 711 specifically finds the word "proactive" as unhelpful in describing the role of an employment tribunal – see para 26 of the Court of Appeal decision.

[224] For a discussion of apparent bias, see paras 4.13 *et seq*.

[225] *Rugamer v Sony Music Entertainment UK Ltd*; *McNicol v Balfour Beatty Rail Maintenance Ltd* [2001] IRLR 644 per Commissioner Howell at para 47, upheld and approved by the Court of Appeal in *McNicol v Balfour Beatty Rail Maintenance Ltd* [2002] EWCA Civ 1074; [2002] IRLR 711 at para 26 (the *Rugamer* and *McNicol* cases were heard before the EAT as conjoined, but only *McNicol* pursued his appeal to judgment in the Court of Appeal). See also the comments of the Immigration Appeal Tribunal in *H v Secretary of State for the Home Department (Iraq)* [2003] UKIAT 00048 where a fresh hearing was ordered since the timing content and nature of some of the questions asked by the adjudicator could have led to a perception of bias. The tribunal there spoke of the need for the adjudicator to refrain from "entering the arena" – para 3. See further *MNM v Secretary of State for the Home Department (Kenya)* [2000] INLR 576; [2000] UKIAT 00005 at para 19.

[226] The passage cited above at para 4.116, n 225 above deals with whether the tribunal is *obliged* to follow this course.

[227] See the comments to this effect by the Immigration Appeal Tribunal in *K v Secretary of State for the Home Department (Côte d'Ivoire)* [2004] UKIAT 00061 at para 42.

Where a tribunal member has asked questions and an issue is taken with the appropriateness of such interventions, either at the hearing or later, there are a number of provisions in the rules that could be referred to as relevant:

- obligation to conduct hearing as informally as possible under r 63(2)(a);
- obligation to conduct hearing in a just way under r 63(2)(b)(i);
- obligation to conduct a hearing in a the way most suitable to clarification and determination of the matters before the tribunal under r 63(2)(b)(ii): in particular could be used to justify questions where the issue has not be raised by the parties or fully discussed;
- power to give directions under r 49(1)(g) on evidential issues, nature of evidence, method of leading evidence and the exclusion of evidence;[228]
- general power to regulate its own procedure under r 52(1);
- the overriding principle in r 4.

4.118   The timing of any interruption can be important. Usually, any questions coming from tribunal members should be put after the witness has been examined, cross-examined and re-examined in full.[229] The reason is that where there is representation, it is usually just to allow that representation to take its full course. It may well be that the questions the tribunal member is keen to ask will be asked by the representative for the patient, for instance, during the questioning process. Since relevant persons are entitled to be represented, it is incumbent on the tribunal members to allow the representative full latitude (as long as that latitude is not being abused – see above on interventions) to examine witnesses as he deems appropriate.

4.119   It might be appropriate for an occasional question to come from a tribunal member during the examination of a witness by a representative, but such questions should only be for the purpose of clarification of an issue the witness has just given evidence on and before the witness moves on and where such clarification is necessary to allow the tribunal member to understand the evidence, or alternatively where a tribunal member has been unable to hear part of the answer of a witness. Anything further might risk the interruption of the flow of the questioning, and therefore the impact of the evidence on the tribunal. However, an argument that a tribunal member is not

---

[228] On directions generally, see paras 7.30 et seq.
[229] The exception to this is, of course, where the tribunal is itself conducting the examination-in-chief or cross-examination of a witness.

permitted to ask a question during, or at the end of, examination of a witness by a representative, on the basis that the representative has control over his own witness, will not be successful.[230] Having said this, if a representative makes it clear to the intervening tribunal member that he intends to cover the area which is the subject-matter of the intervention, the tribunal member should at that point desist from his line of enquiry, although he may return to it at the end of the examination if he feels that it has not been properly investigated.[231] In cases where a party is unrepresented (whether the patient or an MHO or RMO) there is a stronger argument for any intervention to come during the questioning of a witness rather than at the end of the evidence of the witness. The reason for this is that where a party is not represented, the evidence of his witnesses is likely to be delivered as a monologue unless the tribunal interrupts that evidence with appropriate questions to guide the flow of it. This approach in such cases was suggested as proper in the context of immigration proceedings.[232]

Once a tribunal member makes an interruption to evidence to ask   **4.120**
a question, it may be that the answer will lead to further questions, and in such cases, as long as the tribunal member does not stray into other areas not connected with the original question, prolonged follow up questions may be posed, and will not, in such circumstances, necessarily be regarded as excessive.[233]

Although there is a requirement that any proposed questions from   **4.121**
medical or general members are permitted by the legal member, in practice Conveners will usually not insist on each individual question being vetted through him. Most Conveners will discuss their preferred approach to questions with the other members during the pre-hearing meeting. This will usually lead to an agreement that certain members will ask questions on certain issues, and the area of expertise of the medical and general member will naturally influence this discussion.[234] It is clear that one of the main benefits

---

[230] *SW* v *Secretary of State for the Home Department (Adjudicator's questions) Somalia* [2005] UKIAT 00037 at para 27.
[231] *Ibid.*
[232] See the decision of the Immigration Appeal Tribunal in *SW* v *Secretary of State for the Home Department (Adjudicator's questions) Somalia* [2005] UKIAT 00037 at para 22.
[233] In *SW* v *Secretary of State for the Home Department (Adjudicator's questions) Somalia* [2005] UKIAT 00037 the questioning session being examined by the Immigration Appeal Tribunal lasted 15 minutes, but it was held this was not excessive in the circumstances: see para 32 of the judgment (although it should be pointed out that part of the issue in that case was that questions were being routed via an interpreter, which added to the length of the interruption).
[234] On the use by a medical or general member of expertise during the hearing, see paras 5.22 *et seq.*

of the presence of the expertise of the medical and general members on the tribunal is to allow appropriate questions to be put on issues informed by that expertise.[235]

4.122   Another important issue arises here: how far may a tribunal member go in asking questions? Some general guidance can be sought from a line of immigration tribunal cases:

> "Questions should not be asked in a hostile tone. They should not be leading questions which suggest the answer which is desired, nor should they disguise what is the point of concern so as to appear like a trap or a closing of the net. They should be open ended questions, neutrally phrased. They can be persisted in, in order to obtain an answer; but they should not be persisted in for longer than is necessary for the [tribunal member] to be clear that the question was understood, or to establish why it was not being answered, or to pursue so far as necessary the detail underlying vague answers. This will be a matter for the judgment of [tribunal members] and it should not usually take more than a few questions for [a tribunal member] to establish the position to his own satisfaction ... The [tribunal member] can properly put, without it becoming a cross-examination, questions which trouble him or inferences from answers given which he might wish to draw adversely to a party. These questions should not be disproportionate in length to the evidence given as to the complexity of the case and, we repeat, a [tribunal member] should be careful to avoid developing his own theory of the case."[236]

4.123   The difference between the role of a cross-examiner in putting a question and that of a tribunal member should be obvious from the above guidance, which applies equally to mental health tribunals. The role of the cross-examiner may well involve disguising the point of concern, and will certainly involve asking leading (if not hostile) questions. Tribunal members are required to tread much more carefully and, to use a key word here, neutrally.[237] Although the

---

[235] The expertise a Convener can bring consists of the management of the hearing in a fair manner, expertise on any legal points, and expertise in the task of ensuring that any written decision of the tribunal is less likely to face any legal challenge.

[236] WN v Secretary of State for the Home Department [2004] UKIAT 00213, para 38. These comments were endorsed in SW v Secretary of State for the Home Department (Adjudicator's questions) Somalia [2005] UKIAT 00037 at para 28. See also the case of XS (Kosovo – Adjudicator's conduct – psychiatric report) Serbia and Montenegro [2005] UKIAT 00093 at para 32 where the Immigration Appeal Tribunal refers to the need to avoid "an appearance of a dual cross-examination" in other words by both a party and the tribunal. The IAT also criticised the adjudicator in that case for adopting a "hostile theory" which was distinct from the position adopted by the Secretary of State in the case (paras 35–37).

[237] See XS (Kosovo – Adjudicator's conduct – psychiatric report) Serbia and Montenegro [2005] UKIAT 00093 where the Immigration Appeal Tribunal criticised repeated questioning by the adjudicator where the questions were asked in a "disbelieving manner" – para 34.

guidelines above should be followed wherever possible, ultimately the question of whether intervention by a tribunal member has gone too far will be judged against the *Porter* v *Magill* test of apparent bias,[238] or, where no apparent bias is alleged, the test will be whether the tribunal has acted in accordance with the overriding objective.[239] In the context of immigration tribunal proceedings, it has been said that the power to intervene during a hearing should be exercised "sparingly".[240] Collins J in the immigration case of *Muwyngyi* put it in this way:

> "[the tribunal member] must be careful not to enter the arena save as is absolutely necessary to enable him to ascertain the truth and must never adopt or appear to adopt a hostile attitude to any [witness]".[241]

These comments would apply equally in the mental health tribunal context. In addition, tribunal members must be careful when asking questions that the questions are put in an appropriate manner. At the extreme end of the scale, questions should not be put in an aggressive or bullying manner, and should not be hostile.[242] This may seem obvious, but tribunal members should be very careful to treat all witnesses with respect when asking questions, even when that witness has not necessarily afforded the tribunal the same courtesy. Where questioning is deemed to be too aggressive or bullying in its nature, this could lead to a finding, on appeal, of apparent bias[243] but only where the test of whether a reasonable observer, present at the time and not connected with the parties, would reasonably have gained such an impression.[244]   **4.124**

As a matter of good practice, as indicated above, leading questions should be avoided. While representatives are entitled to ask such questions during cross-examination, there is a danger that a leading   **4.125**

---

[238] On this test, see above at paras 4.13 *et seq*. This was made clear in the Immigration Appeal Tribunal case of *T* v *Secretary of State for the Home Department (Algeria)* [2003] UKIAT 00128, paras 7–10.

[239] On the overriding objective generally, see para 1.26.

[240] I A MacDonald and F Webber (eds), *Immigration Law and Practice in the United Kingdom* (7th edn, 2008), para 18.144.

[241] These comments were endorsed by Mr Justice Moses in the High Court case of *R* v *Special Adjudicator, ex p Demeter* [2000] IAR 424 at para 22.

[242] For a case where the Immigration Appeal Tribunal took the view that the questioning of an adjudicator was hostile in tone, see *XS (Kosovo – Adjudicator's conduct – psychiatric report) Serbia and Montenegro* [2005] UKIAT 00093 at para 34.

[243] On bias generally, see paras 4.13 *et seq*. For a case where such a finding was overturned on appeal by the Inner House of the Court of Session in an employment tribunal case, see *Docherty* v *Strathkelvin DC* 1994 SLT 395.

[244] *Ibid*, p 399.

question coming from a tribunal member, even as a direct supplement to the cross-examination of a witness, will have a disproportionate effect. The reason is that a witness might be more tempted to agree with the proposition contained in such a question, out of deference to the authority of the tribunal member as decision-maker, than he might in the case of a similar question from a representative of a party.

4.126   Although the general and medical members of the tribunal are appointed in order to allow them to bring particular expertise to the decision-making process, this does not mean that any questions asked by such members must be confined to these areas of expertise. Once a panel member is appointed, he holds full judicial office, and can ask any relevant question. The same applies to a Convener: he is not restricted to questions that relate to the legal criteria relevant to the case, but can ask about matters such as medication and treatment for the patient. This point is made in the employment tribunal case of *Docherty* v *Strathkelvin District Council*[245] where it was suggested that the lay members on an employment tribunal (one representing employers and the other employees)[246] could ask questions only on issues relating to their own expertise. The Inner House responded:

> "we profoundly disagree ... Whatever interest has led to a lay member being [appointed], once he has been appointed to sit as a member of a tribunal he sits in a judicial capacity, and accordingly is quite entitled to address questions where necessary to witnesses on either side".[247]

Of course, medical and general members of the mental health tribunal are not lay members, but this reasoning is applicable to any tribunal members with subject specialist expertise.

4.127   Finally, it is crucial that, following any evidence given in reply to a question(s) from the tribunal, all parties (or their representatives) are given an opportunity to ask any questions that arise out of that evidence.[248] This applies whether the tribunal questions have come during or after the end of the normal examination process for that witness. Tribunal members should be particularly careful when asking questions of witnesses where the examination of that witness has been completed at an earlier stage in the hearing, and

[245] 1994 SLT 395.
[246] On membership of employment tribunals, see para 5.31.
[247] 1994 SLT 395 at 399.
[248] This rule applies in the public courts as well as in other tribunals: see the Immigration Appeal Tribunal case of *Secretary of State for the Home Department* v *Yogalingam* (01TH02671) (4 January 2002). For employment tribunal cases, see the Court of Appeal case of *Hereford and Worcester County Council* v *Neale* [1986] IRLR 168, on the general duty of employment tribunals to make sure that all parties have a full opportunity to comment on all pertinent issues.

where the tribunal has remembered an unasked question, or where something comes out in later evidence that the tribunal member wishes to put to that witness. The obligation to give an opportunity to the other parties to ask questions on the subject raised persists even here.

Exclusion of an individual during the hearing

The tribunal has certain limited but important rights to exclude an individual from a hearing. However, the title of the rule suggests that such powers should be exercised only in "exceptional circumstances".[249] Having said this, there is no mention in the body of the rule of "exceptional circumstances" as being any part of the test in such cases. Despite this omission, the use of the word "exceptional" in the title of the rule suggests that the power to exclude should be used sparingly.   **4.128**

The test that is to be applied is whether the attendance of any person at the hearing or part of it may cause serious harm to the patient or any other person.[250] Where this is deemed to be the case, the Convener or the tribunal may direct that such a person shall be excluded from the hearing or part of it.[251] The reference in the rule to the Convener or tribunal suggests that the decision can be made by the tribunal at the hearing (in which case it would be raised as a preliminary matter) or by a Convener sitting alone in advance of the hearing date.[252] In either case, usually consideration of the use of this power would follow a request to exclude an individual. However, there is nothing in the rule to suggest that the tribunal cannot act of its own volition in raising the matter.[253] The rule suggests that before deciding whether to issue such a direction, all relevant persons should be invited to make written representations.[254] This provision suggests that usually the tribunal should not make the decision to exclude at a hearing, but should adjourn first (or part-hear evidence) in order to allow written representations to be made. Since this obligation is on the tribunal, its non-adherence cannot be excused under the dispensing power.[255] Of course, where an advance request is made, this will perhaps allow time for written representations in advance   **4.129**

---

[249] Rule 68.
[250] Rule 68(1).
[251] *Ibid.*
[252] On decisions being made by an in-house Convener in advance of a hearing generally, see para 2.11.
[253] In such cases, the tribunal must canvass with the parties this possibility in advance in order to comply with r 52(3)–(4), which is discussed further at para 3.14.
[254] Rule 68(4).
[255] See paras 7.49 *et seq* on the dispensing power.

of a hearing so an advance request for a direction should always be made where possible. The other benefit of the advance request is that if it is granted and intimated prior to the hearing, this will avoid the delicate situation of having to handle the request at a hearing where the party who might be excluded is present.

4.130   Any written representations may be "both as to the necessity of the direction and as to the availability of alternative measures".[256] So, these are the two general grounds of argument against the direction being made. On the question of necessity, there may be a discussion about whether the attendance of the person will cause serious harm to the patient or any other person. Although not stated, it would seem sensible that the party seeking the exclusion direction (or the tribunal) would have to establish/be satisfied that such harm is likely (not just possible) and not necessarily inevitable. This is supported by the reference in r 68(7) to "the harm apprehended". It seems clear that the tribunal/Convener will have to receive evidence on this point. That evidence may take the form of the content of the CTO application or the equivalent, or the content of the mental health reports or some other skilled witness report. It may be based on the events at an earlier hearing, where there is evidence of actual harm having occurred in similar circumstances, although clearly such earlier harm is not necessary to satisfy the likelihood test.

4.131   Where a relevant person seeks to be heard on the application to exclude, he should make his intention known in writing within the period for written representations and the tribunal or Convener may fix an oral hearing.[257] It is submitted that where such a request is made, it would be difficult to envisage a situation in which it should be refused, while complying with the overriding objective to be fair.[258] Even where such a request is not made, the Convener/tribunal should always closely consider an oral hearing on the issue, unless the evidence in favour of exclusion is very strong.

4.132   The question of what constitutes "serious harm" is one of fact and degree, but it would appear that it is not an easy test to satisfy. This conclusion follows not only from the plain meaning of the phrase, but also from the use of the word "exceptional" in the title of the rule, as well as the obvious dangers to the overriding principle of fairness that follow a direction to cut a relevant person out of proceedings, possibly completely denying that person an opportunity

---

[256] Rule 68(4).
[257] Rule 68(5). This provision refers to the tribunal affording an opportunity to be heard, but the rule must apply also to the Convener having this power.
[258] Rule 4. On this objective generally, see para 1.26.

to put his views.[259] Against this background, it would seem that a wish by the applicant (however strongly expressed), that the person should be excluded on any moral ground, should be resisted. It is suggested that some form of serious physical or psychological harm must be likely to arise from the person's attendance. This could be distress, for example on the part of the patient, but the Convener or tribunal would have to be careful to have medical evidence before it suggesting something much more than discomfort or mild upset. The tribunal has the power to appoint a person having appropriate skills or experience to assess whether attendance might cause serious harm, and report on that, and to remunerate that expert's work in doing so.[260] This further suggests the test is a high one, since the question is not one that can necessarily be resolved without hearing skilled evidence.

It may be the case that the patient is the person who, it is claimed, might suffer serious harm as a result of someone else's presence. An example might be where there are allegations of abuse of the patient being made by someone present against another person who intends to be present. It could be argued that the patient's own attendance could cause serious harm to him, perhaps due to his likely exposure to distressing details about his history or family or personal details. Alternatively, the distress that a formal hearing in itself may cause could, irrespective of the evidence likely to be heard, be likely to lead to serious harm. However, where the serious harm argument is made in relation to the patient, the tribunal should tread very carefully in considering whether to make the exclusion direction, and the possibility of "alternative measures" should loom large (see below on this). In fact, the rule recognises that the patient in this situation deserves additional protection, since it obliges the tribunal to invite an unrepresented patient in this position to seek an adjournment of the case in order to obtain legal representation and, where that invitation is accepted, the motion to adjourn must be granted.[261] This is designed to allow the patient to be represented before consideration is even given to whether he is excluded. In a further attempt to protect the patient, the rule reminds the tribunal that in cases where an unrepresented patient is excluded, a curator *ad litem* may be appointed;[262] this part of the rule does not add to or

4.133

---

[259] This would be in contravention of the basic rules of fairness, as discussed in this context at paras 4.06 *et seq* above. Such a result is not, however, inevitable since written views can always be expressed or the excluded person's views can be expressed by someone else in attendance at the hearing.

[260] Rule 68(2).

[261] Rule 68(6).

[262] Rule 68(8).

expand the power to appoint one under r 55 (which expressly refers to this situation), but simply acts as a prompt.[263] However, given the importance of ensuring that a patient participates as fully as possible in the proceedings,[264] it is barely conceivable that a tribunal could grant anything other than an interim order in the absence of the patient or a representative, since at least a curator could be appointed, given the specific and unfettered power to do so in just these circumstances under r 55(2)(c).

4.134   It is clear that the rule only covers the situation where the mere presence of the person would be likely to lead to serious harm. Where the tribunal is looking at likely behaviour detrimentally affecting a hearing, r 69 should be used.[265] Again, this demonstrates the narrow application of r 68.

4.135   Even where the tribunal is satisfied that serious harm would be likely to follow from the mere presence of the individual, the reference to the "availability of alternative measures"[266] is a clear indication than an application for an exclusion direction could be opposed on the basis that there is some way, short of exclusion, in which the evidence and/or representations of that person can be taken. Of course, the rule only allows a direction to prevent the "attendance" of the person,[267] which must refer to the physical attendance of that person at the hearing on the case (or part of it). Alternatives might include taking the evidence or representations of that person separately from the main hearing (after or before it, either on the same day or a different day, and alone or in the presence of everyone other than the person who might be caused serious harm, or a selection of individuals) or allowing that person to submit written evidence. The express power to exclude a person during part of the hearing until that person is due to give evidence[268] could also be used as an alternative measure, and might lead to any serious harm being avoided by keeping witnesses apart. In these cases, the direction should be refused, and instead a separate direction could be issued under, for example, r 49(1)(g)(iii) on the way in which evidence is to be led. Indeed, given the width of that provision (and of the others in r 49) as well as of the general power to regulate procedure as it sees fit,[269] it is difficult to imagine a situation where no alternative measures would be available which

---

[263] On the appointment of a curator *ad litem* generally, see paras 2.54 *et seq.*
[264] This is one of the general principles in s 1 of the 2003 Act: s 1(3)(c).
[265] See the discussion on this rule at paras 4.139 *et seq* below.
[266] Rule 68(4).
[267] Rule 68(1).
[268] Rule 63(7).
[269] Rule 52(1).

would avoid the risk of serious harm while preserving the right of all relevant persons to present their case fully and fairly. Any alternative measures should be applied carefully by the tribunal so that, for example, evidence given at a separate mini-hearing or tendered in writing is available for comment and, if desired, rebuttal, all in circumstances where the risk of serious harm is avoided or minimised; to put it another way, r 68 does not absolve the tribunal/Convener of the obligation to conduct proceedings fairly, in accordance with the overriding objective.[270]

Assuming that the tribunal is satisfied that a direction under the rule is necessary, the direction should be strictly limited in its scope and application so as to prevent only the harm apprehended by attendance.[271] This indicates that the tribunal should consider whether a blanket exclusion is necessary or whether exclusion from part of the proceedings may suffice. However, it will always be easier to justify some alternative measure to take the evidence of that person, leading to a direction under r 49 (see above) rather than a limited r 68 direction.   **4.136**

Although it hardly needs to be expressed, the rule makes it clear that any expert report, as well as any representations made, require to be taken into account before any direction to exclude is made.[272]   **4.137**

Finally, where the serious harm might arise from the disclosure of a document, the appropriate course is to consider withholding that document or report under r 47,[273] rather than excluding the person who may be caused serious harm from exposure to it.   **4.138**

Exclusion of persons disrupting a hearing

Given the nature of some of the issues that may require to be aired at a tribunal hearing, it is not unusual for the tribunal to have to deal with disruption. In addition, the relative informality of proceedings when compared with those in the sheriff court can lead to disruptive behaviour breaking out more readily. The danger of disruption may stem from, for example, difficult relations between a patient and an RMO and/or MHO, or between a named person and the patient. It is not unusual, for instance, to find the patient interrupting the evidence of the RMO, when he hears evidence or representations he disputes or that he perceives as unfair. Indeed, the disinhibition that accompanies some mental illnesses can lead to a patient being more vocal and interventionist than would   **4.139**

---

[270] Rule 4 and see comments on it generally at para 1.26.
[271] Rule 68(7).
[272] *Ibid*.
[273] See this rule discussed at paras 3.184 *et seq*.

otherwise be the case. Such situations will usually be able to be dealt with by firm but sympathetic intervention by the Convener, either to stop the interruption from continuing, or by allowing it to run its course, in the hope of defusing any anger or upset, in either case preventing the interruption from deteriorating into a serious disruption. Any representative of the patient may also have a role to play in defusing the situation. In appropriate cases, the Convener may direct that evidence of a certain kind or relating to a certain situation should not continue, where it is causing distress or upset to the patient or another person, and where the evidence is not strictly necessary for the determination of the case.[274] In other instances, the tribunal could be adjourned briefly to let the participants have a break, in the hope that any disruption may subside. Sometimes, the patient or another person will feel unable to take a full part in the proceedings, and may prefer to leave. Where this happens with a represented relevant person, it may be that the representative can continue on his client's behalf, but in that person's absence. In rare cases, the behaviour of a professional, for example a lawyer or advocacy worker[275] or an RMO or MHO, might be regarded as disruptive but, in such instances, the Convener will almost always be able to restore order, perhaps with the help of a short break in proceedings.

4.140   These are just some of the situations that may arise in cases of disruptive behaviour. However, where the situation cannot be handled in one of the ways mentioned above, and depending on the extent of the disruption, the tribunal can force the exclusion of an individual from the hearing. As with a r 68 direction, such a move should be exceptional since, if someone is at a hearing, and is participating in it, it will be because they are entitled to be there, as a witness, relevant person or additional party; the exclusion of any such person would be difficult to justify in the face of the obligation to act fairly.[276] In addition, while a request to exclude might come from one of the parties, there is nothing in the rule to suggest that the tribunal cannot, of its own volition, raise the issue of possible exclusion.[277]

4.141   There are four situations in which a tribunal might exclude a person under this rule from the whole or part of the hearing:

---

[274] Such a direction could be issued under r 49(1)(g)(iii).
[275] The rule specifically refers to the possibility of exclusion of a representative – r 69(1)(a).
[276] This obligation is present in the overriding objective in r 4 – see this rule commented on generally at para 1.26.
[277] Subject always to the obligation to draw to attention of the parties: r 52(3) and (4).

(1) where that person's conduct has already disrupted the hearing;[278]

(2) where that person's conduct is likely to disrupt the hearing;[279]

(3) where a person's presence at the hearing is likely to make it difficult for any relevant person to present evidence or representations properly;[280] or

(4) where a person has, in some other way, interfered with the administration of justice or is likely to do so.[281]

These powers allow the tribunal to exclude anyone at the hearing, including a relevant person, witness, additional party, patient escort or member of the public. Situation (1) requires there to have been some evidence of disruptive behaviour, which might include excessive interruption of the evidence, shouting, swearing, aggressive behaviour, threatening behaviour, violence or attempted violence, inappropriate questioning of witnesses or a refusal to follow directions issued by the tribunal (for instance by insisting on a line of questioning ruled inadmissible by the tribunal). With the possible exception of threatening behaviour, violence or attempted violence, in all but the most exceptional cases, the tribunal should exclude the person only where at least one warning is given and is not heeded. In some cases, depending on the nature and extent of the disruption, more than one warning may be appropriate. Any other course of action would expose the tribunal to a possible appeal on the ground of procedural impropriety either from a relevant person or from an additional party excluded or from the relevant person or additional party detrimentally affected by the exclusion of a witness or representative. Situation (2) will be more unusual, and there would have to be some information or evidence before the tribunal which would suggest that such behaviour is likely to take place at the hearing. This could be evidence of disruptive behaviour shortly before the start of the hearing, or even at a previous hearing, although the tribunal should be careful not to assume that previous behaviour will necessarily be repeated.

4.142

Situation (3) is different from (1) and (2). Here, the tribunal is considering the possible impact of the mere presence of an individual. That person may not have been disruptive at the hearing; neither might there be any likelihood of disruptive behaviour. Instead, the presence of the person would have some negative impact on a relevant

4.143

---

[278] Rule 69(1)(a).
[279] *Ibid.*
[280] Rule 69(1)(b).
[281] Rule 69(1)(c).

person. This does not mean that a relevant person can simply ask that someone should be excluded since he would prefer that that person is not there; there must be some likelihood of difficulty in presentation of the case of a relevant person caused by the mere presence of that individual. A few points are worth making here. First of all, there must be some likelihood of a difficulty arising, not merely a possibility. Such likelihood might be inferred from the particular circumstances of the situation, or from difficulties facing a relevant person at an earlier hearing. It might be argued that a relevant person would be unable to give evidence in the presence of another relevant person or witness, due to a fear of an angry or aggressive response. It might be said that a witness or relevant person would be unable to mention a relevant incident or point in the presence of another because of fear or embarrassment.

4.144   Finally, situation (4) allows the tribunal to consider in a wider sense the behaviour of a person who might appear at the hearing. The reference to the "administration of justice" would appear to be a reference to interfering in earlier proceedings in the case or interfering in some way with the potential evidence. The word "interference" suggests some underhand or inappropriate behaviour by the person concerned. For instance, it might cover evidence of intimidation attempts by the person concerned towards other witnesses or relevant persons, although, even in such a case, the behaviour would have to justify exclusion, and not just be morally reprehensible or even illegal. This provision will be very rarely, if ever, invoked, and situations (1)–(3) will be far more common (although not, in any ordinary sense, common).

4.145   Where the person to be excluded (on whatever ground) is not a relevant person or his representative (so usually a witness) the test to be applied by the tribunal is not particularly illuminating: the tribunal must have regard to the interests of all relevant persons.[282] However, the overriding objective will apply, so the tribunal will have to act fairly.[283] In the absence of representation for the person who might be excluded, the tribunal may consider some measures to allow the excluded person to be made aware of the content of the evidence led in his absence. This could be done by the tribunal simply reading it back to that person, in the absence of the objector but in the presence of everyone else, including all representatives. There is a danger in simply allowing the excluded person back into the hearing, and ultimately making a decision partly on the basis of the evidence led in the absence of the excluded person, without first considering whether

[282] Rule 69(2)(a).
[283] Rule 4. See para 1.26 on the overriding objective generally.

it is at all feasible to inform the excluded person of the nature of the evidence led; in such a case, the tribunal's decision could be open to challenge on the ground of procedural impropriety. Although there is no obligation to do so where the person being considered for exclusion is not a relevant person, the tribunal should always seek the views of all other parties and from the representative of the person displaying disruptive behaviour, on the possible exclusion of that person, before making a decision. Of course, the immediate exclusion of the person may well be necessary in order for those representations to be taken. The tribunal should be careful to avoid a snap decision, and the Convener has no authority to make that decision without consulting the others on the tribunal.[284]

4.146

There are special provisions in place where the person who is under consideration for exclusion (on whatever ground) is a relevant person. First of all, in such cases, the tribunal not only the interests of all relevant persons, but also whether the relevant person excluded will be adequately represented.[285] Where that person has representation, the decision to exclude might be easier to justify. Where there is no representation for that party (particularly legal representation) the tribunal will have to consider carefully the possible consequences of exclusion; this does not mean that a relevant person who is not represented should never be excluded; only that the tribunal should specifically consider the full impact that such exclusion may have on that party's case. It may be that the answer lies in the duty of the tribunal to conduct questioning (and if necessary cross-examination) of witnesses in the absence of a party.[286] In addition, the tribunal cannot exclude a relevant person without first affording that person and all other relevant persons it thinks fit the opportunity to be heard on the issue.[287] A relevant person under consideration for exclusion must be given sufficient opportunity to consult his representative before a decision is made (this effectively means before representations on possible exclusion are taken).[288] Finally, the tribunal must consider the availability of alternative measures which may allow the relevant person to participate in proceedings.[289] So, it might be possible for the excluded person to give evidence alone after other parties and witnesses have been heard, or the tribunal might direct that the person can give evidence in writing. Such directions could be made under

---

[284] See para 3.48 on the joint role of decision-making in the tribunal.
[285] Rule 69(2)(b).
[286] However, the limited role the tribunal has in such a process should be noted: see comments on this at paras 4.115 *et seq.*
[287] Rule 69(3)(b).
[288] Rule 69(3)(a).
[289] Rule 69(3)(c).

r 49(1)(g)(iii). In such cases, the exclusion of the relevant person may still be justified, because the obligation is only to consider such alternatives. This could well lead to an order to exclude being coupled with an direction under r 49(1)(g)(iii). In fact, it is difficult to imagine a situation where a r 69 order is made with no other provision being offered or put in place to take the evidence of the relevant person, and where the decision of the tribunal would not be open to serious doubt on a procedural impropriety appeal.

4.147   In the case of exclusion of a representative of a relevant person, the tribunal is charged with considering whether the relevant person will be adequately represented upon such exclusion.[290] Given the inquisitorial nature of the tribunal proceedings[291] such lack of representation could be compensated for by the proper questioning of witnesses by the tribunal. Having said this, the role of the tribunal member as questioner is not the same as that of the representative and this may expose such an argument to criticism on appeal.[292] The tribunal may need carefully to consider adjourning the hearing in order to allow the relevant person to obtain alternative representation. Again, this course of action may well be necessary in the interests of fairness, and in the interests of the relevant person concerned.[293]

4.148   Where the relevant person being considered for exclusion is an unrepresented patient, even more protective measures apply. In such a case the tribunal may adjourn the hearing to allow the patient to be represented or to allow a curator *ad litem* to be appointed under r 55(1).[294] Given the importance of ensuring that a patient participates as fully as possible in the proceedings,[295] it is barely conceivable that a tribunal could grant anything other than an interim order in the absence of the patient or a representative, since at least a curator could be appointed, given the specific and unfettered power to do so in just these circumstances under r 55(1)(c).

4.149   In all cases (whether the potentially excluded person is a relevant person or not) the tribunal may make alternative arrangements deemed necessary to allow that person to continue participating in the proceedings; participation via video-link is specifically mentioned, although it is clear that all methods of communication are covered.[296] This could allow the giving of evidence or representations by that

---

[290] Rule 69(2)(b).
[291] On this, see paras 3.05 *et seq* and 4.01 *et seq.*
[292] On this, see paras 4.116 *et seq.*
[293] The latter is a compulsory consideration: r 69(2)(a).
[294] Rule 69(4). The rule later emphasises this possibility, rather unnecessarily, in r 69(6). On the curator *ad litem* generally, see paras 2.54 *et seq.*
[295] This is one of the general principles in s 1 of the 2003 Act: s 1(3)(c).
[296] Rule 69(5).

person separately from the rest of the hearing, whether after the end of the hearing or on a separate occasion, or perhaps by inviting written evidence or representations. While such alternative methods are not compulsory, unless they would lead to an unjustified delay in the proceedings, it seems that it would be difficult to justify an absence of some attempt to put in place an alternative. Clearly, where such an alternative is used, the tribunal should consider whether to and if so how to communicate the content of any evidence taken or representations made in the excluded person's absence, so that the further participation opportunity is meaningful and fair.

Hearings in private or in public

Rule 66(1) creates a presumption that tribunal hearings are to be held   **4.150**
in private. On the face of it, this is contrary to the usual presumption in favour of public hearings and open justice. Article 6(1) of the ECHR provides that individuals are entitled to a fair and public hearing in the determination of their civil rights and obligations. As noted elsewhere in this work, the question as to whether Art 6 is engaged in relation to tribunal proceedings is not entirely settled.[297] The factors which in litigation generally favour public hearings are the deterrence of inappropriate behaviour by the judicial body; the promotion of public confidence, as the public can see that justice is being administered properly and impartially; and the fact that evidence might become available which would not if the proceedings were conducted behind closed doors, and with the identities of parties or witnesses concealed.[298]

Even where Art 6 is engaged, however, Art 6(1) provides, further,   **4.151**
that the public may be excluded from all or part of a trial in the interest of morals, public order or national security in a democratic society, where the interests of juveniles or the protection of the private life of the parties so require, or to the extent strictly necessary in the opinion of the court in special circumstances where publicity would prejudice the interests of justice. In the context of mental health tribunal proceedings, where details of sensitive information

---

[297] See para 4.09. See also the discussion of this point in *Paterson v Kent* 2007 SLT (Sh Ct) 8; [2007] MHLR 20 at paras 43 and 53.

[298] See *R (Mersey Care NHS Trust) v Mental Health Review Tribunal* [2005] 1 WLR 2469 at para 13, and the authorities cited there. The discussion seems to assume that Art 6 applies, but the presumption at common law in favour of public hearings is in any event of long standing: see, eg *Scott v Scott* [1913] AC 417 at 437. Rule 38 of the Tribunal Procedure (First-tier Tribunal) (Health, Education and Social Care Chamber) Rules 2008 (SI 2008/2699) creates a similar presumption in favour of public hearings in England.

as to the psychiatric history and other aspects of the private lives of patients are under discussion, private hearings can be justified on the basis that the protection of the private life of a party necessitates the exclusion of the public from the hearing. At common law it was also the position that in proceedings concerning the interests of the mentally ill, privacy of proceedings could be justified, contrary to the usual presumption in favour of publicity.[299] A presumption in favour of private hearings even in an entire class of case does not necessarily offend against Art 6(1).[300]

4.152   As r 66 creates a presumption that hearings will be in private, the onus is on any party who wishes a public hearing to satisfy the tribunal that it should be public. The only person entitled to make an application to the tribunal for a public hearing is the patient himself.[301] On such an application, the tribunal may make an order that a hearing be held in public. The tribunal may refuse to make an order for a hearing to be held in public where any one of the following requirements is met:

- that a public hearing would fail to safeguard the welfare of the patient or any other person;
- that it would not, in all the circumstances, allow the fair hearing of the case; or
- that it would prejudice the interests of justice.[302]

4.153   The tribunal must refuse to make an order for a public hearing only to the extent necessary to protect the interest which is being protected by the refusal, and only in relation to those parts of a hearing in respect of which any of the requirements set out above is satisfied.[303] This introduces a requirement that the tribunal deals with the application in a proportionate manner. The nature and extent of the restriction on the public nature of the hearing must be no more than is necessary to ensure that the particular interests identified in r 66(4) are protected. The tribunal might require evidence in order to satisfy itself as to whether any of the requirements set out above were met in a particular case. Rule 66(5) envisages that a hearing

[299] See *Scott v Scott*, at passage referred to in n 298 above.

[300] See *B v United Kingdom and P v United Kingdom* (2002) 34 EHRR 19 at para 39, in which the majority rejected a contention that the presumption in favour of private hearings in the Children Act 1989 was contrary to Art 6(1). It was held that the applicable English law was a specific reflection of the general exceptions provided for by Art 6(1).

[301] Rule 66(2).

[302] Rule 66(3) and (4). These requirements themselves reflect some of the general exceptions provided for by Art 6(1).

[303] Rule 66(5).

may be in part public and in part private. A problem which might arise is that evidence being heard publicly in relation to very sensitive clinical matters would be liable to run counter to the welfare of the patient, particularly in high-profile cases. That might involve much of the hearing. It has been observed that a decision to hold a public hearing where it is contemplated that it may be necessary to protect the evidence as to the fundamental issue before the tribunal in such a context would need careful justification.[304] Practical difficulties could arise if a patient's own evidence could be led in chief, but any cross of him touching on his clinical condition would have to be made private.[305] A decision to make or refuse to make an order under r 66(2) is a decision of the tribunal, and as such requires to be recorded in writing, with adequate reasons.[306]

Where a hearing is in private, the President and any member of the Administrative Justice and Tribunals Council or its Scottish Committee will always be entitled to attend.[307] A member of the tribunal or a member of staff of the tribunal will be entitled to attend with the agreement of the Convener.[308] A provision of this sort is necessary to allow for training of new tribunal members, and for the presence of members involved in the appraisal process. An interpreter or other person giving other necessary assistance to a person entitled to attend the hearing will also always be entitled to attend a private hearing.[309]   **4.154**

The tribunal is empowered by r 66(7) to exclude from any hearing or part of a hearing any person, other than a representative of a patient or a relevant person, where it is considering a document which has been withheld from disclosure under r 47.[310] What seems to be envisaged is that a representative of a patient or relevant person will protect the interests of the patient or relevant person in relation to the report, where the patient or relevant person may be excluded from sight of the report or any hearing in which the non-disclosed   **4.155**

---

[304] R (Mersey Care NHS Trust) v Mental Health Review Tribunal [2005] 1 WLR 2469 per Beatson J at para 58. Beatson J also points to the potential situation of the evidence led in the public hearing giving a misleading impression of the case as a whole. A public hearing that would allow a patient to express complaints about a hospital with any evidence of mental illness being heard in private would also require careful consideration.

[305] Ibid per Beatson J at para 59.

[306] See paras 7.10 et seq for the duty to give reasons generally.

[307] Rule 66(6)(a) and (c).

[308] Rule 66(6)(b).

[309] Rule 66(6)(d).

[310] It is perhaps rather odd that this provision appears in r 66 and not in r 47, since the provision is not really aimed at the regulation of the public or private nature of a hearing; it is dealt with here in any event, and r 47 is examined elsewhere – see paras 3.184 et seq.

document is discussed. This is reflected in the provision of r 47(6) permitting the appointment of a curator *ad litem* where a document or any part of it is not disclosed, and the patient does not have a representative to protect his interests. The tribunal requires to inform the person excluded of its reasons for excluding him, and to record those reasons in writing. In practice the reason for exclusion is likely to be related to the need to prevent the person in question from becoming aware of the content of the non-disclosed document. It is suggested that in the interests of consistency, the criteria for excluding a person from a hearing where he may become aware of the content of the document must reflect those which inform the decision as to whether the document is to be disclosed to that person.[311]

4.156   Rule 67 provides for an order limiting the publicity to be given to a hearing in circumstances where an order has been made under r 66. The reference is to r 66 as a whole, rather than just to r 66(2), and the question arises whether the reference is both to a situation where a hearing has been made public in whole or in part and to one where an order has been made excluding a person where there is evidence about a non-disclosed document. Rule 66(7) refers to the tribunal "deciding" to exclude a person, rather than making an order to exclude a person. Only those provisions of r 66 dealing with an application for a public hearing use the word "order". Further, in the circumstances with which r 66(7) is concerned, the hearing may well be a private hearing, and the likelihood of there being publicity about it therefore very limited. These matters favour a construction whereby orders under r 67 will be made only in circumstances where the hearing has been held wholly or partly in public. The factors to be borne in mind in deciding whether to make an order limiting publicity are:

- the need to safeguard the welfare of a patient or any other person;
- the need to protect the private life of any person;
- any representations on the matter which a relevant person has provided in writing;
- the effect of any direction under r 49.[312]

4.157   An order limiting publicity is, again, to be proportionate in that it is to limit publicity only to the extent necessary to protect the interest which the maker of the order is seeking to protect.[313] It may

---

[311] See paras 3.180 *et seq* on non-disclosure requests.
[312] Rule 67(1)(a)–(d).
[313] Rule 67(2).

allow publicity which does not identify the parties. It is suggested that where a tribunal has ordered, for example, that a party should not be identified in any published material, a breach of such an order might in some circumstances constitute contempt of court.[314] A mental health review tribunal is a court for the purposes of the Contempt of Court Act 1981, as is an employment tribunal.[315] The Scottish Mental Health Tribunal would almost certainly be held also to be a court for those purposes, as a body which exercises the judicial, rather than administrative, power of the State. In England, Ord 52 r 1(2)(a) of the Rules of the Supreme Court makes provision for contempt of an inferior court to be punished by a Divisional Court of the Queen's Bench Division. There is no similar provision in the Rules of the Court of Session, and it is not entirely clear by what means proceedings for contempt of a tribunal in Scotland would be brought. It has been suggested that proceedings could be brought by an interested party by petition and complaint to the Court of Session, with intimation to the Lord Advocate for the public interest.[316]

There is no direct equivalent in the Rules of r 14(7) of the English **4.158** tribunal rules,[317] which provides that information about proceedings before the tribunal and the names of any persons concerned in the proceedings shall not be made public. It may be that the drafter of the 2005 Rules envisaged that the general provision for hearings to be held in private would obviate the need for specific provision, and that where a hearing has taken in place in public, the provisions of r 67(3) would suffice.

So far as publication of decisions by the Tribunal is concerned, **4.159** r 73 makes provision for the President to make such arrangements as he considers appropriate for the publication of Tribunal decisions. Decisions may be published electronically.[318] A decision may be published in edited form or subject to deletions.[319] Such editing and deletions are a matter for the Convener rather than the President, and he must bear in mind the need to safeguard the welfare of a patient or any other person; the need to protect the private life of

---

[314] See *Pickering* v *Liverpool Daily Post and Echo* [1991] 2 AC 370 at 425. For the limitations of the law of contempt as a vehicle for enforcing restrictions on publicity under a similar English rule, see *R (Mersey Care NHS Trust)* v *Mental Health Review Tribunal* [2005] 1 WLR 2469, for the discussion at paras 52–55.

[315] *Pickering*; *Peach Grey and Co* v *Sommers* [1995] ICR 549.

[316] See R McInnes with J D Fairley, *Contempt of Court in Scotland* (2000), pp 20–21.

[317] Tribunal Procedure (First-tier Tribunal) (Health, Education and Social Care Chamber) Rules 2008 (SI 2008/2699).

[318] Rule 73(2).

[319] Rule 73(3).

any person; and any representations which any relevant person has provided in writing.[320] Any decision published must be produced so as to protect the anonymity of the patient.[321]

Experts' reports – obligation to disclose

4.160   There are two circumstances in which the report of an expert can be presented to the tribunal, and these are outlined in r 62; in this section, we will consider one of those circumstances, covered by r 62(5)–(8). Of course, in almost every tribunal hearing the opinions of experts (or "skilled witnesses" being a more accurate term)[322] will be presented, namely those of the RMO and the MHO, but we are dealing here with the circumstances in which a report not required or offered to support the application before the tribunal may be presented.

4.161   Where a relevant person obtains a written report from a person having expertise in an area covering an issue before the tribunal, that relevant person must send a copy of the report to the tribunal before the 7-day period in advance of the next tribunal hearing of the case (unless a different period is specified by the tribunal).[323] This is an odd provision, since it requires disclosure of such a report automatically and by all relevant persons. The fact that it covers all relevant persons should not be forgotten; it covers, for instance, the RMO and the MHO. So, where the RMO is a relevant person (for example as a party in an application to extend and vary a CTO or in a challenge to a decision to extend a CTO)[324] he must disclose any written report he receives from, for example, another health professional such as an occupational therapist. The same applies to an MHO who is a party to a CTO application (and therefore is a relevant person in those proceedings)[325] and who might receive a report from another health professional such as a community psychiatric nurse. In practice, this provision is seen as one that covers the patient, and in particular the receipt by the patient of an independent psychiatric report, but the scope of this provision is not so limited. Whoever receives a written report falling within the terms of r 62(5) is obliged to send it to the tribunal, whether it is favourable to the case of that relevant person or not. As has been

---

[320] Rule 73(3)(a)–(c).
[321] Rule 73(4).
[322] See the discussion of the terminology at para 5.104.
[323] Rule 62(5).
[324] In such cases, the RMO is a party, and so is a relevant person: see r 2(1) for the definitions, and para 2.16 for a discussion of "relevant person".
[325] See para 2.16 on the definition of "relevant person".

noted elsewhere, the rule covers only written reports.[326] It would seem sensible to interpret the phrase "written report" widely, to include even a short note, memo, e-mail or letter; a written report need not necessarily be a full report badged as such.

Where the relevant person does not wish to disclose the report, an application must be made to the tribunal for permission not to disclose. Rule 62(6) suggests that a written request should be made in advance of the hearing at which the report would be disclosed, but such an application will be rare, particularly where the report is an independent psychiatric report obtained by the patient. In such cases, the patient's representative will usually have received the report only a few days (or less) before the hearing, and so there will be no time for such an advance application. In such cases, the tribunal will usually hear an oral application at the outset of the hearing. Where this happens, the tribunal should hear the applicant on the reason for failure to comply with r 62(6) and where it is due to mistake, oversight or other excusable cause, the dispensing power[327] should be used to allow an oral application to be made. Given the tight time constraints involved in the CTO application procedure, including where an interim CTO has been granted, lack of time to make a written application due to the arrival time of the report should almost always be accepted as an excusable cause for failure to make available a written application. In practice, lawyers acting for patients will often simply intimate that they do not intend to disclose an independent psychiatric report. This is not the correct course; a request to invoke r 62(6) should be made. As noted elsewhere,[328] privilege arguments can be made in almost every case, meaning that there will rarely, in practice, be a need for a patient to disclose an independent medical report to the tribunal. Sheriff Principal Lockhart of the Sheriffdom of South Strathclyde, Dumfries and Galloway has commented on an *obiter* basis that:

4.162

> "only in very exceptional circumstances, and on specific cause shown, should an independent report obtained by the patient with a view to challenging the [conclusions in the MHO's report] not be made available to the Tribunal. It seems to me to be in the interests of justice that such a report should be available. The Tribunal is concerned with what is best in the interests of the patient".[329]

It is submitted, with respect, that these comments are misguided. For reasons noted elsewhere,[330] privilege arguments are almost always

4.163

---

[326] See para 5.91.
[327] Rule 75. On this power generally, see paras 7.48 *et seq.*
[328] Paragraphs 5.90 *et seq.*
[329] *Beattie v Dunbar* 2006 SCLR 777; [2007] MHLR 7 at para [57].
[330] See paras 5.90 *et seq.*

available to patients in such cases. In addition, there is no mention in the Rules of a test of "very exceptional circumstances" so the introduction of such a test seems unwarranted. The sheriff principal relies on the interests of justice argument as well as the argument that disclosure is (in all but the most exceptional cases) in the best interests of the patient. However, the role of the tribunal in ensuring that the interests of all participants are balanced is far more complex than is suggested by the use of such general tests as the interests of justice and the best interests of the patient, neither of which feature at all in the 2003 Act or the Rules. This complexity is evident throughout the tribunal rules and in the 2003 Act provisions, not least s 1 of the Act which sets out no fewer than 12 principles for the discharge of functions under the Act,[331] all of which apply to, among others, the tribunal.

4.164   Whether the request for permission not to disclose a report is made in writing or orally, the tribunal may afford the relevant person an opportunity to be heard on the request.[332] Although such an opportunity is not obligatory, it would be unwise to refuse a request before such an opportunity is provided; if it is so refused, and if the relevant person is forced to hand over the report, this will almost certainly give rise to an opportunity to appeal on the ground of a procedural impropriety. Where the tribunal is faced with a request not to disclose, it has four choices. First, it can refuse the request and order the disclosure of the whole report.[333] Second, it can grant the request and decide that none of the report need be disclosed.[334] Third, it can grant the request in part, and give permission to the relevant person not to disclose part of the report.[335] Fourth, it can refuse the request in part and order the disclosure of part of the report.[336] One option not available to the tribunal under this rule is to *order* non-disclosure. If it wishes to order the non-disclosure of the entire report or part of it, an order under r 46(2) and (6) (whether on its own initiative or as a result of a request by a relevant person) will be required.[337]

Experts' reports – ordered by the tribunal

4.165   The second circumstance in which an expert report can be presented (other than a routine one in support of an application before the

---

[331] These are contained in s 1(3)–(6) of the 2003 Act.
[332] Rule 62(7).
[333] Rule 62(8)(b).
[334] Rule 62(8)(a).
[335] *Ibid.*
[336] Rule 62(8)(b).
[337] On such orders generally, see paras 3.180 *et seq.*

tribunal) is where one is ordered by the tribunal itself. This is rare, since the parties will usually present their own evidence and it will be unusual for the tribunal to take the view that some additional information not relied upon by any relevant person should be presented. Although, as indicated earlier, the tribunal should generally not adopt its own theory in a case or become involved in gathering evidence,[338] this provision enables the tribunal to order evidence in an area of relevance to the case where the parties have not, for whatever reason, presented this evidence themselves. The power for the tribunal to order an expert report is set out in r 62(1)–(4). It is important to note that these provisions do not apply where the tribunal wishes certain routine further information before it can decide the application or appeal before it: there are provisions in statutory instruments to cover such a situation, discussed elsewhere.[339] In most cases, where information is sought from the MHO or RMO, the power to act in these statutory instruments should be used. However, there may be cases where the tribunal feels that it needs further information that it cannot obtain from the MHO or RMO, and where there is no sign that one of the parties will produce it. In one tribunal case, the power was used to order an independent psychiatric assessment of a patient who had been in hospital for some considerable time, and where such an assessment had not been carried out recently and was not sought by the lawyer acting for the patient.

The test for the ordering of such a report by the tribunal is that,   **4.166** in the opinion of the tribunal, it would be desirable for the tribunal to have the assistance of an expert on an issue in relation to the case.[340] The expert is appointed to inquire into and report on any such matter.[341] In addition, the expert must have the appropriate qualifications to conduct this task.[342] Unless the report produced by the expert (or part of it) falls within the remit of r 47 (allowing the non-disclosure of a document or part of it, discussed elsewhere)[343] the tribunal must supply the parties (not all relevant persons)[344] with a copy of it in advance of the hearing.[345] The tribunal can require that the expert attends the hearing and gives oral evidence.[346] In practice, the appointment of a suitable expert will take place after

---

[338] See para 4.116.
[339] See para 3.144.
[340] Rule 62(1).
[341] *Ibid.*
[342] *Ibid.*
[343] Paragraphs 3.184 *et seq.*
[344] For the difference between a party and a relevant person, see para 2.16.
[345] Rule 62(2).
[346] Rule 62(3).

the hearing, from the tribunal administration's list of available experts, and so the tribunal panel that orders the report should set out carefully and clearly the nature of the report required, the issues to be addressed in it and any qualifications, experience and expertise the chosen expert should possess. Any direction to attend could be contained in the terms of appointment, but again it would seem good practice for the tribunal panel appointing the expert to specify whether or not it wishes the expert to attend. The expert appointed should, as a matter of good practice, carefully review the terms of the decision appointing him, as well as all of the papers that were before the tribunal when the appointment decision was made. In most cases, an examination of the patient by the expert will be necessary.

4.167   Before deciding whether to appoint an expert, the tribunal should canvass the views of all relevant persons, and take those views into account.[347] Failure to do so may constitute a procedural impropriety.

4.168   Where an expert is appointed by the tribunal, the MHTS is responsible for paying the expert any necessary report preparation expenses (presumably including those relating to any examination of the patient) as well as those incurred in the giving of evidence at the later tribunal hearing(s).[348]

Tribunals with sheriff Conveners

4.169   Where the Tribunal is dealing with applications, appeals or references relating to persons who are subject to compulsion orders and restriction orders, or to patients who were "restricted patients"[349] under the predecessor provisions, the Convener of the tribunal must be the President, a sheriff principal, a sheriff, or a part-time sheriff. Paragraph 2 of Sch 2 to the 2003 Act makes provision for a panel of Conveners consisting of sheriffs principal, sheriffs and part-time sheriffs.

---

[347] Rule 52(3)–(4), discussed elsewhere generally at para 3.14.

[348] Rule 62(4).

[349] A "restricted patient" is a person liable to be detained in a hospital immediately before 5 October 2005 under a hospital order or order having the effect of a hospital order made under the Criminal Procedure (Scotland) Act 1995 and who immediately before 5 October 2005 was subject to the special restrictions set out in s 62(1) of the 1984 Act. By virtue of art 20 of the Mental Health (Care and Treatment) (Scotland) Act 2003 (Transitional and Savings Provisions) Order 2005 (SSI 2005/452), a restricted patient is now treated as though a compulsion order under s 57A(2) of the 1995 Act and a restriction order under s 59 of the 1995 Act had been made in respect of him. For a definition of "restricted patient" for this purpose, see art 2 of the same Order.

Paragraph 7(4)[350] of Sch 2 to the 2003 Act provides: 4.170

"In relation to proceedings (other than proceedings relating solely to
an application under ss 255 or 256 of this Act) before the Tribunal in
relation to a patient subject to a compulsion order and a restriction
order, a hospital direction[351] or a transfer for treatment direction[352] the
Convener shall be

(a) the President; or
(b) a person selected by the President from the panel mentioned in
    para 2 above."

Patients who are subject to a compulsion order and restriction order   4.171
together, a hospital direction, or a transfer for treatment direction,
are all patients who have been convicted of offences punishable by
imprisonment. Patients who are subject to both a compulsion order
and a restriction order are patients who have been made subject
without limit of time to special restrictions under Pt 10 of the
2003 Act. The sentencing court will only impose these restrictions
in addition to a compulsion order if satisfied, having regard to the
nature of the offence, the antecedents of the offender, and the risk
that as a result of his mental disorder the offender would commit
offences if set at large, that it is necessary for the protection of the
public from serious harm so to do.[353] The gravity of the concern for
public safety in relation to such a patient is therefore obvious. In the
case of a patient who is subject to a hospital direction, the conviction
must have been on indictment. Parliament has determined that where
cases concerning such patients come before the Tribunal, they should
be dealt with by tribunals chaired by the President, or a member of

---

[350] As amended by para 32 of Sch 1 to the Mental Health (Care and Treatment)
(Scotland) Act 2003 (Modification of Enactments) Order 2005 (SSI 2005/465).
[351] A hospital order may be made under s 59A of the Criminal Procedure (Scotland)
Act 1995 where a person is convicted on indictment in the High Court or on
indictment in the sheriff court of an offence punishable by imprisonment. Where
satisfied as to certain matters by medical evidence, the court may, in addition to
any sentence of imprisonment, impose a hospital direction, authorising detention in
hospital and the provision of treatment to the offender under Pt 16 of the 2003 Act.
The order may authorise detention in a State Hospital where conditions of special
security which can be provided only there are required.
[352] Section 136 of the 2003 Act makes provision for the situation where someone
is serving a sentence of imprisonment. It does not apply to one who has been made
subject to a mental health disposal in the course of criminal proceedings: see
s 136(9). Where a prisoner suffers from a mental disorder, the Scottish Ministers
may make a transfer for treatment direction, providing that certain statutory
criteria are met. The direction may authorise detention in a State Hospital, where
conditions of special security which can be provided only there are required.
[353] Criminal Procedure (Scotland) Act 1995, s 59.

the panel mentioned above, unless the application is only in relation to the named person of such a patient, under s 255 or s 256 of the 2003 Act.

4.172   Matters which may come before the Tribunal include references under ss 210(3), 211(2) or 213(2), or an application under s 214(2), (in relation to patients subject to hospital directions or transfer for treatment directions), and references under ss 185(1), 187(2) or 189(2), or an application under s 191 or 192(2) in relation to patients subject to a compulsion order and a restriction order. The tribunal's powers in relation to a patient subject to a hospital direction or a transfer for treatment direction are set out in s 215, and in s 193 in relation to patients subject to a compulsion order and a restriction order. What these provisions have in common is that, if the tribunal is satisfied that the patient has a mental disorder and that, as a result of the patient's mental disorder, it is necessary, in order to protect any other person from serious harm, for the patient to be detained in hospital, whether or not for medical treatment, the direction or orders relating to the patient are to remain unchanged.[354] Applications simply in relation to the named person of a patient subject to a direction or orders of these types can be dealt with by a tribunal which is chaired by a legal member of the panel, rather than the President or a sheriff.

4.173   There is little in the Rules providing for any speciality in relation to tribunal cases of this sort, save the provisions for intimation to the Scottish Ministers of applications under ss 192 and 214 of the 2003 Act,[355] of certain references,[356] and of applications under s 264 for a declaration that a patient in the State Hospital is being detained in conditions of excessive security, where that patient is a relevant patient in terms of s 273;[357] that is, he is a patient whose detention is authorised by a compulsion order and who is also subject to a restriction order, or whose detention is authorised by a hospital direction or a transfer for treatment direction. There is also provision in r 2 as amended,[358] making the Scottish Ministers a party in such an application under s 264.

4.174   The general provisions of the Rules apply to cases of these types just as they do to any others. In particular, r 63, relating to the informality of the proceedings, and providing a wide discretion as to the conduct of the proceedings, applies. The difficulty and complexity of the

---

[354] For a discussion of the compatibility of similar provisions with Art 5(4) ECHR, see *A v Scottish Ministers* 2002 SC (PC) 63.
[355] See rr 15 and 16.
[356] Rule 30(1)(b).
[357] Rule 17A, inserted by the Mental Health Tribunal for Scotland (Practice and Procedure) (No 2) Amendment Rules 2006 (SSI 2006/171), r 2(3).
[358] Amended by the Mental Health Tribunal for Scotland (Practice and Procedure) (No 2) Amendment Rules 2006 (SSI 2006/171), r 2(2).

issues in these particularly sensitive cases are likely to require perhaps more formality than in some others. In many cases, particularly where applications are made by patients or their named persons, a number of issues are likely to be in contention. The consideration of the "serious harm" test may require complex and detailed evidence, as may the formulation of conditions to be imposed on conditional discharge under s 193(7). It may be necessary to examine in some detail the history of the patient over a lengthy period.

In many cases, particularly where issues are contested between the patient and the Scottish Ministers, it will be of assistance to hold a first hearing specifically for the purpose of seeking to clarify the nature and extent of issues in dispute, and make any necessary directions for the future efficient conduct of the case. It is worth remembering that cases such as these were, under the previous legislation, conducted before the sheriff alone, by way of summary application. They were often the subject of detailed pleadings from both the patient and the Scottish Ministers, which assisted in focusing the points of contention. In the absence of formal pleadings, the Tribunal may seek to clarify the issues by directing parties to lodge a summary, in writing, of their positions, and to direct that those summaries be exchanged. Documents and reports in such cases are frequently more extensive than in the majority of cases that otherwise come before the Tribunal. With that in mind, the Tribunal may choose to direct parties to order and number the papers in a more formal manner than in other proceedings, and in a way similar to that employed in ordinary court proceedings. No definitive guidance can be given here as to the whole range of procedures that the tribunal may employ to try to ensure a hearing focused on the issues between the parties, and carried out in an expeditious manner.

4.175

One issue which has arisen in relation to references under s 189 (where the case of a patient subject to a compulsion order with a restriction order is automatically referred to the Tribunal every 2 years unless some other reference or application has been made to the Tribunal), is the attendance of the Scottish Ministers at hearings. It has been the practice of the Scottish Ministers to produce a written position statement, usually asking for no order to be made, but asking to be given the opportunity to appear in the event that the patient produces medical evidence apparently supportive of the possibility that the tribunal might make an order altering the *status quo*. The volume of matters arising by way of such references has apparently made it difficult for the Scottish Ministers to be represented at every hearing. Even where the patient does not seek any alteration in his position, the tribunal requires to be satisfied in relation to certain matters on the reference before determining to make no order. The writer has experience of a situation where the

4.176

Scottish Ministers were not represented. The patient did not ask for any order to be made, but one of the tribunal members raised an issue as to whether the risk of serious harm identified could properly be attributed to the patient's mental disorder. The tribunal came to be satisfied in relation to that matter on the evidence. Had it not been so satisfied at that stage, it would have been desirable to have had the Scottish Ministers' submissions in relation to the matter, and the tribunal would have had to consider whether it was just to adjourn to permit the Scottish Ministers to make such submissions.

4.177   The proper approach to cases where it is contended that a patient detained in the State Hospital is detained in conditions of excessive security (whether or not that patient is a relevant patient in terms of s 273) has been considered on appeal by Sheriff Principal Lockhart.[359] At the stage when the Tribunal is considering the matter under s 264, the question for the Tribunal is whether the condition of the patient requires his detention in conditions of special security that can be provided only in a State Hospital. Questions of the resources of the Health Board to provide alternative facilities for detention are irrelevant at this stage. The Act provides for further hearings where the Health Board fails, in the face of a decision that the patient is being detained in conditions of excessive security, to give notice that the patient has been transferred to another hospital.[360] This is intended to give the Health Board time to make suitable arrangements. If the Health Board contends that alternative accommodation cannot be found, its remedy is to seek recall of the Tribunal's decision under s 267(2)(b).

4.178   Section 193 of the Act is not easy to construe, and a tribunal is faced with an array of possible disposals, and provisions which combine positive and negative language ("if the tribunal is satisfied of X, but not satisfied of Y") and variously disjunctive and conjunctive language ("if the tribunal is not satisfied of X or Y" and "if the tribunal is not satisfied of X and Y"). The Inner House has sought to clarify the approach that ought to be taken by tribunals to the tests set out in s 193: *Scottish Ministers* v *Mental Health Tribunal for Scotland* ("*JK*").[361] According to the court in *JK*, the section provides a sequential list of tests. The tribunal must first consider s 193(2) and determine whether it ought to make any order at all. The tribunal must reach a clear and reasoned view on s 193(2). If the tests in s 193(2) are met, the tribunal must make no order and

---

[359] *Lothian Health Board* v M 2007 SCLR 478.
[360] Sections 265 and 266.
[361] 2009 SLT 273.

it cannot proceed to exercise any of the powers under s 193(3), (4) and (5). The court sought to clarify the correct approach to the tests in s 193(5)(b)(i) and (ii). The tribunal, if proceeding under s 193(5), must consider not only whether the "serious harm" test is met, but whether there is a continuing necessity for a restriction order. The statute provides no guidance as to how the "continued necessity" test is to be applied. The court, however, provides guidance at para 39: consideration must be given to the antecedents of the patient and the risk that he would commit further offences if at large, and a reasoned conclusion reached as to whether or not these matters (which derive from the tests applicable to the original imposition of the order) remain of relevance. The nature and effect of the restriction order itself on the patient's present circumstances must also be considered. The court also approved *R v Birch*:[362] the "serious harm" test requires the tribunal to consider whether the restriction order is necessary to protect the public from a risk of serious harm, rather than from a serious risk of harm. The reasoning of the court in *JK* has, in however, been criticised in one respect by another Division in *Scottish Ministers v Mental Health Tribunal for Scotland and MM*.[363] Both the appellant and the tribunal in *MM* submitted that the court had erred in what it said at para 34 of its opinion in *JK*. The application of the "continued necessity" test and the construction of, and interaction between, subss (4), (5) and (6) were said to raise difficulties which merited consideration in a suitable case: Lord Reed (*obiter*) in *MM*. All three members of the court in *MM* pointed out difficulties involved in construing s 193, while not offering a solution to those difficulties, as the appeal was decided on the basis that the reasons given by the tribunal were inadequate.

4.179   Where the Scottish Ministers have made directions for the conditional discharge of a patient under s 68(2) of the 1984 Act, and the case thereafter comes before a tribunal for a review under s 189 of the Act, the tribunal has no power to make an order conditionally discharging the patient under s 193(7) or to alter the conditions of discharge. The tribunal's power to impose conditions on conditional discharge arises only at the time when the tribunal itself makes an order for conditional discharge. Where the Scottish Ministers had made directions, the Mental Health Care and Treatment (Scotland) Act 2003 (Transitional and Savings Provisions) Order 2005[364] applied, the tribunal was to be regarded as having

---

[362] (1989) 11 Cr App R (S) 202.
[363] [2009] CSIH 66.
[364] SSI 2005/452.

already made the order for conditional discharge itself, and could not make a further order effectively revoking that already in place: *Scottish Ministers* v *Mental Health Tribunal for Scotland*.[365]

---

[365] 2009 SLT 650.

CHAPTER 5

HEARING PROCEDURE III – THE RULES
OF EVIDENCE[1]

THE ROLE OF EVIDENCE IN TRIBUNAL HEARINGS

Evidence is the name given to any material that may be made available   **5.01**
to the tribunal and from which it may draw conclusions as to matters
of fact. There are two main types of evidence: documentary and oral.[2]
It should be noted that legal submissions or arguments (including
any preliminary points)[3] are not evidence. Evidence will feature in
the vast majority of tribunal hearings, the main exceptions being
those hearings that do not really begin since the hearing requires to
be adjourned for a particular reason. The importance of identifying
material that is evidence is twofold. First, there are certain legal rules
that apply to the permissibility (admissibility), presentation and
assessment of evidence. Many of these rules have been developed in
the context of hearings in the public courts. Most apply to criminal
proceedings in those courts, but there are some rules of civil evidence.
The questions, then, are: which rules apply to tribunal hearings, and
how do they apply? These questions will be considered below. Second,
the tribunal cannot find any fact proven unless it can be established
as such within the rules of evidence. This means that the tribunal
cannot find a single fact proven without evidence being available to

---

[1] Of course, the law of evidence is a complex subject and it is not dealt with in full
in this text; only the main points, as they relate to tribunal proceedings, are dealt
with in sufficient detail to enable the reader to recognise and deal with most issues
as they arise. In the event of a difficult point on the law of evidence arising in any
tribunal case, the material in this chapter should be supplemented by reference to
the main texts on the law of evidence in Scotland: F P Davidson, *Evidence* (2007);
M L Ross and J Chalmers, *Walker and Walker: The Law of Evidence in Scotland*
(3rd edn, 2009); F Raitt, *Evidence: Principles, Policy and Practice* (2008).
[2] There is a third (real evidence) which refers to physical evidence, ie physical
items that are not documents, but it is difficult to imagine any such evidence being
produced for a tribunal hearing, so it is not dealt with here.
[3] On such points, see paras 4.93 *et seq.*

it about that fact. With some very limited exceptions,[4] the tribunal can assume no factual knowledge at all (even if the tribunal members themselves are all possessed of that knowledge) without satisfactory evidence being offered to support it. This means that before any substantive order is made[5] the tribunal needs evidence; without it, the tribunal is powerless. It should be noted here that while the vast majority of hearings in which evidence is led will include the leading of oral evidence (testimony), the tribunal can determine a case purely on the basis of written evidence submitted to it.[6]

5.02   It is clear that the business of the Tribunal is properly classed as civil proceedings for the purposes of the law of evidence. There are several indications of this. First, any appeal from a tribunal decision must proceed through the civil appeal courts, first to the sheriff principal, then to the Inner House of the Court of Session and, ultimately, to the House of Lords.[7] In addition, the equivalent hearings under the Mental Health (Scotland) Act 1984 were conducted in a civil court, the sheriff court, and were conducted according to the civil evidence rules. Third, there are the Rules themselves. For the most part, they contain provisions that have a strong civil court flavour, such as the dispensing power provision,[8] the overriding objective[9] and the stipulations on the lodging, distribution and disclosure of documents.[10] When one considers the tribunal provisions on the rules on evidence too, the mention of the power to exclude evidence as "irrelevant, unnecessary or improperly obtained"[11] is indicative: these

---

[4] The two exceptions are: (1) inferences drawn from facts (see paras 5.123 *et seq* below); even then these are limited in scope and must arise from facts that have been proven; and (2) facts that are within judicial knowledge – see below at paras 5.13 *et seq.*

[5] The term "substantive" in relation to orders (not a term used in the 2003 Act or the Rules, but a term well recognised in civil procedural law) refers to orders where the tribunal is determining the merits of an application or appeal such as granting a CTO application or refusing an application to revoke one. The other type of order that can be made is a "procedural" order, such as a decision to adjourn a hearing or to appoint a curator *ad litem*. It should be borne in mind that evidence will be required before the tribunal can grant even an interim order; this is discussed further at para 4.38.

[6] For circumstances in which this might be possible and appropriate, see the provisions of r 58.

[7] See the 2003 Act, ss 320–324 for the provisions dealing with appeals as far as the Court of Session. For an examination of appeals from a tribunal decision, see Chapter 8.

[8] Rule 75, discussed further at paras 7.48 *et seq.*

[9] Rule 4, discussed further at para 1.26.

[10] Rules 45, 46A and 47 in Pt VII (General Rules) and the various provisions on lodging and intimating applications, reviews, references and appeals of various kinds set out in Pts II–VI.

[11] Rule 49(1)(g)(iv), discussed in more detail at paras 5.02 *et seq* and 5.49 *et seq.*

grounds exist in the civil public courts. This does not mean that the rules of evidence that apply in criminal proceedings can be ignored completely. It is not uncommon for allegations of criminal activity to be levelled at a patient during tribunal hearings. Even in these cases, it seems that some of the rules of evidence to be applied, such as those relating to the burden of proof, are those that apply in civil cases, not criminal.[12] However, there are some examples of instances where it would seem sensible that the rules of evidence that apply in criminal cases apply, and these instances are covered below.[13] Finally, as noted further below, the Rules have avoided the common formulation that applies in other tribunal rules, whereby the rules on admissibility applicable in public court actions are specifically inapplicable.[14]

The Rules do not specify comprehensively which rules of evidence apply to tribunal proceedings. However, there is a very important provision that appears not under the section of the Rules entitled "Evidence",[15] but elsewhere. Rule 49, setting out the directions that the Tribunal may make,[16] provides at r 49(1)(g) that directions can be issued as to: **5.03**

"(i)   any issues on which the Tribunal requires evidence;
(ii)   the nature of the evidence which the Tribunal requires to decide those issues;
(iii) the way in which the evidence is to be led before the Tribunal; and

---

[12] The general position is that allegations of criminal activity within civil proceedings attract the civil burden of proof, namely the balance of probabilities: see *Mullan* v *Anderson (No 1)* 1993 SLT 835; 1993 SCLR 506. On the burden of proof in the context of tribunal proceedings, see paras 5.05 *et seq*.

[13] See the brief reference to the rule against the admissibility of secondary hearsay evidence, below at para 5.45 and the example, also below, of the incriminating statement made by a patient in response to questioning that is not preceded by a caution – see para 5.73.

[14] This inapplicability is reflected in the English tribunal rules: see the Tribunal Procedure (First-tier Tribunal) (Health, Education and Social Care Chamber) Rules 2008 (SI 2008/2699), r 15(2)(a). See also a similar provision in the rules of procedure that apply to employment tribunals across the UK, the Employment Tribunals (Constitution and Rules of Procedure) Regulations 2004 (SI 2004/1861), as amended, Sch 1, reg 14(2). See also the rules of procedure of the Asylum and Immigration Tribunal, the Asylum and Immigration Tribunal (Procedure) Rules 2005 (SI 2005/230), r 51(1). However, unlike in the Employment Tribunal rules, the Asylum and Immigration Tribunal rules (r 51(2)), the English Mental Health Review Tribunal rules (r 15(2) and now SI 2008/2699, r 16(3)) do mirror the Scottish Mental Health Tribunal rules in precluding the Tribunal from forcing a witness to give evidence/produce a document where that witness could not be compelled to do so in court. For the equivalent provision for the Scottish Mental Health Tribunal, see the 2003 Act, Sch 2, para 12(4).

[15] This section of the Rules covers rr 59–62 inclusive.

[16] For commentary on directions under this rule generally, see paras 7.30 *et seq*.

(iv) the exclusion of any evidence which is irrelevant, unnecessary or
improperly obtained."

This is the critical provision on the scope and nature of the evidence
that can be led in tribunal proceedings. Before we can examine this
part of r 49 further in this chapter, we need to consider the rules of
evidence that apply in civil proceedings in the public courts to which
we turn in the next section. One point should be made at the outset:
the direction may only (as with any r 49 directions) be made where
the tribunal considers it to be "necessary or desirable to further the
overriding objective in the conduct of a case".[17] It should also be noted
that the provisions in the Civil Evidence (Scotland) Act 1988 (see
below on hearsay evidence and on statutory shortcuts)[18] specifically
apply to tribunal proceedings.[19] One further general point should
be noted here. In the rules for both employment and immigration
tribunal proceedings[20] as well as those for mental health review
tribunals in England,[21] there are provisions which expressly relieve the
tribunal from complying with the rules of evidence that apply in civil
court proceedings in the public courts. No such provision appears
in the Scottish mental health tribunal rules. In fact, the intentions
of the framers of the Scottish tribunal rules to generally apply those
civil court evidential requirements is clear from two provisions, first
r 49(1)(g)(iv) quoted above, which provides for the exclusion of certain
types of evidence, not their inclusion; second from the appearance of
a provision allowing a person to refuse to give or produce evidence in
the tribunal where that person could refuse to do so in court.[22] The
decision by the framers of the Scottish mental health tribunal rules to
decline to follow this formula which appears in other tribunal rules
must, it is submitted, be taken to be deliberate. It is also notable that

---

[17] Rule 49(1), first para. For a full discussion of the circumstances in which a
direction may be made, see paras 7.30 *et seq.*
[18] Below, at paras 5.38 *et seq* and para 5.37 respectively.
[19] See s 9 of the Act, the interpretation section, and the definition of "civil proceedings": "'civil proceedings' includes, in addition to such proceedings in any of
the ordinary courts of law – ... (c) any proceedings before a tribunal or inquiry,
except in so far as, in relation to the conduct of proceedings before the tribunal or
inquiry, specific provision has been made as regards the rules of evidence which are
to apply".
[20] For employment tribunals, see r 14(2) of the Employment Tribunals (Constitution
and Rules of Procedure) Regulations 2004 (SI 2004/1861) and for immigration
tribunals, see Asylum and Immigration Tribunal (Procedure) Rules 2005 (SI
2005/230), r 51(1).
[21] Tribunal Procedure (First-tier Tribunal) (Health, Education and Social Care
Chamber) Rules 2008 (SI 2008/2699), r 15(2)(a).
[22] Mental Health (Care and Treatment) (Scotland) Act 2003, Sch 2, para 12(4),
discussed below in more detail at paras 5.73 and 5.98.

despite the power on the part of employment tribunals to ignore the
rules of admissibility of evidence, the Employment Appeal Tribunal
has issued general guidelines indicating that:

> "while the tribunal's discretion to admit otherwise inadmissible evidence
> ... is recognised, nevertheless it must be remembered that the rules of
> procedure and evidence have been built up over the years in order to
> guide courts and tribunals as to the fairest and simplest way of dealing
> with and deciding issues".[23]

In other words, even in a set of rules where the tribunal is empowered
to ignore the rules of admissibility of evidence, it should not do so
where this would cause unfairness.

SOME BASIC EVIDENTIAL CONCEPTS

Although concepts such as admissibility, weight and sufficiency   5.04
are best considered below at appropriate points, it is convenient to
examine some others here before moving onto consider some of the
specific grounds for the exclusion of evidence as provided for in the
Rules.

The burden of proof

The burden of proof is a device that deals with the following question: 5.05
which party must prove an issue in question and ultimately, therefore,
the case before the tribunal? The standard of proof (below) deals
with the following question: *to what extent* must that party prove
the issue?

In order to determine which party bears the burden on which   5.06
issue, there is a simple rule. Where a party affirmatively relies upon
a fact and where it is essential to the establishment of an issue before
the tribunal, he will usually bear the legal burden of proving that
fact. If he fails to prove it (fails to discharge the burden), it will be
deemed not to have been established and, where the establishment of
the issue is critical to that party's case, he will lose the case. Another
way of putting it is to say that the burden of proof rests on the party
who would lose on the issue if no other evidence was led, or if at the
end of the case the evidence led by both parties (or all parties) on the
issue is equally persuasive. By contrast, the party who does not bear
the burden of proof on that issue does not need to establish anything
in relation to it. Taking this to extremes, the party who does not

---

[23] P Wood, in *Aberdeen Steak Houses Group plc v Ibrahim* [1988] ICR 550 at
557–558. See also *Snowball v Gardner Merchant Ltd* [1987] ICR 719 at 722 per
Sir Ralph Kilner-Brown.

bear the burden of proof may simply present no evidence at all and may make no argument other than simply stating that he opposes the granting of the application or appeal before the tribunal. Even here, the tribunal could refuse the application or appeal is if is not satisfied that the burden has been discharged. This, of course, is an extremely unlikely scenario, but does demonstrate the importance of the burden of proof. A more likely scenario is one where the patient is opposing the granting of an order by the tribunal, but does not present any evidence of his own; he (or more usually his lawyer) will simply try to undermine the case for the granting of the order by cross-examination of the witnesses for the party supporting an order.[24] The idea that a party not bearing a burden can attack his opponent's case without putting forward any positive evidence of his own is a well established one in the public civil courts. As a matter of professional legal practice, however, it is improper to cross-examine a witness without having a proper basis on which to do so.

5.07   This point was demonstrated recently in a personal injury case, the Scottish House of Lords case of *Thomson* v *Kvaerner Govan Ltd*.[25] The House of Lords, by a majority of 4–1, found that the reliance placed by the lower court upon the inability of the defender's expert to devise an alternative explanation for the accident effectively involved inverting the burden of proof. The court held that, except in one special case,[26] the defenders had no obligation to prove anything. The pursuer (who in this case was in the equivalent position to the applicant/appellant in a tribunal case) bore the burden of proving that the plank in question broke, injuring him, in circumstances demonstrating negligence on the part of the defenders. The fact that the defence expert discredited this explanation did not mean that he had to come up with an alternative explanation himself. It seems that this reasoning is correct, since defenders cannot be seen to be being punished for failing to produce their own theory as to how an accident happened in circumstances negating negligence on their part. They can choose to restrict themselves solely to attacking the account of the pursuer. Where they do so successfully, they win the case.

5.08   Of course, a key issue is the determination of which party bears the burden in any particular case in general terms. In a CTO application, it is clear that the MHO as the applicant bears the burden of establishing that the statutory criteria for the granting of a CTO are met. In the case of an appeal or application to review an order by someone other

---

[24] On cross-examination of witnesses in a tribunal case, see paras 4.52 *et seq.*
[25] [2003] UKHL 45; 2004 SC (HL) 1.
[26] Where there is an argument of *res ipsa loquitur*, but this concept is not applicable in a mental health context.

than the MHO or RMO (for example the patient or named person), it might be thought that the burden lies with the appellant/applicant. However, this is not the case. In terms of Art 5 of the ECHR, the onus is always on the State to justify detention,[27] and so the burden in such cases lies with the MHO/RMO, depending upon who is the opposing party. In many cases, the grounds for a successful appeal or application will involve establishing the non-application of the statutory criteria for the continuation of compulsory measures.

Why is the burden of proof necessary? The main reason is to ensure   5.09
that, in any particular case, there will be a winner. In most cases, the tribunal will be in no doubt as to which party has made out his case. However, sometimes, the case may be evenly balanced. In such a situation, the tribunal can rely on the burden of proof to decide the case – it tilts the scales in one direction or the other in difficult cases. It is also useful in ensuring that the parties are aware of the points on which they must lead convincing evidence. Were it not for the burden of proof, the parties would not know which facts to concentrate on when preparing their case. So, for example, in a CTO application, a patient knows that he does not require to disprove an issue essential to the MHO's case.

The standard of proof

The standard of proof is the benchmark by which judicial bodies   5.10
decide whether a fact is established or not. Its application was recently described by Baroness Hale in the House of Lords:

> "In our legal system, if a judge finds it more likely than not that something did take place, then it is treated as having taken place. If he finds it more likely than not that it did not take place, then it is treated as not having taken place. He is not allowed to sit on the fence. He has to find for one side or the other. Sometimes the burden of proof will come to his rescue: the party with the burden of showing that something took place will not have satisfied him that it did. But generally speaking a judge is able to make up his mind where the truth lies without needing to rely upon the burden of proof."[28]

The standard of proof in civil cases in Scotland is that the essential facts must be established on the *balance of probabilities* (not beyond

---

[27] See the cases of *Hutchison Reid v United Kingdom* (2003) 37 EHRR 9, paras 60 and 63–74; *R (H) v Mental Health Review Tribunal North and East London Region (Secretary of State for Health intervening), ex p H* [2001] 3 WLR 512 and *L v Scottish Ministers*, unreported, First Division, 17 January 2002, available on the Scottish Courts website at www.scotcourts.gov.uk.
[28] *In re B (Children) (Care Proceedings: Standard of Proof)* [2008] UKHL 35; [2009] 1 AC 11; [2008] 3 WLR 1 at para 32.

reasonable doubt – this is the criminal standard). The essential facts are those that the tribunal relies upon during the evaluation process as contributing to the sufficiency (or not) of the case as made out by the party bearing the burden of proof.[29] To cite the most common example, the tribunal considers whether the essential facts, when combined, are sufficient to allow the criteria in s 64(5) of the 2003 Act to be established. However, it should be noted that the tribunal is not applying the test of balance of probabilities directly to the relevant statutory criteria; the test applies to the establishment of individual facts. When applying those facts that have been proven on the balance of probabilities to the criteria, this is a different stage in the process, and the test at that second stage is one of sufficiency, dealt with as a separate subject below.[30] Even where there is an allegation of criminal activity being dealt with by the tribunal, the civil standard applies.[31]

5.11   What does the "balance of probabilities" mean? A number of judges in cases in the civil courts in England have attempted to define this concept. Lord Denning in *Miller* v *Minister of Pensions*[32] put it in this way:

> "If the evidence is such that the tribunal can say 'we think it more probable than not', the burden is discharged – but if the probabilities are equal it is not."[33]

It should be noted that Lord Denning is referring here to each essential factual issue on which the party bears the burden of proof.

Another definition is provided by Lord Simon in the case of *Davies* v *Taylor (No 1)*:[34]

> "proof on a balance of probabilities [is] the burden of showing odds of at least 51 to 49 that such-and-such has taken place or will do so … in other words, is it more likely than not? … If a possibility is conceivable but fanciful, the law disregards it entirely".[35]

This could mean that more than one possible explanation may be put for a particular occurrence and the tribunal might reject them

---

[29] For an examination of the evaluation process, see paras 5.119 *et seq* below.
[30] See paras 5.127 *et seq* below.
[31] See above at n 12. In England this has been recently held to be the case by the Court of Appeal, considering an appeal from a decision of an English mental health review tribunal: *R (N)* v *Mental Health Review Tribunal (Northern Region)* [2006] QB 468.
[32] [1947] 2 All ER 372; 63 TLR 474.
[33] [1947] 2 All ER 372 at 374.
[34] [1974] AC 207; [1972] 3 WLR 801.
[35] [1974] AC 207 at 219.

all as improbable, leaving the party bearing the burden of proof to lose the case.[36] The House of Lords has, in two recent cases, had to consider judicial pronouncements on how the standard of proof operates.[37] There had, in some earlier cases, been suggestions that the standard of proof varies according to the seriousness of the fact being considered. However, the House in both cases made it clear that while the weight of evidence to establish a particular fact on the balance of probabilities might depend on the fact itself, the standard is the same in relation to all facts in all cases. Lord Carswell explains the position in this way:

> "a possible source of confusion is the failure to bear in mind with sufficient clarity the fact that in some contexts a court or tribunal has to look at the facts more critically or more anxiously than in others before it can be satisfied to the requisite standard. The standard itself is, however, finite and unvarying. Situations which make such heightened examination necessary may be the inherent unlikelihood of the occurrence taking place ... the seriousness of the allegation to be proved or, in some cases, the consequences which could follow from acceptance of proof of the relevant fact. The seriousness of the allegation requires no elaboration: a tribunal of fact will look closely into the facts grounding an allegation of fraud before accepting that it has been established. The seriousness of consequences is another facet of the same proposition: if it is alleged that a bank manager has committed a minor peculation, that could entail very serious consequences for his career, so making it the less likely that he would risk doing such a thing. These are all matters of ordinary experience, requiring the application of good sense on the part of those who have to decide such issues. They do not require a different standard of proof or a specially cogent standard of evidence, merely appropriately careful consideration by the tribunal before it is satisfied of the matter which has to be established. ..."[38]

Baroness Hale had this to say on the matter:

> "Neither the seriousness of the allegation nor the seriousness of the con-sequences should make any difference to the standard of proof to be applied in determining the facts. The inherent probabilities are simply something to be taken into account, where relevant, in deciding where the truth lies. ... As to the seriousness of the allegation, there is no logical or

---

[36] This happened in the case of *Rhesa Shipping Co SA v Edmunds (The Popi M)* [1985] 1 WLR 948; [1985] 2 All ER 712.
[37] *In re D (Original Respondent and Cross-appellant) (Northern Ireland)* [2008] UKHL 33; [2008] 1 WLR 1499 and *In re B (Children) (Care Proceedings: Standard of Proof)* [2008] UKHL 35; [2009] 1 AC 11; [2008] 3 WLR 1.
[38] *In re D (Original Respondent and Cross-appellant) (Northern Ireland)* [2008] UKHL 33; [2008] 1 WLR 1499 at para 28.

necessary connection between seriousness and probability. Some seriously harmful behaviour, such as murder, is sufficiently rare to be inherently improbable in most circumstances. Even then there are circumstances, such as a body with its throat cut and no weapon to hand, where it is not at all improbable. Other seriously harmful behaviour, such as alcohol or drug abuse, is regrettably all too common and not at all improbable. Nor are serious allegations made in a vacuum. Consider the famous example of the animal seen in Regent's Park. If it is seen outside the zoo on a stretch of greensward regularly used for walking dogs, then of course it is more likely to be a dog than a lion. If it is seen in the zoo next to the lions' enclosure when the door is open, then it may well be more likely to be a lion than a dog."[39]

5.12   Of course, much of the factual material before the tribunal is often uncontroversial, and will be contained in the documentation before it, whether in a CTO application, mental health reports, independent psychiatric report, social circumstances report, to name a few common examples. The tribunal will always have to consider whether the fact in question is proved, but this is unlikely to present any difficulty where there is no dispute. However, where there is some contradictory evidence offered in connection with a fact, whether in writing also (and sometimes even in documents produced by the same party) or orally during the hearing, the tribunal will have to consider whether the fact has been established on the balance of probabilities. That fact might relate to any issue that is relevant to the case before the tribunal.

Judicial knowledge

5.13   As indicated earlier, the importance of the law of evidence lies at least partly in the notion that no judicial body can find a fact established without evidence to support that finding. Aside from inferences,[40] the only exception to this rule is the concept of judicial knowledge (known as "judicial notice" in England). Although this part of the law of evidence will not commonly be of relevance in tribunal hearings, it could sometimes arise, and in any event it indicates the importance of the requirement of evidence in support of any fact.

There is a related question, namely whether a medical or general member can use his knowledge to supplement or contradict evidence led, as opposed to simply allowing for interpretation of that evidence. This is dealt with below.[41]

---

[39] *In re B (Children) (Care Proceedings: Standard of Proof)* [2008] UKHL 35; [2009] 1 AC 11; [2008] 3 WLR 1 at paras 70 and 72.
[40] On inferences, see paras 5.123 *et seq* below.
[41] At paras 5.22 *et seq*.

Judicial knowledge centres on the idea that certain facts are either   **5.14**
(1) so notorious or (2) so able to be immediately ascertained, that it
would be pointless adducing evidence of them. In both England and
Scotland, the law in this area is similar, therefore cases from both
jurisdictions are relevant here.

Notorious facts

These are facts that will not require to be proven, simply because   **5.15**
no one would seriously dispute them, and to require that they be
established by evidence would be both absurd and time-consuming.
This category is extremely wide and can hardly be quantified. A few
examples will suffice: the fact that night follows day; that a car is
a mechanically propelled vehicle and that a pushbike is not; that
2 weeks is too short for human gestation;[42] that cats are usually kept
for domestic purposes.[43] There are some less obvious examples of
notorious facts. For example, *Taylor* v *Glasgow Corporation*[44] was
a damages action following the death of a child who ate poisonous
berries. It was held by the House of Lords to be within judicial
knowledge that children are prone to be drawn to and tempted
to eat colourful berries whenever they can be reached. The fact of
such a temptation on the part of children generally, was notorious
and so was within judicial knowledge. In *Doyle* v *Ruxton*,[45] for the
purposes of a liquor licensing prosecution, the High Court held that
drinks with certain well-known brand names – such as McEwan's
Export, Guinness, Carlsberg Special Brew and Holsten Pils lager –
are all alcoholic drinks. This fact was deemed to be within judicial
knowledge. On the other hand, the fact that pension funds had
recently, at the time of the hearing, been falling in value was held to
be a fact that is not within judicial knowledge – evidence on this issue
would be required.[46]

The fact that no assumption can be made without evidence,   **5.16**
even where there seems to be a perfectly logical conclusion, can be
demonstrated by the decision in *Kennedy* v *Smith & Ansvar Insurance
Co Ltd*.[47] There, Lord McDonald in the Outer House of the Court of
Session had regard, in an insurance dispute arising out of a road traffic
accident, to evidence suggesting that the driver was unaccustomed to
drinking alcohol and that he had taken alcohol on an empty stomach.
These factors were treated by the court as adminicles of evidence

---

[42] *R* v *Luffe* (1807) 8 East 193.
[43] *Nye* v *Niblett* [1918] 1 KB 23.
[44] [1922] 1 AC 44; [1921] All ER Rep 1.
[45] 1999 SLT 487; 1998 SCCR 467.
[46] *Kennedy* v *Kennedy* 2004 SLT (Sh Ct) 102; 2004 SCLR 777.
[47] 1975 SC 266; 1976 SLT 110.

that supported an inference that the accident had been caused by the driver having been under the influence of alcohol. The Inner House, in overturning the original decision, held that such matters were not within judicial knowledge and that medical evidence on the effect of alcohol in these circumstances should have been led. This could be a relevant consideration in tribunal cases, where the tribunal should be careful not to seek to fill any gaps in the evidence with the knowledge of the medical or general member, no matter how clear the conclusion must be. Although there is the power on the part of the tribunal to draw inferences, as discussed below,[48] these apply in only the most obvious cases, and this does not cover inferences that involve filling any gaps in medical evidence.[49]

Judicial notice after inquiry

5.17   These cases are more difficult and involve a party claiming that a fact is within judicial knowledge since it has been verified by the tribunal after checking with a reliable source. An example is the definition of a word contained in a dictionary – such a definition can be regarded as being within judicial knowledge. In *Inland Revenue Commissioners v Russell*,[50] the word "stepchild" in a tax statute was interpreted by the House of Lords with reference to the dictionary meaning of that word. Another example might be a map or a historical reference work. However, not all reference works fall within this category.[51] For example, in the Outer House case of *Cavin v Kinnaird*,[52] it was held that the stopping distances in the Highway Code could not replace the leading of expert evidence on likely stopping distances. However, such data could be used to "check evidence given in court".[53] More recently, the Inner House has stated, in the context of a medical negligence action, that the content of medical textbooks, no matter how authoritative, are not within judicial knowledge, and such content would obtain any evidential value only if put to a medical witness to be commented upon.[54] In tribunal hearings, a similar rule would apply: where a party seeks to challenge the medical evidence

---

[48] See paras 5.123 *et seq.*
[49] See further discussion of this issue at para 5.123 below.
[50] 1955 SC 237; 1955 SLT 255.
[51] In the case of terminology considered by a tribunal, where there is a statutory meaning for a word or phrase, this will be the meaning to be used, and a dictionary could not be used to assist. Another source of the meaning of a word or phrase in a statute (other than being defined there) might be the meaning ascribed to it by a court in a previous case, perhaps when used in a different, but analogous, statutory provision, whether in Scotland, elsewhere in the UK or even abroad.
[52] 1994 SLT 111; 1993 SCLR 618.
[53] *Ibid* per Temporary Judge Coutts at 113.
[54] *Gerrard v Edinburgh NHS Trust Royal Infirmary* 2005 1 SC 192.

of, for instance, the RMO, opinion evidence will almost always be required from a medical professional and not from, for example, a medical textbook. The reason for this is that in the realm of scientific evidence there is clear room for argument and while the authors of a textbook might have a view on (for example) the classic symptoms of a particular mental disorder, another medical professional may have written a textbook or academic paper offering the opposite or a different viewpoint. The tribunal has no way of being sure, therefore, of how representative the opinion being put before the tribunal actually is. There is no way of testing this since the author of the textbook is not present as a witness and cannot, therefore, be cross-examined.

On the other hand, where a reference work, such as the British National Formulary,[55] is put to a witness, since parts of this would be regarded as purely reference material, it is more likely to be accepted as a source that is within judicial knowledge, but only as far as the purely factual medical material in that publication is concerned.   **5.18**

The content of the law

The content of Scots law, from whatever source, is regarded as being within judicial knowledge. Foreign law is not and has to be proven as if it were a fact. For these purposes, English law is regarded as foreign law. This does not mean, for example, that English law must be ignored by the tribunal where no evidence is led to establish its content. Where Scots and English law are the same, English case law will be within judicial knowledge. However, where the issue before the tribunal is the content of English law, and where Scots law is distinct in the area, the content of English law will require to be proven as a fact.   **5.19**

Judicial knowledge of Scots law extends to relevant Acts of Parliament (both from the Scottish and Westminster Parliaments) case law, Acts of Sederunt and Adjournal and applicable EU law.   **5.20**

It seems possible that the content of Scots law could be regarded as within judicial knowledge as a result of the notorious nature of the law. This was the basis of the decision in *Valentine* v *Macphail*,[56] where a Bench of Five Judges in the High Court held that the fact that a Camic breathalyser machine was an approved device for the purposes of the road traffic legislation was within judicial knowledge as a fact that had been ascertained by the sheriff from earlier cases   **5.21**

---

[55] This publication is produced jointly by the British Medical Association and the Royal Pharmaceutical Society of Great Britain and is presently in its 57th edition, published in March 2009, and can be viewed from www.bnf.org.
[56] 1986 JC 131.

where the relevant order had been produced (in this case it had not). Such uses of notoriety on the content of the law will, however, be rare.

Personal/professional knowledge held by the tribunal member

5.22   Sometimes, a member of a judicial body will attempt to use his own personal knowledge to infer that a fact is established. This is not an example of judicial knowledge. Tribunal members must clear their minds of all personal and professional knowledge and decide the case only on the evidence presented. In the case of the mental health tribunal, the medical member will have professional knowledge of issues relevant to each case. The general member will almost invariably have some experience in a mental healthcare profession or be a former or current mental health service user. Indeed, that is the whole point of the thinking behind the rules on the eligibility criteria for tribunal panel membership. This brings us to consider the use by the medical and general member of their expertise as tribunal members. In order to consider this fully, we need to examine the law surrounding the use of personal knowledge by judges in the public courts, then by considering the rules that apply in other tribunals, mainly arbitral and employment tribunals.

5.23   Turning to public court judges first of all, the starting point is that judges must be very careful in cases where they might be seen to be gathering evidence; in such cases the courts have held that this effectively constitutes the conversion of the judge into a witness. So, in *Hattie* v *Leitch*,[57] where the sheriff examined the locus after the evidence was over, in order to test the accuracy of an account of events given by certain witnesses, he was held to have gathered his own evidence and so his decision was overturned on appeal.[58]

5.24   Another similar example is the case of *Aitken* v *Wood*.[59] This was a criminal case in which the justices were considering a charge of assault. The complainer alleged that she had been assaulted when her arm was seized and compressed by the accused. During her evidence she had indicated that she was willing to show her arm, which was bruised, she alleged, as a result of the assault. However, she did not actually show her arm during her evidence (it is not clear why not – it seems that the question on her willingness to show was not followed up). The justices retired to consider their verdict and during the

---

[57]   (1889) 16 R 1128.
[58]   For an example of an employment tribunal appeal where it was held a lay member had wrongly gathered evidence in relation to the case, see *Halford* v *Sharples* [1992] ICR 146. The position of lay members with some specialist knowledge is discussed below.
[59]   1921 JC 84.

deliberation period they asked to see the complainer in chambers. One of the justices was a doctor. They examined the complainer's arm but there was no evidence of any questions having been put to her or of any exchange of any kind between the complainer and the justices. Neither the prosecution nor defence lawyers were present. The accused was not present. The accused was convicted and appealed. The appeal was successful and his conviction was quashed (cancelled). It was held that there was an irregularity in the proceedings. By examining the arm, the justices were essentially taking fresh evidence. This happened in the absence of the accused, and so was a fatal irregularity.

Of course, the public judge example is not entirely analogous to that of the medical or general member on the tribunal. In an arbitration, however, there is sometimes a skilled decision-maker. Arbitration is common as a method of dispute resolution in commercial contract cases. In such contracts, the parties may agree that any dispute arising out of the contract should be arbitrated. One of the main perceived advantages of arbitration in comparison to litigating a dispute through the public courts is that the arbitrator is usually not a lawyer, but instead is someone with expertise in the subject-matter of the contract. So, he may be a surveyor, or an engineer or an accountant. The idea behind this is that such a decision-maker is more suited to understanding the technical issues arising out of the contract, and so will be less likely to misunderstand the issues inherent in any dispute arising out of the contract, and will be able to take the evidence in a more efficient and less time-consuming manner. A large volume of jurisprudence has arisen around the issue of how far the arbitrator can go in using that knowledge in the decision-making process. The Scottish case of *Dyer* v *Wilsons and Clyde Coal Co Ltd*[60] was an arbitration under the Workmen's Compensation Act 1906 for compensation for incapacity suffered following an accident at work. The arbitrator dismissed the claim as irrelevant on a number of grounds, before first hearing evidence. One of those grounds was that the claimant had applied to work at only five pits. The arbitrator formed the view that such applications did not represent sufficient activity on the part of the claimant so that it could be said (as the claimant did) that work was not available in the area. The arbitrator stated:

> "It is within my knowledge from constant experience of arbitrations under this Act in the western district of Fife that it is not a sufficient test of the market in the Lochgelly district for such work as the claimant was certified to be fit for. There is a market for such work."

5.25

---

[60] 1915 SC 199; 1914 2 SLT 411.

The Inner House sent the case back to the arbitrator for a full hearing. The Lord President said this:

> "I do not say that ... local knowledge could not be used as an element in the proof; but the arbitrator used his local knowledge as the sole evidence in the case."[61]

5.26   There has been some further judicial comment in this area in England. It is clear that the comments there are applicable in similar Scottish cases. Two situations have developed in the English case law. The first involves the issue of the extent to which an arbitrator can use his own expert knowledge to understand the issues and the second involves the extent to which a case can be decided on the basis of an argument or material not placed before the arbitrator during the proceedings.

5.27   The main case here is *Checkpoint Ltd v Strathclyde Pension Fund*.[62] This was a rent review case where the arbitrator specifically relied upon his own personal experience of transactions in the area concerned.

The Court of Appeal, after reviewing the authorities, formulated a new test in these terms:

> "... is the information upon which the arbitrator has relied information of the kind and within the range of knowledge one would reasonably expect the arbitrator to have acquired if, as is required by the terms of the lease, he is experienced in the letting and/or valuation of property which is of a similar nature to the premises, is situated in the same region as the premises and used for purposes similar to those authorised under the lease. If he uses knowledge of that kind he acts fairly; if he draws on knowledge outside that field, then the rule is quite clear".[63]

The court went on to cite, with approval, the following passages from the earlier Court of Appeal case of *Fox v Wellfair Ltd*.[64]

Lord Denning MR:

> "His [the arbitrator's] function is not to supply evidence for the defendants but to adjudicate upon the evidence given before him. He can and should use his special knowledge so as to understand the evidence that is given – the letters which have passed – the usage of the trade – the dealings in the market – and to appreciate the worth of all that he sees upon a view. But he cannot use his special knowledge – or at any rate he should not use

---

[61] See also the Scottish cases of *Black v John Williams & Co* 1923 SC 510 and *Millar and Partners v Edinburgh Corporation* 1978 SC 1.
[62] [2003] EWCA Civ 84.
[63] *Ibid* at para 31.
[64] [1981] 2 Lloyd's Rep 514.

it – so as to provide evidence on behalf of the defendants which they have not chosen to provide for themselves. For then he would be discarding the role of an impartial arbitrator and assuming the role of advocate for the defaulting side. At any rate he should not use his own knowledge to derogate from the evidence of the plaintiffs' experts – without putting his own knowledge to them and giving them a chance of answering it and showing that his view is wrong."[65]

Dunn LJ said this:

"If the expert arbitrator, as he may be entitled to do, forms a view of the facts different from that given in the evidence which might produce a contrary result to that which emerges from the evidence, then he should bring that view to the attention of the parties."[66]

The court in *Checkpoint* continued:

"Thus the question becomes: was the arbitrator supplying evidence of a market and demand in it, or was he adjudicating upon it? Was he evaluating the evidence before him or introducing new and different evidence?"[67]

In considering whether the evidence is new or not, the Court of Appeal in *Checkpoint* again adopted the approach favoured in an earlier case, namely *Winchester City Council* v *Secretary of State for the Environment*,[68] a planning case involving whether a site visit led to the consideration of "any new evidence". In considering the question, Forbes, J said this:[69]

    5.28

"What does 'new evidence' in this context mean? ... I think that what it means is simply this: that, if what is seen on a view raises a point that was either not raised during evidence or argument at the inquiry or, if it was raised, was taken as being so peripheral as to be of virtually no account, then there is a duty to reconvene the inquiry or at least to give an opportunity of making representations. If, however, when [what] is seen on a view simply serves to underline or give greater emphasis to some point that was raised at the inquiry, then no such opportunity need to be given. Any other view of the matter seems to me to result in a multiplicity of opportunities for making further representations."

So, there are two points to be drawn from the *Checkpoint* case:

(1) where the reference clause (arbitration clause in the contract) requires the arbitrator to possess certain skills or expertise (as

---

[65] [1981] 2 Lloyd's Rep 514 at 522.
[66] *Ibid* at 529.
[67] [2003] EWCA Civ 84 at para 33.
[68] (1978) 36 P & CR 455.
[69] *Ibid* at 466–467.

is required of the medical and general member of the mental health tribunal) he may use that skill or expertise to assist in the determination of the case, but;

(2) where his conclusions derive from a consideration of points not put by the parties or put to the parties during the arbitration, the arbitrator should reconvene the arbitration and allow the parties an opportunity to address the arbitral tribunal on those conclusions.[70]

Regarding point (2), it has been stated that an arbitrator who has taken into account unseen material is in effect giving evidence to himself.[71] Tackaberry and Marriott, authors in international arbitration, take the view that the tribunal member should subject the new "evidence" to the same scrutiny as any other piece of factual evidence: the parties should be given an opportunity to comment on it and should be able to "cross-examine" the tribunal member on his view.[72] In fact, the parties should be allowed, if deemed useful, to recall any witnesses who have given evidence or to call new ones, to address the point being made by the tribunal member. Of course, the re-calling of witnesses could be avoided if the tribunal member puts his point while a witness is giving evidence. These comments apply equally to medical and general members of the tribunal.

5.29   Throughout any "rectification" process adopted by the tribunal, it must keep an open mind to the possibility that it might be dissuaded on the "new" point raised by the medical or general member. This will be difficult, but will ultimately be judged on the nature of the procedure adopted to redress the balance and how he puts his point to the parties; the language used by the tribunal member would be best to be in the form of a suggestion rather than a point the member is sure about.

As Tackaberry and Marriott put it, in the context of an arbitrator's view conflicting with the evidence:

"The progenitor of an idea often has a strong emotional link with it. Arbitrators who volunteer new directions of enquiry must try particularly hard to understand any reasoned objection to them: and seek to avoid holding too tightly to the original idea."[73]

---

[70] For a recent case where the arbitrator was held to have failed to follow this course of action, leading to a successful challenge, see *Guardcliffe Properties Ltd* v *City & St James* [2003] EWHC 215.

[71] See Dunn LJ in *Fox* at 658, quoted in J A Tackaberry and A Marriott, *Bernstein's Handbook of Arbitration and Dispute Resolution Practice*, vol 1 (4th edn, 2003) at p 165 (para 2–437)).

[72] See Tackaberry and Marriott, n 71 above.

[73] *Ibid*, p 163 (para 2–431).

However, where the tribunal member reasons to a point in con-   5.30
sequence of a submission by one of the parties, this conclusion
need not be referred back to the parties for comment. This was
the decision of Judge Havelock-Allan QC in the Bristol Mercantile
Court decision in *Al Hahda Trading Co v Tradigrain*.[74] There, the
following was said:

> "It is well settled that a tribunal acts unfairly if it thinks of an argument
> which neither party has raised, keeps the argument up its sleeve and then
> decides the claim on the basis of that argument in its award. But it has
> never been held that a tribunal acts unfairly if it derives a conclusion
> from a submission which one or other party has made without putting
> the conclusion to that party for comment. That is the very function of a
> judicial or quasi-judicial tribunal. If arbitrators were required to consult
> the parties about their interpretation of the submissions made to them,
> arbitrations would never end. Only if the arbitrators consider that they
> have an entirely new point in mind, which neither party has addressed,
> they are obliged to revert to the parties to give them an opportunity of
> dealing with it."[75]

All of the above comments could be applied to the use of specialised
knowledge or new evidence or a point in consequence of a submission,
in relation to the proceedings of the mental health tribunal.

Before coming to address the mental health tribunal more specific-   5.31
ally, however, this kind of question has been covered in another
major statutory tribunal, namely the employment tribunal. Like
arbitrations, employment tribunals include decision-makers who are
not legally qualified. In fact the composition of most employment
tribunals are not dissimilar to that of the mental health tribunal, with
one legally qualified Chairman (equivalent of the Convener) and two
lay members, one with an employer's representative background and
the other with experience as an employee's representative.[76] Usually,
there is no particular attempt to match cases with lay members
according to their specialised knowledge but, on occasion, the lay
member may happen to have such knowledge relevant to the issues
in the case.

In dealing with this type of situation, Harvey distinguishes the use
by lay members of their industrial knowledge in a general way, from
the use of such knowledge in a specialist way. In the former case:

---

[74] [2002] 2 Lloyd's Rep 512.
[75] *Ibid* at para 52.
[76] The chairman does sit alone in some cases, while in others he might sit with only
one lay member. For a full discussion of employment tribunal membership, see
P Elias and B Napier (eds), *Harvey on Employment Law and Industrial Relations*,
para T21–28.

"they may use their expertise for the purpose of explaining and understanding the evidence which they hear, and in order to fill gaps in the
evidence about matters which will be obvious to them but which might
be obscure to a layman".[77]

The authors go on to refer to the case of *Kirton v Tetrosyl Ltd*[78] as an
example of a case in which medical knowledge was used in this way.
To put it another way, the knowledge of the lay member can be used
in order to weigh up, assess or interpret evidence.[79]

5.32   Turning to the use of knowledge in a specialist manner, we can
see, in the following passage, a similar approach to that used in the
Checkpoint and *Fox* cases (above) to the use of specialised knowledge
which is not canvassed before the parties:

"It not infrequently happens that one or other of the lay members will
have a specialised knowledge or experience of a particular matter which
is under consideration in the case they are hearing. It may also happen
that such member will disagree with evidence that has been given ... in
relation to that matter on the ground that it is contrary to his or her own
special knowledge. The tribunal as a whole might then, when the time
comes to give its decision, wish to rely on that member's expertise as a
reason for rejecting the evidence which has been given. Whenever this
situation arises, the member concerned is under an obligation, not only to
disclose his specialist knowledge, but to bring to the attention of the party
whose evidence is disputed ... the facts that cause him to disagree with
the evidence given, so as to give the party an opportunity to deal with the
point or, if necessary, to apply for an adjournment to enable him to do so.
It is only when this procedure is carried out that a tribunal will be entitled
to rely upon the specialised knowledge of its lay member in preference to
evidence that has been given in the case."[80]

5.33   Applying all of this to mental health tribunal decisions, it is clear that
the medical and general members can draw on their own experience
in order to understand, interpret and assess evidence within their
own specialisms, but they cannot use that specialist knowledge
to contradict specialist evidence led from witnesses, unless their
provisional view on the matter is put to the relevant witnesses

---

[77] P Elias and B Napier (eds), *Harvey on Employment Law and Industrial
Relations*, para T888. The author goes on to cite the Employment Appeal Tribunal
case of *Dugdale v Kraft Foods Ltd* [1977] 1 All ER 454 at 459 as authority for this
proposition.
[78] [2002] IRLR 840.
[79] See the comments to this effect by Talbot J in *Hammington v Berker Sportcraft
Ltd* [1980] ICR 248 at 252.
[80] Elias and Napier (eds) (n 77 above), para T889. The author cites the *Dugdale* case
(see preceding footnote) as well as the case of *Hammington v Berker Sportcraft Ltd*
[1980] ICR 248.

and they are provided with an opportunity to comment on that provisional view. In the event that these parameters are exceeded, there is a distinct possibility of a successful appeal on the basis of a procedural impropriety.

There are at least two other uses for the specialist knowledge of   5.34
the medical and general members. The first is to assist the other two members in understanding and focusing the issues relevant to the case which fall within the expertise of that member; this can happen both during the pre-hearing meeting as well as during any adjournment in the hearing and even during deliberations. This will avoid the need for the legal member, and possibly the third member, to ask detailed questions of a background nature. The member with the specialist medical or other knowledge will be able to explain certain concepts and terminology to those untrained in the area. These issues might revolve, for example, around the proper provision of anti-psychotic medication, whether certain community alternatives have been explored fully, whether certain treatments such as occupational therapy or psychological therapies could and should be made available to the patient, and so on. The second use is that such specialist knowledge can lead to the formulation of proper and focused questioning of specialist witnesses. In a sense, only those with specialist knowledge will know which questions to ask, how to ask them in order to secure the desired information and whether an issue is worth exploring further.

This leads to a related point: that the tribunal should not base its decision on whether its members (or one or some of them) would have acted differently to the specialists (RMO and MHO, for example) involved in the case, but instead on whether, objectively viewed (and on the basis of a full understanding of the issues and evidence), the relevant statutory criteria are satisfied.

Finally, it should be noted that the legal member is in a peculiar   5.35
position here. His specialist knowledge is not of fact (and any knowledge he happens to have of fact must be ignored) but of law. This does not mean that he has the final say on any legal issues, only that he will be in a position to explain any legal terminology to the other members (as well as to the other tribunal participants) and his view on the content and effect of the law is likely to hold more influence than that of the other members at the deliberation stage, just as their view on matters falling within their specialisms will likewise be highly regarded and respected.

The best evidence rule

Generally speaking, in any civil case, and therefore in a tribunal case,   5.36
the best evidence available must be produced. This rule applies most

obviously to real evidence (things), which will hardly ever feature in tribunal cases but it does have some application to documentary evidence. It has been made clear that where a document is fundamental to a case, non-production of the original (as opposed to a copy) can be fatal, unless a "no fault" explanation for the absence of the original can be provided. In *Scottish and Universal Newspapers* v *Gherson's Trs*,[81] certain financial records were not produced at all. This was fatal to the admissibility of oral evidence as to their content. The Inner House, in supporting the decision of the Outer House judge, held that the pursuers had failed to take "proper and elementary steps" to retain the documents, and that as the absence of the documents was therefore not due to an absence of fault on the part of the pursuers, the oral evidence was inadmissible. The court also indicated that, in considering such issues, the extent of any prejudice that would result to the other party would be a factor. There is some discussion in the main civil cases on the issue of prejudice, but while prejudice plays a key role in similar criminal cases, it holds less prominence in civil cases. Having said that, there is some emphasis on quality of written evidence since there is a requirement that any statement is signed.[82] The word "statement" here should be interpreted using the definition of that word in the Civil Evidence (Scotland) Act 1988, s 9: "'statement' includes any representation (however made or expressed) of fact or opinion but does not include a statement in a precognition".[83]

This definition is extremely wide, and it seems that any written material prepared by an individual and produced to the tribunal must be signed. There is no mention of whether or not an original signature is required, but it would seem that it is not, since this would create immense difficulties in some cases. For example, the original CTO application is usually retained at the Tribunal headquarters and is not made available to the tribunal members. In any event, there is an emphasis in the Rules on the conduct of proceedings as informally as the circumstances permit,[84] and this would appear to include allowing copies of any signed statement to be a substitute for an original, as long as there is no argument that the copy is not a genuine or accurate one.

5.37   Where the other parties to be represented at the tribunal agree that copies of documents will suffice, it would be wise for the party relying on the copy to enter into a written agreement with the other

---

[81] 1987 SC 27; 1988 SLT 109.

[82] See r 60.

[83] See above at para 5.03 on the application of the 1988 Act to tribunal proceedings.

[84] Rule 63(2)(a). For further discussion of this provision in various contexts, see paras 4.43, 4.67, 4.93, 4.103 and 4.117.

parties in advance, agreeing that the copy is a true replica of the original document. This agreement is called a joint minute, and is used in civil proceedings regularly. Alternatively, certain statutory shortcuts are available in respect of documentary evidence. The relevant provisions are ss 5–6 of the Civil Evidence (Scotland) Act 1988:

s 5: a document which is certified as being part of business records will be taken to be so and no witness need speak to it;

s 6: a document that is authenticated by the author as a true copy of the original will be treated as an original (however, a witness will be needed to speak to it, unless also certified in terms of s 5).

In connection with public records, under s 41 of the Registration of Births, Deaths and Marriages (Scotland) Act 1965, an extract or abbreviated certificate of birth, death or marriage is self-proving.

Hearsay evidence

Hearsay evidence has been defined as: "evidence of what another person has said (orally, in writing or by other physical expression)".[85]

5.38

There are rules to protect against the admission of hearsay evidence, but they apply mainly in criminal cases. The rationale behind any exclusion or limitation of the admissibility of hearsay evidence is that it is not the best evidence available of what was expressed. It is sometimes viewed as an example of the best evidence rule. This means that the other party does not have the opportunity to cross-examine the person(s) who made the statement or had the conversation. In addition, the witness's demeanour is lost – the tribunal cannot assess properly whether or not the witness is credible and reliable[86] if he is not giving evidence himself. The origins of the rule against admission of hearsay evidence to some extent lie in the perception that juries could not be trusted to assess how much weight to give to such evidence.[87]

The position in Scotland in civil cases is regulated by the Civil Evidence (Scotland) Act 1988. The important provisions of this Act are:

5.39

---

[85] M L Ross and J Chalmers, *Walker and Walker: The Law of Evidence in Scotland* (3rd edn, 2009), para 8.1.1.
[86] On credibility, see paras 5.119 *et seq* below; and, on reliability, see paras 5.121 *et seq*.
[87] See the comments by Lord Carswell in *R v Abdroikov* [2007] 1 WLR 2679 at para 55.

"s 2 Admissibility of hearsay.

(1) In any civil proceedings –
   (a) evidence shall not be excluded solely on the ground that it is hearsay;
   (b) a statement made by a person otherwise than in the course of the proof shall be admissible as evidence of any matter contained in the statement of which direct oral evidence by that person would be admissible; and
   (c) the court, or as the case may be the jury, if satisfied that any fact has been established by evidence in those proceedings, shall be entitled to find that fact proved by the evidence notwithstanding that the evidence is hearsay.

...

s 9 Interpretation.

In this Act, unless the context otherwise requires –
... 'statement' includes any representation (however made or expressed) of fact or opinion but does not include a statement in a precognition."

5.40   As already discussed,[88] tribunal proceedings are classed as civil proceedings for the purposes of the 1988 Act, so these provisions apply. One point of general note is that whether the statement maker gives evidence of his own hearsay statement or not, the courts are willing to admit evidence of that statement. In F v *Kennedy (No 2)*[89] a child witness did give evidence. However, the statement in question was not put to him. In *Sanderson v McManus*[90] the child was not called to give evidence at all. In both cases the hearsay evidence was admitted.

Hearsay evidence and a precognition

5.41   As will be seen from the definition of "statement" in the 1988 Act above, it does not include a precognition. The term "precognition" is undefined by the Act, but case law makes it clear that it is an account taken from a witness and put into the words of the statement taker – not the actual words of the witness. If an account is in the words of a witness, it is a statement. This distinction is crucial since a precognition is inadmissible while a statement is admissible.

5.42   The objection to the admissibility of a precognition (which also exists in criminal cases), as Lord Justice-Clerk Thomson put it in the criminal case of *Kerr v HM Advocate*,[91] is that in such cases the account is "filtered through the mind of another".[92] It is unlike a *verbatim* (word-for-word) account and so is not completely

---

[88] See above at para 5.03.
[89] 1993 SLT 1284; 1992 SCLR 750.
[90] 1997 SC (HL) 55; 1997 SLT 629.
[91] 1958 JC 14; 1958 SLT 82.
[92] 1958 JC 14 at 19 per LJ-C Thomson.

reliable evidence of what was actually said. The distinction between the two has been argued in various cases in Scotland. It has been made clear in a number of these cases that it is only the precognition document itself that is inadmissible. In other words, evidence can be led from the precognoscer who may be asked what he recollects of what was *actually* said. This is not a breach of the rule against a precognition. The position was put in this way by Lord Morton of Shuna:

> "It appears to me that in civil proceedings the only reason for the exclusion of a precognition is that what is stated in the precognition is or may be coloured by the mind of the precognoscer who produces in the precognition an edited version of what the witness has said. This would exclude the actual document prepared by the precognoscer but would not exclude evidence of what the witness actually said to the precognoscer prior to the preparation of the document. I am of the opinion that the exception in the definition of 'statement' in the Civil Evidence (Scotland) Act excluding 'a statement in a precognition' means what is recorded in a document prepared by the precognoscer and does not exclude evidence of what the person said to the precognoscer in interview. On that basis Miss Neilson's evidence, for what it is worth, is admissible."[93]

Having said this, it has been made clear by the courts that the account given by the precognoscer in such a situation is not likely to be regarded as a strong piece of evidence.[94] Alternatively, the common law can be relied upon to seek admission of a precognition where the witness has, by the time of the hearing, died.[95]   **5.43**

A precognition might be used in a number of circumstances in a mental health tribunal context. For example, where an incident occurs which involves the patient in circumstances where an official written record is taken by a third party witness, that statement might, in fact, be a precognition. Where that third party is a police officer, it is likely that the statement taken by him will be a statement proper, and not a precognition. However, where the third party witness is, for example, a housing officer, a neighbour, a nurse or a doctor, or even   **5.44**

---

[93] *Anderson v Jas B Fraser & Co Ltd* 1992 SLT 1129 at 1130. See also Lord Clyde in *Cavanagh v BP Chemicals* 1995 SLT 1287, affirmed by Lord Hardie in *Ellison v Inspirations East Ltd* 2003 SLT 291.

[94] See *Cavanagh v BP Chemicals* 1995 SLT 1287, where Lord Clyde commented upon the absence of an exact record of what the witness had said as being a weakening factor; see also *Anderson v Jas B Fraser & Co Ltd* 1992 SLT 1129 per Lord Morton.

[95] For the boundaries of this common law exception, see the cases of *William Thyne (Plastics) Ltd v Stenhouse Reed Shaw (Scotland) Ltd* 1979 SLT (Notes) 93; *Pirie v Geddes* 1973 SLT (Sh Ct) 81; [1975] Crim LR 107; and *Moffat v Hunter* 1974 SLT (Sh Ct) 42.

someone visiting a psychiatric ward, the account of events may well be filtered through the mind of the statement taker, in which case it is a precognition. This would apply to such an account taken from the patient or from any other witness.[96] In such a case, the precognition itself (the document in which it is embodied) is inadmissible. An oral "reading" of the account during the hearing is also inadmissible, as it is taken from an inadmissible document. So, where a witness at the hearing, for example the RMO, seeks to recount an incident taken from a precognition which was collected from, say, a nursing assistant who witnessed and recorded in her own words an incident in which the patient is said to have behaved violently, the RMO's evidence is inadmissible. Where the statement taker, for example the ward manager, gives oral evidence of what the nursing assistant said in her account, that will be admissible hearsay evidence, since it is not coming from the precognition, it is coming from the memory of the ward manager as to what was said to her by the nursing assistant.

Allegations of criminal activity and hearsay evidence

5.45   In many tribunal cases, there will be allegations made against the patient of behaviour that might constitute criminal activity. These will usually be allegations of aggressive, verbally abusive or truculent behaviour, which may amount to the commission of a breach of the peace; or violent or aggressive behaviour, which could constitute an assault. Whether or not the police are involved in such incidents, the patient's representative must take great care when such allegations are expected to be made. As discussed below, the patient will have the protection of the self-incrimination privilege.[97] In addition, there is a rule in criminal proceedings against the admissibility of secondary hearsay evidence. This rule basically excludes hearsay evidence where the purpose of leading it is to establish the truth of the content of the hearsay statement, as opposed to simply that the statement was made. It is probably going too far to say that such evidence is inadmissible in tribunal proceedings, since the proceedings are not criminal in nature and since the fairness of the tribunal proceedings must be viewed as a whole.[98] The tribunal should, however, consider with great care what weight it is proper to give to such evidence,

---

[96] In the case of *HM Advocate* v *McSween* 2007 SLT 645 the High Court suggests that the question of whether a document is a precognition or statement depends partly on the stage in the proceedings reached when the document is compiled. This consideration is not relevant in civil proceedings.

[97] See below at paras 5.78 *et seq.*

[98] For an employment tribunal case in which hearsay evidence consisting of an allegation of a crime was admitted on appeal, see *Coral Squash Club* v *Matthews* [1979] IRLR 390.

given the parallel between criminal proceedings and tribunal cases, both involving considerations of the liberty of individuals.[99] A full discussion of the nature and extent of the secondary hearsay rule is outwith the scope of this text, and the reader is referred to the relevant parts in the main texts on the law of evidence in Scotland.[100]

There are many cases in which second-hand accounts are provided   **5.46** to the tribunal, and in some cases, these are third hand or even fourth hand. Where these accounts do not come from a precognition and where they do not relate to alleged criminal activity and represent secondary hearsay evidence, they will be admissible. However, this does not mean that they have to be accepted; the tribunal should treat such evidence with caution, and if the evidence relates to a critical point, the tribunal may wish to take steps to allow the original statement maker to give evidence to the tribunal. The words of Munby J,[101] as cited below,[102] should be borne in mind.

THE EXCLUSION OF EVIDENCE

At the outset, the idea of the power to exclude evidence must be   **5.47** grasped. A judicial body has the power to declare that certain evidence is inadmissible. This means that the evidence is not permitted to be heard (in the case of oral evidence) or produced (in the case of written evidence). This may be for a number of reasons, and these are discussed below. However, the difference between admissibility of evidence (that is: whether it is permitted to be heard/produced) and the weight to be attached to evidence that is so permitted is a key distinction. If evidence is legally admissible (can be heard or produced) this does not mean that it has to be accepted as influential by the tribunal. If the evidence is inadmissible, the tribunal must simply leave it out of account. Where evidence is heard/produced following an admissibility debate, the evidence is assessed like any other evidence. This involves placing weight on each piece of evidence and feeding that assessment into an overall evaluation process. This evaluation process is discussed below.[103] The important point for the moment is to understand that if the evidence is regarded as inadmissible, it must be ignored; if it is admissible, it must be heard and evaluated.

---

[99] See further on this parallel at para 1.38.

[100] These are listed above, at n 1.

[101] In *R (on the application of DJ) v Mental Health Review Tribunal; R (on the application of AN) v Mental Health Review Tribunal* [2005] EWHC 587 (Admin) at para 129.

[102] See para 5.56 below.

[103] See paras 5.118 *et seq* below.

5.48   We now turn to the circumstances in which evidence may be excluded from consideration by the tribunal (declared inadmissible). In some cases, the authority for exclusion arises from the Rules themselves; in other cases, the general civil law of evidence is the basis for the decision. The basic approach of the law of civil evidence in Scotland is that any evidence is admissible unless one of certain specified rules applies to exclude it. Where such a rule applies to evidence intended to be led, this can lead to the evidence being declared inadmissible (see the previous paragraph on admissibility). This would be done by issuing a direction to that effect.[104] In considering the possible grounds for exclusion of evidence, as a starting point it is convenient to consider those grounds specifically provided for in the Rules. Here, we find three such grounds: irrelevant evidence, improperly obtained evidence and unnecessary evidence.[105] Once these grounds are dealt with, we turn to consider any other available exclusionary devices. If one or more of the exclusionary rules (either from the general civil law or from the Rules) does not apply, the evidence is admissible and must be heard and evaluated.

Irrelevant evidence

5.49   It is essential that all evidence offered is relevant to the question(s) the tribunal is charged with answering. This may seem obvious and simple, and in many cases any evidence offered is clearly relevant. The test for relevance was set out in the case of *Strathmore Group Ltd v Credit Lyonnais* during which Lord Osborne stated: "the ultimate test [of relevance is] whether or not the material in question [has] a reasonably direct bearing on the subject under investigation".[106]

This means that the material must be not only remotely relevant, but also reasonably directly connected with the case in hand. Of course, this will vary from case to case. It seems clear and logical that where evidence sought to be presented is relevant to an issue in dispute, that evidence must be admitted.[107] Conversely, if evidence is deemed irrelevant, it must be excluded (assuming there is an

---

[104] See r 49 on directions, and the discussion at paras 7.30 *et seq*; and on the procedure for the raising admissibility issues, see paras 4.71 *et seq*.

[105] Rule 49(1)(g)(iv).

[106] 1994 SLT 1023 at 1031. The court here was simply referring to this test as approved by the Inner House in *W Alexander and Sons v Dundee Corporation* 1950 SC 123 at 131.

[107] This was the decision of the Court of Appeal in the employment tribunal case of *ALM Medical Services Ltd v Bladon* [2002] EWCA Civ 1085, and there seems no reason for this to be inapplicable in mental health tribunal cases.

argument made to that effect by one of the parties or if the tribunal takes the view that the issue of relevancy should be raised). Lord Justice Buxton put it in this way in an employment tribunal appeal in the Court of Appeal:

> "The first and most important rule of the law of evidence, though one that is not always perceived or observed, is that evidence is only admissible if it indeed is relevant to an issue between the parties ... [the disputed evidence in this case] being irrelevant, it is not evidence in the case at all."[108]

An obvious example, and one that applies regularly in mental health tribunal cases, is evidence relating to events that occurred some time before the hearing at which that evidence is being presented. The reason for the regular presentation of historical evidence, particularly by the MHO or RMO, is that the mechanics of the diagnosis of and treatment for mental disorder rely heavily on the history of the patient's behaviour, symptoms and treatment. Those treating a patient with a mental disorder will routinely rely on the complete history of the patient (in many cases spanning years or even decades) in order to seek to justify their current treatment views. In this way, where the patient has a history of mental illness, the question of relevance takes on a different dimension to that applied in cases where the focus is on a single incident. Examples of cases in which only single incidents are relevant include an accident at work and a road traffic accident, to cite two instances of case types that are regularly litigated through the public civil courts. No lawyer would reasonably suggest that in a civil road traffic case, evidence should be able to be led from others about the history of the allegedly negligent driver's past driving habits. Such material would clearly be ruled as irrelevant under Lord Osborne's test.
　　5.50

On the other hand, in mental health cases, the history of the patient is always an important consideration for the tribunal. This is particularly so in cases which are "cyclical" in nature, in other words where there is said to be a pattern: imposition of compulsory measures, leading to recovery by the patient, leading to the removal of compulsory measures, leading to relapse of the patient, leading to the imposition of compulsory measures, and so on. This is also sometimes known as the "revolving door" patient. This does not mean, however, that in cases where a patient has a history of mental illness, the MHO and RMO possess *carte blanche* to present any evidence at all, no matter how historical it might be. It could be argued, for instance, that particular evidence is based on events so long ago that it would not have a reasonably direct bearing on the
　　5.51

---

[108] *XXX* v *YYY and ZZZ* [2004] EWCA Civ 231 at paras 16 and 22.

issue before the tribunal, which in most cases would be the question of what is to happen to the patient there and then. Even so, evidence might be of events perhaps years before the hearing, but which are so serious or significant that the passage of time does not rob them of their status of having a reasonably direct bearing on consideration of what is to happen to the patient today. The converse applies also: very recent events may have little or no bearing on the issues before the tribunal.

5.52   One common example of how the relevance test might be invoked in a case involving historical evidence relates to evidence of non-compliance by a patient with advice on taking medication. It might be alleged that the patient has a long history of non-compliance with such advice. However, it could be argued that such evidence is irrelevant since it relates to non-compliance, say, 5 or 10 years ago, without any evidence of such an occurrence since then. In such a case, the tribunal will almost always hear the evidence and weigh it, perhaps placing little or no weight on the evidence due to its age. It will weigh it in the light of the whole evidence, including any expert opinion as to the significance to be put on the past events in question. It will be difficult for the tribunal to assess whether the evidence is relevant other than in the light of the whole evidence in the case. A different scenario exists where there has been a constant history of non-compliance over a long period, with little or no break. In such a case, evidence of the whole history is likely to satisfy the relevance test, as this will have a reasonably direct bearing on what might happen in the future since, here, it could be argued that there is a very well-established pattern, which would include allegations of recent instances of non-compliance.

Relevance – collateral evidence

5.53   There is another strand to the rule that evidence must be relevant in order to allow it to be considered. Evidence that is "collateral" to the issues before the tribunal should not be considered relevant. This is often also known as "similar fact" evidence and consists of evidence not directly related to the issues, but where something similar to that under consideration has occurred in the past. The party seeking to lead such evidence will usually be seeking to establish that conduct in the past by the other party (typically the patient) in a similar situation is good evidence of what is likely to have happened on the occasion in question.

5.54   From some early civil cases, it seemed that such evidence was inadmissible as irrelevant to the issues in dispute. For example, in *A v B*[109] the pursuer was suing for damages for allegedly having been

---

[109] *Sub nom Simpson* v *Melvin* (1895) 2 SLT 515.

raped by the defender. The pursuer sought to introduce evidence suggesting that the defender had raped two other women. The evidence was disallowed on the ground that it was collateral. In the course of the case, Lord President Robertson said this:

> "Experience shows that it is better to sacrifice the aid which may be got from the more or less uncertain solution of collateral issues, than to spend a great amount of time, and confuse the jury [or court or tribunal] with what, in the end, even supposing it to be certain, has only an indirect bearing on the matter in hand."[110]

On the other hand, similar fact evidence has been admitted in later Scottish civil cases. For example, in the case of *W Alexander & Sons v Dundee Corporation*[111] the pursuer bus company sought to introduce evidence of previous occasions on which its buses had slid on the stretch of road on which the accident in question had occurred. The aim was to establish that the road was in a slippery condition because of the materials used by the defenders (the local authority) in constructing the road melting and becoming slippery. The evidence was allowed and, in allowing it, Lord Justice-Clerk Thomson said this:

5.55

> "... if it is established that the skidding of these vehicles on these other occasions was truly due to the condition of the road, then it seems to me that that is not a collateral issue at all but something having a direct bearing on the decision of the present case. There no doubt comes a point at which it is possible to say that the bearing of some fact is too indirect and too remote properly to assist the Court [or tribunal] in deciding what the cause of the accident is; but I am quite clear that that point is far from being reached [in this case]".[112]

Another civil case in which similar fact evidence was allowed is *Knutzen* v *Mauritzen*,[113] where the condition of meat delivered was in dispute and where the pursuers sought to adduce evidence from another customer of the defenders who had received meat in a similarly poor state from the same consignment. This evidence was allowed as having a direct bearing on the facts in issue.

---

[110] *Simpson v Melvin* (1895) 2 SLT 515 at 515. This case pre-dates *Moorov v HM Advocate* 1938 JC 68. Corroboration of the evidence of a single witness to one offence can be obtained from the evidence of another single witness to another offence, provided the two offences are linked sufficiently closely in time, character and circumstance. Might *Simpson* be decided differently in the light of *Moorov*? However, the point remains that collateral evidence generally will not be regarded as admissible.
[111] 1950 SC 123; 1950 SLT 76.
[112] 1950 SC 123 at 131.
[113] 1918 1 SLT 85.

5.56   How does all of this apply to tribunal cases? Once again, the routine reliance on historical events by those involved in the treatment of persons with a mental disorder threatens to cloud the issue. Here, the question is usually not whether the evidence is too historical to be relevant but more whether the evidence is sufficiently similar to the issue in question to be regarded as having a reasonably direct bearing on it. An example might illustrate the point. An allegation might be made that 6 months before the admission of the patient to hospital under an emergency detention certificate, he punched someone in a bar during an argument over the result in a football match, while heavily under the influence of alcohol. It also alleged that, shortly before the granting of the certificate, the patient, for no apparent reason, verbally abused a community psychiatric nurse who had paid a home visit to check on his mental well-being. One of the arguments by the MHO seeking a full CTO at a later hearing might be that the patient is aggressive to those seeking to offer psychiatric care, and so is a danger to the safety of others. It could be argued that the incident in the pub is irrelevant, since it does not demonstrate the point being made: aggression towards healthcare professionals. Also, the violence exhibited earlier was physical, not verbal, was displayed while the patient was under the influence of alcohol, and was part of an argument on another matter and so was not spontaneous aggressive behaviour. It could be argued that such behaviour is not sufficiently similar to the behaviour relied upon to detain the patient (and being relied upon as part of the argument in favour of a CTO application) and so is collateral to the application, and as such should be excluded as irrelevant and therefore inadmissible. The English courts have recently issued some guidance on the dangers in using historical evidence in mental health tribunal cases, in particular where the evidence of previous incidents comes in the form of hearsay evidence:[114]

> "If the Tribunal is relying upon hearsay evidence it must take into account the fact that it is hearsay and must have regard to the particular dangers involved in relying upon second, third or fourth hand hearsay. The Tribunal must be appropriately cautious of relying upon assertions as to past events which are not securely recorded in contemporaneous notes, particularly if the only evidence is hearsay. The Tribunal must be alert to the well-known problem that constant repetition in 'official' reports or statements may, in the 'official' mind, turn into established fact something which rigorous forensic investigation shows is in truth nothing more than 'institutional folk-lore' with no secure foundation in either recorded or provable fact. The Tribunal must guard against too quickly jumping to conclusions adverse to the patient in relation to past events where the only direct evidence is that of the patient himself, particularly where there

---

[114] On hearsay evidence, see paras 5.38 *et seq.*

is no clear account in contemporaneous notes of what is alleged to have happened. In relation to past incidents which are centrally important to the decision it has to take the Tribunal must bear in mind the need for proof to the civil standard of proof; it must bear in mind the potential difficulties of relying upon second or third hand hearsay; and, if the incident is really fundamental to its decision, it must bear in mind that fairness may require the patient to be given the opportunity to cross-examine the relevant witness(es) if their evidence is to be relied on at all."[115]

Although this passage appears in an English case, it is clearly equally applicable in a Scottish context, particularly where, unlike in the English system,[116] all of the ordinary rules of civil evidence apply in Scottish cases.

Aside from historical evidence or evidence that is said to be collateral to the point being made, there are instances where an argument could be made to the effect that there is a straight relevancy point. It is important to note that when evidence is presented during, say, a hearing on a CTO application, its relevance to one of the criteria in s 64(5) of the 2003 Act must be established. If the evidence cannot be connected with one of the criteria there, it is irrelevant and should be disallowed. One of the criteria is that a patient's ability to make decisions about the provision of medical treatment is significantly impaired *because of* the mental disorder he is suffering from (emphasis added).[117] Any evidence of such impairment that is not connected to the mental disorder is, therefore, irrelevant, unless such evidence is relevant for the purposes of one of the other criteria. Another example relates to the "significant risk" criterion.[118] Evidence might be presented to the effect that the patient, if in the community, will be likely to present a significant risk to the health, safety or welfare of himself or the safety of others. However, this evidence would be irrelevant if it could not be asserted that the significant risk would be caused by (and only by) a failure to provide the patient with medical treatment that would alleviate an existing mental disorder. It might be the case, for example, that the significant risk would still exist

5.57

---

[115] This is from the judgment of Munby J in R *(on the application of DJ)* v *Mental Health Review Tribunal; R (on the application of AN)* v *Mental Health Review Tribunal* [2005] EWHC 587 (Admin) at para 129. On appeal, the Court of Appeal approved of these comments: R *(N)* v *Mental Health Review Tribunal (Northern Region)* [2006] QB 468 at para 77, although it is noted by the Court of Appeal that the content of the passage was not argued in detail during the appeal proceedings. Munby J's passage above is quoted with approval by R M Jones in *Mental Health Act Manual* (10th edn, 2006) at para 3–070.

[116] Tribunal Procedure (First-tier Tribunal) (Health, Education and Social Care Chamber) Rules 2008 (SI 2008/2699), r 15(2)(a).

[117] See 2003 Act, s 64(5)(d).

[118] *Ibid*, s 64(5)(c).

whether or not such medical treatment was provided. The purpose of the 2003 Act is not to allow the imposition of compulsory measures in respect of individuals who have a mental disorder and happen, for instance, to have a propensity to aggression, violence, untidiness, lack of cleanliness or odd/socially unacceptable behaviour; there must be a causal connection between them. In addition, arguments are sometimes made around issues of the availability of community care resources. For example, it might be argued that the MHO has not done enough to explore the possible commmunity resources. Such an argument might be advanced under the necessity criterion in connection with a hospital-based CTO application. However, arguments around the unavailability of adequate community-based alternatives for a patient are not relevant, since the tribunal is considering necessity on the basis of the options for care that *are* available. See Chapter 5, note 245 for further discussion in this area

It is fair to point out that, in practice, such evidence may well not be objected to as irrelevant and an argument may be made at the submissions stage that the ground has not been made out. However, it is possible that an objection could be made in cases where the evidence *could not* be relevant to one of the criteria, particularly where the objection is to a continuing line of questioning.[119]

Relevance – character attacks

5.58   The law of evidence prevents a party to proceedings from launching a general attack on the character on a witness. The only circumstances in which an attack on character is permitted is where the party launching the attack wishes to expose a lack of credibility in a witness. It would be relevant, for instance, to allege that a patient had been dishonest in the past in his assertions that he had complied with medical advice, in an attempt to cast doubt on similar assertions as made to the tribunal. However, while in general terms such a character attack is permissible, there are limits and, again, such evidence might be ruled irrelevant where it is too remote in time from the hearing or does not have a reasonably direct bearing on the matter in issue, or does not properly relate to the relevant statutory criteria.

5.59   An attempt to attack the character of a witness in order simply to paint a picture of that witness as a generally morally bad or un-desirable person should be regarded as irrelevant, even where the attack is supported by specific allegations, such as allegations of violence, aggression or of criminal or morally reprehensible behaviour. The tribunal has no locus to reach a view on the general character of an individual.

---

[119] On making admissibility objections generally, see paras 4.71 *et seq.*

Improperly obtained evidence

The way in which evidence is recovered (gathered, acquired) takes up   5.60
much more time and space in the rules relating to criminal cases than
those in civil cases. In Scotland, if evidence later relied on in a civil
action is obtained legally, albeit in an "underhand" way, it will be
admissible. The position on illegally obtained evidence is less certain.
Many cases involve divorce actions and breaches of privacy.

It is difficult to see the rules on improperly obtained evidence   5.61
having a major impact in tribunal cases. However, it is dealt with in
some detail here since directions on the exclusion of such evidence are
specifically provided for in the Rules.[120] Possible tribunal applications
of the Rules discussed next are suggested below.[121]

Obtained irregularly but not illegally

The present position is that stated in the cases of *MacNeill* v   5.62
MacNeill[122] and *Watson* v *Watson*.[123] In *MacNeill*, a divorce action
on the ground of adultery, the husband had discovered a letter
lying on the floor in the matrimonial home where it had fallen in
the absence of a letter box. He went there during the period of
separation. The letter was meant to be opened by his wife, who was
not in the home when it was delivered, and was addressed to her by
her lover, using a pseudonym. The husband opened the letter and
saw that it bore evidence of an adulterous relationship between the
author and his wife. It was held that the husband could rely on the
terms of the letter in his divorce action since he had discovered its
content by chance.

In *Watson*, another divorce action based on adultery, the husband   5.63
had discovered in an open bureau in the home where he and his
wife were residing, a torn-up draft letter written by his wife to her
lover, which was "couched in passionate terms".[124] It was held
that this letter was admissible as having been discovered by chance and
the facts that it was torn up and had not been sent were irrelevant.

Obtained illegally

As far as illegally obtained evidence is concerned, the position at   5.64
present is uncertain. The most authoritative case on the issue is the
Inner House decision of *Rattray* v *Rattray*.[125] In this case (again a

---

120 Rule 49(1)(g)(iv).
121 See para 5.68 below.
122 1929 SLT 251.
123 1934 SC 374; 1934 SLT 275.
124 These were the words of the first-instance judge Lord Wark at 1934 SC 374 at
375.
125 (1897) 5 SLT 245.

divorce action based on adultery), the husband sought to rely on a letter passing between his wife and her lover which he (the husband) had stolen from the post office. By the time of the hearing of the divorce action, he had been convicted of the offence of theft of the letter and had served a short period in prison. In a 2–1 decision, the court allowed the evidence to be admitted on the basis that if it was relevant, the court should look at it, notwithstanding the manner in which it was obtained. In spite of this decision, there are indications that the Scottish courts dislike the decision in *Rattray*. So, for example in the case of *MacColl* v *MacColl*,[126] Lord Moncrieff followed *Rattray* with reluctance, but felt that he had to since it was an Inner House decision, and so was binding on him.

5.65   More recently, there seems to have been a move towards a more case-by-case test of fairness. In *Duke of Argyll* v *Duchess of Argyll (No 3)*,[127] yet another divorce case, the husband had obtained certain diaries written by his wife by breaking into his wife's home and stealing them. The diaries were admitted in evidence. However, in proposing the use of the test used by Lord Justice-General Cooper in the criminal case of *Lawrie* v *Muir*,[128] Lord Wheatley in the Outer House said this:

> "There is no absolute rule, it being a question of the particular circum-stances of each case determining whether a particular piece of evidence should be admitted or not. Among the circumstances which may have to be taken into account are the nature of the evidence concerned, the purpose for which it is used in evidence, the manner in which it was obtained, whether its introduction is fair to the party from whom it has been illegally obtained and whether its admission will in fairness throw light on disputed facts and enable justice to be done."[129]

5.66   More recently still, in an immigration case, Lord Cameron (again in the Outer House) suggested that information obtained by immigration officials from an alleged illegal immigrant had been unfairly obtained as a caution had not been administered. Lord Cameron stated that the general test was one of fairness.[130] The driving force in this case was that the liberty of an individual was at stake, so this case would be directly applicable in any mental health tribunal environment, but particularly one where a hospital-based CTO is being sought or challenged. It remains to be seen whether the *Rattray* decision will

---

[126] 1946 SLT 312; 1946 SLT (Notes) 3.
[127] 1963 SLT (Notes) 42.
[128] 1950 JC 19; 1950 SLT 37.
[129] 1963 SLT (Notes) 42.
[130] *Oghonoghor* v *Secretary of State for the Home Department* 1995 SLT 733.

hold good in the future, but it seems unlikely. For the time being, it is the only Inner House authority in the area and therefore remains authoritative.

ECHR and privacy

The right to respect for privacy in Art 8 of the ECHR[131] adds to the question of irregularly obtained evidence in civil cases. This article was applied in *Martin v McGuiness*.[132] One of the questions in that case was the compatibility of the tactics of a private investigator employed to gather evidence to discredit a personal injury claim, with the right to privacy enshrined by Art 8. This particular investigator had approached the home of the pursuer and pretended to the pursuer's wife to be an old acquaintance of her husband. He persisted in his anxiety to see the pursuer when told by his wife that he was not at home. The pursuer heard of the visit when he returned and the view was quickly formed that this had been an attempt by a prospective burglar to prepare for a break-in. An alarm was fitted and the pursuer and his wife continued to be anxious about a possible theft. The investigator also set up a telephoto lens in an adjacent property and filmed the pursuer's movements while he was in the curtilage of his property. A question arose as to the admissibility of pleadings relating to evidence that would be led during the proof in the case (the hearing at which evidence is led) of the observations of the investigator, as a result of his surveillance work. One of the arguments the defenders intended to make at the proof was that the pursuer had been exaggerating the effect of his injuries. Lord Bonomy in the Outer House had no difficulty in holding that the actions of the investigator were in breach of Art 8(1). However, he held that the admissibility of evidence of such surveillance was saved by being "necessary in a democratic society" in terms of Art 8(2). The balance, according to Lord Bonomy, is between:

5.67

> "the interest of the pursuer in the security and integrity of his home as part of his right to respect for his private and family life and the competing interest of the defender in protecting his assets, and the interests of the wider community in protecting theirs".[133]

In this case, the scale was tipped in favour of the latter. No doubt, however, the intrusion in a future case might be more significant and

---

[131] For a discussion of the application of the Human Rights Act 1998 and the ECHR to tribunal proceedings in the context of Arts 5 and 6, see paras 4.06 *et seq*.
[132] 2003 SLT 1424; 2003 SCLR 548.
[133] 2003 SLT 1424 at para 16.

the decision different.[134] There is some ECHR jurisprudence on the issue of surveillance activities, but there is insufficient space here to deal with these.[135]

Applications of the rules on improperly obtained evidence in tribunal cases

5.68   Where evidence is stolen and then presented to the tribunal, the law as set out above will apply. However, such cases will be rare. One example might be the interception and retention of correspondence between a patient and another person (whether another patient or a relative from outwith the hospital). It is worth noting, however, that the provisions for interference with postal and telephone correspondence are carefully prescribed by statute. So far as the provisions of the 2003 Act are concerned, these relate either to patients in the State Hospital or to patients in relation to whom the RMO has certified that the sending of correspondence or making of telephone calls by the patient is likely to cause another named individual distress. Directions may be made by the Scottish Ministers in relation to the use of telephones by patients.[136] Interceptions of communications other than in accordance with the law permitting such interceptions are likely to be regarded as "not in accordance with the law" and therefore in breach of Art 8 ECHR.[137] As noted below, even if an interference with a right protected by Art 8 is in accordance with the law, it must also be in pursuit of one of the aims identified in Art 8(2) and be a necessary and proportionate response.

A possible application of the rule on improperly obtained evidence might be evidence obtained following a search of a patient who is

---

[134] See also the employment case of *McNicol* v *Balfour Beatty Rail Maintenance Ltd* [2002] EWCA Civ 1074; [2002] IRLR 711 at para 15 where Mummery LJ in the Court of Appeal approved (on an *obiter* basis) of a decision of the EAT in a disability discrimination claim that video evidence of the applicant, filmed secretly and taken shortly before the original tribunal hearing was properly admitted by the tribunal, since it was relevant to his credibility where the main question in dispute was whether the applicant had suffered from an impairment. There was no argument on this point in the Court of Appeal and no detailed submission on admissibility was made in the EAT case (reported as *Rugamer* v *Sony Music Entertainment UK Ltd*; *McNicol* v *Balfour Beatty Rail Maintenance Ltd* [2001] IRLR 644: see paras 50–52 for the decision of the EAT on the video evidence).

[135] For a detailed commentary on these authorities, see R Reed and J A Murdoch, *Guide to Human Rights Law in Scotland* (2nd edn, 2008), paras 6.25 *et seq*.

[136] See ss 281–285 of the Act; also the Mental Health (Definition of Specified Person: Correspondence) (Scotland) Regulations 2005 (SSI 2005/466); and the Mental Health (Use of Telephones) (Scotland) Regulations 2005 (SSI 2005/468).

[137] The question of whether an interference of a particular kind with telephone communications (in this case the inclusion of a recorded message) was "in accordance with the law" is not necessarily always entirely straightforward. See *Potter* v *Scottish Ministers* [2007] CSIH 67; 2007 SLT 1019.

suspected of possessing material that might be harmful to him, such as excess medication (as was the situation in one tribunal case) or an implement that might be used to inflict self-harm or to injure others. There are clear statutory powers of search,[138] and if these are regarded as having been breached, such a search could be regarded as an unlawful one and so would probably be subjected to the *Duke of Argyll* test, above. If the search is legal but irregular, the evidence uncovered will be admissible, in accordance with the *MacNeill* and *Watson* cases, also above. In either event, such a search could face a challenge under the Human Rights Act 1998. In such cases, the justification offered for any breach of Art 8(1) would probably consist of an argument that the interference is permitted as being in accordance with the law (assuming the search is legal) and as being necessary in a democratic society "for the protection of health or morals".[139] The outcome would depend on the circumstances of the case.

Unnecessary evidence[140]

The appearance of a provision in the Rules authorising the exclusion of unnecessary evidence might seem odd. On reflection, however, this provision, in the context of tribunal hearings, is sensible. Evidence might be unnecessary for a range of reasons. For example, it might be evidence that is already before the tribunal. Although the level of detail with which a CTO application is framed will vary widely from case to case, most are sufficiently detailed to provide the tribunal members with at least a reasonable understanding of the patient's history, mental state at the time of the application, and reasons for the order being sought. In many cases, the prospect of hearing a lengthy examination-in-chief[141] of the MHO and RMO, during which this information is repeated in oral form, will be an unappetising one. In such a case, the tribunal could be justified in preventing the examiner from adopting this course; by doing so, the tribunal will technically be excluding evidence on the ground that it is unnecessary.[142] In

5.69

---

[138] These are set out in the Mental Health (Safety and Security) (Scotland) Regulations 2005 (SSI 2005/464), regs 4, 5, 6, 8 and 10. See also the Code of Practice, vol 1, Chapter 12, paras 43 and 44. On the status of the Code, see para 1.40. The English Code is more detailed on this issue in the absence of specific statutory provision: see the 2008 *Code of Practice Mental Health Act 1983*, Chapter 16, s 25 and the case of *R v Broadmoor Special Hospital Authority, ex p S* [1998] COD 199 for further guidance on the English position. The English material would be a relevant consideration in any question of the interpretation of the Scottish regulations.

[139] Human Rights Act 1998, Sch 1, Art 8(2). For an Art 8(1) argument in the context of the power of search in England, see the Court of Appeal decision in *R v Broadmoor Special Hospital Authority, ex p S* [1998] COD 199.

[140] See r 49(1)(g)(iv).

[141] On the examination-in-chief generally, see paras 4.47 *et seq.*

[142] For an examination of the practicalities of excluding evidence, see para 5.47.

practice, the tribunal can deal with the situation by saying that it will treat the report as the evidence-in-chief of the author, subject to any additions, alterations or updates that he wishes to give in oral evidence.[143] In other cases, mere repetition of points already covered in oral evidence could be legitimately curtailed by a direction issued by the tribunal.

5.70   Another application of this rule relates to the exclusion of the evidence of a witness in its entirety. This is never a measure which a tribunal will undertake without very careful consideration. The Rules require that the hearing is conducted fairly,[144] and on the face of it the exclusion of the whole evidence a witness intends to give is open to an attack of unfairness; how, it could be argued, could the tribunal determine that it did not need to hear/be presented with certain evidence before it could be sure of its content? There would appear to be nothing in the Rules to prevent the tribunal from seeking an advance summary of the evidence a witness is due to give in order to determine if it is necessary. In addition, one can see that a tribunal might refuse to grant an adjournment of a case, where the request for a delay is made in order to take evidence from a witness who is not available to give evidence at the hearing. The tribunal could take the view that such evidence (and therefore the adjournment) is unnecessary as sufficient evidence is available to make the decision in hand without it. The general power to conduct procedure as the tribunal sees fit[145] could be prayed in aid of such a course of action.

Other grounds for exclusion of evidence

5.71   At first glance, the provisions in the Rules on directions appear to allow for the exclusion of evidence only on certain grounds, namely evidence that is irrelevant, unnecessary or improperly obtained (all dealt with above). However, this is not necessarily the case and there may be scope for arguing in favour of the exclusion of evidence on other grounds. One such argument might focus on the scope of r 49(1)(g)(ii), which allows a tribunal to make directions on the "nature of the evidence which the Tribunal requires to decide those issues". Arguably, while this provision is framed positively, such a direction might exclude certain evidence. The contrary argument is that the framers of the Rules considered exclusionary directions and

---

[143] See the adoption of written material into oral evidence discussed further at para 4.48.
[144] See r 4, discussed at para 1.26.
[145] This is to be found in r 52(1) but this power is not unfettered, as discussed further at paras 3.07 *et seq.*

limited the scope of them in r 49(1)(g)(iv), leaving r 49(1)(g)(ii) to cover only the possibility of positive (inclusionary) directions.

The second source of an argument for other grounds of exclusion of evidence is the suggestion that the list of issues in r 49(1) is not exhaustive. The wording refers to "such directions ... and may *in particular*" (emphasis added).[146] This suggests that the list that follows is illustrative of the type of directions that the tribunal can make, as opposed to a prescription of all of them. Given that there is the power to exclude evidence on certain grounds that are already recognised in the law of evidence, it does not take too much imagination to include such other grounds as applicable to tribunal hearings.

5.72

In fact, a provision in the 2003 Act is relevant here. In Sch 2, Pt 3, para 12(4), the following is stated:

5.73

"A person need not give evidence or produce any document, if, were it evidence which might be given or a document that might be produced in any court in Scotland, the person having that evidence or document could not be compelled to give or produce it in such proceedings."[147]

This provision explicitly opens the door to an argument for the exclusion of any evidence on the same basis as might be sought in relation to similar evidence in any court. Although this provision makes reference to "any court in Scotland" this should, for the most part, be taken to be a reference to the rules that apply in courts with non-criminal jurisdiction. In order for an argument to be made that any rule that applies in criminal court cases should be applicable, there would have to be some allegation of criminal conduct being made by one of the parties or witnesses appearing before the tribunal. This might be the case when, for instance, there is an allegation by an MHO of violent conduct or conduct that might amount to a breach of the peace by the patient on the ward. In such cases, the rules on, for example, the inadmissibility of secondary hearsay could apply in a tribunal hearing.[148] Where there is intended to be an assertion that a patient has confessed to criminal conduct (while on a CTO or not) and no common law caution has been administered in advance, there might be a question over whether that evidence is admissible from the person to whom the incriminating statement or confession was made. This is because in criminal cases, a confession, in order to be admissible, must usually be preceded by a common

---

[146] Rule 49(1), first para.

[147] The wording of this provision requires to be substantially repeated in any witness citation issued by the Tribunal, in relation to the production of any document by a cited witness: see r 59(2)(b).

[148] On the issue of secondary hearsay evidence, see para 5.45.

law caution.[149] Much would depend on the circumstances in which the confession is heard.[150] There is precedent for a caution being administered by officials other than police officers,[151] and for a caution to be required in a non-criminal (immigration) context, where (as in many tribunal cases) the liberty of an individual is at stake.[152] On the other hand, in the context of employment tribunal cases, it has been held that criminal admissibility rules on confessions do not apply.[153] On balance, given that in such cases liberty of the individual is not at stake, it is submitted that the *Oghonoghor* case is a more reliable authority in the context of mental health tribunal cases, but again much will depend on the circumstances of each case.[154] At the end of the day, however, the tribunal should almost always warn someone in this situation of his entitlement not to answer the question about the alleged confession on the ground that the answer might incriminate him,[155] and this may resolve the situation from a practical standpoint, even where the evidence of the confession is decided to be otherwise admissible.

Many of the grounds for the exclusion of evidence which are not specifically covered by r 49, and which might apply in a tribunal context, are to be found in the general law of civil evidence. It is to those grounds that we now turn.

COMPETENCY AND COMPELLABILITY OF WITNESSES

5.74   Rules exist in order to regulate which persons are permitted to give evidence in civil cases and whether they can, even if permitted to do so, be forced to give evidence. There are two key concepts here:

> *competency*: this dictates whether a particular person is permitted, as a matter of law, to give evidence; and

---

[149] The caution content is fixed in the case law for most cases, and must be administered once suspicion crystallises on a suspect: see *Chalmers* v *HM Advocate*, 1954 JC 66, 1954 SLT 177; *Tonge* v *HM Advocate*, 1982 JC 130; 1982 SLT 506; and *HM Advocate* v *Von* 1979 SLT (Notes) 62.

[150] For a borderline case, see *Custerson* v *Westwater* 1987 SCCR 389; and for a case in which a caution was not required, see *Pennycuick* v *Lees* 1992 SLT 763; 1992 SCCR 160.

[151] *Pennycuick* v *Lees* 1992 SLT 763; 1992 SCCR 160, a case involving an investigation by social security officials.

[152] *Oghonoghor* v *Secretary of State for the Home Department* 1995 SLT 733.

[153] *Morley's of Brixton Ltd* v *Minott* [1982] IRLR 270, a decision of the Employment Appeal Tribunal.

[154] For a discussion of the nature of tribunal proceedings in the context of other proceedings, see paras 1.31 *et seq.*

[155] On the self-incrimination privilege, see paras 5.78 *et seq.*

compellability: this concept is applied to discover if a particular witness who is competent can be forced, against his will, to give evidence.

The application of these concepts in the case of the vast majority of   5.75
potential witnesses is not problematic. Most persons are permitted to give evidence and can be compelled to do so, even if they would rather not.[156] There are various categories of witness that are affected by competency and/or compellability considerations. We will now deal with the only such category likely to ever apply to tribunal proceedings.

Witnesses with a mental disorder

A witness who suffers from a mental disorder may in some cases   5.76
be an incompetent witness. Of course, given that in the vast majority of cases tribunals are satisfied that the patient suffers from a mental disorder, this rule might be seen as having some serious consequences. However, the law is clear that insanity is not an automatic bar to giving evidence; such witnesses are competent and compellable as long as they can tell the difference between truth and lies, appreciate the duty to tell the truth and can give coherent testimony.[157] Each case will be different and the tribunal will decide on whether the witness is fit to testify. In so deciding, it might hear evidence from experts.[158] However, this will rarely be an issue, and the preferable way to deal with a situation where a patient is unable to give coherent evidence is to allow that evidence to be given as much as possible, while still dealing with the case in accordance with the overriding objective,[159] and to weigh the evidence appropriately at the evaluation point.[160] It should be noted that although this area is now regulated by provisions dealing with vulnerable witnesses in civil cases in the public courts,[161] the statutory provisions do not

---

[156] Witnesses cited by the Tribunal to attend and give evidence can be prosecuted if they refuse to comply with the citation, without reasonable excuse: see r 59 and the 2003 Act, para 12(3) of Sch 2, all as discussed at paras 3.80 and 4.63.

[157] F Raitt, *Evidence: Principles, Policy and Practice* (2008), para 3–40.

[158] This happened in the criminal case *HM Advocate* v *Stott* (1894) 1 Adam 386. In that case, in directions to the jury, the judge commented on the weight to be attached to such evidence and he advised the jury that limited reliance should be placed on the testimony.

[159] See r 4, explained further at para 1.26.

[160] On the task of evaluating the evidence, see paras 5.118 *et seq* below.

[161] These provisions are contained in the Vulnerable Witnesses (Scotland) Act 2004.

apply to tribunal cases,[162] so the general common law in this area still applies. It seems that the procedures and case law covering the admonishment and the competency test (to the extent, if any, that it survives the purported abolition under s 24 of the 2004 Act) are inapplicable in tribunal cases since they have been developed for evidence that would ordinarily be given under oath. As noted elsewhere, evidence on oath or affirmation will rarely feature in tribunal proceedings,[163] and even where evidence in a tribunal hearing is taken in such a manner, the emphasis on the tribunal seeking to conduct the hearing as informally as the circumstances of the case permit,[164] would seem to exclude such a device in many cases. In addition, regard should be had to the 2003 Act "patient participation" principle.[165]

PRIVILEGE

5.77   In judicial proceedings, witnesses can usually be forced to give evidence or to produce documentation, even if they do not wish to do so. The sanction for failing to comply with an order to do so is almost always the possibility of imposition of a criminal penalty. The tribunal is no exception.[166] However, sometimes a witness can perfectly legally refuse to give evidence on a certain matter, and refuse to produce documents in connection with that matter. Given that the tribunal process (as with any judicial process) is so heavily dependent on evidence in order to allow it to function properly, the occasions on which a witness can lawfully refuse to co-operate are limited in number and are strictly defined. A witness may refuse to co-operate with the tribunal in this way in two main cases: where the privilege against self-incrimination applies and when the solicitor–client privilege applies. When one of these is successfully prayed in aid of a refusal to answer a question or produce a document, the tribunal will find that the witness possesses the "privilege" of not co-operating.

---

[162] See the definition of "civil proceedings" in s 11 of the 2004 Act: "'civil proceedings' includes, in addition to such proceedings in any of the ordinary courts of law, any proceedings to which s 91 (procedural rules in relation to certain applications etc.) of the Children (Scotland) Act 1995 (c. 36) applies".

[163] See para 4.43 on the oath and affirmation.

[164] Rule 63(2)(a), discussed in various contexts at paras 4.43, 4.67. 4.93, 4.103 and 4.117.

[165] 2003 Act, s 1(3)(c).

[166] See the criminal penalties that attach to failure or refusal by a cited witness without reasonable excuse to attend and give evidence or to destroying, altering, concealing or refusing without reasonable excuse to produce a document required in connection with that evidence: 2003 Act, Sch 2, Pt 3, paras 12(3), (5) and (7).

Privilege against self-incrimination

If to answer a question or produce a document would expose a tribunal witness to a real risk of criminal prosecution, the individual can refuse to answer the question or produce the document. Since the scope of this privilege in England is similar to that in Scotland (except in one situation),[167] some relevant English cases will be referred to here. The most obvious example is where a patient is asked to comment on an allegation of violent or aggressive behaviour while on a hospital ward.

5.78

This privilege can only be invoked where there is a *real possibility* of a *criminal* prosecution. If the information might expose the witness to a civil claim, it must be revealed, since the privilege will not, in such a case, apply. It has also been made clear that, for the privilege to apply, the information that would be provided in the event of the question being answered or the document being produced need not be a confession of a crime, but may simply reveal evidence of the individual's involvement in it.[168] The tribunal must assess the risk of prosecution. In order to do so, the tribunal must know what the evidence would consist of in order to decide on what is, essentially, a question of law (whether the privilege exists, justifying a refusal to divulge).[169]

5.79

Once it is aware of the content of the proposed evidence, the tribunal must decide whether there is a realistic prospect of a prosecution, not just whether one would be feasible.[170] If it so decides, the witness should then be given a warning indicating that he is not obliged to answer the question or produce the document on the ground that the answer/production may incriminate him. However, if the chances of self-incrimination represent only a remote possibility, the tribunal should not issue the warning.[171] The role of any representative (particularly a lawyer) involved in the case may be crucial here, since it is not uncommon for a representative to spot a potential problem and then object to a question and ask the

5.80

---

[167] The main difference between Scotland and England in relation to this privilege is that in England the privilege can be claimed where to produce the document or answer the question would "tend to expose" the spouse of that individual to a criminal prosecution (Civil Evidence Act 1968, s 14(1)). There is no such rule in Scotland.

[168] R v *Slaney* (1832) 5 Car & P 212; 172 ER 944.

[169] As Lord Stephen put it in: R v *Cox and Railton* (1884) LR 14 QBD 153; (1881–1885) All ER Rep 68 "the secret must be told in order [that the court may] see whether it ought to be kept" (1884) LR 14 QBD 153 at 175.

[170] See the examples of *Blunt* v *Park Lane Hotel Ltd* [1942] 2 KB 253; and *Rank Film Distributors Ltd* v *Video Information Centre* [1982] AC 380; [1981] 2 WLR 668.

[171] *Singh* v *HM Advocate* 2004 SCCR 604.

judge to issue the warning.[172] Despite any warning, since the privilege belongs to the witness, he may choose to waive it and so can still answer the question if he wishes. In the case of a witness who is not strictly speaking a competent witness on the ground of suffering from a mental disorder,[173] the tribunal may choose to declare any incriminating answer/production of a document inadmissible, as coming from an incompetent witness.

5.81   It should be noted that at the time of the hearing at which the issue is live, the witness must still be in danger of prosecution. So, for example, if there has been a "not guilty" finding or if a witness has been called as an accomplice or if the witness has pled guilty in a criminal court already, the privilege will be lost since there is no chance of self-incrimination *as a result of* the answer or document production.

Solicitor–client privilege

5.82   The communications between a solicitor and his client, written or oral, do not require to be divulged in response to a tribunal direction ordering the production of documents, a witness citation or in response to a question at a hearing. The idea behind this privilege is that a client is supposed to be able to consult his solicitor in confidence. This confidence would be undermined if a client was aware that his solicitor could be forced to betray that confidence by the courts. The privilege also covers communications between a solicitor and an advocate and those between an advocate (the Scottish equivalent of a barrister) and the client. Again, some English case law is relevant here. However, it is probably the case that the privilege is not extended to advisers who are not solicitors or advocates since, in the context of employment tribunals, this has been held to be the case.[174] Although in these cases the main focus has been personnel advisers, there seems no reason in principle for the same not to apply in mental health tribunals to, for instance, advocacy workers.[175]

5.83   The communication must have been made during the existence of a professional relationship. Therefore, where the individual is communicating with a solicitor to see whether he will act for him and the solicitor declines, anything said during the declination is not privileged – see the English case of *Minter* v *Priest*.[176] In Scotland,

---

[172] For a discussion of the rules on making an objection, see paras 4.71 *et seq.*
[173] On this, see above at para 5.76.
[174] See the judgment of the Employment Appeal Tribunal in *New Victoria Hospital* v *Ryan* [1993] IRLR 202, where production of the relevant documents was ordered even although they contained legal advice, partly since they were not authored by legally qualified persons.
[175] On advocacy workers generally, see paras 2.49 *et seq.*
[176] [1930] AC 558.

this point has arisen but was not decided;[177] however, it is likely that the English approach will be followed when the issue does arise.

The privilege is permanent and does not come to an end after the solicitor–client relationship ends. This is clear from the decision of the House of Lords in *R v Derby Magistrates' Court, ex p B*,[178] where the communications that were sought to be relied upon had occurred some 17 years previously and privilege was held to remain attached to them. The extraordinary facts of that case also demonstrate the absolute nature of the privilege. There, the privilege was held to exist despite evidence of the communication between the client and his solicitor being sought by the accused in a murder case, and where it was hoped that evidence of the communication might bolster the accused's defence. This is in contrast to the doctor–patient privilege where it has been held, in the context of a patient detained under the English mental health legislation, that the confidentiality privilege must be balanced against the public interest of the relevant authorities being aware of all relevant facts before deciding whether to release a patient who may then be violent.[179] In that case, it was held that the disclosure of the doctor's report was justified, although this would be so only in the most compelling circumstances.   5.84

The communication must be directly related to the giving of advice.   5.85
If not, the privilege does not attach. In *R v Manchester Crown Court, ex p Rogers*,[180] the Crown in a criminal case sought to establish that the accused had visited his solicitor's office at a certain time on a certain day. The solicitor's note of the time of attendance was not privileged and had to be produced; it was not made in connection with legal advice. Sometimes, the purpose of the disclosure attempt will lead to a decision that the privilege does not apply. For example, where the very question the court is enquiring into is whether or not the communication was made, the privilege flies off. This occurred in the case of *Anderson v Lord Elgin's Trs*.[181] There, the question was whether the pursuer (a solicitor) had delayed unduly in raising an action. To determine that question, the court had to hear evidence on the communications between the pursuer and his client. The privilege was held not to apply. In England, a similar rule applies, and the test has been stated in these terms:

---

[177] *HM Advocate v Davie* (1881) 4 Coup 450.
[178] [1996] AC 487; [1995] 3 WLR 681.
[179] *W v Egdell* [1990] Ch 359.
[180] [1999] 1 WLR 832.
[181] (1859) 21 D 654.

"whether the relevant communication ... is part of the necessary exchange of information of which the dominant purpose is the giving of legal advice as and when appropriate".[182]

5.86   Similarly, where the nature of the solicitor–client relationship is the very issue being probed by the court, the privilege will not apply. The question in the case of *Fraser* v *Malloch*[183] was whether a relationship of solicitor–client had ever formed. The privilege did not apply to communications in that case. Finally, it seems arguable that the privilege covers only communications, not observations made by the solicitor during contact with his client. As Wilkinson puts it:

"A solicitor must refuse to say whether his client confessed to a crime but must answer if asked whether he came to him wearing blood-stained clothing."[184]

This has not been tested in the courts, but not all commentators take the same view as Wilkinson.[185] It would seem that observations must also, logically, be covered and any rule to the contrary would seem artificial. This might apply in a tribunal context where, for instance, a solicitor's consultation with his client is overheard by staff on the ward of the hospital where the patient resides, and where someone at the hearing seeks confirmation from the solicitor as to what the patient told him, for instance where it is claimed that the patient is saying something different in his evidence. Here, even where the panel deems it appropriate to probe the solicitor for his account, the solicitor could (and almost certainly should) legitimately refuse to provide any information, citing the solicitor–client privilege.

5.87   The position is not clear if evidence of the communication comes from another source and is illegally obtained. However, if it is innocently obtained, it seems that it will be admissible – see *McLeish* v *Glasgow Bonding Co Ltd*.[186] Other than the type of situation cited

---

[182] J Richardson (ed), *Archbold: Criminal Pleading, Evidence and Practice 2007* (55th edn, 2006), para 12–7b. Although this is a criminal law text, the law in this area in England is the same in civil and criminal cases, and this text cites examples of both in this area.

[183] (1895) 3 SLT 211.

[184] A B Wilkinson, *The Scottish Law of Evidence* (1986), p 95.

[185] See, for example, the contrary view expressed in M L Ross and J Chalmers, *Walker and Walker: The Law of Evidence in Scotland* (3rd edn, 2009) at para 10.2.4. See also F P Davidson, *Evidence* (2007) at para 13.25, where the author argues: "a legitimate distinction can surely be drawn between what is communicated between [the client] and his legal adviser, and physical details the latter happens to observe".

[186] 1965 SLT 39; 1964 SLT (Notes) 84. See further the discussion on evidence improperly obtained at paras 5.60 *et seq.*

in the previous paragraph, this privilege is unlikely to apply often in the context of tribunal hearings, save in one clear case,[187] but it is worth bearing in mind. It might apply, for instance, where the tribunal asks for information from the solicitor about a change of instructions by his client, where, say, the client had indicated a desire to obtain an independent psychiatric assessment, but had changed his mind and had declined to obtain one. Here, the reasons will have been communicated in the instruction to the lawyer and so is caught by the privilege.

Where the privilege applies, both the solicitor and the patient can refuse to answer questions. It is important to distinguish between evidence provided by the solicitor and representations made by him on behalf of his client. The complexity arises in a tribunal setting since evidence is not usually provided on oath.[188] This can blur the distinction between representations and evidence. Where the solicitor is specifically asked to clarify any matter relating to his client's instructions, he is effectively giving evidence, and can lay claim to the protection of the privilege. However, the tribunal, under its general power to conduct proceedings as it wishes,[189] can insist that a representative states his client's general position on the application, as that is not factual material, and so is not caught by the privilege.   5.88

Of course, where any other party is represented by a solicitor, the privilege applies equally to that party, for example the RMO, MHO, named person or curator *ad litem*. However, such representation is not common, and less common are examples of situations in which the privilege might be invoked. It is worth mentioning also that the privilege applies only to solicitors and advocates, not to any other representative, such as an advocacy worker.[190]   5.89

The admissibility of independent psychiatric reports – the privilege position

As was the case under the 1984 Act system, it is not uncommon to find that the solicitor acting for a patient wishes to have the patient examined by an independent psychiatrist. We consider elsewhere the issue of the circumstances under which such a request should be evaluated.[191] Here, we consider the admissibility issue. Of course, an independent assessment of the mental state of the patient, usually coupled with a view on the future care options, all carried out in   5.90

---

[187] See the potential confidentiality argument that could be used to argue against the release of an independent psychiatric report, discussed at paras 5.90 *et seq*.
[188] On the oath, see para 4.43.
[189] Rule 52(1), discussed further at para 3.07.
[190] On advocacy workers generally, see paras 2.49 *et seq*.
[191] See paras 3.31 *et seq*.

the context of the CTO application, is clearly admissible where it is sought to be tendered by a representative of the patient (usually a solicitor). However, where the independent report substantiates the view expressed by the MHO and RMO, and supports the CTO, the patient's solicitor will, naturally, be reluctant to produce it to the tribunal as such a report will significantly damage any opposition to the granting of the CTO application. The problem arises since, at first glance, the Rules seem to require that such a report, whether favourable to the patient's case or not, must be lodged. Rule 62(5) reads as follows:

> "where any relevant person obtains in relation to an issue before the Tribunal a written report from a person having expertise in any subject relevant to that issue, that relevant person shall send a copy of the report to the Tribunal 7 days prior to the next hearing of the Tribunal or at such period prior to the next hearing of the Tribunal as specified by the Tribunal in a particular case".

5.91   The first point to note about this provision is that it applies only to written reports. So where an independent report is obtained orally, the rule does not apply, and even where an adjournment has been obtained for the specific purpose of obtaining an independent psychiatric report, the patient's solicitor can refuse to disclose the content of any such oral report. Where such a report is obtained in writing, however, the position is less clear. It would seem that the rule applies and that the patient's solicitor must disclose it. On the other hand, there are arguments that can be made in favour of not disclosing. There are two such arguments, either of which, in the authors' view should, where applicable, be regarded as persuasive. Each of these arguments will now be considered.

(1) Post litem motam report argument

5.92   The first involves an argument that the written report is one that falls into the category of reports obtained *post litem motam*. While litigation is under contemplation, any communications between a third party (not the patient) and a solicitor are privileged (see above on the nature of privileged evidence). The communications must be made for the specific purpose of the contemplated litigation in order to be covered by the privilege. These communications are sometimes referred to as communications *post litem motam* ("after an action has been raised"). However, the literal translation is not accurate since litigation need not have actually commenced for this privilege to apply: it needs only to be in contemplation. A communication *post litem motam* is one made when it is in the mind of a party that litigation may occur; in other words, "after it is apparent that

there is going to be a litigious contention".[192] In England, the test is
that the document must be prepared "with a view to litigation"[193]
and although this is slightly different wording, it would seem to
be the same test in substance. This privilege does not just apply
to the solicitor–client relationship (which might be covered by the
communications privilege anyway),[194] but to any communications
between a relevant person and a third party or another relevant
person. The distinction between the solicitor–client communications
privilege and the *post litem motam* privilege (known in England as
the "litigation privilege") has been noted in the House of Lords:

> "The former, covering communications between a client and his legal
> adviser, is available whether or not proceedings are in existence or
> contemplated. The latter embraces a wider class of communications,
> such as those between a legal adviser and potential witnesses [and
> are] privileged only when proceedings are in existence or are con-
> templated."[195]

This privilege (*post litem motam*) has particular application to com-   **5.93**
munications between a solicitor and a potential skilled witness,[196]
and would cover, for example, a letter of instruction to a witness
and the report prepared by the witness. The idea behind this
privilege in such a situation is that the solicitor should be able to
conduct investigations prior to litigation freely, without fear that
he will have to disclose what may be an unfavourable report on
his client's case to his opponent or the court.[197] This, of course,
has particular application in the tribunal context of a written
independent psychiatric report.

It is important to note that litigation should be in contemplation   **5.94**
at the time of the communication. In *Wheeler* v *Le Marchant*,[198]
a surveyor's report made to the solicitor of the defendant had to
be produced by the solicitor since at the time it was prepared, no
litigation was in contemplation, even though one later ensued. In

---

[192] *Admiralty* v *Aberdeen Steam Trawling and Fishing Co* 1909 1 SLT 2 per the
Lord President at 6.
[193] See Lord Jauncey of Tullichettle in the House of Lords case of *Re L (A Minor)
(Police Investigation: Privilege)* [1997] AC 16 at 25, citing for support the main
case in this area in England, *Waugh* v *British Railways Board* [1980] AC 521.
[194] On this privilege, see para 5.101.
[195] As discussed by Lord Nicholls of Birkenhead in *Re L (A Minor) (Police
Investigation: Privilege)* [1997] AC 16 at 33.
[196] On the evidence of such witnesses generally, see the discussion on opinion
evidence below at paras 5.102 *et seq*.
[197] See *Johnstone* v *National Coal Board* 1968 SC 128; 1968 SLT 233, per
LP Clyde (1968 SC 128 at 134).
[198] (1881) LR 17 Ch D 675.

applying this to a tribunal situation, this difficulty is unlikely to arise. Rule 62(5) clearly does not apply until there are Tribunal proceedings under way, since the rule refers to a report "in relation to an issue before the Tribunal". If there are no Tribunal proceedings under way at the time when the report is obtained, it does not fall within the remit of this provision, and so the patient's solicitor need not even draw the Tribunal's attention to the existence of the report, even if the *post litem motam* rule would usually not apply, since the report was prepared in advance of any Tribunal proceedings. An example might be where a patient has gone into a psychiatric ward in a hospital voluntarily, but where relatives of the patient are not convinced of the diagnosis or care plan, so they obtain an independent psychiatric report. Shortly thereafter, the RMO decides to apply for a hospital-based CTO. The report would not be protected by the *post litem motam* privilege, but nevertheless would escape the clutches of r 62(5) as not having been obtained "in relation to an issue before the Tribunal". For the purposes of timing, it would seem that an issue should be regarded as being "before the Tribunal" from the date when a CTO application or appeal against an STDC has been lodged.

5.95   The privilege does not necessarily apply to a communication made with a mixed purpose, only one of which is a contemplated litigation.[199]

5.96   One other leading case is *Hepburn v Scottish Power plc*.[200] This case concerned a house fire, the cause of which was suspected to be a short circuit in the electrical distribution board in the house. The defenders instructed engineers to investigate the cause of the fire. They visited the house with the consent of the householders and took away parts of the distribution board. A new board was then installed and a report was sent to the defenders by the engineers. In this case the Inner House held that the report, although prepared only a few days after the fire, had been prepared *post litem motam*. However, there was an exception to the rule that such documents are always irrecoverable. Where an examination involves the destruction or material alteration of the subject-matter of the examination, so that the party inspecting is in possession of information about the cause of an incident and the other party is not, thereby, in a position to acquire such knowledge, then the report will not be privileged. This exception applied in this case, and so disclosure of the report was ordered. The rationale in this case could apply where, for example, an RMO or MHO seeks to invoke the *post*

---

[199] This situation arose in the House of Lords case of *Waugh v British Railways Board* [1980] AC 521; [1979] 3 WLR 150.
[200] 1997 SC 80; 1997 SLT 859.

litem motam rule in connection with an expert report that he has obtained.[201] Take the example of the RMO who seeks an informal (but written) second opinion from a colleague in a borderline case. He may justify refraining from releasing it on the basis of the *post litem motam* rule. However, where the patient becomes aware of the existence of the report, it might be possible to argue that the *post litem motam* rule should not apply, on the basis of the application of an adapted *Hepburn* argument. The rationale behind that case is essentially the avoidance of a situation whereby one party has unfairly favourable access to information or material. It might just be arguable that the circumstances in which the RMO (or MHO) is able to call upon expert support that is simply not available to the patient or his representative (or at least not available in the case of someone who is not wealthy) and that this advantage could, in a sense, be equalised by the removal of the ability to secrete the expert reports (the advantage) behind the *post litem motam* rule, just as the advantage of one party was equalised using this method in *Hepburn*. Admittedly, the *Hepburn* formula would need to be stretched somewhat to allow this argument to be made. There is one other analogous situation which might assist the maker of this argument. The Crown in a criminal case is arguably in a similar position to the MHO and the RMO in tribunal case. Indeed, as discussed earlier, tribunal cases should be regarded as akin to other types of "citizen versus the State" cases.[202] This lends weight to the idea that criminal procedural law should, where appropriate and logical, be applied by analogy in mental health tribunal cases. The Crown has access to expert services, such as the use of the police force, the forensics service and expert legal advice from a large team of prosecutors and prosecuting counsel (Advocates Depute). The accused has none of this at his fingertips, unless, again, he is very wealthy. Even then there is a home advantage for the Crown, who generally will have the resources and legal entitlement to access the crime scene first, and to the exclusion of any other interested parties, including the accused. To compensate for this huge advantage, the Scottish courts have developed a duty of disclosure on the part of the Crown, so that any evidence gathered by the Crown that might be of advantage to the accused should be disclosed to him and, where it is not, this could represent good grounds for an appeal

---

[201] The rule on the disclosure of expert reports (r 62(5)) applies to all parties, not just the patient; see the full discussion on the application of this rule at paras 4.160 *et seq.*

[202] For a general discussion of a comparison of tribunal cases with other types of case, see paras 1.31 *et seq.*

and for a conviction to be quashed.[203] Again, it is just arguable that the MHO and RMO are in a similarly advantaged position in that they have access to specialist services and expertise all of which places them in a better position to present their case than the patient. This advantage is magnified when one considers that where a patient is suffering from a mental disorder, his ability to redress that advantage is more limited than in the case of an accused person who possesses all of his mental faculties intact. One way of replicating the advantage gained by the Crown in criminal cases would be to deprive the MHO and RMO of the benefit of the *post litem motam* rule. Until these arguments (the *Hepburn* and Crown arguments) can be made, the law remains as it is and MHOs and RMOs can continue to refrain from disclosing expert reports that fall within the scope of r 62(5) for the same reasons (and only for those reasons) as the patient or any other party can.

5.97   It is clear that factual reports do not attract the privilege, while reports concerning litigation do. The distinction was dealt with in *Marks & Spencer* v *British Gas Corporation (No 1)*.[204] This case is also authority for the fact that parts of a report might attract the privilege while other parts do not. In such a case, the parts that do not can be released, but only if these parts are severable (in the *Marks & Spencer* case, this was deemed not possible).

5.98   An argument might be made against the application of the *post litem motam* rule in the context of tribunal proceedings, on the basis that the rule is clearly suited to the more adversarial world of the public court civil action. However, there are three main problems with this argument. The first is that tribunal proceedings are judicial in nature, and often involve decisions on the liberty of individuals. Given that the stakes are, then, very high and that patients are entitled to be legally represented, there seems little reason to deprive a patient of the ability to take full advantage of the legal evidential devices available to someone in, say, a minor road traffic accident damages claim in the public courts, where the stakes are clearly insignificant by comparison. The second is that the rationale behind the *post litem motam* rule – the pursuit of a case without being hindered by the fear of having to produce to the decision-making body material that is adverse to it – applies to a patient facing a tribunal decision as it does to any public court litigant. This point is highlighted when one considers that in the absence of the application of an exclusionary

---

[203] See the cases of *Sinclair* v *HM Advocate* 2005 SLT 553, *McClymont* v *HM Advocate* 2006 SCCR 348 and *Gair* v *HM Advocate* 2006 SCCR 419 (all on disclosure by the Crown of police statements) and *Holland* v *HM Advocate* 2005 SLT 563 (disclosure by the Crown of previous convictions and outstanding charges of Crown witnesses).

[204] 1983 SLT 196.

ground such as the *post litem motam* rule, a solicitor acting for a patient will be under a duty to warn his client that there would be a risk of damaging his case if an independent report is sought since it might (if produced) bolster, or even fill gaps in, the case presented in the CTO application. In such circumstances, the patient is put in the very undesirable position of having seriously to consider declining to obtain an independent medical report, when otherwise he would wish to obtain one. The third reason against the non-application of such a rule in tribunal proceedings on the same basis as with public court proceedings is that the 2003 Act envisages such application, where it is stated:

> "A person need not give evidence or produce any document [in tribunal proceedings] if, were it evidence which might be given or a document that might be produced in any court in Scotland, the person having that evidence or document could not be compelled to give or produce it in such proceedings."[205]

Applying this provision where a report qualifies as one *post litem* **5.99** *motam*, the party holding it cannot be compelled to produce it in any civil public court in Scotland, so cannot be so compelled to do so before a tribunal. This provision is not restricted in its scope, and applies to any civil court exclusionary rule.[206] In England, the equivalent privilege, known as the "litigation privilege", has been held to be inapplicable in certain non-adversarial proceedings.[207] However, it is clear that mental health tribunal proceedings in Scotland, although being in many ways inquisitorial, retain a sufficiently adversarial multi-principled flavour such that this privilege applies to such tribunal proceedings.[208] It should be noted, however, that this argument could not be made by a curator *ad litem* since his role is quite distinct from that of a solicitor. He is appointed by the Tribunal and so the usual rule in r 62(5) will apply to him and he will be obliged to disclose the report unless exceptional reasons apply. He is not, of course, taking instructions from the patient (see para 2.65 on his role as contrasted with that of a solicitor).

---

[205] Mental Health (Care and Treatment) (Scotland) Act 2003, Sch 2, para 12(4).

[206] The reference to "any court in Scotland" should be taken as a reference to any civil court.

[207] *Re L (A Minor) (Police Investigation: Privilege)* [1997] AC 16; and *S County Council* v *B* [2000] Fam 76.

[208] The reason for the exclusion of the privilege in the *Re L* case in proceedings under the Children Act 1989: the welfare of the child is paramount, so this, reasoned the court, made the proceedings non-adversarial in the sense that the parties' interests was not the main touchstone. The same cannot be said in relation to mental health proceedings where there is no paramount interest: in order to comply with the principles in s 1 of the 2003 Act, the tribunal requires to balance a number of interests, none of which can be described as paramount.

5.100   Of course, it could be argued that the ability of the patient to circumvent the application of r 62(5) by the privilege plea in virtually every case deprives that rule of any meaningful purpose, which Parliament cannot have intended. This view, however, is unsustainable. The rule is very wide in its application and does not apply only to an independent psychiatric assessment obtained by the patient. It is clear, as noted elsewhere,[209] that it applies to all expert reports falling within the rule, whether they are produced for the patient or for any other relevant person. Of course, it could be argued by that other person that the *post litem motam* rule, where applicable, can be used by him to argue against the release of expert reports, but the comments on the *Hepburn* case and the Crown analogy, both noted above, and their possible application to block this argument should be noted. Further, it is not clear that Parliament has fully considered the interaction (and conflict) between r 62(5) and the application of the *post litem motam* rule, despite the terms of Sch 2, para 12(4) to the 2003 Act.

(2) Solicitor–client privilege argument

5.101   The second argument that could be levelled at the application of r 62(5) in relation to the production of an independent psychiatric report is that the report is privileged as having arisen out of the solicitor–client relationship. Of course, in such a case, this is not strictly a communication between the solicitor and client, but instead the report will be instructed by the solicitor and the communication will be between the solicitor and the independent expert. However, privilege can still attach to it, as long as it has come into existence in connection with the grant of legal advice. There is authority to this effect in England[210] and, in the absence of Scottish authority on the point, reliance on the English position is sensible.[211] Indeed, the position adopted in England on this point seems rational and in keeping with the underlying aims of the solicitor–client communications privilege in both Scotland and England. In such

---

[209] For a full discussion of the application of that part of the rule, see paras 4.160 *et seq*.

[210] *R v King* [1983] 1 WLR 411, a Court of Appeal decision, cited with approval by P Murphy, *Murphy on Evidence* (11th edn, 2009) at para 14.12 and by C Allen in *Practical Guide to Evidence* (4th edn, 2008) at p 305. The *King* case makes it clear that if the report is obtained before legal advice is sought and is then passed to a solicitor who, at the time of the hearing, has it, the privilege will not apply, except that privilege does still apply to the content of the instructions given by the solicitor to the expert.

[211] It is cited with apparent approval by the main Scottish text on the law of evidence: F P Davidson, *Evidence* (2007) at para 13.29.

cases there will be communications between the client and solicitor in the form of instructions to obtain the report; the communication between the expert and the solicitor is simply a direct by-product of those instructions, and so is regarded as on a par with them, for the purposes of this privilege.

OPINION EVIDENCE

As already commented on, evidence can be categorised according to its inherent nature: oral, documentary and real. There is another way to categorise evidence, and that is according to its source. Here, we can say that there are two types of evidence: evidence as to fact and opinion evidence.   **5.102**

Generally speaking, any witness can (as long as he is a competent witness and the evidence is admissible) give evidence as to fact. However, only skilled witnesses can give opinion evidence. Some common examples of such witnesses are: **5.103**

- a medical consultant in a personal injury case;
- a computer expert in a case alleging the downloading of unlawful pornographic material;
- a valuer in a dispute about what something is worth, eg shares, a pension, a matrimonial home, a car (surveyor, financial adviser, accountant);
- a safety expert on the state of a piece of equipment or premises;
- a technical expert on the workings of a piece of machinery or structure.

Sometimes reference is made to an "expert" witness, however, the better terminology, and the one adopted by *Walker and Walker*, is "skilled witness".[212] A skilled witness need not be regarded as an expert in his field. For example, a psychiatric nurse who looks after a patient on a ward is a skilled witness, but is probably not an expert in psychiatric nursing techniques. The same would apply to, for example, an MHO.   **5.104**

The rule is that only skilled witnesses can give opinion evidence. However, we need to consider in more detail some of the aspects of this important form of evidence. Once again, the rules that apply to such evidence in the public courts are transferable to the tribunal environment. This time, since the rules in public civil and criminal cases are the same, criminal and civil case law is relevant.   **5.105**

---

[212] M L Ross and J Chalmers, *Walker and Walker: The Law of Evidence in Scotland* (3rd edn, 2000), para 16.3.1.

The role of opinion evidence

5.106 The main Scottish case on the role of the skilled witness is *Davie* v *Edinburgh Corporation (No 2)*.[213] In that case, Lord President Cooper stated:

> "Expert witnesses, however skilled or eminent, can give no more than evidence. They cannot usurp the functions of the jury or Judge. ... Their duty is to furnish the Judge or jury with the necessary scientific criteria for testing the accuracy of their conclusions, so as to enable the Judge or jury to form their own independent judgment by the application of these criteria to the facts proved in evidence. The scientific opinion evidence, if intelligible, convincing and tested, becomes a factor (and often an important factor) for consideration along with the whole other evidence in the case, but the decision is for the Judge or jury."[214]

5.107 As a consequence of this rule, it has been made clear in Scotland that an expert cannot give evidence on an issue that the decision-making body is required to determine (this is sometimes referred to as the "ultimate issue"). So, for example, in *Galletly* v *Laird*,[215] expert evidence on the question of whether the content of certain books was indecent or obscene was disallowed. The basis for this was that this question was the very one the court had to answer in considering the criminal charge before it, so a witness could not usurp that function, even an expert one. Also, in *Ingram* v *Macari (No 2)*,[216] the accused was acquitted on a charge of shamelessly indecent conduct (selling certain magazines of a pornographic nature in his shop). The High Court reversed the acquittal and referred the case back to the sheriff to proceed. The sheriff had admitted the evidence of a psychologist and a psychiatrist, who had made special studies of pornography, and who gave evidence on the question of whether the magazines were "liable to deprave and corrupt the morals of the lieges". However, the High Court held that this question was the very one with which the court was concerned and was a question of law, not one that could be resolved by opinion evidence. The opinion evidence had, in this case, been wrongly admitted.

---

[213] *Sub nom Davie* v *Magistrates of Edinburgh* 1953 SC 34; 1953 SLT 54.

[214] 1953 SC 34 at 40. Despite this, it has recently been held by the Inner House that the statutory role of the RMO under the 2003 Act is "plainly of the highest importance" and that the tribunal should "pay close attention to all parts of [the RMO's] evidence". It was also said that "clear and intelligible reasons" should be given for the rejection of an RMO's evidence. See the case of *Scottish Ministers* v *MHTS* 2009 SLT 273 at para 52. The appeal in this case was allowed, partly because of the tribunal's inadequate reasoning.

[215] 1953 JC 16; 1953 SLT 67.

[216] 1983 JC 1; 1983 SLT 61.

Although the general role of the skilled witness is outlined by Lord   **5.108**
President Cooper above, the courts have since scoped out his duties
in more detail. In a further landmark judgment setting out the role of
an expert witness in civil cases, Cresswell J listed these as follows:

> "1. Expert evidence presented to the Court should be and should be seen
> to be the independent product of the expert uninfluenced as to form or
> content by the exigencies of litigation.
>
> 2. An expert witness should provide independent assistance to the
> Court by way of objective unbiased opinion in relation to matters within
> his expertise ... An expert witness ... should never assume the role of
> advocate.
>
> 3. An expert witness should state the facts or assumptions on which his
> opinion is based. He should not omit to consider material facts which
> detract from his concluded opinion ...
>
> 4. An expert witness should make it clear when a particular question or
> issue falls outside his expertise.
>
> 5. If an expert's opinion is not properly researched because he considers
> that insufficient data is available then this must be stated with an indication
> that the opinion is no more than a provisional one ...
>
> 6. If after exchange of reports, an expert witness changes his view on a
> material matter ... such change of view should be communicated ... to
> the other side without delay and when appropriate to the Court.
>
> 7. Where expert evidence refers to photographs, plans, calculations ...
> survey reports or other similar documents there must be provided to the
> opposite party at the same time as the exchange of reports ...".[217]

This case is a civil one, and has been applied in both immigration[218]
and employment[219] tribunal cases. There seems no logical reason not
to apply this guidance in mental health tribunal cases. This means
that such guidelines apply to the evidence of the RMO, MHO or any
other expert who gives evidence in favour of the case for the RMO/
MHO as well as to any expert who provides evidence for the patient
or any other relevant person. Even although the RMO and MHO
will have a direct interest in the outcome of the case (as applicant or
as someone directly involved in the care of the patient) and so in a
sense cannot be described as "independent", these cases still apply to
them since they are classed as skilled witnesses.

In considering the application of the rule that the skilled witness   **5.109**
should not give evidence on the very issue faced by the tribunal, we
encounter a problem. In many cases before the tribunal, the criteria

---

[217] *National Justice Compania Naviera SA v Prudential Assurance Co Ltd* ("The
Ikarian Reefer") 1993 2 Lloyd's Rep 68 at 81.
[218] *Slimani* (01TH00092) (starred), unreported, 12 February 2001.
[219] *Saunder v Birmingham City Council*, unreported, 21 May 2008.

set out in s 64(5) of the 2003 Act will, in some shape or form, be under consideration. As part of the CTO application process, the MHO, RMO and the author of the second mental health report are asked to provide their view on whether the statutory conditions are met. Similarly, with a determination extending the CTO, or in the case of a decision by the tribunal on an application to extend and vary an order, consideration is being given to whether the s 64(5) conditions remain met. While the documentation does not ask if the criteria are met with direct reference to s 64(5), the wording used in the form reflects the wording of the criteria. In addition, the MHO is under a duty to apply for a CTO only when he is in possession of two mental health reports that both cover the s 64(5) criteria.[220] So, the legislation anticipates that the authors of those reports address those criteria specifically. There is a temptation, then, to assume that the skilled witness preparing the application documentation is deciding that the criteria are met and that the tribunal needs only to consider if the factual material set out by the skilled witnesses is accurate. This temptation must be resisted by the tribunal who, at the time or later,[221] come to consider the evidence. This is because the views being expressed are only those of the witnesses, and the tribunal is not obliged to accept them. In fact, in accordance with the case law above, the tribunal is obliged to leave these views on the statutory criteria out of account, and isolate the raw material from the witnesses' opinions. It is for the tribunal to decide, on all of the evidence presented, whether the criteria are met. For instance, the tribunal might accept the evidence of the RMO as credible and reliable in its entirety. However, it may still form the view that in the case being considered, the risk to the safety of others alleged by the RMO is not significant. To put it another way, simply because the RMO says the risk is significant does not mean that this is so. The tribunal must satisfy itself of the existence of the statutory criteria. One reason for this awkward and complex situation is that, unlike in many other cases, the legal criteria that must be fulfilled in tribunal cases require, to a greater or lesser degree, the input of skilled evidence. Another reason is the requirement in the 2003 Act upon the mental health report authors in a CTO application specifically to address the statutory criteria that the tribunal has to be satisfied exist to grant the order.[222] In the context of immigration tribunal cases, it has been commented that:

---

[220] 2003 Act, s 57(3).

[221] In the case of an application to extend a CTO, consideration by the tribunal would generally arise only where there was an appeal lodged by the patient under s 99 or s 100, or where there was a 2-yearly review under s 101(2)(b) of the 2003 Act.

[222] See ss 57(3) and 64(5) of the 2003 Act.

"[immigration tribunals] are entitled to assess the weight to be given to a medical report taking into account the doctor's qualifications, specialisation and experience, the quality of the doctor's reasoning and the extent to which any conclusion is related to established diagnostic criteria and the material on which the opinion is based".[223]

These comments would seem equally applicable to the assessment of such evidence delivered in mental health tribunal cases.

Another way to consider this complex issue is to recognise the importance of separating out the facts and the criteria; they are not one and the same. The MHO will, in making a CTO application, offer a mixture of purely factual evidence (most of which should be contained in the CTO application and any factual report available on the patient) and opinion evidence (the main part of which will be the opinions expressed in the mental health reports that must accompany the application) all of which will be geared to the criteria. Of course, the opinion evidence in particular will, as is noted already, be formulated around the criteria. However, the MHO is not technically offering evidence of the criteria, simply evidence which will support the existence of the criteria. The application of those facts, plus inferences that can be drawn from them,[224] to the criteria, is the task of the tribunal. Taking the example of the significant risk criterion,[225] an RMO might say there is a significant risk in terms of the statutory provision, but the tribunal should not take that to mean that the criterion is established. It should consider (and if not clear on paper should enquire) whether there really is a significant risk, and so should, if necessary, prise behind the RMO's assessment of the risk as "significant". In a sense the RMO is offering a quantification of the risk as significant in his mind, but the question is rather: As a matter of law is the risk significant? The same applies to the issue of significant impairment, when related to the patient's ability to make decisions about medical treatment,[226] and, even more so, to the issue of whether compulsory measures are necessary.[227]

A slightly different consideration applies to the criterion that requires that the patient who is the subject of a CTO application (to cite the most common example of a tribunal application) suffers from a mental disorder[228] and to the criterion regarding the availability of

5.110

5.111

---

[223] I A MacDonald and F Webber (eds), *Immigration Law and Practice in the United Kingdom* (7th edn, 2008), para 18.144. The author refers to a number of cases in support of these comments.
[224] On inferences, see paras 5.123 *et seq*.
[225] 2003 Act, s 64(5)(c).
[226] *Ibid*, s 64(5)(d).
[227] *Ibid*, s 64(5)(e).
[228] *Ibid*, s 64(5)(a).

medical treatment for the disorder.[229] Here, the opinion evidence of the RMO and the other mental health report author carry a more prominent role since the questions here are more heavily reliant on the content of opinion evidence. However, ultimately even the question of whether or not the patient is suffering from a mental disorder is a matter for the tribunal. This is clear when one considers a case in which there is conflicting opinion evidence on the point where, say, an independent psychiatrist in his report disagrees with the RMO on the existence of any disorder. Here, the tribunal will have to choose between the two views. Even where there is no conflicting medical evidence on the point, the tribunal could still reject the evidence of the authors of the mental health reports on the existence of a mental disorder. Franks and Cobb note, in the context of the partial definition of "mental disorder" contained in s 328 of the 2003 Act, that:

> "When considering whether these disorders exist, the Tribunal and Courts *will have regard to* medical evidence." [230] (emphasis added)

5.112   A skilled witness holds no special status *per se*. Such a witness cannot usurp the role of the tribunal and his evidence must be weighed along with all other evidence in the decision-making process. A natural consequence of this is that in a case involving conflicting expert evidence, the tribunal is not obliged simply to choose between the views expressed. The tribunal may decide that no weight can be accorded to evidence tendered and adopt a different view, as long as the view taken is based on other evidence which is accepted, and not on the tribunal's own assumptions.[231] It will also have to explain in the reasons for its decision why it has taken the view that it has.

Who may qualify as a skilled witness?

5.113   In order to qualify as a skilled witness, a person is not required to have a certain minimum level of qualifications or experience. So, for example, an amateur handwriting "expert" was accepted as an opinion witness in *R v Silverlock*.[232] This was further demonstrated in the case of *Hewat v Edinburgh Corporation*,[233] where the Inner House held that the question of whether a hole in a public road could

---

[229] 2003 Act, s 64(5)(b).
[230] R A Franks and D Cobb, *Greens Annotated Acts: Mental Health (Care and Treatment) (Scotland) Act 2003* (2005) at p 366.
[231] Such assumptions must be absent completely from the tribunal's reasoning process – see para 5.123 above.
[232] [1894] 2 QB 766.
[233] 1944 SC 30.

be said to be dangerous was one that could be addressed by a police constable, part of whose duty was to report such dangers. So, as long as the witness can be shown to possess some experience or has informally acquired expertise in the field, the evidence is likely to be admissible. In *White* v *HM Advocate*,[234] experienced police officers were permitted to give evidence as to the amount of a drug which a user might possess for his own consumption (as opposed to for onward sale purposes). Again, in *Wilson* v *HM Advocate*[235] police officers in the drugs squad were allowed to disclose the "received wisdom of persons concerned in drugs enforcement" garnered at seminars and in discussions with customs officers on the question of methods of importation of cannabis resin. So, the important question is not whether the witness possesses certain qualifications, but what the knowledge and experience of the witness is.

Whether a witness is formally qualified or not, it is usually necessary   5.114
to establish during the evidence that the witness is properly (and preferably well) qualified to give opinion evidence about the matter in hand. The first questions asked of a medical witness will be about his studies, degrees, diplomas, research, publications, memberships of professional bodies and experience in the field concerned. It will usually be a simple matter to establish the witness's expertise, given the need for formal qualifications in most scientific or technical fields. Of course, where the witness is the RMO or the other mental health report author, this is not usually done, as the expertise of the witness is assumed. In the case of an independent psychiatrist who has produced a written report, this information will usually be contained in the report, to a greater or lesser degree. Unless the qualifications or experience of a skilled witness are challenged by someone, this should not present a problem; a party will not be permitted to wait until the evidence is over and the witness gone before objecting to the admissibility of his testimony[236] and in any event the matter should be covered in cross-examination. However, where there is more than one skilled witness and where they hold different views on the same point, the depth and nature of the experience of the witness (as well as the extent of exposure to the patient) can be influencing factors on reliability.[237] Each party introducing skilled evidence in such a situation should therefore explore in the oral evidence of his witness their professional credentials. An efficient way to do this would be simply to produce a précis of these credentials on paper for the tribunal, to avoid unnecessary and uncontroversial oral evidence being led.

---

[234] 1986 SCCR 224.
[235] 1987 JC 50; 1988 SCCR 384.
[236] On the timing of objections, see paras 3.115 *et seq*.
[237] On reliability of evidence, see paras 5.121 *et seq* above.

The importance of leading opinion evidence

5.115   Where evidence from a skilled witness is required but not led, this can be fatal, so it is very important to be in a position to judge when such evidence is required and when it is not. The absence of opinion evidence was fatal in the Inner House case of *Columbia Steam Navigation Co v Burns*.[238] The dispute in that case arose out of a collision between two ships. The court was asked to draw certain inferences about the cause of the accident from the nature and extent of damage to one of the vessels. It was held that skilled evidence on the nature and extent of the damage was needed and the inference requested could not be made without it. This links in with the idea that any conclusion reached must be based on evidence, and no assumptions of fact can be made by the tribunal except where within judicial knowledge.[239] As discussed elsewhere,[240] any temptation to compensate for a lack of expert evidence on any point, where such evidence is required, by using the medical expertise on the tribunal is disallowed, and would found a ground of appeal. Of course, this is only a problem where skilled witness evidence is *required*. The view might be taken that the conclusion can be reached by the tribunal by implication from other facts that are satisfactorily established.[241]

Establishing the factual basis for opinion evidence

5.116   Before opinion evidence can competently be led, a factual basis for the expression of such opinions must be established. Thus, in *Blagojevic v HM Advocate*,[242] a case in which the accused disputed the reliability of his confession, expert psychological evidence as to the accused's "suggestibility" was excluded. This was on the technical ground that, since the accused had not himself given evidence as to the nature of his interrogation, there was no proper evidential foundation for opinion evidence regarding the stress or pressure to which the accused had been subjected during his police interviews. The factual evidence must, therefore, be available as a foundation for the opinion evidence based on those facts.[243] In the context of tribunal proceedings also, it is important that the basis of fact is laid for any opinion that is formed. To take a simple example, suppose an independent psychiatrist in his report comes to the conclusion that the patient does not require to be detained in a hospital but could

---

[238] (1895) 2 SLT 449.
[239] On judicial knowledge, see paras 5.13 *et seq* above.
[240] See the full discussion of this at paras 5.22 *et seq.*
[241] On inferences, see paras 5.123 *et seq* below.
[242] 1995 SLT 1189; 1995 SCCR 570.
[243] See also the case of *McD v HM Advocate* 2002 SCCR 896.

be properly looked after in the community now, within supported accommodation, and that the patient should therefore be released. This is pure opinion evidence. The tribunal considering the case could not simply accept that opinion as determinative unless there is evidence that such supported accommodation is in fact available. Absent such evidence, it may well be that the tribunal would have to decide that a hospital-based order is inevitable in terms of the necessity criterion.[244] That factual evidence need not come from the same source, but can come from anywhere. There needs to be a factual basis as a foundation for the opinion evidence.[245] Another example might be a statement from an RMO that if the patient were to be released into the community following the refusal of a CTO application, he would pose a significant risk to the safety of others. Again, this will have to find some basis in fact. Further, that basis in fact must be reasonable given the opinion reached: clearly, if the RMO relies on past suicide attempts by the patient as his basis for a significant risk to the safety of others, this would not make sense, so the factual material relied on does not match the conclusion embodied in the opinion evidence. It should also be borne in mind that the factual basis for the opinion evidence must be accepted by the tribunal as having been established. Where the tribunal is not satisfied that the factual basis for the opinion is established (on the basis of the balance of probabilities) so the opinion itself must be disregarded.

Exception to the rule: opinion evidence from lay witnesses

In some situations, it is possible for a non-skilled witness to provide opinion evidence. However, the scope for such a possibility is narrow. The exception applies only where the witness is able to comment on something that he has seen, heard or sensed and where it would be reasonable for a lay person to offer an opinion on such a matter. For

5.117

---

[244] See s 64(5)(e) of the 2003 Act.

[245] In this example, there may be an argument that resources are lacking, and this can be criticised as a reason for not fulfilling the statutory duty to use the least restrictive option (s 1(4) of the 2003 Act) or for failing in the duties to provide certain services (ss 25 and 26 of the 2003 Act) but, on the other hand, even where a specific and unequivocal duty is placed on the local authority, there is usually still some discretion as to how to apply it: see the cases of *Clunis v Camden and Islington Health Authority* [1998] QB 978 and *R (on the application of K) v Camden and Islington Health Authority* [2002] QB 198, both under the English mental health legislation and more generally the case of *R v London Borough of Barnet, ex p G* [2003] UKHL 57. These cases are considered by H Patrick, *Mental Health, Incapacity and the Law in Scotland* (2006), paras 28.02 and 28.12. The *Clunis* case is cited as relevant in R A Franks and D Cobb, *Greens Annotated Acts: Mental Health (Care and Treatment) (Scotland) Act 2003* (2005) at p 40.

example, in *Kenny v Tudhope*,[246] police officers were permitted to give evidence that the accused's breath smelled of alcohol, his speech was slurred and his eyes glazed, where the charge was one of driving while unfit to do so through the use of drink or drugs. It can be seen, however, that in this example the issue is one upon which most adults could be expected to form a reasonably reliable view, given an awareness of the everyday use and abuse of alcohol and its effects. The same cannot be said for less commonplace occurrences and conditions, and whether expert evidence is required is ultimately a matter of law. One example might be an observation by a lay person that a patient seemed to be acting in a strange and unorthodox manner, although stopping short of whether the patient seemed to be suffering from some form of mental disorder, as this, of course, requires evidence from a skilled witness.

THE EVALUATION OF THE EVIDENCE

5.118   Admissible evidence must be evaluated by the tribunal. This evaluation process is key to the decision-making path of any judicial body. The trouble is that the evaluation process is not (and cannot be) a scientific exercise. Even where the judicial body consists of a single member, the evaluation process will vary wildly and will be difficult to distil into some kind of formulaic process. Where the judicial body is made up of three members, the process becomes even more complex since each member may view any part of the evidence (or any witness) in two or three different ways. It is possible, however, to discuss the evaluation process in very broad terms, by considering five key areas of that process: credibility, reliability, inferences, weight and sufficiency. Each will now be dealt with in turn. Before doing so, it should be remembered that only the evidence that is considered to be admissible will be eligible to be assessed: inadmissible evidence must be ignored completely.

(1) Credibility

5.119   This applies almost exclusively to the assessment of oral evidence and, simply put, the issue here is: "Is the witness telling the truth?". Of course, the answer is not as simple as this. The view might be taken that a witness is telling the truth on some matters and not on others: witnesses do not have to be assessed as complete liars on one hand or paragons of virtue on the other. Where the tribunal takes

---

[246] 1984 SCCR 290.

the view that all or part of the testimony[247] of a witness is untruthful, the law is clear: that evidence should simply be ignored. Of course, where the decision is that the whole of the witness's testimony is untruthful, the tribunal must eliminate everything the witness says from its consideration. A key point about credibility is that the tribunal is *not* permitted to assume that the opposite of what a non-credible witness says must be true.[248] So, if a patient gives evidence to the effect that he takes his medication all of the time, without fail, the tribunal might disbelieve this. However, it is not entitled to assume from this that he does not ever take his medication, or even that he has failed to take it once. Since any disbelieved evidence must simply be put aside and ignored, this means that no positive implication can be taken from it. Of course, if there was evidence from another source that is believed, to the effect that the patient did not always take his medication, the tribunal can conclude from this that the patient had not only lied about his compliance but that he had, in fact, failed to comply.

There is a more fundamental question about credibility, which is: how does one assess whether a witness is telling the truth or not? Again, this is not a scientific exercise. There is no need for the tribunal member to become an amateur psychoanalyst who, for example, scrutinises the mannerisms of the witness to try to deduce whether he is showing any of the classic signs of dishonesty. In fact, such an approach would clearly be inappropriate. There are two main ways to assess credibility. The first is to consider the general demeanour of the witness; does he seem shifty, awkward, overly nervous or hesitant in the delivery of the evidence on the point in question? This can be a difficult assessment to make, as witnesses in a tribunal setting could exhibit all of these as symptoms of the difficult process of giving evidence in a judicial forum and in front of others, and still be telling the truth. The second way to assess credibility is to do so comparatively. In other words, where the evidence of two witnesses conflicts on a particular point, the tribunal could come to the conclusion that it prefers the evidence of one witness over the other. In the context of credibility, this is a diplomatic way of branding a witness as untruthful on a particular point without actually saying so.

5.120

---

[247] "Testimony" is a term that refers to the oral evidence of a witness in judicial proceedings.

[248] There are no Scottish civil cases in this area but, in criminal cases, this has been made clear: *Fisher* v *Guild* 1991 SLT 253; 1991 SCCR 308, HCJ, cf *Winter* v *Heywood* 1995 JC 60; 1995 SLT 586, but the *Winter* decision is doubted in *Brown* v *HM Advocate* 2003 SLT 2. It seems logical that this line of authority should apply in civil cases (and therefore in tribunal proceedings), as the rationale on this point holds equal force in both types of cases.

(2) Reliability

5.121   A more common assessment tool in the context of tribunal hearings is reliability. The question of whether or not a witness is giving his evidence in a reliable fashion can take a number of forms, but the overall question here is: "Is this witness sufficiently well placed to give this evidence?". So, it might be argued that a witness does not possess the requisite qualifications to allow a reliable skilled opinion to be delivered. This might be the case where, for instance, it is argued that a medically qualified witness is insufficiently experienced in cases relating to a particular mental disorder in order to give a reliable opinion on its manifestation in the patient. Skilled (or expert) evidence is discussed elsewhere,[249] but one would have to be very careful when making such an argument. Another possible reliability issue might arise where it is said that a witness is ill equipped to comment on a particular issue because of lack of exposure to the underlying material. For example, a witness might give evidence that a patient had been neglected on a hospital ward. That witness could be asked to explain how that conclusion is reached. Suppose the answer is that the witness visited the patient in that hospital only once in 5 years, and for a 10-minute spell during which the patient was left unobserved by staff. In such a case, it could be argued that the witness's evidence on this point is unreliable. The witness is not, from this very limited perspective, able to provide a reliable assessment of whether the patient had been neglected in the ward. Once again, as with credibility, reliability can be comparative. So, two skilled witnesses may provide conflicting assessments on whether a patient requires to be treated on the ward or in the community. One example of this might be where an RMO is seeking a hospital-based CTO and where an independent psychiatrist recommends a community-based one. The tribunal in this situation might conclude that the RMO's opinion is more reliable than that of the independent psychiatrist, as a result of the RMO's extensive dealings with the patient over a number of years, contrasting with a single 1-hour examination by the independent psychiatrist coupled with scrutiny of the notes. On the other hand, the view might equally be taken that the conclusions of the independent psychiatrist, having applied a fresh mind to the patient's situation, are more firmly grounded in the facts than those of the RMO.

5.122   Sometimes a witness might be regarded as unreliable, simply due to being mistaken on his recollection or interpretation of events. Usually, this view will be taken in a comparative context. For example, the mother of a patient might recollect in her evidence

---

[249] See above at paras 5.102 et seq.

two violent incidents involving her daughter as a patient during the times she was visiting her; the MHO and ward staff might insist that there were four, all of which were recorded in writing at the time. If the tribunal took the view that there had been four incidents, this would not necessarily mean that it was of the view that the patient's mother was lying or was not a good witness on the point; it could simply conclude that she was mistaken and so her evidence should be regarded as unreliable.

(3) Inferences

Part of the evaluation process involves the use of inferences. An   5.123
inference is essentially a conclusion that can naturally be drawn from a fact or combination of facts. However, there is a fine line between drawing a permissible inference and indulging in speculation. An example of an inference might be the conclusion that where a patient has refused during a period of several months prior to the hearing to take anti-psychotic medication by injection, this trend is likely to continue in the future. The tribunal would be entitled to infer this. Having said this, there are a few rules that qualify the ability to infer conclusions from facts. First of all, the conclusions must be obvious and natural consequences of the facts being relied upon. There must be no element of speculation or leaps of logic. Often, inferences are obvious and uncontroversial. Second, if there is evidence that would tend to negative the inference, it must be considered. This does not mean that the inference cannot be made, just that the tribunal requires to consider whether the evidence against the inference is to be accepted. An example might be, in the above scenario, evidence from the patient that he would, in the event of his release under an order in the community, be prepared to take medication by injection. If the tribunal accepts this evidence as credible and reliable, the inference cannot be reached. On the other hand, the view might be taken that the patient's evidence on this point is lacking in credibility as a pretence being put up by him in an effort to be released from hospital. In that event, the tribunal will reject the patient's evidence on this point and can make the inference.

Third, the nature of an inference is such that it is a conclusion   5.124
drawn by the tribunal; this means that there is no need for a witness to reach the inference during evidence to the tribunal. Of course, often witnesses will draw inferences, particularly skilled witnesses, as that is a significant part of what they must do to reach an opinion, but the tribunal is free to draw an inference that no witness has made, as long as that inference is justified. The converse is also true: the tribunal can refuse to draw an inference from certain facts, even

where a witness has or witnesses have done so, either because the inference is unjustified as it is speculative or as a result of credible and reliable evidence countering the inference.

5.125   Finally, an inference cannot be drawn from a negative. A good example is where a patient declines to lodge a report following an independent psychiatric assessment. It might be thought to be natural to conclude from this that the report is negative and that it supports the position of the MHO or RMO. However, this inference cannot be drawn as there is no positive evidence to support it. While this might seem odd, it is logical since there may be reasons for a decision by a patient not to use an independent report that is favourable, for instance where the patient cannot accept part of the report's conclusions or observations and so refuses to permit the lodging of the report by his solicitor, despite its overall positive tenor. In addition, drawing an inference from a negative is dangerous as it is difficult to know how far to go: in the above example, it is difficult to know what the inference could be – that the independent report supported the RMO's position in full? that it was supportive in part? that it was inconclusive? With an inference drawn from positive evidence, the tribunal (and ultimately the appeal court considering whether the inference was properly drawn) can calculate and explain the extent and nature of the inference and so justify it with reference to certain established facts. The inability to draw an inference from a negative applies to the complete absence of evidence too: so where a patient does not give evidence at all, or chooses not to on a particular point, say an allegation of violent conduct, the tribunal cannot infer from the silence of the patient on that point that the violent conduct took place. It may conclude that it did from other evidence, but that conclusion must not be based on or influenced in any way by the silence of the patient.

(4) Weight

5.126   In considering all evidence, whether conflicting or not, the tribunal will be indulging in a weighing process. Each piece of evidence will be mulled over in the private session during which the tribunal deliberates.[250] Where a piece of evidence is accepted as admissible, it will be weighed up. The tribunal as a whole may place particular emphasis on the weight to be taken from a particular piece of evidence, while placing little or no weight on another piece. This does not mean that during deliberations each word of written and oral evidence needs to be minutely examined. In most cases, there

---

[250] The task of the examination of the evidence and its application to the statutory criteria is discussed in detail at paras 7.21 et seq.

will be a large body of evidence that is uncontroversial and that can be accepted by the tribunal as factually correct, and where the weight to be placed on that body of evidence is obvious. This will often lead to the focus of the tribunal being directed to certain key controversial points. For instance, the question of whether the patient poses a significant risk to the health, safety or welfare of himself or safety of another[251] might be amply covered by the written evidence of the MHO and the authors of the mental health reports, and may not be challenged during the hearing by the patient or a representative. Instead, there might be some cross-examination and submissions by the patient's lawyer on the question of whether a hospital-based order is necessary.[252] The tribunal's deliberations, then, will tend to focus on the evidence that can help to answer the latter question; as long as the written evidence and conclusions on significant risk are clear, these are unlikely to merit long discussions by the tribunal. Where no weight is placed on particular evidence, that evidence should simply be ignored, whether it has been heard in full or not.

(5) Sufficiency

Although the tribunal's deliberation and decision-making processes are dealt with elsewhere,[253] we need to consider the concept of sufficiency here. Essentially, this concept requires consideration to be given to whether the party with the burden of proof has discharged that burden by proving the essential facts to the required standard of proof. The key here is the presence of the essential facts. What are these facts? This depends on what the party with the burden of proof in the case wishes the tribunal to do. Where the tribunal is considering whether or not to grant a CTO, the MHO will require to ensure that credible and reliable evidence is available that is sufficient to establish that, on the balance of probabilities, certain facts are established. These facts will be those that are key to each of the s 64(5) criteria, and these will vary according to the nature of the case. So, the tribunal needs to identify the facts that have been established on the balance of probabilities. However, there is one other tool the tribunal has: inferences. These have been dealt with already,[254] and they allow certain conclusions to be reached from facts that the tribunal finds have been established. So, the tribunal takes the proven facts, adds any inferences that have been drawn from them, and the sum total is the material which the tribunal has

5.127

---

[251] 2003 Act, s 64(5)(c).
[252] Ibid.
[253] At paras 4.96 et seq and Chapter 7.
[254] Above, paras 5.123 et seq.

available to it in order to allow it to consider whether the criteria have been met. In a sense, the facts that are accepted as proven on the balance of probabilities, plus the inferences that can be drawn from them, form a pool or resource bank from which the tribunal can draw to allow it to consider whether the statutory criteria have been established. Each fact and inference can be used more than once, and in different combinations for different criteria.

5.128   There is no minimum requirement as to the volume of evidence to be offered on each of the criteria, so one piece of evidence that the tribunal decides allows it to establish one fact may be enough. Of course, the MHO has no way of knowing in advance what the tribunal will decide is sufficient, so as much evidence as is available and relevant will be offered in an attempt to ensure that the tribunal finds each of the criteria established.

5.129   While the issue of sufficiency affects all of the criteria, it is more often a live issue in relation to certain criteria than with others. For instance, where the tribunal is considering whether the absence of medical treatment for the patient's disorder would create a significant risk to the health, safety or welfare of the patient or to the safety of another,[255] the tribunal will need to consider whether sufficient evidence of risk of certain events happening has been led to allow it to reach the view that "significant" risk exists. This leads to a consideration of what is "significant". This is a question of sufficiency and as such is a question of law (as are all of the criteria). The tribunal will consider whether the facts found established (plus any inferences drawn from them) are sufficient to allow the conclusion to be reached that the risk is significant and not minor or of medium severity. So the view might be reached that the evidence, when properly evaluated, points to a small risk. In such a case, there has been insufficient evidence led to allow that criterion to be satisfied. It is important here to recall, as noted earlier, that the decision on significant risk is for the tribunal, not for the parties or even for the RMO as a witness. A witness or party may comment on whether he feels that there is a risk of something happening, and that evaluation, as that belonging to a skilled witness, will be taken account of, but the tribunal must reach its own conclusion from all of the facts and inferences.[256] Another consideration on the same criterion might relate to the meaning of "welfare". The extent to which this word might relate to general cleanliness and personal hygiene could be debated. Again, this is a sufficiency conclusion for the tribunal: is

---

[255] 2003 Act, s 64(5)(c).
[256] For a further discussion of this difficult distinction between opinion evidence and the criteria, see above under "Opinion Evidence" at paras 5.109 et seq.

there sufficient evidence that a significant risk would be caused to the welfare of the patient in the event of that person not obtaining the available medical treatment? Again, the witness should not simply be permitted to state that the welfare of the patient will be at risk, since the witness may be misinterpreting what "welfare" means, and the tribunal may take the view that the patient's welfare will not be at risk at all. Instead, the tribunal should prise under the witness's understanding of what he understands "welfare" to mean. The same applies to any consideration of "safety".

CHAPTER 6

TRIBUNAL APPLICATIONS, APPEALS, REFERENCES AND REVIEWS

The 2003 Act makes provision for the manner in which various **6.01** types of proceedings before the Tribunal are to be initiated and progressed. This chapter deals with the provisions relating to the procedure for applications, appeals, references and reviews, which are contained in, respectively, Pts II, III, IV and V of the Rules. Cases remitted to the Tribunal following a successful appeal to the sheriff principal or the Court of Session, for which provision is made in Pt VI, are covered in the chapter dealing with appeals from the Tribunal.[1]

At first sight, there is no obvious logic to the terms of art chosen **6.02** by the drafters for some of the different means of proceeding as between applications and appeals. Where a patient is dissatisfied with a determination made by an RMO to extend his CTO, he may make an application for its revocation. Where he is unhappy with a decision of the Scottish Ministers to vary a condition of conditional discharge, however, his remedy is to appeal to the Tribunal. What distinguishes those provisions of the Act which allow for appeals to the Tribunal against decisions[2] from those which permit applications to revoke orders or determinations,[3] however, is that the statutory provisions relating to appeals set a time limit within which the appeal must be commenced. Many of the matters against which appeals can be marked are decisions which effect an immediate change in the practical arrangements for the care of a patient, for example appeals against transfers from one hospital to another, or against recall from conditional discharge. It makes sense for any well-founded challenge to be made quickly, both from the point of view of the patient and from that of the institutions involved.

---

[1] Chapter 8.
[2] Sections 125(2), 126(2), 178, 201(1), 204(1), 219(2), 220(2) and 290(1).
[3] Sections 99, 100, 120, 163, 164, 192 and 214(2).

6.03   By contrast, applications for revocation of orders or determinations are not limited to being made within a certain period after the decision complained of. Those relating to applications for revocation can be made (subject to certain restrictions) at any time, in accordance with the need for a patient to be able to seek review of the lawfulness of his continuing detention before a court, in accordance with Art 5(4) ECHR. Some, such as an application for revocation or variation of a CTO,[4] cannot be made within the 3 months following the making of the order in question. If it is considered that the order should not have been made, the appropriate course is to consider whether to appeal from the Tribunal to the sheriff principal or the Court of Session under ss 320 or 322 of the 2003 Act.[5] Applications for revocation are appropriate when it is recognised that the order has been properly made, but it is thought that the evidence would no longer indicate that the criteria for an order are met. Perhaps surprisingly, the 2003 Act does not set out a test for the revocation of any order. In the absence of this, it is suggested that an order should be revoked only where it is concluded by the tribunal that one or more of the criteria in place for the order under scrutiny no longer applies. There are also provisions limiting the scope for repeated applications in relation to the revocation or variation of a CTO where there have previous unsuccessful applications in relation to the same order, aimed at presenting a series of related applications in quick succession.[6]

6.04   Applications which fall to be made by officials such as MHOs and RMOs are applications which they are under a duty to make when certain sets of circumstances arise.[7] Time limits arise for MHOs and RMOs because the power to detain a patient under an earlier certificate or order may be about to come to an end. MHOs have to be alert to the need to apply for a CTO, if it is required, before the expiry of a short-term detention certificate. Applying timeously has the effect, in terms of s 68 of the 2003 Act, of extending the period during which the patient may lawfully be detained under the short-term detention certificate by 5 working days.[8] Similarly, RMOs have to be alert to the need to apply for extensions of compulsion orders before the end of the 6-month

---

[4] Section 100 of the Act.
[5] On such appeals, see paras 8.10 *et seq* and 8.15 *et seq* respectively.
[6] See s 100(6), (7) and (8).
[7] See, for example, s 57(1). Where two medical practitioners are satisfied that that the criteria for making a CTO are met, the MHO is under a duty to apply for a CTO.
[8] For a discussion of the effect of not complying with this time limit, see paras 3.127 *et seq.*

period which would otherwise bring the compulsion order to an end.

APPLICATIONS AND APPEALS

Applications – general

The Rules make provision for each of the different types of application which may be made under the 2003 Act. In relation to each of the types of application which may be made by a patient or named person, it is specified that the application must be made in writing.[9] In relation to the applications (such as those for CTOs) which must be made by officials or medical personnel, there is no specific requirement that the application be in writing, but it is required instead that the application should state the matters mentioned in whichever is the relevant section of the Act.[10] It is clear that this can only be done effectively in written form, and certain applications require in terms of the statute to be accompanied by particular documents. Exceptions to the requirement for writing are made in relation to applications for interim CTOs, which can be made orally at a hearing, or in writing sent to the Tribunal,[11] and applications in relation to the appointment of a named person where that is expedient.[12]

6.05

The Rules themselves give no indication as to the form in which particular applications are to be made, other than that it is specified in relation to each type of application that it must be made. As a matter of practice, however, there are forms for particular types of application and for the submission of medical reports in association with these, where that is appropriate, as in an application for a CTO.[13] In general, the applications which require to be made by officials, such as that for a CTO, or for extension of a compulsion order, are made on proforma forms. The Tribunal provides a very basic form for patients and named persons, indicating the information required as to the identity of the applicant, patient and named person, and providing a space to indicate why the application is being made. There is no requirement that any particular form be used, provided that the necessary information is provided. The

6.06

---

[9] Subject to the exception in r 17(5) in relation to certain applications relating to a named person, which may be made orally where this is expedient. Examples of the requirement for writing in applications by patients and named persons may be found in rr 10, 11, 13, 15, 16, 17(1) and 18.

[10] See, for example, r 6(1), and its reference to the matters specified in s 63(2).

[11] Rule 7.

[12] Rule 17(5).

[13] These are available on the website of the Mental Health Tribunal for Scotland at https://www.mhtscotland.gov.uk/mhts/541.81.211.html.

Tribunal is appropriately flexible in accepting as applications a fairly wide range of correspondence from patients who seek to challenge decisions made about their care, often, at least in the first instance, without the assistance of a lawyer or other representative.

6.07   The provisions relating to applications have certain common features, and it would be otiose simply to repeat here the terms of each of the relevant rules. Each rule specifies what is to be contained in the application. The Rules then make provision for the intimation of the application to relevant persons, and for sending a copy of the application to parties. Slight variations as to the persons on whom intimation is to be made appear in relation to different types of application.[14] Similarly, there are slight variations as to the information that is to be provided in the notice providing intimation, depending on the nature of the application. In some instances, the Clerk is required to fix a hearing as soon as possible. This is obviously necessary in situations of urgency, such as a challenge to a certificate made under s 114(2) or 115(2) of the Act,[15] or to a short-term detention certificate.[16] Each of the rules provides for a notice of response to be sent to the Tribunal by persons wishing to make representations or to lead or produce evidence.

6.08   Specific provision is made in r 8 for an application for a CTO where an application is made under s 63 of the Act and s 68 of the Act applies. Where an application for a CTO has been made before what would otherwise have been the expiry of a short-term detention certificate, s 68 allows for a further 5 working days of lawful detention. The rule provides that where s 68 applies, the Tribunal requires to hold a hearing in order to determine whether an ICTO should be made. If the tribunal determines that it should not be made, it must determine the application. This provision reflects the terms of s 69 of the Act.[17]

6.09   Rules which relate to applications in which a hearing will have been fixed at an early date[18] anticipate the need for a further hearing,

---

[14] Compare, for example, r 5 and r 11.

[15] Rule 11(4).

[16] Rule 5(5). In such cases, the criteria to be considered by the tribunal are slightly different to those to be considered in a CTO application. See s 50(4) of the 2003 Act which refers to s 44(4)(a), (b) and (d) plus the necessity of continuation in hospital (s 50(4)(b)). Section 44(4)(d) refers to significant risk relating to a stay in hospital. It is also relevant to consider that s 44(3)(b) refers to the medical practitioner requiring to form the view that the s 44(4) conditions are *likely* to be met. However, under s 50, the tribunal is considering whether the conditions (minus (c)) *are* met.

[17] For a discussion of the possible consequences of ss 68–69 not being adhered to, see paras 3.127 *et seq.*

[18] Such as applications for a CTO where s 68 applies, or under s 120 for revocation of certificates under ss 114(2) and 115(2).

which is in practical terms very likely to arise where parties have been summoned at short notice, and may not be fully prepared to deal with the matter.[19] In these situations the Tribunal is given particular power to make directions and to take other steps that may be necessary for the proper conduct of the forthcoming hearing. It is not entirely clear that these provisions are necessary, in that these powers are provided elsewhere in the Rules.[20] What these provisions do make clear, where they appear within the body of rules such as r 8 and r 11, is that before fixing a further hearing or exercising any of the specified case management powers, the Tribunal is to afford all the relevant persons who are present the opportunity to be heard.

Rule 19 makes provision as to the content of notices of response. Rule 20 makes general provision for the withdrawal of certain types of applications either at any time before the hearing, by submission of a notice signed by the applicant, or at the hearing on the application. Notwithstanding the terms of the rule, which seems to suggest that written notice will not be required if the application is withdrawn at a hearing, it seems to be the practice of the Tribunal to require the applicant or his legal representative to complete a form indicating that the application has been withdrawn. Rule 20 does not apply to applications under ss 92, 95, 148, 158 and 161, all of which relate to extension and/or variation of compulsion orders; or to applications under s 191, which are applications by the Scottish Ministers for various orders revoking compulsion orders and restriction orders, or for an order conditionally discharging a patient. It is not entirely clear what is intended by the exclusion of these types of applications from r 20. Presumably there are circumstances in which the applicant in one of these types of application will for good reason decide that it should not be pursued. It may be that the drafter intended that the withdrawal of an application of this type should as a matter of policy remain before the tribunal and an explanation given for its withdrawal, having regard to the issues of public protection that may arise where compulsion orders and restriction orders are in issue.

6.10

Amendment of the application or notice of response is dealt with in r 21. In practice, written amendment of applications is rare; alteration to the terms of an application is more likely to arise in the course of a hearing, and to be sought orally, giving rise, sometimes, to the need to adjourn in order to make all relevant parties aware of the proposed alteration. Again, in practice, the terms of notices of response rarely play a material part in the deliberations of the tribunal, and it is unusual for detailed notices of response to be put in, or amendments to be made to them.

6.11

---

[19] For example, r 8(3) and (4) and r 11(9) and (10).
[20] In rr 49, 53 and 55.

Applications made by MHOs, RMOs and the Scottish Ministers

6.12   As mentioned above, there are forms for completion by professional and institutional applicants, and on which the reports from medical practitioners may be included, as in the case of an application for a CTO.[21] Practice in filling in these forms varies as to the quantity of information provided, the detail in which the forms are completed, and the attention given to addressing each of the statutory criteria relevant to the application in question. The forms are designed so as to assist those completing them to address the criteria, by providing text boxes into which information relevant to each of the criteria may be placed.

6.13   It is good practice to provide the tribunal with as much relevant information in these forms as possible. Some tribunals indicate that they will treat the reports in the forms as the evidence-in-chief of their authors, subject to any amendments or updates to be provided orally, thus limiting the time that needs to be taken over oral evidence. All the evidence, whether contained in the reports or given orally, will then be subject to challenge in cross-examination. The scope for dealing with matters in this way, which we would suggest is in accordance with the aim of dealing with proceedings expeditiously,[22] is, however, limited, if the material in the written application is not sufficiently detailed, and a great deal of additional information needs to be elicited in oral evidence.[23]

Applications by patient or named person

6.14   The provisions relating to applications which may be made by patients or named persons follow a recognisable pattern, and it is not necessary or helpful to repeat here the precise terms of the Rules. In addition to the general requirement that applications are to be made in writing, the Rules set out certain basic requirements as to the information that has to be contained in the application. In addition to information as to the identity of the applicant, the patient and the named person, and the place of detention or residence of the patient, where applicable, a brief statement of reasons for the application has to be given. Applications require to be signed by the applicant.

Appeals

6.15   The provisions relating to appeals follow the same basic pattern as those relating to applications by patients. There is provision as

---

[21] These are available at https://www.mhtscotland.gov.uk/mhts/541.81.211.html.

[22] This consideration is part of the overriding principle in r 4.

[23] For further commentary on this point, see para 4.48.

to the basic information required to be given in writing in order to initiate an appeal,[24] as to sending a copy of the appeal to, in this instance, the respondent, with information as to the time and place of the hearing,[25] and for a notice of response.[26] In relation to appeals, the respondent is to intimate whether or not the appeal is to be opposed. There is provision also for withdrawal of opposition to the appeal. It is not specified what the practical effect of withdrawing opposition will be and, in particular, whether the tribunal will simply grant the appeal unopposed and make the order sought in the appeal.

Where an appeal is withdrawn under r 26, no further appeal **6.16** against the same decision will be permitted. In practical terms, the statutory time limits applicable to these appeals would be likely to preclude any such further appeal in any event.

REFERENCES AND REVIEWS

Parts IV and V deal respectively with references and reviews. The **6.17** tribunal is under a duty to review certain determinations in relation to compulsion orders under s 101(2) and 165(2). Where the circumstances specified in those sections exist, the tribunal has no discretion, and requires to review the determination. A review is not a procedure initiated by a party, but one which requires to take place as a matter of law.

The majority of references also come before the tribunal as a matter **6.18** of law. Although a party, whether that be the RMO, the Commission or the Scottish Ministers, refers the matter to the tribunal, once the reference is made, the tribunal requires to consider it. In relation to some of the references under the 2003 Act, the referee has no discretion as to whether to refer the matter, as, for example, where a patient is subject to a compulsion order and a restriction order, and no reference has been made for 2 years and no application under s 191 or s 192 has been made to the Tribunal. The Commission, on the other hand, under ss 98(2) and 162(2) of the 2003 Act, has a discretion to make a reference if it appears to the Commission to be appropriate to do so.

Unsurprisingly, in that context, there is no provision for withdrawal **6.19** of a review or a reference, although there is provision for withdrawal of a notice of response, and for amendment of the reference or notice of response.[27] In relation to each of these procedures, provision is

---

[24] Rule 23.
[25] Rule 24.
[26] Rule 25.
[27] Rules 32 and 37.

made for intimation of the reference or review to the appropriate persons, and for notices of response.[28]

SENDING OF NOTICES AND DOCUMENTS

6.20   Where a relevant person has appointed a representative, any notices required by the various rules associated with applications, appeals, references and reviews will be sent to his representative, in accordance with r 54(5). Similarly, where the rules require the sending to him of documents, that will be effected by service on his representative.

---

[28] Rules 30, 31, 35 and 36.

CHAPTER 7

TRIBUNAL DECISIONS

In the course of proceedings before the tribunal, a variety of decisions   **7.01**
will have to be made, some in relation to preliminary and procedural
matters, and others of a substantive nature, whether making or
refusing interim orders, or reaching a determination which will finally
dispose of the proceedings. This chapter is concerned with the way
in which the tribunal communicates its decisions, and the statutory
and other legal rules concerned with the issuing of written reasons
for such decisions.

Like other courts and tribunals, there are occasions when, rather   **7.02**
than making a substantive order authorising particular measures in
respect of a patient, it will be open to the tribunal to make orders
which deal only with procedural matters. Many of the matters that
come before the tribunal do not require a substantive order to be
made on each occasion the case calls. There may be, for example,
an existing order of some sort authorising care and treatment, but
the patient or his named person is seeking to have that revoked, or
the matter is the subject of a reference to the tribunal under one of
the 2-year review provisions. In such situations, if the tribunal needs
further information to allow it to consider the application properly, it
does not need to make any further order authorising the treatment in
question. It may simply adjourn the case to another date under r 65,
making such directions as it considers appropriate for the purposes
of case management.[1]

Where a CTO is being sought in respect of the patient, it may   **7.03**
not be possible to ensure the appropriate care and treatment of the
patient without making an interim order. Interim orders authorising
the care and treatment of the patient may themselves be accompanied
by orders giving directions regarding the future management of the
case.

---

[1] See paras 7.30 *et seq* on directions.

7.04   Schedule 2, para 13(3) to the 2003 Act provides that a decision of the Tribunal shall be recorded in a document which contains a full statement of the facts found by the Tribunal and the reasons for the decision. This is also reflected in the terms of r 72(7). Not every decision of the Tribunal involves fact finding. Where no order is being made, but an application or reference is simply being adjourned, it is unlikely that the Tribunal will be in a position to make or record any findings of fact, not having heard all (or possibly any) of the evidence. Every decision must, however, be in written form, and it is the intention of the legislation that the reasons for the decision be clear from the written record of the decision, whether that decision is one based on findings of fact, or a purely procedural decision dealing with the management of the matter. The statute makes no distinction in this respect between decisions in which interim orders authorising treatment are pronounced and those in which "full" orders, for example a CTO, are pronounced, or between decisions in which orders are made and those in which an application is adjourned.

7.05   In practice, in most cases, the tribunal will adjourn for a period after hearing evidence and submissions, in order to deliberate and reach a decision. The hearing will then reconvene, and the tribunal will inform those attending of the decision that has been reached. Rule 72(1) makes provision for a decision of the tribunal either to be given at the end of the hearing or to be reserved. Tribunal Conveners will usually try to give some brief indication of the reasons for the decision. It is in any event good practice to try to give those attending an explanation, in ordinary language, as to the basis for the decision. Sometimes, however, there is some merit in not providing reasons orally, or in providing an abridged version of oral reasons, since this might lead to a re-opening of the case, with participants seeking to argue their case further. Much will depend on how the hearing has gone and tribunal members should exercise caution when deciding how detailed the oral delivery of the decision should be. In more complex cases, and in particular in applications for conditional discharge in respect of patients subject to compulsion orders and restriction orders, evidence may have been lengthy, and the tribunal may be unable to issue a decision orally at the end of the hearing. In such an event, the decision will be issued only after the tribunal has had the opportunity to deliberate fully on all of the evidence, and the first intimation of the decision will usually be of the written findings of the tribunal.

7.06   Tribunal decisions are recorded on pre-printed forms relating to the various types of applications and references that may be made under the 2003 Act. The form will be completed so as to indicate in very short form the conclusion of the tribunal relative to the various statutory criteria at issue in each type of application, and indicating the measures authorised by any order. It does not, however, give any reasons for the decision, and would not, on its own, constitute a written decision of the type required by the Act or the Rules. The forms are signed by the tribunal Convener. The findings of the tribunal, where findings are made, and the reasons for the decision, are recorded in writing drafted by the tribunal Convener in a document separate from the forms just mentioned. The practice of the tribunal, depending on the nature of the order being made, is that these may be recorded in the form of an interlocutor with explanatory note, or in a form headed "Findings and Reasons" or "Full Findings and Reasons". Where the decision is one to adjourn the hearing and where (as would usually be the case in such instances) no findings-in-fact are issued, a summary of the proceedings and reasons for the adjournment will be included in a form entitled "Decision" (formerly entitled "Interlocutor"). In any case where directions are to be issued, whether findings-in-fact are also issued or not, these will be recorded in a separate form, again the one headed "Decision". This is a change to the previous practice of including them in the "Full Findings and Reasons" form, in order that the staff at MHTS headquarters can see at a glance any directions issued, so that they can take any action to ensure that they are intimated for implementation.

Schedule 2, para 13(4)(a) to the 2003 Act provides that the Tribunal shall inform each party of its decision. As mentioned above, the Tribunal will, in the ordinary case, inform those present at the hearing of the decision. Not all parties may be present at a hearing. The Tribunal Clerks arrange for distribution of copies of the completed pre-printed forms to parties. Paragraph 13(4)(b) provides that the document containing the statement of findings and reasons is to be sent to each party by the Tribunal "as soon as practicable after completion".[2]   **7.07**

Rule 72 makes further provision in relation to decisions. The decision is to be signed by the Convener and dated.[3] Notice of the decision is to be sent, as soon as reasonably practicable, to the parties and such other relevant person as the tribunal may direct,[4] along with information as to any rights of appeal and applicable time limits.[5] The   **7.08**

---

[2] As amended by Sch 1, para 32(26)(b) to the Mental Health (Care and Treatment) (Scotland) Act 2003 (Modification of Enactments) Order 2005 (SSI 2005/465). As originally enacted, the Act provided that the written reasons were to be sent to all parties as soon as reasonably practicable after a party requested the Tribunal to provide it.
[3] Rule 72(2).
[4] Rule 72(3).
[5] Rule 72(4).

decision is also to be sent to the Commission.[6] Where, following a successful appeal, the case has been remitted from the appellate court to the tribunal for further determination, the decision of the tribunal is also to be sent to that court as soon as reasonably practicable.[7] Unless a decision is made at the end of the hearing, it is to be treated as having been made on the date on which it is sent to the parties. Rule 72(7) reflects the requirements of the 2003 Act, discussed at greater length below, to give a decision in writing, with a statement of the facts found and the reasons for the decision.

7.09   Mere clerical mistakes in a decision in the document in which the decision is recorded may be corrected by the Convener by certificate in writing.[8] Where this is done, or if a decision is altered by an appellate court, the Clerk is to notify parties and the Commission of that change.[9] Where a document requires to be signed by the Convener, but the Convener is by reason of death or incapacity unable to sign it, it may be signed by the other tribunal members or the President, with a certification that the Convener is unable to sign.[10]

THE REQUIREMENT TO GIVE REASONS

7.10   It is important that all those involved in working with the Tribunal system are alert to the importance of the tribunal providing reasons for its decisions that are adequate in law. Those writing the decisions must take care to communicate adequately their reasons for making their decisions on matters of fact and of law. As explained below, failure to give adequate reasons may provide the basis for a successful appeal against the tribunal's decision; however good the underlying reasoning may be, if it is not adequately disclosed, the efforts of the tribunal will be in vain. It is desirable, quite apart from the statutory requirement to give written reasons, that parties be made aware of the basis on which the decisions of the tribunal are made. The requirement to give reasons also assists with focusing the minds of the decision-makers: if they know that they will have to justify themselves in writing, that perhaps assists them in approaching their task with the appropriate rigour, and on concentrating properly on the matter before them. As Lord Clyde has remarked:

> "The advantages of the provision of reasons have been often rehearsed. They relate to the decision-making process, in strengthening that process itself, in increasing the public confidence in it, and in the desirability of

---

[6] Rule 72(5).
[7] *Ibid.*
[8] Rule 72(8).
[9] Rule 72(9).
[10] Rule 72(10).

the disclosure of error where error exists. They relate also to the parties immediately affected by the decision, in enabling them to know the strengths and weaknesses of their respective cases, and to facilitate appeal where that course is appropriate."[11]

It is also important that those practising before the tribunal are alert to written decisions which disclose error on the part of the tribunal, or which fail to make it clear to the parties the basis on which the decision was taken. Where error is disclosed, it may be appropriate to appeal, if the error is of the type giving rise to a right of appeal. As discussed more fully below, a failure to give reasons which make clear how and why the decision was taken may itself be an error of law, and appeal may be appropriate where there is such a failure.

7.11

The terms of Sch 2, para 13(3) to the 2003 Act may be argued to be such as to indicate that the validity of the decision is dependent on compliance by the tribunal with the obligation to give written reasons.[12] The text of the statute is similar to that of the statutory instrument[13] under consideration by Lord Reed in *Chief Constable, Lothian and Borders Police* v *Lothian and Borders Police Board*.[14] The proceedings were for judicial review of a decision of a Police Appeals Tribunal to allow an appeal against the penalty imposed on a police officer in disciplinary proceedings. The tribunal had produced a decision in writing. It consisted only of the terms of the order made, and a statement in the following terms:

7.12

"The Tribunal unanimously determined to make the foregoing order because it considered that the disposal by the Chairman of the Misconduct Hearing in respect of allegation 4 *et separatim* allegation 5 was, in the circumstances, unduly harsh and excessive."

---

[11] *Stefan* v *General Medical Council* [1999] 1 WLR 1293 at 1300, citing Sedley J in *R* v *Higher Education Funding Council ex p Institute of Dental Surgery* [1994] 1 WLR 242 at 256.

[12] This seems to apply to every decision, including a decision to issue or refuse to issue an ICTO: this is confirmed in the Practice Direction: *Issuing of Reasons where Interim Compulsory Treatment Order is Made*, MHTS Practice Direction 1/2007 of 17 May 2007. On Practice Directions generally, see paras 1.29 *et seq*.

[13] Police Appeals Tribunals (Scotland) Rules 1996 (SI 1996/1644), r 16(6) and (7): "(6) The decision of the tribunal shall be recorded not later than 7 days after the date on which it is made in a document which shall contain – (a) the terms of the order made by the tribunal in determining the appeal including any direction as to expenses which the tribunal makes by virtue of paragraph 9(1) of Schedule 3 to the Act; and (b) a statement of the reasons for the decision, and shall be signed and dated by the chairman of the tribunal. (7) The Registrar shall forthwith send a copy of the document to – (a) each party; and (b) the Secretary of State."

[14] 1995 SLT 315.

7.13   Judicial review proceedings were raised, seeking reduction (in ordinary language, a complete, and retrospective, setting aside) of the tribunal's decision on the basis that the decision was unsupported by adequate reasons. It was conceded that the reasons were not adequate in law, but the respondents argued that the court should not quash the decision, but that it should, instead, order the tribunal to give a more detailed statement of its reasons. This submission relied in part on authorities such as *Brayhead (Ascot) Ltd* v *Berkshire County Council*[15] and on a statement by Lord Keith of Kinkel in *London and Clydeside Estates Ltd* v *Aberdeen District Council*[16] that a failure to state reasons in writing could always be put right at a later date without anything more serious than inconvenience.

7.14   After extensive citation and analysis of authorities concerning the legal consequences of a failure to comply with a duty to give reasons, Lord Reed rejected the respondent's submissions on this point, and ordered reduction of the tribunal's decision. He held that the stringency with which a court will require compliance with a statutory duty to give reasons will depend on the court's view of the intention of the particular statute. One relevant question will be whether the purpose of the duty is solely to provide information about the reasons for the decision, or whether it has other purposes, such as to affect the decision-making process, or to maintain public confidence in that process. He found also that where there is a statutory duty to provide reasons as part of the notification of the decision to the parties, the court will usually interpret the legislation as having made the provision of adequate reasons with the decision a condition of the validity of the decision. Lord Reed's derivation of these propositions from the various authorities which he discusses is, it is respectfully submitted, correct.

7.15   Looking at the terms of Sch 2, paras 13(3) and (4) to the 2003 Act, there does not appear to be any relevant distinction to be drawn between them and the terms of the instrument under consideration in *Chief Constable, Lothian and Borders Police*. Paragraph 13(4), as amended, makes it clear that the written reasons are to be provided to parties as part of the notification of the decision. There might have been some scope for argument, given the terms of the statute as originally enacted, to the effect that there was no absolute requirement that the written reasons be provided to parties, and that to that extent *Chief Constable, Lothian and Borders Police* might be distinguished. In addition, the following considerations militate against any view that there might be scope in mental health tribunal proceedings for the provision of supplementary reasons at a date

---

[15] [1964] 2 QB 303.
[16] 1980 SC (HL) 1 at 41–42.

later than that of the initial issue of written reasons. It is plainly the intention of the legislature that the reasons be recorded in writing, and the reference is to recording in "a document". The use of the singular is significant here. Further, the document is to contain a full statement of the facts found by the tribunal and the reasons for the decision. This again would tend to indicate that it was not the intention of the legislature that the tribunal should be permitted to provide supplementary reasons for its decision at some later date. Finally, as a matter of policy, the decisions of the tribunal may have the effect of depriving an individual of his liberty. They are decisions which are usually taken following proceedings in private.[17] It is essential to the maintenance of confidence in the decision-making process that reasons be given which disclose fully the basis on which the decision has been made, and it is appropriate that the giving of reasons in accordance with the statutory obligation be regarded as a condition of the validity of the decision. It would be undesirable in relation to decisions affecting the liberty of vulnerable individuals to permit any possibility of justification of the decisions *ex post facto* by the provision of additional reasons at a later date.

The English courts have allowed a tribunal to amplify its reasons in the context of an application for judicial review, where the evidence subsequently supplied by the tribunal is "merely elucidatory of the reasons contained in the formal decision", rather than providing reasons which differed from those already given.[18] This course of action has been regarded as desirable where a tribunal has authorised the release of a patient, that decision is challenged, and he might remain detained against his will, in circumstances where the matter might be resolved by the issuing of further reasons.[19] It should be noted, however, that while remedy is a matter of discretion in judicial review, it may be open to question as to whether the sheriff principal or the Court of Session has any discretion to proceed in this way in a statutory appeal.

7.16

CONSEQUENCE OF FAILURE TO GIVE REASONS

Although the case before Lord Reed was a judicial review rather than a statutory appeal, such as those for which provision is made in ss 320 and 322 of the 2003 Act, failure to give reasons is relevant to such an appeal, in that a failure to give adequate reasons

7.17

---

[17] Rule 66(1).
[18] *R (Secretary of State for the Home Department)* v *Mental Health Review Tribunal and CH* [2005] MHLR 199 at para 35.
[19] *R (Mersey Care NHS Trust)* v *Mental Health Review Tribunal* [2003] MHLR 354.

is an error in law.[20] Failure to observe the legal prerequisites of a valid decision is perhaps evidently an error of law. Error of law can found an appeal under ss 320 and 322 of the 2003 Act.[21] It is also noteworthy that the duty to give adequate reasons may be characterised as an aspect of the duty to provide a fair hearing; reasons may be inadequate to the extent that procedural unfairness results.[22] Procedural impropriety is, again, a basis for appeal in terms of the 2003 Act.[23] A failure to explain the tribunal's reasoning properly, or to formulate findings-in-fact properly, may make it difficult to demonstrate that the tribunal's decision is supported by the facts found to be established by it.[24]

7.18   Where the tribunal's decision involves the exercise of a discretion, as do many decisions which it is called on to make in exercising its powers under the Rules, it will be difficult to defend the exercise of the discretion as reasonable unless the factors taken into account and the way in which they have been weighed is apparent from the statement of reasons.[25] The decision of Sheriff Principal Kerr in *Laurie* v *Mental Health Tribunal for Scotland*[26] is one in which the absence of any indication that the tribunal had considered whether or not to require the attendance of a witness led the sheriff

---

[20] *R (Iran)* v *Secretary of State for the Home Department* [2005] EWCA Civ 982 at para 9.

[21] Section 324(1) and (2). See the case of *Di Mascio* v *MHTS* 2008 GWD 37–559, where Sh Pr Taylor takes the view that a failure to have sufficient evidence to enable a finding to be made may be an error in law – para 25 of his judgment, available on the Scottish Courts website at: www.scotcourts.gov.uk and on the legal database Westlaw.

[22] *Koca* v *Secretary of State for the Home Department* 2005 1 SC 487 at para 19: "this case falls to be decided in accordance with the overriding requirement that the reclaimer should have been given a fair hearing. That requirement, of course, is not confined to the actual conduct of the hearing itself before the adjudicator but applies also to the process whereby the adjudicator reaches his decision. Both under domestic law, and under the jurisprudence in relation to Art 6 of the European Convention on Human Rights, the duty in relation to providing a fair hearing includes an obligation to ensure that the person whose rights are being affected adversely by a decision of the tribunal or court in question is informed adequately of why his case did not succeed ... we have reached the conclusion that the reasons supplied by [the adjudicator] for her decision are inadequate to the extent that there has been procedural unfairness which requires that the decision be reduced." The Division was dealing with a failure to give reasons for rejecting expert evidence which was *prima facie* supportive of the appellant's position.

[23] Section 324(2)(b). See *Di Mascio* v *MHTS*, n 21 above.

[24] Again, giving rise to potential appeals: s 324(2)(d).

[25] If the Tribunal has acted unreasonably in the exercise of its discretion, that may found an appeal: s 324(2)(c).

[26] [2007] Scot SC 44; 2007 GWD 32–555. See also *Di Mascio* v *MHTS*, n 21 above, at para 23.

principal to conclude that the possibility of doing so had not been considered, and that the tribunal had therefore erred in the exercise of its discretion. In summary, a failure to give adequate reasons may give rise to appeals under any one of the four grounds provided in the 2003 Act.

The failure of a tribunal applying s 193 to give adequate reasons for its decision was considered by the Inner House in *Scottish Ministers* v *Mental Health Tribunal Scotland ("JK")*.[27] The tribunal had not recorded that it had considered the "continued necessity" test in terms of s 193(5)(b)(ii), and the court could not, therefore, be satisfied that the tribunal had focused on the correct principles. Further, it had given no reasons for its rejection of evidence from the RMO that the restriction order was necessary and should not be revoked. There was relevant and significant evidence that the patient had a long history of aggressive and unpredictable behaviour. That evidence did not feature in the tribunal's consideration of the issues before it, and there was no explanation as to why the tribunal had not regarded that evidence as relevant. Similarly, in *Scottish Ministers* v *MHTS and MM*[28] the court allowed an appeal against a decision to revoke a restriction order because the tribunal had failed to explain why it had apparently disregarded the evidence of psychiatrists which militated against revocation of the restriction order. As in *JK*, the tribunal had not made clear whether it had applied itself to continued necessity in terms of s 193(5)(b)(ii).

FORM OF TRIBUNAL DECISIONS

As mentioned above, decisions that are purely procedural in nature may take the form of an order set out on the "Decision" form produced by the tribunal, with the reasons for the decision explained (insofar as that may be necessary) in an attached note. Directions may be given for the future conduct of the case. As mentioned elsewhere in this work,[29] several of the Rules[30] make specific provision for directions to be made where the tribunal is fixing a further hearing. Rules 49 and 52 make more general provision for the giving of directions and the making of other orders for case management purposes. The written order of the tribunal will usually simply specify that the tribunal makes a direction in particular terms. For example, it might in terms of r 49(1)(g) direct

7.19

---

[27] 2009 SLT 273.
[28] [2009] CSIH 66.
[29] See para 3.86 for the most common such direction – ordering additional documents.
[30] For example, r 8(4) and r 11(10).

that the RMO should provide an updated report for the proceedings relating to a particular issue. In a reference relating to a CORO case the tribunal might direct that a report be produced by the RMO setting out the details of the RMO's view in relation to whether, as a result of the patient's mental disorder, there is a risk of serious harm in the event that the patient is not detained, and explanation as to the nature of the harm apprehended. The tribunal may also require certain categories of person to attend the hearing under reference to r 52(2)(b). The procedure for giving directions is flexible, and it is a matter for the tribunal to draft the directions or requirements so that it is clear to all concerned what requires to be done before the next hearing, and, where applicable, in what form evidence is to be produced. Particularly if procedural and interlocutory decisions have been the subject of dispute and debate, some brief explanation should be given as to why a particular procedural course was decided upon, so that the reasons why one course rather than another was chosen will be apparent.

7.20   Where a substantive order is being made, whether a "full" order or an interim order, or a decision is being made to make no order, in circumstances where that decision represents the determination of an application to revoke an order,[31] the tribunal will have to set out clearly its conclusions based on the evidence before it. The form in which this is done varies in practice. Some Conveners favour a style based on that used by a sheriff making findings after a hearing involving evidence, with numbered findings-in-fact followed by an explanation as to how the findings-in-fact have been arrived at under reference to the evidence before the tribunal, and further explanation as to how the facts found support the conclusion reached in law. Others prefer a style whereby the facts found are included in the body of the determination, rather than being enumerated separately at the beginning. What is important is that it must be possible to discern from the written decision what matters have been accepted as fact by the tribunal. Care should be taken to make the decision as clear and readable as possible. With this in mind, it can be helpful to structure the written decision with headings and distinct sections, such as "Findings-in-Fact", "Preliminary and Procedural Issues", "Evidence Considered" and "Discussions and Conclusions".[32]

---

[31] As, for example, where there is an application to revoke an order or a determination, or to seek conditional discharge.

[32] See the case of *Di Mascio* v *MHTS* 2008 GWD 37–559, where Sh Pr Taylor agreed effectively to ignore the headings used in his quest to identify the facts found (para 26 of his judgment which can be found on the Scottish Courts website: www. scotcourts.gov.uk and on the legal database Westlaw).

It is important to be aware of the distinction between findings-in-fact and the evidence which supports those findings. It is also necessary to distinguish between the findings-in-law, or in fact and law, which are necessary to the decision, and which the findings-in-fact in their turn must support. By way of example, a tribunal might find in fact that a patient suffered from schizophrenia, and that schizophrenia is a mental illness. That finding might be made on the basis of the evidence provided by the psychiatrist, that is, the information provided by him in his report and in oral evidence. As a matter of law, a mental illness is a mental disorder. The findings-in-fact mentioned would satisfy, as a matter of law, one of the criteria for making a CTO, namely that the patient suffers from a mental disorder. The decision-maker should consider carefully in relation to each relevant criterion whether he has found facts which, as a matter of law, enable the order in question to be made. He should also be clear as to the evidence on which he is relying in making the finding of fact.

7.21

Simply because an expert says, in terms, that in his opinion one of the statutory criteria for an order being made is met, this is not conclusive of the matter.[33] The tribunal requires to address its mind to the evidence of the expert witness, and determine whether it accepts that evidence, so as to permit it to make a finding-in-fact which would support a finding-in-fact and law that the relevant criterion was met. It is not necessary,[34] and certainly not conclusive of the matter, for an expert to repeat in his evidence the words of the statute in that part of his evidence which is relevant to the determination of whether or not a particular statutory criterion is met. The temptation simply to conclude that because an expert speaks of a criterion being fulfilled, then it must be, is particularly acute when one considers the "significant risk"[35] and the "significant impairment of decision-making capacity"[36] grounds. When it comes to the "necessity" ground,[37] this temptation will

7.22

---

[33] This point is made in the context of expert evidence at paras 5.109 *et seq* and in the context of sufficiency at para 5.129.

[34] See comment by Sh Pr Sir Stephen Young at para 32 in *B v MHTS* 2008 GWD 36–543 (full judgment is available on the Scottish Courts website at: www.scotcourts.gov.uk and on the legal database Westlaw). In this case the sheriff principal was referring to evidence relating to the criterion under s 64(5)(d) of the Act. His comments are applicable equally to evidence which bears to deal with any of the statutory criteria that the tribunal has to consider. It will always be for the tribunal to consider, on the basis of all the available evidence, including any expression of opinion by an expert to that effect, whether there would be, for example, a significant risk to the health, safety or welfare of the patient if medical treatment were not provided.

[35] 2003 Act, s 64(5)(c).

[36] *Ibid*, s 64(5)(d).

[37] *Ibid*, s 64(5)(e).

not apply in the same way. The question of whether the order is necessary is a very broad one. Usually, this question will involve (in tandem with the least restrictive principle) asking whether there is any viable alternative to the order being sought (in the case of a hospital-based CTO, whether a community order can be granted or considered further at a later hearing, or in any case whether the patient can be given appropriate treatment informally, that is voluntarily). However, necessity can mean legal and not factual necessity, for instance where there is no order in place and where, for the protection of those dealing with the patient (and for the protection of the patient's rights) his treatment should be provided with some legal protection. This was successfully argued in one case where the patient had been being treated informally for some time but where the RMO argued that treatment had become more difficult without restraint, and so an order was necessary to give the carers the necessary legal powers to offer full and appropriate care. One more point about the "necessity" ground is that where there are other legal powers available to treat the patient adequately, then they must be used and in such cases the order being sought under the 2003 Act will not be necessary and should not be made.[38] This point was argued unsuccessfully in a tribunal case where a guardianship order was in place under the AWISA but where it was held that legal protection for the patient and the staff caring for him in itself necessitated a CTO. The case was complicated by the fact that the patient lacked the capacity to instruct a solicitor and so a curator *ad litem* had been appointed. This brought the case within the *Bournewood* category.[39]

CONTENT OF TRIBUNAL DECISIONS

7.23   In order for reasons for a decision to be regarded as adequate in law, they must leave the court and the informed reader in no real and substantial doubt as to what the reasons for it were and what were the material considerations which were taken into account in

---

[38] An example that has been given is the situation where the powers under the Adults with Incapacity (Scotland) Act 2000 ("AWISA") are adequate, then an order under the 2003 Act is not necessary: H Patrick, *Mental Health, Incapacity and the Law in Scotland* (2006), para 24.37.

[39] The *Bournewood* decision is a reference to *HL v United Kingdom* (2005) 40 EHRR 32; [2004] MHLR 236, in which it was held that the detention of a patient who lacks capacity to consent to medical treatment on the basis of necessity and voluntary competence alone is a breach of the patient's ECHR rights. See also s 291 of the 2003 Act on applications in relation to the unlawful detention of informal patients.

reaching it.[40] The legal test for adequacy of reasons has also been explained in these terms:

> "The reasons for a decision must be intelligible and they must be adequate. They must enable the reader to understand why the matter was decided as it was and what conclusions were reached on the 'principal important controversial issues', disclosing how any issue of law or fact was resolved."[41]

Differing views have been expressed in relation to the significance of the informed reader of a decision in the context of mental health proceedings. On the one hand, those who receive the decision will probably be familiar with the case papers, and with what has been said orally at the tribunal hearing, so it might be said that it is not necessary for a tribunal to enter into a particularly detailed narration of the evidence it has relied on. On the other, however, patients may not find it easy to recall and analyse exactly what has been said at a tribunal hearing.[42] It would be particularly important for social workers and medical personnel to be aware of the basis on which a patient has been discharged by the tribunal, particularly if they are for any reason contemplating a further application in relation to him shortly after.[43]

7.24

Findings-in-fact must be distinguished from a narration of the evidence. A narration of the oral or written evidence before the tribunal does not by itself indicate what facts the tribunal has found proved on the basis of that evidence, or even the extent to which various parts of the evidence have been accepted or rejected. In relation to any factual matter of importance, the written decision must disclose what was found proved, what evidence the finding is based on, and why that evidence was accepted. As is noted below, it should be borne in mind that there is no requirement for all factual and opinion evidence to be recorded in the findings-in-fact: only the

7.25

---

[40] *Wordie Property Co Ltd* v *Secretary of State for Scotland* 1984 SLT 345 per the Lord President at 348. For approval of that approach in the context of the decisions of statutory tribunals, see *Singh* v *Secretary of State for the Home Department* 2000 SC 219 at 222; *Singh* v *Secretary of State for the Home Department* 1998 SLT 1370 at 1374J.

[41] *South Bucks DC* v *Porter (No 2)* [2004] 1 WLR 1953 per Lord Brown of Eaton-Under-Heywood at para 36; see also *Koca* v *Secretary of State for the Home Department* 2005 1 SC 487 at para 19.

[42] Compare *R* v *Mental Health Review Tribunal, ex p Booth* [2008] EWHC 2356 (Admin); [1998] COD 203 with *R (on the application of H)* v *Ashworth Hospital Authority* [2002] MHLR 314 per Dyson LJ at para 76. For an example of a "reasons" appeal under the 2003 Act, see *Robbins* v *Mitchell* [2007] Scot SC 19.

[43] See *R (H)*, above, and *R* v *East London and City Mental Health NHS Trust, ex p Brandenburg* [2002] 2 QB 235

evidence which the tribunal found to be relevant to the decision in hand need be referred to – irrelevant evidence can be ignored, although care should be taken when considering what should be included and what can be left out since an appeal can be based on a failure properly to take account of material evidence in reaching a decision.[44] Where there is dispute as to a matter of fact, the explanation as to the nature and extent of the available evidence and as to why a particular conclusion on the evidence has been reached will necessarily be more detailed and involved than in cases where there is no controversy. It is not, however, necessary to narrate evidence at length or enter into lengthy, written, consideration of evidence which is not essential to the determination that the tribunal requires to make. In the context of challenges to the reasons given for decisions in immigration appeals, Lord Penrose commented that:

> "nothing could be more destructive of the efficient disposal of immigration appeals than the notion that the adjudicator and the tribunal are under an obligation to carry through a mechanical process of narration of the evidence, analysis of it into classes, and an explanation factor by factor of the relevance or irrelevance, credibility and reliability or otherwise of it".[45]

7.26   The need for clarity as to what evidence has been accepted, what evidence has been rejected, and why, is particularly acute where expert evidence is concerned. Where two or more expert witnesses provide conflicting views, the tribunal needs to decide what evidence it accepts and why, and to explain in its written decision the reasons for its conclusions. A case illustrating the importance of clarity in relation to these matters, and the potential for successful appeal where there is not such clarity on the part of the fact-finder, is *Dingley* v *Chief Constable, Strathclyde Police*.[46] The case involved a dispute between medical experts as to whether multiple sclerosis could be triggered as the result of whiplash injury. The Lord Ordinary was found to have failed to explain what parts of the evidence he accepted, and why. The comments of the Lord President are instructive from the point of view of indicating what tribunals require to do in expressing the reasons for their decisions on disputed expert evidence, and what parties and practitioners are entitled to look for by way of adequate reasons in such situations:

---

[44] An appeal in such a case would not sit easily within any of the grounds for appeal but would probably fall within an appeal on the grounds of procedural impropriety. On appeals generally, see Chapter 8. See the reference below to the *Asif* case (n 43).

[45] *Asif* v *Secretary of State for the Home Department* 1999 SLT 890 at 894, approved in *Singh* v *Secretary of State for the Home Department* 2000 SC 219

[46] 1998 SC 548 (1st Div); 2000 SC (HL) 77.

"Perhaps the essential point is that parties who come to court are entitled to the decision of a judicial tribunal. Such a decision may take account of many rather intangible things such as the demeanour of witnesses and the way that they gave their evidence, but, whatever its components may be, such a decision must be reasoned. As Lord Cooper says, an oracular pronouncement will not do. In this case the parties' expert witnesses gave evidence at length and were subjected to cross-examination. The experts for the pursuer commented on the approach adopted by the defender's experts and *vice versa*. In that situation the Lord Ordinary required to test the experts' evidence and, having done so, to use those parts which he accepted and apply them to the facts of this case. If he did not do this, then it must be inferred that he misdirected himself and his conclusion on the matters of fact is open to review by this court."[47]

Even where expert evidence is led which is not contradicted by expert evidence led by another party, the tribunal will still have to consider whether it is satisfied with that evidence, and to explain why.[48] If the tribunal chooses not to accept uncontradicted evidence, whether of an expert or any other witness, it will have to take some care to explain why it has done so. It should also be clear that the tribunal has addressed the relevant legal tests in relation to the matter before it, and that it has applied and understood the statute properly. In addition to consideration of the criteria, for example, justifying the making of a CTO, it should be clear from the tribunal's decision that it has acted in accordance with the principles in s 1 of the 2003 Act. It may, for example, be of importance to demonstrate in the reasoning that the tribunal has addressed its mind to making a decision that restricts the liberty of the patient to the least extent possible.

7.27

The determination of procedural issues, which may arise either in the course of a hearing leading to a final determination of the case, or at an interlocutory stage, also gives rise to the need to explain in writing the reasons for the decision. Where this has not been done, the appeal court may be ready to infer that the factors material to the determination of these issues have not adequately been considered.

7.28

In the event that a decision is being made by more than one member of the tribunal, as it will be in any case where the Convener is not sitting alone, the decision is to be made by a majority.[49] The Convener's view in this situation has no greater influence than the

7.29

---

[47] 1998 SC 548 per the Lord President (Rodger) at 555.
[48] *Davie* v *Magistrates of Edinburgh* 1953 SC 34 per the Lord President (Cooper) at 40. See also the recent case of *Scottish Ministers* v *MHTS* 2009 SLT 273, where such reasons were not adequate. See para 5.106, n 214, for further details on this case.
[49] Schedule 2, para 13(1).

views of the two other panel members. If there is a tie, the Convener has a second vote as a casting vote.[50] This will arise only where a member has for some reason been unable to continue sitting after a hearing has commenced, and the tribunal comes to be the decision of two members[51] or in the very unlikely event that there are three different views expressed by each of the members on the outcome (for instance, one favours granting the order, another wishes to refuse it and the third wishes to grant it but with the attachment of certain recorded matters). Where there is a difference of view within the tribunal as to the correct decision, that should be recorded in writing. It is usually the role of the Convener, in consultation with the other members, to reduce the reasoning of the tribunal to writing. This means that all three members must be content with the final written reasons before they can be signed by the Convener and released. Where there is a dissenting view, he should take care to record and explain that view also, whether the dissenting view is his own or that of one of the other tribunal members.

DIRECTIONS

7.30   The tribunal may require to consider whether or not to issue a direction. Although a direction can be requested at any time, it is appropriate to deal with this matter in this chapter, since a request for a direction is a request for a decision of the tribunal. A direction is essentially an instruction issued on a particular procedural matter. A direction can be issued at one of two stages of a tribunal case:

(1) in advance of the first hearing; or

(2) during or between hearings.

We will deal with each in turn, before considering other matters related to directions.

Directions issued in advance of the first hearing

7.31   Where a relevant person wishes the tribunal to issue a direction in advance, he should apply for one by writing to MHTS headquarters, as far in advance of the hearing as possible. There is no deadline, but there is a provision requiring that the Clerk (meaning the caseworkers at MHTS headquarters)[52] should intimate the request

---

[50] Schedule 2, para 13(2).
[51] See r 64(3)
[52] On the caseworking staff, see para 2.14. The word "Clerk" is defined in both ways in r 2(1) – see para 2.07.

and invite representations on it from other relevant persons on a 14-day notice period, or a shorter period where specified.[53] Given the tight timescales involved, it would seem that a period of notice of less than 14 days would not be unusual, in order that the direction decision process can be completed before the first hearing.

Advance direction requests will be dealt with by an in-house Convener.[54] The most common such request is a request for a direction under r 46A[55] seeking non-disclosure of a document or part of it. As noted elsewhere in more detail,[56] such a request should be accompanied by full reasons and, where appropriate, supporting evidence. The other type of direction request that might be made in advance would be one seeking to exclude either written or prospective oral evidence as inadmissible. The grounds upon which an admissibility argument could be made and the procedure for making such an argument are discussed elsewhere.[57] A further possible advance request might be made to secure the production of certain documentation at the tribunal, where it is known (or strongly suspected) that it exists, where it is relevant to the case, and where a fruitless request has been made for it to be disclosed voluntarily (or where such a request would be inappropriate or impractical for some reason). In such circumstances, the acquisition of such documents in advance might prevent an adjournment of the tribunal at the first hearing, and so could be justified on the basis of the requirement to act expeditiously, in terms of r 4. Such a direction is specifically authorised.[58]

7.32

Where an advance direction is sought, the request must be made in writing, for obvious reasons. Full reasons and evidence (where appropriate) should be included in order to allow the in-house Convener to make a proper decision. Intimation on the other relevant persons is usually required[59] (on a period of notice of 14 days or such other period as may be specified) and any objections to the direction request must be considered,[60] and this may involve affording an objector an opportunity to be heard.[61] In most cases, written objections will suffice. Where the in-house Convener cannot make a decision on paper and where the hearing is imminent, he may simply refer the request and the objections to the tribunal panel for a

7.33

---

[53] Rule 49(3).
[54] On the role of the in-house Convener, see para 2.11.
[55] On this rule, see paras 3.180 *et seq.*
[56] Para 3.181.
[57] In the former case, see paras 5.47 *et seq*; and in the latter, see paras 4.71 *et seq.*
[58] Rule 49(1)(a).
[59] Rule 49(3).
[60] Rules 49(5) and (6).
[61] Rule 49(5).

decision on the day of the hearing, although this should be avoided where it would (to the detriment of the applicant) defeat the purpose of the advance request. In some cases, a failure to intimate a direction request before the direction is made can be cured by notifying that person of the direction in writing as soon as reasonably practicable.[62] That decision must be one which affects the relevant person concerned, although it is difficult to imagine a direction which can be said not to affect all relevant persons, at least indirectly. Where this provision is not followed, the relevant person upon whom intimation has not been made can seek to cure the problem by applying to have the direction varied or set aside[63] and, if such an application is made, all relevant persons must be heard on it. The rules do not issue guidance on when such remedies (under r 49(8) or r 50) are appropriate, so there seems to be wide discretion here.

Directions issued during the hearing (or between hearings)

7.34   On reading r 49, it would seem that the framers of the Rules intended that directions would be issued only in response to an advance written request. However, on a sensible reading of the rule, this applies only to directions issued under the specific headings mentioned in r 49(1)(a)–(g) inclusive. Where the direction is of a type not listed there (and the list is expressly non-exhaustive), the provision requiring advance written notice[64] does not apply. This is reinforced by the wording of the first paragraph of r 49(1) which refers to the fact that a direction can be issued "at any time". In addition, directions can be issued by the tribunal on its own initiative,[65] and clearly the tribunal does not require to give itself advance written notice. Having said this, it does seem odd that even the list of specific directions in r 49(1)(a)–(g) can only, on the face of it, be issued on advance written notice, since those listed cover many of the directions a party will wish to seek. The view that should be taken is that where a request is made during a hearing, advance written notice is not required, unless there is a relevant person who is not present, and where the view is taken that the direction may affect that person, in which case the notice provisions in r 49 should be complied with. Although this interpretation requires some straining of the wording of the rule, it seems inconceivable that the drafters wished to exclude the possibility of an oral request for a direction at a hearing in the areas covered by r 49(1)(a)–(g). This interpretation is, in essence, a purposive one.

---

[62] Rule 49(8).
[63] Rule 50.
[64] Rule 49(2).
[65] Rule 49(1), first para.

Where an oral request for a direction is made during the hearing, **7.35**
it should be decided there and then where it might affect the future
progress of the proceedings. An example would be where the direction
sought is one that might affect the admissibility of evidence to be
led at the hearing, although, as noted elsewhere,[66] such evidence can
sometimes be heard under reservation, the objection being determined
after the submissions stage.

The Convener should be careful in such cases to canvass the views **7.36**
of all of the relevant persons present on the direction request. Where
a request for a direction leads to one being issued during the course
of the hearing (as opposed to at the end of it), it would seem sensible
for that decision to be intimated orally at the time, in order to allow
the hearing to continue, with the full written direction in identical
terms being issued later.

Sometimes a direction will be issued which will lead to the hearing **7.37**
having to be adjourned. This most often happens in cases where
further written information is required by the tribunal (or at the
request of a relevant person) in order to decide the case.[67]

It is sometimes necessary for the tribunal to issue a direction in **7.38**
order to regulate proceedings. This might occur where a representative
wishes to pursue a line of cross-examination which the tribunal feels
is inappropriate or repetitive or irrelevant. In such cases, a clear
direction should be issued orally by the tribunal, with reasons in
writing in the Directions Form later. However, before considering
whether such a curtailment of the right to cross-examine should
happen, the members of the tribunal should adjourn to deliberate
(or should at least consult briefly there and then and come to a
view) since, as is mentioned elsewhere,[68] this is a decision (although
procedural) which should not be taken by the Convener alone.[69]
This point is reinforced when one considers that such a curtailment
would have to be recorded and justified in the written record of
proceedings, which is a record of decisions made by the tribunal as
a panel.

---

[66] See para 4.74.

[67] This situation is discussed at paras 3.82 *et seq*.

[68] See para 3.48.

[69] For more detail on the right to cross-examination, see para 4.59; and on
intervention by tribunal members during evidence, see paras 4.103 *et seq*. See
also the decision of Sh Pr Sir Stephen Young in *B v MHTS* 2008 GWD 36–543
(judgment is available on the Scottish Courts website at: www.scotcourts.gov.uk
and on the legal database Westlaw). In this case, the Convener prevented further
cross-examination on a particular point on the basis of repetition, apparently
without consulting with the other tribunal members. This was not a live issue in the
appeal, however.

7.39   Finally, a direction can be issued between hearings, since one can be issued "at any time".[70] This will be very unusual, but an issue might arise after a hearing that could not be anticipated, and it might be inefficient simply to wait for the next hearing of the case before the request for a direction is made, perhaps leading to a further adjournment of the case. If such a situation arises, a request for a direction should be made to MHTS headquarters, and will be dealt with by an in-house Convener. The procedure here will be the same as where a request for a direction is made in advance of a hearing.[71]

The subject-matter of directions

7.40   Directions can be issued across a whole range of subject areas, as demonstrated by the breadth of the list in r 49(1)(a)–(g). It should be noted, however, that this list is not exhaustive and the subject-matter is, therefore, unlimited, as long as the direction has a proper basis.

The recording of directions

7.41   Whether the direction is issued in advance of the hearing, orally during the hearing (this is mentioned above) or at the end of the hearing, it should be recorded in writing, since it is a decision of the tribunal. As with a decision on the merits of the case, full reasons should be provided and where representations have been made on the direction application, these should be recorded also, with reasons as to why certain arguments were preferred over others in cases where there was a difference of opinion among relevant persons. The basis on which directions can be issued (see below) should form the foundation of the reasons stated. When framing a direction, the tribunal should be precise and clear on its terms. This applies particularly where the direction requires some action in the future, such as the lodging of documents. The documents should be defined clearly and timescales for lodging and intimating them to other relevant persons should be specified. The persons who need to act on the direction must also be specified by name and address/designation. This means that the MHTS staff who will, in such cases, action the direction will be more likely to do so in the way intended by the tribunal. The direction itself should be recorded in the Directions Form, with the reasons and representations summarised in the Full Findings-in-Fact and Reasons Form. This practice was recently introduced in order to highlight the existence of directions to MHTS caseworkers, so that that they could be acted upon quickly, rather than being buried in the text of a perhaps lengthy Full Findings-in-Fact and Reasons document.

---

[70] Rule 49(1), first para.
[71] See paras 7.31 et seq.

In the event that reasons are not properly recorded, this could constitute a procedural impropriety, which could found the basis of an appeal.[72]   **7.42**

The basis for issuing directions

This is to be found in r 49(1), first para. The tribunal must consider that the direction is: "necessary or desirable to further the overriding objective in the conduct of a case".[73] This wording is very wide, and it is clear that a direction can be issued as one that is necessary or where it is not deemed necessary but is nonetheless desirable. The necessity or desirability must be connected with the furthering of the overriding objective of the case, as provided for in r 4.   **7.43**

It should be noted that the exclusion of evidence (one basis for a direction) need not be *necessary* in order to allow the hearing to take place as fairly, expeditiously and efficiently as possible (the overriding objective under r 4), but could be *desirable* in the aim to meet this end.   **7.44**

Given the wide basis for the issuing of directions, any further comment would be unduly restrictive.   **7.45**

Failure to comply with directions

In the unlikely event that a direction is not complied with, the tribunal can, before or at the hearing, direct that the offending relevant person takes no further part in proceedings.[74] Before taking such action, representations must be invited from the relevant person concerned, with a view to determining whether there is cause for not following this course of action.[75] Such action would be justified only in the most extreme case, where there was no way in which the proceedings could continue with the offending person remaining involved and in the face of a failure to comply. Where possible, at least one further opportunity to comply with the direction should be afforded before exclusion of the relevant person.   **7.46**

Appeal against decisions to issue directions

As noted elsewhere,[76] an appeal can be taken from an earlier decision of a tribunal once the final decision in the case has been issued. There is a question, then, as to whether such an appeal can be taken against a decision to issue a direction and when that appeal   **7.47**

---

[72] For appeals against decisions to issue directions, see para 7.47; and on appeals generally, see Chapter 8. For the need to issue reasons, see paras 7.23 *et seq.*
[73] See r 49(1).
[74] Rule 51(1).
[75] Rule 51(2).
[76] See para 8.02.

can competently be taken. Since a decision to issue a direction qualifies as a decision of the tribunal, and given the ability (at least in relation to appeals based on procedural impropriety) to lodge an appeal based on the conduct of "any hearing",[77] it would seem that an appeal against a decision to issue a direction could be taken after proceedings are over, following the issue of the written decision, and need not be taken, for instance, during a period between hearings. In fact, the list of decisions in the 2003 Act, s 320 against which appeal can be taken is exhaustive, and would seem to exclude the possibility of a competent appeal against a decision which is only procedural in nature.

As to the grounds for an appeal against a decision related to a direction, these are the same as the grounds for an appeal against any other decision of the tribunal, and these are discussed elsewhere.[78]

DISPENSING POWER

7.48   Like most other procedural rules applying to courts and tribunals, the Rules include a provision which empowers the tribunal to relieve a person from what would otherwise be the consequences of failure to comply with one of the rules.[79] The power must be exercised in accordance with the overriding objective in r 4, namely the fair, expeditious and efficient handling of proceedings before the tribunal. The provisions of r 75 provide the tribunal with a broad discretion to excuse failures to comply with provisions of the Rules. In connection with analogous rules, it has been observed that their purpose is to enable the court or tribunal in question "to do justice".[80]

7.49   Relief may be given where, before the tribunal has decided a case, a relevant person has failed to comply with any provision of the Rules.[81] The language of the rule suggests that it is the failure to comply with a provision that must have taken place before the decision has been reached, as opposed to the decision in which the tribunal exercises its dispensing power. It is, however, difficult to figure a potentially significant failure on the part of a relevant person to comply with a provision of the Rules after the tribunal has reached a decision.

---

[77] 2003 Act, s 324(2)(b). This point is discussed elsewhere, at para 8.02.
[78] For an example of a recent appeal against a direction to limit cross-examination, see the decision of *B* v *MHTS* 2008 GWD 36–543, a decision of Sh Pr Sir Stephen Young (full judgment is available on the Scottish Courts website at: www.scotcourts. gov.uk and on the legal database Westlaw). This decision is discussed elsewhere from the cross-examination perspective: para 7.38, n 69.
[79] Rule 75.
[80] *Dalgety's Trs* v *Drummond* 1938 SC 709 at 715.
[81] Rule 75(1).

It is therefore suggested that, while awkwardly drafted, the rule is meant to convey that it is only before the tribunal has reached a decision on the merits of the case that it can exercise its dispensing power. If the dispensing power could be exercised after the decision has been reached, there would be prejudice to the certainty that such a decision provides for parties. If it had been the intention of the drafter that the tribunal could re-open a decision in the exercise of its dispensing power, it is likely that a period would have been specified within which this might be done.

The failure must be due to mistake, oversight or other excusable cause. This form of words is very similar to that which appears in the provisions of other court and tribunal procedural rules.[82] "Mistake" and "oversight" are self-explanatory. "Other excusable cause" broadens the scope of the discretion considerably. Comparable rules have, in the past, referred not to "other excusable cause", but instead have excluded from the scope of the power a discretion to relieve parties from the consequences of "wilful non-observance" of a requirement of the rules in question.[83] By contrast, the use of the phrase "other excusable cause" suggests that even a deliberate decision not to observe the rule, provided that this could for some reason be demonstrated to be excusable, could be founded on in seeking to take advantage of the rule. There may also be situations where it is impossible for some reason to comply with a time limit, for example, but this has not arisen through a mistake or through anything having been overlooked. It might arise through the ill health of a party or representative, or even as a result of technological failure within the office of a representative. Such a circumstance would, it is suggested, fall within the definition of "other excusable cause". Ignorance of the content of a rule can be an excusable cause.[84]

7.50

The failure to comply must have been with a provision of the Rules. If the failure relates to a provision of the 2003 Act, for example to provide with a CTO application medical reports which satisfy the requirements of s 57, r 75 will be of no assistance. The rule may assist, however, where a party has failed to observe a time limit. If a person fails to send a notice of response to the tribunal within the period specified in a notice sent to him of an application, he may still be permitted to make representations or lead or produce evidence, if the tribunal is of the view that it would be in the interests of the just and efficient disposal of the case that he be permitted to do so. It could assist also in a situation where

7.51

---

[82] Compare, for example, r 2.1(1) of the Rules of the Court of Session.
[83] See discussion of r 2.1(1) of the Rules of the Court of Session, and its predecessor provision, in *Annotated Rules of the Court of Session 2007/8*.
[84] *Dalgety's Trs v Drummond* 1938 SC 709 at 715.

an application lacked a feature which was required not by the 2003 Act, but by the Rules only.

7.52   Generally, where a rule contains a dispensing power particularly applicable to that rule, courts have been slow to apply the more general dispensing provision.[85] An example which might arise in relation to the Rules is to be found in r 45(2) and (3). Lists of documents, witnesses and written representations are to be sent to the tribunal 7 days prior to any hearing.[86] Where a relevant person seeks to rely on documents not produced in accordance with r 45(1), the tribunal may allow the documents to be lodged late where good reason is given. This is a more stringent test than that contained in r 75, which provides a broad discretion where the failure results from mistake, oversight or other excusable cause. It is unlikely therefore that a person seeking to produce documents late would be permitted to rely on r 75; rather, he would have to demonstrate in terms of r 45(2) that there was a good reason for the documents to be allowed to be lodged late. The tribunal would also, in terms of r 45(3), have to have regard to whether it was fair to allow documents to be lodged late.[87]

7.53   The tribunal has power to relieve the relevant person from the consequences of his failure, and to give any direction it thinks fit.[88] Where the exercise of the power impacts on the position of another party, the tribunal might, for example, require to give that party further time to prepare his case. Particular provision is made in r 75(2) for the tribunal to take any necessary steps, including the amendment of any document, the giving of any notice or otherwise, to enable the case to proceed as though the failure to comply with the provision had not occurred. It is possible to figure the omission of the identity of a named person from an application by a patient. The tribunal could regard the application as a competent one, notwithstanding the failure to supply the required information, but might require to give notice to the named person, and give him time to become fully involved in the proceedings.

7.54   As with any other decision of the tribunal, a decision on whether or not to exercise the dispensing power must be recorded, with reasons, as part of the full findings and reasons of the tribunal.

---

[85] See, for example: *McGee v Matthew Hall Ltd* 1996 SLT 399; *Thomson v Omal Ltd* 1994 SLT 705. Courts have differed as to whether extraordinary circumstances are required for the exercise of the general dispensing power where a rule contains its own dispensing power: compare *Thomson* with *Semple Cochrane plc v Hughes* 2001 SLT 1121.

[86] Rule 45(1).

[87] Although this is arguably an unnecessary provision; the tribunal requires, at common law, in terms of ECHR jurisprudence and in terms of the overriding objective, to act fairly.

[88] Rule 75(1)(a) and (b).

CHAPTER 8

APPEALS FROM TRIBUNAL DECISIONS

APPEALS – GENERAL

Sections 320 and 322 of the 2003 Act make provision respectively for appeal to the sheriff principal and the Court of Session from decisions of the tribunal. Almost all of the decisions which can be appealed under s 320 are decisions on the merits of the application or other matter before the tribunal relating to the status of the patient in the sense of his liability to detention, or the conditions of his detention. Examples include a refusal to revoke an STDC,[1] a decision to make or refuse to make a CTO,[2] and a decision to revoke a compulsion order under s 193(3) and (4) of the 2003 Act.[3] Appeals may also be made against decisions of the tribunal about the appointment of named persons.[4]

8.01

There is no provision for an immediate appeal against procedural decisions such as those to adjourn, or to make directions as to the way in which a future hearing is to proceed. The legislature must be taken to have intended that cases should proceed to a conclusion on the merits without interruption caused by appeals on procedural matters. It is, however, noteworthy that s 324(2)(b) makes it a ground of appeal against the ultimate decision in the proceedings that there has been a procedural impropriety in the conduct of any hearing by the tribunal on the application. In proceedings which culminate in, for example, a decision to refuse an application for revocation of a determination extending a CTO, there may have been a number of hearings, none involving any positive order being made in relation to the determination complained of. This provision seems to contemplate the possibility of founding in an

8.02

---

[1] 2003 Act, s 320(1)(a).
[2] *Ibid*, s 320(1)(b).
[3] *Ibid*, s 322(1)(a).
[4] *Ibid*, s 320(1)(t) and (u).

appeal against the eventual decision on the merits on procedural irregularity at an earlier hearing in the application. Applications for a CTO, by contrast, are unlikely to involve hearings which do not give rise directly to potentially appealable decisions. The application may be refused, an interim order may be made, or a CTO may be made, and any of these decisions may be appealed under s 320 of the 2003 Act.

8.03   The provision for appeal to the sheriff principal against an interim CTO has been used in only one case, so far as the authors are aware, and although the interim order had expired by the time of the appeal hearing, the sheriff principal held that the appeal should proceed.[5] Given that provision for this type of appeal exists, it would be appropriate to use it where there has been a procedural irregularity in the conduct of the hearing leading to the interim CTO, rather than seeking to rely on the impropriety in an appeal against a "full" CTO.[6] Alternatively, an argument aimed at the competency of the interim order (as took place in M v Murray) could found an appeal.

8.04   Section 321 provides a right of appeal from the sheriff principal to the Court of Session. The decisions which may be appealed directly to the Court of Session are those involving restricted patients, and which will have been dealt with by a panel chaired by a sheriff.[7]

8.05   Section 324, which makes general provision in relation to appeals, is unusual in providing that the tribunal may be a party to an appeal under s 320 or s 322, or in any appeal from the sheriff principal to the Court of Session under s 321.[8] The court (the sheriff principal or the Court of Session, as the case may be) may order the tribunal to be represented in any such appeal.[9] The normal position in Scots law is that a tribunal is deemed to be *functus officio* when it is has issued its decision and to have no further *locus* to appear or be represented in any challenge to that decision.[10]

---

[5] *M v Murray* 2009 Scot (D) 8/15, a decision of Sh Pr Lockhart.

[6] See the comments of Sh Pr Sir Stephen Young in *B v MHTS* 2008 GWD 36–543 (full judgment available on the Scottish Courts website at: www.scotcourts.gov.uk and on the legal database Westlaw).

[7] On restricted patient hearings generally, see paras 4.169 *et seq.*

[8] 2003 Act, s 324(3).

[9] *Ibid*, s 324(4).

[10] *Mackintosh v Arkley* (1868) 6 M (HL) 141, commented on by Lord Rodger of Earlsferry in *Tehrani v Secretary of State for the Home Department* 2007 SC (HL) 1 at para 87. Sh Pr Bowen commented on this matter in *AG v Mental Health Tribunal for Scotland* [2007] MHLR 1, indicating that he would not expect the tribunal to appear in appeals as a matter of routine. He did, however, construe the statute as intending that the tribunal has a right to appear, without the need to apply to be made a party to the appeal.

The grounds on which an appeal from a decision of the   **8.06**
tribunal may proceed are limited to those four specified in s 324(2),
namely that the decision is based on an error of law; that there
has been a procedural impropriety in the conduct of any hearing
by the tribunal on the application; that the tribunal has acted
unreasonably in the exercise of its discretion; and that the tribunal's
decision was not supported by the facts found by the tribunal to be
established.

There is a degree of overlap between certain of the permitted   **8.07**
grounds of appeal. A procedural impropriety resulting in unfairness
will be an error of law, as will an unreasonable exercise of discretion,
if it can be characterised as perverse. Procedural irregularity may
encompass unfair procedure such as a failure to permit both parties
to be fully heard. It might also involve a failure to comply with
the procedural requirements of the Rules. Error of law is a very
broad category, and comprehends any misdirection in law. It would
allow for an appeal on the ground that a decision was unlawful
because it was incompatible with one of the ECHR rights.[11] It
would also cover a failure properly to understand and apply the
2003 Act or any associated subordinate legislation, including the
Rules, to the circumstances of a given case. It is an error of law to
make a finding of fact if there is no evidence at all to support it, or
if the finding is perverse, in the sense that no reasonable tribunal
could have reached it on the available evidence. A failure to give
adequate reasons for a decision is an error of law. It represents a
failure to provide a fair hearing, which would be both an error of

---

[11] For a useful discussion of errors of law likely to be encountered in statutory
appeals (from immigration tribunals), see R (Iran) v Secretary of State for the Home
Department [2005] EWCA Civ 982 per Brooke LJ at paras 9 et seq. Brooke LJ gave
a non-exhaustive, but very useful, summary of the errors of law most commonly
encountered in practice, as follows:

  i) Making perverse or irrational findings on a matter or matters that were
     material to the outcome ("material matters");
  ii) Failing to give reasons or any adequate reasons for findings on material
     matters;
  iii) Failing to take into account and/or resolve conflicts of fact or opinion on
     material matters;
  iv) Giving weight to immaterial matters;
  v) Making a material misdirection of law on any material matter;
  vi) Committing or permitting a procedural or other irregularity capable of
     making a material difference to the outcome or the fairness of the pro-
     ceedings;
  vii) Making a mistake as to a material fact which could be established by objective
     and uncontentious evidence, where the appellant and/or his advisers were not
     responsible for the mistake, and where unfairness resulted from the fact that
     a mistake was made.

law itself, and a procedural impropriety.[12] It is suggested that, while the statute itself does not in terms[13] require that an error of law must have been material to the decision complained of, the court will have to be satisfied as to that before allowing the appeal. It is sometimes said that the court will not act in vain by setting aside a decision simply because of an error which could have had no bearing on that decision.[14]

8.08   If the court allows an appeal under any of ss 320, 321 or 322, the disposals open to it are those set out in s 324(5). It requires to set aside the flawed decision. If it can do so on the facts found by the tribunal, it may substitute its own decision. If it cannot do so, it may remit the matter to the tribunal for consideration anew. The court may, in that latter case, specify that the tribunal should be differently constituted from when it made the decision under appeal, and may issue such other directions about the consideration of the case as it considers appropriate.

8.09   Part VI of the Rules makes specific provision for cases remitted to the tribunal by the court under s 324(5)(b)(ii). The provisions are brief, and apply the Rules to remitted cases as they apply to cases before the tribunal, subject to any directions made by the court under s 324(6). In a remitted case, the tribunal is to consider and determine which of the rules is to apply to the remitted case, and issue such directions as it sees fit.[15]

APPEALS TO THE SHERIFF PRINCIPAL

8.10   While there are numerous miscellaneous statutory appeals from various administrative bodies and tribunals to the sheriff sitting alone, the provision in s 320 is relatively unusual in making provision for appeal from a judicial tribunal directly to the sheriff principal. The appeal is made by way of summary application.[16]

8.11   The initial writ should be in accordance with Form 1 in the Summary Applications Rules.[17] There is no specific provision as to the persons to whom the writ should be intimated and, in terms of

---

[12] See discussion at paras 7.17 et seq.

[13] Unlike, for example, certain of the provisions discussed in R (Iran), above.

[14] See, for example, Lord Wilberforce's comments in Malloch v Aberdeen Corporation 1971 SC (HL) 85 at 118.

[15] Rule 40(2).

[16] In terms of Act of Sederunt (Summary Applications, Statutory Applications and Appeals etc Rules) 1999 (SI 1999/929), r 1.2, as amended, "summary application" is defined by reference to s 3(p) of the Sheriff Courts (Scotland) Act 1907.

[17] Act of Sederunt (Summary Applications, Statutory Applications and Appeals etc Rules) 1999 (SI 1999/929), as amended.

r 2.5 of the Summary Applications Rules, the sheriff may make an order for intimation on any person who appears to have an interest in the summary application. In practice, intimation is made to the parties who have been directly involved in the proceedings before the tribunal. For example, if the appeal is against a CTO, the appeal will be brought by the patient or named person, and intimated to the MHO. It is submitted, however, that all persons who were parties to the proceedings before the tribunal (as defined in r 2 of the 2005 Rules), including the named person, should receive intimation. The appeal is also, as a matter of practice, intimated to the tribunal, given that the tribunal has a right to be represented at the appeal, as set out above.

In the summary application, the appellant should specify in the craves the orders he wishes the court to make. These should be framed by reference to the powers of the court in terms of s 324. An appellant might, for example, crave the court to set aside the decision of the tribunal of a given date, granting a CTO in respect of the patient. The writ should set out concisely the matters that the appellant is relying on, and specify which of the grounds in s 324(2) is being founded on. The pleas in law also should refer to the nature of the error being founded on. An appellant's writ might include a plea that "the tribunal's decision to grant a CTO having been based on an error of law, the decision should be set aside".   8.12

No regulations have been made under s 324(7), providing a time limit for appeal to the sheriff principal from the tribunal, and the provisions of r 2.6 of the Summary Applications Rules apply, prescribing a period of 21 days after intimation of the decision complained of.   8.13

If the sheriff principal considers that the appeal to him raises an important or difficult question of law, he may remit it to the Court of Session either *ex proprio motu* or on the motion of any party to the appeal.[18] If the sheriff principal decides to do so, the sheriff clerk must transmit the process to the Court of Session within 4 days, and send written notices to the parties that he has done so.[19]   8.14

APPEALS FROM THE SHERIFF PRINCIPAL

Decisions of the sheriff principal on appeals to him under s 320 may, under s 321, be appealed to the Court of Session. Again, it does not appear that any regulations have been made under s 324(7), making provision for time limits for appeals under s 321. In the absence   8.15

---

[18] 2003 Act, s 320(4).
[19] SI 1999/929, as amended, r 3.30.4.

of such provision, r 40.4(1) of the Rules of the Court of Session provides for a period of 21 days for appeal from an inferior court. The appeal is marked by a note of appeal in Form 40.4 marked on the interlocutor sheet, minute of court or other written record containing the decision appealed against.[20]

APPEALS TO THE COURT OF SESSION

8.16 Appeals to the Court of Session from the tribunal are governed by Chapter 41, Pt III of the Rules of the Court of Session. The appeal should be drafted in accordance with Form 41.19, and contain the information specified in r 41.19. Regulations[21] have been made under s 324(7) in relation to appeals from the tribunal to the Court of Session, specifying a period of 21 days from either the date on which the party was informed of the decision or, if he had requested a copy of the document mentioned in para 13(3) of Sch 2 to the 2003 Act, the date on which he received the document.[22]

SUSPENSION OF TRIBUNAL DECISION PENDING APPEAL

8.17 Section 323 of the 2003 Act makes provision in certain cases for the suspension of certain decisions of the tribunal, pending the determination of an appeal by the Scottish Ministers to the Court of Session. The decisions to which this provision relate concern restricted patients. On a motion by the Scottish Ministers, the Court of Session may order that the patient shall continue to be detained, be subject to a compulsion order and a restriction order, or a transfer for treatment order, until the appeal has been finally determined.

JUDICIAL REVIEW

8.18 A full discussion of the law and practice of judicial review in Scotland, and the many, and developing, bases of law on which an application for judicial review may be founded, is beyond the scope of this work.[23] Judicial review is the modern process by which applications

---

[20] RCS, r 40.4(2).
[21] Mental Health (Period for Appeal) (Scotland) (No 2) Regulations 2005 (SSI 2005/441).
[22] This reflects the wording of the 2003 Act, Sch 2, para 13, prior to amendment by SSI 2005/465; the position is now that the tribunal must send the written findings and reasons to every party as soon as reasonably practicable after it is completed.
[23] Readers are referred to O'Neill, *Judicial Review in Scotland: A Practitioner's Guide* (1999); Clyde and Edwards, *Judicial Review* (2000); and to Chapter 58 of the annotated Rules of the Court of Session.

to the supervisory jurisdiction of the Court of Session are to be made. The origins of judicial review in the supervisory jurisdiction of the Court of Session, and the scope of the modern remedy in Scotland, were discussed and analysed at length by the First Division in *West* v *Secretary of State for Scotland*[24] which remains the leading authority as to the circumstances in which judicial review will be competent, subject to what is said below about the role of the court in determining a judicial review application where it is alleged that a Convention right has been infringed.

An application for judicial review, classically, does not provide a mechanism for appeal, but examines the lawfulness of the process by which a decision has been made. The position is now complicated in applications for judicial review which are based on alleged breaches of human rights, as the court assesses for itself whether, on the merits, a decision is incompatible with a Convention right, rather than merely scrutinising the process by which the decision has been reached.[25]   **8.19**

The principles set out in *West* may be summarised as follows: **8.20**

- The Court of Session has power, in the exercise of its supervisory jurisdiction, to regulate the process by which decisions are taken by any person or body to whom a jurisdiction, power or authority has been delegated or entrusted by statute, agreement or any other instrument.

- The only purpose for which the supervisory jurisdiction may be exercised is to ensure that the person or body does not exceed or abuse that jurisdiction, power or authority or fail to do what the jurisdiction, power or authority requires. The "jurisdiction" of the inferior tribunal or administrative decision-maker in this context means the "power to decide" which is vested in that body, for example by the statute constituting it. Exceeding its proper jurisdiction may involve stepping outside it, or failing to observe its limits, or departing from the rules of natural justice, or a failure to understand the law, or the taking into account of matters which ought not to have been taken into account. The categories of what may amount to an excess or abuse of jurisdiction are not closed, and they are capable of being adapted in accordance with the development of administrative law.

- The competency of the application does not depend upon any distinction between public law and private law, nor is it confined to those cases which English law has accepted as amenable

---

[24] 1992 SC 385.
[25] *R (SB)* v *Governors of Denbigh High School* [2007] 1 AC 100; *Belfast City Council* v *Miss Behavin' Ltd* [2007] 1 WLR 1420: see particularly Baroness Hale of Richmond at para 31.

to judicial review, nor is it correct in regard to issues about competency to describe judicial review under Chapter 58 of the Rules of Court as a public law remedy.

- The cases in which the exercise of the supervisory jurisdiction is appropriate involve a tri-partite relationship, between the person or body to whom the jurisdiction, power or authority has been delegated or entrusted, the person or body by whom it has been delegated or entrusted and the person or persons in respect of or for whose benefit that jurisdiction, power or authority is to be exercised.

8.21   The tribunal is a body to which certain powers have been given by statute, and those powers are exercised in respect of individuals who, in principle, may have title and interest to seek review of its decisions. It is important to note, however, that judicial review, or an application to the supervisory jurisdiction of the Court of Session, is a remedy of last resort, and will not normally succeed where there is a statutory remedy in relation to the decision complained of, such as a statutory right of appeal.[26] Judicial review will therefore be inappropriate in relation to any decision which can be appealed to the sheriff principal or to the Court of Session in terms of s 320 or s 322.

8.22   The tribunal does, however, make decisions in addition to those specified as appealable – for example, procedural decisions to continue, or to refuse to continue, certain applications, and decisions to make directions in relation to future procedure. If there had been a procedural impropriety or misdirection in law at a procedural stage, it is likely that this could be founded on in an appeal against the ultimate decision on the merits of the case. With this in mind, an application for judicial review of the procedural decision might well fail as unnecessary or premature, and possibly incompetent, given the potential for a statutory appeal. The comments in para 8.02 relating to the terms of s 324(2)(b) are relevant here.

---

[26] Rule 58.3(2); *Tarmac Econowaste* v *Assessor for Lothian Region* 1991 SLT 77 (cannot ignore statutory appeals framework); *Chowdry, Petitioner* 1999 SLT 697; *Abdulla* v *Secretary of State for the Home Department* [2007] CSOH 34. Similarly, if an appeal would have been available but for the expiry of a time-limit, judicial review will be excluded unless there are exceptional circumstances: *Mensah* v *Secretary of State for the Home Department* 1992 SLT 177; *Alagon* v *Secretary of State for the Home Department* 1995 SLT 381; *Choi* v *Secretary of State for the Home Department* 1996 SLT 590; *Sangha* v *Secretary of State for the Home Department* 1997 SLT 545; *Ingle* v *Ingle's Tr* 1999 SLT 650; *Mahmood* v *Secretary of State for the Home Department* [2005] CSOH 52. See comment in *Abdulla*, above, on *Alagon* and *Sangha*.

An example of a decision which can be challenged only by judicial **8.23** review is that of an administrative decision of the tribunal – for example to set, or not to set a hearing in a particular case. A failure to set a hearing within the appropriate timescale was the basis of the only application for judicial review of the tribunal which has so far resulted in a written decision from the Court of Session.[27]

---

[27] *Smith* v *MHTS* 2006 SLT 347; [2007] MHLR 17.

APPENDIX 1

MENTAL HEALTH (CARE AND TREATMENT)
(SCOTLAND) ACT 2003
(asp 13)

SELECTED PARTS

Part 1

Introductory

1 Principles for discharging certain functions

(1) Subsections (2) to (4) below apply whenever a person who does not fall within subsection (7) below is discharging a function by virtue of this Act in relation to a patient who has attained the age of 18 years.

(2) In discharging the function the person shall, subject to subsection (9) below, have regard to the matters mentioned in subsection (3) below in so far as they are relevant to the function being discharged.

(3) The matters referred to in subsection (2) above are—

    (a) the present and past wishes and feelings of the patient which are relevant to the discharge of the function;

    (b) the views of—

        (i) the patient's named person;

        (ii) any carer of the patient;

        (iii) any guardian of the patient; and

        (iv) any welfare attorney of the patient,

which are relevant to the discharge of the function;

    (c) the importance of the patient participating as fully as possible in the discharge of the function;

    (d) the importance of providing such information and support to the patient as is necessary to enable the patient to participate in accordance with paragraph (c) above;

    (e) the range of options available in the patient's case;

    (f) the importance of providing the maximum benefit to the patient;

337

(g) the need to ensure that, unless it can be shown that it is justified in the circumstances, the patient is not treated in a way that is less favourable than the way in which a person who is not a patient might be treated in a comparable situation;

(h) the patient's abilities, background and characteristics, including, without prejudice to that generality, the patient's age, sex, sexual orientation, religious persuasion, racial origin, cultural and linguistic background and membership of any ethnic group.

(4) After having regard to—
(a) the matters mentioned in subsection (3) above;
(b) if subsections (5) and (6) below apply, the matters mentioned there; and
(c) such other matters as are relevant in the circumstances,
the person shall discharge the function in the manner that appears to the person to be the manner that involves the minimum restriction on the freedom of the patient that is necessary in the circumstances.

(5) Whenever a person who does not fall within subsection (7) below is discharging a function by virtue of this Act (other than the making of a decision about medical treatment) in relation to a patient, the person shall have regard, in so far as it is reasonable and practicable to do so, to—
(a) the needs and circumstances of any carer of the patient which are relevant to the discharge of the function and of which the person is aware; and
(b) the importance of providing such information to any carer of the patient as might assist the carer to care for the patient.

(6) Whenever a person who does not fall within subsection (7) below is discharging a function by virtue of this Act in relation to a person who is, or has been, subject to—
(a) detention in hospital authorised by a certificate granted under section 36(1) of this Act (any such certificate being referred to in this Act as an "emergency detention certificate");
(b) detention in hospital authorised by a certificate granted under section 44(1) of this Act (any such certificate

being referred to in this Act as a "short-term detention certificate");

(c) an order made under section 64(4)(a) of this Act (any such order being referred to in this Act as a "compulsory treatment order"); or

(d) an order made under section 57A(2) of the 1995 Act (any such order being referred to in this Act as a "compulsion order"),

the person who is discharging the function shall have regard to the importance of the provision of appropriate services to the person who is, or has been, subject to the certificate or order concerned (including, without prejudice to that generality, the provision of continuing care when the person is no longer subject to the certificate or order).

(7) A person falls within this subsection if the person is discharging the function by virtue of being—

(a) the patient;

(b) the patient's named person;

(c) the patient's primary carer;

(d) a person providing independent advocacy services to the patient under section 259 of this Act;

(e) the patient's legal representative;

(f) a curator *ad litem* appointed by the Tribunal in respect of the patient;

(g) a guardian of the patient; or

(h) a welfare attorney of the patient.

(8) In subsection (3)(a) above, the reference to wishes and feelings of the patient is a reference to those wishes and feelings in so far as they can be ascertained by any means of communication, whether human or by mechanical aid (whether of an interpretative nature or otherwise), appropriate to the patient.

(9) The person need not have regard to the views of a person mentioned in subsection (3)(b) above in so far as it is unreasonable or impracticable to do so.

(10) In subsection (3)(d) above, the reference to information is to information in the form that is mostly likely to be understood by the patient.

(11) In this section, a reference to "discharging", in relation to a power, includes a reference to exercising the power by taking no action; and "discharge" shall be construed accordingly.

...

PART 3

THE MENTAL HEALTH TRIBUNAL FOR SCOTLAND

21 The Mental Health Tribunal for Scotland

(1) There shall be a tribunal to be known as the Mental Health Tribunal for Scotland (in this Act referred to as "the Tribunal").

(2) The Tribunal shall discharge such functions as are conferred on it by virtue of this Act.

(3) Regulations may make such provision in connection with the Tribunal as the Scottish Ministers consider appropriate.

(4) Schedule 2 to this Act (which makes provision as respects the Tribunal and its proceedings) shall have effect.

...

PART 5

EMERGENCY DETENTION

Emergency detention certificate

36 Emergency detention in hospital

(1) Where—

  (a) a medical practitioner carries out a medical examination of a patient;

  (b) the patient does not fall within subsection (2) below; and

  (c) subsection (3) below applies,

  the medical practitioner may, before the expiry of the appropriate period, grant an emergency detention certificate authorising, if the condition mentioned in subsection (7) below is satisfied, the measures mentioned in subsection (8) below.

(2)[1] The patient falls within this subsection if, immediately before the medical examination mentioned in subsection (1)(a) above is carried out, the patient is subject to—

  (a) an emergency detention certificate;

  (b) a short-term detention certificate;

---

[1] As amended by Mental Health (Care and Treatment) (Scotland) Act 2003 (Modification of Enactments) Order 2005 (SSI 2005/465), Sch 1, para 32(2).

   (c) an extension certificate;

   (d) section 68 of this Act; or

   (e) a certificate granted under section 114(2) or 115(2) of this Act.

(3) Subject to subsection (6) below, this subsection applies where—

   (a) there is no conflict of interest in relation to the medical examination;

   (b) the medical practitioner considers that it is likely that the conditions mentioned in subsection (4) below are met in respect of the patient;

   (c) the medical practitioner is satisfied that the conditions mentioned in subsection (5) below are met in respect of the patient; and

   (d) the medical practitioner has consulted a mental health officer and that mental health officer has consented to the grant of an emergency detention certificate.

(4) The conditions referred to in subsection (3)(b) above are—

   (a) that the patient has a mental disorder; and

   (b) that, because of the mental disorder, the patient's ability to make decisions about the provision of medical treatment is significantly impaired.

(5) The conditions referred to in subsection (3)(c) above are—

   (a) that it is necessary as a matter of urgency to detain the patient in hospital for the purpose of determining what medical treatment requires to be provided to the patient;

   (b) that if the patient were not detained in hospital there would be a significant risk—

     (i) to the health, safety or welfare of the patient; or

     (ii) to the safety of any other person; and

   (c) that making arrangements with a view to the grant of a short-term detention certificate would involve undesirable delay.

(6) If it is impracticable for the medical practitioner to consult or seek consent under paragraph (d) of subsection (3) above, that paragraph need not be satisfied for the subsection to apply.

(7) The condition referred to in subsection (1) above is that the measure mentioned in subsection (8)(b)(i) below is authorised by the certificate only if, before the patient is admitted under authority of the certificate to a hospital, the certificate is given to the managers of that hospital.

(8) The measures referred to in subsection (1) above are—

    (a) the removal, before the expiry of the period of 72 hours beginning with the granting of the emergency detention certificate, of the patient to a hospital or to a different hospital; and

    (b) the detention of the patient in hospital for the period of 72 hours beginning with—

        (i) if, immediately before the certificate is granted, the patient is not in hospital, the first admission under authority of the certificate of the patient to hospital;

        (ii) if, immediately before the certificate is granted, the patient is in hospital, the granting of the certificate.

(9) Regulations may specify—

    (a) the circumstances in which there is to be taken to be; and

    (b) the circumstances in which there is not to be taken to be,

a conflict of interest in relation to the medical examination.

(10) The emergency detention certificate—

    (a) shall state the medical practitioner's reasons for believing the conditions mentioned in subsections (4) and (5) above to be met in respect of the patient; and

    (b) shall be signed by the medical practitioner.

(11) If a medical practitioner grants an emergency detention certificate in respect of a patient who, immediately before the certificate is granted, is in hospital, the medical practitioner shall, as soon as practicable after granting the certificate, give the certificate to the managers of that hospital.

(12) In subsection (1) above "appropriate period" means—

    (a) in a case where the medical examination of the patient is completed at least 4 hours before the end of the day (or, if it takes place on two days, the later of the days) on which it is carried out, the period beginning with completion of the examination and ending with the end of that day;

    (b) in any other case, the period of 4 hours beginning with the completion of the medical examination.

37 Notification by medical practitioner

(1) Subject to subsection (3) below, a medical practitioner who grants an emergency detention certificate shall, when the certificate is given to the managers of the hospital in which the patient is to be detained under authority of the certificate,

give notice to them of the matters mentioned in subsection (2) below.

(2) Those matters are—

    (a) the reason for granting the certificate;

    (b) whether consent of a mental health officer was obtained to the granting of the certificate;

    (c) if the certificate was granted without consent to its granting having been obtained from a mental health officer, the reason why it was impracticable to consult a mental health officer;

    (d) the alternatives to granting the certificate that were considered by the medical practitioner; and

    (e) the reason for the medical practitioner determining that any such alternative was inappropriate.

(3) If it is impracticable for notice to be given when the certificate is given to the managers, the medical practitioner shall give notice as soon as practicable after that time.

Duties on hospital managers

38 Duties on hospital managers: examination, notification etc.

(1) This section applies where a patient is detained in hospital under authority of an emergency detention certificate.

(2) As soon as practicable after the period of detention authorised by the certificate begins as mentioned in section 36(8)(b) of this Act, the managers of the hospital shall make arrangements for an approved medical practitioner to carry out a medical examination of the patient.

(3) The managers of the hospital shall—

    (a) before the expiry of the period of 12 hours beginning with the giving of the certificate to them, inform the persons mentioned in subsection (4) below of the granting of the certificate; and

    (b) before the expiry of the period of 7 days beginning with the day on which they receive notice under section 37 of this Act—

        (i) give notice to the persons mentioned in subsection (4) below of the matters notified to them under that section; and

        (ii) if the certificate was granted without consent to its granting having been obtained from a mental health officer, give notice of those matters to the persons mentioned in subsection (5) below.

(4) The persons referred to in subsection (3)(a) and (b)(i) above are—

(a) the patient's nearest relative;

(b) if that person does not reside with the patient, any person who resides with the patient;

(c) if—

(i) the managers know who the patient's named person is; and

(ii) that named person is not any of the persons mentioned in paragraphs (a) and (b) above,

the patient's named person; and

(d) the Commission.

(5) The persons referred to in subsection (3)(b)(ii) above are—

(a) if the managers know where the patient resides, the local authority for the area in which the patient resides; or

(b) if the managers do not know where the patient resides, the local authority for the area in which the hospital is situated.

Revocation of certificate

39[2] Approved medical practitioner's duty to revoke emergency detention certificate

Where a medical examination has been carried out under section 38(2) of this Act and an approved medical practitioner is not satisfied—

(a) that the conditions mentioned in section 36(4)(a) and (b) and (5)(b) of this Act continue to be met in respect of the patient; or

(b) that it continues to be necessary for the detention in hospital of the patient to be authorised by the certificate,

the approved medical practitioner shall revoke the certificate.

40 Revocation of emergency detention certificate: notification

(1) Where an approved medical practitioner revokes a certificate under section 39 of this Act, the practitioner shall, as soon as practicable after doing so, inform—

---

[2] As amended by Mental Health (Care and Treatment) (Scotland) Act 2003 (Modification of Enactments) Order 2005 (SSI 2005/465), Sch 1, para 32(3).

(a) the patient; and

(b) the managers of the hospital in which the patient is detained,

of the revocation.

(2) The managers of the hospital shall, as soon as practicable after being informed of the revocation, inform the persons mentioned in section 38(4) and (5) of this Act of the revocation.

Suspension of authority to detain

41 Suspension of authority to detain

(1) Where—

   (a) a patient is subject to an emergency detention certificate; and

   (b) the patient's responsible medical officer grants a certificate specifying a period during which the emergency detention certificate shall not authorise the measure mentioned in section 36(8)(b) of this Act,

the emergency detention certificate does not authorise that measure during that period.

(2) A period specified in a certificate granted under subsection (1) above may be expressed as—

   (a) the duration of—

      (i) an event; or

      (ii) a series of events; or

   (b) the duration of—

      (i) an event; or

      (ii) a series of events,

and any associated travel.

(3) If the responsible medical officer considers that it is necessary—

   (a) in the interests of the patient; or

   (b) for the protection of any other person,

a certificate granted under subsection (1) above may include conditions such as are mentioned in subsection (4) below; and any such conditions shall have effect.

(4) Those conditions are—

   (a) that, during the period specified in the certificate, the patient be kept in the charge of a person authorised in writing for the purpose by the responsible medical officer;

   (b) such other conditions as may be specified by the responsible medical officer.

42 Certificate under section 41: revocation

(1) Subsection (2) below applies where a certificate is granted under section 41(1) of this Act in respect of a patient.

(2) If the patient's responsible medical officer is satisfied that it is necessary—

(a) in the interests of the patient; or

(b) for the protection of any other person,

that the certificate be revoked, the responsible medical officer may revoke the certificate.

(3) Where a responsible medical officer revokes a certificate under subsection (2) above, the responsible medical officer shall, as soon as practicable after doing so, inform—

(a) the patient;

(b) if the certificate includes a condition such as is mentioned in section 41(4)(a) of this Act, any person authorised in accordance with that condition; and

(c) the managers of the hospital in which the patient is detained,

of the revocation.

(4) The managers of the hospital shall, as soon as practicable after being informed of the revocation, inform the persons mentioned in section 38(4) and (5) of this Act of the revocation.

Effect of emergency detention certificate on compulsory treatment order

43 Effect of subsequent emergency detention certificate on compulsory treatment order

(1) This section applies where—

(a) a patient is subject to a compulsory treatment order; and

(b) an emergency detention certificate is granted in respect of the patient.

(2) The compulsory treatment order shall, subject to subsection (3) below, cease to authorise the measures specified in it for the period during which the patient is subject to the emergency detention certificate.

(3) If the measure mentioned in section 66(1)(b) of this Act is specified in the compulsory treatment order, the compulsory treatment order shall continue to authorise that measure during the period mentioned in subsection (2) above.

PART 6

SHORT-TERM DETENTION

Short-term detention certificate

44 Short-term detention in hospital

(1) Where—

    (a) an approved medical practitioner carries out a medical examination of a patient;

    (b) the patient does not fall within subsection (2) below; and

    (c) subsection (3) below applies,

the approved medical practitioner may, before the expiry of the period of 3 days beginning with the completion of the medical examination, grant a short-term detention certificate authorising, if the condition mentioned in subsection (6) below is satisfied, the measures mentioned in subsection (5) below.

(2)[3] The patient falls within this subsection if, immediately before the medical examination mentioned in subsection (1)(a) above is carried out, the patient is subject to—

    (a) a short-term detention certificate;

    (b) an extension certificate;

    (c) section 68 of this Act; or

    (d) a certificate granted under section 114(2) or 115(2) of this Act.

(3) This subsection applies where—

    (a) there is no conflict of interest in relation to the medical examination;

    (b) the approved medical practitioner considers that it is likely that the conditions mentioned in subsection (4) below are met in respect of the patient;

    (c) the approved medical practitioner consults a mental health officer; and

    (d) the mental health officer consents to the grant of a short-term detention certificate.

(4) The conditions referred to subsection (3)(b) above are—

    (a) that the patient has a mental disorder;

---

[3] As amended by Mental Health (Care and Treatment) (Scotland) Act 2003 (Modification of Enactments) Order 2005 (SSI 2005/465), Sch 1, para 32(4).

(b) that, because of the mental disorder, the patient's ability to make decisions about the provision of medical treatment is significantly impaired;

(c) that it is necessary to detain the patient in hospital for the purpose of—

(i) determining what medical treatment should be given to the patient; or

(ii) giving medical treatment to the patient;

(d) that if the patient were not detained in hospital there would be a significant risk—

(i) to the health, safety or welfare of the patient; or

(ii) to the safety of any other person; and

(e) that the granting of a short-term detention certificate is necessary.

(5) The measures referred to in subsection (1) above are—

(a) the removal, before the expiry of the period of 3 days beginning with the granting of the short-term detention certificate, of the patient to a hospital or to a different hospital;

(b) the detention of the patient in hospital for the period of 28 days beginning with—

(i) if, immediately before the certificate is granted, the patient is not in hospital, the beginning of the day on which admission under authority of the certificate of the patient to hospital first takes place;

(ii) if, immediately before the certificate is granted, the patient is in hospital, the beginning of the day on which the certificate is granted;

(c) the giving to the patient, in accordance with Part 16 of this Act, of medical treatment.

(6) The condition referred to in subsection (1) above is that the measure mentioned in subsection (5)(b)(i) above is authorised by the certificate only if, before the patient is admitted to hospital under authority of the certificate, the certificate is given to the managers of that hospital.

(7) If an approved medical practitioner grants a short-term detention certificate in respect of a patient who, immediately before the certificate is granted, is in hospital, the approved medical practitioner shall, as soon as practicable after granting the certificate, give the certificate to the managers of that hospital.

(8) Regulations may specify—
    (a) the circumstances in which there is to be taken to be; and
    (b) the circumstances in which there is not to be taken to be,
a conflict of interest in relation to the medical examination.

(9) The short-term detention certificate—
    (a) shall state the approved medical practitioner's reasons for believing the conditions mentioned in subsection (4) above to be met in respect of the patient; and
    (b) shall be signed by the approved medical practitioner.

(10) Before granting the short-term detention certificate, the approved medical practitioner shall, subject to subsection (11) below, consult the patient's named person about the proposed grant of the certificate; and the approved medical practitioner shall have regard to any views expressed by the named person.

(11) The approved medical practitioner need not consult a named person as mentioned in subsection (10) above in any case where it is impracticable to do so.

45 Mental health officer's duty to interview patient etc.

(1) Subject to subsection (2) below, before deciding whether to consent for the purposes of section 44(3)(d) of this Act, a mental health officer shall—
    (a) interview the patient;
    (b) ascertain the name and address of the patient's named person;
    (c) inform the patient of the availability of independent advocacy services under section 259 of this Act; and
    (d) take appropriate steps to ensure that the patient has the opportunity of making use of those services.

(2) If it is impracticable for the mental health officer to—
    (a) interview the patient; or
    (b) ascertain the name and address of the patient's named person,
the mental health officer shall comply with the requirements in subsection (3) below.

(3) Those requirements are—
    (a) recording the steps taken by the mental health officer with a view to complying with the duty concerned; and
    (b) before the expiry of the period of 7 days beginning with the day on which the mental health officer is consulted by an approved medical practitioner under section 44(3)(c)

of this Act, giving a copy of the record to the approved medical practitioner.

Duties on hospital managers

46 Hospital managers' duties: notification

(1)[4] This section applies where a patient is subject to a short-term detention certificate.

(2) The managers of the hospital shall as soon as practicable after the production to them of the short-term detention certificate, give notice of its granting to—

(a) the patient;

(b) the patient's named person;

(c) any guardian of the patient; and

(d) any welfare attorney of the patient.

(3) The managers of the hospital shall, before the expiry of the period of 7 days beginning with the day on which the certificate is granted, give notice of its granting, and send a copy of it, to—

(a) the Tribunal; and

(b) the Commission.

Extension certificate

47 Extension of detention pending application for compulsory treatment order

(1) Where—

(a)[5] a patient is subject to a short-term detention certificate;

(b) an approved medical practitioner carries out a medical examination of the patient; and

(c) subsections (2) and (3) below apply,

the approved medical practitioner may, before the expiry of the period of 24 hours beginning with the completion of that medical examination, grant a certificate (any such certificate being referred to in this Act as an "extension certificate") authorising the measures mentioned in subsection (4) below.

(2) This subsection applies where—

---

[4] As amended by Mental Health (Care and Treatment) (Scotland) Act 2003 (Modification of Enactments) Order 2005 (SSI 2005/465), Sch 1, para 32(5).

[5] As amended by *ibid*, Sch 1, para 32(6).

    (a) there is no conflict of interest in relation to the medical examination; and

    (b) the approved medical practitioner considers—

        (i) that the conditions mentioned in paragraphs (a) to (d) of section 44(4) of this Act are met in respect of the patient; and

        (ii) that because of a change in the mental health of the patient, an application should be made under section 63 of this Act for a compulsory treatment order.

(3) This subsection applies where—

    (a) no application has been made under section 63 of this Act;

    (b) it would not be reasonably practicable to make an application under that section before the expiry of the period of detention authorised by the short-term detention certificate; and

    (c) subject to subsection (6) below—

        (i) the approved medical practitioner consults a mental health officer about the proposed grant of an extension certificate; and

        (ii) the mental health officer consents to the granting of the extension certificate.

(4) The measures referred to in subsection (1) above are—

    (a) the detention in hospital of the patient for the period of 3 days beginning with the expiry of the period for which the short-term detention certificate authorises the detention of the patient in hospital; and

    (b) the giving to the patient, in accordance with Part 16 of this Act, of medical treatment.

(5) Regulations may specify—

    (a) the circumstances in which there is to be taken to be; and

    (b) the circumstances in which there is not to be taken to be,

a conflict of interest in relation to the medical examination.

(6) An approved medical practitioner need not consult or seek consent under subsection (3)(c) above in any case where it is impracticable to do so.

(7) In reckoning the period of days mentioned in subsection (4)(a) above, there shall be left out of account any day which is not a working day.

(8) In this section "working day" means a day which is not—

(a) Saturday;

(b) Sunday; or

(c) a day which is a bank holiday under the Banking and Financial Dealings Act 1971 (c.80) in Scotland.

48 Extension certificate: notification

(1) An approved medical practitioner who grants an extension certificate shall, before the expiry of the period of 24 hours beginning with the granting of the certificate, give the certificate to the managers of the hospital in which the patient is detained and give notice to the persons mentioned in subsection (2) below—

(a) of the granting of the extension certificate;

(b) of the approved medical practitioner's reasons for believing the conditions mentioned in paragraphs (a) to (d) of section 44(4) of this Act to be met in respect of the patient;

(c) as to whether consent of a mental health officer was obtained to the granting of the certificate; and

(d) if the certificate was granted without consent to its granting having been obtained from a mental health officer, the reason why it was impracticable to consult a mental health officer.

(2) Those persons are—

(a) the patient;

(b) the patient's named person;

(c) the Tribunal;

(d) the Commission;

(e) any guardian of the patient;

(f) any welfare attorney of the patient; and

(g) the mental health officer.

Revocation of certificates

49 Responsible medical officer's duty to review continuing need for detention

(1)[6] Where a patient is subject to a short-term detention certificate or an extension certificate, the patient's responsible medical officer shall, from time to time, consider—

---

[6] As amended by Mental Health (Care and Treatment) (Scotland) Act 2003 (Modification of Enactments) Order 2005 (SSI 2005/465), Sch 1, para 32(7).

(a) whether the conditions mentioned in paragraphs (a), (b) and (d) of section 44(4) of this Act continue to be met in respect of the patient; and

(b) whether it continues to be necessary for the detention in hospital of the patient to be authorised by the certificate.

(2) If, having complied with subsection (1) above, the responsible medical officer is not satisfied—

(a) that the conditions referred to in paragraph (a) of that subsection continue to be met in respect of the patient; or

(b) that it continues to be necessary for the detention in hospital of the patient to be authorised by the certificate,

the responsible medical officer shall revoke the certificate.

(3) The responsible medical officer shall, as soon as practicable after revoking a certificate under subsection (2) above, give notice of its revocation to—

(a) the patient;

(b) the patient's named person;

(c) any guardian of the patient;

(d) any welfare attorney of the patient; and

(e) the mental health officer who was consulted under section 44(3)(c) of this Act.

(4) The responsible medical officer shall, before the expiry of the period of 7 days beginning with the day on which the certificate is revoked, give notice of its revocation to—

(a) the Tribunal; and

(b) the Commission.

50 Patient's right to apply for revocation of short-term detention certificate or extension certificate etc.

(1)[7] Where a patient is subject to a short-term detention certificate or an extension certificate—

(a) the patient; or

(b) the patient's named person,

may apply to the Tribunal for revocation of the certificate.

(2) Before determining an application under subsection (1) above, the Tribunal shall afford the persons mentioned in subsection (3) below the opportunity—

---

[7] As amended by Mental Health (Care and Treatment) (Scotland) Act 2003 (Modification of Enactments) Order 2005 (SSI 2005/465), Sch 1, para 32(8).

(a) of making representations (whether orally or in writing); and

(b) of leading, or producing, evidence.

(3) Those persons are—

(a) the patient;

(b) the patient's named person;

(c) any guardian of the patient;

(d) any welfare attorney of the patient;

(e) the approved medical practitioner who granted the short-term detention certificate;

(f) the mental health officer who was consulted under section 44(3)(c) of this Act;

(g) if the patient has a responsible medical officer, that responsible medical officer;

(h) any curator *ad litem* appointed in respect of the patient by the Tribunal; and

(i) any other person appearing to the Tribunal to have an interest in the application.

(4) On an application under subsection (1) above, the Tribunal shall, if not satisfied—

(a) that the conditions mentioned in paragraphs (a), (b) and (d) of section 44(4) of this Act continue to be met in respect of the patient; or

(b) that it continues to be necessary for the detention in hospital of the patient to be authorised by the certificate,

revoke the certificate.

(5) Where, before a short-term detention certificate is revoked under subsection (4) above an extension certificate has been granted in respect of the patient, the revocation of the short-term detention certificate shall have the effect of revoking the extension certificate, notwithstanding that there has been no application under subsection (1) above in relation to the extension certificate.

51 Commission's power to revoke short-term detention certificate or extension certificate

Where—

(a)[8] a patient is subject to a short-term detention certificate or an extension certificate; and

---

[8] As amended by Mental Health (Care and Treatment) (Scotland) Act 2003 (Modification of Enactments) Order 2005 (SSI 2005/465), Sch 1, para 32(9).

(b) the Commission is satisfied—

    (i) that not all of the conditions mentioned in paragraphs (a), (b) and (d) of section 44(4) of this Act continue to be met in respect of the patient; or

    (ii) that it does not continue to be necessary for the detention in hospital of the patient to be authorised by the certificate,

the Commission may revoke the certificate.

52 Revocation of short-term detention certificate or extension certificate: notification

Where the Commission revokes a certificate under section 51 of this Act, it shall, as soon as practicable after doing so, give notice of the revocation to—

(a) the patient;

(b) the patient's named person;

(c) any guardian of the patient;

(d) any welfare attorney of the patient;

(e) the managers of the hospital in which the patient is detained;

(f) the mental health officer who was consulted under section 44(3)(c) of this Act; and

(g) the Tribunal.

Suspension of detention

53 Suspension of measure authorising detention

(1) Where—

    (a) a patient is subject to a short-term detention certificate; and

    (b) the patient's responsible medical officer grants a certificate specifying a period during which the short-term detention certificate shall not authorise the measures mentioned in section 44(5)(b) of this Act,

the short-term detention certificate does not authorise that measure during that period.

(2) A period specified in a certificate granted under subsection (1) above may be expressed as—

    (a) the duration of—

        (i) an event; or

        (ii) a series of events; or

   (b) the duration of—

      (i) an event; or

      (ii) a series of events,

   and any associated travel.

(3) If the responsible medical officer considers that it is necessary—

   (a) in the interests of the patient; or

   (b) for the protection of any other person,

a certificate granted under subsection (1) above may include conditions such as are mentioned in subsection (4) below; and any such conditions shall have effect.

(4) Those conditions are—

   (a) that, during the period specified in the certificate, the patient be kept in the charge of a person authorised in writing for the purpose by the responsible medical officer;

   (b) such other conditions as may be specified by the responsible medical officer.

54 Certificate under section 53: revocation

(1) Subsection (2) below applies where a certificate is granted under section 53(1) of this Act in respect of a patient.

(2) If the patient's responsible medical officer is satisfied that it is necessary—

   (a) in the interests of the patient; or

   (b) for the protection of any other person,

that the certificate be revoked, the responsible medical officer may revoke the certificate.

(3) Where a responsible medical officer revokes a certificate under subsection (2) above, the responsible medical officer shall, as soon as practicable after doing so, give notice of the revocation to—

   (a) the patient;

   (b) the patient's named person;

   (c) the mental health officer;

   (d) if the certificate includes a condition such as is mentioned in section 53(4)(a) of this Act, any person authorised in accordance with that condition; and

   (e) the Commission.

Effect of short-term detention certificate on emergency detention certificate

55[9] Effect of subsequent short-term detention certificate on emergency detention certificate

If a short-term detention certificate is granted in respect of a patient who is subject to an emergency detention certificate, the emergency detention certificate shall, on the granting of the short-term detention certificate, be revoked.

Effect of short-term detention certificate on compulsory treatment order

56 Effect of subsequent short-term detention certificate on compulsory treatment order

(1) Subsection (2) below applies where—

(a) a patient is subject to a compulsory treatment order; and

(b) a short-term detention certificate is granted in respect of the patient.

(2) The compulsory treatment order shall cease to authorise the measures specified in it for the period during which the patient is subject to the short-term detention certificate.

PART 7

COMPULSORY TREATMENT ORDERS

CHAPTER I

APPLICATION FOR, AND MAKING OF, ORDERS

Pre-application procedures

57 Mental health officer's duty to apply for compulsory treatment order

(1) Where subsections (2) to (5) below apply in relation to a patient, a mental health officer shall apply to the Tribunal

---

[9] As amended by Mental Health (Care and Treatment) (Scotland) Act 2003 (Modification of Enactments) Order 2005 (SSI 2005/465), Sch 1, para 32(10).

under section 63 of this Act for a compulsory treatment order in respect of that patient.

(2) This subsection applies where two medical practitioners carry out medical examinations of the patient in accordance with the requirements of section 58 of this Act.

(3) This subsection applies where each of the medical practitioners who carries out a medical examination mentioned in subsection (2) above is satisfied—

  (a) that the patient has a mental disorder;

  (b) that medical treatment which would be likely to—

    (i) prevent the mental disorder worsening; or

    (ii) alleviate any of the symptoms, or effects, of the disorder,

    is available for the patient;

  (c) that if the patient were not provided with such medical treatment there would be a significant risk—

    (i) to the health, safety or welfare of the patient; or

    (ii) to the safety of any other person;

  (d) that because of the mental disorder the patient's ability to make decisions about the provision of such medical treatment is significantly impaired; and

  (e) that the making of a compulsory treatment order is necessary.

(4) This subsection applies where each of the medical practitioners who carries out a medical examination mentioned in subsection (2) above submits to the mental health officer a report (any such report being referred to in this Act as a "mental health report")—

  (a) stating that the medical practitioner submitting the report is satisfied that the conditions mentioned in paragraphs (a) to (e) of subsection (3) above are met in respect of the patient;

  (b) stating, in relation to each of the conditions mentioned in paragraphs (b) to (e) of subsection (3) above, the medical practitioner's reasons for believing the condition to be met in respect of the patient;

  (c) specifying (by reference to the appropriate paragraph (or paragraphs) of the definition of "mental disorder" in section 328(1) of this Act) the type (or types) of mental disorder that the patient has;

  (d) setting out a description of—

(i) the symptoms that the patient has of the mental disorder; and

(ii) the ways in which the patient is affected by the mental
disorder;

(e) specifying the measures that should, in the medical
practitioner's opinion, be authorised by the compulsory
treatment order;

(f) specifying the date or dates on which the medical practitioner carried out the medical examination mentioned in
subsection (2) above; and

(g) setting out any other information that the medical practitioner considers to be relevant.

(5) This subsection applies where—

(a) for the purposes of subsection (4)(c) above each of the
mental health reports specifies at least one type of mental
disorder that is also specified in the other report;

(b) for the purposes of subsection (4)(e) above each of the
mental health reports specifies the same measures; and

(c) one of the mental health reports (being a report by an
approved medical practitioner) states the views of that
medical practitioner as to—

(i) subject to subsection (6) below, whether notice should
be given to the patient under section 60(1)(a) of this
Act; and

(ii) whether the patient is capable of arranging for a
person to represent the patient in connection with the
application under section 63 of this Act.

(6) A medical practitioner may state the view that notice should
not be given under section 60(1)(a) of this Act only if, in the
opinion of that medical practitioner, the giving of notice would
be likely to cause significant harm to the patient or any other
person.

(7) Where a mental health officer is required by subsection (1)
above to make an application for a compulsory treatment order,
the mental health officer shall make the application before the
expiry of the period of 14 days beginning with—

(a) in the case where each of the mental health reports specifies
the same date (or dates) for the purposes of subsection
(4)(f) above, that date (or the later, or latest, of those
dates); or

(b) in the case where each of those reports specifies for those
purposes a different date (or different dates), the later (or
latest) of those dates.

58 Medical examination: requirements

(1) The requirements referred to in section 57(2) of this Act are set out in subsections (2) to (6) below.

(2) Subject to subsection (4) below and to regulations under subsection (5) below—

   (a) each medical examination of the patient shall be carried out by an approved medical practitioner; and

   (b) subject to subsection (6) below, each such examination shall be carried out separately.

(3) Where the medical examinations are carried out separately, the second shall be completed no more than five days after the first.

(4) The patient's general medical practitioner may carry out one of the medical examinations of the patient although not an approved medical practitioner.

(5) Except in circumstances specified in regulations, there must not be a conflict of interest in relation to the medical examination; and regulations shall specify the circumstances in which there is to be taken to be such a conflict of interest.

(6) The medical examinations need not be carried out separately if—

   (a) where the patient is capable of consenting to the examinations, the patient consents to the examinations being carried out at the same time; or

   (b) where the patient is incapable of consenting to the examinations—

      (i) the patient's named person;

      (ii) any guardian of the patient; or

      (iii) any welfare attorney of the patient,

   consents to the examinations being carried out at the same time.

59 Mental health officer's duty to identify named person

Where a mental health officer is required by 57(1) of this Act to make an application under section 63 of this Act in respect of a patient, the mental health officer shall, as soon as practicable after the duty to make the application arises, take such steps as are reasonably practicable to ascertain the name and address of the patient's named person.

60 Application for compulsory treatment order: notification

(1) Where a mental health officer is required by section 57(1) of this Act to make an application under section 63 of this Act in respect of a patient, the mental health officer shall, as soon as practicable after the duty to make the application arises (and, in any event, before making the application) give notice that the application is to be made—

    (a) subject to subsection (2) below, to the patient in respect of whom the application is to be made;

    (b) to the patient's named person; and

    (c) to the Commission.

(2) If the view set out in one of the mental health reports by virtue of section 57(5)(c) of this Act is that notice should not be given under paragraph (a) of subsection (1) above, the mental health officer—

    (a) need not give such notice; but

    (b) may, if the mental health officer considers it appropriate to do so, give such notice.

61 Mental health officer's duty to prepare report

(1) This section applies where a mental health officer is required by section 57(1) of this Act to make an application under section 63 of this Act in respect of a patient.

(2) The mental health officer shall, before the date on which, by virtue of section 57(7) of this Act, the application is to be made—

    (a) subject to subsection (3) below, interview the patient;

    (b) if the patient has not been given notice under section 60(1)(a) of this Act, inform the patient that the application is to be made;

    (c) inform the patient of—

        (i) the patient's rights in relation to the application; and

        (ii) the availability of independent advocacy services under section 259 of this Act;

    (d) take appropriate steps to ensure that the patient has the opportunity of making use of those services; and

    (e) prepare in relation to the patient a report in accordance with subsection (4) below.

(3) If it is impracticable for the mental health officer to comply with the requirement in subsection (2)(a) above, the mental health officer need not do so.

(4) The report shall state—

    (a) the name and address of the patient;

    (b) if known by the mental health officer, the name and address of—

        (i) the patient's named person; and

        (ii) the patient's primary carer;

    (c) the steps that the mental health officer has taken in pursuance of the requirements imposed by subsection (2) above;

    (d) if it was impracticable for the mental health officer to comply with the requirement in subsection (2)(a) above, the reason for that being the case;

    (e) in so far as relevant for the purposes of the application, details of the personal circumstances of the patient;

    (f) the mental health officer's views on the mental health reports relating to the patient;

    (g) if known by the mental health officer, details of any advance statement that the patient has made (and not withdrawn); and

    (h) any other information that the mental health officer considers relevant to the determination by the Tribunal of the application.

62 Mental health officer's duty to prepare proposed care plan

(1) This section applies where a mental health officer is required by section 57(1) of this Act to make an application under section 63 of this Act in respect of a patient.

(2) The mental health officer shall, before the date on which, by virtue of section 57(7) of this Act, the application is to be made, prepare a plan (a "proposed care plan") relating to the patient.

(3) Before preparing the proposed care plan, the mental health officer shall consult—

    (a) the medical practitioners who provided the mental health reports relating to the patient;

    (b) subject to subsection (7) below, the persons mentioned in subsection (4) below; and

    (c) such other persons as the mental health officer considers appropriate.

(4) The persons referred to in subsection (3)(b) above are persons who appear to the mental health officer to provide—

(a) medical treatment of the kind that it is proposed to specify, by virtue of paragraph (d) of subsection (5) below, in the proposed care plan;

(b) community care services, or relevant services, of the kind that it is proposed to specify, by virtue of paragraph (e) of that subsection, in that plan; or

(c) other treatment, care or services of the kind that it is proposed to specify, by virtue of paragraph (f) of that subsection, in that plan.

(5) The proposed care plan shall specify—

(a) (by reference to the appropriate paragraph (or paragraphs) of the definition of "mental disorder" in section 328(1) of this Act), the type (or types) of mental disorder which the patient has;

(b) the needs of the patient for medical treatment that have been assessed by the medical practitioners who submitted the mental health reports relating to the patient;

(c) in so far as relevant for the purposes of the application—

(i) where the patient is a child, the needs of the patient that have been assessed under section 23(3) of the Children (Scotland) Act 1995 (c.36);

(ii) where the patient is not a child, the needs of the patient that have been assessed under section 12A(1)(a) of the Social Work (Scotland) Act 1968 (c.49);

(d) the medical treatment which it is proposed to give to the patient in relation to each of the needs specified by virtue of paragraph (b) above (including the names of the persons who would give the treatment and the addresses at which the treatment would be given);

(e) any community care services or relevant services which it is proposed to provide to the patient in relation to each of the needs specified by virtue of paragraph (c) above (including the names of the persons who would provide such services and the addresses at which such services would be provided);

(f) in so far as relevant for the purposes of the application—

(i) any treatment or care (other than treatment or care specified, by virtue of paragraph (d) above, in the proposed care plan); or

(ii) any service (other than a service specified, by virtue of paragraph (e) above, in the proposed care plan),

which it is proposed to provide to the patient (including the names of the persons who would provide such treatment, care or service and the addresses at which such treatment, care or service would be provided);

(g) which of the measures mentioned in section 66(1) of this Act it is proposed that the compulsory treatment order should authorise;

(h) where it is proposed that the compulsory treatment order should authorise the detention of the patient in hospital, the name and address of the hospital;

(i) where it is proposed that the compulsory treatment order should authorise any of the measures mentioned in section 66(1)(c) to (h) of this Act, details of the measure (or measures);

(j) where it is proposed that the compulsory treatment order should specify—

(i) any medical treatment specified, by virtue of paragraph (d) above, in the proposed care plan;

(ii) any community care services, or relevant services, specified, by virtue of paragraph (e) above, in the proposed care plan; or

(iii) any treatment, care or service specified, by virtue of paragraph (f) above, in the proposed care plan,

that medical treatment, those services or that treatment, care, or service, as the case may be;

(k) where it is proposed that the compulsory treatment order should authorise measures other than the detention of the patient in hospital, the name of the hospital the managers of which should have responsibility for appointing the patient's responsible medical officer; and

(l) the objectives of—

(i) the medical treatment which it is proposed, by virtue of paragraph (d) above, to give to the patient;

(ii) any community care services or relevant services which it is proposed, by virtue of paragraph (e) above, to provide to the patient;

(iii) any treatment, care or service which, by virtue of paragraph (f) above, it is proposed to provide to the patient; and

(iv) the measures (other than detention of the patient in hospital) that it is proposed that the compulsory treatment order should authorise.

(6) The proposed care plan shall be signed by the mental health officer.

(7) The mental health officer need not consult any person such as is mentioned in subsection (4) above in any case where it is impracticable to do so.

(8) In this section "child" has the same meaning as in section 23(3) of the Children (Scotland) Act 1995 (c.36).

Application for order

63 Application for compulsory treatment order

(1) An application to the Tribunal for a compulsory treatment order may be made by, and only by, a mental health officer.

(2) An application—

  (a) shall specify—

    (i) the measures that are sought in relation to the patient in respect of whom the application is made;

    (ii) any medical treatment, community care services, relevant services or other treatment, care or service specified in the proposed care plan by virtue of section 62(5)(j)of this Act; and

    (iii) where it is proposed that the order should authorise measures other than the detention of the patient in hospital, the name of the hospital the managers of which should have responsibility for appointing the patient's responsible medical officer; and

  (b) shall be accompanied by the documents that are mentioned in subsection (3) below.

(3) Those documents are—

  (a) the mental health reports;

  (b) the report prepared under section 61 of this Act; and

  (c) the proposed care plan,

relating to the patient.

Making of order etc.

64 Powers of Tribunal on application under section 63: compulsory treatment order

(1) This section applies where an application is made under section 63 of this Act.

(2) Before determining the application, the Tribunal shall afford the persons mentioned in subsection (3) below the opportunity—
  (a) of making representations (whether orally or in writing); and
  (b) of leading, or producing, evidence.

(3) Those persons are—
  (a) the patient;
  (b) the patient's named person;
  (c) any guardian of the patient;
  (d) any welfare attorney of the patient;
  (e) the mental health officer;
  (f) the medical practitioners who submitted the mental health reports which accompany the application;
  (g) if the patient has a responsible medical officer, that officer;
  (h) the patient's primary carer;
  (i) any curator *ad litem* appointed in respect of the patient by the Tribunal; and
  (j) any other person appearing to the Tribunal to have an interest in the application.

(4) The Tribunal may—
  (a) if satisfied that all of the conditions mentioned in subsection (5) below are met, make an order—
    (i) authorising, for the period of 6 months beginning with the day on which the order is made, such of the measures mentioned in section 66(1) of this Act as may be specified in the order;
    (ii) specifying such medical treatment, community care services, relevant services, other treatment, care or service as the Tribunal considers appropriate (any such medical treatment, community care services, relevant services, other treatment, care or service so specified being referred to in this Act as a "recorded matter");
    (iii) recording (by reference to the appropriate paragraph (or paragraphs) of the definition of "mental disorder" in section 328(1) of this Act) the type (or types) of mental disorder that the patient has; and
    (iv) if the order does not authorise the detention of the patient in hospital, specifying the name of the hospital the managers of which are to have responsibility for

appointing the patient's responsible medical officer; or

(b) refuse the application.

(5) The conditions referred to in subsection (4)(a) above are—
  (a) that the patient has a mental disorder;
  (b) that medical treatment which would be likely to—
    (i) prevent the mental disorder worsening; or
    (ii) alleviate any of the symptoms, or effects, of the disorder,
    is available for the patient;
  (c) that if the patient were not provided with such medical treatment there would be a significant risk—
    (i) to the health, safety or welfare of the patient; or
    (ii) to the safety of any other person;
  (d) that because of the mental disorder the patient's ability to make decisions about the provision of such medical treatment is significantly impaired;
  (e) that the making of a compulsory treatment order in respect of the patient is necessary; and
  (f) where the Tribunal does not consider it necessary for the patient to be detained in hospital, such other conditions as may be specified in regulations.

(6) Subject to subsection (7) below, an order under subsection (4)(a) above may, in addition to, or instead of, specifying some or all of the measures sought in the application to which the order relates, specify measures other than those set out in that application.

(7) The Tribunal may specify in the order under subsection (4)(a) above measures other than those set out in the application only if, before making the order—
  (a) subject to subsection (8) below, the Tribunal gives notice to the persons mentioned in subsection (3) above—
    (i) stating what it is proposing to do; and
    (ii) setting out what those measures are;
  (b) the Tribunal affords those persons the opportunity—
    (i) of making representations (whether orally or in writing) in relation to the proposal; and
    (ii) of leading, or producing, evidence.

(8) Where the duty under subsection (7)(a) above arises during a hearing of the application, notice need not be given under that

subsection to any person mentioned in subsection (3) above who is present at the hearing.

(9) Before making regulations under subsection (5)(f) above, the Scottish Ministers shall consult such persons as they consider appropriate.

65 Powers of Tribunal on application under section 63: interim compulsory treatment order

(1) This section applies where an application is made under section 63 of this Act.

(2) Subject to subsections (3) and (4) below and to section 69 of this Act, on the application of any person having an interest in the proceedings, or *ex proprio motu*, the Tribunal may, if satisfied as to the matters mentioned in subsection (6) below, make an order (an "interim compulsory treatment order")—

    (a) authorising for such period not exceeding 28 days as may be specified in the order such of the measures mentioned in section 66(1) of this Act as may be so specified; and

    (b) if the order does not authorise the detention of the patient in hospital, specifying the name of the hospital the managers of which are to have responsibility for appointing the patient's responsible medical officer.

(3) The Tribunal may not make an interim compulsory treatment order if its effect, when taken with any other interim compulsory treatment order made in respect of the patient, would be to authorise measures in respect of the patient for a continuous period of more than 56 days.

(4) Before making an interim compulsory treatment order, the Tribunal shall afford the persons mentioned in subsection (5) below the opportunity—

    (a) of making representations (whether orally or in writing); and

    (b) of leading, or producing, evidence.

(5) Those persons are—

    (a) the persons referred to in section 64(3)(a) to (e) and (g) to (i) of this Act;

    (b) the medical practitioners who submitted the mental health reports which accompany the application under section 63 of this Act; and

(c) any other person appearing to the Tribunal to have an interest in that application.

(6) The matters referred to in subsection (2) above are—

(a) that the conditions mentioned in paragraphs (a) to (d) of section 64(5) of this Act are met in respect of the patient; and

(b) that it is necessary to make an interim compulsory treatment order.

66 Measures that may be authorised

(1) Subject to subsection (2) below, the measures referred to in sections 64(4)(a)(i) and 65(2)(a) of this Act are—

(a) the detention of the patient in the specified hospital;

(b) the giving to the patient, in accordance with Part 16 of this Act, of medical treatment;

(c) the imposition of a requirement on the patient to attend—

(i) on specified or directed dates; or

(ii) at specified or directed intervals,

specified or directed places with a view to receiving medical treatment;

(d) the imposition of a requirement on the patient to attend—

(i) on specified or directed dates; or

(ii) at specified or directed intervals,

specified or directed places with a view to receiving community care services, relevant services or any treatment, care or service;

(e) the imposition of a requirement on the patient to reside at a specified place;

(f) the imposition of a requirement on the patient to allow—

(i) the mental health officer;

(ii) the patient's responsible medical officer; or

(iii) any person responsible for providing medical treatment, community care services, relevant services or any treatment, care or service to the patient who is authorised for the purposes of this paragraph by the patient's responsible medical officer,

to visit the patient in the place where the patient resides;

(g) the imposition of a requirement on the patient to obtain the approval of the mental health officer to any proposed change of address; and

(h) the imposition of a requirement on the patient to inform the mental health officer of any change of address before the change takes effect.

(2) Regulations may make provision for measures prescribed by the regulations to be treated as included among the measures mentioned in subsection (1) above.

(3) In this section—

"directed" means in accordance with directions given by the patient's responsible medical officer; and

"specified" means specified in the compulsory treatment order or, as the case may be, the interim compulsory treatment order.

67 Order authorising detention: ancillary authorisation

(1) Where a compulsory treatment order or an interim compulsory treatment order—

(a) authorises the detention of a patient in a hospital specified in the order; or

(b) imposes a requirement on a patient to reside at a place specified in the order,

this section authorises the removal, before the expiry of the period of 7 days beginning with the appropriate day, of the patient in respect of whom the order is made to that hospital or, as the case may be, place.

(2) In subsection (1) above, "appropriate day" means the day on which—

(a) a compulsory treatment order or, as the case may be, an interim compulsory treatment order authorising detention of a patient in hospital is made; or

(b) a compulsory treatment order is varied so as to authorise the detention of a patient in the hospital specified in the order.

Extension of short-term detention: special case

68 Extension of short-term detention pending determination of application

(1) Where—

(a) the detention of a patient in hospital is authorised by—

(i) a short-term detention certificate; or

(ii) an extension certificate; and

(b) before the expiry of the period of detention so authorised, an application is made under section 63 of this Act,

the measures mentioned in subsection (2) below are authorised.

(2) Those measures are—

(a) the detention in hospital of the patient for the period of 5 days beginning with the expiry of the period for which the certificate authorises the detention of the patient in hospital; and

(b) the giving to the patient, in accordance with Part 16 of this Act, of medical treatment.

(3) In reckoning the period of days mentioned in subsection (2)(a) above, there shall be left out of account any day which is not a working day.

(4) In this section "working day" has the meaning given by section 47(8) of this Act.

Time limit for Tribunal's determination: special case

69 Time limit for determining application etc. where section 68 applies

Where section 68 of this Act applies, the Tribunal shall, before the expiry of the period of 5 days referred to in section 68(2)(a) of this Act—

(a) determine whether an interim compulsory treatment order should be made; and

(b) if it determines that an interim compulsory treatment order should not be made, determine the application.

Effect of making of orders on short-term detention

70 Effect of subsequent order on short-term detention certificate

If a compulsory treatment order, or an interim compulsory treatment order, is made in respect of a patient who is in hospital under authority of a short-term detention certificate, the certificate shall, on the making of the order, be revoked.

*Application of Chapter where patient subject to hospital direction
or transfer for treatment direction*

**71 Application of Chapter where patient subject to hospital
direction or transfer for treatment direction**

Where a patient is subject to—

(a) a hospital direction; or

(b) a transfer for treatment direction,

this Chapter shall have effect in accordance with Schedule 3 to
this Act.

CHAPTER 2

INTERIM COMPULSORY TREATMENT ORDERS:
REVIEW AND REVOCATION

**72 Interim compulsory treatment order: responsible medical
officer's duty to keep under review**

(1) Where a patient is subject to an interim compulsory treatment
order, the patient's responsible medical officer shall from time
to time consider—

(a) whether the conditions mentioned in paragraphs (a) to (d)
of section 64(5) of this Act continue to apply in respect of
the patient; and

(b) whether it continues to be necessary for the patient to be
subject to an interim compulsory treatment order.

(2) If, having considered the matters mentioned in paragraphs (a)
and (b) of subsection (1) above, the responsible medical officer
is not satisfied—

(a) that the conditions mentioned in paragraphs (a) to (d) of
section 64(5) of this Act continue to apply in respect of the
patient; or

(b) that it continues to be necessary for the patient to be
subject to an interim compulsory treatment order,

the responsible medical officer shall make a determination
revoking the interim compulsory treatment order.

(3) A determination under this section shall be made as soon as
practicable after the duty to make it arises.

73 Commission's power to revoke interim compulsory treatment order

(1) This section applies where a patient is subject to an interim compulsory treatment order.

(2) If the Commission is satisfied—

    (a) that not all of the conditions mentioned in paragraphs (a) to (d) of section 64(5) of this Act continue to apply in respect of the patient; or

    (b) that it does not continue to be necessary for the patient to be subject to an interim compulsory treatment order,

the Commission may revoke the interim compulsory treatment order.

74 Revocation under section 72 or 73: notification

(1) Where a patient's responsible medical officer makes a determination under section 72 of this Act, the responsible medical officer shall, as soon as practicable after doing so—

    (a) give notice of the determination; and

    (b) send a statement of the reasons for it,

to the Commission and to the persons mentioned in subsection (3) below.

(2) Where the Commission makes a determination under section 73 of this Act, it shall, as soon as practicable after doing so—

    (a) give notice of the determination; and

    (b) send a statement of the reasons for it,

to the patient's responsible medical officer and to the persons mentioned in subsection (3) below.

(3) The persons referred to in subsections (1) and (2) above are—

    (a) the patient;

    (b) the patient's named person;

    (c) any guardian of the patient;

    (d) any welfare attorney of the patient;

    (e) the mental health officer; and

    (f) the Tribunal.

75 Effect of subsequent compulsory treatment order on interim compulsory treatment order

If a compulsory treatment order is made in respect of a patient who is subject to an interim compulsory treatment order, the interim compulsory treatment order shall, on the making of the compulsory treatment order, be revoked.

CHAPTER 3

COMPULSORY TREATMENT ORDERS: CARE PLAN

76   Care plan: preparation, placing in medical records etc.

(A1)[10]   This section applies where a compulsory treatment order is made in respect of a patient.

(1) As soon as practicable after a patient's responsible medical officer is appointed under section 230 of this Act, the responsible medical officer shall—

  (a) prepare a plan (any such plan being referred to in this Act as a "care plan") relating to the patient; and

  (b) ensure that the patient's care plan is included in the patient's medical records.

(2) The care plan shall set out—

  (a) the medical treatment—

   (i) which it is proposed to give; and

   (ii) which is being given,

  to the patient while the patient is subject to the compulsory treatment order; and

  (b) such other information relating to the care of the patient as may be prescribed by regulations.

(3) Subject to subsection (4)(b) below, a patient's responsible medical officer may from time to time amend the patient's care plan.

(4) Regulations may prescribe—

  (a) circumstances in which a patient's responsible medical officer is required to amend the patient's care plan;

  (b) information in a care plan which may not be amended.

(5) Where a patient's responsible medical officer amends the patient's care plan—

---

[10] Inserted by Mental Health (Care and Treatment) (Scotland) Act 2003 (Modification of Enactments) Order 2005 (SSI 2005/465), Sch 1, para 32(11).

(a) the responsible medical officer shall ensure that, as soon as practicable after it is amended, the amended care plan is included in the patient's medical records; and

(b) subsections (2) to (4) above and this subsection shall apply as if references to the care plan were references to the amended care plan.

CHAPTER 4

REVIEW OF ORDERS

Mandatory reviews by responsible medical officer

77 First mandatory review

(1) This section applies where a compulsory treatment order is made in respect of a patient.

(2) The patient's responsible medical officer shall, during the appropriate period, carry out a review in respect of the order (such review being referred to in this Part of this Act as the "first review") by complying with the requirements in subsection (3) below.

(3) Those requirements are—

  (a) to—

    (i) carry out a medical examination of the patient; or

    (ii) make arrangements for an approved medical practitioner to carry out such a medical examination;

  (b) to consider—

    (i) whether the conditions mentioned in paragraphs (a) to (d) of section 64(5) of this Act continue to apply in respect of the patient; and

    (ii) whether it continues to be necessary for the patient to be subject to a compulsory treatment order; and

  (c) to consult—

    (i) the mental health officer;

    (ii) such persons as are mentioned in subsection (4) below as the responsible medical officer considers appropriate; and

    (iii) such other persons as the responsible medical officer considers appropriate.

(4) The persons referred to in subsection (3)(c)(ii) above are—

(a) persons who appear to the responsible medical officer to provide medical treatment of the kind that is set out in the patient's care plan;

(b) if any community care services or relevant services are set out in that plan, persons who appear to the responsible medical officer to provide services of that kind;

(c) if any other treatment, care or service is set out in that plan, persons who appear to the responsible medical officer to provide treatment, care or a service of that kind.

(5) In subsection (2) above, "appropriate period" means the period of 2 months ending with the day on which the compulsory treatment order ceases to authorise the measures specified in it.

78 Further mandatory reviews

(1) This section applies where a compulsory treatment order is extended—

(a) by a determination under section 86 of this Act; or

(b) by virtue of an order under section 103 of this Act.

(2) The patient's responsible medical officer shall, during the period mentioned in subsection (3) below, carry out a review in respect of the compulsory treatment order (such review being referred to in this Part of this Act as a "further review") by complying with the requirements set out in section 77(3) of this Act.

(3) The period referred to in subsection (2) above is the period of 2 months ending with the day on which the compulsory treatment order as extended by the determination, or by virtue of the order under section 103 of this Act, ceases to authorise the measures specified in it.

Revocation of order by responsible medical officer or Commission

79 Responsible medical officer's duty to revoke order: mandatory reviews

(1) This section applies where a patient's responsible medical officer is carrying out—

(a) the first review of the compulsory treatment order to which the patient is subject; or

(b) a further review of that order.

(2) If, having regard to any views expressed by persons consulted under section 77(3)(c) of this Act for the purpose of the review being carried out, the responsible medical officer is not satisfied—

(a) that the conditions mentioned in paragraphs (a) to (d) of section 64(5) of this Act continue to apply in respect of the patient; or

(b) that it continues to be necessary for the patient to be subject to a compulsory treatment order,

the responsible medical officer shall make a determination revoking the compulsory treatment order.

(3) A determination under this section shall be made as soon as practicable after the duty to make it arises.

80 Revocation of order: responsible medical officer's duty to keep under review

(1) This section applies where a patient is subject to a compulsory treatment order.

(2) Without prejudice to the duties imposed on the patient's responsible medical officer by sections 77(2), 78(2), 79(2) and 93(2) of this Act, the responsible medical officer shall from time to time consider—

(a) whether the conditions mentioned in paragraphs (a) to (d) of section 64(5) of this Act continue to apply in respect of the patient; and

(b) whether it continues to be necessary for the patient to be subject to a compulsory treatment order.

(3) If, having considered the matters mentioned in paragraphs (a) and (b) of subsection (2) above, the responsible medical officer is not satisfied—

(a) that the conditions mentioned in paragraphs (a) to (d) of section 64(5) of this Act continue to apply in respect of the patient; or

(b) that it continues to be necessary for the patient to be subject to a compulsory treatment order,

the responsible medical officer shall make a determination revoking the compulsory treatment order.

(4) A determination under this section shall be made as soon as practicable after the duty to make it arises.

81 Commission's power to revoke order

(1) This section applies where a patient is subject to a compulsory treatment order.

(2) If the Commission is satisfied—

   (a) that not all of the conditions mentioned in paragraphs (a) to (d) of section 64(5) of this Act continue to apply in respect of the patient; or

   (b) that it does not continue to be necessary for the patient to be subject to a compulsory treatment order,

   it may make a determination revoking the compulsory treatment order.

82 Revocation of order: notification

(1) Where a patient's responsible medical officer makes a determination under section 79 or 80 of this Act, that officer shall—

   (a) give notice of the determination; and

   (b) send a statement of the reasons for it,

   to the Commission and to the persons mentioned in subsection (3) below.

(2) Where the Commission makes a determination under section 81 of this Act, it shall—

   (a) give notice of the determination; and

   (b) send a statement of the reasons for it,

   to the patient's responsible medical officer and to the persons mentioned in subsection (3) below.

(3) The persons referred to in subsections (1) and (2) above are—

   (a) the patient;

   (b) the patient's named person;

   (c) any guardian of the patient;

   (d) any welfare attorney of the patient;

   (e) the mental health officer; and

   (f) the Tribunal.

(4) Notice under subsection (1) or (2) above—

   (a) to the persons mentioned in paragraphs (a) to (d) of subsection (3) above shall be given as soon as practicable after the determination is made and, in any event, before the expiry of the period of 7 days beginning with the day on which the determination is made; and

(b) to—

    (i) the Commission;

    (ii) the patient's responsible medical officer; and

    (iii) the persons mentioned in paragraphs (e) and (f) of that subsection,

shall be given before the expiry of the period of 7 days beginning with the day on which the determination is made.

Further steps to be taken where order not revoked

83 Mandatory reviews: further steps to be taken where order not revoked

(1) This section applies where a patient's responsible medical officer is carrying out—

    (a) the first review of the compulsory treatment order to which the patient is subject; or

    (b) a further review of that order.

(2) If, having regard to any views expressed by persons consulted under section 77(3)(c) of this Act for the purpose of the review being carried out, the patient's responsible medical officer is satisfied—

    (a) that the conditions mentioned in paragraphs (a) to (d) of section 64(5) of this Act continue to apply in respect of the patient; and

    (b) that it continues to be necessary for the patient to be subject to a compulsory treatment order,

the responsible medical officer shall comply with the requirements in subsection (3) below.

(3) Those requirements are—

    (a) to consider whether it will continue to be necessary for the patient to be subject to a compulsory treatment order after the day on which the order to which the patient is subject will cease (unless extended) to authorise the measures specified in it;

    (b) to assess the needs of the patient for medical treatment;

    (c) to consider—

        (i) whether the compulsory treatment order should be varied by modifying the measures, or any recorded matter, specified in it; and

(ii) if the order should be varied, what modification is appropriate;

(d) to consider any views expressed on the matters mentioned in paragraphs (a) to (c) above by persons consulted under section 77(3)(c) of this Act.

Extension of order by responsible medical officer

84 Responsible medical officer's duty where extension of order appears appropriate

(1) This section applies where a patient's responsible medical officer is carrying out—

(a) the first review of the compulsory treatment order to which the patient is subject; or

(b) a further review of that order.

(2) If, having regard to any views expressed by persons consulted under section 77(3)(c) of this Act for the purpose of the review being carried out, it appears to the responsible medical officer—

(a) that it will continue to be necessary for the patient to be subject to a compulsory treatment order after the day on which the order will cease (unless extended) to authorise the measures specified in it; and

(b) that the order should not be varied by modifying the measures, or any recorded matter, specified in it,

the responsible medical officer shall give notice to the mental health officer that the responsible medical officer is proposing to make a determination under section 86 of this Act extending the order.

85 Mental health officer's duties: extension of order

(1) The mental health officer shall, as soon as practicable after receiving notice under section 84(2) of this Act, comply with the requirements in subsection (2) below.

(2) Those requirements are—

(a) subject to subsection (3) below, to interview the patient;

(b) to inform the patient—

(i) that the patient's responsible medical officer is proposing to make a determination under section 86 of this Act extending the compulsory treatment order to which the patient is subject for the period mentioned in section 86(2) of this Act;

    (ii) of the patient's rights in relation to such a determination; and

    (iii) of the availability of independent advocacy services under section 259 of this Act;

(c) to take appropriate steps to ensure that the patient has the opportunity of making use of those services; and

(d) to inform the patient's responsible medical officer—

    (i) of whether the mental health officer agrees, or disagrees, that the determination that is proposed should be made;

    (ii) if the mental health officer disagrees, of the reason why that is the case; and

    (iii) of any other matters that the mental health officer considers relevant.

(3) If it is impracticable for the mental health officer to comply with the requirement in subsection (2)(a) above, the mental health officer need not do so.

86 Responsible medical officer's duty to extend order

(1) If, having regard to—

(a) any views expressed by persons consulted under section 77(3)(c) of this Act for the purpose of the review being carried out; and

(b) any views expressed by the mental health officer under section 85(2)(d) of this Act for the purpose of that review,

the responsible medical officer is satisfied as to the matters mentioned in section 84(2)(a) and (b) of this Act, the responsible medical officer shall make a determination extending the compulsory treatment order for the period mentioned in subsection (2) below.

(2) The period referred to in subsection (1) above is—

(a) where a determination is made in respect of the first review, the period of 6 months beginning with the day on which the compulsory treatment order will cease (unless extended) to authorise the measures specified in it;

(b) where a determination is made in respect of the first further review, the period of 12 months beginning with the expiry of the period mentioned in paragraph (a) above;

(c) where a determination is made in respect of a subsequent further review, the period of 12 months beginning with the expiry of the period of 12 months for which the order is extended as a result of the immediately preceding further review.

87 Determination extending order: notification etc.

(1) Where a patient's responsible medical officer makes a determination under section 86 of this Act, that officer shall, as soon as practicable after the determination is made and, in any event, before the day on which the compulsory treatment order will cease, if it is not extended by the determination, to authorise the measures specified in it, comply with the requirements in subsection (2) below.

(2) Those requirements are—
   (a) to prepare a record stating—
      (i) the determination;
      (ii) the reasons for it;
      (iii) whether the mental health officer agrees, or disagrees, with the determination or has failed to comply with the duty imposed by section 85(2)(d)(i) of this Act;
      (iv) if the mental health officer disagrees with the determination, the reasons for the disagreement;
      (v) (by reference to the appropriate paragraph (or paragraphs) of the definition of "mental disorder" in section 328(1) of this Act) the type (or types) of mental disorder that the patient has; and if there is a difference between that type (or types) and the type (or types) of mental disorder recorded in the compulsory treatment order in respect of which the determination is made, what that difference is; and
      (vi) such other matters as may be prescribed by regulations;
   (b) to submit the record to the Tribunal; and
   (c) at the same time as the responsible medical officer submits the record to the Tribunal, to give notice of the determination and send a copy of the record—
      (i) subject to subsection (3) below, to the patient;
      (ii) to the patient's named person;
      (iii) to the mental health officer; and
      (iv) to the Commission.

(3) If the responsible medical officer considers that there would be a risk of significant harm to the patient, or to others, if a copy of the record were sent to the patient, that officer need not send a copy to the patient.

(4) At the same time as the responsible medical officer submits the record to the Tribunal, that officer shall send to the Tribunal, and to the persons mentioned in subsection (2)(c)(ii) to (iv) above, a statement of the matters mentioned in subsection (5) below.

(5) Those matters are—
   (a) whether the responsible medical officer is sending a copy of the record to the patient; and
   (b) if the responsible medical officer is not sending a copy of the record to the patient, the reason for not doing so.

Extension and variation of order: application by responsible medical officer

88 Responsible medical officer's duty where extension and variation of order appear appropriate

(1) This section applies where a patient's responsible medical officer is carrying out—
   (a) the first review of the compulsory treatment order to which the patient is subject; or
   (b) a further review of that order.

(2) If, having regard to any views expressed by persons consulted under section 77(3)(c) of this Act for the purpose of the review being carried out, it appears to the responsible medical officer—
   (a) that it will continue to be necessary for the patient to be subject to a compulsory treatment order after the day on which the order will cease (unless extended) to authorise the measures specified in it; but
   (b) that the order should be varied by modifying the measures, or any recorded matter, specified in it,
   the responsible medical officer shall comply with the requirement in subsection (3) below.

(3) That requirement is to give notice to the mental health officer—
   (a) that the responsible medical officer is proposing to make an application to the Tribunal under section 92 of this Act for an order under section 103 of this Act—

(i) extending the compulsory treatment order for the period mentioned in subsection (4) below; and

(ii) varying that order by modifying the measures, or a recorded matter, specified in it; and

(b) of the modification of the measures, or any recorded matter, specified in that order that the responsible medical officer is proposing.

(4) The period referred to in subsection (3) above is—

(a) where the application is made in respect of the first review, the period of 6 months beginning with the day on which the compulsory treatment order will (unless extended) cease to authorise the measures specified in it;

(b) where the application is made in respect of the first further review, the period of 12 months beginning with the expiry of the period mentioned in paragraph (a) above;

(c) where the application is made in respect of a subsequent further review, the period of 12 months beginning with the expiry of the period of 12 months for which the order is extended as a result of the immediately preceding further review.

89 Mental health officer's duties: extension and variation of order

(1) The mental health officer shall, as soon as practicable after receiving notice under section 88(3) of this Act, comply with the requirements in subsection (2) below.

(2) Those requirements are—

(a) subject to subsection (3) below, to interview the patient;

(b) to inform the patient of the matters mentioned in subsection (4) below;

(c) to inform the patient of the availability of independent advocacy services under section 259 of this Act;

(d) to take appropriate steps to ensure that the patient has the opportunity of making use of those services; and

(e) to inform the patient's responsible medical officer—

(i) of whether the mental health officer agrees, or disagrees, that the application that is proposed should be made;

(ii) if the mental health officer disagrees, of the reason why that is the case; and

(iii) of any other matters that the mental health officer considers relevant.

(3) If it is impracticable for the mental health officer to comply with the requirement in subsection (2)(a) above, the mental health officer need not do so.

(4) The matters referred to in subsection (2)(b) above are—

(a) that the patient's responsible medical officer is proposing to make an application to the Tribunal under section 92 of this Act for an order—

(i) extending the compulsory treatment order to which the patient is subject for the period mentioned in section 88(4) of this Act; and

(ii) varying the compulsory treatment order by modifying the measures or a recorded matter specified in it;

(b) the modification of the measures or any recorded matter specified in that order that the responsible medical officer is proposing; and

(c) the patient's rights in relation to such an application.

90 Responsible medical officer's duty to apply for extension and variation of order

(1) If, having regard to—

(a) any views expressed by persons consulted under section 77(3)(c) of this Act for the purpose of the review being carried out; and

(b) any views expressed by the mental health officer under section 89(2)(e) of this Act for the purpose of that review, the responsible medical officer is satisfied as to the matters mentioned in section 88(2)(a) and (b) of this Act, the responsible medical officer shall comply with the requirement in subsection (2) below.

(2) That requirement is to make an application to the Tribunal under section 92 of this Act for an order—

(a) extending the compulsory treatment order for the period mentioned in section 88(4) of this Act; and

(b) varying that order by modifying the measures, or a recorded matter, specified in it.

(3) An application made under section 92 of this Act, by virtue of subsection (1) above, for an order mentioned in subsection (2) above shall be made as soon as practicable after the duty to make it arises.

91 Application for extension and variation of order: notification

Where, by virtue of section 90(1) of this Act, an application is to be made under section 92 of this Act, the patient's responsible medical officer shall, as soon as practicable after the duty to make the application arises (and, in any event, before making the application), give notice that the application is to be made to—

(a) the patient;

(b) the patient's named person;

(c) any guardian of the patient;

(d) any welfare attorney of the patient;

(e) the mental health officer; and

(f) the Commission.

92 Application to Tribunal

An application under this section to the Tribunal by a patient's responsible medical officer for an order extending and varying a compulsory treatment order—

(a) shall state—

   (i) the name and address of the patient;

   (ii) the name and address of the patient's named person;

   (iii) the modification of the measures, or any recorded matter, specified in the compulsory treatment order that is proposed by the responsible medical officer;

   (iv) the reasons for seeking that modification;

   (v) whether the mental health officer agrees, or disagrees, that the application should be made, or has failed to comply with the duty imposed by section 89(2)(e)(i) of this Act; and

   (vi) if the mental health officer disagrees, the reason for that disagreement; and

(b) shall be accompanied by such documents as may be prescribed by regulations.

Variation of order: application by responsible medical officer

93 Responsible medical officer's duties: variation of order

(1) This section applies where a patient is subject to a compulsory treatment order.

(2) Without prejudice to the duties imposed on the patient's responsible medical officer by sections 77(2), 78(2) and 83(2)

of this Act, the responsible medical officer shall from time to time consider whether the compulsory treatment order should be varied by modifying the measures, or any recorded matter, specified in it.

(3) If it appears to the responsible medical officer that the compulsory treatment order should be varied as mentioned in subsection (2) above, the responsible medical officer shall, as soon as practicable, comply with the requirements in subsection (4) below.

(4) Those requirements are—
    (a) to assess the needs of the patient for medical treatment;
    (b) to consider what modification, if any, of the measures, or any recorded matter, specified in the compulsory treatment order is appropriate;
    (c) to consult—
      (i) the mental health officer; and
      (ii) such persons as the responsible medical officer considers appropriate.

(4A)[11] If, having regard to any views expressed by persons consulted under subsection (4)(c) above, it continues to appear to the responsible medical officer that the compulsory treatment order should be varied as mentioned in subsection (2) above, the responsible medical officer shall, as soon as practicable, notify the mental health officer—
    (a) that the responsible medical officer is proposing to make an application to the Tribunal under section 95 of this Act for an order under section 103 of this Act varying the compulsory treatment order; and
    (b) the modification of the measures, or any recorded matter, specified in that order that the responsible medical officer is proposing.

(4B)[12] The mental health officer shall, as soon as practicable after being notified under subsection (4A) above, comply with the requirements in subsection (4C) below.

(4C)[13] Those requirements are—

---

[11] Inserted by Mental Health (Care and Treatment) (Scotland) Act 2003 Modification Order 2004 (SSI 2004/533), art 2(2)(a).
[12] *Ibid.*
[13] *Ibid.*

(a) subject to subsection (4D) below, to interview the patient;

(b) to inform the patient of the matters mentioned in subsection (4E) below;

(c) to inform the patient of the availability of independent advocacy services under section 259 of this Act;

(d) to take appropriate steps to ensure that the patient has the opportunity of making use of those services; and

(e) to inform the patient's responsible medical officer—

(i) of whether the mental health officer agrees, or disagrees, that the application that is proposed should be made;

(ii) if the mental health officer disagrees, of the reason why that is the case; and

(iii) of any other matters that the mental health officer considers relevant.

(4D)[14] If it is impracticable for the mental health officer to comply with the requirement in subsection (4C)(a) above, the mental health officer need not do so.

(4E)[15] The matters referred to in subsection (4C)(b) above are—

(a) that the patient's responsible medical officer is proposing to make an application to the Tribunal under section 95 of this Act for an order varying the compulsory treatment order by modifying the measures or a recorded matter specified in it;

(b) the modification of the measures or any recorded matter specified in that order that the responsible medical officer is proposing; and

(c) the patient's rights in relation to such an application.

(5)[16] If, having regard to any views expressed by persons consulted under subsection (4)(c) above and any views expressed by the mental health officer under subsection (4C)(e) above, the responsible medical officer is satisfied that the compulsory treatment order should be varied as mentioned in subsection (2) above, the responsible medical officer shall make an application to the Tribunal under section 95 of this Act for an order under

---

[14] As inserted by Mental Health (Care and Treatment) (Scotland) Act 2003 (Modification Order 2004 (SSI 2004/533), art 2(2)(a).

[15] As amended by *ibid*, art 2(2)(b).

[16] *Ibid*.

section 103 of this Act varying the compulsory treatment order in that way.

(6) An application made under section 95 of this Act, by virtue of subsection (5) above, for an order mentioned in that subsection shall be made as soon as practicable after the duty to make it arises.

94 Application by responsible medical officer for variation of order: notification

Where, by virtue of section 93(5) of this Act, an application is to be made under section 95 of this Act, the patient's responsible medical officer shall, as soon as practicable after the duty to make the application arises (and, in any event, before making the application), give notice that the application is to be made to the persons mentioned in section 91(a) to (f) of this Act.

95[17] Application to Tribunal by responsible medical officer

An application under this section to the Tribunal by a patient's responsible medical officer for an order varying a compulsory treatment order—

(a) shall state
  (i) the matters mentioned in section 92(a)(i) to (vi) of this Act; and
  (ii) whether the mental health officer agrees, or disagrees, that the application should be made, or has failed to comply with the duty imposed by section 93(4C)(e)(i) of this Act; and
  (iii) if the mental health officer disagrees, the reason for that disagreement; and
(b) shall be accompanied by such documents as may be prescribed by regulations.

Recorded matters: reference to Tribunal by responsible medical officer

96 Recorded matters: reference to Tribunal by responsible medical officer

(1) This section applies where a patient is subject to a compulsory treatment order which specifies one or more recorded matters.

---

[17] As amended by Mental Health (Care and Treatment) (Scotland) Act 2003 Modification Order 2004 (SSI 2004/533), art 2(3).

(2) Without prejudice to the duties imposed on the patient's responsible medical officer by sections 77(2), 78(2) and 83(2) of this Act and subject to subsection (6) below, if it appears to the responsible medical officer that any recorded matter specified in the compulsory treatment order is not being provided, the responsible medical officer shall, as soon as practicable, consult—

(a) the mental health officer; and

(b) such other persons as the responsible medical officer considers appropriate.

(3) If, having regard to any views expressed by persons consulted under subsection (2) above, the responsible medical officer is satisfied that a recorded matter specified in the compulsory treatment order is not being provided, the responsible medical officer shall make a reference to the Tribunal.

(4) A reference under subsection (3) above—

(a) shall state—

(i) the name and address of the patient;

(ii) the name and address of the patient's named person; and

(iii) the reason for making the reference; and

(b) shall be accompanied by such documents as may be prescribed by regulations.

(5) A reference under subsection (3) above shall be made as soon as practicable after the duty to make it arises.

(6) Subsections (2) to (5) above do not apply where—

(a) the responsible medical officer is required, by virtue of section 79 or 80 of this Act, to revoke the compulsory treatment order; or

(b) the responsible medical officer is making an application under section 92 or 95 of this Act in respect of the compulsory treatment order.

97 Reference to Tribunal under section 96(3): notification

Where a patient's responsible medical officer is required by section 96(3) of this Act to make a reference to the Tribunal, the responsible medical officer shall, as soon as practicable after the duty to make the reference arises, give notice that the reference is to be made to the persons mentioned in section 91(a) to (f) of this Act.

Reference to Tribunal by Commission

98 Reference to Tribunal by Commission

(1) This section applies where a patient is subject to a compulsory treatment order.

(2) If it appears to the Commission that it is appropriate to do so, it may make a reference to the Tribunal in respect of the compulsory treatment order to which the patient is subject.

(3) Where a reference is to be made under subsection (2) above, the Commission shall, as soon as practicable, give notice that a reference is to be made to—

(a) the patient's responsible medical officer; and
(b) the persons mentioned in section 91(a) to (e) of this Act.

(4) A reference under subsection (2) above shall state—

(a) the name and address of the patient;
(b) the name and address of the patient's named person; and
(c) the reason for making the reference.

Applications by patient etc.

99 Application by patient etc. for revocation of determination extending order

(1) Where a patient's responsible medical officer makes a determination under section 86 of this Act, subject to subsection (3) below, either of the persons mentioned in subsection (2) below may make an application under this section to the Tribunal for an order under section 103 of this Act revoking the determination.

(2) Those persons are—

(a) the patient;
(b) the patient's named person.

(3) Subsection (1) above does not apply where the Tribunal is required, by virtue of section 101 of this Act, to review the determination.

100 Application by patient etc. for revocation or variation of order

(1) This section applies where a patient is subject to a compulsory treatment order.

(2) Either of the persons mentioned in subsection (3) below may, subject to subsections (4) and (6) below, make an application

under this section to the Tribunal for an order under section 103 of this Act—

(a) revoking the compulsory treatment order; or

(b) varying that order by modifying—

    (i) the measures; or

    (ii) any recorded matter,

specified in it.

(3) Those persons are—

(a) the patient;

(b) the patient's named person.

(4) An application under this section may not be made during the period of 3 months beginning with the making of any of the orders mentioned in subsection (5) below.

(5) Those orders are—

(a) the compulsory treatment order;

(b) an order in respect of the compulsory treatment order made under section 102 of this Act;

(c) an order in respect of the compulsory treatment order made, by virtue of section 92 of this Act, under section 103 of this Act.

(6) If—

(a) an application under this section for revocation of a compulsory treatment order is refused; or

(b) an application is made under this section for variation of a compulsory treatment order,

the person who made the application shall not be entitled to make more than one further application under this section in respect of the compulsory treatment order during the period mentioned in subsection (8) below.

(7) If an application under section 99 of this Act for revocation of a determination under section 86 of this Act is refused, the person who made the application shall not be entitled to make more than one application under this section in respect of the compulsory treatment order which is the subject of the determination during the period mentioned in subsection (8) below.

(8) The period referred to in subsections (6) and (7) above is—

(a) where the application mentioned in subsection (6)(a) or (b) or (7) above is made before the expiry of the period of

6 months beginning with the day on which the compulsory treatment order was made, that period of 6 months; or

(b) where that application is made before the expiry of—

(i) the period of 6 months beginning with the expiry of the period mentioned in paragraph (a) above, that period of 6 months; or

(ii) any subsequent period of 12 months that begins with, or with an anniversary of, the expiry of the period of 6 months mentioned in subparagraph (i) above, that subsequent period of 12 months.

Review by Tribunal of determination extending order

101 Tribunal's duty to review determination under section 86

(1) This section applies where a patient's responsible medical officer makes a determination under section 86 of this Act.

(2) If—

(a) the record submitted to the Tribunal under section 87(2)(b) of this Act states—

(i) that there is a difference between the type (or types) of mental disorder that the patient has and the type (or types) of mental disorder recorded in the compulsory treatment order in respect of which the determination is made; or

(ii) that the mental health officer disagrees with the determination or has failed to comply with the duty imposed by section 85(2)(d)(i) of this Act; or

(b)[18] the conditions in subsection (3) are satisfied in relation to the compulsory treatment order to which the determination relates,

the Tribunal shall review the determination.

(3)[19] The conditions mentioned in subsection (2)(b) above are—

(a) that the order was made 2 or more years before the renewal day;

(b) that this section did not require the Tribunal to review the previous determination made under section 86 of this Act in relation to the order; and

(c) that, in the period of 2 years ending with the day before the renewal day, no application has been made to the

---

[18] Substituted by Adult Support and Protection (Scotland) Act 2007, s 68.
[19] Inserted by *ibid*, s 68(b).

Tribunal under section 92, 99, 95 or 100 in relation to the order.

(4)[20] In subsection (3) above, the renewal day is the first day on which the order, had it not been extended by the determination, would not authorise the measures specified in it.

Powers of Tribunal

102 Powers of Tribunal on review under section 101

(1) On the review of a determination under section 101 of this Act, the Tribunal may make an order under this section—

(a) revoking the determination;

(b) revoking both the determination and the compulsory treatment order;

(c) confirming the determination; or

(d) confirming the determination and varying the compulsory treatment order by modifying—

(i) the measures; or

(ii) any recorded matter,

specified in it.

(2) Before making a decision under subsection (1) above, the Tribunal shall allow the persons mentioned in subsection (3) below the opportunity—

(a) of making representations (whether orally or in writing); and

(b) of leading, or producing, evidence.

(3) Those persons are—

(a) the patient;

(b) the patient's named person;

(c) any guardian of the patient;

(d) any welfare attorney of the patient;

(e) the mental health officer;

(f) the patient's responsible medical officer;

(g) the patient's primary carer;

(h) any curator *ad litem* appointed in respect of the patient by the Tribunal; and

(i) any other person appearing to the Tribunal to have an interest in the determination.

---

[20] Inserted by Adult Support and Protection (Scotland) Act 2007, s 68(b).

103 Powers of Tribunal on application under section 92, 95, 99 or 100

(1) Where an application is made under section 92 of this Act, the Tribunal may make an order—

    (a) extending the compulsory treatment order to which the application relates for the period mentioned in section 88(4) of this Act and varying the compulsory treatment order by modifying—

        (i) the measures; or

        (ii) any recorded matter,

        specified in it;

    (b) extending the compulsory treatment order for that period;

    (c) refusing the application; or

    (d) refusing the application and revoking the compulsory treatment order.

(2) Where an application is made under section 99 of this Act, the Tribunal may make an order—

    (a) revoking the determination to which the application relates;

    (b) revoking—

        (i) the determination; and

        (ii) the compulsory treatment order to which the determination relates;

    (c) confirming the determination; or

    (d) confirming the determination and varying the compulsory treatment order by modifying—

        (i) the measures; or

        (ii) any recorded matter,

        specified in it.

(3) Where an application is made under section 100(2)(a) of this Act, the Tribunal may make an order—

    (a) revoking the compulsory treatment order to which the application relates;

    (b) varying the compulsory treatment order by modifying—

        (i) the measures; or

        (ii) any recorded matter,

        specified in it; or

    (c) refusing the application.

(4) Where an application is made under section 95 or 100(2)(b) of this Act, the Tribunal may make an order—

   (a) varying the compulsory treatment order to which the application relates by modifying—

     (i) the measures; or

     (ii) any recorded matter,

     specified in it;

   (b) refusing the application; or

   (c) refusing the application and revoking that order.

(5) Before making a decision under any of subsections (1) to (4) above, the Tribunal shall afford the persons mentioned in subsection (6) below the opportunity—

   (a) of making representations (whether orally or in writing); and

   (b) of leading, or producing, evidence.

(6) Those persons are—

   (a) the persons mentioned in section 102(3)(a) to (h) of this Act; and

   (b) any other person appearing to the Tribunal to have an interest in the application.

104 Powers of Tribunal on reference under section 96 or 98

(1) Where a reference is made under section 96 or 98 of this Act, the Tribunal may make an order—

   (a) varying the compulsory treatment order in respect of which the reference is made by modifying—

     (i) the measures; or

     (ii) any recorded matter,

     specified in it; or

   (b) revoking the compulsory treatment order.

(2) Before making an order under subsection (1) above, the Tribunal shall allow the persons mentioned in subsection (3) below the opportunity—

   (a) of making representations (whether orally or in writing); and

   (b) of leading, or producing, evidence.

(3) Those persons are—

   (a) the persons mentioned in section 102(3)(a) to (h) of this Act; and

   (b) any other person appearing to the Tribunal to have an interest in the reference.

105 Interim extension etc. of order: application under section 92

(1) This section applies where an application is made under section 92 of this Act.

(2) Subject to section 107 of this Act, on the application of any person having an interest in the proceedings, or *ex proprio motu*, the Tribunal may, if it considers—

   (a) that it will be unable to determine the application before the compulsory treatment order to which the application relates ceases to authorise the measures specified in it; and

   (b) that it is appropriate, pending its determining the application, to—

      (i) extend the order; or

      (ii) extend and vary the order by modifying the measures, or any recorded matter, specified in it,

make an interim order extending, or extending and varying, the compulsory treatment order for such period not exceeding 28 days as may be specified in the order of the Tribunal.

106 Interim variation of order: application, reference or review under Chapter

(1) This section applies where—

   (a) an application is made under section 92, 95, 99 or 100 of this Act;

   (b) a reference is made under section 96 or 98 of this Act; or

   (c) the Tribunal is reviewing a determination under section 101 of this Act.

(2) Subject to section 107 of this Act, on the application of any person having an interest in the proceedings, or *ex proprio motu*, the Tribunal may, if it considers that it is appropriate to do so pending its—

   (a) determining the application or reference; or

   (b) making its decision on the review;

make an interim order varying the compulsory treatment order by modifying the measures, or any recorded matter, specified in it, for such period not exceeding 28 days as may be specified in the order of the Tribunal.

107 Limit on Tribunal's power to make interim orders

The Tribunal may not make an interim order under section 105 or 106 of this Act if the effect of making the order would be that interim orders under either, or both, of those sections would be in force for a continuous period of more than 56 days.

108 Tribunal's order varying compulsory treatment order

Where the Tribunal makes—

(a) an order under section 102, 103, 104 or 106 of this Act varying a compulsory treatment order; or

(b) an order under section 103 or 105 of this Act extending and varying such an order,

the Tribunal shall specify in its order the modifications made by its order to the measures, and any recorded matter, specified in the compulsory treatment order.

109 Ancillary powers of Tribunal

(1) This section applies where—

(a) an application is made to the Tribunal under section 92, 95, 99 or 100 of this Act;

(b) the Tribunal is, under section 101 of this Act, reviewing a determination; or

(c) a reference is made to the Tribunal under section 96 or 98 of this Act.

(2) Regulations may prescribe circumstances in which the Tribunal may require—

(a) the patient's responsible medical officer; or

(b) the mental health officer,

to prepare and submit to the Tribunal reports on such matters as may be prescribed.

Effect of interim orders on calculation of time periods in Chapter

110 Effect of interim orders on calculation of time periods in Chapter

(1) Subject to subsection (2) below, in calculating, for the purpose of this Chapter, the day on which a compulsory treatment order—

(a) ceases;

(b) will cease; or

(c) would have ceased,

to authorise the measures specified in it, there shall be left out of account any period for which the order is extended (or extended and varied) by an interim order under section 105 of this Act.

(2) Subsection (1) above does not apply as respects calculating that day for the purpose of that section.

Meaning of "modify"

111 Meaning of "modify"

In this Chapter, any reference to modifying measures, or recorded matters, specified in a compulsory treatment order, includes a reference to—

(a) amending those measures or recorded matters;

(b) removing from the order any measure or recorded matter;

(c) adding to the order any measure or recorded matter;

(d) specifying a recorded matter in an order which does not specify a recorded matter.

CHAPTER 5

BREACH OF ORDERS

Failure to attend for medical treatment

112 Failure to attend for medical treatment

(1) Subject to subsection (2) below, where—

(a) a patient is subject to—

(i) a compulsory treatment order; or

(ii) an interim compulsory treatment order,

that imposes on the patient a requirement mentioned in section 66(1)(c) of this Act ("the attendance requirement"); and

(b) the patient fails to comply with the attendance requirement,

the patient's responsible medical officer may exercise the power conferred by subsection (3) below.

(2) The responsible medical officer may exercise the power conferred by subsection (3) below only if—

(a) the responsible medical officer has consulted a mental health officer; and

(b) the mental health officer consents to the power being exercised.

(3) The responsible medical officer may take, or may cause a person authorised for the purpose by the responsible medical officer to take, the patient into custody and convey the patient—

    (a) to the place the patient is required to attend by the attendance requirement; or

    (b) to any hospital.

(4) Subject to subsection (5) below, where by virtue of subsection (3) above the patient is conveyed to the place the patient is required to attend or a hospital—

    (a) if the order to which the patient is subject authorises the measure mentioned in section 66(1)(b) of this Act, the patient may be detained there for so long as is necessary for the purpose of giving to the patient any medical treatment that could have been given to the patient had the patient complied with the attendance requirement;

    (b) if the order to which the patient is subject does not authorise that measure, the patient may be detained there for so long as is necessary to determine whether the patient is capable of consenting to medical treatment and, if so, whether the patient consents to receive any medical treatment.

(5) The patient may not be detained by virtue of subsection (4) above for more than a period of 6 hours beginning with the arrival of the patient in the place or hospital.

Non-compliance generally with order

113 Non-compliance generally with order

(1) Where—

    (a) a patient is subject to—

        (i) a compulsory treatment order; or

        (ii) an interim compulsory treatment order,

    that does not authorise the detention of the patient in hospital;

    (b) the patient fails to comply with any measure authorised by the order; and

    (c) subsection (2) or (3) below applies,

the power conferred by subsection (4) below may be exercised.

(2) This subsection applies if the patient's responsible medical officer considers that—

(a) reasonable steps have been taken to contact the patient following the patient's failure to comply with the measure;

(b) if contact has been made with the patient, the patient has been afforded a reasonable opportunity to comply with the measure; and

(c) if the patient were to continue to fail to comply with the measure, it is reasonably likely that there would be a significant deterioration in the patient's mental health.

(3) This subsection applies if the patient's responsible medical officer considers that—

(a) if the patient were to continue to fail to comply with the measure, it is reasonably likely that there would be a significant deterioration in the patient's mental health; and

(b) it is necessary as a matter of urgency that the power conferred by subsection (4) below be exercised.

(4) The patient's responsible medical officer may take, or may cause a person authorised for the purpose by the responsible medical officer to take, the patient into custody and convey the patient to a hospital.

(5) Where the power conferred by subsection (4) above is exercised in relation to a patient, the patient may be detained in hospital for the period of 72 hours beginning with the arrival by virtue of that subsection of the patient in hospital.

(6) As soon as reasonably practicable after the patient has been conveyed to a hospital, the responsible medical officer shall—

(a) carry out a medical examination of the patient; or

(b) make arrangements for an approved medical practitioner to carry out such an examination.

114 Compulsory treatment order: detention pending review or application for variation

(1) Subsection (2) below applies where—

(a) a patient who is subject to an order such as is mentioned in subsection (1)(a)(i) of section 113 of this Act is detained in hospital by virtue of subsection (5) of that section;

(b) the patient has been examined under subsection (6) of that section;

(c) the patient's responsible medical officer—

(i) is considering under subsection (2) of section 93 of this Act whether that order should be varied by modifying the measures specified in it; or

(ii) by virtue of subsection (5) of that section, is required to make an application to the Tribunal; and

(d) the patient's responsible medical officer considers that if the patient does not continue to be detained in hospital it is reasonably likely that there will be a significant deterioration in the patient's mental health.

(2) Subject to subsections (3) and (4) below, the responsible medical officer may grant a certificate authorising the continued detention in hospital of the patient for the period of 28 days beginning with the granting of the certificate.

(3) The power in subsection (2) above may be exercised only if—

(a) the responsible medical officer has consulted the mental health officer; and

(b) the mental health officer consents to the power being exercised.

(4) Before granting a certificate under subsection (2) above the responsible medical officer shall, if it is practicable to do so, consult the patient's named person.

(5) A certificate under subsection (2) above—

(a) shall state the responsible medical officer's reasons for believing that paragraph (d) of subsection (1) applies in the patient's case; and

(b) shall be signed by the responsible medical officer.

115 Interim compulsory treatment order: detention pending further procedure

(1) Subsection (2) below applies where—

(a) a patient who is subject to an order such as is mentioned in subsection (1)(a)(ii) of section 113 of this Act is detained in hospital by virtue of subsection (5) of that section;

(b) the patient has been examined under subsection (6) of that section;

(c) the patient's responsible medical officer considers that if the patient does not continue to be detained in hospital it is reasonably likely that there will be a significant deterioration in the patient's mental health; and

(d) on the expiry of the period of detention authorised by subsection (5) of that section the period for which the order authorises the measures specified in it will not have expired.

(2) Subject to subsections (3) and (4) below, the responsible medical officer may grant a certificate authorising the continued detention in hospital of the patient for the period beginning with the granting of the certificate and ending with the expiry of the period for which the order authorises the measures specified in it.

(3) The power in subsection (2) above may be exercised only if—

(a) the patient's responsible medical officer has consulted a mental health officer; and

(b) the mental health officer consents to the power being exercised.

(4) Before granting a certificate the responsible medical officer shall, if it is practicable to do so, consult the patient's named person.

(5) A certificate under subsection (2) above—

(a) shall state the responsible medical officer's reasons for believing that subsection (1)(c) above applies in the patient's case; and

(b) shall be signed by the responsible medical officer.

116 Certificate under section 114(2) or 115(2): notification

(1) This section applies where a certificate is granted under section 114(2) or 115(2) of this Act in respect of a patient.

(2) The managers of the hospital in which the patient is detained shall, as soon as practicable after the granting of the certificate, give notice of its granting to—

(a) the patient;

(b) the patient's named person;

(c) any guardian of the patient; and

(d) any welfare attorney of the patient.

(3) The managers of the hospital in which the patient is detained shall, before the expiry of the period of 7 days beginning with the granting of the certificate, give notice of its granting, and send a copy of it, to—

(a) the Tribunal; and

(b) the Commission.

Revocation of certificates

117 Certificate under section 114(2): responsible medical officer's duty to revoke

(1) Where—

    (a) a patient's responsible medical officer grants, by virtue of subsection (1)(c)(i) of section 114 of this Act, a certificate under subsection (2) of that section; and

    (b) the responsible medical officer determines that the order should not be varied as mentioned in section 93(2) of this Act, the responsible medical officer shall revoke the certificate.

(2) Where—

    (a) a patient's responsible medical officer grants, by virtue of subsection (1)(c)(ii) of section 114 of this Act, a certificate under subsection (2) of that section; and

    (b) the responsible medical officer is not satisfied that if the patient does not continue to be detained in hospital it is reasonably likely that there will be a significant deterioration in the patient's mental health,

the responsible medical officer shall revoke the certificate.

118 Certificate under section 115(2): responsible medical officer's duty to revoke

Where—

    (a) a patient's responsible medical officer grants a certificate under section 115(2) of this Act; and

    (b) the responsible medical officer is not satisfied that if the patient does not continue to be detained in hospital it is reasonably likely that there will be a significant deterioration in the patient's mental health,

the responsible medical officer shall revoke the certificate.

119 Revocation of certificate granted under section 114(2) or 115(2): notification

Where a patient's responsible medical officer revokes, under section 117 or 118 of this Act, a certificate, the responsible medical officer shall—

(a) as soon as practicable after the revocation, give notice of the revocation to the persons mentioned in subsection (2) of section 116 of this Act; and

(b) before the expiry of the period of 7 days beginning with the revocation, give notice of the revocation to the persons mentioned in subsection (3) of that section.

120 Certificates under sections 114(2) and 115(2): patient's right to apply to Tribunal

(1) This section applies where a certificate is granted under section 114(2) or 115(2) of this Act in respect of a patient.

(2) On the application of the patient or the patient's named person, the Tribunal shall, if not satisfied that if the patient does not continue to be detained in hospital it is reasonably likely that there will be a significant deterioration in the patient's mental health, revoke the certificate.

Effect of section 113(5) on order

121 Effect of section 113(5) on order

(1) Subject to subsection (2) below, where a patient is detained in hospital under section 113(5) of this Act, the compulsory treatment order or, as the case may be, interim compulsory treatment order to which the patient is subject shall cease, during the period mentioned in that section, to authorise the measures specified in it.

(2) If the measure mentioned in section 66(1)(b) of this Act is specified in the order, the order shall continue to authorise that measure during the period referred to in subsection (1) above.

Effect of certificate under section 114(2) on order

122 Effect of certificate under section 114(2) on order

(1) Subject to subsection (2) below, where a certificate is granted under section 114(2) of this Act in respect of a patient, the compulsory treatment order to which the patient is subject shall cease, during the period mentioned in that section, to authorise the measures specified in it.

(2) If the measure mentioned in section 66(1)(b) of this Act is specified in the order, the order shall continue to authorise that measure during the period referred to in subsection (1) above.

Effect of certificate under section 115(2) on order

123 Effect of certificate under section 115(2) on order

(1) Subject to subsection (2) below, where a certificate is granted under section 115(2) of this Act in respect of a patient, the interim compulsory treatment order to which the patient is subject shall cease, during the period mentioned in that section, to authorise the measures specified in it.

(2) If the measure mentioned in section 66(1)(b) of this Act is specified in the order, the order shall continue to authorise that measure during the period referred to in subsection (1) above.

. . .

PART 17

PATIENT REPRESENTATION ETC.

CHAPTER I

NAMED PERSON

Meaning of "named person"

250 Nomination of named person

(1) Where a person who has attained the age of 16 years (a "nominator") nominates in accordance with subsection (2) below another person who has attained that age to be the nominator's named person, that person is, subject to subsections (3) and (6) below, the nominator's named person.

(2) A person is nominated in accordance with this subsection if—

(a) the nomination is signed by the nominator;

(b) the nominator's signature is witnessed by a prescribed person;

(c) the prescribed person certifies that, in the opinion of the prescribed person, the nominator—

  (i) understands the effect of nominating a person to be the nominator's named person; and

  (ii) has not been subjected to any undue influence in making the nomination.

(3) A nomination under subsection (1) above may be revoked by the nominator in accordance with subsection (4) below.

(4) The nomination of a named person is revoked in accordance with this subsection if—

(a) the revocation is signed by the nominator;

(b) the nominator's signature is witnessed by a prescribed person;

(c) the prescribed person certifies that, in the opinion of the prescribed person, the nominator—

  (i) understands the effect of revoking the appointment of a person as named person; and

  (ii) has not been subjected to any undue influence in making the revocation.

(5) The nomination of a named person shall be effective notwithstanding the nominator's becoming, after making the nomination, incapable.

(6) A person nominated under subsection (1) above may decline to be the nominator's named person by giving notice to—

(a) the nominator; and

(b) the local authority for the area in which the nominator resides,

to that effect.

(7) In this section—

"incapable" means incapable by reason of mental disorder or of inability to communicate because of physical disability; but a person shall not fall within this definition by reason only of a lack or deficiency in a faculty of communication if that lack or deficiency can be made good by human or mechanical aid (whether of an interpretative nature or otherwise); and

"prescribed person" means a person of a class prescribed by regulations.

251 Named person where no person nominated or nominated person declines to act

(1) Subject to subsections (2) to (5) below, where, in the case of a person who has attained the age of 16 years, there is no person who is by virtue of section 250 of this Act the person's named person, the person's primary carer shall, unless the person's primary carer has not attained the age of 16 years, be the person's named person.

(2) Where a person's primary carer has not attained the age of 16 years, but the person has a carer who has attained that age, that carer shall be the person's named person.

(3) Where—
   (a) a person does not have a primary carer; or
   (b) a person's primary carer has not attained the age of 16 years,

   but the person has two or more carers who have attained the age of 16 years, those carers may agree which of them is to be the named person of the person.

(4) Where, by virtue of subsection (2) or (3) above, a carer is a person's named person, the references in subsections (5) and (6) below to a person's primary carer shall be construed as references to that carer.

(5) If—
   (a) the person has no primary carer; or
   (b) the person's primary carer declines in accordance with subsection (6) below to be the person's named person,

   the person's nearest relative shall be the person's named person.

(6) A person's primary carer declines in accordance with this subsection to be the person's named person by giving notice to—
   (a) the person; and
   (b) the local authority for the area in which the person resides,

   to that effect.

252 Named person in relation to child

(1) The named person of a person who has not attained the age of 16 years ("the child") shall be—

   (a)[21] subject to subsection (2) below, in a case where a relevant person has parental rights and parental responsibilities in relation to the child, that person;

   (b) in a case where the child is in the care of a local authority by virtue of a care order made under section 31 of the Children Act 1989 (c.41), that authority; or

   (c) in any other case, where the child's primary carer has attained the age of 16 years, that person.

(2)[22] Subject to subsection (3) below, where two or more relevant persons have parental rights and parental responsibilities in relation to the child, the named person of the child shall be—

   (a) if those persons agree that one of them is to be the named person of the child, that person; or

   (b) if those persons do not so agree, the one of them—

      (i) who provides, on a regular basis, all, or most, of the care for, and support to, the child;

      (ii) in a case where the child is in hospital, who provided all, or most, of that care for, and support to, the child before the child was admitted to hospital.

(3)[23] If—

   (a) one of the persons who has parental rights and parental responsibilities in relation to the child is a local authority; and

   (b) the local authority has those rights and responsibilities by virtue of an order under section 86(1) of the Children (Scotland) Act 1995 (c.36) (orders transferring parental rights and parental responsibilities),

the relevant local authority shall be the child's named person.

(4)[24] In this section—

"parental responsibilities", in relation to a child, has the meaning given by section 1(3) of the Children (Scotland) Act 1995 (c.36); and

"parental rights", in relation to a child, has the meaning given by section 2(4) of that Act;

---

[21] As amended by Mental Health (Care and Treatment) (Scotland) Act 2003 (Modification of Enactments) Order 2005 (SSI 2005/465), Sch 1, para 32(20)(a).
[22] As amended by *ibid*, Sch 1, para 32(20)(b).
[23] As amended by *ibid*, Sch 1, para 32(20)(c).
[24] As amended by *ibid*, Sch 1, para 32(20)(d)(ii).

"relevant person" means—

(a) a local authority; or

(b) a person who has attained the age of 16 years.

253 Declaration in relation to named person

(1) Subject to subsection (4) below and to section 257 of this Act, where a person who has attained the age of 16 years ("the declarer") makes a declaration in writing in accordance with subsection (2) below stating that a person specified in the declaration shall not be the declarer's named person, that person shall not be the declarer's named person.

(2) A declaration is made in accordance with this subsection if—

(a) signed by the declarer; and

(b) witnessed by a prescribed person who certifies that, in the opinion of the prescribed person, the declarer—

(i) understands the effect of making the declaration; and

(ii) has not been subjected to any undue influence in making the declaration.

(3) A declaration under this section shall be effective notwithstanding the individual's becoming, after making the declaration, incapable.

(4) A declaration under subsection (1) above may be revoked by the declarer in accordance with subsection (5) below.

(5) A declaration is revoked in accordance with this subsection if the revocation is—

(a) signed by the declarer; and

(b) witnessed by a prescribed person who shall certify that, in the opinion of the prescribed person, the declarer—

(i) understands the effect of revoking the declaration; and

(ii) has not been subjected to any undue influence in making the revocation.

(6) In this section, "incapable" and "prescribed person" have the same meaning as in section 250 of this Act.

254 Meaning of "nearest relative"

(1) In this Act, "nearest relative", in relation to a person (the "relevant person"), means—

(a) subject to subsection (3) below, in a case where only one person falls within the list set out in subsection (2) below, that person;

(b) subject to subsections (3) and (4) below, in a case where two or more persons fall within that list, the person falling within the paragraph first appearing in the list set out in subsection (2) below.

(2) The list mentioned in subsection (1) above is—

(a)[25] the relevant person's spouse or civil partner;

(b) a person such as is mentioned in subsection (7) below;

(c) the relevant person's child;

(d) the relevant person's parent;

(e) the relevant person's brother or sister;

(f) the relevant person's grandparent;

(g) the relevant person's grandchild;

(h) the relevant person's uncle or aunt;

(i) the relevant person's niece or nephew;

(j) the person mentioned in subsection (8) below.

(3)[26] If the relevant person's spouse or civil partner—

(a) is permanently separated (either by agreement or under an order of a court) from the relevant person; or

(b) has deserted, or has been deserted by, the relevant person and the desertion continues,

subsection (2)(a) above shall be disregarded for the purposes of subsection (1) above.

(4) Where two or more persons fall within the paragraph first appearing on the list set out in subsection (2) above, the nearest relative shall be—

(a) if those persons agree that one of them should be the nearest relative, that person; or

(b) if those persons do not so agree, the person determined in accordance with the following rules—

(i) brothers and sisters of the whole blood shall be preferred over brothers and sisters of the half-blood; and

(ii) the elder or eldest, as the case may be, shall be preferred.

(5) A relevant person's nearest relative may decline to be the named person of the relevant person by giving notice to—

(a) the relevant person; and

(b) the local authority for the area in which the relevant person resides,

to that effect.

---

[25] As amended by Civil Partnership Act 2004, Sch 28(4), para 69(2).

[26] As amended by *ibid*, Sch 28(4), para 69(3).

(6) For the purposes of subsection (2) above—

(a) a relationship of the half-blood shall, subject to subsection (4)(b)(i) above, be treated as a relationship of the whole blood;

(b) the stepchild of a person shall be treated as the child of that person;

(c) if the relevant person is ordinarily resident in the United Kingdom, the Channel Islands or the Isle of Man, any person who is not so resident shall be disregarded; and

(d) any person who is under 16 years of age shall be disregarded.

(7) The person referred to in subsection (2)(b) above is a person who—

(a) is living with the relevant person—

(i) as husband and wife; or

(ii)[27] in a relationship which has the characteristics of the relationship between civil partners; and

(b)[28] has been living with the relevant person for a period of at least 6 months or, if the relevant person is for the time being in hospital, or in a care home service, had been living with the relevant person for such period when the relevant person was admitted to hospital or to a care home service.

(8) The person referred to in subsection (2)(j) above is a person who—

(a) is living with the relevant person and has been living with the relevant person for a period of at least 5 years; or

(b)[29] if the relevant person is in hospital or in a care home service, had been living with the relevant person for such period when the relevant person was admitted to hospital or to a care home service.

Mental health officer's duties etc.

255 Named person: mental health officer's duties etc.

(1) Subsection (2) below applies where—

---

[27] As amended by Civil Partnership Act 2004, Sch 28(4), para 69(4).

[28] As amended by Mental Health (Care and Treatment) (Scotland) Act 2003 (Modification of Enactments) Order 2005 (SSI 2005/465), Sch 1, para 32(21)(a)(i) and (ii).

[29] As amended by *ibid*, Sch 1, para 32(21)(b)(i) and (ii).

(a) a mental health officer is discharging any function by virtue of this Act or the 1995 Act in relation to a patient; and

(b) it is necessary for the purposes of the discharge of the function to establish whether the patient has a named person.

(2) The mental health officer shall take such steps as are reasonably practicable—

(a) to establish whether the patient has a named person; and

(b) if so, to ascertain who that person is.

(3) Subsection (4) below applies where the mental health officer—

(a) establishes that the patient does not have a named person; or

(b) is unable to establish whether the patient has a named person.

(4) The mental health officer—

(a) shall make a record of the steps taken under subsection (2)(a) above; and

(b) may apply to the Tribunal for an order under section 257 of this Act.

(5) Where the mental health officer makes a record under subsection (4)(a) above, the mental health officer shall, as soon as practicable, give a copy of the record to—

(a) the Tribunal; and

(b) the Commission.

(6) Where by virtue of subsection (2) above—

(a) the mental health officer—

  (i) establishes that the patient has a named person; and

  (ii) ascertains the name of that person ("the apparent named person"); but

(b) the mental health officer considers that it is inappropriate for the apparent named person to be the patient's named person,

the mental health officer shall apply to the Tribunal for an order under section 257 of this Act.

(7) Where—

(a) a mental health officer is discharging any function by virtue of this Act in relation to a patient; and

(b) it appears to the mental health officer—

(i) that the patient does not have a named person; or

(ii) that the patient has a named person ("the apparent named person") but the mental health officer considers that it is inappropriate for the apparent named person to be the patient's named person,

the mental health officer may apply to the Tribunal for an order under section 257 of this Act.

Applications to Tribunal by patient etc.

256 Named person: application by patient etc.

(1) Where—

(a) it appears to a person mentioned in subsection (2) below (any such person being referred to in this section as "the applicant") that a patient does not have a named person;

(b) the applicant considers that though the patient has a named person it is inappropriate that that person be the patient's named person; or

(c) circumstances of such description as may be prescribed by regulations exist,

the applicant may apply to the Tribunal for an order under section 257 of this Act in relation to the patient.

(2) Those persons are—

(a) the patient;

(b) the patient's responsible medical officer;

(c) if the patient is a child, any person who has parental responsibilities in relation to the patient;

(d) if the patient is in hospital, the managers of the hospital;

(e) any welfare attorney of the patient;

(f) any guardian of the patient;

(g) any relative of the patient; and

(h) any other person having an interest in the welfare of the patient.

(3) In subsection (2)(c) above, "child" and "parental responsibilities" have the same meanings as they have in Part I of the Children (Scotland) Act 1995 (c.36).

Tribunal's powers

257 Named person: Tribunal's powers

(1) Where—

  (a) an application is made under section 255(4)(b) or (7)(b)(i) or 256(1)(a) of this Act; and

  (b) the Tribunal is satisfied that the patient does not have a named person,

  the Tribunal may, subject to subsection (4) below, make an order appointing the person specified in the order to be the patient's named person.

(2) Where—

  (a) an application is made under section 255(6) or (7)(b)(ii) or 256(1)(b) of this Act; and

  (b) the Tribunal is satisfied that it is inappropriate for the named person ("the acting named person") to be the patient's named person,

  the Tribunal may, subject to subsection (4) below, make an order declaring that the acting named person is not the named person or appointing the person specified in the order to be the patient's named person in place of the acting named person.

(3) Where an application is made under section 256(1)(c) of this Act, the Tribunal may, subject to subsection (4) below, make such order as it thinks fit.

(4) It shall not be competent for the Tribunal to make an order under this section appointing a person who has not attained the age of 16 years to be a patient's named person.

Interpretation of Chapter

258 Interpretation of Chapter

In this Chapter, other than section 252, "person" means a natural person.

CHAPTER 2

ADVOCACY ETC.

Advocacy

259 Advocacy

(1) Every person with a mental disorder shall have a right of access to independent advocacy; and accordingly it is the duty of—

    (a) each local authority, in collaboration with the (or each) relevant Health Board; and

    (b) each Health Board, in collaboration with the (or each) relevant local authority,

to secure the availability, to persons in its area who have a mental disorder, of independent advocacy services and to take appropriate steps to ensure that those persons have the opportunity of making use of those services.

(2) Each relevant Health Board and local authority shall, for the purposes of subsection (1) above, collaborate with the local authority or, as the case may be, Health Board in relation to which it is the relevant Board or authority.

(3) For the purposes of subsections (1) and (2) above—

    (a) a Health Board is, in relation to a local authority, a "relevant" Health Board if its area or part of its area is the same as or is included in the area of the local authority; and

    (b) a local authority is, in relation to a Health Board, a "relevant" local authority if its area or part of its area is the same as or is included in the area of the Health Board.

(4) In subsection (1) above, "advocacy services" are services of support and representation made available for the purpose of enabling the person to whom they are available to have as much control of, or capacity to influence, that person's care and welfare as is, in the circumstances, appropriate.

(5) For the purposes of subsection (1) above, advocacy services are "independent" if they are to be provided by a person who is none of the following—

    (a) a local authority;

    (b) a Health Board;

    (c) a National Health Service trust;

(d) a member of—

    (i) the local authority;

    (ii) the Health Board;

    (iii) a National Health Service trust,

in the area of which the person to whom those services are made available is to be provided with them;

(e) a person who—

    (i) in pursuance of arrangements made between that person and a Health Board, is giving medical treatment to;

    (ii) in pursuance of those arrangements, is providing, under the National Health Service (Scotland) Act 1978 (c.29), treatment, care or services for; or

    (iii) in pursuance of arrangements made between that person and a local authority, is providing, under Part II of the Social Work (Scotland) Act 1968 (c.49) (promotion of social welfare) or any of the enactments specified in section 5(1B) of that Act, services for,

the person to whom the advocacy services are made available;

(f) in relation to a patient detained in a state hospital or a person who (by virtue of any of the means specified in subsection (11)(b) below) is no longer detained there, the State Hospitals Board for Scotland or a member of that Board.

(6) In subsection (5)(d) above the reference to the area of a National Health Service trust is a reference to the Health Board area in which the trust discharges its functions.

(7) It is the duty of the State Hospitals Board for Scotland (the "State Hospitals Board") to secure the availability to persons who are patients detained in a state hospital of the services referred to in subsection (1) above and, in relation to those persons, to take the steps there referred to.

(8) It is the duty of—

(a) the State Hospitals Board, in collaboration with each relevant local authority and Health Board; and

(b) each relevant local authority and Health Board, in collaboration with the State Hospitals Board,

to secure the availability to relevant persons of the services referred to in subsection (1) above, and, in relation to those persons, to take the steps there referred to.

(9) Each relevant local authority and Health Board shall, for the purposes of subsection (8)(a) above, collaborate with the State Hospitals Board and with each other.

(10) The State Hospitals Board shall, for the purposes of subsection (8)(b) above, collaborate with each relevant local authority and Health Board.

(11) For the purposes of subsections (8) to (10) above—

(a) a local authority or Health Board is a relevant local authority or, as the case may be, Health Board if there is residing in its area a relevant person;

(b) a relevant person is a person with a mental disorder who, having been detained as a patient in a state hospital, is (by virtue of section 127 or 193(7) of this Act) no longer detained there.

Information

260 Provision of information to patient

(1) This section applies where a patient—

(a) is detained in hospital by virtue of—
(i) this Act; or
(ii) the 1995 Act; or

(b) though not detained in hospital, is subject to—
(i) an emergency detention certificate;
(ii) a short-term detention certificate;
(iii) a compulsory treatment order;
(iv) an interim compulsory treatment order;
(v) an assessment order;
(vi) a treatment order;
(vii) a hospital direction;
(viii) a transfer for treatment direction;
(ix) an interim compulsion order; or
(x) a compulsion order.

(2) The appropriate person shall—

(a) take all reasonable steps—
(i) to ensure that the patient understands the relevant matters at each of the times mentioned in subsection (3) below;
(ii) to ensure that the patient is supplied with material appropriate to the patient's needs (and in a form that is appropriate to those needs and permanent) from which

the patient may refresh the patient's understanding of those matters; and

   (iii) to inform the patient of the availability under section 259 of this Act of independent advocacy services at each of those times; and

(b) take appropriate steps to ensure that the patient has the opportunity of making use of those services.

(3) Those times are—

(a) as soon as practicable after—

   (i) where the patient is detained in hospital, the beginning of such detention; or

   (ii) where the patient is not so detained, the making of the order;

(b) as soon as practicable after any occasion on which the patient reasonably requests to be informed of those matters; and

(c) such other times as may be prescribed by regulations.

(4) Where material is supplied to the patient under subsection (2)(a)(ii) above, the appropriate person shall, as soon as practicable after such material is supplied, take all reasonable steps to ensure that the patient's named person is supplied with a copy of such material in a form that is appropriate to the person's needs.

(5) In this section—

"the appropriate person" means—

(a) where the patient is detained in hospital, the managers of the hospital;

(b) where by virtue of a certificate granted under any provision of this Act, the authorisation to detain the patient in a hospital is suspended, the managers of the hospital in which, but for the certificate, the patient would be authorised to be detained;

(c) in any other case, the managers of the hospital specified in the order; and

"the relevant matters" means—

(a) the provision of this Act or the 1995 Act by virtue of which—

   (i) the patient is being detained; or

   (ii) the order has effect;

(b) the consequences of the operation of that provision;

(c) the powers that the patient's responsible medical officer and the Tribunal each has in relation to revoking that provision;

(d) any right to make an application, or appeal, to the Tribunal that the patient has by virtue of that provision;

(e) the powers exercisable by the Tribunal in the event of any such right being exercised;

(f) how the patient may exercise any such right;

(g) the functions that the Commission has that appear to be relevant to the patient's case;

(h) how the patient may obtain legal assistance as respects any such right.

261 Provision of assistance to patient with communication difficulties

(1) This section applies where—

(a) a patient is detained in hospital by virtue of—

(i) this Act; or

(ii) the 1995 Act; or

(b) though not detained in hospital, a patient is subject to—

(i) an emergency detention certificate;

(ii) a short-term detention certificate;

(iii) a compulsory treatment order;

(iv) an interim compulsory treatment order;

(v) an assessment order;

(vi) a treatment order;

(vii) a hospital direction;

(viii) a transfer for treatment direction;

(ix) an interim compulsion order; or

(x) a compulsion order,

and the patient has difficulty in communicating or generally communicates in a language other than English.

(2) The appropriate person shall take all reasonable steps to secure that, for the purpose of enabling the patient to communicate during each of the events mentioned in subsection (3) below—

(a) arrangements appropriate to the patient's needs are made; or

(b) the patient is provided with assistance, or material, appropriate to the patient's needs.

(3) Those events are—

    (a) any medical examination of the patient carried out for the purpose of assessing the patient's mental disorder;

    (b) any review under this Act or the 1995 Act of the patient's detention; or

    (c) any proceedings before the Tribunal relating to the patient.

(4) As soon as practicable after taking any steps under subsection (2) above, the appropriate person shall make a written record of the steps.

(5) In this section "the appropriate person" has the meaning given by section 260(5) of this Act.

Access to medical practitioner

262 Access to medical practitioner for purposes of medical examination

(1) This section applies where a patient is detained in hospital by virtue of—

    (a) this Act; or

    (b) the 1995 Act.

(2) A duly authorised medical practitioner may, for any of the purposes mentioned in subsection (3) below, visit the patient at any reasonable hour and carry out a medical examination of the patient in private.

(3) Those purposes are—

    (a) advising the patient or, as the case may be, the patient's named person about the making of applications to the Tribunal in respect of the patient under this Act; and

    (b) providing to the patient or, as the case may be, the patient's named person information as respects the condition of the patient for the purpose of—

        (i) any such application (or proposed application); or

        (ii) any other proceedings before the Tribunal in respect of the patient in which the patient or, as the case may be, the patient's named person is taking part (or considering whether to take part).

(4) For the purposes of subsection (2) above and subject to subsection (5) below, a medical practitioner is duly authorised if authorised for the purposes of this section by—

    (a) the patient; or

    (b) the patient's named person.

(5) Authorisation given for the purposes of this section by the patient's named person may be rescinded by the patient at any time when the patient is not incapable.

(6) In subsection (5) above, "incapable" has the same meaning as in section 250(7) of this Act.

263 Inspection of records by medical practitioner

(1) A duly authorised medical practitioner may, for any of the purposes mentioned in subsection (3) below, require any person holding records relating to—

   (a) the detention of; or
   (b) medical treatment given at any time to,

   a patient whose detention in hospital is authorised by virtue of this Act or the 1995 Act to produce them for inspection by the medical practitioner.

(2) A duly authorised medical practitioner may, for any of the purposes mentioned in subsection (3) below, require any person holding records relating to medical treatment given at any time to a patient who is subject to—

   (a) a compulsory treatment order; or
   (b) a compulsion order,

   that does not authorise the detention of the patient in hospital to produce them for inspection by the medical practitioner.

(3) Those purposes are—

   (a) advising the patient or, as the case may be, the patient's named person about the making of applications to the Tribunal in respect of the patient under this Act;
   (b) providing to the patient or, as the case may be, the patient's named person information as respects the condition of the patient for the purpose of—
      (i) any such application (or proposed application); or
      (ii) any other proceedings before the Tribunal in respect of the patient in which the patient or, as the case may be, the patient's named person is taking part (or considering whether to take part).

(4) For the purposes of subsections (1) and (2) above and subject to subsection (5) below, a medical practitioner is duly authorised if authorised for the purposes of this section by—

   (a) the patient; or
   (b) the patient's named person.

(5) Authorisation given for the purposes of this section by the patient's named person may be rescinded by the patient at any time when the patient is not incapable.

(6) In subsection (5) above, "incapable" has the same meaning as in section 250(7) of this Act.

. . .

PART 18

MISCELLANEOUS

Code of practice

274 Code of practice

(1)[30] The Scottish Ministers shall, in accordance with this section, draw up, give effect to and publish a code of practice giving guidance to any person discharging functions by virtue of this Act or Part VI (mental disorder) of the 1985 Act as to—

(a) the discharge of such of those functions; and

(b) such matters arising in connection with the discharge of those functions,

as they think fit.

(2) The Scottish Ministers shall, before giving effect to a code of practice drawn up under subsection (1) above—

(a) consult such persons as they think fit; and

(b) lay a draft of the code before the Scottish Parliament.

(3) A code of practice drawn up under subsection (1) above shall be given effect by being—

(a) confirmed by order made; and

(b) brought into force on a day appointed,

by the Scottish Ministers.

(4)[31] Any person discharging functions by virtue of this Act or Part VI (mental disorder) of the 1985 Act shall have regard (so far as they are applicable to the discharge of those functions by

---

[30] As amended by Mental Health (Care and Treatment) (Scotland) Act 2003 Modification Order 2004 (SSI 2004/533), art 2(8)(a).

[31] As amended by *ibid*, art 2(8)(b).

that person) to the provisions of any code of practice published under subsection (1) above for the time being in force.

(5)[32] The references in subsections (1) and (4) above to a person discharging functions by virtue of this Act or Part VI (mental disorder) of the 1995 Act do not include references to—

(a) any court;

(aa)[33] a prosecutor;

(b) the Tribunal; and

(c) the Commission.

(6) The Scottish Ministers may, from time to time, revise the whole or part of any code of practice published under subsection (1) above; and if a code is so revised, the Scottish Ministers shall publish the revised code.

(7) Subsections (2) to (6) above apply to a code of practice revised under subsection (6) above as they apply to a code of practice published under subsection (1) above.

Advance statements

275 Advance statements: making and withdrawal

(1) An "advance statement" is a statement complying with subsection (2) below and specifying—

(a) the ways the person making it wishes to be treated for mental disorder;

(b) the ways the person wishes not to be so treated,

in the event of the person's becoming mentally disordered and the person's ability to make decisions about the matters referred to in paragraphs (a) and (b) above being, because of that, significantly impaired.

(2) An advance statement complies with this subsection if—

(a) at the time of making it, the person has the capacity of properly intending the wishes specified in it;

(b) it is in writing;

(c) it is subscribed by the person making it;

(d) that person's subscription of it is witnessed by a person (the "witness") who is within the class of persons prescribed

[32] As amended by Mental Health (Care and Treatment) (Scotland) Act 2003 Modification Order 2004 (SSI 2004/533), art 2(8)(c)(i).
[33] Inserted by *ibid*, art 2(8)(c)(ii).

by regulations for the purposes of this paragraph and who signs the statement as a witness to that subscription; and

(e) the witness certifies in writing on the document which comprises the statement that, in the witness's opinion, the person making the statement has the capacity referred to in paragraph (a) above.

(3) An advance statement may be withdrawn by the person who made it by a withdrawal complying with this subsection; and a withdrawal so complies if—

(a) at the time of making it the person has the capacity properly to intend to withdraw the statement; and

(b) it is made by means of a document which, were it an advance statement, would comply with paragraphs (b) to (e) of subsection (2) above.

276 Advance statements: effect

(1) If the Tribunal is satisfied as to the matters set out in subsection (2) below, it shall, in making any decision in respect of a patient who is a person who has made and not withdrawn an advance statement, have regard to the wishes specified in the statement.

(2) Those matters are—

(a) that, because of mental disorder, the ability of the person who made the advance statement to make decisions about the matters referred to in paragraphs (a) and (b) of subsection (1) of section 275 of this Act is significantly impaired;

(b) that the statement complies with subsection (2) of that section;

(c) that any measures or treatment which might or will be authorised by virtue of the decision referred to in subsection (1) above or might or will, by virtue of that decision, no longer be authorised correspond to any wishes specified in the statement; and

(d) that, since the person made the statement, there has been no change of circumstances which, were the person to have been considering making the statement at the time the Tribunal is making the decision referred to in subsection (1) above, would have been likely to cause the person not to make the statement or to make a substantially different one.

(3) A person giving medical treatment authorised by virtue of this Act or the 1995 Act to a patient who is a person—

   (a) who has made and not withdrawn an advance statement; and

   (b) whose ability to make decisions about the matters referred to in paragraphs (a) and (b) of subsection (1) of section 275 of this Act is, because of mental disorder, significantly impaired,

   shall have regard to the wishes specified in the advance statement.

(4) Before making a decision under section 236(2)(c), 239(1)(c) or 241(1)(c) of this Act in relation to a patient who is a person who has made and not withdrawn an advance statement, a designated medical practitioner shall have regard to the wishes specified in the statement.

(5) For the purposes of subsections (1) and (2) above and (in the case where medical treatment is to or might be given to a patient otherwise than by virtue of any such decision as is referred to in subsection (1) above or is to be given to the patient by virtue of such a decision which was made in ignorance of the existence or the withdrawal of an advance statement) of subsections (3) and (4) above—

   (a) an advance statement shall be taken to comply with subsection (2) of section 275 of this Act; and

   (b) a withdrawal of an advance statement shall be taken to comply with subsection (3) of that section,

   unless the contrary appears.

(6) For the purposes of subsections (3) and (4) above in the case where the medical treatment is authorised by virtue of a decision such as is referred to in subsection (1) above—

   (a) an advance statement shall be taken to comply with subsection (2) of section 275 of this Act; and

   (b) a withdrawal of an advance statement shall be taken to comply with subsection (3) of that section,

   if the Tribunal was satisfied when making the decision that the statement or, as the case may be, the withdrawal so complies.

(7) If, in respect of a patient who is a person who has made and not withdrawn an advance statement—

   (a) the Tribunal makes such a decision as is referred to in subsection (1) above authorising measures which conflict with the wishes specified in the statement;

(b) a person having functions under this Act gives medical treatment authorised by virtue of this Act or the 1995 Act to the person and that treatment conflicts with those wishes;

(c) a designated medical practitioner makes such a decision as is referred to in subsection (4) above and it conflicts with those wishes; or

(d) such measures, treatment or decision which could have been so authorised, given or, as the case may be, made are not so authorised or is not so given or made, with the consequence that there is a conflict with those wishes,

then the Tribunal, person having those functions or, as the case may be, designated medical practitioner shall comply with the requirements set out in subsection (8) below.

(8) Those requirements are—

(a) recording in writing the circumstances in which those measures were or treatment or decision was authorised, given or made or, as the case may be, not authorised, given or made, and the reasons why;

(b) supplying—

(i) the person who made the statement;

(ii) that person's named person;

(iii) that person's welfare attorney;

(iv) that person's guardian; and

(v) the Commission,

with a copy of that record; and

(c) placing a copy of that record with that person's medical records.

. . .

PART 22

APPEALS

320 Appeal to sheriff principal against certain decisions of the Tribunal

(1) This section applies to the following decisions of the Tribunal—

(a) a decision under section 50(4) of this Act refusing an application for revocation of a short-term detention certificate;

(b) a decision under section 64(4)(a) or (b) of this Act making or refusing to make a compulsory treatment order;

(c) a decision to make an interim compulsory treatment order under section 65(2) of this Act;

(d) a decision to make an order under section 102(1)(c) or (d) of this Act confirming the determination of a patient's responsible medical officer extending a compulsory treatment order;

(e) a decision to make an order under section 103(1)(a) or (b) of this Act on an application by the patient's responsible medical officer for an order extending and varying a compulsory treatment order;

(f) a decision to make an order under section 103(2)(c) or (d) of this Act on an application for revocation of the determination of a patient's responsible medical officer extending a compulsory treatment order;

(g) a decision to make an order under section 103(3)(b) or (c) of this Act on an application under section 100(2)(a) of this Act to revoke a compulsory treatment order;

(h) a decision to make an order under section 103(4)(a) of this Act on an application by a patient's responsible medical officer to vary a compulsory treatment order;

(i) a decision to make an order under section 103(4)(b) of this Act refusing an application under section 100(2)(b) of this Act to vary a compulsory treatment order;

(j) a decision to make an order under section 104(1)(a) of this Act varying a compulsory treatment order;

(k) a decision not to revoke under section 120(2) of this Act a certificate granted under section 114(2) or 115(2) of this Act;

(l) a decision to make or refuse to make an order under section 125(5) or 126(5) of this Act preventing a transfer or requiring that a transferred patient be returned;

(m) a decision to make an order under section 166(1)(c) or (d) of this Act confirming the determination of a patient's responsible medical officer extending a compulsion order;

(n) a decision to make an order under section 167(1)(a) of this Act on an application by the patient's responsible medical officer for an order extending a compulsion order;

(o) a decision to make an order under section 167(2)(a) or (b) of this Act on an application by the patient's responsible medical officer for an order extending and varying a compulsion order;

(p) a decision to make an order under section 167(3)(c) or (d) of this Act on an application for revocation of the determination of a patient's responsible medical officer extending a compulsion order;

(q) a decision to make an order under section 167(4)(b) or (c) of this Act on an application under section 164(2)(a) of this Act;

(r) a decision to make an order under section 167(5)(a) of this Act on an application by a patient's responsible medical officer to vary a compulsion order;

(s) a decision to make an order under section 167(5)(b) of this Act refusing an application under section 164(2)(b) of this Act to vary a compulsion order;

(t) a decision to make or refuse to make an order under section 257(1) of this Act appointing a person to be a patient's named person;

(u) a decision to make or refuse to make an order under section 257(2) of this Act declaring an acting named person not to be a named person or appointing a person to be a patient's named person in place of an acting named person;

(v) a decision to make an order under section 257(3) of this Act;

(w) a decision, in relation to a patient who is not subject to a restriction order, a hospital direction or a transfer for treatment direction—

 (i) to make or refuse to make an order under section 264(2), 265(3) or 266(3) of this Act;

 (ii) under section 267(2) of this Act to recall or refuse to recall an order made under section 264, 265 or 266 of this Act;

 (iii) to make or refuse to make an order under section 268(2), 269(3) or 270(3) of this Act;

 (iv) under section 271(2) of this Act to recall or refuse to recall an order made under section 268, 269 or 270 of this Act; and

(x) a decision granting or refusing an application for an order requiring the managers of the hospital to cease to detain a patient under section 291 of this Act.

(2) A relevant party to proceedings before the Tribunal may appeal to the sheriff principal against a decision to which this section applies.

(3) An appeal to the sheriff principal under subsection (2) above shall be to the sheriff principal—

   (a) of the sheriffdom in which the person to whom the decision relates is resident at the time when the appeal is lodged;

   (b) where the person to whom the decision relates is detained in a hospital at the time when the appeal is lodged, of the sheriffdom in which the hospital is situated; or

   (c) in any other case, of any sheriffdom.

(4) If the sheriff principal to whom an appeal is made considers that the appeal raises an important or difficult question of law that makes it appropriate to remit the appeal to the Court of Session the sheriff principal may—

   (a) *ex proprio motu*; or

   (b) on the motion of any party to the appeal,

   do so.

(5) Subject to subsections (6) to (9) below, in this section "relevant party" means—

   (a) the person to whom the decision relates;

   (b) that person's named person;

   (c) any guardian of the person;

   (d) any welfare attorney of the person;

   (e) the mental health officer; and

   (f) that person's responsible medical officer.

(6) Where the person to whom the decision relates is a person to whom subsection (7) below applies, "relevant party" means—

   (a) the person to whom the decision relates;

   (b) that person's named person;

   (c) any guardian of the person;

   (d) any welfare attorney of the person; and

   (e) the Scottish Ministers.

(7) This subsection applies to a patient who is subject to—

   (a) a compulsion order and a restriction order;

   (b) a hospital direction; or

   (c) a transfer for treatment direction.

(8) Where the appeal is against a decision mentioned in paragraph (w) of subsection (1) above, "relevant party" means—

(a) the person to whom the decision relates;

(b) that person's named person;

(c) any guardian of the person;

(d) any welfare attorney of the person;

(e) the Commission; and

(f) the relevant Health Board (within the meaning of section 273 of this Act).

(9) Where the appeal is against a decision mentioned in paragraph (x) of subsection (1) above, "relevant party" means—

(a) the person to whom the decision relates;

(b) that person's named person;

(c) any guardian of the person;

(d) any welfare attorney of the person;

(e) the managers of the hospital; and

(f) if the person who applied for the order does not fall within paragraphs (a) to (d) above, the person who applied for the order.

321 Appeal to Court of Session against decisions of sheriff principal

(1) A relevant party to an appeal to the sheriff principal under section 320(2) of this Act may appeal to the Court of Session against the decision of the sheriff principal allowing or refusing the appeal.

(2) In subsection (1) above, "relevant party" has the same meaning as in section 320 of this Act.

322 Appeal to Court of Session against certain decisions of the Tribunal

(1) This section applies to the following decisions of the Tribunal—

(a) a decision to make an order revoking a compulsion order under section 193(3) or (4) of this Act;

(b) a decision to make an order revoking a restriction order under section 193(5) of this Act;

(c) a decision to make an order varying a compulsion order under section 193(6) of this Act;

(d) a decision to make an order conditionally discharging a patient under section 193(7) of this Act;

    (e) a decision, under section 193 of this Act, to make no order under that section;

    (f) a decision, under section 215(2) of this Act, to make no direction;

    (g) a decision to make a direction under section 215(3) or (4) of this Act;

    (h) a decision to make or refuse to make an order under section 219(5) or 220(5) of this Act preventing a transfer or requiring that a transferred patient be returned; and

    (i) a decision, in relation to a patient who is subject to a restriction order, a hospital direction or a transfer for treatment direction—

        (i) to make or refuse to make an order under section 264(2), 265(3) or 266(3) of this Act;

        (ii) under section 267(2) of this Act to recall or refuse to recall an order made under section 264, 265 or 266 of this Act;

        (iii) to make or refuse to make an order under section 268(2), 269(3) or 270(3) of this Act; or

        (iv) under section 271(2) of this Act to recall or refuse to recall an order made under section 268, 269 or 270 of this Act.

(2) A relevant party to proceedings before the Tribunal may appeal to the Court of Session against a decision to which this section applies.

(3) Subject to subsection (4) below, in this section "relevant party" means—

    (a) the person to whom the decision relates;

    (b) that person's named person;

    (c) any guardian of the person;

    (d) any welfare attorney of the person; and

    (e) the Scottish Ministers.

(4) Where the appeal is against a decision mentioned in paragraph (i) of subsection (1) above, "relevant party" means—

    (a) the person to whom the decision relates;

    (b) that person's named person;

    (c) any guardian of the person;

    (d) any welfare attorney of the person;

    (e) the Commission;

    (f) the relevant Health Board (within the meaning of section 273 of this Act); and

    (g) the Scottish Ministers.

323 Suspension of decision of Tribunal pending determination of certain appeals

(1) Where the Scottish Ministers appeal under section 322(2) of this Act against any decision of the Tribunal under section 193 of this Act, or a decision of the Tribunal to make a direction under section 215(3) or (4) of this Act, the Court of Session may, on the motion of the Scottish Ministers, order—

(a) that the patient in respect of whom the Tribunal's decision was made shall continue, subject to subsection (2) below, to be detained; and

(b) that both the compulsion order and restriction order or, as the case may be, the hospital direction or transfer for treatment direction to which the patient is subject shall continue to have effect accordingly.

(2) An order under subsection (1) above has the effect of continuing the patient's detention—

(a)[34] in a case where no appeal is made to the Supreme Court against the decision of the Court of Session under section 322(2) of this Act, until the expiry of the time allowed to so appeal to the Supreme Court; or

(b) in a case where such an appeal is made, until it is abandoned or finally determined.

324 Appeals: general provisions

(1) An appeal—

(a) to the sheriff principal under section 320(2) of this Act; or

(b) to the Court of Session under section 322(2) of this Act,

may be made only on one or more of the grounds mentioned in subsection (2) below.

(2) The grounds referred to in subsection (1) above are—

(a) that the Tribunal's decision was based on an error of law;

(b) that there has been a procedural impropriety in the conduct of any hearing by the Tribunal on the application;

(c) that the Tribunal has acted unreasonably in the exercise of its discretion;

(d) that the Tribunal's decision was not supported by the facts found to be established by the Tribunal.

---

[34] As amended by Constitutional Reform Act 2005, Sch 9, para 83.

(3) The Tribunal may be a party to an appeal under section 320(2) or 322(2) and in any appeal from the decision of the sheriff principal under section 321(1).

(4) The court may, where it considers it appropriate, order the Tribunal to be represented at any hearing of an appeal under section 320(2), 321(1) or 322(2).

(5) In allowing an appeal under section 320(2), 321(1) or 322(2) of this Act the court—

(a) shall set aside the decision of the Tribunal; and
(b) shall—
   (i) if it considers that it can properly do so on the facts found to be established by the Tribunal, substitute its own decision; or
   (ii) remit the case to the Tribunal for consideration anew.

(6) If the court remits a case under paragraph (b)(ii) of subsection (5) above, the court may—

(a) direct that the Tribunal be differently constituted from when it made the decision; and
(b) issue such other directions to the Tribunal about the consideration of the case as it considers appropriate.

(7) Regulations may specify the period within which an appeal under section 320(2), 321(1) or 322(2) of this Act shall be made.

(8) In this section, "the court" means the sheriff principal or the Court of Session as the case may be.

PART 23

GENERAL

...

328 Meaning of "mental disorder"

(1) Subject to subsection (2) below, in this Act "mental disorder" means any—

(a) mental illness;
(b) personality disorder; or

(c) learning disability,

however caused or manifested; and cognate expressions shall be construed accordingly.

(2) A person is not mentally disordered by reason only of any of the following—

(a) sexual orientation;

(b) sexual deviancy;

(c) transsexualism;

(d) transvestism;

(e) dependence on, or use of, alcohol or drugs;

(f) behaviour that causes, or is likely to cause, harassment, alarm or distress to any other person;

(g) acting as no prudent person would act.

329 Interpretation

(1)[35] In this Act, unless the context otherwise requires—

"the 1995 Act" means the Criminal Procedure (Scotland) Act 1995 (c.46);

"advance statement" has the meaning given by section 275 of this Act;

"approved medical practitioner" has the meaning given by section 22(4) of this Act;

"assessment order" means an order made under section 52D(2) of the 1995 Act;

"care home service" has the meaning given by section 2(3) of the Regulation of Care (Scotland) Act 2001 (asp 8);

"care plan", in relation to a patient, means a plan prepared under subsection (1)(a) of section 76 of this Act; and includes a reference to a care plan amended by virtue of subsection (3) or (4)(a) of that section;

"carer", in relation to a person, means an individual who, otherwise than—

(a) by virtue of a contract of employment or other contract with any person; or

(b) as a volunteer for a voluntary organisation,

provides, on a regular basis, a substantial amount of care for, and support to, the person; and includes, in the case where the

---

[35] As amended by Mental Health (Care and Treatment) (Scotland) Act 2003 (Modification of Enactments) Order 2005 (SSI 2005/465), Sch 1, para 32(24)(a).

person is in hospital, an individual who, before the person was admitted to hospital, provided, on a regular basis, a substantial amount of care for, and support to, the person;

"the Commission" means the Mental Welfare Commission for Scotland;

"community care services" has the meaning given by section 5A(4) of the Social Work (Scotland) Act 1968 (c.49);

"compulsion order" means an order made under section 57A(2) of the 1995 Act;

"compulsory treatment order" means an order made under section 64(4)(a) of this Act;

"designated medical practitioner" has the meaning given by section 233(2) of this Act;

"emergency detention certificate" means a certificate granted under section 36(1) of this Act;

"extension certificate" means a certificate granted under section 47(1) of this Act;

"guardian" means a person appointed as a guardian under the Adults with Incapacity (Scotland) Act 2000 (asp 4) who has power by virtue of section 64(1)(a) or (b) of that Act in relation to the personal welfare of a person;

"Health Board" means a board constituted by order under section 2(1)(a) of the National Health Service (Scotland) Act 1978 (c.29);

"hospital" means—

(a) any health service hospital (as defined in section 108(1) of the National Health Service (Scotland) Act 1978 (c.29));
(b) any independent health care service; or
(c) any state hospital;

"hospital direction" means a direction made under section 59A of the 1995 Act;

"independent health care service" has the meaning given by section 2(5) of the Regulation of Care (Scotland) Act 2001 (asp 8);

"interim compulsion order" means an order made under section 53(2) of the 1995 Act;

"interim compulsory treatment order" means an order made under section 65(2) of this Act;

"local authority" means a council constituted under section 2 of the Local Government etc. (Scotland) Act 1994 (c.39);

"managers", in relation to a hospital, means—

(a) in the case of a hospital vested in the Scottish Ministers for the purposes of their functions under the National Health Service (Scotland) Act 1978 (c.29), the Health Board or Special Health Board responsible for the administration of the hospital;

(b) in the case of a hospital vested in a National Health Service trust, the directors of the trust;

(c) in the case of an independent health care service which is registered under Part 1 of the Regulation of Care (Scotland) Act 2001 (asp 8), the person providing the service; and

(d) in the case of a state hospital—

(i) where the Scottish Ministers have delegated the management of the hospital to a Health Board, Special Health Board, National Health Service trust or the Common Services Agency for the Scottish Health Service, that Board, trust or Agency;

(ii) where the management of the hospital has not been so delegated, the Scottish Ministers;

"medical practitioner" means registered medical practitioner;

"medical records" has the meaning given by section 77(1) of the Regulation of Care (Scotland) Act 2001 (asp 8);

"medical treatment" means treatment for mental disorder; and for this purpose "treatment" includes—

(a) nursing;

(b) care;

(c) psychological intervention;

(d) habilitation (including education, and training in work, social and independent living skills); and

(e) rehabilitation (read in accordance with paragraph (d) above);

"mental health officer" means a person appointed (or deemed to be appointed) under section 32(1) of this Act, and "the mental health officer", in relation to a patient, means a mental health officer having responsibility for the patient's case;

"mental health report" has the meaning given by section 57(4) of this Act;

"named person" means the person who is, in relation to another person, that other person's named person by virtue of any of sections 250 to 254 and 257 of this Act;

"National Health Service trust" means a body established by order under section 12A(1) of the National Health Service (Scotland) Act 1978 (c.29);

"notice" means notice in writing;

"patient" means a person who has, or appears to have, a mental disorder;

"primary", in relation to a carer, means the individual who provides all, or most, of the care for, and support for, the person;

"prison" includes any prison other than a naval, military or air force prison;

"recorded matter" has the meaning given by section 64(4)(a) (ii) of this Act;

"regulations" means regulations made by the Scottish Ministers;

"relevant services" has the meaning given by section 19(2) of the Children (Scotland) Act 1995 (c.36);

"restriction order" means an order made under section 59 of the 1995 Act;

"short-term detention certificate" means a certificate granted under section 44(1) of this Act;

"Special Health Board" means a board constituted by order under section 2(1)(b) of the National Health Service (Scotland) Act 1978 (c.29);

"state hospital" means a hospital provided under section 102(1) of the National Health Service (Scotland) Act 1978 (c.29);

"transfer for treatment direction" has the meaning given by section 136 of this Act;

"treatment order" means an order made under section 52M of the 1995 Act;

"the Tribunal" means the Mental Health Tribunal for Scotland;

"voluntary organisation" means a body, other than a public or local authority, the activities of which are not carried on for profit;

"welfare attorney" means an individual authorised, by a welfare power of attorney granted under section 16 of the Adults with Incapacity (Scotland) Act 2000 (asp 4) and registered under section 19 of that Act, to act as such; and

"young offenders institution" has the same meaning as in the Prisons (Scotland) Act 1989 (c.45).

(2) In this Act, unless the context otherwise requires, a reference to the Tribunal is, where the power conferred by paragraph 7(1) of Schedule 2 is exercised, to be construed as a reference to the tribunal concerned.

(3) References in this Act to the giving of medical treatment to a person include references to medical treatment being performed on a person.

(4)[36] References in this Act to a patient's responsible medical officer are references to the approved medical practitioner who is for the time being—

  (a) appointed under section 230(i) or 3(a) of this Act; or
  (b) authorised under section 230(3)(b) of this Act,
     in respect of the patient.

...

SCHEDULE 2

(introduced by section 21)

THE MENTAL HEALTH TRIBUNAL FOR SCOTLAND

PART 1

MEMBERS OF THE TRIBUNAL ETC.

1 Members

(1) The Scottish Ministers shall appoint as members of the Tribunal—

  (a) a panel of persons who have such legal—

    (i) qualifications;
    (ii) training; and
    (iii) experience,

    as may be prescribed in regulations for the purposes of serving as legal members of the Tribunal;

---

[36] Substituted by Mental Health (Care and Treatment) (Scotland) Act 2003 (Modification of Enactments) Order 2005 (SSI 2005/465), Sch 1, para 32(24)(b).

(b) a panel of persons who have such qualifications, training and experience—

(i) in medicine; and

(ii) in the diagnosis and treatment of mental disorder,

as may be prescribed in regulations for the purposes of serving as medical members of the Tribunal; and

(c) a panel of persons who have—

(i) such qualifications, training, skills and experience in caring for, or providing services to, persons having a mental disorder; or

(ii) experience of such description,

as may be prescribed in regulations for the purposes of serving as general members of the Tribunal.

(2) A person is disqualified from appointment as, and being, a member of the Tribunal if the person—

(a) is a member of the Scottish Parliament;

(b) is a member of the Scottish Executive or a junior Scottish Minister; or

(c) is of such other description as may be prescribed in regulations.

2 Shrieval panel

There shall be a panel consisting of each person who for the time being holds the office of—

(a) sheriff principal;

(b) sheriff; or

(c) part-time sheriff,

for the purposes of serving as sheriff conveners of the Tribunal.

3 The President

(1) The Scottish Ministers shall appoint a person to be known as the President of the Mental Health Tribunal for Scotland (the "President").

(2) The President—

(a) shall preside over the discharge of the Tribunal's functions; and

(b) may serve as a Convener of the Tribunal.

(3) The Scottish Ministers may not appoint a person to be the President unless that person has such—

(a) qualifications;

(b) training; and

(c) experience,

as may be prescribed by regulations.

(4) The following provisions of this schedule apply (with the necessary modifications) to the President as they apply to a member of the Tribunal—

(a) paragraph 1(2);

(b) paragraph 4;

(c) paragraph 5; and

(d) paragraph 6.

(5) The functions of the President may, if the President is absent or otherwise unable to act, be discharged by one of the members of the panel mentioned in paragraph 1(1)(a) above appointed for that purpose by the Scottish Ministers.

(6) Regulations may make provision as to the delegation by the President of any of the President's functions to any of the members of the Tribunal or its staff.

(7) Regulations made under sub-paragraph (6) above may include provision for different functions to be delegated to different persons for different areas.

4 Terms of office etc.

(1) Subject to this paragraph and paragraph 5 below, each member of the Tribunal shall hold office in accordance with the terms of such member's instrument of appointment.

(2) An appointment as a member of the Tribunal shall, subject to sub-paragraphs (3) and (4) below, last for 5 years.

(3) A member of the Tribunal—

(a) may at any time resign office by notice to the Scottish Ministers;

(b)[37] ...

(c) shall vacate office on becoming disqualified from being a member of the Tribunal by virtue of paragraph 1(2) above.

---

[37] Repealed by Smoking, Health and Social Care (Scotland) Act 2005, Sch 3, para 1.

(4) A member of the Tribunal's appointment shall come to an end upon the member's being removed from office under paragraph 5(1) below.

(5) A member of the Tribunal whose appointment comes to an end by operation of sub-paragraph (2) above may be reappointed and, except in the circumstances set out in sub-paragraph (6) below, shall be reappointed.

(6) The circumstances referred to in sub-paragraph (5) above are that—

  (a) the member of the Tribunal has declined that re-appointment;

  (b)[38] ...

  (c) the President has made a recommendation to the Scottish Ministers against the reappointment;

  (d) there has, since the member of the Tribunal was last appointed, been a reduction in the number of members of the panel to which the member belongs required by the Tribunal to discharge its functions;

  (e) since the member of the Tribunal was last appointed, the member has, without reasonable excuse, failed to comply with the terms of the member's appointment; or

  (f) the member of the Tribunal does not have such quali-fications, training, skills or experience as are for the time being prescribed under paragraph 1(1) above for appointment to the panel to which the member of the Tribunal belongs.

5

(1) A member of the Tribunal may be removed from office only by order of the disciplinary committee constituted under sub-paragraph (3) below.

(2) The disciplinary committee may order the removal from office of a member of the Tribunal only if, after investigation carried out at the request of the Scottish Ministers, it finds that the member is unfit for office by reason of inability, neglect of duty or misbehaviour.

(3) The disciplinary committee shall consist of—

  (a) a Senator of the College of Justice or a sheriff principal (who shall preside);

---

[38] Repealed by Smoking, Health and Social Care (Scotland) Act 2005, Sch 3, para 1.

(b) a person who is a solicitor or an advocate of at least ten years' standing; and

(c) one other person,

all appointed by the Lord President of the Court of Session.

(4) Regulations—

    (a) may make provision—

        (i) enabling the disciplinary committee, at any time during an investigation, to suspend a member of the Tribunal from office; and

        (ii) as to the effect and duration of such suspension; and

    (b) shall make such further provision as respects the disciplinary committee (including in particular provision for the procedure of the committee) as the Scottish Ministers consider necessary or expedient.

6 Remuneration and pensions etc.

(1) The Scottish Ministers may pay, or make provision for paying, to, or in respect of, each member of the Tribunal such remuneration, expenses, pensions, allowances and gratuities (including by way of compensation for loss of office) as the Scottish Ministers may determine.

(2) Sub-paragraph (1) above, so far as relating to pensions, allowances and gratuities, shall not have effect in relation to persons to whom Part I of the Judicial Pensions and Retirement Act 1993 (c.8) applies, except to the extent provided by virtue of that Act.

PART 2

ORGANISATION AND ADMINISTRATION OF THE TRIBUNAL

7 Organisation and administration of the functions of the Tribunal

(1) The functions of the Tribunal shall be discharged by such number of tribunals as may be determined from time to time by the President.

(2) The Tribunal shall sit at such times and in such places as the President may determine.

(3) Subject to sub-paragraph (4) below, and to any rules made under paragraph 10(1) below, a tribunal constituted under sub-paragraph (1) above shall consist of—

(a) a Convener who shall be—
   (i) the President; or
   (ii) a member selected by the President from the panel mentioned in paragraph 1(1)(a) above; and
(b) a member selected by the President from each of the panels mentioned in paragraph 1(1)(b) and (c) above.

(4)[39] In relation to proceedings (other than proceedings relating solely to an application under section 255 or 256 of this Act) before the Tribunal in relation to a patient subject to a compulsion order, a hospital direction or a transfer for treatment direction, the Convener shall be—

(a) the President; or
(b) a person selected by the President from the panel mentioned in paragraph 2 above.

(5) Subject to the provisions of this Act, regulations made under section 21 of this Act and rules made under paragraph 10 below, the President shall secure that the functions of the Tribunal are discharged efficiently and effectively.

(6) The President may—

(a) give such directions; and
(b) issue such guidance,

about the administration of the Tribunal as appear to the President to be necessary or expedient for the purpose of securing that the functions of the Tribunal are discharged efficiently and effectively.

8   Staff and accommodation

(1) The Scottish Ministers may appoint such staff and provide such accommodation for the Tribunal as they may determine.

(2) The Scottish Ministers may pay, or make provision for paying, to, or in respect of, the Tribunal's staff, such remuneration, expenses, pensions, allowances and gratuities (including by way of compensation for loss of employment) as the Scottish Ministers may determine.

(3) The persons mentioned in sub-paragraph (4) below shall, in so far as it is reasonably practicable to do so, provide, in response to a request by the President, accommodation for the holding of hearings by the Tribunal.

---

[39] As amended by Mental Health (Care and Treatment) (Scotland) Act 2003 (Modification of Enactments) Order 2005 (SSI 2005/465), Sch 1, para 32(26)(a).

(4) The persons referred to in sub-paragraph (3) above are—

    (a) a Health Board;

    (b) the State Hospitals Board for Scotland;

    (c) a local authority.

9 Finance

Such expenses of the Tribunal as the Scottish Ministers may determine shall be defrayed by the Scottish Ministers.

PART 3

TRIBUNAL PROCEDURE

10 Rules

(1) The Scottish Ministers may make rules as to the practice and procedure of the Tribunal.

(2) Such rules may, without prejudice to the generality of sub-paragraph (1) above, include provision for or in connection with—

    (a) the composition of the Tribunal for the purposes of its discharge of particular functions;

    (b) where the functions of the Tribunal are being discharged by more than one tribunal—

        (i) determining by which tribunal any proceedings are to be dealt with; and

        (ii) transferring proceedings from one tribunal to another;

    (c) the form of applications to the Tribunal;

    (d) the recovery and inspection of documents;

    (e) the persons who may appear on behalf of the parties;

    (f) enabling specified persons other than the parties to appear or be represented in specified circumstances;

    (g) requiring specified persons to give notice to other specified persons of specified matters in such form and by such method as may be specified;

    (h) as to the time within which any notice by virtue of sub-paragraph (g) above shall be given;

    (i) enabling any matters that are preliminary or incidental to the determination of proceedings to be determined by the Convener alone or with such other members of the Tribunal as may be specified;

(j) enabling hearings to be held in private;

(k) enabling the Tribunal (or the Convener, with such other members of the Tribunal as may be specified, as the case may be) to exclude the person to whom the proceedings relate from attending all or part of hearings;

(l) enabling specified proceedings or specified matters that are preliminary or incidental to the determination of proceedings to be determined in specified circumstances without the holding of a hearing;

(m) enabling the Tribunal to hear and determine concurrently two or more sets of proceedings relating to the same person;

(n) the recording, publication and enforcement of decisions and orders of the Tribunal;

(o) the admissibility of evidence to the Tribunal;

(p) enabling matters to be referred to the Commission;

(q) enabling the Tribunal to commission medical and other reports in specified circumstances;

(r) requiring specified proceedings, or specified matters that are preliminary or incidental to the determination of proceedings, to be determined, or other specified actions to be taken, within specified periods;

(s) the circumstances in which a curator *ad litem* may be appointed.

(3) In sub-paragraph (2) above, "specified" means specified in the rules.

11 Practice directions

Subject to rules made under paragraph 10 above the President may give directions as to the practice and procedure to be followed by the Tribunal in relation to any matter.

12 Evidence

(1) The Tribunal may by citation require any person to attend, at such time and place as is specified in the citation, for the purpose of—

(a) giving evidence; or

(b) producing any document in the custody, or under the control, of such person which the Tribunal considers it necessary to examine.

(2) In relation to persons giving evidence the Tribunal may administer oaths and take affirmations.

(3) A person who is cited to attend the Tribunal and—

    (a) refuses or fails—

        (i) to attend; or

        (ii) to give evidence; or

    (b) alters, conceals or destroys, or refuses to produce, a document which such person may be required to produce for the purposes of proceedings before the Tribunal,

shall, subject to sub-paragraph (4) below, be guilty of an offence.

(4) A person need not give evidence or produce any document if, were it evidence which might be given or a document that might be produced in any court in Scotland, the person having that evidence or document could not be compelled to give or produce it in such proceedings.

(5) It shall be a defence for a person charged with contravening sub-paragraph (3) above to show that the person has a reasonable excuse for such contravention.

(6) A person guilty of an offence under sub-paragraph (3)(a) above shall be liable on summary conviction to a fine not exceeding level 5 on the standard scale.

(7) A person guilty of an offence under sub-paragraph (3)(b) above shall be liable—

    (a) on summary conviction to a fine not exceeding the statutory maximum;

    (b) on conviction on indictment to imprisonment for a term not exceeding 2 years or a fine or both.

13 Decisions of the Tribunal

(1) Subject to sub-paragraph (2) below, where a decision is to be made by more than one member of the Tribunal, the decision of the Tribunal shall be made by majority.

(2) If there is a tie, the Convener shall have a second vote as a casting vote.

(3) A decision of the Tribunal shall be recorded in a document which contains a full statement of the facts found by the Tribunal and the reasons for the decision.

(4)[40] The Tribunal shall—

(a) inform each party of its decision; and

(b) as soon as practicable after completion of the document mentioned in sub-paragraph (3) above, send a copy to each party.

13A[41] Withdrawn applications to be disregarded for certain purposes

For the purposes of sections 101(3)(c), 189(2)(a)(ii) and (b)(ii) and 213(2)(a)(ii) and (b)(ii) of this Act, an application to the Tribunal which is withdrawn by the applicant before it is determined is to be treated as having not been made.

PART 4

REPORTS, INFORMATION ETC.

14 Annual report

(1) The President shall, in respect of each period of 12 months beginning on 1st April, prepare a written report as to the Tribunal's discharge of its functions during that period.

(2) The President shall submit each report prepared under sub-paragraph (1) above, as soon as practicable after the period to which it relates, to the Scottish Ministers.

(3) The Scottish Ministers shall lay before the Scottish Parliament a copy of each report submitted to them under sub-paragraph (2) above.

15 Disclosure of information

The President shall, at such times and in respect of such periods as the Scottish Ministers may specify, provide to—

(a) the Scottish Ministers;

(b) such persons as the Scottish Ministers may specify,

such information relating to the discharge of the Tribunal's functions as the Scottish Ministers may direct.

---

[40] As amended by Mental Health (Care and Treatment) (Scotland) Act 2003 (Modification of Enactments) Order 2005 (SSI 2005/465), Sch 1, para 32(26)(b)(i) and (ii).
[41] Inserted by Adult Support and Protection (Scotland) Act 2007, s 73.

16 Allowances etc. for attendance at hearings of the Tribunal and preparation of reports

(1) The Tribunal may pay to any person (other than a member of the Tribunal or a member of the staff of the Tribunal) such allowances and expenses as the President shall determine for the purposes of, or in connection with, the person's attendance at hearings of the Tribunal.

(2) The Tribunal may pay to any person (other than a member of the Tribunal or a member of the staff of the Tribunal) such amounts as the President shall determine in connection with any report prepared by the person in accordance with rules made under paragraph 10(2)(q) above.

APPENDIX 2

MENTAL HEALTH TRIBUNAL FOR SCOTLAND (PRACTICE AND PROCEDURE) (NO 2) RULES 2005 (SSI 2005/519)

Part 1

INTRODUCTION

1 Citation and commencement

These Rules may be cited as the Mental Health Tribunal for Scotland (Practice and Procedure) (No 2) Rules 2005 and shall come into force on 14th November 2005.

2 Interpretation

(1) In these Rules—

"the Act" means the Mental Health (Care and Treatment) (Scotland) Act 2003;

"appellant" means a person who appeals to the Tribunal under or by virtue of any of the sections of the Act specified in Part III of these Rules;

"applicant" means a person who makes an application to the Tribunal under the Act;

"Clerk" means a member of staff of the Tribunal employed to carry out the administration of the Tribunal or to act as clerk at a hearing of the Tribunal;

"Convener" means the President or a person selected by the President from the panel mentioned in paragraph 1(1)(a) or 2 of Schedule 2 to the Act;

"electronic communication" has the meaning given to it by section 15(1) of Electronic Communications Act 2000 and "electronic signature" has the same meaning as in section 7 of that Act;

"hearing" means a sitting of the Tribunal for the purpose of enabling the Tribunal to take a decision on any matter relating to the case before it;

"notice" means notice in writing;

"the overriding objective" means the overriding objective described in rule 4;

"party" means—

(a) the person who initiated the proceedings before the Tribunal;

(b) the patient to whom the proceedings relate;

(c) the named person of the patient to whom the proceedings relate;

(d) any person whose decision (which shall include any direction or order, determination or grant of a certificate, but does not include a decision by a court) is the subject of the proceedings before the Tribunal;

(e) any person added as a party under rule 48; and

(f) in the case of proceedings under sections 264 to 267 of the Act—

(i) the relevant Health Board; and

(ii) in the case where those proceedings relate to a relevant patient, the Scottish Ministers;[1]

"patient" means the patient to whom the proceedings relate;

"relevant person" means any party and any other person who sends a notice of response under Part II, IV or V of these Rules indicating a wish to make representations or to lead or produce evidence;

"President" means the President of the Tribunal;

"referee" means a person who makes a reference to the Tribunal under the Act;

"relevant Health Board" and "relevant patient" are to be interpreted in accordance with section 273 of the Act;[2]

"respondent" means the person who made the decision which is the subject of appeal under or by virtue of Part III of these Rules;

"Tribunal" means the Mental Health Tribunal for Scotland and "tribunal" means a tribunal constituted under sub-paragraph

---

[1] Inserted by Mental Health Tribunal for Scotland (Practice and Procedure) (No 2) Amendment Rules 2006 (SSI 2006/171), r 2(2)(a)(ii).

[2] Inserted by *ibid*, r 2(2)(b).

(1) of paragraph 7 of Schedule 2 to the Act to discharge the functions of the Tribunal; and

"working day" means a day which is not—

(a) a Saturday;

(b) a Sunday; or

(c) a day which is a bank holiday in Scotland under the Banking and Financial Dealings Act 1971.

(2) Any reference in these Rules to a rule is a reference to a rule in these Rules, and in any rule a reference to a paragraph or sub-paragraph is, unless otherwise expressly provided, a reference to a paragraph or sub-paragraph in the rule.

(3) Where the time specified by these Rules for doing any act ends on a Saturday, Sunday or a day which is a bank holiday in Scotland under the Banking and Financial Dealings Act 1971 that act is done in time if it is done on the next day which is not a Saturday, Sunday or bank holiday.

3 Scope of the Rules

These Rules apply to the following proceedings:—

(a) applications to the Tribunal;

(b) references to the Tribunal;

(c) appeals to the Tribunal;

(d) reviews by the Tribunal; and

(e) cases remitted to the Tribunal under section 324(5)(b)(ii) of the Act.

4 The overriding objective

The overriding objective of these Rules is to secure that proceedings before the Tribunal are handled as fairly, expeditiously and efficiently as possible.

PART II

APPLICATIONS TO THE TRIBUNAL

Short-term detention

5 **Application for revocation of short-term detention certificate or extension certificate under section 50 of the Act**

(1) An application to the Tribunal for revocation of a short-term detention certificate under section 50 of the Act shall be made in writing.

(2) The application shall state—

(a) the name and address of the applicant;

(b) the name and address of the patient;

(c) the name and address of the patient's named person;

(d) the name and address of the hospital where the patient is detained; and

(e) a brief statement of the reasons for the application.

(3) The applicant shall sign the application.

(4) The Clerk shall send a copy of the application to the parties.

(5) Upon receipt of the application the Clerk shall fix a hearing as soon as possible.

(6) The Clerk shall send notice of the application to the following persons—

(a) the patient;

(b) the patient's named person;

(c) any guardian of the patient;

(d) any welfare attorney of the patient;

(e) the approved medical practitioner who granted the short-term certificate;

(f) the mental health officer who was consulted under section 44(3)(c) of the Act;

(g) if the patient has a responsible medical officer, the responsible medical officer;

(h) any curator *ad litem* appointed in respect of the patient by the Tribunal; and

(i) any other person appearing to the Tribunal to have an interest in the application.

(7) Notice under paragraph (6) shall inform the persons—

    (a) of the case number of the application (which must from then on be referred to in all correspondence relating to the application);

    (b) that they are being afforded the opportunity—

        (i) of making representations (whether orally or in writing); and

        (ii) of leading, or producing evidence;

    (c) of the date, time and place of the hearing; and

    (d) that if they wish to make representations or lead or produce evidence, they must respond to the notice within the period specified in the notice.

(8) If a person mentioned in paragraph (6) wishes to make representations (whether orally or in writing) or to lead or produce evidence, that person shall within the period specified in the notice—

    (a) send a notice of response to the Tribunal; and

    (b) send to the Tribunal a copy of any documents the person intends to rely upon at the hearing.

(9) The Clerk shall send a copy of each notice of response and any documents received under paragraph (8) to each party.

(10) Where at the hearing on an application to which this rule applies the Tribunal does not decide the application, it shall fix a further hearing.

(11) The Tribunal may on fixing a further hearing under paragraph (10) do any of the following as it thinks fit:—

    (a) it may give directions as to—

        (i) any issues on which the Tribunal requires evidence;

        (ii) the nature of the evidence which the Tribunal requires to decide those issues;

        (iii) the way in which the evidence is to be led before the Tribunal;

        (iv) the exclusion of any evidence which is irrelevant, unnecessary or improperly obtained;

        (v) the dates by which any documents or other evidence upon which any relevant person is intending to rely shall be sent to the Tribunal;

        (vi) the date by which a relevant person shall send any written representations on the case to the Tribunal; and

(vii) any other matter as is necessary to enable the Tribunal to decide the application as soon as possible;

(b) take any steps required by rule 53 to secure the needs of a person with communication difficulties;

(c) appoint a curator *ad litem* as necessary to meet the circumstances narrated in rule 55(2);

(d) decide any request or interim application made by any relevant person in relation to the case before the Tribunal.

(12) Before fixing a further hearing and doing any of those things referred to in paragraph (11), the Tribunal shall afford the relevant persons who are present an opportunity to be heard.

Compulsory treatment orders

6 Application for compulsory treatment order under section 63 of the Act

(1) An application for a compulsory treatment order shall state the matters specified in section 63(2) of the Act.

(2) The Clerk shall send a copy of the application and any accompanying documents mentioned in section 63(3) of the Act to the patient and the patient's named person.

(3) The Clerk shall send a notice of the application to the following persons:—

(a) the patient;

(b) the patient's named person;

(c) any guardian of the patient;

(d) any welfare attorney of the patient;

(e) the mental health officer;

(f) the medical practitioners who submitted the mental health reports which accompany the application;

(g) if the patient has a responsible medical officer, that officer;

(h) the patient's primary carer;

(i) any curator *ad litem* appointed in respect of the patient by the Tribunal; and

(j) any other person appearing to the Tribunal to have an interest in the application.

(4) Notice under paragraph (3) shall inform the persons—

  (a) of the case number of the application (which must from then on be referred to in all correspondence relating to the application);

  (b) that an application has been made by the mental health officer;

  (c) of the measures that are sought in relation to the patient in respect of whom the application is made;

  (d) of the date, time and place of the hearing; and

  (e) that they are being afforded the opportunity—

    (i) of making representations (whether orally or in writing); and

    (ii) of leading, or producing, evidence,

  in relation to the making of an order under section 63 of the Act.

(5) If a person mentioned in paragraph (3) wishes to make representations (whether orally or in writing) or to lead or produce evidence, that person shall send a notice of response to the Tribunal within 14 days of receipt of the notice under that paragraph or within such other period specified in that notice.

(6) The Clerk shall send a copy of each notice of response to each party.

7 Application for interim compulsory treatment order under section 65 of the Act

An application under section 65 of the Act for an interim compulsory treatment order may be made orally at a hearing of the Tribunal or in writing sent to the Tribunal.

8 Determination of application for compulsory treatment order where section 68 of the Act applies: special case

(1) This rule applies where an application is made under section 63 of the Act and section 68 of the Act applies.

(2) Before the expiry of the period of 5 days referred to in section 68(2)(a) of the Act, the Tribunal shall hold a hearing ("a first hearing") in order to determine whether an interim compulsory order should be made and, if it determines it should not be made, to determine the application.

(3) Where the Tribunal—

(a) makes an interim compulsory treatment order that authorises the detention of the patient in hospital; and

(b) does not determine that a compulsory treatment order should not be made,

it shall fix a further hearing.

(4) The Tribunal may on fixing a further hearing under paragraph (3), do any of the following as it thinks fit:—

    (a) it may give directions as to—

        (i) any issues on which the Tribunal requires evidence;

        (ii) the nature of the evidence which the Tribunal requires to decide those issues;

        (iii) the way in which the evidence is to be led before the Tribunal; the exclusion of any evidence which is irrelevant, unnecessary or improperly obtained;

        (iv) the dates by which any documents or other evidence upon which any relevant person is intending to rely shall be sent to the Tribunal;

        (v) the date by which a relevant person shall send any written representations on the case to the Tribunal; and

        (vi) any other matter as is necessary to enable the Tribunal to decide the application as soon as possible;

    (b) take any steps required by rule 53 to secure the needs of a person with communication difficulties;

    (c) appoint a curator *ad litem* as necessary to meet the circumstances narrated in rule 55(2);

    (d) decide any request or interim application made by any relevant person in relation to the case before the Tribunal.

(5) Before fixing a further hearing and doing any of those things referred to in paragraph (4), the Tribunal shall afford the relevant persons who are present an opportunity to be heard.

9 Application for extension and variation of compulsory treatment order under section 92 of the Act and variation of compulsory treatment order under section 95 of the Act

(1) An application for extension and variation of a compulsory treatment order under section 92 of the Act and an application for variation of a compulsory treatment order under section 95

of the Act shall state the matters mentioned in section 92(a) or, as the case may be, 95(a), of the Act.

(2) The Clerk shall send a copy of the application and any accompanying documents prescribed by virtue of section 92(b) or, as the case may be, section 95(b), of the Act to the patient and the patient's named person.

(3) The Clerk shall send notice of the application to—

   (a) the patient;
   (b) the patient's named person;
   (c) any guardian of the patient;
   (d) any welfare attorney of the patient;
   (e) the mental health officer;
   (f) the patient's responsible medical officer;
   (g) the patient's primary carer;
   (h) any curator *ad litem*; and
   (i) any other person appearing to the Tribunal to have an interest in the application.

(4) Notice under paragraph (3) shall inform the persons—

   (a) of the case number of the application (which must from then on be referred to in all correspondence relating to the application);
   (b) that the application has been made and the orders sought in the application;
   (c) of the terms of the existing compulsory treatment order;
   (d) of the date, time and place of the hearing; and
   (e) that they are being afforded the opportunity—
      (i) of making representations (whether orally or in writing); and
      (ii) of leading, or producing, evidence.

(5) If a person mentioned in paragraph (3) wishes to make representations (whether orally or in writing) or to lead or produce evidence, that person shall send a notice of response to the Tribunal within 14 days of receipt of the notice under that paragraph or within such other period specified in that notice.

(6) The Clerk shall send a copy of each notice of response to each party.

10 Application by patient etc. under section 99 of the Act for revocation of determination extending compulsory treatment order and for revocation or variation of a compulsory treatment order under section 100 of the Act

(1) An application under section 99 or 100 of the Act shall be made in writing.

(2) The application shall state—
   (a) the name and address of the applicant;
   (b) the name and address of the patient;
   (c) the name and address of the patient's named person;
   (d) where the patient is detained, the name and address of the hospital where the patient is detained;
   (e) where the patient is required to reside at a specified place, the address of that specified place; and
   (f) a brief statement of the reasons for the application.

(3) The applicant shall sign the application.

(4) The Clerk shall send a copy of the application to the patient's responsible medical officer.

(5) The Clerk shall send notice of the application to—
   (a) the patient;
   (b) the patient's named person;
   (c) any guardian of the patient;
   (d) any welfare attorney of the patient;
   (e) the mental health officer;
   (f) the patient's responsible medical officer;
   (g) the patient's primary carer;
   (h) any curator *ad litem*; and
   (i) any other person appearing to the Tribunal to have an interest in the application.

(6) Notice under paragraph (5) shall inform the persons—
   (a) of the case number of the application (which must from then on be referred to in all correspondence relating to the application);
   (b) that the application has been made;
   (c) of the orders sought in the application;
   (d) of the terms of the existing compulsory treatment order;
   (e) of the date, time and place of the hearing; and
   (f) that they are being afforded the opportunity—
      (i) of making representations (whether orally or in writing); and
      (ii) of leading, or producing, evidence.

(7) If a person mentioned in paragraph (5) wishes to make representations (whether orally or in writing) or to lead or produce evidence, that person shall send a notice of response

to the Tribunal within 14 days of receipt of the notice or within such other period specified in the notice.

(8) The Clerk shall send a copy of each notice of response to each party.

11 Application by patient etc. under section 120 of the Act for revocation of certificates under sections 114(2) and 115(2) of the Act

(1) An application under section 120 to the Tribunal for revocation of a certificate under section 114(2) or 115(2) of the Act shall be made in writing.

(2) The application shall state—
   (a) the name and address of the applicant;
   (b) the name and address of the patient;
   (c) the name and address of the patient's named person, if known;
   (d) where the patient is detained, the name and address of the hospital where the patient is detained;
   (e) where the patient is required to reside at a specified place, the address of that specified place; and
   (f) a brief statement of the reasons for the application.

(3) The applicant shall sign the application.

(4) Upon receipt of the application the Clerk shall fix a hearing as soon as possible.

(5) The Clerk shall send a copy of the application together with notice of the application to the parties.

(6) Notice under paragraph (5) shall inform the parties—
   (a) of the case number of the application (which must from then on be referred to in all correspondence relating to the application); and
   (b) of the date, time and place of the hearing.

(7) If a party wishes to make representations (whether orally or in writing) or to lead or produce evidence, that person shall within the period specified in the notice—
   (a) send a notice of response to the Tribunal; and
   (b) send to the Tribunal a copy of any document the person intends to rely upon at the hearing.

(8) The Clerk shall send a copy of any notice of response and any documents received under paragraph (7) to each party.

(9) Where at the hearing on an application to which this rule applies the Tribunal does not decide the application, it shall fix a further hearing.

(10) The Tribunal may on fixing a further hearing under paragraph (9) do any of the following as it thinks fit:—

    (a) it may give directions as to—

        (i) any issues on which the Tribunal requires evidence;

        (ii) the nature of the evidence which the Tribunal requires to decide those issues;

        (iii) the way in which the evidence is to be led before the Tribunal;

        (iv) the exclusion of any evidence which is irrelevant, unnecessary or improperly obtained;

        (v) the dates by which any documents or other evidence upon which any relevant person is intending to rely shall be sent to the Tribunal;

        (vi) the date by which a relevant person shall send any written representations on the case to the Tribunal; and

        (vii) any other matter as is necessary to enable the Tribunal to decide the application as soon as possible;

    (b) take any steps required by rule 53 to secure the needs of a person with communication difficulties;

    (c) appoint a curator *ad litem* as necessary to meet the circumstances narrated in rule 55(2);

    (d) decide any request or interim application made by any relevant person in relation to the case before the Tribunal.

(11) Before fixing a further hearing and doing any of those things referred to in paragraph (10), the Tribunal shall afford the relevant persons who are present an opportunity to be heard.

Compulsion orders

12 Application by responsible medical officer under sections 149, 158 and 161 of the Act

(1) An application by a patient's responsible medical officer to the Tribunal—

    (a) for an extension of a compulsion order following first review under section 149 of the Act shall state the matters mentioned in section 149(a) of the Act;

    (b) for extension and variation of a compulsion order under section 158 of the Act shall state the matters mentioned in section 158(a) of the Act; and

    (c) for an order varying a compulsion order under section 161 of the Act shall state the matters mentioned in section 158(a) of the Act.

(2) The Clerk shall send a copy of the application and any accompanying documents prescribed in respect of each application by regulations under section 149(b), 158(b) or, as the case may be, 161(b) of the Act to the patient and the patient's named person.

(3) The Clerk shall send notice of the application to—

    (a) the patient;

    (b) the patient's named person;

    (c) any guardian of the patient;

    (d) any welfare attorney of the patient;

    (e) the mental health officer;

    (f) the patient's responsible medical officer;

    (g) the patient's primary carer;

    (h) any curator *ad litem* appointed in respect of the patient by the Tribunal; and

    (i) any other person appearing to the Tribunal to have an interest in the application.

(4) Notice under paragraph (3) shall inform the persons—

    (a) of the case number of the application (which must from then on be referred to in all correspondence relating to the application);

    (b) that the application has been made and the orders sought in the application;

    (c) of the terms of the existing order;

    (d) of the date, time and place of the hearing, if known;

    (e) that they are being afforded the opportunity—

        (i) of making representations (whether orally or in writing); and

        (ii) of leading, or producing, evidence.

(5) If a person mentioned in paragraph (3) wishes to make representations (whether orally or in writing) or to lead or produce evidence, that person shall send a notice of response to the Tribunal within 14 days of receipt of the notice or such other period specified in the notice.

(6) The Clerk shall send a copy of each notice of response to each party.

13 Application by patient etc. for revocation of determination extending compulsion order under section 163 of the Act, for revocation or variation of a compulsion order under section 164 of the Act and under section 120 of the Act for revocation of a certificate under section 114(2) of the Act as applied with modifications by section 177 of the Act

(1) An application for revocation of a determination extending a compulsion order under section 163 of the Act or for revocation and variation of a compulsion order under section 164 of the Act shall be made in writing and shall state—

 (a) the name and address of the applicant;

 (b) the name and address of the patient;

 (c) the name and address of the patient's named person;

 (d) where the patient is detained, the name and address of the hospital where the patient is detained;

 (e) where the patient is required to reside at a specified place, the address of that specified place; and

 (f) a brief statement of the reasons for the application.

(2) The applicant shall sign the application.

(3) The Clerk shall send notice of the application to—

 (a)   the patient;

 (b) the patient's named person;

 (c) any guardian of the patient;

 (d) any welfare attorney of the patient;

 (e) the mental health officer;

 (f) the patient's responsible medical officer;

 (g) the patient's primary carer;

 (h) any curator *ad litem* appointed in respect of the patient by the Tribunal; and

 (i) any other person appearing to the Tribunal to have an interest in the application.

(4) Notice under paragraph (3) shall inform the persons—

 (a) of the case number of the application (which must from then on be referred to in all correspondence relating to the application);

 (b) that the application has been made and the orders sought in the application;

(c) of the terms of the existing order;

(d) of the date, time and place of the hearing;

(e) that they are being afforded the opportunity—

    (i) of making representations (whether orally or in writing); and

    (ii) of leading, or producing, evidence.

(5) If a person mentioned in paragraph (3) wishes to make representations (whether orally or in writing) or to lead or produce evidence, that person shall send a notice of response to the Tribunal within 14 days of receipt of the notice under that paragraph or within such other period specified in that notice.

(6) The Clerk shall send a copy of each notice of response to each party.

(7) Rule 11 shall apply to an application under section 120, as applied by section 177, of the Act for revocation of a certificate under section 114(2) of the Act; the reference in paragraph (1) of that rule to section 120 shall be read as a reference to section 120 as modified by section 177 of the Act.

Compulsion orders and restriction orders

14 Application under section 191 of the Act by the Scottish Ministers for an order under section 193 of the Act

(1) An application under section 191 of the Act by the Scottish Ministers for an order under section 193 of the Act shall state the matters mentioned in section 191(a) of the Act.

(2) The Clerk shall send a copy of the application and any accompanying documents prescribed by virtue of section 191(b) of the Act to the patient and the patient's named person.

(3) The Clerk shall send notice of the application to the following persons:—

(a) the patient;

(b) the patient's named person;

(c) the patient's primary carer;

(d) any guardian of the patient;

(e) any welfare attorney of the patient;

(f) any curator *ad litem* appointed by the Tribunal in respect of the patient;

(g) the Scottish Ministers;

(h) the patient's responsible medical officer;

(i) the mental health officer; and

(j) any other person appearing to the Tribunal to have an interest.

(4) Notice under paragraph (3) shall inform the persons—

(a) of the case number of the application (which must from then on be referred to in all correspondence relating to the application);

(b) that the application has been made and the order, or orders, sought in the application;

(c) of the terms of the existing order;

(d) of the date, time and place of the hearing, if known;

(e) that they are being afforded the opportunity—

(i) of making representations (whether orally or in writing); and

(ii) of leading, or producing, evidence.

(5) If a person mentioned in paragraph (3) wishes to make representations (whether orally or in writing) or to lead or produce evidence, that person shall send a notice of response to the Tribunal within 14 days of receipt of the notice under that paragraph or within such other period specified in that notice.

(6) The Clerk shall send a copy of each notice of response to each party.

15 Application by patient etc. under section 192 of the Act for order under section 193 of the Act

(1) An application under section 192 of the Act for an order under section 193 of the Act shall be made in writing and shall state—

(a) the name and address of the applicant;

(b) the name and address of the patient;

(c) the name and address of the patient's named person;

(d) where the patient is detained, the name and address of the hospital where the patient is detained;

(e) where the patient is required to reside at a specified place, the address of that specified place;

(f) the name of the patient's responsible medical officer;

(g) the order sought; and

(h) a brief statement of the reasons for the application.

(2) The applicant shall sign the application.

(3) The Clerk shall send a copy of the application to the patient's responsible medical officer and the Scottish Ministers.

(4) The Clerk shall send notice of the application to the following persons:—
   (a) the patient;
   (b) the patient's named person;
   (c) the patient's primary carer;
   (d) any guardian of the patient;
   (e) any welfare attorney of the patient;
   (f) any curator *ad litem* appointed by the Tribunal in respect of the patient;
   (g) the Scottish Ministers;
   (h) the patient's responsible medical officer;
   (i) the mental health officer; and
   (j) any other person appearing to the Tribunal to have an interest.

(5) Notice under paragraph (4) shall inform the persons—
   (a) of the case number of the application (which must from then on be referred to in all correspondence relating to the application);
   (b) that the application has been made and the order sought in the application;
   (c) of the terms of the existing order;
   (d) of the date, time and place of the hearing;
   (e) that they are being afforded the opportunity—
      (i) of making representations (whether orally or in writing); and
      (ii) of leading, or producing, evidence.

(6) If a person mentioned in paragraph (4) wishes to make representations (whether orally or in writing) or to lead or produce evidence, that person shall send a notice of response to the Tribunal within 14 days of receipt of the notice under that paragraph or within such other period specified in that notice.

(7) The Clerk shall send a copy of each notice of response to each party.

Hospital directions and transfer for treatment directions

16 Application by patient and named person for revocation of hospital direction or transfer for treatment direction under section 214(2) of the Act

(1) An application under section 214(2) of the Act shall be made in writing.

(2) The application shall state—

    (a) the name and address of the applicant;

    (b) the name and address of the patient;

    (c) the name and address of the patient's named person;

    (d) the name and address of the hospital where the patient is detained;

    (e) the direction which the applicant seeks to revoke; and

    (f) a brief statement of the reasons for the application.

(3) The applicant shall sign the application.

(4) The Clerk shall send a copy of the application to the patient's responsible medical practitioner and the Scottish Ministers.

(5) The Clerk shall send notice of the application to the following persons:—

    (a) the patient;

    (b) the patient's named person;

    (c) the patient's primary carer;

    (d) any guardian of the patient;

    (e) any welfare attorney of the patient;

    (f) any curator *ad litem* appointed by the Tribunal in respect of the patient;

    (g) the Scottish Ministers;

    (h) the patient's responsible medical officer;

    (i) the mental health officer; and

    (j) any other person appearing to the Tribunal to have an interest.

(6) Notice under paragraph (5) shall inform the persons—

    (a) of the case number of the application (which must from then on be referred to in all correspondence relating to the application);

    b) that the application has been made and the direction which it seeks to revoke;

    (c) of the terms of the existing direction;

    (d) of the date, time and place of the hearing;

(e) that they are being afforded the opportunity—

    (i) of making representations (whether orally or in writing); and

    (ii) of leading, or producing, evidence.

(7) If a person mentioned in paragraph (5) wishes to make representations (whether orally or in writing) or to lead or produce evidence, that person shall send a notice of response to the Tribunal within 14 days of receipt of the notice or within such other period specified in that notice.

(8) The Clerk shall send a copy of each notice of response to each party.

Named person

17 Application by mental health officer under section 255, and patient etc. under section 256, of the Act for appointment of named person

(1) Subject to paragraph (5) of this rule, an application under section 255 or section 256 for appointment of a named person shall be made in writing.

(2) The Clerk shall send a copy of the application—

    (a) if the application is made under section 255, to the patient, the patient's apparent named person, if applicable, and any person whom it is proposed in the application should be the patient's named person; or

    (b) if the application is made under section 256, to the mental health officer, the patient, the patient's named person, if applicable, and any person whom it is proposed in the application should be the patient's named person,

together with notice of the case number of the application (which must from then on be referred to in all correspondence relating to the application).

(3) If a person mentioned in paragraph (2) wishes to make representations (whether orally or in writing) or lead or produce evidence, that person shall send a notice of response to the Tribunal within 14 days of receipt of the copy application under that paragraph or within such other period specified in a notice sent with the copy application.

(4) The Clerk shall send a copy of each notice of response to each party and any person whom it is proposed in the application should be the patient's named person.

(5) Where it considers it expedient to do so, the Tribunal may permit an application to which this rule applies to be made by oral request and, in that event, the Tribunal shall take such steps as are reasonably practical to inform the persons mentioned in paragraph (2) of the application and to allow them to be heard on the application.

17A[3] Application that detention in state hospitals is in conditions of excessive security

(1) An application to the Tribunal for an order under section 264(2) of the Act (detention in conditions of excessive security: state hospitals) shall be made in writing.

(2) The application shall state—
  (a) the name and address of the applicant;
  (b) the name and address of the patient;
  (c) the name and address of the patient's named person;
  (d) the address where the patient resided ordinarily immediately before the making of the order or direction by which their detention in hospital is authorised;
  (e) the order or direction under the authority of which the patient is detained in hospital, including, where the order is a compulsion order, whether or not the patient is subject to a restriction order; and
  (f) a brief statement of the reasons for the application.

(3) The applicant shall sign the application.

(4) The Clerk shall send a notice of the application to the following persons:—
  (a) the patient;
  (b) the patient's named person;
  (c) the relevant Health Board;
  (d) the patient's responsible medical officer;
  (e) the managers of the state hospital in which the patient is detained;
  (f) the mental health officer;
  (g) any guardian of the patient;
  (h) any welfare attorney of the patient;
  (i) any curator *ad litem* appointed by the Tribunal in respect of the patient;

---

[3] Inserted by Mental Health Tribunal for Scotland (Practice and Procedure) (No 2) Amendment Rules 2006 (SSI 2006/171), r 2(3).

(j) the Commission;

(k) in the case of a relevant patient, the Scottish Ministers; and

(l) any other person appearing to the Tribunal to have an interest in the application.

(5) Notice under paragraph (4) shall inform the persons—

(a) of the case number of the application (which must from then on be referred to in all correspondence relating to the application);

(b) of the date, time and place of the hearing; and

(c) that they are being afforded the opportunity—

(i) of making representations (whether orally or in writing); and

(ii) of leading, or producing, evidence,

in relation to the making of an order under section 264(2) of the Act.

(6) If a person mentioned in paragraph (4) wishes to make representations (whether orally or in writing) or to lead, or produce, evidence, that person shall send a notice of response to the Tribunal within 21 days of receipt of the notice under that paragraph or within such other period specified in that notice.

(7) The Clerk shall send a copy of each notice of response to each party.

17B[4] Detention in state hospitals in conditions of excessive security: hearings under sections 265(2) and 266(2) of the Act

(1) This rule applies where section 265(2)or 266(2) of the Act applies.

(2) The Clerk shall, within seven days of the end of the period specified in the order made under section 264(2) or, as the case may be, 265(3) of the Act, send notice of the hearing to the persons mentioned in rule 17A(4).

(3) Notice under paragraph (2) shall inform the persons —

(a) of the date, time and place of the hearing, which, as far as practicable, shall be within 21 days of the end of the period specified in the order made under section 264(2) or, as the case may be, section 265(5) of the Act; and

---

[4] Inserted by Mental Health Tribunal for Scotland (Practice and Procedure) (No 2) Amendment Rules 2006 (SSI 2006/171), r 2(3).

(b) that they are being afforded the opportunity—
    (i) of making representations (whether orally or in writing); and
    (ii) of leading, or producing evidence,

in relation to a hearing under section 265(2) or, as the case may be, 266(2)of the Act.

(4)[5] If a person sent notice under paragraph (2) wishes to make representations (whether orally or in writing) or to lead, or produce, evidence, that person shall send a notice of response to the Tribunal within 7 days of receipt of the notice under that paragraph or within such other period specified in that notice.

(5)[5] The Clerk shall send a copy of each notice of response to each party.

17C[6] Application under section 267 of the Act for recall of an order under sections 264 to 266 of the Act

(1) An application to the Tribunal under section 267(2) of the Act for a recall of an order made under section 264(2), 265(3) or 266(3) of the Act shall be made in writing.

(2) The application shall state—
    (a) the name and address of the applicant;
    (b) the name and address of the patient;
    (c) the order to which the application relates; and
    (d) a brief statement of the reasons for the application.

(3) The applicant shall sign the application.

(4) The Clerk shall send a notice of the application to the persons mentioned in rule 17A(4).

(5) Notice under paragraph (4) shall inform the persons—
    (a) of the date, time and place of the hearing; and
    (b) that they are being afforded the opportunity—
        (i) of making representations (whether orally or in writing); and
        (ii) of leading, or producing, evidence

---

[5] Paragraph numbering corrected from original SSI text which shows these paragraphs as "(3)" and "(4)" respectively.
[6] Inserted by Mental Health Tribunal for Scotland (Practice and Procedure) (No 2) Amendment Rules 2006 (SSI 2006/171), r 2(3).

in relation to an application under section 267(2) for recall of an order made under section 264(2), 265(3) or, as the case may be, 266(3) of the Act.

(6) If a person sent notice under paragraph (4) wishes to make representations (whether orally or in writing) or to lead, or produce, evidence, that person shall send a notice of response to the Tribunal within 21 days of receipt of the notice under that paragraph or within such other period specified in that notice.

(7) The Clerk shall send a copy of each notice of response to each party.

Informal patients

18 Application to Tribunal under section 291 of the Act in relation to unlawful detention

(1) An application to the Tribunal under section 291 for an order requiring the managers of the hospital to cease to detain the patient shall be made in writing.

(2) The application shall state —
   (a) the name and address of the applicant;
   (b) the name and address of the patient;
   (c) the name and address of the patient's named person, if known;
   (d) the name and address of the hospital where the patient is apparently detained; and
   (e) a brief statement of the reasons for the application.

(3) The applicant shall sign the application.

(4) The Clerk shall send a copy of the application to the hospital managers and the patient.

(5) The Clerk shall notify the hospital managers—
   (a) of the case number of the application (which must from then on be referred to in all correspondence relating to the application);
   (b) that an application has been made;
   (c) of the date, time and place of the hearing;
   (d) that they are being afforded the opportunity—
      (i) of making representations at the hearing (whether orally or in writing); and
      (ii) of leading, or producing, evidence.

(6) If the hospital managers wish to make representations (whether orally or in writing) or lead or produce evidence, they shall send a notice of response to the Tribunal as soon as reasonably practicable or within such other period specified in that notice.

(7) The Clerk shall send a copy of the notice of response to each party.

19 Notice of response under Part II

A notice of response by any of the persons who are given notice under this Part shall be made in writing and shall state—

(a) the name and address of the person;

(b) the case reference number;

(c) whether the person wishes to make representations, either orally or in writing; and

(d) whether the person wishes to lead, or produce, evidence.

20 Withdrawal of application

(1) Where an application is made to the Tribunal under section 50, 63, 99, 100, 120, 163, 164, 192 or 214 of the Act, an applicant may withdraw that application—

(a) at any time before the hearing of the application by sending to the Clerk a notice signed by the applicant; or

(b) at the hearing on the application.

(2) On receipt of any such notice, the Clerk shall send a copy to the relevant persons.

(3) Where an applicant gives notice under paragraph (1), the Tribunal may terminate the proceedings without making any order.

21 Amendment of application or notice of response

(1) A relevant person may, at any time before notification of the date of the hearing of the application, amend the application or the notice of response by sending notice of any amendment to the Clerk.

(2) A relevant person may amend the application or the notice of response with the permission of the Tribunal at any time after receiving notification of the date of the hearing or, with the permission of the Convener, at the hearing itself.

(3) On receipt of any amendment, the Clerk shall send a copy to the parties.

PART III

APPEALS TO THE TRIBUNAL

22 Scope of this Part

This Part applies to appeals to the Tribunal under, or by virtue of, the following sections of the Act:—

(a) 125(2) (appeal where patient subject to compulsory treatment order against transfer to hospital other than state hospital);

(b) 126(2) (appeal where patient subject to compulsory treatment order against transfer to state hospital);

(c) 178 (appeal where patient subject to compulsion order against transfers to state hospital or hospital other than state hospital);

(d) 201(1) (appeal against variations of conditions imposed on conditional discharge);

(e) 204(1) (appeal against recall from conditional discharge);

(f) 219(2) (appeal against transfer to hospital other than state hospital);

(g) 220(2) (appeal against transfer to state hospital); and

(h) 290(1) (appeal by patient under regulations against proposed removal from Scotland).

23 Initiating appeals to the Tribunal

(1) An appeal to the Tribunal shall be made in writing and shall state—

(a) the name and address of the appellant;

(b) the name and address of the patient;

(c) the name and address of the patient's named person;

(d) where the patient is detained, the name and address of the hospital where the patient is detained;

(e) where the patient is required to reside at a specified place, the address of that specified place;

(f) the matter which is being appealed;

(g) a brief statement setting out the reasons for the appeal.

(2) The appellant shall sign the appeal.

24 Notice of the appeal

(1) The Clerk shall send a copy of the appeal to—

(a) the patient;

    (b) the patient's named person; and

    (c) the respondent.

(2) The Clerk shall send a notice of the appeal to the respondent.

(3) The notice shall inform the respondent—

    (a) of the case number of the appeal (which must from then on be referred to in all correspondence relating to the appeal);

    (b) of the date, time and place of the hearing; and

    (c) that if the respondent wishes to make representations or lead or produce evidence, the respondent should send a notice of response to the Tribunal within the period specified in the notice.

25 Notice of response under Part III

(1) If the respondent wishes to make representations (whether orally or in writing) or lead or produce evidence, the respondent shall send a notice of response to the Tribunal within 21 days of receipt of the notice by the respondent under rule 24 or within such other period specified in that notice.

(2) The notice of response shall state—

    (a) the name and address of the respondent;

    (b) the case reference number;

    (c) whether the respondent wishes to make representations, either orally or in writing;

    (d) whether the respondent wishes to lead, or produce, evidence;

    (e) whether the respondent intends to oppose the appeal and the basis of the opposition.

(3) The Clerk shall send a copy of the notice of response to parties.

26 Withdrawal of appeal

(1) An appellant may withdraw their appeal—

    (a) at any time before the hearing of the appeal by sending to the Clerk a notice signed by the appellant; or

    (b) at the hearing of the appeal.

(2) On receipt of any such notice, the Clerk shall send a copy to the respondent.

(3) No further appeal may be brought by the appellant in relation to the decision which was the subject of the appeal withdrawn.

27 Withdrawal of opposition

(1) The respondent may withdraw their opposition to the appeal—
   (a) at any time before the hearing of the appeal by sending to the Clerk a notice signed by the respondent; or
   (b) at the hearing on the appeal.

(2) On receipt of any such notice, the Clerk shall send a copy to the appellant.

28 Amendment of appeal or notice of response

(1) A party may, at any time before notification of the date of the hearing of the appeal, amend the appeal or the notice of response by sending a notice of any amendment to the Clerk.

(2) A party may amend the appeal or the notice of response with the permission of the Tribunal at any time after receiving notification of the date of the hearing or with the permission of the Convener at the hearing itself.

(3) On receipt of any amendment, the Clerk shall send a copy to any other party.

PART IV

REFERENCES TO THE TRIBUNAL

29 Scope of this Part

This Part applies to references to the Tribunal under the following sections of the Act—

(a) 96(3) (reference on recorded matters by responsible medical officer);

(b) 98(2) (reference by Commission where patient subject to compulsory treatment order);

(c) 162(2) (reference by Commission where patient subject to compulsion order);

(d) 185(1) (reference by Scottish Ministers where patient subject to compulsion order and restriction order);

(e) 187(2) (reference by Scottish Ministers required by Commission where patient subject to a compulsion order and a restriction order);

(f) 189(2) (reference by Scottish Ministers where no reference made for two years and patient subject to compulsion order and a restriction order);

(g) 210(3) (reference by Scottish Ministers following report by responsible medical officer);

(h) 211(2) (reference by Scottish Ministers required by Commission where patient subject to a hospital direction or transfer for treatment direction);

(i) 213(2) (reference by Scottish Ministers where no reference has been made for two years where patient subject to a hospital direction or a transfer for treatment direction); and

(j) 290(1) (reference by Commission under regulations against proposed removal of a patient from Scotland).

30 Notice of reference

(1) The Clerk shall send notice of the reference—

    (a) under section 96(3), 98(2), 162(2) or under regulations under section 290(1) of the Act, as the case may be, to—

        (i) the patient;

        (ii) the patient's named person;

        (iii) any guardian of the patient;

        (iv) any welfare attorney of the patient;

        (v) the mental health officer;

        (vi) the patient's responsible medical officer;

        (vii) the patient's primary carer;

        (viii) any curator *ad litem* appointed in respect of the patient by the Tribunal; and

        (ix) any other person appearing to the Tribunal to have an interest in the reference.

    (b) under section 185(1), 187(2), 189(2), 210(3), 211(2) or 213(2) of the Act, as the case may be, to—

        (i) the patient;

        (ii) the patient's named person;

        (iii) the patient's primary carer;

        (iv) any guardian of the patient;

        (v) any welfare attorney of the patient;

        (vi) any curator *ad litem* appointed by the Tribunal in respect of the patient;

        (vii) the Scottish Ministers;

        (viii) the patient's responsible medical officer;

        (ix) the mental health officer; and

        (x) any other person appearing to the Tribunal to have an interest.

(2) The notice shall inform the persons—

    (a) of the case number of the reference (which must from then on be referred to in all correspondence relating to the reference);

    (b) that they are being afforded the opportunity—

        (i) of making representations (whether orally or in writing); and

        (ii) of leading, or producing evidence; and

    (c) of the date, time and place of the hearing.

31 Notice of response

(1) If any person mentioned in rule 30 wishes to make representations (whether orally or in writing) or lead or produce evidence, that person shall send a notice of response to the Tribunal within 21 days of receipt of the notice under that rule or within such other period specified in that notice.

(2) The notice of response shall state—

    (a) the name and address of the person making the response;

    (b) the case reference number;

    (c) whether the person wishes to make representations, either orally or in writing;

    (d) whether the person wishes to lead, or produce, evidence; and

    (e) a statement of the facts and contentions on which the person intends to rely.

(3) The Clerk shall send a copy of each notice of response to each party.

32 Withdrawal of notice of response

(1) A person who has sent a notice of response under rule 31 may withdraw the notice of response—

    (a) at any time before the hearing by sending to the Clerk a notice signed by the person; or

    (b) at the hearing.

(2) On receipt of any such notice, the Clerk shall send a copy of that notice to each party.

33 Amendment of reference or notice of response

(1) A referee or a person who has sent a notice of response under rule 31, as the case may be, may at any time before notification

of the date of the hearing, amend the reference or notice of response by sending notice of any amendment to the Clerk.

(2) A referee or such a person may amend the reference or notice of response with the permission of the Tribunal at any time after receiving notification of the date of the hearing or with the permission of the Convener at the hearing itself.

(3) On receipt of any amendment, the Clerk shall send a copy to each party.

Part V

REVIEWS

34 Scope of this Part

This Part applies to reviews by the Tribunal under section 101(2) (review of determination extending compulsory treatment order under section 86 of the Act) and 165(2) (review of determination by responsible medical officer extending compulsion order under section 152 of the Act) of the Act.

35 Notice of review

(1) Where the Tribunal intend to review a determination under section 101(2) or 165(2) of the Act, the Clerk shall send notice of review to the following persons:—
  (a) the patient;
  (b) the patient's named person;
  (c) any guardian of the patient;
  (d) any welfare attorney of the patient;
  (e) the mental health officer;
  (f) the patient's responsible medical officer;
  (g) the patient's primary carer;
  (h) any curator *ad litem* appointed in respect of the patient by the Tribunal; and
  (i) any other person appearing to the Tribunal to have an interest in the determination.

(2) The notice shall inform the persons—
  (a) of the case number of the review (which must from then on be referred to in all correspondence relating to the review);
  (b) that a review is to be made by the Tribunal and of the reason for the review;
  (c) of the date, time and place of the hearing; and

   (d) that they are being afforded the opportunity—
      (i) of making representations (whether orally or in writing); and
      (ii) of leading, or producing, evidence.

36 Notice of response

(1) If any person mentioned in rule 35(1) wishes to make representations (whether orally or in writing) or lead or produce evidence, that person shall send a notice of response to the Tribunal within 21 days of receipt of the notice under that rule or within such other period specified in that notice.

(2) The notice of response shall state—
   (a) the name and address of the person making the response;
   (b) the case reference number;
   (c) whether the person wishes to make representations, either orally or in writing;
   (d) whether the person wishes to lead, or produce, evidence;
   (e) a statement of the facts and contentions on which the person intends to rely.

(3) The Clerk shall send a copy of each notice of response to each party.

37 Withdrawal of notice of response

(1) A person who has sent a notice of response under rule 36 may withdraw their notice of response—
   (a) at any time before the hearing by sending to the Clerk a notice signed by the person; or
   (b) at the hearing.

(2) On receipt of any such notice, the Clerk shall send a copy to each party.

38 Amendment of notice of response

(1) A person who has sent a notice of response under rule 36 may, at any time before notification of the date of the hearing, amend the notice of response by sending notice of any amendment to the Clerk.

(2) Such a person may amend the notice of response with the permission of the Tribunal at any time after receiving notification of the date of the hearing or with the permission of the Convener at the hearing itself.

(3) On receipt of any amendment, the Clerk shall send a copy to each party.

PART VI

CASES REMITTED TO THE TRIBUNAL

39 Scope of this Part

This Part applies to cases remitted to the Tribunal by the court under section 324(5)(b)(ii) of the Act.

40 Application of these Rules

(1) Subject to any directions made by the court under section 324(6) of the Act and by the Tribunal under paragraph (2), these Rules shall apply to cases remitted to the Tribunal as they do to cases before the Tribunal.

(2) After the case is remitted, the Tribunal shall consider and determine which of these Rules shall apply to that case and issue such directions as it thinks fit.

PART VII

GENERAL RULES

41 Scope of this Part

(1) This Part applies generally to cases before the Tribunal.

(2) The cases referred to in paragraph (1) include an application, reference, appeal or review before the Tribunal, and to any case referred to in Part VI, as the Tribunal may determine.

42 Disqualification

(1) A person shall be disqualified from serving as a member of a tribunal in any case if that person—

(a) is employed by or contracted to provide services in or to the hospital or independent health care service in which the patient is or may be detained;

(b) is directly involved in providing medical treatment, community care services, relevant services or any other treatment, care or service to that patient; or

(c) has a personal or professional connection with the patient.

(2)[7] For the purposes of paragraph (i)(a), unless a person works wholly or mainly in a hospital or independent health care service, that person shall not be regarded as being employed by or contracted to provide services in or to that hospital or independent health care service.

43 Interim or preliminary matters

(1) The Tribunal may, either on the written request of a relevant person or on its own initiative, consider and determine any interim or preliminary matter in relation to the case including any matter for which specific provision is made in this Part.

(2) Any matter referred to in paragraph (1) may be considered by the Convener alone or with such other members as the Tribunal may direct.

(3) Before determining such a matter, the Tribunal or the Convener, as the case may be, may—

(a) send notice to any of the relevant persons inviting them to make written representations within such period as may be specified; or

(b) summon any of the relevant persons to appear before the Tribunal or Convener for a preliminary hearing and may give any necessary directions relating to their appearance.

44 Misconceived case

(1) A case before the Tribunal is misconceived if it is—

(a) outwith the jurisdiction of the Tribunal;

(b) made otherwise than in accordance with these Rules and has no reasonable prospect of success; or

(c) frivolous or vexatious.

(2) Where a case appears to the Clerk to be misconceived, the Clerk shall refer the case to a Convener.

(3) The Convener may decide whether the case is misconceived either alone or with such other members as the Tribunal may direct.

---

[7] Inserted by Mental Health Tribunal for Scotland (Practice and Procedure) (No 2) Amendment Rules 2008 (SSI 2008/396), r 2(2).

(4) Before dismissing a case as misconceived, the Convener may—

(a) send notice of the proposed dismissal to the relevant persons inviting them to make written representations within 28 days or such other period as may be specified by the Convener;

(b) afford the relevant persons an opportunity to be heard.

(5) The Convener may where appropriate, on dismissing a misconceived application refer the matter to the Commission.

(6) Rule 72 shall apply to a decision made under this rule.

45 Lodging of documents etc.

(1) Except as otherwise provided in these Rules or as specified by the Tribunal in a particular case, a relevant person shall send to the Tribunal seven days prior to any hearing—

(a) a list of documents and the documents that the relevant person wishes to lead as evidence;

(b) a list of witnesses whom the relevant person wishes to call; and

(c) any written representations the relevant person wishes to make.

(2) Where a relevant person seeks to rely upon documents not produced in accordance with paragraph (1), the Tribunal may allow the documents to be lodged late where good reason is given.

(3) In determining whether to allow documents to be lodged late, the Tribunal shall have regard to whether to do so is fair in all the circumstances.

46[8] Distribution of documents

(1) Except as otherwise provided for in these Rules, the Clerk shall as soon as reasonably practicable send a copy of any document received in relation to the proceedings to the parties.

(2) At the request of any relevant person, or on its own initiative, the Tribunal or a Convener may determine whether a document should also be sent to any other person.

---

[8] As substituted by Mental Health Tribunal for Scotland (Practice and Procedure) (No 2) Amendment Rules 2008 (SSI 2008/396), r 2(3).

46A[9] Requests to the Tribunal for non-disclosure of documents

(1) A request for non-disclosure of any document or part of it in connection with proceedings before the Tribunal shall be made in writing by the person sending the document when that document is sent to the Tribunal, indicating the words and passages for which non-disclosure is claimed and giving reasons in each instance.

(2) If so directed by the Convener or the Tribunal, the person making the request under paragraph (1) shall, where practicable, supply a disclosable version of the relevant document.

(3) On receipt of a request under paragraph (1), the Convener or the Tribunal shall determine whether the request shall be intimated to any person and the Clerk shall intimate the request to such a person inviting that person—

   (a) to make written representations within such period as may be specified; or

   (b) to make representations at a hearing on such date as specified in the notice.

(4) On considering the request and accompanying reasons, and after taking into account any representations received in response to any intimation of that request under paragraph (3), the Convener or Tribunal may—

   (a) where the Convener or Tribunal is satisfied that all or any part of the document should not be disclosed, direct that the document or any part of the document should not be disclosed;

   (b) where a disclosable version has been provided under paragraph (2), direct that the version will be disclosed in place of the relevant document; or

   (c) reject the request.

(5) The Tribunal shall notify the person who made the request under paragraph (1) and any person to whom the request was intimated under paragraph (3) and who made representations that such a decision has been made and the reasons for that decision.

47[10] Withholding documents or reports from disclosure at initiative of the Tribunal in exceptional circumstances

---

[9] As substituted by Mental Health Tribunal for Scotland (Practice and Procedure) (No 2) Amendment Rules 2008 (SSI 2008/396), r 2(3).
[10] Ibid.

(1) This rule applies to documents or reports received by the Tribunal where the Convener or the Tribunal is concerned that disclosure of all or any part of the contents of a document or report—

    (a) may cause serious harm to the patient or any other person such that it would be wrong to disclose it to the patient or another person; but

    (b) that in all the circumstances it would nevertheless not be unfair if the document or report or that part of it is considered by the Tribunal.

(2) The Convener or the Tribunal may appoint a person having appropriate skills or experience to—

    (a) assess whether disclosure of the document or report to a patient or another person may cause serious harm; and

    (b) report to the Convener or the Tribunal, as the case may be, on the matter.

(3) The Tribunal shall pay to an expert appointed under paragraph (2) such an amount in respect of necessary expenses incurred in preparing and producing any report, as the President shall direct.

(4) If the Convener or the Tribunal is satisfied, taking into account the report of any expert appointed under paragraph (1), the Convener or the Tribunal, as the case may be, shall determine whether the document, report or any part of it, is not to be disclosed and may direct that—

    (a) the document or report may be considered by the Tribunal; and

    (b) all or any part of its contents must not be disclosed to such persons as specified by the Convener or the Tribunal.

(5) The Tribunal shall notify the representative of the patient or other person to whom the document, report or any part of it is not to be disclosed, that such a decision has been made, and the reasons for that decision.

(6) Where a decision is made under this rule not to disclose a document, report or any part of it to a patient and the patient does not have a representative to represent their interests, a curator *ad litem* may be appointed under rule 55(1).

48 Additional parties and relevant persons

(1) Any person who has an interest in the case may send to the Tribunal a written request for leave to enter the proceedings stating—

(a) the person's name and address;

(b) the nature of the person's interest and the person's reasons for the request.

(2) The Tribunal may refer the request to a Convener to decide or decide the matter itself at a hearing.

(3) On receipt of a request under paragraph (1), the Clerk shall send a copy to the parties inviting them to make written representations within such period as may be specified by the Convener.

(4) At the request of any party in writing within that period, the Tribunal may afford the parties an opportunity to be heard either by the Convener alone or with such other members as the Tribunal may direct.

(5) The Tribunal or the Convener, as the case may be, shall consider any representations made, and if satisfied that the person has an interest in the case, and that it is reasonable to do so, may grant the request and direct that the person shall be treated as a party or as a relevant person and the request treated as their notice of response.

(6) On granting a request under paragraph (5), the Tribunal or the Convener, as the case may be, shall consider whether any decision already taken in the case requires to be reconsidered in the light of the person's notice of response.

49 Directions

(1) Except as otherwise provided for in these Rules, the Tribunal may at any time, either on the request of a relevant person or on its own initiative, give such directions as the Tribunal considers necessary or desirable to further the overriding objective in the conduct of a case and may in particular—

(a) direct a relevant person to provide any further particulars or to produce any documents which may reasonably be required;

(b) direct that a relevant person shall supply a list of documents and a list of witnesses whom that relevant person wishes to call to give evidence at the hearing;

(c) give directions as to the dates by which any documents or other evidence on which any relevant person wishes to rely shall be sent to the Tribunal;

(d) give a direction as to the date by which a relevant person shall send any written representations on the case to the Tribunal;

(e) direct that the parties or the relevant persons should provide a statement of agreed facts;

(f) give directions restricting the reporting, recording, photography or filming of any hearing;

(g) give directions as to—

(i) any issues on which the Tribunal requires evidence;

(ii) the nature of the evidence which the Tribunal requires to decide those issues;

(iii) the way in which the evidence is to be led before the Tribunal; and

(iv) the exclusion of any evidence which is irrelevant, unnecessary or improperly obtained.

(2) Where a request is made by a relevant person for a direction under paragraph (1), it shall be made in writing specifying the direction sought and the basis for the request.

(3) On receipt of such a request, the Clerk shall intimate the request to the relevant persons inviting them to make written representations within 14 days or such other period as the Tribunal may specify.

(4) The requirement in the foregoing paragraph to intimate a request to the relevant persons does not require intimation to the person who made the request.

(5) Where a party objects to the request, the Tribunal shall consider the objection and, if the Tribunal considers it necessary in order to decide the request, may afford the relevant persons an opportunity to be heard either by the Convener alone or with such other members as the Tribunal may direct.

(6) The Tribunal shall, in deciding whether to make a direction, consider any representations made.

(7) A direction under this rule may, if appropriate, include a statement of the possible consequences of failure to comply mentioned in rule 51.

(8) A direction made without prior intimation to a relevant person whom it affects shall as soon as reasonably practicable be notified in writing to that relevant person by the Tribunal.

50 Varying or setting aside of directions

(1) Where a direction that affects a person is given by the Tribunal without prior intimation to that person, that person may request that the Tribunal to vary it or set it aside, but the Tribunal must not do so without first intimating the request to the relevant persons and considering any representations made by them.

(2) The requirement in paragraph (1) to intimate a request to the relevant persons does not require intimation to the person who made the request.

51 Failure to comply with directions

(1) If any direction given to a relevant person under rule 49 is not complied with by that relevant person, the Tribunal may, before or at the hearing, direct that the relevant person concerned take no further part in proceedings.

(2) The Tribunal shall not exercise its powers under paragraph (1) unless it has given the relevant person concerned an opportunity to show cause why the Tribunal should not proceed to give such a direction.

52 Other case management powers

(1) Subject to the provisions of the Act and these Rules, the Tribunal may regulate its own procedure.

(2) The Tribunal may in any proceedings—

(a) on the request of any relevant person or on its own initiative, extend the time appointed by these Rules for doing any act even if the time appointed has expired if—

(i) it would not be reasonable to expect the relevant person concerned to comply or, as the case may be, to have complied with the time limit; or

(ii) not to extend the time limit would be contrary to the interests of the patient;

(b) require a relevant person (other than the patient) or a relevant person's representative or the patient's named person to attend a hearing; and

(c) hold a hearing and receive evidence by telephone, through video link or by using any other method of communication if the Tribunal is satisfied that this would be fair in all the circumstances.

(3) Except where a rule or other enactment provides otherwise, the Tribunal may exercise its powers on the request of any relevant person or on its own initiative.

(4) Where the Tribunal proposes to exercise a power on its own initiative—

(a) it may give any person likely to be affected an opportunity to make representations;

(b) where it does so it must specify the period within which and the manner in which any representations must be made; and

(c) it shall take any representations into account, when deciding whether to proceed to do so.

(5) Where there are two or more sets of proceedings pending before the Tribunal which relate to the patient, the Tribunal may, on the request of a relevant person or on its own initiative—

(a) suspend the whole or part of any proceedings or decision either generally or until a specified date or event;

(b) hear and determine the proceedings concurrently, and give any directions necessary to enable it to do so.

(6) The Tribunal may, on the request of a relevant person or on its own initiative, on cause shown, suspend the whole or part of any proceedings or decision either generally or until a specified date.

53 Assistance to persons with communication difficulties

(1) This rule applies where—

(a) a person taking part in proceedings before the Tribunal has difficulty in communicating or generally communicates in a language other than English; and

(b) assistance is not required to be given under section 261 of the Act.

(2) Where a person requires assistance to enable that person to take part in proceedings before the Tribunal, that person shall at the earliest opportunity notify the Tribunal of that requirement.

(3) Where a relevant person becomes aware that a person requires assistance to enable that person to take part in proceedings before the Tribunal, the relevant person shall at the earliest opportunity notify the Tribunal of that requirement.

(4) Where this rule applies, the Tribunal shall take all reasonable steps to secure that arrangements appropriate to the person's needs are made.

54 Representation

(1) A relevant person who initiates proceedings before the Tribunal or who wishes to take part in such proceedings shall as soon as practicable give notice to the Tribunal of the name and address of any representative appointed by the relevant person and if

none has as yet been appointed, whether the relevant person intends to appoint a representative or to conduct the case without such assistance.

(2) If at any time a relevant person wishes to be represented by a person other than a representative whose details have been notified to the Tribunal, the relevant person shall notify the Tribunal of the name and address of that person.

(3) At any hearing a relevant person may conduct the relevant person's own case (with assistance from any person if the relevant person wishes) or may be represented by any person whether or not legally qualified.

(4) If the Tribunal is satisfied that there is a good reason, it may refuse to permit a particular person to assist or represent a relevant person at a hearing.

(5) References in these Rules (however expressed) to the sending of any notice or other documents to a relevant person shall be construed as references to the sending of any notice or other documents to the relevant person's representative.

55 Curator *ad litem*

(1) Where the circumstances in paragraph (2) apply, a curator *ad litem* may be appointed by the Tribunal or a Convener.

(2) Those circumstances are—

(a) that the patient does not have the capacity to instruct a solicitor to represent the patient's interests in proceedings before the Tribunal;

(b) that where the Tribunal or a Convener has made a decision not to disclose a document or report or part of it to the patient under rule 47, and the patient does not have a representative to represent their interests; or

(c) that the patient has been excluded from any hearing or part of it under rule 68 or 69 and the patient does not have a representative to represent their interests.

(3) The Tribunal or the Convener, as the case may be, may appoint a person having appropriate skills or experience to—

(a) assess whether the circumstances in paragraph (2)(a) may apply; and

(b) provide a report on the matter.

(4) The Tribunal shall pay to an expert appointed under paragraph (3) such an amount in respect of necessary expenses incurred

in preparing and producing any report, as the President shall direct.

(5) The Tribunal shall provide all necessary information to a curator *ad litem* appointed to enable the curator *ad litem* to represent the patient's interests in proceedings before the Tribunal.

56 Notices

(1) Where these Rules require notice of proceedings before the Tribunal to be served upon a person who initiated those proceedings, such a notice shall not require to be served, but in such a case a notice of hearing shall be sent intimating the date, time and place of the hearing and giving such directions as the Tribunal shall consider appropriate in the circumstances.

(2) Where a person has notified the Tribunal in writing that that person does not wish to receive any notices or documents from the Tribunal in relation to proceedings before it specified in the notification, these Rules do not require any such notices or documents to be sent to that person.

(3) Except where the relevant persons have already been notified of the date of the hearing under notice provided under Parts II to V of these Rules, the Clerk shall send to each relevant person, not less than 7 days before the date fixed (or such shorter period as the Tribunal or the Convener may decide is appropriate) notice of hearing intimating the date, time and place of the hearing and giving such directions as the Tribunal shall consider appropriate in the circumstances.

(4) The Clerk shall include with a notice of hearing, information and guidance in a form approved by the President, as to—

(a) the right of a relevant person to make representations in writing;

(b) the attendance at the hearing of the relevant persons and witnesses, including a statement explaining the consequences of non-attendance;

(c) the sending of documents;

(d) the right of representation or assistance by another person;

(e) the need to notify the Clerk if a relevant person or a witness requires assistance as referred to in rule 53;

(f) the right of the parties to receive a copy of a decision of the Tribunal;

(g) the availability of general procedural advice in relation to proceedings from the Office of the Mental Health Tribunal for Scotland; and

(h) the availability of other sources of advice.

57 Alteration of hearing

(1) The Tribunal may, on receipt of a written request from a relevant person, or on its own initiative, alter the date, time or place of any hearing and shall give the relevant persons as much notice as is reasonably practicable of any such alteration.

(2) The Tribunal shall not, without good cause, alter any date under paragraph (1) to a date before the date originally fixed.

58 Power to decide case without a hearing

(1) Except as otherwise provided for in the Act, this rule applies where—

(a) the relevant persons agree in writing;

(b) the Tribunal considers that having regard to the nature of the issues raised in the case, sufficient evidence is available to enable it come to a decision; and

(c) to do so will not, in the view of the Tribunal, be contrary to the interests of the patient.

(2) Subject to paragraph (3), the Tribunal may decide the case without a hearing.

(3) Before making a decision under paragraph (2), the Tribunal must consider any representations in writing submitted by relevant persons.

Evidence

59 Production of documents etc.

(1) Subject to the provisions of the Act and paragraph (2) of this rule, the Tribunal may on the request of any relevant person or on its own initiative send a citation to any person requiring that person to attend and produce any document in the custody, or under the control of, such person which the Tribunal considers it necessary to examine.

(2) The citation must explain that—

(a) it is an offence under paragraph 12(3) of Schedule 2 to the Act for a person who is cited to attend the Tribunal—

    (i) to refuse or fail to attend; and

    (ii) to alter, conceal or destroy or refuse to produce, a document which such person is required to produce for the purposes of the proceedings before the Tribunal;

(b) a person need not produce any document if, were it a document that might be produced in any court in Scotland, the person having that document could not be compelled to produce it in such proceedings;

(c) it is a defence under paragraph 12(5) of Schedule 2 to the Act for a person charged with contravening paragraph 12(3) to show that the person has a reasonable excuse for such contravention.

(3) No person shall be required to attend and produce a document in compliance with a citation unless the necessary expenses of that person's attendance are paid or tendered to them by the relevant person who requested their attendance or by the Tribunal, as the President shall direct.

(4) A person receiving a citation under this rule may apply in writing to the Tribunal for the citation to be varied or set aside and the Convener may vary or set aside the citation as they see fit.

(5) The Clerk shall send a copy of the decision under paragraph (4) to the person making the application under that paragraph and the relevant persons.

(6) It shall be a condition of the production of any document under this rule that a relevant person must use the document provided only for the purposes of the proceedings.

(7) In giving effect to this rule, the Tribunal shall take into account—

(a) the need to protect any matter that relates to intimate personal or financial circumstances or was communicated or obtained in confidence; and

(b) any request for non-disclosure made under rule 46A(1).[11]

60 Evidence of witnesses — general rule

Evidence before the Tribunal may be given orally or by signed statement but the Tribunal may at any stage of the proceedings

---

[11] As amended by Mental Health Tribunal for Scotland (Practice and Procedure) (No 2) Amendment Rules 2008 (SSI 2008/396), r 2(4).

require the personal attendance of any witness to give oral evidence.

61 Attendance of witnesses

(1) Subject to the provisions of the Act, the Tribunal may on the written request of any relevant person or on its own initiative send a citation to a person requiring that that person attends as a witness.

(2) A request by a relevant person under paragraph (1) shall give the name and address of each person in respect of whom the request is made.

(3) The citation must explain that—

    (a) it is an offence under paragraph 12 of Schedule 2 to the Act to refuse or fail, without reasonable excuse, to comply with it;

    (b) a person need not give evidence as a witness if the person could not be compelled to give that evidence in proceedings in any court in Scotland.

(4) No person shall be required to attend as a witness in compliance with a citation unless—

    (a) that person has been given 5 working days' notice of the hearing or such other period of notice, which must be at least 48 hours' notice, as shall be specified in the citation; and

    (b) the necessary expenses of that person's attendance are paid or tendered to them by the relevant person who requested their attendance or by the Tribunal, as the President shall direct.

62 Experts' reports

(1) The Tribunal may, if any issue arises in relation to any proceedings on which, in the opinion of the Tribunal, it would be desirable for the Tribunal to have the assistance of an expert, appoint a person having appropriate qualifications to inquire into and report on any matter.

(2) Subject to rule 47, the Tribunal shall supply the parties with a copy of any written report received under paragraph (1) in advance of the hearing.

(3) The Tribunal may direct that the expert shall attend the hearing and give oral evidence.

(4) The Tribunal shall pay to an expert appointed under this rule such an amount in respect of necessary expenses incurred in

preparing and producing any written report, and for attendance at the hearing as the President shall direct.

(5) Subject to the following paragraphs, where any relevant person obtains in relation to an issue before the Tribunal a written report from a person having expertise in any subject relevant to that issue, that relevant person shall send a copy of the report to the Tribunal 7 days prior to the next hearing of the Tribunal or at such period prior to the next hearing of the Tribunal as specified by the Tribunal in a particular case.

(6) A relevant person may send a request to the Tribunal for permission not to send a report to the Tribunal under paragraph (5), giving reasons for the request and, pending consideration of that request, the copy report need not be produced

(7) The Tribunal may afford the relevant person making the request an opportunity to be heard either by the Convener alone or with such other members as the Tribunal may direct.

(8) The Tribunal shall, in deciding the request, consider any representations made, and may either—

  (a) give permission to the relevant person not to send part or all of the report in question; or

  (b) order that part or all of the report be sent to the Tribunal within such time as the Tribunal may specify.

The hearing

63 Procedure

(1) At the beginning of any hearing the Convener shall explain the manner and order of proceedings and the procedure which the Tribunal proposes to adopt.

(2) The Tribunal may, in accordance with the overriding objective, conduct the hearing—

  (a) as informally as the circumstances of the case permit; and

  (b) in the manner the Tribunal considers—

    (i) to be just; and

    (ii) most suitable to the clarification and determination of the matters before the Tribunal.

(3) The relevant persons shall be entitled to make representations and to lead or produce evidence.

(4) At any hearing the Tribunal may, if satisfied that it is just and reasonable to do so, permit a relevant person to rely on matters

not stated in the application, reference, appeal, review, written representations or notice of response and to lead or produce any evidence not previously notified to the other relevant persons.

(5) Having considered the circumstances of the relevant persons and whether (and to what extent) they are represented, the Convener—

    (a) may, in order to assist resolution of any disputed fact, put questions to the relevant persons and to witnesses or may allow another member of the Tribunal to put such questions; and

    (b) shall, to the extent the Convener considers it necessary for the just conduct of the hearing, explain any legal terms or expressions which are used.

(6) The Tribunal may require any witness to give evidence on oath or affirmation.

(7) The Tribunal may exclude from the hearing any person who is to appear as a witness in the case until such time as they give evidence if it considers it is fair in all the circumstances to do so.

64 Absence of a member of the Tribunal

(1) Except as provided for otherwise in these Rules, a tribunal shall not decide any question unless all members are present and, if any member is absent, the case shall be adjourned or referred to another tribunal.

(2) If a member of a tribunal ceases to be a member of the Tribunal or is otherwise unable to act before that tribunal has commenced hearing the case, the President may allocate the hearing of that case to a differently constituted tribunal.

(3) If, after the commencement of any hearing, a member other than the Convener is absent, the case may, with the consent of the parties, be heard by the other two members and, in that event, the tribunal shall be deemed to be properly constituted.

65 Adjournment of the hearing

(1) The Tribunal may on the request of a relevant person or on its own initiative, adjourn a hearing in order that further information or evidence may be obtained or for such other purpose as it sees fit.

(2) Where a relevant person requests an adjournment under paragraph (1), the Tribunal shall consider any representations made by any other relevant person before deciding whether or not the hearing will be adjourned.

(3) When a hearing is adjourned under paragraph (1), the Tribunal may give directions under rule 49 regarding the future conduct of the case as it considers appropriate and may, in particular, require any relevant person to intimate to the Tribunal by a specified date any matter to be relied upon by that person at the further hearing.

(4) The Tribunal shall notify the relevant persons of the date for the resumed hearing except that if the date, time and place of the resumed hearing are announced before the adjournment, no further notice shall be required.

66 Hearings in public or private

(1) Subject to the provisions of this rule, hearings shall be held in private.

(2) Where a patient applies in writing for a hearing to be held in public, the Tribunal may make an order that a hearing be held in public.

(3) The Tribunal may refuse to make an order under paragraph (2) where any of the requirements of paragraph (4) is met.

(4) The requirements are that a public hearing—
   (a) would fail to safeguard the welfare of the patient or any other person;
   (b) would not, in all the circumstances, allow the fair hearing of the case; or
   (c) would prejudice the interests of justice.

(5) The Tribunal shall refuse to make an order under paragraph (2) only to the extent necessary to protect the interest which is being protected by the refusal and only in relation to those parts of a hearing in respect of which any of the requirements of paragraph (4) is satisfied.

(6) The following persons shall be entitled to attend a hearing, even although it may be held in private—
   (a) the President;
   (b) any member of the Tribunal, or a member of staff of the Tribunal, with the agreement of the Convener;

(c)[12] a member of the Administrative Justice and Tribunals Council or of its Scottish Committee; and

(d) an interpreter or other person giving other necessary assistance to a person entitled to attend the hearing.

(7) The Tribunal may exclude from any hearing or any part of a hearing, any person, other thana representative of the patient or a relevant person, where it is considering a document or report withheld from disclosure in accordance with rule 47, and in any case where the Tribunal decides to so exclude such a person, it shall inform the person excluded of its reasons and record those reasons in writing.

67 Publicity

(1) Where the Tribunal has made an order under rule 66, the Tribunal may on the request of a relevant person or on its own initiative make an order that any publicity to be given to the hearing should be limited, where the President or the Convener considers it appropriate bearing in mind—

(a) the need to safeguard the welfare of a patient or any other person;

(b) the need to protect the private life of any person;

(c) any representations on the matter which a relevant person has provided in writing; and

(d) the effect of any direction under rule 49.

(2) An order under paragraph (1) shall limit publicity only to the extent necessary to protect the interest which is being protected by the order.

(3) An order under paragraph (1) may allow publicity that does not identify the parties.

68 Excluding persons from hearings in exceptional circumstances

(1) Where the Convener or the Tribunal is satisfied that attendance of any person at the hearing or part of it may cause serious harm to the patient or any other person, the Convener or the Tribunal, as the case may be, may make a direction that such a person shall be excluded from the hearing or any part or it.

---

[12] As amended by Mental Health Tribunal for Scotland (Practice and Procedure) (No 2) Amendment Rules 2008 (SSI 2008/396), r 2(5).

(2) The Convener or the Tribunal, as the case may be, may appoint a person having appropriate skills or experience to—

(a) assess whether such attendance by the patient or another person may cause serious harm; and

(b) report on the matter.

(3) The Tribunal shall pay to an expert appointed under paragraph (2) such an amount in respect of necessary expenses incurred in preparing and producing any report, as the President shall direct.

(4) Where the Convener or the Tribunal is considering making a direction under this rule, the Clerk shall invite the relevant persons to make written representations both as to the necessity of the direction and as to the availability of alternative measures, within such period as may be specified by the Convener.

(5) At the request of any relevant person in writing within that period, the Tribunal may afford the relevant persons an opportunity to be heard either by the Convener alone or with such other members as the Tribunal may direct.

(6) If the patient is the person who may be the subject of a direction under this rule, and does not have legal representation, the Tribunal shall invite the patient to seek an adjournment of the Tribunal's consideration of the matter, in order to obtain legal representation and, if the patient does seek such an adjournment, shall grant it.

(7) A direction under paragraph (1) shall exclude the patient or other person only to the extent strictly necessary to prevent the harm apprehended by attendance and may be made only after taking into account any report under paragraph (2) and any representations made under paragraph (4) or (5).

(8) Where such a direction excluding the patient is made and the patient does not have a representative to represent their interests, a curator *ad litem* may be appointed under rule 55(1).

69 Exclusion of persons disrupting hearing

(1) Without prejudice to any other powers the Tribunal may have, the Tribunal may exclude from any hearing, or part of it—

(a) any person (including a relevant person or the relevant person's representative) whose conduct has disrupted, or is likely, in the opinion of the Tribunal, to disrupt the hearing;

(b) any person whose presence is likely, in the opinion of the Tribunal, to make it difficult for any relevant person to make representations or present evidence necessary for the proper conduct of the hearing; or

(c) any person whose conduct has otherwise interfered with the administration of justice or is likely to do so.

(2) In deciding whether to exercise the power conferred by paragraph (1) the Tribunal shall have regard to—

(a) the interests of the relevant persons; and

(b) in the case of the exclusion of a relevant person or relevant person's representative, whether the relevant person will be adequately represented.

(3) Before the Tribunal decides to exclude a relevant person, the Tribunal shall—

(a) allow the relevant person's representative sufficient opportunity to consult the relevant person;

(b) afford the relevant person concerned and any other relevant person as it thinks fit, an opportunity to be heard; and

(c) consider the availability of alternative measures which may enable the relevant person concerned to continue to participate in proceedings.

(4) Where the relevant person concerned is the patient, and that patient does not have a representative present to represent the patient's interests, the Tribunal may, before making a decision under paragraph (1), adjourn the hearing to allow—

(a) the patient to obtain representation; or

(b) a curator *ad litem* to be appointed under rule 55(1).

(5) The Tribunal may make such alternative arrangements as may be necessary to enable a person excluded to continue to participate in the proceedings, including allowing the proceedings to continue through video-link or other method of communication.

(6) Where the Tribunal decides to exclude a patient under this rule and the patient does not have a representative to represent their interests, a curator *ad litem* may be appointed under rule 55(1).

70 Failure of a relevant person to attend

(1) If a relevant person fails to be present or represented at a hearing, the Tribunal may, if satisfied that the relevant person was duly notified of the hearing and that there is no good reason for such absence, hear and decide the proceedings in that relevant

person's absence and may give such directions as the Tribunal thinks fit.

(2) Before deciding any case in the absence of a relevant person, the Tribunal shall consider any representations in writing submitted by that relevant person in response to the notice of hearing.

(3) Where the relevant person concerned is a party, the Tribunal shall afford that party an opportunity to be heard either by the Convener alone or with such other members as the Tribunal may direct to explain the absence and to advise whether the party wishes to proceed.

71 Inability to attend

(1) If the Convener is satisfied that any relevant person is unable, through illness, age, incapacity or other sufficient cause to attend the hearing, the Convener may make such arrangements as may appear best suited in all the circumstances of the case, for deciding the case fairly, and in particular may arrange—

   (a) for the relevant person to provide a signed statement, or evidence in such form as the Tribunal thinks fit;

   (b) for taking the evidence of expert or other witnesses on behalf of the relevant person;

   (c) for enabling the relevant person to make representations on the evidence; and

   (d) for the case to be decided in the absence of the relevant person.

(2) Arrangements under paragraph (1) may include arrangements to take evidence and hear representations by video-link.

72 Decision of the Tribunal

(1) A decision of the Tribunal may be given at the end of the hearing or reserved.

(2) The decision shall be signed by the Convener and dated.

(3) The Tribunal shall, as soon as reasonably practicable, send notice of the decision to the parties and such other relevant person as the Tribunal may direct.

(4) Information in such form as the President may approve, shall be sent with the notice referred to in paragraph (3), explaining any right of appeal against the Tribunal's decision under sections 320 and 322 of the Act, including any time limits which may apply.

(5)[13] Where a decision has been made by the Tribunal, whether at a hearing or otherwise, the Clerk shall, within 21 days of the date on which the decision is signed by the Convener, send a copy of the decision to the Commission and where the case was remitted to the Tribunal by a court, to that court.

(5A)[14] Paragraph 5B applies to decisions made by the Tribunal in relation to applications or references under sections 50(1), 63(1), 92, 95, 98(2), 99(1), 100(2), 120(2), 149, 158, 161, 162(2), 163(1), 164(2), 185(1), 187(2), 189(2), 191, 192(2), 210(3), 211(2), 213(2), 214(2), 255(4), (6) and (7), 256(1), 264(2), 267(2), 268(2), 271(2) and 291(2) of the Act but does not apply in relation to any such applications which are not granted by the Tribunal.

(5B)[15] Where a copy of a decision is sent to the Commission under paragraph (5) the Clerk shall at the same time send to the Commission a copy of:—

(a) the application or reference (as the case may be); and
(b) in the case of application, any mental health report that is required under the Act to accompany that application.

(6) Other than where a decision is made at the end of the hearing, a decision shall be treated as having been made on the date on which it is sent to the parties.

(7) The Tribunal shall record the decision in a document which contains a full statement of the facts found by the Tribunal and the reasons for the decision.

(8) Clerical mistakes or errors arising from an accidental slip or omission in the document referred to in paragraph (7), may at any time be corrected by the Convener by certificate in writing.

(9) If a document is corrected by certificate under paragraph (8), or if a decision is altered in any way by order of an appellate court, the Clerk shall send a notice to each of the parties and to the Commission advising of that change.

(10) Where this rule requires a document to be signed by the Convener, but the Convener is unable, by reason of death or

---

[13] As amended by Mental Health Tribunal for Scotland (Practice and Procedure) (No 2) Amendment Rules 2008 (SSI 2008/396), r 2(6).
[14] Added by *ibid*, r 2(7).
[15] *Ibid*.

incapacity to sign it, the document shall be signed by the other members of the tribunal, whom failing the President, who shall certify that the Convener is unable to sign.

73 Publication

(1) The President must make such arrangements as the President considers appropriate for the publication of Tribunal decisions.

(2) Decisions may be published electronically.

(3) A decision may be published in an edited form, or subject to any deletions, where the Convener considers it appropriate bearing in mind—

    (a) the need to safeguard the welfare of a patient or any other person;

    (b) the need to protect the private life of any person;

    (c) any representations on the matter which any relevant person has provided in writing.

(4) A decision of the Tribunal shall be published in such a manner as to protect the anonymity of the patient.

Miscellaneous

74 Performance of the Tribunal's functions

The President may authorise any member of the staff of the Tribunal to exercise such administrative functions under these Rules as the President shall specify.

75 Relief from failure to comply with the Rules

(1) Where before the Tribunal has decided a case, a relevant person has failed to comply with any provision of these Rules, which is shown to be due to mistake, oversight or other excusable cause, the Tribunal may—

    (a) relieve the relevant person from the consequences of that failure; and

    (b) give any direction as it thinks fit.

(2) In particular, where it considers that any relevant person may have been prejudiced by such failure, the Tribunal may take any necessary steps including the amendment of any document, the giving of any notice or otherwise, to enable the case to

proceed as if the failure to comply with the provision had not occurred.

76 Signature of documents

(1) Any requirement in these Rules for a document to be signed by a person shall be satisfied, in the case of a document which is transmitted by electronic communication in accordance with these Rules, by electronic signature of the person who is required to sign the document.

(2) Any requirement in these Rules for an application or appeal to be signed by an applicant or appellant shall be satisfied if signed by the legal representative of the applicant or appellant.

77 Proof of documents

Any document purporting to be a document duly executed or issued by the President, or Convener on behalf of the Tribunal shall, unless the contrary is proved, be deemed to be a document so executed or issued as the case may be. Method of delivering and receipt of notices and documents

78 Method of delivering and receipt of notices and documents

(1) Any notice or document required or authorised by these Rules to be sent to the Tribunal, may be sent to or presented at the Office of the Mental Health Tribunal for Scotland, or such other office as may be notified by the Tribunal.

(2) All notices and documents required by these Rules to be sent by the Tribunal or the Clerk or given to any person may—

    (a) in the case of a relevant person—

        (i) be sent by post or delivered (by courier or otherwise) to the address specified by that relevant person;

        (ii) transmitted by fax to a specified fax number, where the relevant person has agreed in writing that the relevant person will accept documents transmitted to that fax number; or

        (iii) transmitted by electronic communication to a specified address for such communications where the relevant person has agreed in writing that the relevant person will accept documents transmitted in that manner to that specified address,

    (b) in the case of any other person, to the person's last known address or in any manner specified for that purpose by the

Tribunal or person to whom the notice or document is directed.

(3) Any notice or document sent to a person in accordance with this rule shall, unless the contrary is proved, be deemed to be received—

    (a) where the document is sent by post, on the second day after the day on which it was sent; and

    (b) in any other case, on the day on which the document was transmitted or delivered to that person.

(4) A notice or document sent or given to the authorised representative of a relevant person shall be deemed to have been sent or given to that relevant person.

(5) A relevant person may at any time by notice to the Tribunal change the address to which notices and documents are to be sent to the relevant person.

79 Transfer of case

(1) Where a tribunal is satisfied, in relation to a case which it is hearing that that case could be better considered by a tribunal in another geographical area, it may request the President to arrange for such other tribunal to dispose of the case.

(2) Where the functions of the Tribunal are being discharged by more than one tribunal, the President shall determine by which tribunal any case is to be dealt with.

(3) Where this rule applies, the President shall transfer the case from one tribunal to another where necessary.

(4) Where a case has been transferred in terms of this rule, any matters already decided in the case shall not require to be further considered by the tribunal to which the case is transferred.

80 Transitional provision

(1) Where, before the date on which these Rules come into force, notice of an application for an interim compulsory treatment order has been sent under rule 7(3) of the rules revoked by rule 81 ("the old Rules"), but the period specified in accordance with rule 7(3)(f) of the old Rules expires on or after the date on which these rules come into force, then the provisions of rule 7(4) to (6) of the old Rules shall, notwithstanding rule 81, continue to apply in respect of that application.

(2) Where, before the date on which these Rules come into force, written representations have been invited by the Convener under

rule 47(4) of the old Rules, but a determination as to whether a document, report or any part of it, is not to be disclosed has not yet been made by the Tribunal or the Convener then the provisions of rule 47 of the old Rules shall, notwithstanding rule 81, continue to apply in respect of the determination of that question.

(3) Where before the date on which these Rules come into force a copy of a written request to alter the date of a hearing has been sent by the Clerk under rule 57(3) of the old Rules, but the Tribunal has not yet made a decision as to whether the date of the hearing will be altered, then the provisions of rule 57(4) of the old Rules shall, notwithstanding rule 81, continue to apply in respect of the decision of the question.

81 Revocation

The Mental Health Tribunal for Scotland (Practice and Procedure) Rules 2005 are revoked.

APPENDIX 3

REGULATIONS

MENTAL HEALTH (COMPULSORY TREATMENT ORDERS – DOCUMENTS AND REPORTS TO BE SUBMITTED TO THE TRIBUNAL) (SCOTLAND) REGULATIONS 2005
(SSI 2005/366)

Citation, commencement and interpretation

1.—(1) These Regulations may be cited as the Mental Health (Compulsory treatment orders – documents and reports to be submitted to the Tribunal) (Scotland) Regulations 2005 and shall come into force on 5th October 2005.

(2) In these Regulations, any reference to a numbered section is a reference to the section bearing that number in the Mental Health (Care and Treatment) (Scotland) Act 2003.

Documents to accompany application to Tribunal under sections 92, 95 and 96

2. The documents prescribed for the purpose of sections 92(b) (application to Tribunal for extension and variation of compulsory treatment order), 95(b) (application to Tribunal for variation of compulsory treatment order) and 96(4)(b) (reference to Tribunal because of non provision of a recorded matter) are–

(a) a copy of the patient's care plan as first prepared under section 76(1)(a)(preparation of a care plan); and

(b) a copy of any such care plan amended by virtue of section 76(3) or (4)(a).

Application for extension and variation of a compulsory treatment order: report to be prepared and submitted to Tribunal under section 109

3. Where the Tribunal is considering an application made under section 92 (application for an order extending and varying a compulsory treatment order), and is not satisfied that it has sufficient information to enable it to make a decision the Tribunal may require, under section 109(2) (power to require preparation and submission of reports), the mental health officer to prepare and submit to it a report–

(a) on the steps that the mental health officer has taken to comply with the requirements imposed by section 89(2) (mental health officer's duties to patient etc);

(b) giving the views of the mental health officer on the application and the reasons for those views;

(c) giving, if known to the mental health officer, the views of the patient and the patient's named person on the application and the reasons for those views;

(d) giving, in so far as the mental health officer considers relevant for the purposes of the application, details of the personal circumstances of the patient;

(e) giving, if known to the mental health officer, details of any advance statement that the patient has made (and not withdrawn); and

(f) giving any other information which the mental health officer considers may assist the Tribunal in considering the application.

Application for variation of a compulsory treatment order: reports to be prepared and submitted to Tribunal under section 109

4. Where the Tribunal is considering an application made under section 95 (application for an order varying a compulsory treatment order) and is not satisfied that it has sufficient information to enable it to make a decision, the Tribunal may require, under section 109(2), the mental health officer to prepare and submit to it a report–

(a) on the steps that the mental health officer has taken to comply with the requirements imposed by section 93(4C)) (mental health officer's duties to patient etc);

(b) giving the views of the mental health officer on the application and the reasons for those views;

(c) giving, if known to the mental health officer, the views of the patient and the patient's named person on the application and the reasons for those views;

(d) giving, in so far as the mental health officer considers relevant for the purposes of the application, details of the personal circumstances of the patient;

(e) giving, if known to the mental health officer, details of any advance statement that the patient has made (and not withdrawn); and

(f) giving any other information which the mental health officer considers may assist the Tribunal in considering the application.

Applications by the patient etc. for revocation of determination extending compulsory treatment order and revocation or variation of compulsory treatment order: reports to be prepared and submitted to Tribunal under section 109

5. Where the Tribunal is considering an application made under section 99(1) (application for revocation of determination extending compulsory treatment order) or section 100(2) (application for revocation or variation of compulsory treatment order), and is not satisfied that it has sufficient information to enable it to make a decision the Tribunal may require, under section 109(2)–

(a) the mental health officer to prepare and submit to it a report–

(i) giving the views of the mental health officer on the application and the reasons for those views;

(ii) giving, if known to the mental health officer, details of any advance statement that the patient has made (and not withdrawn); and

(iii) giving any other information which the mental health officer considers may assist the Tribunal in considering the application; and

(b) the patient's responsible medical officer to prepare and submit to it a report–

(i) giving the views of the responsible medical officer on the application and the reasons for those views; and

(ii) giving any other information which the responsible medical officer considers may assist the Tribunal in considering the application.

Review of determination extending compulsory treatment order: reports to be submitted to Tribunal under section 109

6.—(1) Where the Tribunal is, under section 101, reviewing a determination made by the patient's responsible medical officer under section 86 (determination extending compulsory treatment order) and is not satisfied that it has sufficient information to enable it to make a decision the Tribunal may require, under section 109(2)–

    (a) the mental health officer to prepare and submit to it a report–

        (i) on the steps that the mental health officer has taken in pursuance of the requirements imposed by section 85(2) (mental health officer's duties to patient etc.);

       (ii) giving the views of the mental health officer on the determination and the reasons for those views;

     (iii) giving, if known to the mental health officer, the views of the patient and the patient's named person on the determination and the reasons for those views;

     (iv) giving, in so far as the mental health officer considers relevant for the purposes of the review, details of the personal circumstances of the patient;

      (v) giving, if known to the mental health officer, details of any advance statement that the patient has made (and not withdrawn); and

     (vi) giving any other information which the mental health officer considers may assist the Tribunal in considering the determination; and

    (b) the patient's responsible medical officer to prepare and submit to it a report on the extent to which the objectives of any medical treatment, community care services, other relevant services, or any other treatment, care or service included in the patient's care plan are being met.

(2) In this regulation "care plan" means the patient's current care plan prepared under section 76(1), whether or not amended by virtue of subsections (3) or (4)(a) of that section.

Reference concerning non-provision of a recorded matter: report to be prepared and submitted to Tribunal under section 109

7. Where the Tribunal is considering a reference under section 96 (reference regarding the non-provision of a recorded matter) and is not satisfied that it has sufficient information to enable it to make a decision, the Tribunal may require, under section 109(2), the mental health officer to prepare and submit to it a report–

    (a) giving the views of the mental health officer on the non-provision of the recorded matter; and

    (b) giving any other information which the mental health officer considers may assist the Tribunal in considering the application.

Reference by Mental Welfare Commission for Scotland: reports to be prepared and submitted to Tribunal under section 109

8. Where the Tribunal is considering a reference made under section 98(2) (reference by Mental Welfare Commission for Scotland) and is not satisfied that it has sufficient information to enable it to make a decision, the Tribunal may require, under section 109(2)–

(a) the mental health officer to prepare and submit to it a report–

  (i) giving the views of the mental health officer on the reference and the reasons for those views;

  (ii) commenting on the relevancy to the Tribunal's consideration of any advance statement that the patient has made (and not withdrawn), if available to the mental health officer; and

  (iii) giving any other information which the mental health officer considers may assist the Tribunal in determining the reference; and

(b) the patient's responsible medical officer to prepare and submit to it a report–

  (i) giving the views of the responsible medical officer on the reference and the reasons for those views; and

  (ii) giving any other information which the responsible medical officer considers may assist the Tribunal in considering the reference.

MENTAL HEALTH (COMPULSION ORDERS – DOCUMENTS AND REPORTS TO BE SUBMITTED TO THE TRIBUNAL) (SCOTLAND) REGULATIONS 2005
(SSI 2005/365)

Citation, commencement and interpretation

1.—(1) These Regulations may be cited as the Mental Health (Compulsion orders – documents and reports to be submitted to the Tribunal) (Scotland) Regulations 2005 and shall come into force on 5th October 2005.

(2) In these regulations–

  (i) "the 1995 Act" means the Criminal Procedure (Scotland) Act 1995; and

(ii) unless the context otherwise requires, any reference to a numbered section is a reference to the section bearing that number in the Mental Health (Care and Treatment) (Scotland) Act 2003.

Documents to accompany application to Tribunal under section 149

2. The documents prescribed for the purpose of section 149(b) (documents to accompany application to Tribunal by responsible medical officer for extension of compulsion order) are–

(a) a copy of the patient's–
  (i) Part 9 care plan as first prepared under section 137(2)(a) (preparation of Part 9 care plan); and
  (ii) amended Part 9 care plan;
(b) a copy of any written evidence given by a medical practitioner under section 57A(2)(a) of the 1995 Act (evidence of medical practitioners prior to making of compulsion order by court); and
(c) a copy of any report by the mental health officer prepared in accordance with section 57C(2)(b) of the 1995 Act (report by mental health officer prior to making of compulsion order by court).

Documents to accompany application to Tribunal under section 158

3. The documents prescribed for the purpose of section 158(b) (documents to accompany application to Tribunal by responsible medical officer for order extending and varying a compulsion order) are–

(a) where the application is made following a first review of the compulsion order, the documents prescribed in regulation 2.
(b) where the application is made other than following a first review of the compulsion order, a copy of the patient's amended Part 9 care plan.

Documents to accompany application to Tribunal under section 161

4. The documents prescribed for the purpose of section 161(b) (documents to accompany application to Tribunal by responsible medical officer for order varying a compulsion order) are–

(a) where the application is made during the period of six months beginning with the day on which the compulsion order is made–

(i) a copy of the patient's–

    (aa) Part 9 care plan as first prepared under section 137(2)(a) (preparation of Part 9 care plan); and

    (bb) amended Part 9 care plan;

(ii) a copy of any written evidence given by a medical practitioner under section 57A(2)(a) of the 1995 Act (evidence of medical practitioners prior to making of compulsion order by court); and

(iii) a copy of any report by the mental health officer prepared in accordance with section 57C(2)(b) of the 1995 Act (report by mental health officer prior to making of compulsion order by court); or

(b) where the application is made in any period for which a compulsion order has been extended, a copy of the patient's amended Part 9 care plan.

Application for extension of compulsion order following first review: reports to be prepared and submitted to Tribunal under section 173

5. Where the Tribunal is considering an application made under section 149 and is not satisfied that it has sufficient information to enable it to make a decision, the Tribunal may require, under section 173(2) (power to require preparation and submission of reports)–

(a) the mental health officer to prepare and submit to it a report–

    (i) on the steps that the mental health officer has taken to comply with the requirements imposed by section 147(2) (mental health officer's duties to patient etc);

    (ii) giving the views of the mental health officer on the application and the reasons for those views;

    (iii) giving, if known to the mental health officer, the views of the patient and the patient's named person on the application and the reasons for those views;

    (iv) giving, in so far as the mental health officer considers relevant for the purposes of the review, details of the personal circumstances of the patient;

    (v) giving, if known to the mental health officer, details of any advance statement that the patient has made (and not withdrawn); and

    (vi) giving any other information which the mental health officer considers may assist the Tribunal in considering the application; and

(b) the patient's responsible medical officer to prepare and submit to it a report–

    (i) stating the basis on which the responsible medical officer is satisfied that the conditions mentioned in section 139(4) (conditions applying to patient) continue to apply and the reasons for that view;

    (ii) specifying, by reference to the appropriate sub-paragraph of section 328(1) (meaning of "mental disorder"), the type (or types) of mental disorder that the patient has;

    (iii) stating why the responsible medical officer considers that it continues to be necessary for the patient to be subject to the compulsion order;

    (iv) on the extent to which the objectives of any medical treatment, community care services, other relevant services, or any other treatment, care or service included in the patient's Part 9 care plan are being met; and

    (v) giving any other information which the responsible medical officer considers may assist the Tribunal in considering the application.

Application for extension and variation of compulsion order: report to be prepared and submitted to Tribunal under section 173

6. Where the Tribunal is considering an application made under section 158 and is not satisfied that it has sufficient information to enable it to make a decision, the Tribunal may require, under section 173(2), the mental health officer to prepare and submit to it a report–

    (i) on the steps that the mental health officer has taken to comply with the requirements imposed by section 155(2) (mental health officer's duties to patient etc);

    (ii) giving the views of the mental health officer on the application and the reasons for those views;

    (iii) giving, if known to the mental health officer, the views of the patient and the patient's named person on the application and the reasons for those views;

    (iv) giving, in so far as the mental health officer considers relevant for the purposes of the review, details of the personal circumstances of the patient;

    (v) giving, if known to the mental health officer, details of any advance statement that the patient has made (and not withdrawn); and

(vi) giving any other information which the mental health officer considers may assist the Tribunal in considering the application.

Application for variation of compulsion order: report to be submitted to Tribunal under section 173

7. Where the Tribunal is considering an application made under section 161 (application for order varying a compulsion order) and is not satisfied that it has sufficient information to enable it to make a decision, the Tribunal may require, under section 173(2), the mental health officer to prepare and submit to it a report–

(a) on the steps that the mental health officer has taken to comply with the requirements imposed by section 159(4C) (mental health officer's duties to patient etc);

(b) giving the views of the mental health officer on the application and the reasons for those views;

(c) giving, if known to the mental health officer, the views of the patient and the patient's named person on the application;

(d) giving, in so far as the mental health officer considers relevant for the purposes of the application, details of the personal circumstances of the patient;

(e) giving, if known to the mental health officer, details of any advance statement that the patient has made (and not withdrawn); and

(f) giving any other information which the mental health officer considers may assist the Tribunal in considering the application.

Application for revocation of determination extending compulsion order or revocation or variation of compulsion order: reports to be submitted to Tribunal under section 173

8. Where the Tribunal is considering an application made under sections 163(1) (revocation of determination extending compulsion order) or 164(2) (revocation or variation of compulsion order) and is not satisfied that it has sufficient information to enable it to make a decision, the Tribunal may require, under section 173(2)–

(a) the mental health officer to prepare and submit to it a report–

(i) giving the views of the mental health officer on the application and the reasons for those views;

(ii) giving, if known to the mental health officer, details of any advance statement that the patient has made (and not withdrawn); and

(iii) giving any other information which the mental health officer considers may assist the Tribunal in considering the application; and

(b) the patient's responsible medical officer to prepare and submit to it a report–

(i) giving the views of the responsible medical officer on the application and the reasons for those views; and

(ii) giving any other information which the responsible medical officer considers may assist the Tribunal in considering the application.

Review of determination extending compulsion order: reports to be submitted to Tribunal under section 173

9. Where the Tribunal is reviewing, under section 165(2) (grounds for review of determination), a determination made under section 152(2) extending a compulsion order and is not satisfied that it has sufficient information to enable it to make a decision, the Tribunal may require, under section 173(2)–

(a) the mental health officer to prepare and submit to it a report–

(i) on the steps that the mental health officer has taken to comply with the requirements imposed by section 151(2) (mental health officer's duties to patient etc);

(ii) giving the mental health officer's views or further views on the determination and the reasons for those views;

(iii) giving, if known to the mental health officer, the views of the patient and the patient's named person on the determination and the reasons for those views;

(iv) giving, in so far as the mental health officer considers relevant for the purposes of the review, details of the personal circumstances of the patient;

(v) giving, if known to the mental health officer, details of any advance statement that the patient has made (and not withdrawn); and

(vi) giving any other information which the mental health officer considers may assist the Tribunal in considering the determination; and

(b) the patient's responsible medical officer to prepare and submit to it a report on the extent to which the objectives of any medical treatment, community care services, other relevant services, or any other treatment, care or service included in the patient's Part 9 care plan are being met.

MENTAL HEALTH (CONFLICT OF INTEREST) (SCOTLAND) (NO 2) REGULATIONS 2005
(SSI 2005/380)

Citation, commencement and interpretation

1.—(1) These Regulations may be cited as the Mental Health (Conflict of Interest) (Scotland) (No 2) Regulations 2005 and shall come into force on 5th October 2005.

(2) For the purposes of these Regulations–

"cohabitee" in relation to a medical practitioner, includes a person, whether of the same sex or not, who is living with that medical practitioner in a relationship which has the characteristics of the relationship between husband and wife; and

"independent health care service" has the same meaning as in section 2(5) of the Regulation of Care (Scotland) Act 2001.

(3) In these Regulations, any other reference to a numbered section is a reference to the section bearing that number in the Mental Health (Care and Treatment) (Scotland) Act 2003.

Conflict of interest in relation to medical examination – short term detention in hospital

2. Subject to regulation 3, the circumstances in which there is to be taken to be a conflict of interest in relation to the medical examination for the purposes of sections 44 (short term detention in hospital) and 47 (extension of short-term detention in hospital) are where the approved medical practitioner is–

(a) related to the patient in any degree specified in the Schedule; or

(b) employed by or contracted to provide services in or to an independent health care service in which the patient will be detained if detention is authorised under either section 44 or, as the case may be, section 47.

Circumstances in which there is not a conflict of interest – short term detention in hospital

3. Notwithstanding regulation 2, the circumstances in which there is not to be taken to be a conflict of interest in relation to the medical examination for the purposes of sections 44 and 47, are where failure by the approved medical practitioner to carry out the medical examination would result in a delay which would involve serious risk to the health, safety or welfare of the patient or to the safety of other persons.

Conflict of interest in relation to medical examination – compulsory treatment order

4.—(1) The circumstances in which there is to be taken to be a conflict of interest in relation to the medical examination for the purposes of section 58(5) (requirements for medical examinations relating to compulsory treatment orders) are where–

(a) either medical practitioner is related to the patient in any degree specified in the Schedule;

(b) the two medical practitioners are related to each other in any degree specified in the Schedule;

(c) it is proposed that the compulsory treatment order should authorise the detention of the patient in an independent health care service and either medical practitioner is employed by or contracted to provide services in or to that independent health care service; or

(d) it is proposed that the compulsory treatment order should authorise the detention of the patient in a hospital other than an independent health care service and both medical practitioners are employed by or contracted to provide services in or to that hospital.

(2) For the purposes of paragraph (1)(d), unless a medical practitioner works wholly or mainly in a hospital, that practitioner shall not be regarded as being employed by or contracted to provide services in or to that hospital.

Permitted conflicts of interest – compulsory treatment order

5.—(1) For the purposes of section 58(5), the circumstances in which a medical examination of a patient may be carried out even although there is a conflict of interest in relation to that medical examination are–

(a) where the conflict of interest is in terms of regulation 4(1)(c) or (d);

(b) failure to carry out the medical examination would result in delay which would involve serious risk to the health, safety or welfare of the patient or to the safety of other persons; and

(c) if one of the medical practitioners is a consultant, the other does not work directly with or under the supervision of that consultant.

Revocation

6. The Mental Health (Conflict of Interest) (Scotland) Regulations 2005 are hereby revoked.

SCHEDULE   **Regulations 2 and 4**

PROHIBITED DEGREES OF RELATIONSHIP

Child
Grandchild
Parent
Grandparent
Wife
Husband
Sister
Brother
Daughter-in-law
Son-in-law
Mother-in-law
Father-in-law
Sister-in-law
Brother-in-law
Cohabitee
Child, grandchild, parent, grandparent, sister or brother of a cohabitee.

For the purposes of this Schedule–

(a) a relationship of the half-blood shall be treated as a relationship of the whole blood; and

(b) the stepchild of a person shall be treated as the child of that person.

MENTAL HEALTH (CONTENT AND AMENDMENT OF CARE PLANS) (SCOTLAND) REGULATIONS 2005 (SSI 2005/309)

Citation, commencement and interpretation

1.—(1) These Regulations may be cited as the Mental Health (Content and amendment of care plans) (Scotland) Regulations 2005 and shall come into force on 5th October 2005.

(2) In these Regulations, any reference to a numbered section is a reference to the section bearing that number in the Mental Health (Care and Treatment) (Scotland) Act 2003.

Content of care plan

2.—(1) The information relating to the care of a patient, which is prescribed for the purpose of section 76(2)(b) (information to be included in care plan in addition to the medical treatment), is–

(a) full details of the compulsory treatment order and the day on which the order was made;

(b) the objectives of the medical treatment referred to in section 76(2)(a) (medical treatment to be set out in care plan);

(c) details of any community care services or other relevant services and the objectives of those services–

(i) which it is proposed to give; and

(ii) which are being given,

to the patient;

(d) details of any other treatment, care or service (other than that described in section 76(2)(a) or in paragraph (c) of this regulation) and the objectives of that treatment, care or service–

(i) which it is proposed to give; and

(ii) which is being given,

to the patient;

(e) the name and other appropriate contact details of the patient's responsible medical officer;

(f) the name and other appropriate contact details of the patient's mental health officer;

(g) the period of 2 months ending with the date by which–

(i) the first mandatory review under section 77(2) (carrying out of first review of compulsory treatment order by responsible medical officer); or

(i)   which it is proposed to give; and
(ii)   which are being given,

to the patient;

(d) details of any other treatment, care or service (other than that described in section 137(3)(a) or in paragraph (c) of this regulation) and the objectives of that treatment, care or service–

(i) which it is proposed to give; and

(ii) which is being given,

to the patient;

(e) the name and other appropriate contact details of the patient's responsible medical officer;

(f) the name and other appropriate contact details of the patient's mental health officer;

(g) the period of 2 months ending with the date by which–

(i) the first mandatory review under section 139(2) (carrying out of first review of compulsion order by responsible medical officer); or

(ii) any further mandatory review under section 140(2) (carrying out of further review of compulsion order by responsible medical officer),

of the patient's compulsion order must take place;

(h) the dates on which such reviews have taken place;

(i) the date of the patient's conviction;

(j) the offence of which the patient was convicted; and

(k) if the patient is subject to–

(i) the notification requirements in Part 2 of the Sexual Offences Act 2003; or

(ii) a sexual offences prevention order under section 105 of that Act,

and if so the notification period or the period specified in the order.

(2) Where the Part 9 care plan is required to be amended in any of the circumstances prescribed in regulation 3, the information in the care plan shall be amended to take account of those circumstances.

Amendment of Part 9 care plan

3.—(1) The circumstances prescribed for the purpose of section 137(5)(a) (circumstances in which Part 9 care plan must be amended) are–

(a) where the Tribunal has made an order under–

  (i) section 166(1)(d) (confirmation of determination and variation of compulsion order);

  (ii) section 167(1)(a) (extension of compulsion order);

  (iii) section 167(2)(a) (extension and variation of compulsion order);

  (iv) section 167(3)(d) (confirmation of determination and variation of compulsion order);

  (v) section 167(4)(b) (variation of compulsion order);

  (vi) section 167(5)(a) (variation of compulsion order); or

  (vii) section 171(1)(a) (variation of compulsion order);

(b) where the Tribunal has made an interim order under–

  (i) section 168(2)(b)(i) (extension of compulsion order);

  (ii) section 168(2)(b)(ii) (extension and variation of compulsion order); or

  (iii) section 169(2) (variation of compulsion order);

(c) where the patient's responsible medical officer has–

  (i) granted a certificate under either section 127(1)(b) or 128(1)(b) (periods during which measures are not authorised) specifying a period exceeding 28 days;

  (ii) revoked such a certificate under section 129(2)(c) (grounds for revocation of certificate);

  (iii) made a determination extending a compulsion order under section 152(2) (extension of compulsion order following further review); or

  (iv) carried out any further mandatory review under section 140(2) (carrying out of further review of compulsion order by responsible medical officer); and

(d) where a patient ceases to be subject to a notification requirement under Part 2 of the Sexual Offences Act 2003 or where a sexual offences prevention order to which that patient is subject under section 105 of that Act is varied, renewed or discharged.

MENTAL HEALTH (SOCIAL CIRCUMSTANCES REPORTS) (SCOTLAND) REGULATIONS 2005
(SSI 2005/310)

Citation and commencement

1. These Regulations may be cited as the Mental Health (Social Circumstances Reports) (Scotland) Regulations 2005 and shall come into force on 5th October 2005.

Social circumstances report

2. A social circumstances report shall set out the following information, where it is relevant to the care of the patient–

(a) the reasons for the use of compulsory powers;

(b) the views of the patient with respect to the use of compulsory powers;

(c) if the patient is unable to give a view, and only if available to the mental health officer, the views of the patient's named person, carer, guardian and welfare attorney with respect to the use of compulsory powers;

(d) the patient's state of mental health;

(e) the patient's state of physical health;

(f) the patient's mental health history;

(g) an assessment of the risk of harm to the patient and to others;

(h) the patient's personal history including details of employment, finances and accommodation prior to the use of compulsory powers;

(i) details of the patient's family situation including whether the patient has children, dependents and caring responsibilities;

(j) details of the patient's regular social contacts;

(k) the patient's ability to care for himself or herself;

(l) the care being provided to the patient prior to the use of compulsory powers;

(m) any matters which would require the local authority to make inquiries into the patient's case under section 33 of the Mental Health (Care and Treatment) (Scotland) Act 2003;

(n) any alternatives to the use of compulsory powers which were considered and ruled out;

(o) any history of offending, including consideration of victims and those affected;

(p) any history of substance misuse;

(q) ethnic, cultural and religious factors;

(r) whether the patient has difficulty in communicating; and

(s) any plan which has been put in place to deal with any of the above.

APPENDIX 4

PRACTICE DIRECTIONS AND GUIDANCE NOTES*

MHTS PRACTICE DIRECTION 1/2006

GRANTING OF A CTO WHERE PATIENT IS SUBJECT TO A HOSPITAL DIRECTION OR TRANSFER FOR TREATMENT DIRECTION

Schedule 3 to the Mental Health (Care and Treatment) (Scotland) Act 2003 ("the 2003 Act") applies the provisions for the application for and making of a CTO in relation to patients subject to a hospital direction (HD) or transfer for treatment direction (TTD) subject to certain specified modifications. Issues have arisen in relation to the date the CTO will come into effect and the granting of interim CTOs in such cases.

The Tribunal can make a CTO in relation to a patient who is subject to a HD or a TTD. The CTO will only authorise the measures specified in it if the direction ceases to have effect within 28 days of the CTO being made.

Commencement of the CTO

The CTO will authorise the measures specified in it for 6 months beginning with the day on which the HD or TTD ceases to have effect.

Section 217 of the 2003 Act provides that where a patient is released under Part 1 of the Prisoners and Criminal Proceedings (Scotland) Act 1993 ("the 1993 Act") or otherwise the direction to which the patient is subject shall cease to have effect.

If a CTO is granted when the patient is still subject to a HD or TTD then the Tribunal should take steps to make it clear in the

---

* The Publishers wish to thank the Mental Health Tribunal for Scotland for permission to reproduce the material contained in this Appendix.

Tribunal decision when the CTO actually takes effect as the CTO will not normally come into effect on the date the CTO is granted but on the date the HD or TTD ceases to have effect. The Tribunal will therefore require information as to when the patient is to be released e.g. the patients earliest date of liberation (EDL) under the 1993 Act.

Interim CTO not competent

Members should also note that where the patient is subject to a HD or a TTD and an application is made for a CTO it is not competent for the Tribunal to grant an interim CTO (see paragraph 3 of Schedule 3 to the 2003 Act).

Members are expected to familiarise themselves with the relevant statutory provisions in relation to applications for a CTO where the patient is subject to a HD or TTD.

PRESIDENT
10 November 2006

MHTS PRACTICE DIRECTION 1/2007

ISSUING OF REASONS WHERE INTERIM COMPULSORY TREATMENT ORDER IS MADE

Paragraph 13(3) of Schedule 2 to the 2003 Act provides that a decision of the Tribunal shall be recorded in a document which contains a full statement of the facts found by the Tribunal and the reasons for the decision. This requirement is repeated in rule 72(7) of the Mental Health Tribunal for Scotland (Practice and Procedure) (No. 2) Rules 2005 ("the Rules").

A copy of the document referred to in paragraph 13(3) requires to be sent to each party as soon as practicable after completion (see paragraph 13(4) of Schedule 2 to the 2003 Act and rule 72(3) of the Rules.

There is a statutory right to appeal a decision to make an interim compulsory treatment order under section 65(2) of the 2003 Act (see section 320(1)(c) of the 2003 Act.

In the light of the above provisions where a Tribunal makes an interim order under section 65(2) of the 2003 Act the Tribunal should prepare a document containing statements of fact and reasons. The statements of fact and reasons need not be lengthy and are not expected to be as full as they would be where a final decision is reached e.g. to make a Compulsory Treatment Order. The Tribunal should however make sure that it is clear the basis on which the conditions mentioned in section 64(5)(a) to (d) are met in respect of the patient and why it is necessary to make an interim compulsory treatment order (see section 65(2) and (6) of the 2003 Act).

The Tribunal Clerk at the hearing will have copies of the blank template which should be completed when an interim compulsory treatment order is made.

EILEEN DAVIE
PRESIDENT
17 May 2007

PRESIDENT'S GUIDANCE 1/07

DOCTORS GIVING EVIDENCE TO TRIBUNAL WHEN RMO CANNOT ATTEND

This guidance applies to any application requiring a report by the RMO.

Where the RMO is unable to attend the hearing a colleague whom the RMO considers appropriate may attend in order to give oral evidence in support of the report by the RMO.

The person attending must have direct and up to date knowledge of the patient.

PRESIDENT
17 September 2007

GUIDANCE TO TRIBUNAL MEMBERS NO 1/2009

SAME PANEL REQUESTS AND DIRECTIONS

Purpose of this Guidance

1. The purpose of this guidance is to clarify the circumstances in which it is appropriate to make a request for the same panel to be re-convened at a future hearing or to make a direction for the same panel to be re-convened.

Same Panel Direction

2. A direction is an order of the Tribunal and requires to be followed by the Tribunal Administration, unless the direction is overturned on

good grounds by another tribunal or by a Convener sitting alone. Directions should therefore only be made where appropriate.

The only circumstance where there is a legal requirement for the same panel to hear a case is where evidence has been led before the tribunal and the hearing has been adjourned **without a final decision having been made (i.e. the case is "part heard")**. It would not be considered appropriate to make a same panel direction where a hearing had been concluded by, for example, the making of an interim order, or where the only issue determined by the tribunal was one of procedure.

Same panel directions must be stated on a separate Directions sheet with full reasons for the direction being made.

Same Panel Requests

3. Where a same panel request is made the Tribunal Administration will endeavour to accommodate that request but is under no obligation to do so. Same panel requests could appropriately be made, for example, in circumstances where it is considered that it would be beneficial to the patient, as having the same panel might limit the stress on the part of the patient. Full reasons must be given as to why it is considered necessary to make a same panel request. It is anticipated that the need for same panel requests is likely to arise infrequently. Where, for example, an interim order has been made, in the event that the same panel was re-convened to consider making a further order that same panel would still require to be satisfied that the criteria in the 2003 Act were still met, and so would still require to hear evidence afresh. Neither the 2003 Act nor the Tribunal's rules require the same panel to be re-convened in such circumstances. It was clearly envisaged that a different panel could sit and consider the case. Members should also be mindful that patients may feel they are better served by a different panel looking at the evidence afresh and thus no perception arises that the issues have been pre-judged as a result of a decision made at an earlier hearing.

Attached to this Guidance are examples of circumstances in which it would be considered that same panel requests and directions are appropriate and inappropriate.

DR JOE MORROW
PRESIDENT
28 May 2009

Examples of where same panel requests and directions would be considered to be appropriate, and where inappropriate:

1. Where evidence has been led to enable a procedural decision to be taken, and the hearing has been adjourned but no substantive decision has been made, the tribunal has not made a substantive order.

A same panel request or Direction would NOT be considered to be appropriate

2. Where evidence has been led and no decision has been made by the Tribunal, then the same panel requires to continue to consider the case. If the same panel did not continue to consider the case then any evidence already heard by the tribunal would require to be reheard, as all members of the Tribunal require to hear all the evidence led before a decision is made.

A same Panel Direction SHOULD be given in these circumstances.

3. The legal requirement for the same panel only applies where the hearing is part heard. If for example an interim compulsory treatment order has been made (which of course requires the tribunal to be satisfied that the statutory criteria in section 64(4) of the Act are met on the evidence before the tribunal) there is no legal requirement for the same panel to consider the application at the next hearing.

A same panel request or Direction would NOT be considered to be appropriate.

4. When only a preliminary or procedural matter has been dealt with and decided upon by the tribunal panel there is no requirement for the same panel to consider the case at the next hearing. Such an example would be a section 101(2)(b) review (2 year review of determination extending CTO) where there is an order in place and the tribunal simply makes a decision to allow an adjournment for an independent medical report or a curator *ad litem* to be appointed.

A same panel request or Direction would NOT be considered to be appropriate.

5. **Where a patient requests the same panel, the tribunal should consider the reasons for the request. When granting a request, those reasons and the reasons for granting the request must be given. The tribunal should balance any perceived benefit to the patient in having the same panel, against possible future perception that the same panel might have pre-judged the issue.**

GUIDANCE TO TRIBUNAL MEMBERS NO 2/2009
DIRECTIONS

Purpose of this Guidance

1. The purpose of this guidance is to assist panels when making directions.

General Comment

2. The authority to give directions is contained within rule 49 of the Mental Health Tribunal for Scotland (Practice and Procedure) (No 2) Rules 2005. Rule 49 is set out in full at the end of this guidance note and should be referred to when making a direction.

Directions are an extremely important power given to Tribunals. Rule 49 provides that directions can be made on the request of a relevant person or on the Tribunal's own initiative.

Where a request for a direction is made by a relevant person prior to a Tribunal hearing, the request must be in writing. On receipt of a request, the clerk will intimate the request to relevant persons inviting them to make written representations within a specified period. At the end of that period, the case papers will usually be placed before an in-house convener sitting at a Standing Tribunal. This will enable directions to be issued in advance of Tribunal hearings, with the expectation that directions will be complied with in time for the Tribunal hearing.

Tribunals may wish to make directions. Tribunals can make directions they consider necessary or desirable "to further the overriding objective in the conduct of a case". The authority to issue directions is one which allows a wide discretion and can be used extremely effectively. Rule 49 gives examples of directions which might be issued, but the list is by no means exhaustive.

Rule 51(1) provides that if any direction given to a relevant person under rule 49 is not complied with by that relevant person, the Tribunal may, before or after the hearing, direct that that relevant person concerned take no further part in proceedings. This power, however, shall not be exercised unless the relevant person has been given an opportunity to show cause why the Tribunal should not proceed to give such a direction.

Guidance on Issuing Directions

3. In order for a direction to be effective, it must comply with the provisions of rule 49. Failure to comply with rule 49 will render a direction ineffective and may result in confusion, delay and an

adjournment of the patient's case. The following should be noted when making directions:—

(i) Form of Direction

A direction must be in writing. It MUST be made on a separate directions template, which will be made available by the clerk.

The purpose of directions is to have action taken. A direction MUST NOT be contained ONLY within the body of the determination. If stated there, it MUST ALSO be stated on a separate directions template. If a direction is contained only within the body of a determination, it will not be processed by MHTS Administration.

(ii) Responsibility for Complying with Direction

A direction must specify who is required to take a particular action in order to comply with the direction. It must name the person, or the organisation, responsible for complying with the direction. If an organisation is to be responsible, some thought should be given as to the person who, or the position within the organisation which, is to be responsible, and that person or position should be specified (for example, the hospital manager of A.N. Other Trust).

(iii) Direction Instruction

If the direction is for someone to do something, or for someone to produce something, there must be clarity and specification as to what has to be done or what has to be produced.

(iv) Time for Compliance

A time limit for compliance with a direction must be stated. Consideration should be given to realistic time scales, as a direction with little prospect of compliance will simply result in delays and adjournments.

A time limit to do or produce something within a time scale *from the date of intimation of the direction* is likely to be more effective than one which provides that something should be done or produced *before, or within a time scale prior to, the next hearing*. Hearings are often not set at the time when a direction is given, and a direction linked to the date of a hearing is likely to lead to uncertainty. A time scale from the date of intimation of the direction will also enable MHTS Administration to more easily monitor compliance with directions and to take appropriate follow up action where necessary.

All directions require to be detailed and unambiguous. There should be no ambiguity as to

- who is under an obligation to comply with the direction;
- what the direction is; and
- when compliance requires to be effected.

DR JOE MORROW
PRESIDENT
10 July 2009

Rule 49:

"(1) Except as otherwise provided for in these rules, the Tribunal may at any time, either on the request of a relevant person or on its own initiative, give such directions as the Tribunal considers necessary or desirable to further the overriding objective in the conduct of a case and may in particular

(a) direct a relevant person to provide any further particulars or to produce any documents which may reasonably be required;

(b) direct that a relevant person shall supply a list of documents and a list of witnesses whom that relevant person wishes to call to give evidence at the hearing;

(c) give directions as to the dates by which any documents or other evidence on which any relevant person wishes to rely shall be sent to the Tribunal;

(d) give a direction as to the date by which a relevant person shall send any written representations on the case to the Tribunal;

(e) direct that the parties or the relevant persons should provide a statement of agreed facts;

(f) give directions restricting the reporting, recording, photography or filming of any hearing;

(g) give directions as to—

(i) any issues on which the Tribunal requires evidence;

(ii) the nature of the evidence which the Tribunal requires to decide those issues;

(iii) the way in which the evidence is to be led before the Tribunal; and

(iv) the exclusion of any evidence which is irrelevant, unnecessary or improperly obtained.

(2) Where a request is made by a relevant person for a direction under paragraph (1), it shall be made in writing specifying the direction sought and the basis for the request.

(3) On receipt of such a request, the Clerk shall intimate the request to the relevant persons inviting them to make written representations within 14 days or such other period as the Tribunal may specify.

(4) The requirement in the foregoing paragraph to intimate a request to the relevant persons does not require intimation to the person who made the request.

(5) Where a party objects to the request, the Tribunal shall consider the objection and, if the Tribunal considers it necessary in order to decide the request, may afford the relevant persons an opportunity to be heard either by the Convener alone or with such other members as the Tribunal may direct.

(6) The Tribunal shall, in deciding whether to make a direction, consider any representations made.

(7) A direction under this rule may, if appropriate, include a statement of the possible consequences of failure to comply mentioned in rule 51.

(8) A direction made without prior intimation to a relevant person whom it affects shall as soon as reasonably practicable be notified in writing to that relevant person by the Tribunal."

GUIDANCE TO CURATORS *AD LITEM*

1.   This Guidance refers where a curator *ad litem* is appointed by the Mental Health Tribunal for Scotland ("the Tribunal") or a Convener in terms of rule 55 of the Mental Health Tribunal for Scotland (Practice and Procedure) (No.2) Rules 2005 ("the Rules").

2. The curator is appointed in a personal capacity and should appear personally before the Tribunal unless there are exceptional circumstances which prevent this.

3. The appointment of a curator will be made on a case by case basis from the List of Curators maintained by the Tribunal. Inclusion in the List of Curators maintained by the Tribunal does not guarantee that a curator will be appointed with any particular frequency.

Section 1 principles

4. While a curator *ad litem* is not subject to a statutory duty to have regard to the principles specified in section 1 of the Mental Health (Care and Treatment) (Scotland) Act 2003 ("the 2003 Act") when discharging any function under the 2003 Act, good practice suggests that the principles should be taken into account by a curator when representing the interests of a patient in proceedings before the Tribunal.

5. It is recognised that there can be a tension between the role of a curator and the principle of patient participation in Tribunal proceedings. On occasion the patient may attend and wish to make

representations at a hearing when a curator has been appointed. Good practice would suggest that such a situation is handled sensitively to ensure that the patient is allowed to participate as fully as possible.

Timescales

Visiting the patient

6. Where a curator *ad litem* is appointed by the Tribunal or a Convener the curator should normally visit the patient within 3 working days of the appointment. It is expected that in accepting the appointment the curator can meet this timescale in the interests of the patient and in the efficient and effective management of the Tribunal.

7. If after visiting the patient the curator is of the view that the patient is capable of instructing a solicitor to represent his/her interests in proceedings before the Tribunal the curator should contact the Tribunal in writing and inform the Tribunal that the appointment of a curator is not necessary in order that the appointment can be revoked by the Tribunal.

8. If at any time during the proceedings before the Tribunal the curator is of the view that the patient is capable of instructing a solicitor the curator should inform the Tribunal that the appointment is no longer necessary in order that the appointment can be revoked by the Tribunal.

Instructing an independent medical report

9. In the event that the curator is of the view that it is necessary to instruct an independent medical report the curator should endeavour to instruct the report within 5 working days of the appointment. The curator should advise the Tribunal that a report has been instructed and when the report is likely to be available.

10. Where a date has been set for a Tribunal hearing and the curator is of the view that it will not be possible to complete necessary investigation and enquiry by the date of the hearing the curator should advise the Tribunal of this at least 7 days before the date of the hearing so that consideration can be given to whether the hearing should proceed.

Remuneration

11. The curator will be remunerated in accordance with the Tribunal's Scale of Fees for Curators *ad litem* (attached at Annex A). The curator should submit a professional account for payment of fees and outlays to the Tribunal as soon as possible after the conclusion of the proceedings.

12. The Tribunal's prior approval in writing should be obtained before the curator incurs expenditure of an exceptional nature.

13. In the event of any dispute in relation to a professional account submitted the curator or the Tribunal may refer the account to the Auditor of Court for taxation.

DR JOE MORROW
PRESIDENT
November 2008

APPENDIX 5

STATEMENT OF PRINCIPLES OF JUDICIAL ETHICS FOR THE SCOTTISH JUDICIARY

1. INTRODUCTION

1.1 While the Scottish Judiciary have an honourable tradition of high standards of judicial conduct, that has been achieved without the benefit of written guidance. However, in recent years written guidance has been developed in many other jurisdictions. Furthermore, recognition of the need for guidance in relation to judicial conduct has emerged in the international context with the development of the *Bangalore Principles of Judicial Conduct*, endorsed at the 59th session of the United nations Human Rights Commission at Geneva in April 2003. Against this background, it is now considered that it is appropriate for such guidance to be available in Scotland.

1.2 There are several sources from which the ethical standards which, it is considered, should be observed by judges derive. First, the terms of the judicial oath, taken by judges in Scotland on their appointment, require the judge to "do right to all manner of people after the laws and usages of this Realm, without fear or favour, affection or ill-will". Second, there is an undoubted public interest in the maintenance of respect for the law and the judges who apply it. Third, Article 6 of the European Convention for the Protection of Human Rights and Fundamental Freedoms confers the right to a fair and public hearing within a reasonable time by an independent and impartial tribunal established by law. Furthermore, it is also appropriate to bear in mind the lucid observations of Mr Justice Thomas, a Judge of the Supreme Court of Queensland in *Judicial Ethics in Australia*, 2nd edition (1997) p. 9), which have implications far beyond that jurisdiction. There, of judges, he said:

> "We form a particular group in the community. We comprise a select part of an honourable profession. We are entrusted, day after day, with the exercise of considerable power. Its exercise has dramatic effects upon the lives and fortunes of those who come before us. Citizens cannot be sure that they or their fortunes will not some day depend upon our judgment. They will not wish such power to be reposed in anyone whose honesty, ability or personal standards are questionable. It is necessary for the continuity of the system of law as we know it, that there be standards of conduct, both in and out of court, which are designed to maintain confidence in those expectations."

1.3 In the development of this document, importance has been attached to the several principles set out in the *Bangalore Principles* themselves and therefore acknowledgement is due to those responsible for their formulation. We would also wish to acknowledge our debt to those who compiled the *Guide to Judicial Conduct* issued by the Judges' Council of England and Wales. The guidance which follows in this document has bene formulated particularly in the light of these sources.

1.4 As regards the character of what follows, it should be understood that it is not intended to be prescriptive, like the contents of a statute; it is of the nature of guidance and should be seen as such. As was pointed out in the *Guide to Judicial Conduct* compiled by the Judges' Council of England and Wales, paragraph 1.6.2:

> "The primary responsibility for deciding whether a particular activity or course of conduct is appropriate rests with the individual judge and what follows is not intended to be prescriptive, unless stated to be. There may be occasion when the overall interests of justice require a departure from propositions as literally stated in the guide. It is also acknowledged that there is a range of reasonably held opinions on some aspects of the restraints that come with the acceptance of judicial office."

2. THE SCOPE OF APPLICATION OF THIS STATEMENT OF PRINCIPLES

2.1 It is hoped that the principles set out in this guide will be of assistance to all judicial office holders exercising their offices within Scotland. These comprise:

(a) All judges of the Court of Session, whether sitting in that court, or as judges of the High Court of Justiciary, or as members of any other court in which such judges may sit;

(b) Sheriffs Principal;

(c) Sheriffs;

(d) The Chairman and other members of the Scottish Land Court;

(e) Temporary judges, or retired judges of the Court of Session;

(f) Acting Sheriffs Principal;

(g) Part-time Sheriffs;

(h) Justices of the Peace;

(i) Stipendiary Magistrates;

(j) Members of tribunals who exercise the functions of their office wholly or mainly in Scotland.

It is considered that certain of the restraints that must be accepted by the holders of full-time judicial appointments cannot reasonably be imposed upon the holders of part-time appointments. In what follows, it should be assumed that any particular guidance is applicable to all judicial office holders, unless it is stated to be limited to the holders of full-time judicial appointments. For the sake of convenience, all judicial office holders are referred to here as "judges". In the test, reference is made to "a judge's family". That expression is intended to include the judge's spouse or civil partner, child, including child by affinity, or adoption, and any other person who forms part of the same household as the judge, who is a close relative, companion or employee. A judge's "spouse or civil partner" is intended to include any person who is in a relationship with the judge which, but for the absence of marriage or civil partnership has the character of a relationship between two persons who are married, or in a civil partnership.

3. THE SIX *BANGALORE PRINCIPLES* THEMSELVES

3.1 These are stated in this way:

(1) Judicial independence is a prerequisite to the rule of law and a fundamental guarantee of a fair trial. A judge shall therefore uphold and exemplify judicial independence in both its individual and institutional aspects.

(2) Impartiality is essential to the proper discharge of the judicial office. It applies not only to the decision itself but also to the process by which the decision is made.

(3) Integrity is essential to the proper discharge of the judicial office.

(4) Propriety, and the appearance of propriety, are essential to the performance of all of the activities of a judge.

(5) Ensuring equality of treatment to all before the courts is essential to the due performance of the judicial office.

(6) Competence and diligence are prerequisites to the due performance of judicial office.

3.2 It will be appreciated that there may be some degree of overlap as between guidance derived from one of these principles and that derived from another. However, that is inherent in the scope of the principles. Nevertheless, it is considered that they constitute a clear focus for the arrangement of appropriate guidance.

4. JUDICIAL INDEPENDENCE

4.1 Judicial independence is a cornerstone of our system of government in a democratic society and a safeguard for the freedom and rights of a citizen under the rule of law. The judiciary, whether viewed as a whole, or as its individual members, must be seen to be independent of the legislative and executive arms of government. The relationship between the judiciary and the other arms of government, however, should be one of mutual respect, each recognising the proper rôle of the others. Accordingly, judges should always take care that their conduct, official or private, does not undermine their institutional or individual independence, or the public appearance of independence.

4.2 Judicial independence implies that any judge shall exercise the judicial function on the basis of the judge's own assessment of the facts of the case, in accordance with a conscientious understanding of the law, and without reference to any extraneous influences, whether inducements, pressures, threats, or other interference, direct or indirect, from any quarter, or for any reason. Thus the judge should be immune to the effects of publicity, whether favourable or unfavourable. However, that does not mean being immune to an awareness of the profound effect that judicial decisions may have, not only upon the lives of people before the court, but sometimes upon issues of great concern to the public in general.

4.3 For any judge, consultation with colleagues when points of difficulty arise is of great assistance and important in the maintenance of standards. However, in actually performing judicial duties, the judge should be independent of judicial colleagues and is solely responsible for his or her own decisions, which that judge is obliged to make independently, save where sitting with another judge or judges.

4.4 The principle of judicial independence requires the acceptance of certain restraints upon the extent to which a judge may be involved in other interests. There is normally no objection to any judge holding shares in commercial companies, or enjoying the proceeds of other ordinary investments, or the benefits or profits of property owned by him or her. However, there is a long-standing tradition that no judge with a full-time appointment should hold a commercial directorship. This restraint applies to any directorship in an organisation whose primary purpose is profit-related. It applies whether the directorship is in a public or private company, and whether or not it is remunerated. Any person holding such a directorship is therefore expected to resign from it on appointment to full-time judicial office. The only recognised exception to this rule is that such a judge may properly take part in the management of family assets, including land or family businesses, and may hold a directorship in a private company for this purpose, or in a company formed for the management of property in which he or she has a common interest. However, caution should be exercised even where private companies are solely owned by the judge and his or her family. A judge with a full-time appointment may continue to hold directorship in organisations the primary purpose of which is not profit-related and whose activities are of an uncontroversial character. However, if any judge is involved in charitable activities, including holding the directorship of a charity, he or she should be on guard against circumstances arising which may be seen to cast doubt upon their independence.

4.5 It is a cardinal feature of judicial independence that any judge should have no party political involvement of any kind, other than the exercising of his or her right to vote. If, at the time of appointment, a judge is a member of any political party or organisation, such a tie should then be severed. Thereafter the judge should do nothing which could give rise to any suggestion of political partisanship, such as involvement in party political controversy. Conventional political involvement on the part of a member of the family of a judge is not objectionable, provided that the judge remains aloof from it.

4.6 Many aspects of the administration of justice and the functioning of the judiciary are the subject of public consideration and debate in a range of contexts. Appropriate judicial contribution to this consideration and debate may be desirable. It may contribute to the public understanding of the administration of justice and to public confidence in the judiciary. However, care should be exercised to ensure that such contribution remains within proper bounds. In this connection, it should be borne in mind that a judge should avoid involvement in political controversy, unless the controversy itself directly affects the operation of the courts, the independence of the judiciary, or the administration of justice. It should also be appreciated that the place at which, or the occasion on which a judge speaks may cause the public to associate the judge with a particular organisation, interest group, or cause, which is to be avoided. Further, judges may hold conflicting views on such matters; in these circumstances, the expression of collective judicial viewpoint may be the preferable course, in order to avoid the damaging effect of open controversy between judges. That viewpoint should normally be expressed by the head of the judiciary.

4.7 A judge should not comment publicly upon any judgment once it has been published, even to clarify supposed ambiguity in it. A judgment may attract unfair, inaccurate or ill-informed comment, or criticism, which may reflect upon the competence, integrity or independence of a judge or the judiciary. Should a public response be appropriate it should come from the head of the judiciary.

4.8 A judge holding a full-time judicial appointment should not normally accept appointment to a governmental committee, commission, or other position that is concerned with issues of fact or policy relating to matters other than the improvement of the law, the legal system or the administration of justice. However, it is consistent with judicial office for any judge to serve in these capacities if the reason for the appointment is the need to harness to the task in question the special skills which a judge possesses, characteristically the ability to dissect and analyse evidence, appraise witnesses, exercise a fair and balanced judgment and write a clear and coherent report. However, he or she should not accept such an appointment where it is considered that the purpose sought to be served by it is to lend the respectability of the office of a judge, or the reputation of the holder, to some political end not acceptable to the public as a whole.

4.9 While attempts to corrupt the judiciary are virtually unknown in this jurisdiction, a judge should be circumspect in the acceptance of any gift, hospitality or favour from any source. Where the benefit sought to be conferred upon the judge is not commensurate with an existing family or social relationship between him or her and the donor, or host, it should normally be declined. However, it is recognised that a judge may, from time to time, legitimately be entertained by legal and other professional or public organisations, in furtherance of good relations between those organisations and the judiciary as a whole. In this connection, it is useful to distinguish between gifts and hospitality unrelated to judicial office, for example from family and close friends, and gifts and hospitality which in any way relate, or might appear to relate to judicial office.

5. THE PRINCIPLE OF IMPARTIALITY

5.1 A judge should strive to ensure that his or her conduct, both in and out of court, maintains and enhances the confidence of the public, the legal profession and litigants in the impartiality of the judge and the judiciary. Because a judge's primary task and responsibility is to discharge the duties of office, it follows that he or she should, so far as is reasonable, avoid extra-judicial activities that are likely to cause the judge to have to refrain from sitting in a case, because of a reasonable apprehension of bias, or because of a conflict of interest that would arise from the activity. Thus, for example, a judge should take care about the place at which and the occasion on which he or she speaks publicly, so as not to cause the public to associate the judge with any particular organisation, group, or cause. The participation in such activities should not be in circumstances which may give rise to a perception of partiality towards some particular organisation, group or cause.

5.2 Plainly a judge, or member of his or her family, must have no pecuniary interest in the outcome of any litigation pending before him, or pertaining to any aspect of it. Furthermore, he or she should carefully consider whether such a litigation may involve the decision of a point of law which itself may affect their personal interest in some different context, or the interest of any business of which a judge holding a part-time appointment may be a member. It may be that the pecuniary interest which a judge, or a member of his or her family, may possess in the outcome of some particular litigation is so limited that the litigants would have no objection to the judge handling the case. An example of such an interest might be the holding of shares in a public company, which is involved in litigation. In such a case, it may be reasonable for the interest to be declared, thus affording litigants the opportunity of objecting to his or her handling of the case. Where litigants have no objection to such an interest, it is conceived that normally the interest declared can thereafter properly be ignored. However, on the other hand, there may be exceptional circumstances in which a declared interest, to which litigants do not object, is nevertheless of such a nature as to cause the judge to decline to proceed, although it is thought that such situations will be rare.

5.3 Where there exists some reason, apart from pecuniary interest, why a judge should not handle a case on its objective merits, or reasonably appear to be unable to do so, he or she should recuse themselves. Thus, for example, a meaningful acquaintance with a litigant, or a person known to be a significant witness in the case might constitute such an objection. Other examples of such reasons are set out in the judgment of the court in *Locabail (UK) Ltd* v *Bayfield Properties Ltd* (CA) [2000] QB 451 at p. 480. Thus, prior to the commencement of a hearing, a judge should carefully consider whether he, she, or any member of their family, has any pecuniary or other interest in the outcome of the litigation, or whether there may exist some reason, other than such interest, why he or she could not try the case on its objective merits, or reasonably appear to be unable to do so. If it is concluded that he, she, or a family member, possesses such an interest, that state of affairs should be declared at the earliest opportunity. If, before a hearing has begun, the judge is alerted to some matter which might, depending on the full facts, throw doubt on his or her fitness to sit, the judge should enquire into the full facts, so far as they are then ascertainable, in order to consider the position and, if so advised, to make a disclosure in the light of them. If a judge has embarked upon a hearing in ignorance of a relevant matter, which emerges during the course of the hearing, he or she should discuss with the parties what has then come to their knowledge at the earliest possible opportunity, so that any problem can be resolved with the minimum of disruption and expense.

5.4 In the interests of judicial impartiality, a judge should be circumspect as regards contact with those legal practitioners who appear regularly in his or her court. In particular, he or she should not conduct themselves in such a way as to give rise to a suspicion that they might be inclined to favour the submissions of a particular practitioner.

5.5 In this area, the circumstances and situations which may arise are so varied that great reliance must be placed on the judgment of the judge, applying the law, his or her judicial instincts and conferring with a colleague, where possible and appropriate.

5.6 Apart from family relationships, personally friendship with, or personal animosity towards, a party would also be a compelling reason for disqualification. Friendship may be distinguished from acquaintanceship, which may or may not be a sufficient reason for disqualification, depending on the nature and extent of such acquaintanceship. A current or recent business association with a party would usually mean that a judge should not sit on a case. However, for this purpose, a business association would not normally include that of insurer and insured, bank and customer, or council tax payer and council. Judges should disqualify themselves from any case in which their own solicitor, accountant, doctor, dentist or other professional adviser is a party to the case. But friendship or past professional association with counsel or a solicitor acting for a party is not generally to be regarded as a sufficient reason for disqualification. The fact that a family member of the judge is partner in, or employee of, a firm of solicitors engaged in a case before the judge does not necessarily require disqualification. In such a situation, it is a matter of considering all the circumstances, including the extent of the involvement in the case of the person in question. Past professional association with a party as a client need not of itself be a reason for disqualification, but the judge must assess whether the particular circumstances could create an appearance of bias. Where it comes to the notice of a judge, in advance of a hearing well known to the judge, all the circumstances should be considered, including whether the credibility of the witness is in issue, the nature of the issue to be decided and the closeness of the friendship. A judge should not normally sit on a case in which a member of the judge's family appears as advocate.

5.7 Judges should, however, be careful to avoid giving encouragement to attempts by a party to use procedure for disqualification illegitimately. If the mere making of an insubstantial objection were sufficient to lead a judge to decline to hear a case, parties would be encouraged to attempt to influence the composition of the Bench, or to cause needless delay and the burden on colleagues would be increased. It is thought that a previous finding or previous findings by a judge against a party, including findings on credibility, will rarely provide a ground for disqualification. The possibility that a judge's comments in an earlier case, particularly if offered gratuitously, might reasonably be perceived as personal animosity cannot be excluded, but that possibility is likely to occur only very rarely.

5.8 If circumstances which may give rise to a suggestion of bias, or appearance of bias, are present and they are to be disclosed to the parties, that should be done ideally well before the hearing. The judge should bear in mind the difficult position in which parties, and their advisers, are placed by disclosure on the day of the hearing, when making a decision as to whether to proceed. Disclosure should, of course, be to all parties, and, save when the issue has been resolved by correspondence before the hearing, discussion between the judge and parties as to what procedure to follow should normally be in open court, unless the case itself is to be heard in chambers. The consent of the parties is a relevant and important factor, but the judge should avoid putting them in a position in which it might appear that their consent is sought to cure a substantial ground of disqualification. Even where the parties consent to the judge sitting, if the judge, on balance, considers that recusal is the proper course, the judge should so act. Conversely, there are likely to be cases in which the judge has thought it appropriate to bring the circumstances to the attention of the parties but, having considered any submissions, is entitled to and may rightly decide to proceed, notwithstanding the lack of consent. Furthermore, it should be recognised that the urgency of a situation may be such that a hearing is required in the interests of justice, notwithstanding the existence of arguable grounds in favour of disqualification.

5.9 So far as a part-time judge is concerned, he or she should be alert to the possibility that outside activities may create a perception of bias when dealing with particular cases. Careful judgment is required in this respect. The part-time judge may, by virtue of professional practice, have links with professional firms or other parties which might make it inappropriate to hear a case. It may be that the risk of a need for recusal arising may be greater in certain locations than in others.

6. THE PRINCIPLE OF INTEGRITY

6.1 In general, judges are entitled to exercise the rights and freedoms available to all citizens. While appointment to judicial office brings with it limitations on the private and public conduct of a judge, there is a public interest in judges participating, in so far as their office permits, in the life and affairs of the community. Moreover, it is necessary to strike a balance between the requirements of judicial office and the legitimate demands of the judge's personal and family life. Judges however require to accept that the nature of their office exposes them to considerable scrutiny and puts constraints on their behaviour, which other people may not experience. Thus judges should avoid situations which might reasonably be expected to lower respect for their judicial office. In particular, they should avoid situations which might expose them to charges of hypocrisy by reason to things done in their private life. Behaviour which might be regarded as merely unfortunate, if engaged in by someone who is not a judge, might be seen as unacceptable if engaged in by a person who is a judge and who, by reason of that office, has to pass judgment on the behaviour of others. An example of this would be the need for a judge to observe all of the requirements of the law.

6.2 With a view to maintaining the respect which should be paid to the holder of any judicial office by the public, judges should at all times be honest in all their dealings. They should ensure that, while publicly exercising their office, they conduct themselves in a manner consistent with the authority and standing of a judge. Since it is necessary for the proper performance of the duties of a judge to maintain, at least, a reasonable working relationship with those who appear in his or her court, they should refrain from conduct which would undermine that relationship. The dignity of the court should at all times be maintained. Thus discourtesy, or overbearing conduct, towards those appearing in court as counsel, or witnesses, is to be avoided. The judge should seek to be courteous, patient, tolerant and punctual and should respect the dignity of all. He or she should try to ensure that no one in court is exposed to any display or bias or prejudice.

7. THE PRINCIPLE OF PROPRIETY

7.1 A judge should avoid impropriety and the appearance of impropriety in all of that judge's activities. As a subject of constant public scrutiny, a judge should accept personal restrictions that might be viewed as burdensome by the ordinary citizen and should do so freely and willingly. As already stated, a judge should conduct himself or herself in a way that is consistent with the dignity of the legal profession who practice regularly in the judge's court, the judge should avoid situations which might reasonably give rise to the suspicion or appearance of favouritism or partiality. A judge holding a full-time appointment should not allow the use of his residence by a member of the legal profession to receive clients, or other members of the legal profession, for business purposes. A judge should not use or lend the prestige of the judicial office which he or she holds to advance his or her own private interests, the interests of a member of the judge's family, or of anyone else, nor should the judge knowingly convey, or permit others to convey the impression that anyone is in a special position improperly to influence the judge in the performance of judicial duties. Confidential information acquired by a judge in his or her judicial capacity should not be used or disclosed by the judge for any purpose not related to the judge's judicial duties. A judge holding a full-time appointment should not practice [sic] law whilst the holder of judicial office.

7.2 It is considered appropriate that a judge may write, lecture, teach and participate in activities concerning the law, the legal system, the administration of justice and related matters. However, a judge holding a full-time appointment should not generally receive any remuneration for such activities, except for fees and royalties as an author or editor. Where a judge is offered a fee for the activities described, such fee should go to charity. There is, of course, no objection to a judge accepting reasonable reimbursement of the cost of any necessary travel and accommodation required in attending lectures, seminars, etc.

8. THE PRINCIPLE OF EQUALITY

8.1 A judge should be aware of, and understand, diversity in society and differences arising from various sources, including but not limited to race, colour, gender, religion, national origin, caste, disability, age, marital status, sexual orientation, social and economic status and other like matters. The judge should not, by words or conduct, manifest any bias or prejudice towards any person or group on such grounds. The judge should carry out judicial duties without any differentiation on such grounds. The judge should also require lawyers in proceedings before the court to refrain from manifesting, by words or conduct, bias or prejudice based on such grounds, except such as may be legally relevant to any issue in the proceedings, or which may be the subject of legitimate advocacy.

9. THE PRINCIPLE OF COMPETENCE AND DILIGENCE

9.1 It is a judge's professional duty to do what he or she reasonably can to equip themselves to discharge their judicial duties with the high degree of competence that the public expect. This means that the judge should take all reasonable steps to maintain and enhance the knowledge and the skills necessary for the proper performance of judicial duties, including availing themselves of the training that may be offered to them. A judge with a full-time appointment should devote his or her professional activity to judicial duties and not to engage in conduct incompatible with the diligent discharge of such duties. In particular, any judge, other than a lay judge, should maintain and enhance their knowledge of the law and usages which they require to apply. Lay judges are not themselves expected to possess a professional knowledge of the law, since they receive advice on law from other sources. However, they have an obligation to avail themselves of the training that may be offered to them in other areas of their responsibilities. It is recognised that, in the context of adversarial procedure, as operated in the Scottish courts, a judge is entitled to rely heavily for the ascertainment of the law upon the submissions made to the court by those who appear. However, if experience in a particular case demonstrates that such reliance is misplaced, a judge should act by drawing to the attention of those involved in the case that he or she considers that they have not been furnished with an adequate exposition of the law to be applied. If such a course is necessary, it should be followed by according to those involved an adequate opportunity to remedy the shortcomings in submissions which the judge has perceived. While it is recognised that judges have a legitimate part to play in the development of the law, it should not be forgotten that their constitutional duty is to apply the law as it is, however unsatisfactory it may be. However, if a judge considers that the state of the law is unsatisfactory, he or she is quite entitled to draw attention to that fact publicly, or refer the matter to the Scottish Law Commission, or other appropriate authority.

9.2 Since the public have certain legitimate expectations as to the decision making of the court, it is important that these should be met. Written decisions should be formatted in such a way as to render them comprehensible to the public, so far as that is consistent with the handling of what may be very complex legal and factual issues. Judges should carefully consider whether they have a sound basis for making critical observations in their judgments. They should do so only if they consider that the public interest requires it to be done in a judgment, as opposed to in some other way. In addition, it is expected that there should not be any undue delay in the issue of judicial decisions. The time reasonably required to formulate a decision is plainly dependent on the nature, number and complexity of the issue with which the judge has to deal; and on the workload imposed upon him in relation to other cases. Accordingly, no absolute time limit can be specified. However, if the presiding judge in the court in which a judge sits has prescribed a period within which decisions ought to be issued, that requirement should, so far as possible, be respected.

INDEX